MANDARIN CHINESE
A Functional Reference Grammar

MANDARIN CHINESE
A Functional Reference Grammar

Charles N. Li

and

Sandra A. Thompson

UNIVERSITY OF CALIFORNIA PRESS

Berkeley   Los Angeles   London

University of California Press

Berkeley and Los Angeles, California

University of California Press, Ltd.

London, England

Copyright © 1981 by The Regents of the University of California

First Paperback Printing 1989

Library of Congress Cataloging in Publication Date

Li, Charles N.   1940–
  Mandarin Chinese.

Bibliography: p. 677
  Includes index.
  1. Chinese language—Grammar.   I. Thompson,
Sandra A., joint author.   II. Title.
PL1107.L5   1981   495.1'82421   80–6054
ISBN 0–520–04286–7 (cloth)
ISBN 0–520–06610–3 (PBK)

Printed in the United States of America

4   5   6   7   8   9 (PBK)

Contents

Preface to the Paperback Edition

In the Preface to the hardback edition, we wrote: "It is in the hope that our effort may spur others on to further discoveries in the study of Chinese that we offer our analyses here." In the intervening years, there have been many cogent and useful debates of the ideas and analyses put forth in the book, and much valuable work on the grammar of Chinese has appeared. We are not rewriting the grammar in the light of this new research at the present time, but we do wish to acknowledge some of the relevant discussion.

We are grateful to Professor James McCawley for a lengthy and careful discussion of many points raised in his seminar on the structure of Chinese, which used *Mandarin Chinese* as a textbook. We are also grateful to Maric-Claude Paris,[1] Zhang Zhanyi,[2] and Paul Yang[3] for their insightful reviews commenting on various issues addressed in *Mandarin Chinese*.

The relevant literature on Chinese grammar which has appeared since our book went to press has been too extensive for us to list here. Six general studies, however, should be mentioned: Helen T. Lin's *Essential Grammar for Modern Chinese* (Boston: Cheng and Tsui, 1981), Beverly Hong's *Situational Chinese* (Beijing: New World, 1983), Chauncey Chu's *A Reference Grammar of Mandarin Chinese for English Native Speakers* (New York: Peter Lang, 1983), Shou-hsin Teng's *Readings in Chinese Transformational Syntax* (Taipei: Crane, 1985), and Jerry Norman's *Chinese* (Cambridge: Cambridge University Press, 1988). In addition, a number of excellent articles have appeared in *Language, Studies in Language, Journal of Chinese Linguistics, Journal of Chinese Language Teachers Association, Cahiers de Linguistique Asie Orientale, Computational Analyses of Asian and African Languages,* and *Zhongguo Yuwen.*

Mandarin Chinese emphasizes the study of grammar in its normal discourse context. Some of the research mentioned above also takes this perspective, and at least one recent work shows very clearly how the choice of anaphor type, discussed in chapter 24, can be shown to be highly determined by the structure of the discourse in which the anaphors are used.[4] We oursleves are continuing to probe Chinese grammar from a discourse perspective, and we look forward to more studies along these lines.

Since some of the discussion of *Mandarin Chinese* has centered on the status of the examples we use, a comment on that point is in order. As is well known, Mandarin is a lingua franca, used by millions of speakers not only as a first language but also as a second language in much of China as well as among Chinese people abroad. As such, it is a language in which wide variation in usage is tolerated, since speakers all know that a number of languages and dialects influence the form of Mandarin. In such a situation, as we noted in the Preface to the 1981 hardback edition, it is to be expected that not all the examples we have used will seem equally "natural" to all speakers. Though Li is a native speaker of Mandarin, and all the examples are natural to him, some will sound strange to other ears. But every example in this book was either taken directly from a conversation in which we participated or checked with other native speakers for "naturalness"; each is therefore a possible utterance which some speaker might use or has used.

More important, certain utterances which are unnatural in some discourse contexts are perfectly natural in others. If a native speaker is asked to decide whether an utterance is "acceptable," the answer may depend on whether the respondent can place the utterance in an appropraite discourse context. In languages that have inflectual morphology, the "acceptability" of a given utterance taken in isolation may be easier to judge. For example, the English utterance "Sara lack confidence" is easily judged "unacceptable" independent of context because the verb is not properly inflected. But in languages such as Chinese, which has essentially no inflection, the notion of "acceptability" is much more controversial in most cases, particularly when the utterance is judged apart from its context. In general, then, the issue is whether an utterance is appropriate in a given context, at least for some speakers, not whether it is "acceptable" in isolation.

In anticipation of dispute over the appropriateness of some of our sample utterances, we provided a large number of examples to illustrate our analysis of each construction in *Mandarin Chinese*. Our approach was designed to reduce the inclination to complain that an analysis is not supported because this or that example doesn't sound quite "natural."

The paperback edition of *Mandarin Chinese* will greatly expand the accessibility of this book, especially for students. We reiterate our hope that it will continue to stimulate others to contribute to a deeper understanding of the grammar of this fascinating language.

Charles N. Li
Sandra A. Thompson

Santa Barbara, California
October 1988

1. *Cahiers de Linguistique Asie Orientale* 11, no. 2 (Dec. 1982).
2. *Journal of the Chinese Language Teachers Association* 19, no. 2 (May 1983).
3. *Journal of Asian Studies* 42, no. 3 (1983).
4. Chen Ping, *Referent Introducing and Tracking in Chinese Narrative,* (Ph.D. dissertation, University of California, Los Angeles, 1986).

Preface

The aim of this reference grammar is to provide, for the first time, a description of Mandarin in functional terms. We attempt as much as possible to discuss the structural properties of sentences in the language in terms of the pragmatic situations in which they are used, that is, with an eye toward their entire communicative context. It is our conviction that only in terms of these functional factors can the grammar of a language be understood.

This grammar is explicitly designed for students and teachers of Mandarin, who are not necessarily linguists. Thus, we have tried to minimize the use of technical linguistic terminology, and those terms that do occur in the book are carefully defined. On the other hand, most of the analyses in this book are original. It is our hope, then, that linguists who are interested in a functional approach to the study of language will also find this book useful. We have attempted to present the empirical facts of Mandarin faithfully, describe the steps of our reasoning concisely, state the generalizations we arrive at clearly, and, whenever possible, provide a functional explanation of these generalizations. Needless to say, a grammar of any language is bound to be incomplete, and ours is no exception. It is in the hope that our effort may spur others on to further discoveries in the study of Chinese that we offer our analyses here.

It is worth noting that the written language in China is a heterogeneous mixture of the classical tradition based on the written literature before the twentieth century and modern colloquial Mandarin speech. Since the promulgation of Putonghua in mainland China, there has been a noticeable reduction of the classical component in most of the written material produced in the People's Republic of China. Nevertheless, a "classical" phrase or usage still makes its appearance here and there. We wish to make it clear that the classical language is not included in the scope of our analyses.

We are indebted to the work of a number of linguists and scholars who have contributed to the study of the Chinese language. Some of our examples are drawn from their writings, and some of our ideas can be traced either directly or indirectly to our predecessors and contemporaries in the study of Mandarin. To all of them, we owe our gratitude. Where we have drawn on their ideas, we have acknowledged this in the notes to each chapter, but we have not attempted to document the sources of our examples, which come largely from conversations in which we have participated and from our own knowledge of the language, as well as from the writings of other linguists and scholars.

The preparation of this grammar has been partially supported by a U.S. Office of Education grant, OEG-G007701660, 1977–1979, and by the University of California, Los Angeles and Santa Barbara. We are grateful to Phoebe Bissell, Donna Childers, Lila Margolis, and Nancy Warfield for their clerical assistance, to Li Ming-ming, Chang Hsiang-wen, Peter Pan, Wu Yenna, and R. McMillan Thompson for their help in discussing many of our examples with us, and to Wu Yenna, Barbara Fox, and R. McMillan Thompson for reading and commenting on the manuscript.

Conventions Used in Examples

1. (x): x is an optional element.

2. $\begin{Bmatrix} x \\ y \end{Bmatrix}$: either x or y.

3. *: an utterance that is either structurally or semantically unacceptable to native speakers.

4. *(x): to be acceptable the example must include x.

5. (*x): to be acceptable the example must not include x.

6. ?: an utterance that is odd but not necessarily unacceptable.

7. Glosses and translations:

   a. Each Mandarin example has two lines of English below it. In the line immediately below the Mandarin example, we have attempted to gloss each Mandarin element with the clearest and most literal English equivalent possible. In the second line we offer a translation of the whole utterance into idiomatic English, attempting to preserve the "flavor" of the Mandarin utterance as much as we can.

   b. Mandarin elements may often have more than one possible English gloss. In cases where the choice of gloss is context sensitive, we have used the gloss appropriate to the given context. For example, *duō* can be glossed either as 'much' or as 'many'; in a sentence such as

(i)   tā   yǒu   hěn   <u>duō</u>   shū
            s/he   exist   very   <u>many</u>   book

S/He has a lot of books.

duō would be glossed as 'many' because it occurs with *shū* 'book', whereas in a sentence such as

(ii)   tā   yǒu   hěn   <u>duō</u>   qián
           3sg   exist   very   <u>much</u>   money

S/He has a lot of money.

duō would be glossed as 'much' because it occurs with *qián* 'money'.

c. Mandarin nouns in general do not indicate singularity versus plurality. We gloss all Mandarin nouns as singular nouns in English.

d. Mandarin has no grammatical category of *tense*, which means that many examples could be translated as either past or present tense in English. Rather than offering both possibilities for each such example, we have chosen arbitrarily to give either a past or a present tense translation. In each case, the discussion within which the examples are presented should make it clear whether a given construction could equally well be translated with an English present or past tense or whether the translation given is the only one it could have.

e. Mandarin pronouns make no distinction between masculine and feminine. We have glossed *tā* as '3sg' and translated it as 's/he'.

f. We have adopted the usage that is now conventional in linguistic scholarship of colons in glosses where it takes more than one English word to gloss a given Mandarin word. For example:

(i)   yīdiǎn
        a:little

(ii)   hǎoxiē
        a:lot

8. Pinyin: the transcription system we use is *pīnyīn* (literally 'spell sound'), the official romanization system of the People's Republic of China, which is

also the most widely used system in the media and scholarly writings on Chinese in the West (see the Introduction):

a. Syllables whose basic tone is third tone are given the third-tone diacritic even in environments where the third tone would change to second tone by tone sandhi. So, for example, we represent a word such as *xiǎo-niǎo* 'small bird, birdie' with two third tones, whereas in normal pronunciation, the tones should be *xiáo-niǎo*, reflecting the application of the tone sandhi rule changing a third tone to a second tone before a third tone.

b. There are two types of neutral-tone syllables (see the Introduction). Syllables of the first type always have the neutral tone, such as the aspect markers *-zhe*, *-le*, *-guo*, and the sentence-final particles *le*, *ne*, *ba*, and so forth; these are simply represented with no tone mark at all. Syllables of the second type, however, may vary between a full-tone pronunciation and a neutral-tone pronunciation. This variation may depend either on dialect differences or on the type of sentence in which the syllable occurs. The best example of variation due to dialect differences involves the pronunciation of the second syllable of many disyllabic words. For example, the word for 'clothes' is pronounced as *yīfu*, with the second syllable having a neutral tone, by some speakers and as *yīfú*, where the second syllable has a full tone, by other speakers, including most of those whose speech is influenced by Min and Yue languages. We have been arbitrary in representing such words: sometimes they are written with their full tone and sometimes with no tone mark. An example illustrating the influence of the sentence context in determining whether a syllable is pronounced with a full tone or a neutral tone is the variation in the pronunciation of *shì* 'be'. In a simple copula sentence, for instance, *shì* normally has no tone:

(i) wǒ   <u>shi</u>   Zhāngsān
    I   be   Zhangsan

I am Zhangsan.

As a marker of affiirmation, however, *shì* is typically pronounced with its full falling tone:

(ii) wǒ   <u>shì</u>   xǐhuān   chī   Zhōngguó   fàn
    I   be   like   eat   China   food

It's true that I like to eat Chinese food.

We represent syllables such as these with their full tones, with the understanding that in some contexts they will be destressed and have a neutral tone.

c. Exceptions to the generalization given just above are *bu* 'not' and *yi* 'one': not only can the pronunciation of these two syllables vary between a full tone and a neutral tone, but each has *different* full tones, depending on the tone of the syllable that follows. For the description of this variation for *bu* and *yi*, see Chao (1968:568). We have chosen not to mark these two syllables with tone diacritics, with the understanding that their pronunciation varies according to the sentences in which they occur.

9. Hyphens: We have attempted to be consistent in using hyphens between syllables in a Mandarin word only when each syllable has an independent meaning or use. Exceptions to this convention occur only in the chapter on compounds, where the structures of compound words are being analyzed. An example illustrating our use of hyphens is *chūbǎn* 'publish'. Although *chū* means 'put forth' and *bǎn* means 'board', we write *chūbǎn* as one word with no hyphen because the meaning 'publish' no longer has anything to do with 'put forth' and 'board'. Similarly, a word such as *xuéxiào* 'school' is written without a hyphen because, although *xué* 'learn, study' may occur independently, *xiào* 'school' may not. A word like *kàn-jiàn* 'see-perceive', on the other hand, is written with a hyphen because the two parts can function independently. It is impossible to be totally consistent on this matter, but we have tried to follow this principle to the best of our ability.

10. ∼: This is a symbol used to gloss an undefinable object of a verb-object compound. An example is *bāng-máng* 'help-∼ = to help'. The second syllable *máng* functions as an object of the verb *bāng* 'help'; but *máng* does not have any independent semantic content within the compound *bāng-máng*.

Abbreviations

ABBREVIATION	TERM	WHERE INTRODUCED, DISCUSSED, AND DEFINED
ASSOC	associative (*-de*)	4.2.2
BA	*bǎ*	15
BEI	*bèi*	16
CL	classifier	4.2.1
COMP	comparative	19
CRS	Currently Relevant State (*le*)	7.1
CSC	complex stative construction (*de*)	22
D.O.	direct object	4.3.1.B
DUR	durative aspect (*-zhe, zài*)	6.2
EXP	experiential aspect (*-guo*)	6.3
FW	Friendly Warning (*ou*)	7.4
GEN	genitive (*-de*)	4.2.2
I.O.	indirect object	10
NOM	nominalizer (*de*)	20
NP	noun phrase	4.2
ORD	ordinalizer (*di-*)	3.1.2A
PFV	perfective aspect (*-le*)	6.1
PL	plural (*-men, -xie*)	3.1.2.C, 4.2.1
Q	question (*ma*)	18.5
REx	Response to Expectation (*ne*)	7.2
RF	Reduce Forcefulness (*a/ya*)	7.5
RVC	resultative verb compound	3.2.3.A
SA	Solicit Agreement (*ba*)	7.3
3sg	third person singular pronoun	

CHAPTER 1

Introduction

The word *Mandarin* denoting the major dialect family of China is an established linguistic term in the West. In popular as well as linguistic usage, the term also represents the speech of Beijing, which for centuries has been recognized as the standard language of China because of the political and cultural significance of that city. China did not officially establish a common language for the nation until 1955, however, when the government of the People's Republic of China proclaimed a national language embodying the pronunciation of the Beijing dialect, the grammar of northern Mandarin, and the vocabulary of modern vernacular literature. This national language has since been known as *Pǔtōnghuà*, which means the 'common language'. The style and vocabulary of Putonghua aim at being close to the language of workers and farmers. During the early fifties, Taiwan also adopted the policy of promoting a uniform language based on the Beijing dialect; in Taiwan it is called *Guóyǔ*, literally 'national language'. Our term *Mandarin* is meant to include both Putonghua and Guoyu.

Since both Putonghua and Guoyu are based on the Beijing dialect, they are quite similar except in certain areas of vocabulary, which can be attributed in part to the political differences between the mainland and Taiwan. On the other hand, both Putonghua and Guoyu are far from being "uniform," for China has a large population spread over a vast geographical area, and consequently numerous other dialects inevitably influence and affect the versions of Putonghua and Guoyu spoken by people from different regions. Thus, a truly uniform language in a country such as China can exist only in theory, not in reality. This is not to downplay the success of Putonghua and Guoyu in facilitating communication among speakers of mutually unintelligible Chinese dialects and in promoting universal education. Nevertheless, it is important for us to point out that when one speaks of "the language"of China, one refers merely to an ideal, and that there will always be some variation between "the Mandarin language" of one person and "the Mandarin language" of another person. What we are attempting to describe and explain in this book is a Mandarin language that is as devoid of the idiosyncracies of individual speakers as possible. We intend the generalizations and explanations offered in this book to be applicable to the speech of all speakers of Putonghua and Guoyu, even if some of the illustrative examples may strike some readers as slightly odd. Each example that is not marked with an asterisk (*) is something that could be or has been said by at least some speakers of Mandarin.

Whenever a generalization or an explanation may be affected by dialectal interference, we try to point it out. Since the dialect situation in China is complex, we will briefly describe it here.

1.1 The Chinese Language Family

It is traditional to speak of the different varieties of Chinese as "dialects," even though they may be different from one another to the point of being mutually unintelligible.[1] It is often pointed out, for example, that Cantonese and Mandarin differ from each other roughly as the Romance "languages" Portuguese and Rumanian do. On the one hand, because Portuguese and Rumanian are spoken in different countries, they are referred to as different "languages." On the other hand, because Cantonese and Mandarin are spoken in the same country, they are called different "dialects." We will continue the tradition and refer to them as dialects.

The classification of the varieties of Chinese into dialects is based primarily on a comparison of their sound structure. The classification into seven major dialect groups as shown in table 1.1 is now generally accepted (see Egerod [1967]). The map shows the geographical spread and the locales of the representatives of the different dialect groups, as well as some major cities in China.

The greatest variations in terms of phonology, syntax, and vocabulary occur in the southern region of the country. The dialects of the Mandarin group, divided into four subgroups, not only can claim the largest percentage of China's population, but also have a higher degree of mutual intelligibility.

The Chinese language family is genetically classified as an independent branch of the Sino-Tibetan language family. The other major branches of the Sino-Tibetan language family are Tibetan, the languages of Tibet; Lolo-Burmese, the languages of Burma and scattered areas in Southern China, Southeast Asia, and the Tibetan borderland; and Karen, the languages of lower Burma and the southern border region between Thailand and Burma. Thus, geographically, the Sino-Tibetan languages are spoken in East Asia and Southeast Asia, with Chinese covering most of the East Asian mainland.

TABLE 1.1
THE SEVEN MAJOR DIALECT GROUPS IN CHINESE

	DIALECT FAMILIES	REPRESENTATIVE LOCALE	PERCENTAGE OF THE TOTAL POPULATION
Mandarin	Northern	Běijīng	70
	Northwestern	Tàiyuán	
	Southwestern	Chéngdū	
	Lower Yangzi	Nánjīng	
Wú	I	Sūzhōu	8.4
	II	Wēnzhōu	
Xiāng	Old	Shuāngfèng	5
	New	Chángshā	
Gàn		Nánchāng	2.4
Hakka		Méixiàn	4
Mǐn	Northern	Fúzhōu	1.5
	Southern	Cháozhōu	
Yuè	Yuè-hǎi	Zhōngshān	5
	Qīn-lián	Liánzhōu	
	Gāo-léi	Gāozhōu	
	Sì-yì	Táishān	
	Guèi-nán	Yùlín	

1.2 The Phonology of Mandarin

Following the traditional approach to the phonological description of Chinese, we will present the structure of the Mandarin syllable in terms of the initials, the finals, and the tones. [2]

1.2.1 Initials

The *initial* represents the consonantal beginning of a syllable. Since Mandarin does not have consonant clusters (sequences of consonants), the consonantal beginning of a syllable can only be a single consonant. There are, however, Mandarin syllables that do not have any initial consonant. For those syllables the tradition is to describe their initials as "zero." The initials of Mandarin are provided in table 1.2 in terms of the International Phonetic Alphabet (IPA) and Pinyin, the national phonetic alphabet adopted in China. Including the zero initial, Mandarin has twenty-two initials.

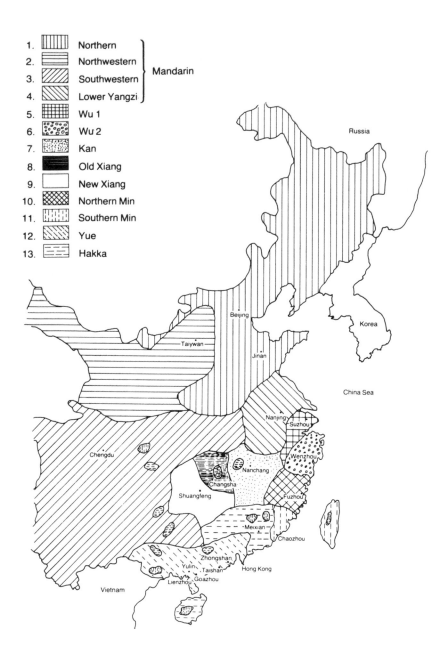

1. ▥ Northern
2. ▤ Northwestern
3. ▨ Southwestern   } Mandarin
4. ▧ Lower Yangzi
5. ▦ Wu 1
6. ⬮ Wu 2
7. ⬚ Kan
8. ■ Old Xiang
9. □ New Xiang
10. ▩ Northern Min
11. ⊞ Southern Min
12. ▨ Yue
13. ☰ Hakka

Russia

Beijing

Korea

Taiywan

Jinan

China Sea

Nanjing

Suzhou

Wenzhou

Chengdu

Nanchang

Changsha

Fuzhou

Shuangfeng

Meixian

Chaozhou

Zhongshan

Yulin   Taishan   Hong Kong

Lienzhou   Goazhou

Vietnam

Chinese Dialect Map

TABLE 1.2
INITIALS

MANNER OF ARTICULATION / PLACE OF ARTICULATION	UNASPIRATED STOPS		ASPIRATED STOPS		UNASPIRATED AFFRICATES		ASPIRATED AFFRICATES		NASALS		FRICATIVES		VOICED CONTINUANTS	
	IPA	Pinyin	IPA	Pinyin	IPA	Pinyin	IPA	Pinyin	IPA	Pinyin	IPA	Pinyin	IPA	Pinyin
Bilabials	p	b	pʰ	p					m	m				
Labio-dentals											f	f		
Dental-alveolars	t	d	tʰ	t	ts	z	tsʰ	c	n	n	s	s	l	l
Retroflexes					ʈʂ	zh	ʈʂʰ	ch			ʂ	sh	ɻ	r
Palatals					tɕ	j	tɕʰ	q			ɕ	x		
Velars	k	g	kʰ	k							x	h		

1.2.2 Finals

The *final* is the part of the syllable excluding the initial. There are thirty-seven finals in Mandarin, and they are listed in table 1.3 in IPA symbols. The rules showing the correspondences between the IPA vowels and the Pinyin vowels are shown in table 1.4.

TABLE 1.3
FINALS

1, ʐ, ɚ	A	ə	o		ai	ei	au	ou	an	ən	aŋ	əŋ	
i	iA			iɛ			iau	iou	iɛn	in	iaŋ	iŋ	
u	uA		uo		uai	uei			uan	uən	uaŋ	uŋ	uəŋ
y				yɛ					yɛn	yn			

The velar nasal, [ŋ], occurs only as part of a final, never as an initial. In Pinyin, it is represented by *ng*. The finals, as can be seen from table 1.4, are composed mainly of vowels. The only two consonants that occur in a Mandarin syllable final are the velar nasal, [ŋ], and the alveolar nasal, [n], and these may occur only at the end of a final.

1.2.3 Tones

The tone system of Mandarin is relatively simple in comparison with those of the southern Chinese dialect groups. There are four tones in Mandarin. Each tone may be described as a relative, contrastive pitch pattern associated with a syllable. The four tones are shown in table 1.5. The symbols in the second column from the right are known as *tone letters,* devised by Y.R. Chao. They provide a simplified time-pitch graph of the voice. The vertical line on the right serves as a reference for pitch height. The time-pitch graph is drawn from left to right so that the point farthest to the left on the graph represents the initial point of the tone, and the graph always ends at the vertical line serving as the reference of pitch height. The number represents the pitch register according to a scale of five levels, 1 being the lowest and 5 being the highest. Thus the 55 number means the pitch register of the syllable remains at level 5 throughout, whereas the 214 number indicates that the pitch register of the syllable begins at level 2, lowers to level 1, and then rises to level 4. If we take the syllable *yi* in Mandarin and place the four tones on it, we obtain a paradigm of four different morphemes, as shown in the far-right column in table 1.5. The four tones are indicated by four diacritic marks in Pinyin, as illustrated in the examples.

TABLE 1.4
CORRESPONDENCES BETWEEN IPA AND PINYIN VOWELS

IPA VOWEL SYMBOLS	PINYIN SYMBOLS	CONTEXT	EXAMPLES
[A]		all	lā = [lĀ] 'pull'
[a]	a	all	bān = [pān] 'move'
[ɛ]		between { [i] [y] } and [n]	lián = [liɛ́n] 'connect' yuǎn = [yɛ̌n] 'far'
[o]	o	all	mó = [mó] 'grind'
[u]		before [ŋ] or after [a]	lóng = [lúŋ] 'dragon' láo = [láu] 'toil'
[ɣ]		all	lè = [lɣ̀] 'happy'
[e]		before [i]	léi = [léi] 'thunder'
[ɛ]	e	after [i] or [y]	liè = [liɛ̀] 'arrange in order' lüè = [lyɛ̀] 'vile'
[ə]		before [h] or [ŋ]	gēn = [kən] 'root' gēng = [kəŋ] 'till'
[ɚ]	er	all	ér = [ɚ] 'son'
[e]	φ	after [Cu]	duì = [tuèi] 'correct'
[ə]	φ	after [Cu]	dūn = [tuən] 'squat'
[i]		with any initial except zero	lí = [lí] 'depart'
[ɿ]	i	after [tʂ], [tʂʰ], [ʂ], [ʐ]	shī = [ʂɻ̄] 'poetry'
[ʅ]		after [ts], [tsʰ], [s]	sī = [sɿ̄] 'think' [cī] = [tsʰʅ̄] 'female'
[u]		with any initial except zero	lú = [lú] 'stove'
[y]	u	after [tɕ], [tɕʰ], [ɕ]	xū = [ɕȳ] 'false' qù = [tɕʰỳ] 'go'
[y]	ü	after [n] and [l]	lǘ = [lý] 'donkey' nǚ = [nỹ] 'daughter'
[y]	yu	after zero initial	yú = [ǘ] 'fish' yuán = [yɛ́n] 'garden'
[i]	y	after zero initial but not in isolation	yào = [iàu] 'want'
[i]	yi	in isolation	yī = [ī] 'one'
[u]	w	after zero initial but not in isolation	wén = [uə́n] 'smell'
[u]	wu	in isolation	wǔ = [ǔ] 'five'

TABLE 1.5

TONES

TONE	DESCRIPTION	PITCH	GRAPH	EXAMPLE
1	high level	55	⌐	yī 'clothes'
2	high rising	35	⌐	yí 'to suspect'
3	dipping/falling-rising	214	⌄	yǐ 'chair'
4	high falling	51	⌐	yì 'meaning'

One of the most interesting phenomena involving tones in the Chinese dialects is called *tone sandhi*.[3] Tone sandhi may be described as the change of tones when syllables are juxtaposed. To put it differently, a syllable has one of the tones in the language when it stands alone, but the same syllable may take on a different tone without a change in meaning when it is followed by another syllable. The most important tone sandhi rules in Mandarin involve the third tone.

(i) *Tone sandhi rule 1:* When a third-tone syllable is followed by a syllable with any tone other than another third tone, the third-tone syllable changes to a low-tone syllable with the pitch contour 21. For example, *mǎ* 'horse' has the third tone in isolation, but when it is followed by another syllable such as *chē* 'vehicle', the sequence is pronounced with the following tone sequence: ⌐ ⌐

(ii) *Tone sandhi rule 2:* When a third-tone syllable is followed by another third-tone syllable, the first one changes into a second tone. For example, *gǎn* 'to chase' and *guǐ* 'demon' both have third tones. When they are in sequence, *gǎn guǐ* 'to exorcise demons', *gǎn* is changed from third tone to second tone.

Another tone sandhi rule in Mandarin involves the second tone, which changes into the first tone when it is preceded by either the first or the second tone and followed by any one of the four tones.

(iii) *Tone sandhi rule 3:* When a second-tone syllable is preceded by either a first tone or second-tone syllable and followed by a syllable with any one of the four tones, it changes into the first tone. For example:

(1)   ⌐   ⌐   ⌐   ⌐   ⌐   ⌐
     shéi   lái   chī ?   ⟶   shéi   lái   chī ?
     who   come   eat   who   come   eat

Who'll come to eat?

(2) ⌐ ⟋   ⟋   ⌐ ⌐   ⟋

　　san nián　−　jí　⟶　san nián　−　jí
　　three year　−　grade　　three year　−　grade

third grade

The spelling in our examples, however, will not reflect the application of any of these tone sandhi rules.

If a syllable has a weak stress or is unstressed, it loses its contrastive, relative pitch and therefore does not have one of the four tones described above. In such a case, the syllable is said to have a *neutral tone*. According to Chao (1968:36), the pitch of the neutral tone is:

.| half-low after first tone: *ta-de* 'he-GEN = his'

·| middle after second tone: *hóng-de* 'red-NOM = red one'

'| half-high after third tone: *wǒ-de* 'I-GEN = my'

| low after fourth tone: *lü-de* 'green-NOM = green one'

Suffixes and grammatical particles typically have a neutral tone. In Pinyin, a syllable with a neutral tone receives no diacritic mark.

1.2.4 Phonetic Effects of the Retroflex Suffix

The addition of the suffix *-er* involves a set of complicated changes in the final of the root morpheme. We will not state these rules here; a detailed listing of all the finals with the retroflex suffix can be found in Chao (1968:47−50). The use of the retroflex suffix is common among natives of Beijing. It is rare, however, among speakers of Putonghua or Guoyu from other locales. In most instances, the retroflex suffix, even when it is used, has become purely an articulatory feature without any semantic significance.

Notes

1. For a more detailed discussion of the Chinese language family and its cultural setting, see Forrest (1948) and Li and Thompson (1979c).
2. For detailed treatments, see Chao (1968:18−56), Lyovin (1972), and Cheng (1973).
3. For further discussion, see Cheng (1973), Howie (1976), and Zee (1980).

CHAPTER 2

Typological Description

There are many respects in which languages of the world are alike: for example, they all have ways of expressing denial (negation), existence, and causation, of asking questions, of modifying nouns and verbs, and of combining simple sentences into complex ones; yet at the same time there are many interesting ways in which languages differ from one another. Both the similarities and the differences are important, because an understanding of both tells us what a language is, what it can be like, what properties it must have, and what properties it need not have. The study of these similarities and differences is known as *language typology*.

In this chapter we will examine the position of Mandarin with respect to four typological parameters that are especially revealing of the basic structure of Mandarin as compared with those of other languages. These four parameters are:

1. The structural complexity of words
2. The number of syllables per word
3. The basic orientation of the sentence: "topic" versus "subject"
4. Word order

2.1 The Structural Complexity of Words: Mandarin as an Isolating Language

When any of the Chinese dialects, including Mandarin, is compared to nearly any other language, one of the most obvious features to emerge is the relative simplicity of the words of Chinese. That is, a typical word is not made up of component parts, called *morphemes*, but is, rather, a single morpheme. In Mandarin, there are a great number of compound words that are equivalent to such compounds as *gas mask* and *wool sweater* in English. Some Chinese dialects, though, do not even have a great number of compounds. In short, there is very little morphological complexity in any of the Chinese languages. This is not to say there is none; in fact, chapter 3 concerns itself with some of the ways Mandarin combines morphemes into words. When we compare the relatively rich inventory of suffixes and prefixes found in languages such as Latin, Turkish, Ojibwa, and even English, however, it is clear that Mandarin is quite striking in its general lack of complexity in word formation. Such a language has been referred to as an *isolating* language, a language in which it is generally true that each word consists of just one morpheme and cannot be further analyzed into component parts.

For the sake of comparison, let us consider some of the types of morphemes that many languages have which are not found in Mandarin.

2.1.1 Morphemes Occurring with Nouns

A. Case Markers

Many languages have morphemes that signal the grammatical function the noun has in the sentence: subject, direct object, indirect object, adverb, and so on. In Turkish, for instance, the underlined suffixes added to the word *ev-* 'house' signal the grammatical function of the word in a sentence as follows:

(1) ev   subject
     ev-i   direct object
     ev-e   direction ('to the house')
     ev-in   possessive ('of the house')
     ev-de   location ('in the house')

In Mandarin, of course, such functions are generally expressed by means of word order and prepositions.

B. Number Markers

Languages often mark nouns for a singular/plural (or singular/dual/plural) distinction, as in the English *cow/cows*. In most such languages, it is obligatory to make this distinction; but the category of number is not at all a necessary one, as shown by the fact that Mandarin does not need to mark it. For instance, *shū* can refer to either 'book' or 'books' in Mandarin. Significantly, if the concept of plurality is expressed in Mandarin, it is typically expressed by a separate word, such as *yìxiē* 'some', or *xǔduō* 'many', and involves no morphological complexity *within* a word. The one place where Mandarin must mark plurality is with pronouns; the suffix *-men* serves this function:

(2) tā   's/he'   tā-men   'they'
    nǐ   'you'   nǐ-men   'you (plural)'
    wǒ   'I'   wǒ-men   'we'

This same suffix *-men* may occasionally be found to express plurality with nouns referring to people, as in *háizi-men* (see section 3.1.2.C.2 of chapter 3) 'child-PL = children' or *kèren-men* 'guest-PL = guests', but its use with nouns is very rare.

2.1.2 Morphemes Occurring with Verbs

A. Agreement Markers

Many languages mark verbs morphologically to agree with the noun class into which the subject or direct object falls. This agreement usually indicates whether the subject or the direct object is first person, second person, or third person, singular or plural. For example, in Turkish, the verb meaning 'saw' is *gördü* if the subject is third person singular ('he', 'John', 'the girl', etc.) and *gördü-ler* if the subject is third person plural ('they', 'the Johnsons', 'the boys', etc.). In Swahili the verb may have agreement morphemes for both the subject and the direct object, as shown in the following example:

(3)   agreement   agreement
       Hamisi   a   —   me   —   ki   —   leta   chakula
       Hamisi   past   buy   food

Hamisi has bought food.

Agreement may serve several functions in a language, including the function of highlighting certain properties of subjects or direct objects. Again, some of these functions are taken over by various other devices in Mandarin, such as word order.

B. Tense and Aspect Markers

Most languages have morphemes for signaling the time of a reported event relative to the time of speaking (tense) or the duration or completion of a reported event relative to other events (aspect), as in the English sentences in (4), where the *a* sentence is in the present tense and progressive aspect, and the *b* sentence is in the past tense.

(4)   *a.* I <u>am</u> walk − <u>ing</u>

    b. I walk − <u>ed</u>

As we will show below in chapter 6, Mandarin has no markers for tense, though it does have aspect morphemes, including:

(5)   <u>-le</u>   'perfective'
    <u>-guo</u>   'experienced action'
    <u>-zhe</u>   'durative'

To sum up, we can state that Mandarin does not manifest a high degree of morphological complexity in terms of the types of grammatical morphemes which we have discussed and illustrated. The richness of a language with respect to these types of morphemes, called *inflectional* morphemes, is what determines whether a language is classified as isolating.

It should be noted, however, that there are other types of morphological combinations languages can manifest. One of those is compounding, and here Mandarin is relatively rich. We will take up the formation of compounds in detail in chapter 3.

2.2 Monosyllabicity: The Number of Syllables per Word

The Chinese dialects are sometimes referred to as *monosyllabic*, meaning that the vast majority of words are one syllable in length.[1] The question is: Is this an accurate typological characterization of Mandarin?

In order to answer this question, clearly we must first resolve the question of what constitutes a *word* in Mandarin. If ''word'' is equated with ''character'' in the writing system, then Mandarin can be claimed to be rigidly monosyllabic, since each character corresponds to only one syllable in the spoken language. Tying the notion of word to a written symbol is, however, somewhat arbitrary. A word should be a unit in the spoken language characterized by syntactic and semantic independence and integrity. Thus polysyllabic forms such as the following will constitute single words even though they are written with two or three characters. Some of the words in (6) can be broken into morphemes, however, and some cannot (see chapter 3):

(6)   <u>xuéxiào</u>   'school'
    <u>qiézi</u>   'eggplant'
    <u>yóuqī</u>   'paint'

pútáo	'grape'
túshūguǎn	'library'
kěshi	'but'
jiàoduì	'proofread'
fāmíng	'invent'
liánhé	'join'

Although classical Chinese appears to have been a monosyllabic language, modern Mandarin is no longer monosyllabic. Indeed, Mandarin has a very large number of polysyllabic words. There are several reasons why we adopt this point of view regarding the notion of word.

First of all, cross-linguistically, defining a word in Mandarin according to its syntactic and semantic independence and integrity is more in line with the way ''word'' is viewed in other languages and not so narrowly tied to the Chinese writing system.

Second, pedagogically, this position tends to be in accord with the perception of most people attempting to learn the Mandarin language. For example, on learning the Mandarin form for 'fruit', *shuǐguǒ*, the English-speaking student is likely to think of it as a single word rather than as two words. Further, the standard textbooks and dictionaries of Mandarin assume the position we are taking by romanizing such forms as those given in (6) as single words. To give an idea of the proportion of such words in the vocabulary, we found that on ten random pages in F. F. Wang's *Mandarin Chinese Dictionary* (1967), a dictionary of spoken Mandarin, out of a total of 129 entries, 87, or 67 percent, are entered as polysyllabic words with no spaces or hyphens between the syllables. This suggests that well over half of the forms he takes to be words are polysyllabic.

Third, historically, the position we are taking allows us to explain why Mandarin has the highest proportion of polysyllabic words of all the Chinese dialects. The explanation concerns the fact that the ancestor language of the modern Chinese dialects was a monosyllabic language. Because of phonological changes that have taken place, most extensively in Mandarin but much less extensively in the southern dialects, many formerly distinct syllables have become homophonous in Mandarin. Thus, where Cantonese, for example, still has a distinction between *yiu* 'want' and *yeuhk* 'medicine', Mandarin has only the single form *yào*. The threat of too many homophonous syllables has forced the language to increase dramatically the proportion of polysyllabic words, principally by means of the compounding processes discussed in chapter 3.

Because of considerations of typology, pedagogy, and history, then, we suggest that Mandarin is not ''monosyllabic.'' This is not to say that there will be 100 percent agreement among speakers or even certainty on the part of one speaker as to whether a given form, such as *kàn-jiàn* 'see', for example, should be regarded as one word or two; there are such questionable cases in every language, and perhaps more of them in Mandarin because of the nature of compounding. This issue is discussed in more depth in section 3.2 of chapter 3.

2.3 Topic Prominence

One of the most striking features of Mandarin sentence structure, and one that sets Mandarin apart from many other languages, is that in addition to the grammatical relations of "subject" and "direct object," the description of Mandarin must also include the element "topic." Because of the importance of "topic" in the grammar of Mandarin, it can be termed a *topic-prominent* language.

Basically, the topic of a sentence is what the sentence is about. It always comes first in the sentence, and it always refers to something about which the speaker assumes the person listening to the utterance has some knowledge, as in the following examples:

(7) Zhāngsān   wǒ   yǐjīng   jiàn   —   guo   le
     Zhangsan   I   already   see   —   EXP   CRS

Zhangsan, I've already seen (him).

(8) zhèi   —   kē   shù   yèzi   hěn   dà
     this   —   CL   tree   leaf   very   big

This tree, (its) leaves are very big.

Furthermore, a topic can always optionally be followed by a pause in speech, which serves to set the topic, that which is being talked about, apart from the rest of the sentence. What distinguishes topic from subject is that the subject must always have a direct semantic relationship with the verb as the one that performs the action or exists in the state named by the verb, but the topic need not. Looking again at examples (7) and (8), we can see that they both have subjects in addition to their topics: the subject in (7), the one who does the seeing, is *wǒ* 'I', while the subject in (8), the one that is very big, is *yèzi* 'leaf'. The topic need not have this kind of direct semantic relationship with the verb.

Topics and subjects are further discussed in section 4.1 of chapter 4. Here, we will simply point out that topic-prominent sentence structure is a significant typological feature of Mandarin in terms of which it can be compared to other languages, such as English. Nearly all English sentences must have a subject, and the subject is easy to identify in an English sentence, since it typically occurs right before the verb and the verb agrees with it in number:

(9)   *a*. That guy <u>has</u> money.

      b. Those guys <u>have</u> money.

In Mandarin, on the other hand, the concept of subject seems to be less significant, while the concept of topic appears to be quite crucial in explaining the structure of ordinary sentences in the language. The subject is not marked by position, by agreement, or by any case marker, and, in fact, in ordinary conversation, the subject may be missing altogether, as in examples (10) and (11):

(10)   zuótiān   niàn   −   le   liǎng   −   ge
        yesterday   read   −   PFV   two   −   CL

                     zhōngtou   −   de   shū
                     hour   −   GEN   book

        Yesterday, (I) read for two hours.

(11)   hǎo   lěng   a
        very   cold   RF

        (It's) very cold.

Both the one who did the reading in (10) and what it is that is cold in (11) are inferred from the context, but do not need to be expressed syntactically by subjects, as they do in English.

The third feature, then, that characterizes Mandarin typologically is its topic prominence, that is, the fact that the notion "topic" is crucial in explaining how Mandarin sentence structure works.

2.4 Word Order

2.4.1 The Word-Order Typology

Languages of the world have been shown by Greenberg (1963*a*) to fall into three main groups with respect to the order of the verb and the nouns in a simple sentence: given a simple transitive sentence with a subject and a direct object, then, the verb can occur before both the subject and the direct object, between them, or after them both. Since in the vast majority of languages the subject comes before the object,[2] we can represent these three basic word-order types in a simple way as: *VSO*, *SVO*, and *SOV*. Thus, for example, a language in which the typical word order for most sentences is to have the verb at the end would be an SOV, or verb-final, language. Japanese is such a language, since sentences such as the following are the norm:

(12) John — · ga   hon   — o <u>kaita</u>
      John —   TOPIC book —   wrote

   John wrote a book.

This is not to say that other word orders cannot occur in Japanese, only that putting the verb at the end of a sentence is typical and characteristic of that language. By the same token, one can state that English is an SVO language, in which the verb typically follows the subject and precedes the object, as in this example:

(13) John <u>wrote</u> a book.

The significance of Greenberg's word-order typology, however, goes far beyond just establishing the relative order of nouns and verbs. He also shows that, to a very large extent, the order of the verb with respect to the direct object correlates with the order of certain other elements; the most important of these correlations can be phrased as follows:

(i) *Greenberg's word-order correlation:* The order of the verb and the direct object tends to correlate with the order of modified element and modifying element in the following way: (*a*) If the direct object *follows* the verb then modifiers of the nouns tend to *follow* the noun and modifiers of the verb tend to *follow* the verb. And conversely: (*b*) If the object *precedes* the verb then modifiers of the noun tend to *precede* the noun and modifiers of the verb tend to *precede* the verb. That is, the order of all types of modifiers in relation to their heads (the words they modify) follows the same order as that of the verb and its direct object.

   Thus, to take just one example, in Japanese the order of direct object and verb is OV; accordingly, we would expect adverbs to precede the verbs they modify. And this is exactly what happens, as illustrated by the preverbal position of *Tokyo-de* 'in Tokyo' in the following sentence:

(14)	John	—	wa	Tokyo	—	de	Mary	—
	John	—	TOPIC	Tokyo	—	in	Mary	—

ni	at	—	ta
I.O.	meet	—	PAST

John met Mary in Tokyo.

In English, on the other hand, where the object follows the verb, the adverbial phrase *in Tokyo* also follows the verb, as can be seen in the English translation of (14) just above.

In addition to the principle regarding modifiers and heads, Greenberg shows that a number of other features tend to correlate with the relative position of verb and object. These correlations are summarized in table 2.1.

TABLE 2.1
FEATURES THAT CORRELATE WITH THE RELATIVE POSITION OF VERB AND OBJECT

VO LANGUAGES	OV LANGUAGES
Head Modifier	Modifier/Head
Verb/Adverb	Adverb/Verb
Noun/Adjective[1]	Adjective/Noun
Noun/Relative Clause	Relative Clause/Noun
Noun/Possessive[2] ('of the box')	Possessive/Noun
Other correlations	
Auxiliary/Verb ('can', 'have')	Verb/Auxiliary
Preposition/Noun	Noun/Postposition[3]
No sentence-final question particle	Sentence-final question particle

1. English is an exception with respect to this correlation, since adjectives regularly precede the noun, as in *bumpy road*.

2. English is also a partial exception to this correlation in that, in general, possessives follow the head in a construction with an inanimate possessor, as in:

    (i) the corner of the box

but precede it in a construction with an animate possessor, as in:

    (ii) the boy's box

3. A *postposition* in an OV language may be a case suffix (see section 2.1), or it may signal the same kinds of semantic relationships as do prepositions in VO languages, namely, location, possession, direction, and the like.

2.4.2 Word Order in Mandarin

Mandarin is not an easy language to classify in terms of word order, for three reasons. We will mention these reasons here and then discuss each one in more detail below.

First, the notion of subject is not a structurally well-defined one in the grammar of Mandarin.

A second and closely related fact is that the order in which basic words and phrases occur is governed to a large extent by considerations of meaning rather than of grammatical functions. This means that sentences with verbs at the beginning, in the middle, and at the end can be found in Mandarin. Languages that are relatively easy to characterize in Greenberg's terms are always those in which word order is determined primarily on strictly grammatical grounds (i.e., independent of principles of meaning), such as French and Turkish.

Third, whether it is taken to be verb medial or verb final, Mandarin is inconsistent with respect to the features that *correlate with* VO or OV order according to Greenberg's typological scheme. For example, sample texts reveal a greater number of VO than OV sentences, yet modifiers must precede their heads, which is an OV feature.

Let us now examine in more detail each of these three problems in determining word order for Mandarin.

The first problem has to do with the fact that Mandarin is a language in which "subject" is not a structurally definable notion. In fact, as is pointed out in section 2.3 of this chapter, it seems sensible to regard Mandarin as a topic-prominent rather than a subject-prominent language, since the basic structure of sentences can be more insightfully described in terms of the topic-comment relation rather than in terms of the subject-predicate relation. Consider again a typical sentence containing both a topic and a subject:

(15) nèi — kuài tián wǒmen jiā — féi
      that — piece field we add — fertilizer

That field (topic), we fertilize.

In this sentence, according to the criteria discussed in section 2.3 above, the topic is *nèi-kuài tián* 'that field', the subject is *wǒmen* 'we', and the verb *jiā-féi* 'fertilize' is a verb-object compound (see section 3.2.5 of chapter 3), in which the object component, *féi* 'fertilizer', cannot occur independently as a word (the independent word for 'fertilizer' is *féiliào*). The point for the present discussion is that in a language in which such sentences are part of the repertory of basic sentence types, clearly it is no simple matter to determine the basic word order according to Greenberg's criteria: the verb, which is a verb-object compound, is preceded by two nouns, but neither the label SOV nor OSV characterizes sentences like (15). Indeed, the first noun, *nèi-kuài tián* 'that field', cannot occur after the verb, *jiā-féi* 'fertilize', although the English translation suggests that they are in a verb-object relation. Thus, the first problem stems from the fact that the word-order typology cannot accommodate the notion of topic as part of a structural description of sentences.

A second problem in determining the basic word order for Mandarin is the related fact that it is primarily factors of meaning (i.e., *semantic* factors) rather than grammatical ones which determine the order of major constituents with respect to the verb. Thus, preverbal position is a signal for definiteness for topics, subjects, and objects, that is, for whether these topics, subjects, and objects are already known to both the speaker and the hearer. In addition, pre- and postverbal position signals a meaning difference for certain adverbial expressions.

Let us briefly illustrate these two points. First, we have said that definiteness (see section 4.2.5 of chapter 4 for a detailed discussion of definiteness) is partially signaled by preverbal position for topics, subjects, and objects. Since topics (as in [15]) may not be indefinite, they are always preverbal, but subjects and objects may appear on either side of the verb. Looking at subjects first, we find that presentative sentences (see chapter 17) allow postverbal subjects, as in (16)*b*:

(16) *a.*   <u>rén</u>   lái   LE³
         person   come   PFV/CRS

     The person(s) has/have come.

    b.   lái   —   le   <u>rén</u>   le

        come   —   PFV   person   CRS

     <u>Some person(s)</u> has/have come.

Sentence (16) *a* can best be interpreted as 'The person(s) whom you and I are expecting has/have come'. In other words, the preverbal subject is interpreted as *definite* (known to both the speaker and the hearer), while the postverbal subject of (16) *b* is interpreted as *indefinite* (not known to the hearer at least; hence 'some person[s]').

Roughly the same is true of objects. In (17) *a* it can be seen that the unmarked postverbal object may be taken as indefinite, while any of the three possible preverbal positions renders it definite, as in (17) *b-d*:[4]

(17) *a.*   wǒ   zài   mǎi   <u>shū</u>   le
     I   DUR   buy   book   CRS

I am buying <u>a book</u>.

b.   wǒ   bǎ   <u>shū</u>   mǎi   LE
     I   BA   book   buy   PFV/CRS

I bought <u>the book</u>.

c.   <u>shū</u>   wǒ   mǎi   LE
     book   I   buy   PFV/CRS

<u>The book</u>, I bought it (topic/contrastive).

d.   wǒ   <u>shū</u>   mǎi   LE
     I   book   buy   PFV/CRS

I bought <u>the book</u> (contrastive).

(See section 4.3.1.B of chapter 4 for further discussion of these preverbal orders.)

Second, to illustrate the semantic difference bewteen pre- and postverbal position for adverbial expressions, we can examine time phrases and locative phrases.[5]

A. Time Phrases

Preverbal time phrases tend to signal punctual time, while postverbal time phrases tend to signal durative time (see chapter 8 on adverbs). The following sentences illustrate this semantic tendency:

(18) *a.*   wǒ   <u>sān</u>   —   <u>diǎnzhōng</u>
     I   three   —   o'clock

         kāi   —   huì
         hold   —   meeting

I have a meeting <u>at three o'clock</u>.

   b.   *wǒ   kāi   –   huì   <u>sān</u>   <u>–</u>

        I   hold   –   meeting   three   –

             <u>diǎnzhōng</u>
              o'clock

(19) *a.*   wǒ   shuì   –   le   <u>sān</u>   <u>–</u>

        I   sleep   –   PFV   three   –

             <u>ge</u>   <u>zhōngtou</u>
             CL   hour

   I slept <u>for three hours</u>.

   b.   *wǒ   <u>sān</u>   –   <u>ge</u>   <u>zhōngtou</u>   shuì   LE

        I   three   –   CL   hour   sleep   PFV/CRS

In (18), the compound verb, *kāi-huì* 'have a meeting', has a punctual meaning. Thus (18) *a*, in which the time phrase occurs preverbally, is acceptable, whereas (18) *b*, in which the same time phrase occurs postverbally, is unacceptable. In (19), in which the verb, *shuì* 'sleep', is durative, the opposite holds true: the postverbal time phrase is acceptable, but the preverbal one is not.

B. Locative Phrases

In general, preverbal position signals location of actions, while postverbal position signals location of a person/thing as a result of the action (see chapter 11 on locative and directional phrases):

(20) *a.*   tā   <u>zài</u>   <u>zhuōzi</u>   –   <u>shang</u>   tiào

        3sg   at   table   –   on   jump

   S/He jumped (up and down) on the table.

   b.   tā   tiào   <u>zài</u>   <u>zhuōzi</u>   –   <u>shang</u>

        3sg   jump   at   table   –   on

   S/He jumped onto the table.

c.

tā	zài	zhuōzi	—	shang	xiě
3sg	at	table	—	on	write

S/He is writing (something) at the table.

d.

tā	xiě	zài	zhuōzi	—	shang
3sg	write	at	table	—	on

S/He is writing (something) onto the table.

Sentences *a* and *c* of (20) show a locative phrase in the preverbal position, which indicates the location of the action. Sentences *b* and *d* show a locative phrase in the postverbal position, which indicates the location of a person/thing as a result of the action.

The preceding discussion illustrates how semantic factors influence the order of noun phrases with respect to the verb. Thus, "basic" word order is difficult to establish in Mandarin because of the association of meaning with constituent ordering.

Before leaving this point, however, let us see what happens if we select some criterion according to which we might try to pick either VO or OV order as basic for Mandarin. One such criterion, which most linguists would consider reasonable, might be the *basic* pragmatic value for subjects and objects, the basic value for subjects being definite, for objects, indefinite. According to this criterion, the basic word order for Mandarin will be SVO for sentences that have subjects and objects. Corroborating this observation are the facts that a sample text count yields more SVO than SOV sentences and that in most complex sentences the subject precedes the verb.

Unfortunately, we cannot be entirely happy even with the results of applying this criterion, because we must still face the third problem in determining a word order for Mandarin: according to Greenberg's discussion, certain features should correlate with the order in which the direct object and verb occur. Mandarin can be seen to have some of the features of an SOV language and some of those of an SVO language, with more of the former than of the latter. Table 2.2 lists the SOV and SVO features of Mandarin. Here are some examples illustrating the SVO features:

(i) SVO sentences occur:

(21)

wǒ	xǐhuān	tā
I	like	3sg

I like him/her.

TABLE 2.2
SOV AND SVO FEATURES OF MANDARIN

SVO LANGUAGE FEATURES	SOV LANGUAGE FEATURES
VO sentences occur	OV sentences occur
prepositions exist	Prepositional phrases precede the V, except for time and place phrases (see above)
auxiliaries precede the V	Postpositions exist
complex sentences are almost always SVO	Relative clauses precede the head noun
	Genitive phrases precede the head noun
	Aspect markers follow the V
	Certain adverbials precede the V

(ii) Prepositions exist:

(22)   tā   cóng   Zhōngguó   lái   le
        3sg   from   China   come   CRS

S/He has come from China.

(iii) Auxiliaries precede the V:

(23)   tā   néng   shuō   Zhōngguó   —   huà
        3sg   can   speak   China   —   speech

S/He can speak Chinese.

(iv) Complex sentences are almost always SVO:

(24)   wǒ   tīngshuō   nǐ   mǎi   —   le
        I   hear   you   buy   —   PFV

                tā   —   de   shū   —   diàn
                3sg   —   GEN   book   —   store

I heard that you bought his/her bookstore.

Example sentences illustrating each of the SOV features are:
(i) SOV sentences occur:

(25)   Zhāngsān   bǎ   tā   mà   LE
       Zhangsan   BA   3sg   scold   PFV/CRS

Zhangsan scolded him/her.

(ii) Prepositional phrases precede the V, and postpositions exist (if we consider locative particles to be postpositions):

(26)   tā   zài   chúfáng   —   lǐ   chǎo   fàn
        3sg   at   kitchen   —   in   fry   rice

S/He's frying rice in the kitchen.

(iii) Relative clauses precede the head noun (see chapter 20), and genitive phrases precede the head noun:

(27)   huì   jiǎng   guóyǔ   de   nèi   —   ge
        know   speak   Chinese   NOM   that   —   CL

        xiǎohái   shì   wǒ   —   de   érzi
        child   be   I   —   GEN   son

The child who knows how to speak Chinese is my son.

(iv) Aspect markers follow the V:

(28)   wǒ   qù   —   guo   Táiběi
        I   go   —   EXP   Taipei

I have been to Taipei.

(v) Certain adverbials precede the verb:

(29)   tā   mǎn   bu   zàihu
        3sg   completely   not   care

S/He is completely indifferent.

(30)   nǐ   <u>màn-man-de</u>   chī
        you   slowly   eat

   You eat slowly.

Mandarin, then, is a language that has many SVO features as well as many SOV features.

   In work attempting to explain these facts, it has been noticed that, in fact, Mandarin has many more SOV features than any of the other Chinese dialects, which suggests that Mandarin, but not the other Chinese dialects, is gradually undergoing a change from being an SVO language to being an SOV language.[6] If Mandarin is indeed in the process of becoming an SOV language, this would then explain why it has both SVO as well as SOV characteristics. The implications of this gradual change for the grammar of present-day Mandarin will be noted at several points in this book.

   We have discussed the word-order issue in detail because it is one of the most important typological parameters and because it has been such a useful parameter in characterizing some of the important differences between languages of the world—for instance, Japanese (verb final), Thai (verb medial), and Berber (verb initial). For the three reasons given above, however, we find that the question ''What is the basic word order of Mandarin?'' is a difficult one to answer. In other words, there are VSO languages, SVO languages, SOV languages, and languages for which no basic word order can be established. Mandarin appears to be in this last category. In determining that it does *not* fit neatly into the basic word-order categories, we have observed that in Mandarin, the positions of elements in a sentence interact with other features of the language, such as the notion of topic and the expression of definiteness and directionality, and we have noted that Mandarin may be undergoing a change from an SVO to an SOV word order.

   In summary, we have seen that Mandarin can be described typologically according to four major criteria: it is an isolating but not a monosyllabic language; it is topic prominent; and it belongs to none of the standard word-order types that universal grammarians have discussed.

Notes

   1. For further discussion, see Rygaloff (1973:10-14).
   2. It should be noted, however, that there are also languages whose basic word order has the subject following rather than preceding the object. Malagasy (VOS) is such an example.

3. For a discussion of LE and the glosses PFV and CRS, see chapters 6 and 7.

4. For more discussion, see Mullie (1932), Chao (1968:76), Li (1971), Tai (1973, 1978), Li and Thompson (1975*a*, 1978*a*), Teng (1975*a*, 1979*a*), and Light (1979).

5. For further discussion, see Tai (1973), Huang (1978), and Light (1979).

6. See, in particular, Li and Thompson (1974*a*, 1974*b*, and 1974*c*) and Hashimoto (1976).

CHAPTER 3

Word Structure

3.1 Morphological Processes

Morphology concerns the internal structure of words.[1] The internal structure of words is described in terms of *morpheme*, referring to the smallest meaningful element in language. If a word consists of only one morpheme, its internal structure is merely a sequence of sounds (phonological segments), and the only relevant processes will be phonological. If, on the other hand, a word consists of two or more morphemes, the internal structure of the word becomes more complicated, and many interesting questions can be posed: What is the nature of the morphemes forming the word? Are they free (can they occur independently as a word), or are they bound (can they not occur independently as a word)? If they are not free, are they affixes (suffix, prefix, infix)? Do the morphemes change their phonological shapes (tones, segments) and meaning as they combine to form the word? It is obvious from these questions that Mandarin compounds such as *lā-cháng* 'pull-long = to lengthen by pulling', *fēng-chē* 'wind-vehicle = windmill', *rè-xīn* 'hot-heart = enthusiastic', *zǎo-wǎn* 'early-late = sooner or later' belong to the realm of morphology. Indeed, compounds constitute a broad and important area in the grammar of Mandarin. They will be treated in section 3.2. of this chapter. In this section, we will discuss two other morphological processes: reduplication and affixation.

3.1.1 Reduplication

As a morphological process, *reduplication* means that a morpheme is repeated so that the original morpheme together with its repetition form a new word.[2]. Such a new word is generally semantically and/or syntactically distinct from the original morpheme. Let us illustrate with an example. In section 6.4 of chapter 6 on aspect, it is stated that a volitional verb may be reduplicated to signal delimitative aspect; that is, the reduplication of an action verb has the semantic effect of signaling that the actor is doing something "a little bit." Thus, the meaning of a reduplicated action verb is often translated with 'a little'.

(1) *a.* qǐng   nǐ   <u>cháng</u>   zhèi   –   ge   cài
         please you   taste   this   –   CL   dish

          Please taste this dish.

    b. qǐng   nǐ   <u>cháng-chang</u> zhèi   –   ge   cài
            please you   taste-taste   this   –   CL   dish

          Please taste this dish a little.

A verb reduplicated usually remains a verb, and an adjective reduplicated usually remains an adjective. Phonologically, the only consistent effect of reduplication occurs with monosyllabic morphemes. When the reduplicated morpheme is monosyllabic, the second syllable takes a neutral tone. *Cháng-chang* 'taste a little' in sentence (1) *b* is an example.[3]

The various types of reduplication are presented in the following sections.

A. Reduplication of Volitional Verbs

As we have said, the semantic function of reduplicating the volitional verb in a sentence is to signal the actor's doing something "a little bit." Adjectival verbs (e.g., *róngyì* 'easy'), resultative verb compounds (e.g., *dǎ-kū* 'hit-cry = hit someone to cause that person to cry') and nonvolitional verbs (e.g., *wàng* 'forget') do not undergo this delimitative aspect reduplication. For example,

(2) <u>jiāo-jiao</u>   'teach-teach = teach a little'
     <u>shuō-shuo</u>   'say-say = say a little'
     <u>xiē-xie</u>   'rest-rest = rest a little'
     <u>bèi-bei</u>   'recite-recite = recite a little'
     <u>zǒu-zou</u>   'walk-walk = walk a little'
     <u>mó-mo</u>   'grind-grind = grind a little'

In addition, when a monosyllabic volitional verb is reduplicated to signal the delimitative aspect, the morpheme *yi* 'one' may occur between the original monosyllabic volitional verb and its repetition without any change in meaning. Thus, the forms in (2) may optionally occur with *yi*; for example, *jiāo-yi-jiāo* 'teach-one-teach = teach a little', *xiē-yi-xiē* 'rest-one-rest = rest a little', *zǒu-yi-zǒu* 'walk-one-walk = walk a little', and *mó-yi-mó* 'grind-one-grind = grind a little'. The phonological effect of the insertion of *yi* 'one' is that the repeated syllable has a full tone, whereas *yi* 'one' always has a neutral tone. The syntactic effect is that *yi* 'one' plus the repeated syllable function as a postverbal adverbial phrase (see section 6.4 of chapter 6 for further discussion).

Some disyllabic verbs can undergo reduplication, and some cannot. When a volitional verb is disyllabic, the reduplicated verb does not change phonologically; for instance,

(3) qǐngjiào-qǐngjiào   'inquire-inquire = inquire a little' (polite)
    tǎolùn-tǎolùn   'discuss-discuss = discuss a little'
    máfán-máfán   'bother-bother (someone with something) = bother someone with something a little'
    pīpíng-pīpíng   'criticize-criticize = criticize a little'
    yánjiū-yánjiū   'research-research = research a little'
    zhùyì-zhùyì   'pay attention=pay attention = pay a little attention'
    kǎolǜ-kǎolǜ   'consider-consider = consider a little'

Even if a disyllabic verb can undergo reduplication, however, it usually cannot take *yi* 'one' with the reduplication. For instance, whereas *tǎolùn-tǎolùn* is acceptable, **tǎolùn-yi-tǎolùn* is not:

(4) *wǒmen tǎolùn   —   yi   —   tǎolùn   zhèi   —
     we   discuss   —   one   —   discuss   this   —

         ge   wèntí
         CL   problem

Let us consider some verbal notions that can be expressed by either a disyllabic verb or a monosyllabic verb: *wèn* 'ask'/*xùnwèn* 'ask'; *zhǎo* 'find, look for'/*xúnzhǎo* 'find, look for'; *mà* 'scold'/*zhòumà* 'scold'. All of the monosyllabic forms can undergo reduplication to acquire the meaning of the delimitative aspect, but all of their disyllabic counterparts are odd under reduplication:

(5) *a.*   nǐ   mà   —   (yi —)   ma   tāmen
           you   scold   —   (one —)   scold   they

You scold them a little.

b. *nǐ <u>zhòumà — zhòumà</u> tāmen
  you scold — scold they

(6) *a.* nǐ <u>wèn — (yi —) wen</u> tā
    you ask — (one —) ask 3sg

You ask him/her a little.

b. *nǐ <u>xùnwèn — xùnwèn</u> tā
  you ask — ask 3sg

(7) *a.* wǒmen <u>zhǎo — (yi —) zhao</u> rén
    we look:for — (one —) look:for person

We're looking for someone a little.

b. *wǒmen <u>xúnzhǎo — xúnzhǎo</u> rén
  we look:for — look:for person

If a volitional verb is a verb-object compound (see section 3.2.5 of this chapter) whose components are separable, then the reduplication involves only the first component—the verb of the verb-object compound—and the second syllable of the reduplicated monosyllabic verb takes on the neutral tone; for example,

(8) <u>shuì-jiào</u> 'to sleep'; <u>shuì-shui-jiào</u> 'sleep a little'
    <u>dǎ-liè</u> 'to hunt'; <u>dǎ-da-liè</u> 'hunt a little'[3]
    <u>xǐ-zǎo</u> 'to bathe'; <u>xǐ-xi-zǎo</u> 'bathe a little'
    <u>tiào-wǔ</u> 'to dance'; <u>tiào-tiao-wǔ</u> 'dance a little'
    <u>jū-gōng</u> 'to bow'; <u>jū-ju-gōng</u> 'bow a little'

If a volitional verb is a verb-object compound whose components are inseparable, then the entire compound must be reduplicated in order to be in the delimitative aspect; for instance,

(9) <u>xiǎo-xīn</u> 'be careful'; <u>xiǎo-xīn-xiǎo-xīn</u> 'be careful a little'
    <u>xiào-láo</u> 'to serve'; <u>xiào-láo-xiào-láo</u> 'render a little service'
    <u>bào-yuàn</u> 'to bear grudge'; <u>bào-yuàn-bào-yuàn</u> 'bear a little grudge'
    <u>ké-sòu</u> 'to cough'; <u>ké-sòu-ké-sòu</u> 'cough a little'

B. Reduplication of Adjectives

Adjectives can be reduplicated either as modifiers of nouns or as manner adverbs, which are modifiers of verbs. When an adjective is reduplicated as a noun modifier, the semantic effect is that the original meaning of the adjective becomes more vivid. Thus, the semantic difference between (10) *a* and (10 *b* is that (10) *b* offers a more vivid description of the noun:

(10) *a.* hóng   —   de   —   huā
          red   —   NOM   —   flower

       flowers that are red

     b. hóng   —   hong   —   de   —   huā
          red   —   red   —   NOM   —   flower

       flowers that are really red (more vivid description)

Manner adverbs can also be formed from reduplicated adjectives (see chapter 8 on adverbs):

(11)   tā   màn-man-de   gǔn
        3sg   slowly   roll

    S/He rolled slowly.

(12)   wǒmen   shū-shu-fù-fu-de   tǎng   zài   nàr
          we   comfortably   lie   at   there

    We lay there comfortably.

When an adjective is disyllabic, the reduplication strategy is to reduplicate each syllable independently, as in (13):

(13) shūfù   'comfortable'   shū-shu-fù-fù   'comfortable'
     gānjìng   'clean'   gān-gan-jìng-jìng   'clean'
     qīngchǔ   'clear'   qīng-qing-chǔ-chǔ   'clear'
     hútú   'muddleheaded'   hú-hu-tú-tú   'muddleheaded'
     kuàilè   'happily'   kuài-kuai-lè-lè   'happy'
     zhěngqí   'orderly'   zhěng-zheng-qí-qí   'orderly'
     pǔtōng   'ordinary'   pǔ-pu-tōng-tōng   'ordinary'

As these examples show, in this type of reduplication, the second syllable is unstressed and therefore takes on the neutral tone.

It should be noted that not all adjectives can undergo reduplication. There does not, however, appear to be any rule governing which adjectives can be reduplicated and which adjectives cannot. Let us look at some contrasting pairs of examples:

(14) jiǎndān 'simple'; jiǎn-jian-dān-dān 'simple'
      fùzá 'complex'; *fù-fu-zá-zá
      chéngshí 'honest'; chéng-cheng-shí-shí 'honest'
      jiǎohuá 'sly'; *jiǎo-jiao-huá-huá
      pàng 'fat'; pàng-pang 'fat'
      shòu 'thin'; *shòu-shou
      jìng 'quiet'; jìng-jing 'quiet'
      chǎo 'noisy'; *chǎo-chao
      guījū 'well behaved'; guī-gui-jū-jū 'well behaved'
      yěmán 'barbarous'; *yě-ye-mán-man
      yuán 'round'; yuán-yuan 'round'
      fāng 'square'; fāng-fang 'square'
      cháng 'long'; ??cháng-chang
      hóng 'red'; hóng-hong 'red'
      fěnhóng 'pink'; *fěn-fen-hóng-hóng
      píngfán 'commonplace'; píng-ping-fán-fán 'commonplace'
      zhòngyào 'important'; *zhòng-zhong-yào-yào

In general, there are many more disyllabic adjectives than monosyllabic adjectives which cannot undergo reduplication. The following are some additional examples of disyllabic adjectives that cannot be reduplicated:

(15) měilì 'beautiful'; *měi-mei-lì-lì
      wěidà 'majestic'; *wěi-wei-dà-dà
      chǒulòu 'ugly'; *chǒu-chou-lòu-lòu
      féiwò 'fertile'; *féi-fei-wò-wò
      xìnggǎn 'sexy'; *xìng-xing-gǎn-gǎn
      jùtǐ 'concrete'; *jù-ju-tǐ-tǐ
      chōuxiàng 'abstract'; *chōu-chou-xiàng-xiàng
      jīběn 'basic'; *jī-ji-běn-běn
      róngyì 'easy'; *róng-rong-yì-yì
      kùnnán 'difficult'; *kùn-kun-nán-nán
      yánzhòng 'serious, grave'; *yán-yan-zhòng-zhòng
      fūqiǎn 'superficial'; *fū-fu-qiǎn-qiǎn
      fāngbiàn 'convenient'; *fāng-fang-biàn-biàn

yōuyǎ 'elegant'; *yōu-you-yǎ-yǎ
fǔbài 'corrupt'; *fǔ-fu-bài-bài
yúbèn 'stupid'; *yú-yu-bèn-bèn
xiánmíng 'sagacious'; *xián-xian-míng-míng
pínqióng 'impoverished'; *pín-pin-qióng-qióng
yǒushàn 'friendly'; *yǒu-you-shàn-shàn
tòumíng 'transparent'; *tòu-tou-míng-míng
gāncào 'arid'; *gān-gan-cào-cào
cháoshī 'humid'; *cháo-chao-shī-shī
xiǎnmíng 'obvious'; *xiǎn-xian-míng-míng

C. Reduplication of Measure Words

The reduplication of measure words (see section 4.2.1 of chapter 4) yields the meaning 'every'. For instance, *bàng* 'pound' is a measure word. When it is reduplicated, *bàng-bang*, it means 'every pound', as in:

(16)   bàng-bang   ròu   dōu   yào   chá
         every pound   meat   all   want   examine

Every pound of meat needs to be examined.

Since most classifiers (again see section 4.2.1 of chapter 4) are measure words either historically or contemporaneously, most of them can be reduplicated to signify 'every'. For example:

(17) *a*. tiáo-tiao   xīnwén   'every item of news' (where tiáo is the classifier
         for xīnwén 'news,' as in yi-tiáo xīnwén 'one item of news')

   b. gè-ge rén 'every person' (where gè is the classifier for rén 'person')

   c. fèn-fen bàozhi 'every newspaper' (where fèn is the classifier for
        bàozhi 'newspaper')

   d. zuò-zuo shān 'every mountain' (where zuò is the classifier for shān
        'mountain')

   e. jiàn-jian yīfu 'every dress' (where jiàn is the classifier for yīfu 'dress,
        clothes')

   f. kē-ke shù 'every tree' (where kē is the classifier for shù 'book') *g.* mén-men pào 'every cannon' (where mén is the classifier for pào 'cannon')

h. zhāng-zhang zhǐ 'every sheet of paper' (where zhāng is the classifier for zhǐ 'paper')

i. piān-pian wénzhāng 'every article' (where piān is the classifier for wénzhāng 'article [in a journal]')

The vast majority of monosyllabic measure words can be reduplicated to signify 'every', but polysyllabic measure words cannot undergo reduplication. For example, *gōnglǐ* 'kilometer', *jiālún* 'gallon', *xīngqi* 'week', and *guànzi* 'jug' cannot be reduplicated.

There are also a few monosyllabic classifiers and measure words that cannot be reduplicated. For example, the measure words for time, *tiān* 'day' and *nián* 'year,' can be reduplicated, as in:

(18)   tiān-tian   'every day'
        nián-nian   'every year'

but *yuè* 'month' and *miǎo* 'second' cannot be reduplicated:

(19)   *yuè-yue
        *miǎo-miao

The reduplication of certain monosyllabic classifiers appears odd in some dialects but not in others. For instance, *zhī* is a classifier for certain animals, such as *jī* 'chicken'. In Mandarin (20) is odd, but its Cantonese counterpart is perfectly natural in Cantonese. Hence, it is possible that (20) might appear natural in certain Mandarin dialects also.

(20) *zhī-zhi jī 'every chicken'

D. Reduplication of Kinship Terms

A number of kinship terms involve reduplication; but the reduplicated morphemes in those kinship terms are mostly *bound* morphemes—morphemes that cannot occur as independent words. The only exceptions are *bà* 'father' and *mā* 'mother'. The kinship terms that are bound morphemes, however, may occur with other morphemes to form terms of address: for instance, *dà-jiě* 'big sister' can be a term of address for one's elder sister, but the general term denoting an elder sister is a reduplicated form, *jiě-jie*. Those kinship terms that do not involve reduplication are bisyllabic, such as *zǔfù* 'paternal grandfather', *biǎogē* 'elder male first cousin', *biǎomèi* 'younger female first cousin', *tángdì* 'younger male first cousin from the paternal side', *zhínǚ* 'a brother's daughter', *nǚxu* 'son-in-law', *wàisheng* 'children of a sister', *sūnzi* 'grandson of male lineage', *jiěfu* 'husband of elder sister'.

The following are the reduplicated kinship terms:

(21)

bàba	'father'	mā-ma	'mother'
gē-ge	'elder brother'	dì-di	'younger brother'
jiě-jie	'elder sister'	mèi-mei	'younger sister'
yé-ye	'paternal grandpa'	nǎi-nai	'paternal grandma'
bó-bo	'elder brother of father'	shú-shu	'younger brother of father'
gū-gu	'paternal aunt'	jiù-jiu	'maternal uncle'
lǎo-lao	'maternal grandma'	gōng-gong	'husband's father'
pó-po	'husband's mother'		

E. Miscellaneous Reduplicated Terms

Some of the reduplicated terms presented here do not exist without the reduplication—for example, *máomao yǔ* does not have a counterpart in **máoyǔ*—and some of them are onomatopoeic terms, such as *dīngdang-dīngdang*:

(22)

línglingsuìsuì de dōngxi	'odds and ends'
máomao yǔ	'drizzle'
lěng bingbīng	'cold as ice'
dīngdang-dīngdang	'sound of ringing bells'
bēngbeng cuì	'crackling crisp'
gāng-gang	'just now'
piān-pian	'in a prejudiced or determined manner'
cháng-chang	'often'

3.1.2 Affixation

Affixes are bound morphemes that are added to other morphemes to form larger units. Often affixes are grammatical morphemes indicating number, aspect, and so on. Compared to Indo-European languages, Mandarin has few affixes. The scarcity of affixes in Mandarin accounts for one of the earliest observed typological characteristics of the language—that Mandarin is an isolating language (see chapter 2). Of the three types of affixes—prefixes, suffixes, and infixes—prefixes and infixes are extremely rare in Mandarin, while suffixes are slightly more numerous.

A. Prefixes

An affix that precedes the morpheme to which it is added is called a *prefix*. There are only a few prefixes in Mandarin:

A.1 *lǎo-/xiǎo-*

Lǎo- and *xiǎo-* are typically prefixed to people's surnames to form nicknames. When *lǎo-* and *xiǎo-* are added to a surname, say, *Zhāng*, to yield *lǎo-Zhāng* and *xiǎo-Zhāng*, they have a slightly different connotation, particularly when they are contrasted against each other. Both are used as nicknames signaling familiarity, but *lǎo-Zhāng*, at least for some speakers, is a slightly more respectful term than *xiǎo-Zhāng*. This subtle connotative nuance can be attributed to the adjectival words *lǎo* 'old' and *xiǎo* 'small, young' from which the prefixes *lǎo-* and *xiǎo-* are derived. *Lǎo-* can also be added to the numbers ranging from two to ten to indicate the order of seniority, usually among children in a family: for example, *lǎo-èr* 'number two', *lǎo-wǔ* 'number five'. Number one, however, is signaled by *lǎo-dà*, where *dà* means 'big'.[4]

A.2 *dì-*

This prefix is added to numerals to form ordinal numbers—for example, *dì-yī* 'first', *dì-liù* 'sixth', *dì-yi-wàn* 'ten thousandth'. It is glossed as *ORD* in examples.

A.3 *chū-*

This prefix is added to the numerals one to ten to denote the first ten days of a lunar month—for instance, *chū-èr* 'the second', *chū-shí* 'the tenth'. *Chū-yī*, *chū-èr*, *chū-sān* containing the numeral *yī* 'one', *èr* 'two', *sān* 'three' can, however, also denote the first year, the second year, and the third year of secondary education, equivalent to the seventh grade, the eighth grade, and the ninth grade in the United States.

There are a number of words that can be viewed either as compounds or as words containing a prefix. We have chosen to present them as the latter.

A.4 *kě-*

Kě- occurs with a number of verbs to form adjectives. Its meaning may be described as '-able', as in these examples:

(23)	kě-ài	'lovable'	ài	'to love'
	kě-xiào	'laughable'	xiào	'to laugh'
	kě-kào	'dependable'	kào	'to depend'

kě-kǒu	'palatable'	kǒu	'mouth'
kě-néng	'possible'	néng	'can'
kě-xìn	'credible'	xìn	'believe'
kě-chī	'edible'	chī	'eat'
kě-pà	'dreadful'	pà	'fear'

Some of the verbs to which *kě-* is prefixed are no longer free morphemes, and the meanings of these terms have become idiomatic. Thus, *kě* in these idioms is a prefix only in the etymological sense:

(24) kě-xí   'unfortunately'
     kě-jiàn   'it is evident that'
     kě-lián   'pitiable, pity'

A.5 *hǎo-/nán-*

Hǎo- and *nán-* as prefixes have opposite meanings. As independent morphemes, *hǎo* means 'good, well', and *nán* means 'hard, difficult'. As prefixes, they may each be added to the same set of verbs to form adjectives. Here are some examples:

(25) hǎo-kàn   'good-look = pretty', kàn 'look'
     nán-kàn   'hard-look = ugly'
     hǎo-wén   'good-smell = fragrant', wén 'smell'
     nán-wén   'hard-smell = smelly'
     hǎo-tīng   'good-listen = euphonious', tīng 'listen'
     nán-tīng   'hard-listen = cacophonous'
     hǎo-shòu   'good-sustain = comfortable', shòu 'sustain'
     nán-shòu   'hard-sustain =miserable'
     hǎo-shuō   'good-say = easy to say', shuō 'say'
     nán-shuō   'hard-say = hard to say'
     hǎo-yòng   'good-use = easy to use,' yòng 'use'
     nán-yòng   'hard-use = hard to use'
     hǎo-chī   'good-eat = delicious,' chī 'eat'
     nán-chī   'hard-eat = unpalatable'

B. Infixes

An *infix* is a bound morpheme that is inserted within a word to form another word. The only forms that could be considered infixes in Mandarin occur with resultative verb compounds. They are *-de-* 'obtain' and *-bu-* 'not' and are traditionally called *potential infixes* of the resultative verb compound because of the meaning of the compound when the infix is present, as in (26):

(26) shuō − de − qīngchu 'say−obtain−clear = can say clearly'
　　shuō − bu − qīngchu 'say−not−clear = cannot say clearly'

The resultative verb compound is treated in detail in section 3.2.3 of this chapter.

C. Suffixes

An affix that follows the morpheme to which it is added is called a *suffix*. Mandarin has more suffixes than either prefixes or infixes. The most frequently occurring suffixes are the aspect markers, *-le* 'perfective', *-zhe* 'durative', *-guo* 'experiential'. The aspect markers, discussed in detail in chapter 6, are an important and intricate area of the Mandarin grammar. Other grammatical morphemes that occur as suffixes are the possessive (genitive) marker *-de* (glossed as *GEN*), presented in section 4.2 of chapter 4, and the manner adverb marker *-de*, discussed in section 8.2.1 of chapter 8. In this section we will discuss suffixes other than the aforementioned grammatical morphemes.

C.1 *-er*

The retroflex suffix, *-er*, is the only nonsyllabic suffix in Mandarin. It merges with the syllable preceding it to form a new syllable ending in the retroflex sound, as in these examples:

(27) niǎo + er:　niǎor 'bird'
　　gēn + er:　gēr 'root'
　　guǐ + er:　guǐr 'ghost'

The rules governing the phonology of the merging of the retroflex suffix with the preceding syllable are presented in detail in *A Grammar of Spoken Chinese* by Y. R. Chao (1968). The range and frequency of occurrence of the retroflex suffix varies from dialect to dialect within the Mandarin dialect family. It is most prominent in the dialect of Běijīng.

Etymologically, *-er* was a diminutive suffix for nouns; but it has lost its semantic content in modern Mandarin, and its distribution in the Běijīng dialect has been extended to other parts of speech, including some place words, time words, verbs, and classifier/measure words, as a purely phonological phenomenon. For instance:

(28) Place words: z<u>hèr</u> 'here'
                               n<u>àr</u> 'there'
     Verbs: w<u>ár</u> 'to play'
                               hu<u>ǒr</u> 'to be angry'
     Time words: j<u>īr</u> 'today'
                               m<u>iér</u> 'tomorrow'
     Classifier/measure
     words: b<u>ěr</u> 'classifier for books, notebooks, albums, and
                               so forth'
                               pi<u>àr</u> 'a slice, a flake'

Basically, the retroflex suffix remains a nominal suffix as it once was when it served as a diminutive suffix. It occurs freely with monosyllabic nouns, less freely with compound nouns. Today, its usage in both Putonghua, the national language of the People's Republic of China, and in the Mandarin spoken in Taiwan is far less common than its usage in the Běijing dialect described in Chao (1968) and the major textbooks.

C.2 -men

The suffix -men is pronounced with neutral tone and is restricted to human nouns and pronouns only.[5] When a human noun takes on this suffix, it becomes a plural noun. It is entirely optional and would generally be used only when there is some reason to emphasize the plurality of the noun. For example:

(29) <u>lǎoshī-men</u>   'teachers'
     <u>xuéshēng-men</u>   'students'
     <u>péngyǒu-men</u>   'friends'
     <u>tóngbao-men</u>   'fellow countrymen'
     <u>xiōngdì-men</u>   'brothers'
     <u>jiěmèi-men</u>   'sisters'

A monosyllabic human noun does not take this plural suffix. Thus, the following examples are unacceptable:

(30) *<u>zéi-men</u>   'thieves'
     *<u>guān-men</u>   'officials'
     *<u>bīng-men</u>   'soldiers'

The suffix -*men* also occurs as a plural marker with pronouns:

(31) <u>wǒ-men</u>   'I-plural = we'
     <u>nǐ-men</u>   'you-plural'
     <u>tā-men</u>   's/he-plural = they'

C.3 -*xué*

-*Xué* is the Mandarin counterpart of the English suffix '-ology', as in *zoology*, *psychology*, and the like:

(32) <u>dòngwù-xué</u>   'animal−ology = zoology'
     <u>xīnlǐ-xué</u>   'psychology:(of someone)−ology = psychology (as a discipline)'
     <u>shēngwù-xué</u> 'living:things−ology = biology'
     <u>dìzhí-xué</u>   'earth:property−ology = geology'
     <u>shèhuì-xué</u>   'society−ology = sociology'
     <u>wùlǐ-xué</u>   'matter:principle−ology = physics'
     <u>huà-xué</u>   'transform−ology = chemistry'
     <u>lìshǐ-xué</u>   'history: (of something)−ology = history (as a discipline)'
     <u>zhíwù-xué</u>   'plant−ology = botany'
     <u>yǔyán-xué</u>   'language−ology = linguistics'
     <u>wén-xué</u>   'literature−ology = the study of literature'
     <u>yī-xué</u>   'remedy−ology = the study of medicine'
     <u>zhé-xué</u>   'philosophy−ology = philosophy (as a discipline)'
     <u>fǎ-xué</u>   'law−ology = law (as a discipline)'
     <u>jīngjì-xué</u>   'economy−ology = economics'
     <u>gōngchéng-xué</u> 'engineering−ology = the study of engineering'

C.4 -*jiā*

The suffix -*jiā* is equivalent to the English suffix '-ist'. For example:

(33) <u>kēxué-jiā</u>   'science-ist = scientist'
     <u>wùlǐxué-jiā</u>   'physics-ist = physicist'
     <u>yùndòng-jiā</u> 'athletics-ist = athlete'
     <u>lǐlùn-jiā</u>   'theory-ist = theorist'
     <u>zhèngzhì-jiā</u> 'politics-ist = politician'
     <u>zuò-jiā</u>   'create-ist = writer'
     <u>xiǎoshuō-jiā</u> 'novel-ist = novelist'

C.5 -huà

The suffix -huà creates verbs from nouns and adjectives. It is semantically equivalent to the English suffix '-ize'.

(34) <u>yǎng-huà</u> 'oxygen-ize = oxidize'
  <u>Měi-huà</u> 'American-ize = Americanize'
  <u>gōngyè-huà</u> 'industry-ize = industrialize'
  <u>jīxiè-huà</u> 'machinery-ize = mechanize'
  <u>tóng-huà</u> 'similar-ize = assimilate'
  <u>è-huà</u> 'undesirable-ize = deteriorate'
  <u>fǔ-huà</u> 'corrupt-ize = to become corrupt'
  <u>měi-huà</u> 'beautiful-ize = beautify'
  <u>yáng-huà</u> 'Western-ize = Westernize'

There are two other syllables we must mention here because they appear to be suffixes, even though they are not really suffixes anymore in present-day Mandarin.

C.6 -zi

Etymologically, -zi was a suffix derived from zǐ 'child'. It can no longer be used productively. It always has the neutral tone, and it constitutes the obligatory second syllable of a large number of nouns when they occur as independent words. Those nouns that must take -zi as their second syllable do not constitute a semantic class or a category of words which can be described in any other fashion. Thus, speakers of Mandarin must memorize this group of nouns that obligatorily cooccur with -zi. Here are some examples:

(35)
<u>tīzi</u>	'ladder'	<u>chúzi</u>	'cook'
<u>guǐzi</u>	'ghosts (derogatory name for Caucasians)'	<u>húzi</u>	'beard'
		<u>dèngzi</u>	'stool'
<u>érzi</u>	'son'	<u>lúzi</u>	'stove'
<u>làzi</u>	'hot pepper'	<u>kuàizi</u>	'chopstick'
<u>zhuōzi</u>	'table'	<u>wàzi</u>	'sock'
<u>shūzi</u>	'comb'	<u>màozi</u>	'hat'
<u>kùzi</u>	'pants'	<u>tíngzi</u>	'pavilion, kiosk'
<u>yǐzi</u>	'chair'	<u>bāozi</u>	'a round dumpling'
<u>dīngzi</u>	'nail'	<u>piànzi</u>	'swindler'
<u>jiǎozi</u>	'elongated dumpling'	<u>lǘzi</u>	'donkey'

jiàzi	'a frame, a scaffold'	shīzi	'lion'
hóuzi	'monkey'	xiāngzi	'chest, suitcase'
diànzi	'cushion'	qiánzi	'plier'
píngzi	'vase, bottle'	hézi	'box'
chuízi	'hammer'	fēngzi	'lunatic,
běnzi	'notebook'		schizophrenic'
tùzi	'rabbit'	wūzi	'room'
dùzi	'abdomen'	yínzi	'silver'
táozi	'peach'	júzi	'orange'
yuànzi	'courtyard'	dāizi	'a retarded person'
liàozi	'yardage of cloth'	pánzi	'tray, plate'

C.7 -tou

Another neutral-tone syllable that is a suffix only in the historical sense, -tou, occurs in modern Mandarin with a number of nouns that are bound morphemes. Again, these nouns with their historical suffix -tou must be learned by speakers of Mandarin. The following are some examples:

(36)
màntou	'Chinese bread'	mùtou	'wood'
gútou	'bone'	pīntou	'paramour'
lóngtou	'faucet'	shítou	'stone'
yùtou	'taro root'	shétou	'tongue'
niàntou	'idea'	pàitou	'grand style'
hòutou	'back'	qiántou	'front'
wàitou	'outside'	lǐtou	'inside'
xiàtou	'below'	shàngtou	'above'

There is a separate, productive usage of the suffix -tou with monosyllabic action verbs in the following context:

(37) $\left\{ \begin{array}{l} \underline{y\check{o}u} \\ \text{exist} \\ \underline{m\acute{e}i \; (y\check{o}u)} \\ \text{not exist} \end{array} \right\}$ action verb − tou

$\left\{ \begin{array}{l} \text{It is worth V-ing.} \\ \text{It is not worth V-ing.} \end{array} \right\}$

For example,

(38)   nàr   yǒu   shénme   kàn   −   tou?
       there   exist   what   see   −   tou

What's worth seeing over there?

(39)   nèi   −   dun   fàn   yǒu   chī   −   tou
       that   −   CL   meal   exist   eat   −   tou

That meal is worth eating.

(40)   zhèi   −   zhǒng   yīnyuè   méi   yǒu   tīng   −   tou
       this   −   kind   music   not   exist   hear   −   tou

This kind of music is not worth listening to.

It is reasonable to wonder why Mandarin should have so many nouns that possess the meaningless syllables -zi and -tou. Just as with parallel verb compounds (see section 3.2.3), the answer has to do with the history of the Chinese language. Briefly, in Mandarin, more than in any of the other dialects, tonal distinctions and final consonants have been lost, with the result that many single-syllable words that had been distinct at earlier stages of the language now would be homophones. The response to this impending massive homophony in Mandarin has been a strong tendency to develop disyllabic words. The existence of this large class of modern two-syllable words ending in the now-meaningless syllables -zi and -tou is one example of this tendency.

One interesting corollary of this historical fact is that many of the noun morphemes that must take -zi or -tou when they occur as independent words may drop these ''suffixes'' when they combine with another morpheme in a compound (see the discussion of compounds in section 3.2 of this chapter for many more examples):

(41) <u>mùtou</u>   'wood'
     *<u>mù</u>

but:

<u>mù</u> − bǎn   'wooden board'
<u>mù</u> − tàn   'charcoal'

(42) háizi   'child'
     *hái

but:

xiǎo − hái   'small child'
nǚ − hái   'female child = girl'

(43) xiézi   'shoe'
     *xié

but:

pí − xié   'leather shoe'
bù − xié   'cloth shoe'
tuō − xié   'remove shoes'

3.2 Compounds

Numerous studies of compounds in Mandarin Chinese are available. Two of the most extensive of these can be found in Chao (1968) and Lu (1965). There is, however, a great deal of disagreement over the definition of *compound*. The reason is that, no matter what criteria one picks, there is no clear demarcation between compounds and noncompounds. Chinese has very few incontrovertible polysyllabic morphemes, and most of those that do exist are borrowed from other languages—for example, *pútáo* 'grape', *húdié* 'butterfly', *bōli* 'glass', *méiguì* 'rose'. Other than the few clear cases of polysyllabic morphemes, the polysyllabic words in Chinese are inevitably composed of several morphemes. The definition of a compound is made difficult by the following facts. Sometimes a component morpheme is from classical Chinese and no longer functions as a free morpheme in modern spoken Mandarin; for example, in *fǒuzé* 'otherwise', the second part, *zé*, meaning 'then' in Classical Chinese, is no longer used in modern spoken Mandarin. Sometimes the meanings of the component morphemes are totally unrelated to the meaning of the entire word; for example, in *fēngliú* 'amorous', *fēng* is a morpheme meaning 'wind', and *liú* is a morpheme meaning 'flow'. Sometimes the meaning of a polysyllabic word can only indirectly be connected with the literal meanings of the component morphemes, as, for example, in *ròumá* 'flesh-numb = disgusting'. Sometimes the meaning of a polysyllabic word can only be metaphorically related to the meanings of its component morphemes, as in *xiǎoxīn* 'small-heart = be careful'. Fortunately, though, the definition of a compound is really not a crucial issue for students of Mandarin. It is important only to linguists analyzing the Mandarin lexicon because it serves to delimit the domain of their studies. Thus, we may consider as compounds all polysyllabic units that have certain properties of single words and that can be analyzed into two or more meaningful elements, or morphemes, even if these morphemes cannot occur independently in modern Mandarin. According to this characterization, then, *kāi-guān* 'open-close = switch' is a compound because it is like a single word in that it refers to a single object. Similarly, *chōu-yān* 'extract-smoke' is a compound because it behaves like a single word in certain respects discussed below in section 3.2.5. The combination *hē tāng* 'drink soup', on the other hand, because it has none of the properties of a single word, is not considered a compound; it is, rather, a phrase consisting of a verb plus its direct object.

3.2.1 The Meanings of Compounds

Let us first examine the relatedness between the meaning of a compound and the meanings of its component morphemes.

The relatedness between the meaning of a compound and those of its components can vary from close to nonexistent. Although not all compounds are idiomatic in meaning, the situation concerning the meaning of compounds by and large parallels that of idioms. One factor that plays a role in the semantic relation between an idiom and its components is time. Idioms are continuously being formed. At the time of the formation of a new idiom, not only are the speakers aware of the literal and idiomatic senses of the term, but they also know the connection between them. As time moves on, this semantic connection begins to recede from the realm of the knowledge of the native speakers until, finally, it is totally lost. A good example in English is *understand*. The semantic relation between the compositional meaning of *under* and *stand*, on the one hand, and the idiomatic meaning, 'to comprehend', on the other, is no longer relevant to present-day speakers of English. For the English example *hit below the belt*, though, the relation between the literal meaning and the idiomatic meaning is still apparent to most speakers of English. In the case of Mandarin compounds, the time element is related to a speaker's knowledge of the classical language. A morpheme in a Mandarin compound may come from the classical language; if one is not familiar with the classical language, such a morpheme will be obsolete and, therefore, meaningless. For example, *qūzú* 'to chase' is composed of two morphemes from Classical Chinese, *qū* 'drive' and *zú* 'pursue', neither of which exists any longer as a morpheme in modern Mandarin. Thus, the problems concerning compounds in Mandarin are often related through the written language to Classical Chinese. Later on in this section we will examine the various types of compounds according to the semantic relations between their components. At this point, let us look at some examples that exhibit various degrees of relatedness between the meaning of the compound and the meaning of its component morphemes.

(i) There may be no apparent semantic connection between the meaning of the compound and the meaning of its constituents in the modern language. Such compounds exhibit the highest degree of idiomaticity. Very few compounds in Mandarin, however, are of this type. Examples include:

(44) fēng-liú   'wind-flow = amorous'
     huā-shēng   'flower-born = peanut'
     féi-zào   'fat-black = soap'
     dà-yì   'great-idea = negligent'
     xīn-shuǐ   'fuel-water = salary'
     xiǎo-shuō   'small-talk = novel'
     dà-biàn   'great-convenience = defecate/feces'
     shāng-fēng   'hurt-wind = catch cold'

(ii) There may be a metaphorical, figurative, or inferential connection between the meaning of the compound and the meanings of its component parts.

(45) máo-dùn   'spear-shield = contradictory'
     shǒu-yìng   'hand-hard = tough'
     kāi-guān   'open-close = switch'
     xū-xīn   'empty-mind = modest'
     rè-xīn   'hot-heart = enthusiastic'
     diàn-yǐng   'electric-image = movie'
     huǒ-chái   'fire-firewood = match'
     tiān-qì   'heaven-breath = weather'
     gōng-lù   'public-way = highway'
     qīng-shì   'light-look = look down upon'
     zhòng-shì   'weighty-look = take as important'
     hòu-rén   'late-people = posterity'
     rù-shén   'enter-spirit = fascinated'

(iii) The meaning of the compound may be directly related or identical to the meanings of its components.

(46) xǐ-zǎo   'wash-bath = take a bath'
     gān-jìng   'dry-clean = clean'
     fēi-jī   'fly-machine = airplane'

jìn-bù	'advance-step = make progress'
chéng-qiáng	'city-wall = city wall'
chē-mǎ	'vehicle-horse = traffic'
yī-kào	'lean-depend on = depend on'
hū-xī	'exhale-inhale = breathe'
mǎn-zú	'full-sufficient = be content'
nián-qīng	'year-light = youthful'
dǎ-tīng	'make-hear = inquire'
zhī-dào	'know-way = know'
jiāng-lái	'future-come = in the future'
chéng-rèn	'receive-recognize = admit'
dēng-huǒ	'lamp-fire = illumination'

We have provided three classes of compounds to illustrate the degree of relatedness between the meaning of a compound and the meanings of its parts, the first class illustrating the lowest degree, the third the highest. This classification is useful for the purpose of illustration; in reality, however, the degree of relatedness between the meaning of a compound and the meaning of its parts forms a continuum.

3.2.2 Nominal Compounds

The semantic relations between the constituents of nominal compounds cannot be exhaustively listed. In fact, among languages that use nominal compounds extensively, such as English, Afrikaans, and Mandarin, it is known that native speakers can create new ones in their speech whenever the speech context is appropriate, and the semantic relation between the constituents of the innovated nominal compounds—that is, the meaning of the nominal compounds—is heavily dependent on the speech context. For example, imagine a speech context in which you and your friend are eating hot dogs with mustard, and you notice a yellow spot on the shirt of your friend. You may say: "You've got a *mustard stain* on your shirt". The nominal compound *mustard stain*, then, means a stain caused by mustard. Consider another context: you and your friend are discussing plant diseases on a farm where, among other plants, mustard is being grown, and the green mustard plants have many black marks on them. In such a context, you may ask your friend: "What are we going to do about those *mustard stains*?" In this context, the compound *mustard stains* means the stains on the mustard plants. If nominal compounds can be created whenever the context is appropriate and if the semantic relations between the constituents cannot be exhaustively enumerated, one may ask the question: Why should anyone provide a list of the semantic relations between the constituents of compounds when such a list cannot in principle ever be complete? The answer is that there are certain more prevalent semantic relations between the constituents of nominal compounds, and it is pedagogically and heuristically useful to describe them. One consequence of enumerating those prevalent semantic relations is that one sees that the same set of relations seem to hold for all languages utilizing productive nominal compounds.

In the following description of the most common semantic relations between the elements in a nominal compound, N_1 will stand for the first noun in the compound, and N_2 for the second.

(i) N_1 denotes the place where N_2 is located:

(47) chuáng-dān(zi)   'bed-sheet'
     mù-bēi   'tomb-monument = tombstone'
     tái-dēng   'table-lamp'
     tián-shǔ   'field-mouse'
     bàngōngshì-zhuōzi   'office-desk'
     kètīng-shāfa   'living:room sofa'
     hé-mǎ   'river-horse = hippopotamus'
     hǎi-gǒu   'sea-dog = seal'

(ii) N_1 denotes the place where N_2 is applied:

(48) chún-gāo   'lip-ointment = lipstick'
     yǎn-yào   'eye-medicine'
     zhǐjia-yóu   'nail-oil = nail polish'
     yá-gāo   'tooth-paste'

(iii) N_2 is used for N_1:

(49) qiāng-dàn   'gun-bullet = bullet'
     pào-dàn   'artillery-bullet = artillery shell'
     yī-jià(zi)   'clothes-rack'
     dēng-zhào(zi)   'lamp-shade'
     mǎ-fáng   'horse-house = manger'
     bùgào-bǎn   'bulletin-board'

(iv) N_2 denotes a unit of N_1:

(50) tiě-yuánzǐ   'iron-atom'
     qīngqì-fènzi   'hydrogen-molecule'
     zhèngfǔ-jīguān   'government-administrative:unit'

(v) N$_2$ denotes a piece of equipment used in a sport, N$_1$:

> (51) pīngpāng-qiú   'Ping:Pong ball'
>   lěiqiú-bàng(zi)   'baseball-cudgel = baseball bat'
>   wǎngqiú-pāi(zi)   'tennis-racket'
>   lánqiú-kuāng(zi)   'basketball-hoop'

(vi) N$_2$ denotes a protective device against N$_1$:

> (52) yǔ-mào   'rain-hat'
>   yǔ-yī   'rain-clothes = raincoat'
>   tàiyang-yǎnjìng   'sun-glasses'
>   dúqì-miànzhào   'poison:gas mask'

(vii) N$_2$ is caused by N$_1$:

> (53) yóu-jí   'oil-stain'
>   hàn-bān   'sweat-spot = freckle'
>   shuǐ-hén   'water-mark'
>   dòu-chuāng   'smallpox-pustules'

(viii) N$_2$ denotes a container for N$_1$:

> (54) shū-bāo   'book-container = satchel'
>   jiǔ-bēi(zi)   'wine-cup'
>   mǐ-dài(zi)   'rice-bag'
>   nǎi-píng(zi)   'milk-bottle'
>   chá-bēi   'tea-cup'
>   fàn-guō(zi)   'rice-pot'
>   lāxī-xiāng   'trash-can'
>   bǐnggān-hé(zi)   'biscuit-box'

(ix) N$_1$ and N$_2$ are parallel:

> (55) huā-mù   'flower-tree = vegetation'
>   jiā-xiāng   'home-village = hometown'
>   guó-jiā   'country-home = nation'
>   shuǐ-tǔ   'water-earth = climate'
>   fù-mǔ   'father-mother = parents'

jūn-zhǔ	'king-master = monarch'
zǐ-nǚ	'son-daughter = children'

(x) N_2 denotes a product of N_1:

(56)	fēng-mì	'bee-honey = honey'
	jī-dàn	'chicken-egg'
	cán-sī	'silkworm-silk'
	māo-fèn	'cat-scat'
	fēng-là	'bee-wax = beeswax'
	Xiānggǎng-chūpǐn	'Hong:Kong-product'

(xi) N_2 is made of N_1:

(57)	dàlǐshí-dìbǎn	'marble-floor'
	shízi-lù	'pebble-road'
	cǎo-xié	'straw-shoe'
	zhǐ-lǎohǔ	'paper-tiger'
	mùtou-zhuōzi	'wood-table'
	tóng-xiàng	'bronze-statue'
	mián-bèi	'cotton-quilt'

(xii) N_2 denotes a place where N_1 is sold:

(58)	bǎihuò-gōngsī	'hundred:merchandise-company = department store'
	fàn-guǎn	'food-tavern = restaurant'
	túshū-guǎn	'book-tavern = library'
	cài-chǎng	'food-market'
	qìyóu-zhàn	'gasoline-station'
	yào-diàn	'drug-store'

(xiii) N_2 denotes a disease of N_1:

(59)	yāo-bìng	'kidney-disease'
	fèi-bìng	'lung-disease = tuberculosis'
	cháng-yán	'intestine-inflammation'
	pífu-zhěngzi	'skin-rash'
	xīnzàng-bìng	'heart-disease'

(xiv) N$_1$ denotes the time for N$_2$:

(60) chūn-tiān   'spring-day = spring'
      xià-jì   'summer-season = summer'
      chén-wù   'morning-fog'
      qiū-yuè   'autumn-moon'
      dōng-yè   'winter-night'
      yè-xiào   'night-school'

(xv) N$_1$ is the source of energy of N$_2$:

(61) diàn-dēng   'electric-lamp'
      qì-chē   'steam-vehicle = automobile'
      fēng-chē   'wind-vehicle = windmill'
      yuánzǐ-néng   'atom-energy = atomic energy'

(xvi) N$_1$ is a metaphorical description of N$_2$:

(62) gǒu-xióng   'dog-bear = bear'
      lù-niǎo   'deer-bird = cassowary'
      lóng-chuán   'dragon-boat'
      shé-zhèng   'snake-formation'
      hǔ-jiàng   'tiger-general = brave general'
      guǐ-liǎn   'ghost-face'

(xvii) N$_2$ is a component of N$_1$:

(63) qìchē-lúnzi   'automobile-wheel'
      jiǎotāchē-lóngtou 'bicycle-handlebar'
      jī-máo   'chicken-feather'
      niú-jiǎo   'bull-horn'
      fēijī-wěiba   'airplane-tail'

(xviii) N$_2$ is a source of N$_1$:

(64) shuǐ-yuán   'water-source'
      yán-jǐng   'salt-well'
      méi-kuàng   'coal-mine'
      yóu-jǐng   'oil-well'

(xix) N_2 is an employee or an officer of N_1:

(65) dàxué-xiàozhǎng   'university-president'
     yínháng-zǒngcái   'bank-director'
     zhèngfǔ-guānyuán   'government-official'
     gōngsī−jīnglǐ   'company-manager'
     kōngjūn-zǒngsīlìng   'air:force commander:in:chief:

(xx) N_1 denotes a proper name for N_2, which may be a location, an organization, an institution, or a structure:

(66) Běijīng-dàxué   'Beijing-University'
     Shànghǎi-lù   'Shanghai-Road'
     Yángzǐ-jiāng   'Yangtze-River'
     Měiguó-guóhuì   'America-Congress'

(xxi) N_2 denotes a person who sells or delivers N_1:

(67) yán-shāng   'salt-merchant'
     bǎoxiǎn-dàilǐrén   'insurance-agent'
     shuǐguǒ-xiǎofàn   'fruit-peddler'

The above list of twenty-one types of nominal compounds by no means constitutes an exhaustive categorization; one can still think of nominal compounds that are not accounted for in the above listing. The important thing to note, though, is that the compounding process of linking noun and noun together to form a nominal compound having the effect of designating an object with a name is a productive and creative one. As we said before, the only constraint is a pragmatic one, and that is that the context must be appropriate for naming a certain object. These twenty-one semantic relations between the noun components of nominal compounds should assist us in our effort to understand the more commonly used nominal compounds. As we can see from the examples, some are highly idiomatic in the sense that the meaning of the compound is hardly related to the meanings of the component nouns; some are very literal in that the meaning of the compound clearly reflects the meanings of the component nouns. We have tried to pick some of the more nonidiomatic compounds as our examples in order to illustrate the productive aspect of these compounding processes.

One class of nominal compounds listed above which deserves some attention is class (ix), where the constituents are in a "parallel" relationship. This parallel relationship may range from synonymy to some sort of vague semantic similarity such as both nouns referring to the same type of object. For example, *dào-zéi* 'robber thief' is a case of synonymy; *huā-mù* 'flower tree = vegetation' is a case where 'flower' and 'tree' may be described as the same type of object: both are plants commonly seen in gardens or in the countryside. The compounds in this class are the least productive. Each one must be memorized, and the creation of new parallel compounds is restricted, even when the meaning of the compound is practically literal, not idiomatic. In addition, a compound of this class is usually an irreversible compound: the order of the constituents is fixed. For example, *dào-zéi* 'robber thief' cannot be **zéi-dào*; *niú-mă* 'cattle-horse = livestock' cannot be **mă-niú*; *qián-cái* 'money wealth' cannot be **cái-qián*; *huā-mù* 'flower tree' cannot be **mù-huā*. To distinguish this class of fixed compounds from conjoined nouns, we observe that there is often a pause between conjoined nouns and that, furthermore, their order of appearance is free; for example, *zázhì, bàozhì* 'magazines and newspapers' and *bàozhì, zázhì* 'newspapers and magazines' are phrases of conjoined nouns and not compounds. The comma signals the possibility of a pause in speech, and there is no restriction in the relative order of the two nouns.

Finally, we should mention that there are also nominal compounds whose components belong to other parts of speech besides nouns. For example, *kāiguān* 'open-shut = switch' is a nominal compound composed of two verbs, *kāi* 'open' and *guān* 'shut'; *fēijī* 'airplane' has two constituents, one a verb, *fēi* 'to fly', and one a noun, *jī* 'machine'. Nominal compounds of this type, however, are predominantly idiomatic, and they usually do not represent the results of productive compounding processes.

3.2.3 Verbal Compounds

There are two basic semantic relations between the constituents of verb compounds. Hence, in terms of the semantic relations between the constituents, the vast majority of verb compounds can be classified into two types: the resultative verb compound and the parallel verb compound. Given the appropriate verb, one can freely create new resultative verb compounds and new parallel verb compounds. The resultative verb compounds are especially important in Mandarin, as they are widely used in both speech and writing; we will begin our presentation with them.

A. Resultative Verb Compounds

The *resultative verb compound*, or *RVC*, is always composed of two elements, although each element may be a compound itself.[6] A two-element verb compound is called a resultative verb compound if the second element signals some *result* of the action or process conveyed by the first element. There are several different kinds of results that can be expressed by an RVC:

(i) Cause:

(68) wǒ   bǎ   chá   —   bēi   dǎ   —   pò   LE
      I   BA   tea   —   cup   hit   —   broken PFV/CRS

I broke the teacup.

(69) tā   bǎ   mén   lā   —   kāi   LE
      3sg   BA   door pull   —   open PFV/CRS

S/He pulled the door open.

(ii) Achievement:

(70) wǒ   bǎ   nèi   —   ge   zì
      I   BA   that —   CL   character

      xiě   —   qīngchu   LE
      write —   clear   PFV/CRS

I wrote that character clearly.

(71) tā   mǎi   —   dào   —   le
      3sg   buy   —   arrive —   PFV

      nèi   —   běn   zìdiǎn
      that —   CL   dictionary

S/he managed to buy that dictionary.

(iii) Direction:

(72) tā   tiào —   guò   —   qu   LE
      3sg   jump —   cross —   go   PFV/CRS

S/He jumped across.

(73) tāmen   pǎo   —   chū   —   lái   LE
      they   run   —   exit   —   come   PFV/CRS

They came running out.

(iv) "Phase":

(74) tā   —   de   qián   yòng   —   wán   LE
      3sg   —   GEN   money use   —   finish PFV/CRS

His/Her money is all used up.

(75) bǎ   diànshì   guān   —   diào
      BA   TV   close   —   away

Turn off the TV.

Because the directional and "phase" types of RVCs have certain unique structural properties, they will be discussed separately below.

RVCs have several important characteristics. First, they can occur in the *potential* form. The potential form of an RVC involves the insertion of *-de-* 'obtain' or *-bu-* 'not' between the two constituents. The insertion of *-de-* has the effect of giving the compound an affimative potential meaning, 'can', whereas the insertion of *-bu-* gives the compound a negative potential meaning, 'cannot'. For example:

(76) *a.*   tā   tiào   —   de   —   guò   —   qù
            3sg   jump   —   obtain   —   cross   —   go

S/He can jump across.

b.   tā   tiào   —   bu   —   guò   —   qù
       3sg   jump   —   not   —   cross   —   go

S/He cannot jump across.

The English renditions of the Mandarin sentences (76) *a* and (76) *b* with the auxiliary verbs 'can' and 'cannot' do not completely convey the meanings of the Mandarin potential forms. The presence of the infix *-de-* in an RVC means that the action or process denoted by the first constituent of the compound *can* have the result denoted by the second constituent of the compound. The presence of the negative infix -*bu*- signals that the action *cannot* have the result. Although we will use the glosses 'can' and 'can't', their actual meanings can perhaps be better conveyed by 'achievable' and 'unachievable'. Thus (76) *a* means that s/he jumps and can achieve getting across, and (76) *b* means that s/he jumps but fails to achieve getting across. This semantic property can be easily understood if we view the function of -*de*- and -*bu*- as similar to that of adverbial elements in Mandarin: the material that follows them is in their ''scope'' (see chapter 8 on adverbs). That is, just as with adverbs and with the negative particle, the meanings 'achievable' and 'unachievable' include the part of the RVC which follows the -*de*- or the -*bu*-, but not what precedes them. So it is only natural that (76) *a* conveys the idea of being able to get across by jumping and (76) *b* the idea of not being able to get across by jumping.[7]

Now that the semantic function of the scope of the adverblike elements -*de*- and -*bu*- is clear, we can see why the auxiliary verb *néng* 'can' may not always be interchangeable with -*de*- and -*bu*- in a resultative verb sentence.[8] To illustrate, let's look again at the potential forms in (76) *a* and *b*. These sentences explicitly mean that the subject initiates the action of jumping, but (76) *a* claims that, in addition to this, s/he is able to get across, while (76) *b* claims that, in spite of this, s/he is not able to get across. Thus it follows that if the subject has, let's say, a broken ankle and can't jump at all, then (76) *b* cannot be used to express this inability. Instead, *bu néng* 'can't' would have to be used:

(77) tā   bu   néng   tiào   —   guò   —   qù
      3sg   not   can   jump   —   cross —   go

  S/He can't jump across (because s/he can't jump).

As Light (1977:35) puts it, to use an RVC, the agent must have initiated the primary action referred to by the compound, while the use of *néng* 'can' only suggests the possibility of initiating the action.

The second characteristic of the RVC is that, unlike most action verbs in Mandarin, which can be reduplicated to indicate delimitative aspect (see section 6.4 of chapter 6 on aspect), RVCs cannot be reduplicated. For example, we have *cháng* 'to taste', *cháng-chang* 'have a taste'; *huódòng* 'take action', *huódong-huódong* 'take some action'; but reduplicated RVCs are unacceptable: **lā-kāi-lā-kāi* 'pull-open—pull-open'; **tiào-guoqu-tiào-guoqu* 'jump-across—jump-across'. Once again, the fact that they cannot be reduplicated to indicate delimitative aspect is directly due to the fact that the primary communicative function of an RVC is to comment on whether the *result* of an action did or did not, can or cannot, take place. Delimitative aspect has to do with doing an action "just a little bit" and is thus incompatible with any comment on its result.

The third characteristic of the RVC is that, except for directional verbs, as noted below, no aspect markers, measure words, or any elements other than the potential infix (-de- and -bu-) may intervene between the two constituents. This property of the RVC distinguishes it from the verb-object compound, which will be described in the next section.

A.1 Directional RVCs

Directional RVCs can be schematized as in (78):[9]

$$(78) \qquad V_1 \qquad - \qquad V_2$$
$$\text{displacement} \qquad \text{direction}$$

An example is sentence (73), repeated here:

(73)   tāmen   pǎo   —   chū   —   lái   LE
          they   run   —   exit   —   come   PFV/CRS

They came running out.

The first verb of the compound, *pǎo* 'run', implies a displacement, and the second verb of the compound, which may itself be a compound, as *chū-lái* 'come out' is, signals the direction in which the subject moves as the result of the displacement.

Let us first discuss the displacement verb. The most obvious type of displacement verb is a verb signaling motion, such as *zǒu* 'walk', *pǎo* 'run', *liú* 'flow', *fēi* 'fly', *gǔn* 'roll'. Another type of displacement verb is an action verb that inherently implies that the direct object undergoes a change of location: for example, *bān* 'remove', *rēng* 'throw', *sòng* 'send, give', *jì* 'to mail', *lǐng* 'lead (to somewhere)', *jǔ* 'lift', *tuī* 'push'. A third type of displacement verb is an action verb that may cause the direct object to undergo displacement; for instance, *dǎ* 'to hit, beat' is not a verb that inherently implies displacement on the part of the direct object, but it is possible that the action of beating or hitting will cause the direct object to move. Thus, we have the RVC *dǎ-chū-lái* 'hit-exit-come = hit someone so that s/he comes out', or the resultative compound *dǎ-jìn-qù* 'hit-enter-go = hit someone so that s/he goes in'.

As for the directional verb, V_2, of the RVCs represented by (78), it can be one of three types.

(i) The first type of directional verb includes *lái* 'come' and *qù* 'go'. As directional verbs in RVCs, *lái* 'come' means 'toward the speaker', and *qù* 'go' means 'away from the speaker'. For example, consider their occurrence in the following two sentences:

(79) tā   sòng – lái   – le   yi   – ge
      3sg   send – come   – PFV   one – CL

      xiāngzi
      suitcase

S/He sent over (toward the speaker) a suitcase.

(80) tā   ná   – qù   – le   liǎng – běn
      3sg   bring – go   – PFV   two   – CL

      shū
      book

S/He took (away from the speaker) two books.

The directional RVC in sentence (79) is *sòng-lái*, where the first part, *sòng* 'send', is a displacement verb that inherently implies a displacement of the direct object, and the second part, *lái*, signals that the displacement is toward the speaker of the sentence. Similarly, the first part of the RVC in sentence (80), *ná* 'bring, take', is a displacement verb that signals a displacement of the direct object, and the second part of the compound signals that the displacement is away from the speaker of the sentence.

   (ii) The second type of directional verb includes the following eight verbs, each of which has a directional meaning when it occurs in an RVC in addition to a verbal meaning when it occurs as an independent verb.[10] In (81) we indicate in the gloss first the independent meaning and then the directional meaning:

(81) shàng   'ascend - up'
      xià   'descend - down'
      jìn   'enter - in'
      chū   'exit - out'
      qǐ   'rise - up'
      huí   'return - back'
      guò   'cross - over'
      kāi   'open - apart, away'

In glossing examples in this book, we will use the independent meaning.

The following sentences illustrate the use of these eight verbs as directional verbs in RVCs:

(82)   tā   <u>dài   —   shàng</u>   —   le   tā   —   de   màozi
       3sg   wear —   ascend   —   PFV   3sg   —   GEN   hat

       S/He put on his/her hat.

(83)   wǒ   <u>fàng   —   xià</u>   wǒ   —   de   shūbāo   le
       I   put   —   descend   I   —   GEN   satchel   CRS

       I laid down my satchel.

(84)   tā   <u>shuō   —   chū</u>   yi   —   ge   bìmì   le
       3sg   speak —   exit   one   —   CL   secret   CRS

       S/He told a secret.

(85)   wǒ   <u>shōu   —   huí</u>   wǒ   —   de   qìche   le
       I   gather —   return   I   —   GEN   car   CRS

       I took back my car.

(86)   tā   <u>zǒu   —   jìn</u>   yi   —   ge   qiú   —   chǎng   le
       3sg   walk —   enter   one   —   CL   ball   —   park   CRS

       S/He walked into a ball park.

(87)   wǒ   <u>tí   —   qǐ</u>   nèi   —   jian   shì   le
       I   mention —   rise   that   —   CL   matter   CRS

       I brought up that matter.

(88)   tā   <u>tiào   —   guò</u>   nèi   —   tiáo   hé   le
       3sg   jump —   cross   that   —   CL   river   CRS

       S/He jumped over that river.

(89)   qǐng   nǐ   <u>tuī   —   kāi</u>   zhèi   —   ge   mén
       please you   push   —   open   this   —   CL   door

Please push this door open.

(iii) The third type of directional verb is formed with a type (ii) directional verb followed by a type (i) directional verb. Thus, if we take any type (ii) directional verb, say, *shàng* 'ascend', and combine it with either member of type (i), we obtain two new double directional verbs: *shàng-lái* 'ascend-come = up toward the speaker'; *shàng-qù* 'ascend-go = up away from the speaker'. Since there are eight members in type (ii) and two members in type (i), we have for this third type sixteen directional verbs. The semantic difference between members of this type and members of type (ii) is that this type of directional verb clarifies the direction of the motion with respect to the speaker, that is, whether it is toward or away from the speaker. For example, in sentence (90), because of the presence of *lái* 'come toward the speaker', we can infer that the speaker was located inside the structure Zhangsan was entering:

(90)   Zhāngsān   <u>zǒu   —   jìn   —   lái</u>   LE
       Zhangsan   walk   —   enter —   come   PFV/CRS

Zhangsan entered (toward the speaker).

Similarly, because of the presence of *qù* 'go away from the speaker', we can infer that the speaker of (91) was located outside the structure Zhangsan was entering:

(91)   Zhāngsān   <u>zǒu   —   jìn   —   qù</u>   LE
       Zhangsan   walk   —   enter —   go   PFV

Zhangsan entered (away from the speaker).

One member of this class may be used with verbs that do not indicate displacement in space, and that is *xià-qù* 'descend-go = down away from the speaker'. The nondisplacement verbs it can occur with in an RVC are all *durative*; that is, the verbal notion may endure for a period of time. When *xià-qù* occurs with such verbs in an RVC it has the meaning 'continue', which can be seen as a metaphoric extension of its directional meaning into the domain of time. Here are some examples:

(92) <u>kàn-xià-qù</u>   'read-continue = keep reading'
     <u>huó-xià-qù</u>   'live-continue = go on living'
     <u>xiě-xià-qù</u>   'write-continue = go on writing'

Of the three types of directional verbs in resultative compounds, the first and the third (that is, those that involve *lái* 'come' or *qù* 'go') allow themselves to be separated, with the direct object of the verb intervening between the displacement verb and the directional verb. Consider, for example, an RVC with a type (i) directional verb, *ná-lái* 'take-come = bring toward the speaker': it is split in (93) by the direct object, *yi-liǎng yínzi* 'one tael of silver':

(93)   tā   <u>ná   –   le</u>   yi   –   liǎng   yínzi   lái
       3sg   take   –   PFV   one   –   tael   silver   come

    S/He brought one tael of silver (toward the speaker).

Similarly, the RVC *gǎn-chū-qù* 'herd-exit-go' (with a type [iii] directional verb) is split in (94) by the direct object *liǎng-zhī gǒu* 'two dogs':

(94)   tā   <u>gǎn   –   le</u>   liǎng   –   zhī   gǒu   <u>chū   –   qù</u>
       3sg   herd   –   PFV   two   –   CL   dog   exit   –   go

    S/He herded two dogs out (away from the speaker).

For an RVC containing the third type of directional verb, a further variation involving separation of the constituents of the compound is possible. Recall that the third type of directional verb involves two constituents: a directional verb of the second type followed by a directional verb of the first type. If that second verb is *lái*, then not only can we place the direct object between the displacement verb and the entire directional verb, but we can also place the direct object between the last directional-verb constituent and the type (ii) directional verb.

Schematically, we can represent both of these types of separation in directional RVCs as follows:

(95) *a.* V_1 +   direct object   + V_2

               displacement   type (i) or (iii)
               verb   directional verb

b.　　V₁ + type (ii) directional verb + direct object + type (i) directional verb, if it is *lái*

For example, take the RVC *duān-shàng-lái* 'serve-ascend-come': (96) *a* and *b* illustrate the two different separations of the constituents of this compound.

(96) *a.*

tā	duān	—	le	yi	—	wǎn	tāng
3sg	serve	—	PFV	one	—	bowl	soup

shàng	—	lái	le
ascend	—	come	CRS

S/He served up a bowl of soup (toward the speaker).

b.

tā	duān	—	shàng	yi	—	wǎn	tāng
3sg	serve	—	ascend	one	—	bowl	soup

lái	le
come	CRS

S/He served up a bowl of soup (toward the speaker).

c.

tā	duān	—	shàng	—	lái	—	le	yi
3sg	serve	—	ascend	—	come	—	PFV	one

—	wǎn	tāng
—	bowl	soup

S/He served up a bowl of soup (toward the speaker).

With ordinary direct objects, if the type (i) directional verb is *qù*, however, then the (95) *b* option is not available:

(97) *a.*

tāmen	gǎn	tā	chū	—	qù	le
they	chase	3sg	exit	—	go	CRS

They chased him/her out (away from the speaker).

b.

*tāmen	gǎn	—	chū	tā	qù	le
they	chase	—	exit	3sg	go	CRS

As far as we can ascertain, there is no semantic distinction between a directional RVC that is split by the direct object and one that is intact. Thus, for instance, sentences *a*, *b*, and *c* of (96) are synonymous. It should be obvious that when a directional RVC is split as in (96) *a*, the compound can no longer occur in the potential form, since it will be impossible to place the potential infixes *-de-* and *-bu-*. When an RVC is split as in schema (95) *b*, however, the compound may occur in the potential form; the potential infix will be placed between the displacement verb and the type (ii) directional verb:

(98) tā   <u>duān — de — shàng</u> yi   — wǎn tāng lái
      3sg serve — can — ascend one — bowl soup come

S/He can serve up one bowl of soup (toward the speaker).

Chao (1968) has observed that when the direct object of an RVC composed of a displacement verb and a type (i) or type (iii) directional verb indicates a place, the compound *must* be split. If the directional verb is of type (i), the locational object will obligatorily be placed between the displacement verb and the directional verb; if the directional verb is of type (iii), the compound must be split according to the format of (95) *b*. For example, consider, first, the RVC with a type (i) directional verb *shàng-qù* 'ascend-go' in sentences *a* and *b* of (99):

(99) *a*. wǒmen <u>shàng</u>   shān   <u>qù</u>
           we   ascend   mountain   go

Let's get up the mountain.

   b. *wǒmen <u>shàng</u>   —   <u>qù</u>   shān
          we   ascend   —   go   mountain

In (99), the direct object, *shān* 'mountain', is a place noun, and thus the compound, *shàng-qù*, must be split; when it is not split, the sentence, as illustrated by (99) *b*, is ungrammatical.

Consider next the RVC with a type (iii) directional verb *pǎo-jìn-qù* 'run-enter-go' in sentences *a*, *b*, and *c* of (100):

(100) *a*. tā   <u>pǎo</u>   —   <u>jìn</u>   wūzi   qù   le
            3sg run   —   enter house   go   CRS

S/He ran into the house (away from the speaker).

b.	*tā	pǎo	wūzi	jìn	—	qù	le
	3sg	run	house	enter	—	go	CRS

c.	*tā	pǎo	—	jìn	—	qù	wūzi	le
	3sg	run	—	enter	—	go	house	CRS

In (100), the direct object, *wūzi* 'house', is again a place noun. The compound must be split according to the format of (95) *b*. Hence, (100) *a*, but neither (100) *b* nor (100) *c*, is acceptable.

A.2 Phase RVCs

There are certain RVCs in which the second verb expresses something more like the *type* of action described by the first verb or the degree to which it is carried out than its result. For convenience, we will refer to these as *phase* RVCs. The following are different types of phase RVCs grouped together according to the second part, which expresses the phase of the action in the first verb.

(i) *-Wán* 'finish', which indicates the completion of an action:

(101)	chàng-wán	'sing-finish = finish singing'
	niàn-wán	'study-finish = finish studying'
	nòng-wán	'do-finish = finish doing'
	tuō-wán	'take off—finish = finish taking off'

(ii) *-Zháo* 'be on target':

(102)	cāi-zháo	'guess-be on target = guess right'
	shuō-zháo	'say-be on target = say (it) right'
	yòng-zháo	'use-be on target = get to use'
	zhǎo-zháo	'search-be on target = find'

(iii) *-Zhù* 'hold on':

(103)	zhàn-zhù	'stand-hold on = stand still'
	zhuā-zhù	'grab-hold on = grab onto'
	tíng-zhù	'stop-hold on = stop'
	guǎn-zhù	'control-hold on = control'
	liú-zhù	'keep-hold on = detain'

(iv) *-Dào*: The meaning of *-dào* in the following RVCs is derived from its independent verbal meaning 'arrive'. It can be vaguely described as 'reach, succeed' and thus has a meaning similar to the meaning of *-zháo* in (ii).

(104) kàn-dào   'see-arrive = succeed in seeing'
       zhǎo-dào   'search-arrive = succeed in searching'
       mèng-dào   'dream-arrive = dream of'
       xiǎng-dào   'think-arrive = think of'

(v) *-Hǎo*: As an independent verb, *hǎo* means 'good'. As the second verb of an RVC, it has the meaning of 'completing the task signaled by the first verb', similar to but not identical with the meaning of *-wán* 'finish'.

(105) xiě-hǎo   'write-complete task = complete the task of writing'
       zuò-hǎo   'do-complete task = complete the task of doing'
       tián-hǎo   'fill out-complete task = complete the task of filling out'
       suàn-hǎo   'calculate-complete task = complete the task of calculating'

A.3 Metaphorical RVCs

This type of RVC involves a result, V_2, which is often used in a metaphorical sense. A V_2 typically used in the metaphorical sense is *sǐ* 'dead', as for example, in:

(106) lèi-sǐ   'tire-dead = tire to death'
       qì-sǐ   'anger-dead = anger to death'
       xià-sǐ   'frighten-dead = frighten to death'

Whether these compounds convey their literal meanings or their metaphorical meanings depends on the pragmatic context, of course.

There is also a directional verb, *chū-lái* 'exit−come', which is used in a figurative sense, meaning 'find out', or 'come out', to form RVCs with verbs of inquiry, verbs of perception, or verbs of saying. With verbs of inquiry, we have, for example, such RVCs as:

(107) wèn-chū-lái   'question-exit-come = find out by questioning'
       chá-chū-lái   'investigate-exit-come = find out by investigating'
       sōu-chū-lái   'search-exit-come = find out by searching'

With verbs of perception, we have such RVCs as:

(108) kàn-chū-lái   'see-exit-come = find out by looking'
      wén-chū-lái   'smell-exit-come = find out by smelling'
      xiǎng-chū-lái 'think-exit-come = find out by thinking'

With verbs of saying, we have such RVCs as:

(109) shuō-chū-lái   'speak-exit-come = get something out by saying it'
      hǎn-chū-lái   'yell-exit-come = yell out'

A.4 RVCs Obligatorily in Potential Form

There are a few result verbs, V_2, whose presence in a RVC means that the compound can occur only in the potential form. These result verbs include the following:

(i) -*Guò* 'surpass', as in:

(110) shuō-de-guò   'talk-can-surpass = can outtalk'
      dǎ-bu-guò   'fight-can't-surpass = can't outfight'
      pǎo-de-guò   'run-can-surpass = can outrun'
      chī-bu-guò   'eat-can't-surpass = can't outeat'

(ii) -*Qǐ* 'to afford', as in:

(111) mǎi-de-qǐ   'buy-can-afford = can afford to buy'
      chī-bu-qǐ   'eat-can't-afford = cannot afford to eat'
      zhù-de-qǐ   'live-can-afford = can afford to live'
      chuān-bu-qǐ 'wear-can't-afford = cannot afford to wear'
      kàn-de-qǐ   {'see-can-afford = can afford to see'}
               {'have regard for (someone)'}
      kàn-bu-qǐ   {'see-can't-afford = cannot afford to see'}
               {'don't have any regard for (someone)'}

(iii) -*Liǎo*: This verb has lost the meaning of 'finish', which it had at an earlier stage of the language. It can combine with most verbs to form RVCs, but the resultative compounds formed with -*liǎo* must occur in the potential form, as in these examples:

(112) gài-de-liǎo   'can cover'
      zuò-bu-liǎo   'cannot seat'

| cún-de-liǎo | 'can save (money, goods)' |
| chī-bu-liǎo | 'cannot finish eating' |

The major types of RVCs have been presented in this section. Our discussion, however, has by no means been exhaustive. There are a great many RVCs that must be learned one by one because their meaning cannot be derived from those of their constituents plus the relation between their components: for example, *kàn-kāi* 'see-open = be understanding, see the light'; *kǎo-qǔ* 'take an exam-obtain = be admitted (to a school)'; *ná-dìng* 'take-settle = make up one's mind'.

B. Parallel Verb Compounds

Parallel verb compounds are similar in nature to parallel nominal compounds. The two verbs that constitute a parallel verb compound either are synonymous or signal the same type of predicative notions. Analogous to the parallel nominal compounds, the parallel verb compounds may be simply represented by this scheme:

(113) V_1 V_2

The vast majority of parallel verb compounds have developed as the Mandarin language, which once contained a predominance of monosyllabic words, has gained an ever-increasing number of polysyllabic words (see chapter 2 on typological description and the concluding paragraphs of the discussion of suffixes in section 3.1.2.C in this chapter). For example, the notion 'fortunate' was expressed by the monosyllabic word xìng at an earlier stage of the language; in modern Mandarin, this notion is expressed by the parallel compound *xìng-fú* 'fortunate-blessed = fortunate'. The notion 'celebrate' was formerly qìng, but is *qìng-zhù* 'celebrate-bless = celebrate' in modern Mandarin. In some instances, the monosyllabic word is in free variation with the compound. For example, *mǎi* 'buy' and *gòu-mǎi* 'buy-buy = buy' are interchangeable in modern Mandarin. Often the rhythm of the sentence may determine which form is preferred. For instance, (114) *a* and *b* are synonymous:

(114) *a.*   wǒ   —   de   gōngsī   gòu   —   mǎi   shāngpǐn
              I   — GEN   company   buy   merchandise

My company buys merchandise.

b.	wǒ	–	de	gōngsī	<u>mǎi</u>	shāngpǐn
	I	–	GEN	company	buy	merchandise

My company buys merchandise.

The *a* sentence, with the compound *gòu-mǎi*, is stylistically preferred, perhaps partly because it preserves the rhythm of the sentence:

(115)   /ˊ   /ˊ   /ˊ   /ˊ

The constituents of most parallel verb compounds are of the same syntactic category—they may be both adjectival verbs, both action verbs, both verbs of perception, and so forth. There are a few exceptions, including *yóng-gǎn* 'brave-dare = brave', *chéng-shóu* 'complete-ripe = mature', *piāo-bái* 'bleach-white = bleach', *tān-wū* 'desire greedily filthy = take graft'. As expected, the parallel verb compound itself shares the semantic and syntactic properties of its constituents: if the constituents are both adjectives, the compound is also adjectival, as in *měi-lì* 'beautiful-beautiful = beautiful', *píng-jìng* 'peaceful-quiet = peaceful and quiet'; if the constituents are transitive verbs, the compound is also a transitive verb, as is e.g., *píng-pàn* 'comment: on-judge = judge'. The following are some more examples of parallel verb compounds:

(i) V_1 and V_2 are synonymous or nearly synonymous:

(116)	<u>cí-shàn</u>	'benevolent'	<u>pí-fá</u>	'tired'
	<u>jiān-nán</u>	'difficult'	<u>pín-qióng</u>	'poor'
	<u>dān-dú</u>	'alone'	<u>hán-lěng</u>	'cold'
	<u>xū-wěi</u>	'fake'	<u>qí-guài</u>	'strange'
	<u>guāi-qiǎo</u>	'clever'	<u>huī-huáng</u>	'luminous, splendid'
	<u>jiàn-zhú</u>	'build'	<u>jiǎn-chá</u>	'examine (something)'
	<u>qiān-yí</u>	'remove'	<u>mó-cā</u>	'rub'
	<u>yí-huò</u>	'suspect'	<u>bāng-zhù/fú-zhù</u>	'help'
	<u>guī-huí</u>	'return to'	<u>zhì-liáo</u>	'cure'
	<u>fáng-shǒu</u>	'defend'	<u>chǒng-bài</u>	'worship'

(ii) V_1 and V_2 are similar in meaning:

(117)	<u>tòng-kǔ</u>	'painful-bitter = painful and bitter'
	<u>zhēn-què</u>	'real-certain = authentic'

bēi-shāng	'sad-hurt = grieved'
pò-jiù	'broken-old = broken and old (worn out)'
yuán-huá	'round-smooth = round and smooth'
xián-míng	'virtuous-enlightened = virtuous and enlightened'
guǎng-dà	'extensive-big = vast'
piāo-liú	'drift-flow = drift'
xiǎn-yǎng	'manifest-display = show off'
fàng-qì	'loosen-abandon = give up'
fēn-sàn	'separate-disperse = separate and disperse'
fú-yǎng	'support-care for = support and care for'
tì-huàn	'replace-change = replace'

3.2.4 Subject-Predicate Compounds

The *subject-predicate compound*, as its name suggests, is composed of two elements, whose relation is one in which the first element is the subject of the second verbal element.[11] Since a simple declarative sentence may also be composed of a subject followed by a verbal element, one may wonder how a subject-predicate compound is distinct from a subject-predicate sentence. There are several characteristics of the subject-predicate compound that make it distinct from a simple sentence. First, the compound is always a verb, although occasionally it may also serve as a noun. Second, a number of subject-predicate compounds have idiomatic meanings. Third, most of them contain at least one bound morpheme, that is, a morpheme that cannot occur in isolation as a word and must combine with some other morpheme to form a word. The major difference between a compound and a simple declarative sentence is, of course, the various syntactic properties that a sentence has. For example, we can negate a sentence by placing the negative morpheme between the subject and the predicate; we can form an A-not-A question by using the predicate as the A element; we can insert time adverbs between the subject and the predicate; and so forth. A compound, being a word, would not be able to undergo these processes. There are, however, certain subject-predicate compounds that can function either as compounds or as simple subject-predicate declarative sentences. For example, consider *tóu-téng* 'head-ache', which can function as a single adjectival verb; that is, we can view it as a compound on the basis of the following evidence.

(i) Like most stative verbs, it can be modified by an intensifier, such as *hĕn* 'very':

(118)   Zhāngsān   hĕn   tóu   —   téng
         Zhangsan   very   head   —   ache

Zhangsan has a severe headache.

(ii) Like the regular verb of a sentence, it can be negated:

(119) Zhāngsān   bu   tóu   –   téng
       Zhangsan   not   head –   ache

Zhangsan doesn't have a headache.

(iii) Like the regular verb of a sentence, it can be modified by an adverb, such as *cháng-chang* 'often':

(120) Zhāngsān   cháng   –   chang   tóu   –   téng
       Zhangsan   often   head –   ache

Zhangsan often has headaches.

(iv) Like the regular verb of a sentence, it can be the A element in an A-not-A question:

(121) Zhāngsān   tóu   –   téng   bu   tóu   –   téng ?
       Zhangsan   head –   ache   not   head –   ache

Does Zhangsan have a headache?

On the other hand, the same unit, *tóu téng* 'head ache', can also function as a simple declarative sentence in which the subject is the noun *tóu* 'head' and the predicate is the verb *téng* 'ache'. Parallel to the properties illustrated by sentences (118)–(121), we can show that *téng* 'ache' is the verb and *tóu* 'head' the subject with sentences (122)–(125):

(i) *Téng* is modified by the intensifier *hěn* 'very':

(122)   tóu   hěn   téng
        head   very   ache

(My) head aches a lot.

(ii) *Téng* is negated:

(123)   tóu   bu   téng
        head   not   ache

(My) head doesn't ache.

(iii) *Téng* is modified by an adverb, such as *cháng-chang* 'often':

(124)   tóu   cháng   —   chang   téng
         head   often   ache

(My) head often aches.

(iv) *Téng* serves as the A element in an A-not-A question:

(125)   tóu   téng   bu   téng ?
         head   ache   not   ache

Does (your) head ache?

There are only a few subject-predicate compounds that can also function as simple declarative sentences. Obviously, the constituents of those compounds that can are not bound morphemes. Examples other than *tóu-téng* 'head-ache' include *tóu-hūn* 'head-dizzy' and *yǎn-huā* 'eye-fuzzy = fuzzy visioned'.

An examination of the subject-predicate compound yields the observation that the predicate constituent is in most cases an adjectival verb. Only a few cases of action verbs serving as the predicate constituent can be found; for example, in *bīng-biàn* 'soldier-rebel = to mutiny', *biàn* is an action verb; in *qì-chuǎn* 'breath-pant = have asthma', *chuǎn* is an action verb; in *dì-zhèn* 'earth-quake = to have an earthquake', *zhèn* is an action verb. The majority of subject-predicate compounds, which are composed of a subject and a stative predicate, are stative verbs; and, in general, those subject-predicate compounds that are composed of a subject and an action verb also function as action verbs.

The following are examples of subject-predicate compounds:

(126) zuǐ-yìng   'mouth-hard = argumentative'
       yǎn-hóng   'eye-red = covetous'
       liǎn-nèn   'face-tender = bashful'
       shǒu-jǐn   'hand-tight = stingy'
       shǒu-qín   'hand-diligent = diligent (in manual work)'
       shǒu-dú   'hand-poisonous = vicious'
       xīn-suān   'heart-sore = distressed'
       xīn-ruǎn   'heart-soft = softhearted'
       dǎn-hán   'gall-cold = fearful'
       dǎn-xiǎo   'gall-small = cowardly'
       dǎn-dà   'gall-big = brave'
       mìng-kǔ   'life-bitter = unfortunate'

xìng-jí	'temper-anxious = impatient'
nián-qīng	'age-light = young'
shēng-zhāng	'noise−open up = to make noise (about it)'

3.2.5 Verb-Object Compounds

The *verb-object compound*, as its name indicates, is composed of two constituents having the syntactic relation of a verb and its direct object.[12] The vast majority of verb-object compounds are verbs. Like the subject-predicate compound, which must be distinguished from subject-predicate sentences, the verb-object compound forces us to establish criteria for distinguishing verb-object compounds from verb-object phrases. There are several conditions under which a verb-object construction is classified as a compound in traditional Chinese grammar (see Chao [1968:415]). Any one of these properties will render a verb-object construction a compound:

1. One or both of the constituents being bound morphemes
2. Idiomaticity of the meaning of the entire unit
3. Inseparability or limited separability of the constituents

For example, *gé-mìng* 'remove the mandate−life = revolution' satisfies all three conditions. First, *gé* is a bound morpheme. Second, the meaning of the construction is idiomatic, that is, it is not derivable from the meaning of the constituents. Third, the construction is inseparable, that is, nothing may intervene between the constituents. To take another example, in *shāng-fēng* 'hurt-wind = catch cold', neither of the constituents are bound, but the meaning of the entire unit is idiomatic, and there is limited separability of the two constituents: thus one could modify the second constituent, *fēng*, with *dà* 'big' and produce the construction:

(127) shāng-dà-fēng   'hurt-big-wind = catch a bad cold'

One could also put a perfective aspect marker such as *-le* after the first constituent, *shēng*:

(128) shāng-le-fēng   'caught cold'

We cannot, however, place the second constituent in the sentence-initial position as a topic, as we can the syntactic direct object of a verb:

(129) *a.*   *fēng,   shāng   LE
              wind,   hurt   PFV/CRS

b.   xiāzi,   zhuā   —   dào   le
       shrimp,   catch   —   succeed   CRS

The shrimp, (I) have caught it.

Consider a third example, *shuì-jiào* 'sleep-sleep = sleep'; the second constituent is a bound morpheme, which occurs only in this compound. The meaning of *shuì-jiào* is synonymous with *shuì*, which occurs freely as a verb. There is practically no constraint on the separability of the two constituents, though. In other words, syntactically, the compound *shuì-jiào* behaves completely like a phrase composed of a verb and an object. For instance, the second constituent, like the object of a verb in a sentence, can be modified:

(130)   shuì   —   yi   —   jiào
         sleep   —   one   —   sleep

Take a nap.

(131)   shuì   —   le   sān   —   ge   zhōngtóu   de   jiào
         sleep —   PFV   three —   CL   hour   NOM   sleep

(I) slept for three hours.

The first constituent, like the verb in a sentence, can take an aspect marker:

(132)   wǒ   shuì   —   le   —   jiào   le
         I   sleep   —   PFV   —   sleep   CRS

I've slept.

The second constituent can be placed in the sentence-initial position, usually when it is modified, to become a topic:

(133)   zhèi   yi   jiào,   shuì   de   zhēn   hǎo
         this   one   sleep   sleep   CSC   real   well

I had a real good sleep.

The three examples of verb-object compounds given above illustrate that the verb-object compounds do not form a uniform group with respect to the three properties stated earlier. We know that idiomaticity of compounds is always a matter of degree. (The issue of idiomaticity is also discussed above in section 3.2.2 on nominal compounds.) The examples show that even the inseparability of the constituents varies among the verb-object compounds. Some, a small minority, are completely inseparable. These are usually highly idiomatic, and their constituents are bound. The vast majority of verb-object compounds allow their constituents to be separated. In general, separation of the constituents of verb-object compounds may be classified as one of the following types.

(i) Separation by an aspect marker:

(134) Zhāngsān   bì   —   le   —   yè   le
      Zhangsan   finish — PFV —   instruction CRS

Zhangsan has graduated. (bì-yè 'finish-instruction = graduate')

(135) tā   hái   méi   lǐ   —   guo   —   fǎ
       3sg   still   not   arrange — EXP   —   hair

S/He still hasn't ever had a haircut. (lǐ-fǎ 'arrange-hair = have a haircut')

(ii) Separation by a measure phrase:

(136) tā   gěi   wǒ   xíng   —   le   yí   —   ge   lǐ
       3sg   to   I   perform — PFV one —   CL   salutation

S/He saluted me once. (xíng-lǐ 'perform-salutation = salute')

(137) wǒ   kòu   —   le   liǎng   —   ge   tóu
       I   knock   —   PFV   two   —   CL   head

I kowtowed twice. (kòu-tóu 'knock-head = kowtow')

(138) tā   liú   —   guo   yi   —   cì   bīng
       3sg   glide   —   EXP   one   —   time   ice

S/He skated once. (liú-bīng 'glide-ice = skate')

(iii) Separation by other modifiers of the object constituent:

(139) nǐ   bié   shēng   tā   —   de   qì
       you   don't   grow   3sg   —   GEN   anger

Don't be angry with him/her! (shēng-qì 'grow-anger = be angry')

(140) tā   yòu   sù   shénme   kǔ?
       3sg   again   tell   what   bitterness

What is s/he complaining about? (sù-kǔ 'tell-bitterness = complain')

(iv) Placing the object constituent of the compound in a position preceding the verb constituent:

(141) tā   lián   wǔ   dōu   bu   tiào
       3sg   even   dance   all   not   dance

S/He won't even dance. (tiào-wǔ 'dance-dance = to dance')

(142) zhèi   —   ge   huǎng   wǒmen   bu   néng   shuō
       this   —   CL   lie   we   not   can   say

This lie we cannot tell. (shuō-huǎng 'say-lie = to lie')

In general, (iv) represents the most drastic type of separation of the constituents of a verb-object compound. Consequently, many verb-object compounds cannot undergo the (iv) type of separation.

Since there is no general principle to tell us which verb-object compounds can undergo what sort of separation processes, the separability of each verb-object compound will have to be learned individually. We have said, however, that most of the verb-object compounds can undergo separation of their constituents, and we have also noted that (iv), placing the object constituent in front of the verb constituent, is not widely applicable. Thus, we can state that, by and large, verb-object compounds may undergo separation processes (i), (ii), and (iii).

Another important characteristic shared by the vast majority of verb-object compounds is that they don't take a direct object. Of course, a great number of verb-object compounds function as intransitive verbs; they would not be expected to take a direct object. Even when they have what might appear to a speaker of

English to be transitivelike meanings, though, they usually don't take a direct object. Here are some examples:

(143) <u>kāi-dāo</u>   'open-knife = operate on'
       <u>xiào-láo</u>   'render-effort = serve'
       <u>mǎn-yì</u>   'full-sentiment = be satisfied with'
       <u>zhào-xiàng</u>   'reflect-image = photograph'
       <u>xíng-lǐ</u>   'perform-salutation = salute'
       <u>jié-hūn</u>   'tie-marriage = marry'
       <u>kāi-wánxiào</u>   'make-joke = joke with, make fun of'

What would be the direct object of the English equivalents of these verb-object compounds appears in Mandarin either as a benefactive phrase (with *gěi*) or in a coverb phrase (see chapter 10 for benefactives and chapter 9 for coverbs). In each of the following three sentences, we see a benefactive noun phrase marked by the benefactive marker *gěi* 'to, for' with a verb-object compound verb that has an apparently transitive meaning:

(144)   yīshēng   gěi   tā   <u>kāi dāo</u>
        doctor   to   3sg   operate

The doctor operated on him/her.

(145)   wǒ   gěi   tā   <u>zhào-xiàng</u>
        I   to   3sg   photograph

I photographed him/her.

(146)   wǒ   gěi   tā   <u>xíng-lǐ</u>
        I   to   3sg   salute

I saluted him/her.

In these sentences, (147)−(149), we find a coverb phrase:

(147)   wǒ   gēn   tā   <u>jié-hūn</u>
        I   with   3sg   marry

I'll marry him/her.

(148)   wǒ   duì   tā   xiào-láo
         I   to   3sg   serve

I served him/her.

(149)   wǒ   gēn   tā   kāi-wánxiào
         I   with   3sg   joke

I am joking with him/her.

Another way to express what might be taken to be the direct object of some verb-object compounds with transitive meanings is to use a possessive phrase before the object constituent. Here are two illustrations:

(150)   wǒ   kāi   tā   —   de   wánxiào
         I   make   3sg   —   GEN   joke

I made fun of him/her.

(151)   wǒ   bāng   tā   —   de   máng
         I   help   3sg   —   GEN   ~

I helped him/her. (bāng-máng 'help- ~ = to help')

Some examples of other verb-object compounds that allow what could be understood as their direct object to be expressed as a possessive phrase before the object constituent are: chī-dòufu 'eat-bean:curd = to tease', chī-cù 'eat-vinegar = to be jealous of', shòu-zuì 'receive-retribution = suffer, be wronged'.

(152)   tā   chī   wǒ   —   de   dòufu
         3sg   eat   I   —   GEN   bean:curd

S/He is teasing me.

(153)   nǐ   chī   tā   —   de   cù
         you   eat   3sg   —   GEN   vinegar

You are jealous of him/her.

There are a few verb-object compounds with transitive meanings which do take a direct object—for example, *guān-xīn* 'involve-heart = be concerned about', *huái-yí* 'harbor-doubt = be suspicious of', *zhù-yì* 'fix-attention = pay attention to', *chū-bàn* 'issue-edition' = publish, *tí-yì* 'suggest-proposal = propose', *dé-zuì* 'obtain-offense = offend', as in:

(154)　wǒ　　hěn　　guānxīn　　tā
　　　　I　　very　concerned　3sg

I am very concerned about him/her.

(155)　tā　　　zhùyì　　　nèi　　−　　jiàn　　shì
　　　　3sg　pay:attention　that　　−　　CL　　matter

S/He is paying attention to that matter.

At the beginning of this section, we noted that the vast majority of verb-object compounds function as verbs. There are also some verb-object compounds that function as nouns and adverbs. Here are some examples:

(i) Verb-object compounds as nouns:

(156) dāng-jú　　　　'be at-situation = authority'
　　　 dǒng-shì　　　'arrange-affair = member of board'
　　　 dāng-chāi　　'be at-order = messenger'
　　　 lǐng-shì　　　'lead-affair = consul (in foreign service)'
　　　 chǎo-fàn　　　'fry-rice = fried rice'
　　　 xíng-zhèng　　'execute-policy = administration'
　　　 zhěn-tóu　　　'rest-head = pillow'

(ii) Verb-object compounds as adverbs:

(157) dāng-shí　　　'be at-time = at the time'
　　　 zhào-cháng　'follow-normal = as usual'
　　　 dào-dǐ　　　'reach-bottom = in the end'
　　　 zhào-yàng　　'follow-pattern = likewise'
　　　 zhuǎn-yǎn　　'turn-eye = instantly'

The following sentences illustrate the use of these adverbs:

(158) wǒmen zhào-cháng gōngzuò
      we   as:usual   work

We work as usual.

(159) tā   dāng — shí   bu   zài   Měiguó
      3sg   at:the:time   not   at   America

At the time s/he was not in America.

(160) nǐ   dào — dǐ   yào   shénme?
      you   in:the:end   want   what

What do you want in the end?

We will sum up this section on the verb-object compound with a historical note. We have observed that idiomaticity and separability of the verb-object compound cannot be predicted on a regular basis. Some verb-object compounds are highly idiomatic; some, less idiomatic; some, not very idiomatic. Similarly, some verb-object compounds are completely inseparable; some are separable to a certain degree; others are almost like a regular verb-plus-object phrase in terms of separability. In other words, for both idiomaticity of meaning and separability of constituents, the behavior of verb-object compounds forms a continuum, with any specific compound falling at some point on the continuum. This continuum can be seen as a result of the fact that verb-object compounds are historically formed from verb-plus-object phrases: that is, certain verb-plus-object phrases have fused together through time to become compounds either as the verb or the object or both have lost their independent free morpheme status, or as the construction developed idiomatic meaning. Since such fusing processes in a language are never abrupt but are instead gradual, occurring over a long period of time as a verb-plus-object phrase develops into a completely fused word that is inseparable and completely idiomatic in meaning (such as dān-xīn 'bear-heart = to worry'), different verb-object compounds may be at different points along this path. The result of this historical process at any given time is a continuum. We have seen many examples exhibiting different degrees of idiomaticity in meaning and different degrees of separability of their constituents. What is reflected here as a continuum with regard to the two properties of verb-object compounds in Mandarin is a general phenomenon in all languages: all aspects and structures of a language change in time, and while structural change from one type to another is always time-consuming, not all members of one structural type undergoing a change march shoulder to shoulder in their rate of change.

3.2.6 Antonymous Adjectives Forming Nominal Compounds

The semantic relation between the adjectives in this class of compounds is one of antonymy. The compound formed by two antonymous adjectives is, however, a noun, and the meaning of this noun is a quality whose bipolar extremes are signaled by the two adjectival constituents.

$$(161) \quad V_1 \quad - \quad V_2$$
$$\qquad\quad \text{adjective} \quad \text{adjective}$$

V_1 and V_2 are antonyms, and the combination is a noun.

The following examples are illustrations:

(162) hǎo-huài   'good-bad = quality'
       dà-xiǎo   'big-small = size'
       cháng-duǎn   'long-short = length'
       lěng-rè   'cold-hot = temperature'
       gāo-ǎi   'tall-short = height'
       kuài-màn   'fast-slow = speed'
       hòu-báo   'thick-thin = thickness'
       zhēn-jiǎ   'true-false = truthfulness'

It is obvious from the above examples that the antonymous compounds always have the constituent indicating the positive pole preceding the constituent indicating the negative pole. This convention for the ordering of the constituents of these compounds is irreversible.

3.2.7 Minor Types of Compounds

In this chapter, we have presented all the major types of compounds in Mandarin Chinese: nominal compounds composed of nouns, resultative verb compounds, parallel verb compounds, autonymous adjective compounds functioning as nouns, subject-predicate compounds, and verb-object compounds. There are a small number of other compounds in Mandarin which don't belong to any of these major types. We will now cite some examples for each of these minor types.

(i) Adjective-noun compound:

(163) <u>xiāng-cài</u>   'fragrant-vegetable = coriander (plant)'
      <u>xiāng-shuǐ</u>   'fragrant-water = perfume'
      <u>rè-xīn</u>   'hot-heart = enthusiastic'
      <u>chòu-dòufu</u>   'smelly-bean:curd = fermented bean curd'
      <u>xū-xīn</u>   'empty-heart = modest'
      <u>huáng-yóu</u>   'yellow-oil = butter'
      <u>dà-mén</u>   'big-door = main door'
      <u>dà-yān</u>   'great-smoke = opium'
      <u>dà-yì</u>   'big-idea = negligent'
      <u>gāo-zú</u>   'high-foot = student (honorific)'
      <u>měi-shú</u>   'beautiful-art = fine art'
      <u>xiǎo-zhàng</u>   'small-account = tip'
      <u>xiǎo-biàn</u>   'minor-convenience = urine, urinate'

(ii) Adverb compounds:

(164) <u>fǎn-zhèng</u>   'reverse-right = anyway'
      <u>gāng-cái</u>   'just-just = just now'
      <u>gēn-běn</u>   'root-root = fundamentally, utterly'
      <u>xiàng-lái</u>   'toward-come = ever'
      <u>zuǒ-yòu</u>   'left-right = approximately'
      <u>zǎo-wǎn</u>   'early-late = sooner or later'

(iii) Noun−measure word/classifier compounds (a generalization one can make about these compounds is that they always indicate a collective or plural noun):

(165) <u>bù-pǐ</u>   'clothes-yardage = material'
      <u>mǎ-pī</u>   'horse-classifier = horses'
      <u>shū-běn</u>   'book-classifier = books'
      <u>chuán-zhī</u>   'boat-classifier = boats'
      <u>yín-liǎng</u>   'silver-tael = quantity of silver'
      <u>dēng-zhǎn</u>   'lamp-classifier = lamps'

(iv) Noun-verb compounds (not to be confused with subject-predicate compounds):

(166) <u>qiāng-bì</u>   'gun-kill = execute by gunfire'
      <u>fēng-xíng</u>   'wind-go = be in fashion'

kǒu-shì	'mouth-exam = oral examination'
lì-yòng	'profit-use = exploit'
bù-xíng	'step-go = walk'

(v) Adverb-verb compounds:

(167)

zì-dòng	'self-move = automatic'
zì-zhì	'self-govern = autonomous (government)'
zì-shā	'self-kill = commit suicide'
hòu-rén	'after-people = posterity'
hòu-shì	'after-affair = funeral affairs'
xiān-tiān	'first-nature = natural endowment'

The vast majority of these minor types of compounds are idioms, as shown by the glosses and the meanings given in the above examples. It is only for the purpose of analysis and illustration that we are presenting them as compounds composed of two separate parts. One who is learning Mandarin will have to memorize all of these compounds and their meanings individually and independent of the nature of their composition.

Notes

1. Much of the discussion in this chapter is adapted from Lu (1965), Chao (1968), Kratochvil (1968), and unpublished work of Benjamin T'sou.

2. For this section, we have benefited from some ideas in unpublished work of Tsang Chui-lim. For further discussion, see also Wang (1947).

3. If the monosyllabic morpheme has the third tone, then the tone sandhi rule applies even though the second syllable of the reduplicated word has the neutral tone, and the third tone of the first syllable becomes a second tone (see the Introduction for a discussion of tone sandhi), though, as stated there, we do not represent that sandhi in our Pīnyīn.

4. Lǎo occurs in a few animal terms, such as lǎohǔ 'tiger', lǎoshu 'mouse, rat', lǎoyīng 'eagle, hawk'. In these terms, however, lǎo has no independent meaning at all. Historically, the lǎo in these terms may be derived from the prefix lǎo-, but in the present-day language, the lǎo in these terms is no longer a separate morpheme and therefore not functioning as a prefix. Each of these terms is a single morpheme in contemporary Mandarin.

5. It has been reported, however, that some dialects allow the suffix -men to occur with nonhuman nouns, including inanimate nouns.

6. For an extensive taxonomic discussion of RVCs, the reader is referred to Chao (1968) and Cartier (1972) and the references cited therein. For an informative discussion of RVCs from a pedagogical point of view, see Light (1977). Our discussion also owes much to Lu (1977) and Teng (1977).

7. Certain RVCs appear to be unable to occur in the potential form, such as:

(i) *a.* | tā | è | — | bìng | le |
   | 3sg | hungry | — | sick | CRS |

S/He got sick from hunger.

   b. | ?tā | è | — | de | — | bìng |
   | 3sg | hungry | — | can | — | sick |

(?S/He can get sick from hunger.)

(ii) *a.* | wǒ | zǒu | — | lèi | le |
   | I | walk | — | tired | CRS |

I got tired from walking.

   b. | ?wǒ | zǒu | — | bu | — | lèi |
   | I | walk | — | can't | — | tired |

(?I can't get tired from walking.)

Such RVCs should not, however, be viewed as exceptions to the general rule that RVCs can occur in the potential form; rather, the sentences seem strange because the meanings 'achievable' and 'unachievable' of *-de-* and *-bu-* imply some effort on the part of the subject, and people do not generally make an effort to achieve such negative results as getting sick or tired.

8. This discussion is adapted from Light (1977).
9. For discussions of directional verbs, see Lin (1977) and Lu (1977).
10. Chao (1968:461) gives a ninth member of this class of directional verbs, *lǒng* 'gather together'; but *lǒng* occurs only in a few idiomatic compounds that do not have any of the properties of the RVCs: for example, *kào-lǒng* 'lean to the Communist side', *lā-lǒng* 'to make political allies'.
11. For further discussion, see Teng (1974*b*).
12. In writing this section we have found Ch'i (1974) helpful.

CHAPTER 4

Simple Declarative Sentences

By *simple sentence* we mean any sentence that has just one verb in it. By contrast, sentences with more than one verb are called *complex sentences*—several types of complex sentences are discussed in chapters 20−24.

In this chapter, we will introduce the basic properties of simple declarative sentences in Mandarin by discussing the elements that comprise them. These elements include the topic, the subject, the noun phrase, and the verb phrase.

4.1 Topic and Subject

In chapter 2 the topic-prominent nature of Mandarin sentences was discussed as a feature that distinguishes Mandarin typologically from many other languages. In this section, the concepts of topic and subject will be presented in more detail.

4.1.1 Characterization of Topic

What is a topic? In chapter 2 the topic was characterized as what the sentence is about. Although it may be an intuitive matter to determine all of the implications of ''what the sentence is about,'' this is essentially a correct characterization. Another way of talking about ''what the sentence is about'' is to say that a topic sets a spatial, temporal, or individual framework within which the main predication holds.[1]

In addition, the topic always refers either to something that the hearer already knows about—that is, it is *definite*—or to a class of entities—that is, it is *generic* (see section 4.2.5 of this chapter for a discussion of definite and generic noun phrases).

Whereas in English nouns are usually marked by articles, which signal whether they are definite or indefinite, in Mandarin this distinction does not need to be marked at all, though *nèi-* 'that' may be used to signal definiteness and *yi-* 'one' may be used to signal indefiniteness. Nouns that are unmarked for definiteness are always interpreted as definite or generic when they are topics, however, and an indefinite noun phrase with *yi-* 'one' or any other numeral in general does not occur as a topic:[2]

(1)	<u>gǒu</u>	wǒ	yǐjing	kàn	–	guo	le
	dog	I	already	see	–	EXP	CRS

$\left\{\begin{array}{l}\text{The dog I have already seen.}\\ \text{Dogs (generic) I have already seen.}\\ \text{(not: A dog I have already seen.)}\end{array}\right\}$

(2)	<u>nèi</u>	–	<u>zhī</u>	<u>gǒu</u>	wǒ	yǐjing	kàn	–	guo	le
	that	–	CL	dog	I	already	see	–	EXP	CRS

That dog I have already seen.

(3)	*<u>yi</u>	–	<u>zhī</u>	gǒu	wǒ	yǐjing	kàn	–	guo le
	one	–	CL	dog	I	already	see	–	EXP CRS

We have given two semantic characteristics of topics: they set a framework in naming what the sentence is about, and they must be either definite or generic. Now we might ask whether there are any formal properties that topics share. The answer is that there are two. First, a topic always occurs in sentence-initial position (unless it is preceded by a connector that links it to the preceding sentence). Second, a topic can be separated from the rest of the sentence (called the *comment*) by a pause or by one of the *pause particles*—*a* (or its phonetic variant *ya*), *me*, *ne* or *ba*—although the use of the pause or the pause particle is optional.[3] Thus sentence (2) above, for example, could also be expressed as:

(4)	nèi	–	zhī gǒu	$\left\{\begin{array}{l}\underline{a}\\ \underline{me}\\ \underline{ne}\end{array}\right\}$,	wǒ	yǐjing	kàn	–	guo	le[4]
	that	–	CL dog		I	already	see	–	EXP	CRS

That dog, I have already seen.

These pause particles may be called *topic markers* since they serve to mark the topic. Topic markers, however, including the simple pause, are not necessary. A cursory survey of Mandarin speech suggests that they are not commonly used at all. There are also dialect variations in terms of the acceptability of some of the topic markers given in sentence (4).

A topic, then, is typically a noun phrase (or a verb phrase) that names what the sentence is about, is definite or generic, occurs in sentence-initial position, and may be followed by a pause or a pause particle.

4.1.2 Characterization of Subject

The *subject* of a sentence in Mandarin is the noun phrase that has a "doing" or "being" relationship with the verb in that sentence. The precise nature of this relationship depends on the semantic makeup of the verb. In fact, each verb requires a specific type of noun phrase to be its subject in a simple sentence. For example, in English a verb such as *elapse* requires a temporal noun phrase as its subject, that is, a noun phrase that expresses a time period; a verb such as *breathe* requires an animate noun phrase as its subject, that is, a noun phrase that refers to something that has life; and a verb such as *happen* requires an abstract noun phrase as its subject, that is, a noun phrase that refers to something other than material objects. Thus the underlined noun phrases in the following sentences are subjects:

(5) <u>wǒ</u>   xǐhuan   chī   píngguǒ
      I   like   eat   apple

I like to eat apples.

(6) <u>Zhāngsān</u>   dǎ   wǒ   le
      Zhangsan   hit   I   CRS

Zhangsan hit me.

(7) <u>nèi   —   suǒ   fángzi</u>   hǎo   guì
      that —   CL   house   very expensive

That house is very expensive.

The one doing the liking in (5) is *wǒ* 'I', the one doing the hitting in (6) is *Zhāngsān*, and the thing being expensive in (7) is *nèi-suǒ fángzi* 'that house'.

4.1.3 Comparison of Topic and Subject

On the basis of the above characterizations of topics and subjects, we can see how these two elements are actually used in simple declarative sentences.[5] Subjects and topics are most easily distinguished in sentences that contain one of each, so we will begin with those.

A. Sentences with Both Subject and Topic

Let us look at sentence (2) again:

(2)	nèi	−	zhī	gǒu	wǒ	yǐjing	kàn	−	guo	le
	that	−	CL	dog	I	already	see	−	EXP	CRS

That dog I have already seen.

In this sentence we can identify the topic as *nèi-zhī gǒu* 'that dog', since it tells what the sentence is about, it is definite, it occurs in sentence-initial position, and it could be followed by a pause particle. It is not the subject, however, since it has no "doing" or "being" relationship with the verb *kàn* 'see'. Instead, the noun that has such a relationship with *kàn* 'see' is *wǒ* 'I'. Sentence (2), then, has both a topic (*nèi-zhī gǒu* 'that dog') and a subject (*wǒ* 'I').

B. Sentences in Which the Subject and the Topic Are Identical

In many sentences the topic noun phrase is the same as the subject noun phrase. Let us look at (5) again:

(5)	wǒ	xǐhuān	chī	píngguǒ
	I	like	eat	apple

I like to eat apples.

In this sentence *wǒ* 'I' is the *subject*, since it is in a "doing" relationship with the verb *xǐhuān* 'like'. It is also, however, the *topic* of the sentence, since it satisfies all the conditions for being the topic as well as for being the subject: it is definite, it is what the sentence is about, and it can be followed by a pause.

C. Sentences with No Subject

There are many sentences in Mandarin which have a topic but not a subject. In those sentences, the subject is understood. Consider sentence (8):

(8)	nèi	−	běn	shū	chūbǎn	LE
	that	−	CL	book	publish	PFV/CRS

That book, (someone) has published it.

In (8), *nèi-běn shū* 'that book' is clearly the topic; but it is not the subject because it is not in a ''doing'' relationship with the verb *chūbǎn* 'publish'. In other words, the book does not publish itself; someone or some institution publishes it. Often sentences such as (8) have been given a passive translation in English, such as 'That book has been published'. Whereas a translator has the freedom to choose any construction in the target language that provides, in his/her opinion, an appropriate rendition of the meaning of the sentence in the source language, it is important to be aware that Mandarin sentences such as (8) are not passive constructions. They are simply topic-comment constructions in which the subject of the verb is not present. Some other examples to (8) are given below:

(9) *a.*   fángzi   zào   —   hǎo   LE
           house   build   —   finish   PFV/CRS

The house, (someone) has finished building it.

     b.   yīfu   tàng   —   wán   LE
           cloth   iron   —   finish   PFV/CRS

The clothing, (someone) has finished ironing it.

     c.   fàn   zhǔ   —   jiāo   —   le   yidiǎn
           rice   cook   —   burnt   —   PFV   a:bit

The rice, (we) burned it a little bit.

     d.   zhèi   —   ge   tímù   zuì   hǎo   buyào
           this   —   CL   topic   most   good   don't

                      tí   —   chū   —   lái
              bring:up   —   exit   —   come

This topic, (you'd) better not bring it up.

D. Sentences with No Topic

There are two types of sentences with no topic. One type of sentence is without a topic because the topic is understood from the communicative context in which the sentence occurs (see section 24.1 of chapter 24). Such sentences typically occur as answers to questions:

(10) A: nǐ   kàn   —   guo   Lǐsi   méiyǒu ?
           you   see   —   EXP   Lisi   not

       Have you seen Lisi?

     B: méi   kàn   —   guo
           not   see   —   EXP

       (I) haven't.

In (10), B's answer does not need to contain the subject/topic *wǒ* 'I' because it was just referred to by *nǐ* 'you' in the preceding question, and, in Mandarin, topics that are understood usually do not need to be expressed. Consider another example:

(11) A: júzi   huài   le   ma ?
           orange   spoiled   CRS   Q

       Are the oranges spoiled?

     B: huài   le
           spoiled   CRS

       (They) are spoiled.

Again, neither *júzi* 'orange' nor a pronoun referring to it need be mentioned in B's response to A because it is understood from the context. Another such example would be the case of an imperative, or command (see chapter 14). In a command, it is always understood that the subject/topic is the hearer, so, again, it need not appear in the sentence.

(12)   jìn   —   lái
         in   —   come

     Come in!

     The second type of sentence without a topic is one in which no noun phrase is definite or generic, or in which the definite or generic noun phrase is not what the sentence is about. In such sentences, the subject is usually an indefinite noun phrase, which cannot occur in sentence-initial position and cannot be a topic. Instead, the indefinite subject noun phrase must be placed after the verb. These sentences are called *presentative sentences* because they are structured to "present" the indefinite noun phrase in discourse. They are discussed in detail in chapter 17. In the following examples, the indefinite subjects are underlined:

(13)   jìn   —   lái   —   le   <u>yi</u>   —   <u>ge</u>   <u>rén</u>
        enter   —   come   —   PFV   one   —   CL   person

    A person came in.

(14)   yǒu   <u>rén</u>   zài   dǎ   —   diànhuà
        exist   person   DUR   hit   —   telephone

           gěi   Zhāngsān
           to   Zhangsan

    Someone is making a phone call to Zhangsan.

(15)   xià   <u>yǔ</u>   le
        descend   rain   CRS

    It's raining.

In (13), the one who is doing the entering is *yi-ge rén* 'a person'. It is clearly the subject of the verb *jìn-lái* 'enter-come = come in', but is not the topic because it is neither definite nor generic, nor is it in sentence-initial position. It introduces a previously unknown entity into the discourse. In (14), *rén* 'person' is the subject of the verb *dǎ-diànhuà* 'hit-telephone', but it is not the topic because it is preceded by the existential verb *yǒu* 'exist'.

Sentence (14) also contains a definite noun, *Zhāngsān*, but it is not the topic because it is not what the sentence is about. In (15), *yǔ* 'rain' is the subject of the verb *xià* 'descend'. Since (15) represents the only way to express the thought 'It's raining' in Mandarin, the fact that *yǔ* 'rain' is the subject of the verb *xià* 'descend' is often overlooked. Observe that in (16), *nèi-chǎng yǔ* 'that-CL rain = that rain' is both the subject and the topic of the sentence with the verb *xià* 'descend':

(16)   nèi   —   chǎng   yǔ   xià   —   de   hěn   dà
        that   —   CL   rain   descend   —   CSC   very   big

That rain came down hard.

Topics and subjects, then, can be distinguished on the basis of whether the noun has a "doing" or "being" relationship with the verb; in sentences such as (2), both a topic noun phrase and a subject noun phrase can be identified, while in sentences such as (5)–(7), one noun phrase plays both the topic and the subject role. In other sentences, such as (8) and (9), only a topic but not a subject exists, and in still other sentences, such as (13)–(15), only a subject but not a topic exists.

4.1.4 Double-Subject Sentences

One type of sentence containing both a topic and a subject deserves special mention, the *double-subject sentence*, of which the following are examples.[6] In these examples, the topic is underlined twice and the subject once:

(17)   xiàng   bízi   cháng
        elephant   nose   long

{Elephants' noses are long. }
{Elephants have long noses. }

(18)   Zhāngsān   nǔ   —   péngyǒu   duō
        Zhangsan   girl   —   friend   many

Zhangsan has lots of girlfriends.

(19)   zhèi   —   ge   nǔhái   yǎnjing   hěn   dà
        that   —   CL   girl   eye   very   big

{This girl's eyes are very big.}
{This girl has very big eyes. }

(20)   wǔ   —   ge   píngguǒ   liǎng   —   ge   huài   le
        five   —   CL   apple   two   —   CL   spoil   CRS

(Of) the five apples, two are spoiled.

(21) zhèi — bān xuésheng tā zuì cōngmíng
      this — class student 3sg most intelligent

(In) that class of students, s/he is the most intelligent.

(22) jiājù jiù — de hǎo
      furniture old — NOM good

Furniture, old is good.

Sentences like (17)−(22) have been called double-subject constructions because earlier investigators, not thinking about such a notion as "topic," analyzed such sentences as having two subjects, as shown in (23):

(23) xiàng bízi cháng
      elephant nose long
            Subject   Predicate

      Subject   Predicate

With the concept of topic, however, we can see that these sentences are just a subset of topic-comment sentences in which there happens to be a particular semantic relationship between the topic and the subject, which we may call *part-whole*. That is, in all the sentences that one might call double-subject constructions, the topic is the *whole* of which the subject is a *part*. Thus, in (17)−(19) above, the subject is *possessed* by the topic, while in (20)−(22), the topic names a class and the subject names a *subset* of that class.

Double-subject constructions, then, involve topics and subjects in a part-whole relationship with each other, but in every other respect they are just like all the other topic-comment sentences being considered: the topic is the definite noun phrase that is what the sentence is about, and the subject is the noun phrase in a "doing" or "being" relationship with the verb.

4.1.5 Comparison with Chao's Analysis

In his *Grammar*, Chao (1968:67-104) discusses the notions of subject and topic, but he arrives at a different labeling system from the one being adopted here. Because of the importance of his *Grammar*, a brief comparison of the two approaches might be useful to readers who wish to consult both his work and this one.

Chao's discussion makes it clear that he does not distinguish between topic and subject. For him, most Mandarin sentences consist of a subject (the first noun phrase) and a predicate (the rest of the sentence), but the *meaning* or *function* of "subject" and "predicate" is "topic" and "comment," respectively. That is, Chao views "topic," not as a grammatical entity distinct from "subject," but, rather, as a way to talk about the meaning that the subject noun phrase conveys.

The problem with this approach is that if the first noun phrase in the sentence is the subject, which has the meaning or function of topic, there can be no distinction between topic and subject. So in a sentence like (24),

(24)   nèi   —   kē   shù   yèzi   hěn   dà
      that   —   CL   tree   leaf   very   big

    That tree, (its) leaves are very big.

Chao would call *nèi-kē shù* 'that tree' the *main subject* (which has a topic meaning) and *yèzi* 'leaf' the *minor subject*.

In contrast, we consider topic and subject to be two different types of notions. Although given noun phrase may serve as both the topic and the subject in certain sentences, the notions need to be kept distinct for two reasons. First, only by recognizing the role of topic in Mandarin sentences can we appreciate Mandarin as a topic-prominent language and the importance of topic prominence as a typological criterion for classifying languages according to their differences and similarities. Second, only by recognizing topics in Mandarin sentences can we come to understand the role that topics play in discourse, as discussed below in sections 4.1.8 and 4.1.9.

4.1.6 Time and Locative Phrases

We have said that topics must occur in sentence-initial position. There are, however, two other types of elements that often occur in sentence-initial position: time phrases and locative phrases. Should these be considered topics as well? We think they should. Here are some examples, the first three of time phrases, the last three of locative phrases:

(25)   zuótian   xuě   xià   de   hěn   jǐn
      yesterday   snow   descend   CSC   very   incessant

    Yesterday it snowed incessantly.

(26) | nèi | — | nián | tā | hěn | jǐnzhāng |
|---|---|---|---|---|---|
| that | — | year | 3sg | very | anxious |

That year s/he was very anxious.

(27) | shàng | — | ge | yuè | tiānqi | fēichang | mèn |
|---|---|---|---|---|---|---|
| last | — | CL | month | weather | extremely | humid |

Last month the weather was extremely humid.

(28) | qiáng | — | shang | pá | — | zhe | hěn | duō | bìhǔ |
|---|---|---|---|---|---|---|---|---|
| wall | — | on | climb | — | DUR | very | many | salamander |

The wall has a lot of salamanders crawling on it.

(29) | xìnfēng | — | lǐ | zhuāng | — | bu | — | jìn |
|---|---|---|---|---|---|---|---|
| envelope | — | in | fit | — | can't | — | enter |
| zhèi | — | xiē | zhàopiàn | | | | |
| this | — | several | photo | | | | |

These photos won't fit in this envelope.

(30) | zài | Táiběi | kéyi | chī | de | hěn | hǎo |
|---|---|---|---|---|---|---|
| at | Taipei | can | eat | CSC | very | good |

(In) Taipei one can eat really well.

The reason these sentence-initial time and locative phrases are considered to be topics is simply that they have all the properties of topics: they set the frame within which the rest of the sentence is presented, they are definite, referring to places and times about which the hearer already knows, and they may be followed by a pause particle.

4.1.7 Further Examples

In order to have a firm grasp of the topic-comment structure in Mandarin, it is important for one to understand the openness of the relationship between the topic and the comment. As long as the comment expresses something about the topic in the perception of the speaker and the hearer, the sentence will be meaningful. In the following section, further examples are presented to illustrate the topic-comment relation:

(31) miàn   wǒ   zuì   xǐhuān   chī   là   de
      noodle   I   most   like   eat   spicy   NOM

Noodles, I like to eat spicy ones the best.

(32) zhèi   —   jian   shì   nǐ   bu   néng
      this   —   CL   matter   you   not   can

      guāng   máfan   yi   —   ge   rén
      only   bother   one   —   CL   person

This matter, you can't deal with it by bothering only one person.

(33) nèi   —   zhǒng   dòuzi   yi   —   jīn
      that   —   kind   bean   one   —   catty

      sān   —   shí   kuài   qián
      three   —   ten   dollar   money

That kind of bean, one catty is thirty dollars.

(34) nèi   —   chang   huǒ   xìngkuī   xiāofang   —   duì
      that   —   CL   fire   fortunate   fire   —   brigade

      lái   de   kuài
      come   CSC   fast

That fire, fortunately the fire brigade came quickly.

(35) lán   —   qiú   wǒ   dǎ   de   bu   tài   hǎo
      basket   —   ball   I   play   CSC   not   too   good

Basketball I don't play too well.

(36) zhèi   —   běn   xiǎoshuō   Zhāngsān   kàn   —   wán   le
      this   —   CL   novel   Zhangsan   read   —   finish   CRS

This novel, Zhangsan has finished it.

(37)

lù	—	shang	de	shé	wǒ	xiǎng	shi
road	—	on	NOM	snake	I	think	be

bu	huì	yǎo	rén	de
not	likely	bite	person	NOM

The snake on the road, I think it won't bite people.

(38)

nèi	—	ge	háizi	(tā	—	de)	yīfu	dōu	pò	le
that	—	CL	child	(3sg	—	GEN)	clothes	all	torn	CRS

That child, his/her clothes are all torn.

(39)

lúzi	—	lǐ	de	huǒ	wǒ	ràng	tā
stove	—	in	NOM	fire	I	let	3sg

zìji	miè	—	diào
self	extinguish	—	off

The fire in the stove, I'll let it go out by itself.

(40)

dàxué	xiànzài	duōbàn	shi	nán	—	nǚ
university	now	most	be	boy	—	girl

tóng	xiào
one	school

Universities, most are coeducational these days.

(41)

bào	—	shang	de	xiāoxi,	shìjiè	—	shang
paper	—	on	NOM	news	world	—	on

de	qíngxíng	hěn	bu	hǎo
NOM	situation	very	not	good

(According to) the news in the paper, the situation in the world is really not good.

(42)

zhèi	—	ge	dōngxi	míngzi	jiào	"diànshì"
this	—	CL	thing	name	call	television

This thing is called a "television."

(43) hūnyīn   de   shì   wǒ   zìjǐ   zuò   —   zhǔ
      marriage NOM   affair   I   self   act   —   master

The matter of marriage, I'll be my own boss.

Sometimes the topic can be a verb or a verb phrase functioning as a noun phrase:

(44) zhù ,   Táiběi   zuì   fāngbiàn;   chī,   háishi   Xiānggǎng   hǎo
      live   Taipei   most   convenient   eat   still   Hong Kong   good

Housing, Taipei is most convenient; eating, Hong Kong is still better.

(45) dào   Měiguó   liúxué   zhèngfǔ   zǎo   guīdìng
      to   America   study:abroad   government   early   stipulate

       —   le   bànfǎ
       —   PFV   procedure

(For) studying abroad in the United States, the government long ago set
up procedural regulations.

(46) tiāntiān   mǎi   cài ,   wǒ   zhēn   bu   zhīdào
      every:day   buy   food   I   really   not   know

                  gāi   mǎi   shénme   hǎo
                  should buy   what   good

Buying food every day, I really don't know what to buy that's good.

(47) chū   —   qu   hē   chá   wǒ   qǐng   nǐ
      exit   —   go   drink   tea   I   invite   you

Going out for tea, I'll invite (treat) you.

Sometimes, an entire clause can be the topic:

(48)

lìshĭ	—	xì	kāi	—	huì	wŏ	kĕyi
history	—	department	hold	—	meeting	I	can

	gēn	Lĭsì	tí	—	yi	—	tí
	with	Lisi	mention	—	one	—	mention

(When) the history department has its meeting, I can mention(it) to Lisi.

(49)

Zhāngsān	míngtiān	qù	Mĕiguó	wŏ	juéde	hĕn	qíguài
Zhangsan	tomorrow	go	America	I	feel	very	strange

Zhangsan's going to the United States tomorrow, I feel is very strange.

Notice that in sentences like (44)–(49), in which either a verb phrase or an entire clause is functioning as topic, the same conditions for topic hold as when a simple noun phrase is the topic: the phrase or clause tells what the sentence is about or sets a frame for the sentence, the phrase or clause can be followed by a topic particle, and the phrase or clause must refer to information that is already known to both the hearer and the speaker. For example, a sentence like (49) could not be used unless the hearer already knew about the fact that Zhangsan was going to America the next day.

Sometimes the topic may be found, not at the beginning of the entire sentence, but at the beginning of the clause of which it is a part (see chapters 21 and 23):

(50)

wŏ	xiăng	nèi	—	jian	yīfu	wŏ	chuān	—
I	think	that	—	CL	clothes	I	wear	—

	qĭ	—	lái	hĕn	hăo	—	kàn
	rise	—	come	very	good	—	look

I think that outfit looks very good on me.

(51)

wŏ	hĕn	băo	le ,	suŏyi	júzi	wŏ	bu	chī	le
I	very	full	CRS	so	orange	I	not	eat	CRS

I'm very full, so the orange I'm not going to eat.

Sentence (50) is a complex sentence whose subordinate clause has a topic and a subject. Whether a subordinate clause of a complex sentence can have a topic that is distinct from the subject depends on the main verb of the complex sentence. In general, only verbs of saying (such as *shuō* 'say', *tíyì* 'suggest') and verbs of mental activity (such as *juéde* 'feel', *xiǎng* 'think') allow a subordinate clause with a topic distinct from the subject. Sentence (51) involves sentence linking or conjunction, *suǒyi* 'so' being the link between the two clauses; the second clause contains both a topic and a subject.

4.1.8 Topic as a Discourse Element

As we have mentioned, there are several important reasons for distinguishing topic from subject.[7] One is that they behave differently in individual sentences. Even more significant, however, is the fact that the topic is essentially a discourse element and functions in a special way in the discourse. By *discourse*, we mean the context in which a given sentence occurs, whether it is a conversation, a paragraph, a story, or some other kind of language situation.

A. The Preceding Discourse

One of the functions of the topic with respect to the preceding discourse is simply to relate the material in the sentence of which it is a part to some preceding sentence. Here is a conversational example:

(52) A.　　wǒ　　zài　　Xīnguó　　xuéxiào　　jiāoshū
　　　　　　I　　　at　　　Xinguo　　school　　　teach

　　　I teach at Xinguo School.

　　　B.　ou!　Xīnguó xuéxiào ,　　nàr　　yǒu　　yi　　－　　wèi
　　　　　Oh!　Xinguo　school　　there　　exist　　one　　－　　CL

　　　　　Zhāng　Xiānsheng　nǐ　　rènshi　bu　rènshi ?
　　　　　Zhang　　Mr.　　　you　　know　　not　know

　　　Oh! Xinguo School, do you know a Mr. Zhang there?

The topic in B's utterance is 'Xinguo school', which clearly picks up on what A had just said. It is in this sense, then, that topics function in discourse to relate one sentence to a preceding one.

Another function of topics in a discourse is to introduce a *subtopic*—an idea that is related to, but slightly different from, what has been discussed. For example, if A and B have been discussing an upcoming move, getting a loan, signing papers, and when the move will take place, B could say to A:

(53)

xīn	de	dìfang	lí	zhèli	yuǎn	bu	yuǎn ?
new	NOM	place	from	here	far	not	far

Is the new place far from here?

In this case, *xīn de dìfang* 'the new place' is the topic (and the subject); although it has not been explicitly mentioned in the speech situation prior to the uttering of (53), it has been implicit in the discussion of moving and thus qualifies as already known to both the hearer and the speaker.

Finally, a third way in which topics relate to the previous discourse is in *re*introducing a topic that had been mentioned earlier but then dropped. So, for example, if A and B in the conversational situation described for sentence (53) have finished talking about the new house and the move and have gone on to other matters, A could return to the first idea by saying:

(54)

nà	xīn	fángzi	wǒ	xiǎng	nǐ	kàn	—
that	new	house	I	think	you	see	—

le	yídìng	hěn	xǐhuān
PFV	certainly	very	like

As for that new house, I think that once you've seen it, you'll certainly like it.

In English, reintroduced topics are typically marked with the expression *as for*, as shown in the translation of (54).

B. The Following Discourse

One way in which topics interact with material that follows is through contrast; that is, when a speaker wants to contrast two items, s/he places them as the topics of contrasting sentences. Here is an example:

(55)

yīfu	xīn	de	hǎo ;	péngyóu	jiù	de	hǎo
clothes	new	NOM	good	friend	old	NOM	good

Clothes, new ones are good; friends, old ones are good.

4.1.9 Topic and Coreference in Discourse

Consider (56), a short excerpt from a story:

(56) <u>John</u> went to college in California. <u>He</u> majored in linguistics.

The underlined subjects of the two sentences in (56) are said to be *coreferential* because they refer to the same person. In general, any two noun phrases having identical reference are coreferential. In English, when two coreferential noun phrases occur in two consecutive but separate sentences, the coreferential noun phrase in the second sentence is normally represented by a pronoun, as shown in (56). In Mandarin, however, normally the coreferential noun phrase in the second sentence is not mentioned, although it may also be present as a pronoun (see chapter 24 on pronouns in discourse). Sentence (57) is the most natural Mandarin counterpart of (56):

(57)	Zhāngsān	shì	zài	Jiāzhou	niàn	de
	Zhangsan	be	at	California	study	NOM

	dàxué	zhuānxiū	yŭyánxué
	college	major	linguistics

Zhangsan went to college in California. (He) majored in linguistics.

An important discourse property of the topic in Mandarin is that when the topic and subject are distinct, the topic has priority over the subject in determining the reference of a missing noun phrase in the sentence that follows. Let us illustrate with example (58):

(58)	<u>nèi</u>	—	<u>kē</u>	shù	yèzi	dà ;	(suŏyĭ)	wŏ
	that	—	CL	tree	leaf	big	(so)	I

	bu	xīhuān_____
	not	like

That tree, the leaves are big; (so) I don't like <u>it</u>.

The missing noun phrase in the second sentence of (58) is the direct object of the verb, *xīhuān* 'like'. It can only be understood to refer to the topic of the preceding sentence, *nèi-kē shù* 'that tree', and not to its subject, *yèzi* 'leaf'.

Consider another example, (59):

(59)

nèi	—	kuài	tián	dàozi	zhǎng	de	hěn
that	—	piece	land	rice	grow	CSC	very

dà	;	(suǒyǐ)	_____	hěn	zhíqián
big		(so)		very	valuable

That piece of land (topic), rice grows very big; (so) it (the land) is very valuable.

Here the missing noun phrase in the second sentence of (59) is the subject of the verb, *zhíqián* '(is) valuable'. Again, it refers to the topic, *nèi-kuài tián* 'that piece of land', and not to the subject, *dàozi* 'rice', of the preceding sentence.

The reason that the topic has priority over the subject in determining coreference in successive clauses is the discourse nature of the topic. The topic being what the sentence is about, it is normal for several sentences to be saying something about the same thing, or to share the topic. Thus a topic can easily extend its scope across sentence boundaries. On the other hand, when a subject is not simultaneously a topic, its role is likely to be restricted to the sentence in which it occurs. It is important to note that the verb of the second sentence in (58), *xǐhuān* 'like', occurring in an isolated sentence, is a verb that semantically could have either the topic of the first sentence, *nèi-kē shù* 'that tree', or the subject of the first sentence, *yèzi* 'leaf', as its direct object. Similarly, the verb of the second sentence in (59), *zhíqián* '(is) valuable', occurring in an isolated sentence, could in principle have either the topic of the first sentence, *nèi-kuài tián* 'that field', or the subject of the first sentence, *dàozi* 'rice', as its subject. Since, however, the missing noun phrases in (58) and (59) are interpreted as coreferential only to the topic and not to the subject in the preceding sentence, we know that the meanings of (58) and (59) result from the topic's having priority over the subject in determining coreference.

4.2 The Noun Phrase

A noun phrase can be characterized in terms of its function as well as its form. A noun phrase functions to label something, which can be a person, a thing, a class of things, an activity, an event, or an abstract quality or concept. A noun phrase can therefore occur with a verb in a sentence as a topic, subject, direct object, indirect object, or object of a preposition. Of course, a noun phrase can also be used in any situation where a label is called for as an appropriate utterance, such as in answering a question like "What's that?" or "What are you studying?"

In form, a noun phrase will consist of at least a pronoun, such as *wǒ* 'I' or *wǒmen* 'we', or a noun. This noun can be a simple noun: for example, *mǎ* 'horse', *pútáo* 'grape'; or it can be a compound noun: for example, *shūbāo* 'book bag', *diàndēng* 'electric light'. The noun phrase can also consist of a noun plus other elements, all of which must occur in front of that noun. Those elements are (1) classifier phrases/measure phrases, (2) associative phrases, and (3) modifying phrases. When a noun occurs with one of these elements, it is called a *head noun*. Let us look at each of these elements in turn.

4.2.1 Classifier Phrases/Measure Phrases

To a speaker of English, one of the most striking features of the Mandarin noun phrase is the classifier.[8] A *classifier* is a word that *must* occur with a number (e.g., *yí* 'one', *bàn* 'half', *shí* 'ten') and/or a demonstrative (i.e., *zhèi* 'this', *nèi* 'that', *něi* 'which'), or certain quantifiers (such as *zhěng* 'whole', *jǐ* 'how many/a few', *mǒu yi* 'a certain', and *měi* 'every') before the noun. For example, the underlined forms in (60) are all classifiers:

(60) *a.*　　sān　　　—　　　<u>ge</u>　　rén
　　　　　three　　　—　　　CL　　person

　　　three people

　　b.　　zhèi　　　—　　　<u>zhǎn</u>　　dēng
　　　　　this　　　　—　　　CL　　　　lamp

　　　this lamp

　　c.　　　　jǐ　　　　—　　　<u>jiàn</u>　　yīfu
　　　　{ how:many }　　—　　　CL　　　garment
　　　　{ a:few   }

　　　{ how many }　garments
　　　{ a few   }

　　d.　　wǔ　　　—　　　<u>jià</u>　　fēijī
　　　　　five　　　—　　　CL　　airplane

　　　five airplanes

e. nèi — <u>tiáo</u> niú
      that — CL cow

that cow

f. zhèi — jǐ — <u>mén</u> pào
      this — few — CL cannon

these few cannons

g. nèi — liù — <u>běn</u> shū
      that — six — CL book

those six books

h. zhěng — <u>ge</u> fángzi
      whole — CL house

the whole house

The choice of classifier is determined by the noun. Mandarin has several dozen classifiers, most of which can be found in Chao (1968:sec. 7.9). We will refer to the combination of demonstrative and/or number or quantifier plus the classifier as the *classifier phrase*. Thus, in (60) *a*, *sān-ge*, *c*, *jǐ-jian*, *f*, *zhèi-jǐ-mén*, *g*, *nèi-liù-běn*, are all classifier phrases.

If the noun itself denotes a measure, it does not take a classifier; examples include: *kuài* 'piece', *lǐ*, 'mile', *jīn*, 'tael', *liǎng* 'ounce', *chǐ* 'foot', and *tiān* 'day'; thus the *a* phrases in (61) and (62) are acceptable, but the *b* phrases are not:[9]

(61) *a.* sān tiān
           three day

three days

b. *sān — <u>ge</u> tiān
      three — CL day

(62) *a.* bā kuài
           eight piece

eight pieces

b.   *ba*   —   <u>ge</u>   kuài
    eight   —   CL   piece

In fact, not only does a measure word generally not take a classifier, but any measure word can *be* a classifier. In each of the examples in (63)−(68), the *a* phrase shows a measure word functioning as a noun without a classifier, and the *b* phrase shows the same measure word functioning as a classifier with another noun.

(63) *a.*   shí   <u>bàng</u>
       ten   pound

    ten pounds

    b.   shí   <u>bàng</u>   ròu
         ten   pound   meat

    ten pounds of meat

(64) *a.*   liù   <u>lǐ</u>
       six   mile

    six miles

    b.   liù   <u>lǐ</u>   lù
         six   mile   road

    six miles of road

(65) *a.*   yi   —   bǎi   <u>liǎng</u>
       one   —   hundred   ounce

    100 ounces

    b.   yi   —   bǎi   <u>liǎng</u>   yínzi
         one   —   hundred   ounce   silver

    100 ounces of silver

(66) *a.*   wǔ   —   shí   <u>chǐ</u>
       five   —   ten   foot

    fifty feet

b.	wǔ	—	shí	<u>chǐ</u>	bù
	five	—	ten	foot	cloth

fifty feet of cloth

(67) a.
	nèi	<u>jīn</u>
	that	tael

that tael

b.	nèi	<u>jīn</u>	yáng	—	ròu
	that	tael	lamb	—	meat

that tael of lamb

(68) a.
	sān	<u>jiālún</u>
	three	gallon

three gallons

b.	sān	<u>jiālún</u>	qìyóu
	three	gallon	gasoline

three gallons of gasoline

The measure words provided in (63)−(68) indicate standards for length, weight, area, or volume. Measure words can also indicate aggregates or containers, however, as in these examples:

(i) Aggregate measures:

(69) a.
	yi	<u>qún</u>	yáng
	one	flock	sheep

a flock of sheep

b.	nèi	<u>duī</u>	lāxī
	that	pile	garbage

that pile of garbage

c.   jī   héng   guǒ   —   shù
{ how:many } row   fruit   —   tree
{   a:few   }

{ how many } rows of fruit trees
{   a few   }

d.   zhèi   shí   duì   yīngwǔ
        this   ten   pair   parrot

these ten pairs of parrots

e.   qī   dǎ   jīdàn
        seven   dozen   egg

seven dozen eggs

f.   zhěng   chuàn   zhūzi
        whole   string   pearl

the/a whole string of pearls

g.   yi   tào   jiājù
        one   set   furniture

a set of furniture

h.   liǎng   zhuō   kè
        two   table   guest

two (banquet) tables of guests

i.   zhèi   bān   xuésheng
        this   class   student

this class of students

(ii) Container measures:

(70) *a.*

wu	—	shí	<u>píng</u>	yóu
five	—	ten	bottle	oil

fifty bottles of oil

b.

bā	—	shí	—	sì	<u>bēi</u>	jiǔ
eight	—	ten	—	four	glass	wine

eighty-four glasses of wine

c.

zhèi	liǎng	<u>xiāng</u>	júzi
this	two	box	orange

these two cases of oranges

d.

zhěng	<u>hé</u>	táng
whole	box	candy

the/a whole box of candy

e.

yi	<u>guō</u>	fàn
one	pot	rice

a pot of rice

f.

jǐ	<u>gāng</u>	cù
{how:many / a:few}	vat	vinegar

{how many / a few} vats of vinegar

When the noun is abstract, the measure classifier may also be abstract:

(71)   jǐ   jù   huà
        { how:many }   sentence   speech
        {   a:few   }

        { how many }   sentences (literally 'how many/a few sentences
        { a few   }   of speech')

Another type of measure word is one that denotes an instance or occurrence of an event. *Chǎng*, which literally means 'arena', can be used in this way, as in (72):

(72) *a.*   nèi   —   chǎng   qiú   hěn   jǐnzhāng
            that   —   CL   ball   very   tense

That ball game was very tense.

  b.   nèi   —   chǎng   huǒ   méi   rén   sǐ
            that   —   CL   fire   not   person   die

In that fire no one died.

  c.   zuótian   yǒu   yi   —   chǎng   diànyǐng
          yesterday exist   one   —   CL   movie

Yesterday there was a movie.

Other examples of measure classifiers indicating an instance or occurrence of an event are given in (73)−(75), where the classifiers at issue are underlined:

(73)   nèi   —   pán   qí   tā   xià   de   hěn   hǎo
       that   —   CL   chess   3sg   descend   CSC   very   good

That game of chess s/he played very well.*

(74)   tāmen   jìnxíng   —   le   jǐ   —   cì   huìtán
       they   hold   —   PFV   a:few   —   time   talk

They held several talks.

*Cf. *pánzi* 'tray', *xià-qí* 'play chess'.

(75) dào Xīnjiāpō yi   tiān yŏu   jĭ   —   bān fēijī ?
      to   Singapore one day   exist how:many —   trip plane

How many flights a day are there to Singapore?

Another type of measure word includes nouns denoting either body parts or enclosed areas. They typically occur with *yi* 'one' with a special meaning, 'a _____ful of'. Examples of this type of measure word are presented in (76):

(76) *a*. liǎn   'face'

       yi   liǎn   huī
      one   face   dust

    a faceful of dust

   b.   tóu   'head'

       yi   tóu   bái   fǎ
      one   head   white   hair

    a headful of white hair

   c. wūzi   'house'

       yi   wūzi   zéi
      one   house   thief

    a houseful of thieves

   d. dì   'ground, floor'

       yi   dì   miànfěn
      one   floor   flour

    a floorful of flour

e. dùzi 'stomach'

yi   dùzi   qì
one   stomach   anger

a stomachful of grievance

The most frequently used classifier in Mandarin is -*ge*. It is gradually becoming the general classifier and replacing the more specialized ones. For example, the "proper" classifier for *cài* 'a course of food' is -*dào*, as in *nèi-dào cài* 'that course of food'; the "proper" classifier for *dàpào* 'artillery piece' is -*mén*, as in *zhèi-mén dàpào* 'this artillery piece'; however, many native speakers of Mandarin have replaced -*dào*, -*mén*, and others with the general classifier, -*ge*. For these speakers, *nèi-ge cài* 'that course of food' and *zhèi-ge dàpào* 'this artillery piece' are perfectly acceptable.

On the other hand, many nouns still require special classifiers. By and large, which nouns occur with which classifier must be memorized, though there is a slight amount of regularity with respect to the meanings of groups of nouns taking the same classifier. For instance, the class of nouns that require the classifier -*tiáo* includes many that refer to elongated objects, such as *shé* 'snake', *shéngzi* 'rope', *lù* 'road', *hé* 'river', *yǐba* 'tail', *yú* 'fish', as well as most four-legged mammals. Such nouns as *xīnwén* 'news', *fǎlù* 'law', however, also require the classifier -*tiáo*, whereas nouns referring to such elongated objects as *máobǐ* 'brush-pen', and *jiàn* 'arrow' take a different classifier, -*zhī*.

Finally, there is a classifier that signals plurality, -*xiē*, which occurs with the numeral *yi* 'one' to mean 'several' or with the demonstratives *nèi* 'that', *zhèi* 'this', and *něi* 'which', as follows:

(77) *a*.   yi   —   xiē   wánjù
            one   —   PL   toy

      some toys

      b.   něi   —   xiē   dōngxi
            which   —   PL   thing

      which things

c.	nèi	—	xiē	kǒuhào
	that	—	PL	slogan

those slogans

4.2.2 Associative Phrases

Associative phrase denotes a type of modification where two noun phrases (NPs) are linked by the particle -*de*. The first noun phrase together with the particle -*de* is the associative phrase. The second noun phrase is the head noun being modified, as schematized in (78):

(78)   NP — de   NP
      associative phrase   head noun

The name *associative phrase* indicates that two noun phrases are "associated" or "connected" in some way; the precise meaning of the association or connection is determined entirely by the meanings of the two noun phrases involved. One very important associative meaning is that of possession. Thus, one type of associative phrase is the possessive, or genitive, phrase:

(79) *a.*

wǒ	—	de	chènshān
I	—	GEN	shirt

my shirt

b.

tāmen	—	de	jiā
they	—	GEN	home

their home

c.

tùzi	—	de	ěrduō
rabbit	—	GEN	ear

(a) rabbit's ear

We gloss the -*de* of the genitive/possessive phrase as *GEN*. Here, of course, the meanings of the two noun phrases in each example make the concept of possession

the most natural connection between them. Many other types of semantic association between two noun phrases are also possible, however. In each of the following
examples, the semantic nature of the association follows from the meanings of the
two noun phrases involved. We gloss this broader associative meaning as *ASSOC*
'associative':

(80) *a.* Zhōngguó   —   de   rénkǒu
           China   —   ASSOC   population

          China's population

    b. nèi   —   ge   fàndiàn   —   de   cài
           that   —   CL   restaurant   —   ASSOC   food

          the food of that restaurant

    c. xuéxiào   —   de   jiào   —   yuán
           school   —   ASSOC   teach   —   personnel

          school's teaching staff

    d. kēxué   —   de   fāzhǎn
          science —   ASSOC   development

          the development of science

    e. chènshān   —   de   kòuzi
           shirt   —   ASSOC   button

          the buttons on (the) shirt

    f. Táiwan   —   huà   —   de   yǔfǎ
           Taiwan   —   speech   —   ASSOC   grammar

          (the) grammar of Taiwanese

    g. nèi   —   ge   zì   —   de   yìsi
           that   —   CL   word   —   ASSOC   meaning

          the meaning of that word

h. chénggōng   —   de   xīwàng
      success   —   ASSOC   hope

hopes for success

i. yèwǎn   —   de   tiānkōng
      night   —   ASSOC   sky

the nighttime sky

j. jiàokēshū   —   de   shōujù
      textbook   —   ASSOC   receipt

a receipt for the textbook

The *-de* of an associative phrase signaling a possessive/genitive relation can be omitted when the possessive/genitive relation is between two human relatives and the noun in the associative phrase is a personal pronoun. For example, the *-de* in the underlined associative phrase can be omitted in (81):

(81) *a.*   wǒ   bu   xīhuan   <u>nǐ   (-de)   mèimei</u>
            I   not like   you (-GEN) younger:sister

I don't like your younger sister.

b.   Zhāngsān   xiàng   <u>tā   (-de)   māma</u>
       Zhangsan   resemble   3sg   (-GEN)   mother

Zhangsan looks like his mother.

c.   wǒ   zuótiān   pèngjian   <u>wǒ   (-de)   shúshu</u>
       I   yesterday encounter   I   (-GEN)   uncle (paternal)

I ran into my uncle yesterday.

There are other cases where the -*de* of the associative phrase can be omitted.[10] For example, in (82), the two noun phrases linked by -*de* do not refer to two human relatives, yet -*de* may be deleted:

(82) *a.*

wǒ	kàn	—	guo	nǐ	—	de
I	read	—	EXP	you	—	GEN

nèi	—	běn	shū
that	—	CL	book

I have read that book of yours.

b.

wǒ	kàn	—	guo	nǐ	nèi
I	read	—	EXP	you	that

—	běn	shū
—	CL	book

I have read that book of yours.

4.2.3 Modifying Phrases

The third kind of element that can occur before a noun in a noun phrase is a modifying phrase. A modifying phrase can be either a relative clause or an attributive adjective.

A. Relative Clauses

A relative clause is simply a nominalized clause placed in front of a noun to modify it. Nominalizations and relative clauses are discussed in detail in section 20.2.1 of chapter 20 on nominalization; here are three examples:

(83)

Zhāngsān	mǎi	de	qìchē	hěn	guì
Zhangsan	buy	NOM	car	very	expensive

The car that Zhangsan bought was very expensive.

(84)

qí	zìxíngchē	de	rén	děi	xiǎoxīn
ride	bicycle	NOM	person	must	careful

People who ride bicycles must be careful.

(85)   nà   shi   <u>wǒ   gěi   nǐ   de</u>   shū
        that   be   I   give   you   NOM   book

That's the book I gave you.

The most important semantic function of a relative clause is to clarify further the reference of the head noun.

B. Attributive Adjectives

An adjective functions attributively (as opposed to predicatively, described in A.1 of section 4.3.1 of this chapter) when it modifies a noun in a noun phrase.[11] A modifying phrase, then, may consist of just an attributive adjective, as illustrated by the underlined phrases in the following examples:

(86)   tā   shi   yi   —   ge   <u>hǎo</u>   rén
        3sg   be   one   —   CL   good   person

S/he is a good person.

(87)   <u>guó   —   lì</u>   dàxué   xuéfèi
        country   —   establish   university   tuition

                bǐjiao   piányi
                relatively cheap

At the national universities tuition is relatively low.

(88)   tāmen   yòng   de   dōu   shi   <u>tiānrán</u>   yánsè
        they   use   NOM   all   be   natural   color

They use only natural colors.

(89)   bié   shuō   <u>jiǎ</u>   huà
        don't   say   false   speech

Don't make false statements.

Some adjectives can appear either in a relative clause (that is, with the nominalizer *de*) or as a simple attributive adjective (that is, without the *de*), as shown in (90)–(94):

(90) *a.*   hóng   de   huā
            red   NOM   flower

        a flower that is red

    b.   hóng   huā
           red   flower

        a red flower

(91) *a.*   yìng   de   xiàngpí
             hard   NOM   rubber

        rubber that is hard

    b.   yìng   xiàngpí
           hard   rubber

        hard rubber

(92) *a.* yuán   de   zhuōzi
           round   NOM   table

        a table that is round

    b. yuán   zhuōzi
           round   table

        a round table

(93) *a.*   jiù   de   shǒushi
           old (used)   NOM   jewelry

        jewelry that is secondhand

b.   jiù   shŏushi
      old (used)   jewelry

used jewelry

(94) *a.*   xiăo   de   júzi
        small   NOM   orange

an orange that is small

b.   xiăo   júzi
      small   orange

a small orange

In general, adjectives that modify a noun without the particle *de* tend to be more closely knit with the noun. The consequence is that the adjective-plus-noun phrase tends to acquire the feature of being a *name* for a category of entities. The relative clause usage of adjectives, on the other hand, always has the function of further clarifying or delineating the reference of the head noun.

What determines when a name is called for, of course, concerns our perception and categorization of entities in the world. If a type of entity is likely to be perceived as an integral and relevant category by speakers of Mandarin, then they are more disposed toward giving a name to that category of entities. As a general rule, the more people are disposed toward naming a category of entities, the more they are likely to refer to that category of objects by using the formula *adjective + noun*, where the adjective specifies the type of entity referred to by the noun. For example, it is perfectly natural to perceive red flowers as a category and quite reasonable to name a group of flowers according to their color; hence, we have *hóng huā* 'red flower' where *de* is absent. On the other hand, it is less likely that we should perceive ''comfortable chairs'' as a relevant category of items in our world, and therefore we are not likely to name such a group of entities. Thus, *shūfu yĭzi* 'comfortable chair' is not acceptable, and the use of *de* after *shūfu* 'comfortable' is obligatory.

For some examples, the naming effect of an adjective-plus-noun phrase is more obvious. Consider (95):

(95) *a.*   hútú   de   jiàoshòu
         muddleheaded   NOM   professor

a professor who is muddleheaded

b.   hútú   jiàoshòu
        muddleheaded   professor

$\begin{Bmatrix} \text{a muddleheaded professor} \\ \text{Professor Muddleheaded} \end{Bmatrix}$

In (95) *b*, one of the possible interpretations, 'Professor Muddleheaded', is a name for a certain professor who is widely known for being muddleheaded. One can imagine such a usage in a cartoon or a humorous story. There are, of course, many phrases composed of adjective plus noun which have become idiomatized as names, such as, for example,

(96) *a*. huáng   —   dòu
          yellow   —   bean

          soybean

    b. xiǎo   —   māoxióng
          small   —   panda

          lesser panda

    c. xiāng   —   yān
          fragrant   —   smoke

          cigarette

    d. gān   —   liáng
          dry   —   food

          precooked staple food

    e. lěng   —   zhàn
          cold   —   war

          cold war

Whereas some adjectives can modify a noun either with or without the particle *de*, a large number of adjectives can modify a noun only with the nominalizing particle *de*. First, all reduplicated adjectives, which acquire a more vivid descriptive force as a result of the reduplication (see section 3.1.1 of chapter 3), must occur with *de*. For example:

(97) *a.*   hóng   –   hong   de   huā
           red   –   red   NOM   flower

        a red flower

    b.   *hóng   –   hong   huā
           red   –   red   flower

(98) *a.*   gān-gan-jìng-jìng   de   xiézi
               clean   NOM   shoe

        clean shoes*

    b.   *gān-gan-jìng-jìng   xiézi
            clean   shoe

Aside from reduplicated adjectives, there are many regular adjectives that cannot modify noun without *de*. Sentences (99)–(104) are examples:

(99) *a.*   shūfu   de   yĭzi
          comfortable   NOM   chair

        a comfortable chair

    b.   *shūfu   yĭzi
          comfortable   chair

(100) *a.*   piàoliang   de   nǚ   –   háizi
           beautiful   NOM   female   –   child

         a beautiful girl

    b.   *piàoliang   nǚ   –   háizi
          beautiful   female   –   child

*Cf. *gānjing* 'clean'.

(101) *a.* róngyì   de   wèntí
               easy   NOM   problem

an easy problem

       b. *róngyì   wènti
              easy   problem

(102) *a.* pàng   de   rén
               fat   NOM   person

fat people

       b. *pàng   rén
              fat   person

(103) *a.* gāo   de   nán   —   háizi
              tall   NOM   male   —   child

a tall boy

       b. *gāo   nán   —   háizi
              tall   male   —   child

(104) *a.* fùzá   de   xiànxiàng
             complex   NOM   phenomenon

a complex phenomenon

       b. *fùzá   xiànxiàng
             complex   phenomenon

In addition to whether the adjective-plus-noun combination forms a useful name, another factor that plays a role in determining whether an adjective may modify a noun without the particle *de* concerns literary style. If the head noun is more literary and has a closer affinity to written Classical Chinese, then a modifying adjective is more likely to be able to occur without the nominalization particle *de*. For example, consider the adjective *zhòngyào* 'important'. Sentence (105) *b* shows that it cannot occur without *de* when it modifies the noun *rén* 'person'; but

(105) *c* shows that it can occur without *de* when it modifies the noun *rénwù* 'personage', which is a literary term that has its origin in Classical Chinese writings:

(105) *a.* zhòngyào   de   rén
            important   NOM   person

an important person

b. *zhòngyào   rén
      important   person

c. zhòngyào   rénwù
      important   personage

an important person

As another example, consider the adjective *gāo* 'tall'. In (103) we showed that *gāo* must take *de* when it modifies *nán-háizi* 'male-child = boy'. We can generalize this claim by stating that *gāo* must occur with *de* when it modifies most animate nouns: *boy, girl, man, woman, people,* and so forth. In (106), though, we see that *gāo* occurs without *de*, and the head noun it modifies is *hàn* 'adult male'. The reason is that *hàn* is a literary term from Classical Chinese:

(106) gāo   hàn
       tall   adult:male

a tall male

The reason behind the absence of *de* when an adjective modifies a literary noun phrase from Classical Chinese is that in Classical Chinese adjectives never occur with *de* when they modify noun phrases. Thus (106) and (105) *c* represent Classical Chinese grammar operating in modern Mandarin.

In summary, there is no rule that can predict when an adjective modifying a noun may occur without the nominalization particle *de*. There are two factors that may serve as useful guidelines, but they are by no means rules that can be rigidly applied.

4.2.4 The Order of Elements in a Noun Phrase

It was stated at the beginning of the section on noun phrases that all the elements in a noun phrase except the noun are optional. If more than one of these elements appears, however, their order is fixed according to one of the following schemas:

(107) *a.* associative phrase + classifier/measure phrase + relative clause + adjective + noun

    b. associative phrase + relative clause + classifier/measure phrase + adjective + noun[12]

Here are some examples illustrating these patterns:

(108) *a.*

wǒ	–	de	nèi	–	ge	hǎo	péngyou
I	–	GEN	that	–	CL	good	friend

that good friend of mine

b.

nèi	–	ge	zuò	mǎimai	de	rén
that	–	CL	do	business	NOM	person

that person who is in business

c.

zuò	mǎimai	de	nèi	–	ge	rén
do	business	NOM	that	–	CL	person

that person who is in business

d.

wǒ	–	de	nèi	–	ge
I	–	GEN	that	–	CL

zhù	zāi	Měiguó	de	hǎo	péngyou
live	at	America	NOM	good	friend

that good friend of mine who lives in the United States

e.

nǐmen	xuéxiào	–	de	nèi	–	wèi	cóng
you:PL	school	–	ASSOC	that	–	CL	from

Zhōngguó	lái	de	kēxuéjiā
China	come	NOM	scientist

that scientist at your school who came from China

f.

wǒ	—	de	zhù	zāi	Měiguó
I	—	GEN	live	at	America

de	nèi	—	ge	péngyou
NOM	that	—	CL	friend

that friend of mine who lives in the United States.

g.

nǐmen	xuéxiào	—	de	cóng	Zhōngguó
you:PL	school	—	ASSOC	from	China

lái	de	nèi	—	wèi	kēxuéjiā
come	NOM	that	—	CL	scientist

that scientist at your school who came from China

As a rule, such long and complex noun phrases as those shown in (108) *d–g* are not commonly used.

Examples such as those in (80) *b* and *g* might appear to be counterexamples to the ordering schemas shown in (107); these two examples were:

(80) *b.*

nèi	—	ge	fàndiàn	—	de	cài
that	—	CL	restaurant	—	ASSOC	food

the food of that restaurant

g.

nèi	—	ge	zì	—	de	yìsi
that	—	CL	word	—	ASSOC	meaning

the meaning of that word

The order of elements in (80) *b* and *g* is:

(109) classifier phrase + associative phrase + noun

whereas, according to the schemas in (107), an associative phrase must always precede a classifier phrase.

The reason that the phrases in (80) *b* and *g* do not actually violate the schemas in (107) is that the latter describe the order of elements in a noun phrase when each of these elements is understood to be directly related to the head noun, the noun farthest to the right. The classifier phrases in (80) *b* and *g*, however, go with the nouns next to them and not with the head nouns. In other words, *nèi-ge* 'that' in (80) *b* goes with *fàndiàn* 'restaurant', not with *cài* 'food', and in (80) *g* it goes with *zì* 'word', not with *yìsi* 'meaning'. These relationships can be represented in the form of a diagram:

(110)

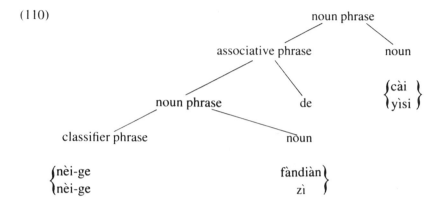

4.2.5 Definiteness and Referentiality

The notions "definite noun phrase" and "indefinite noun phrase" were briefly introduced in chapter 2.[13] In order to understand how these notions are manifested in Mandarin grammar, we must first examine the notion of reference. Noun phrases may be either referential or nonreferential. A noun phrase is *referential* when it is used to refer to an entity. This entity may be physical or conceptual, real or hypothetical, singular or plural. The underlined noun phrases in the following sentences are all referential because they are being used to refer to, or name, some entity:

(111)   Zhāngsān   shì   wǒ   —   de   péngyǒu
         Zhangsan   be   I   —   GEN   friend

Zhangsan is my friend.

(112)   mén   —   kǒu   zuò   —   zhe   yi   —
         door   —   mouth sit   —   DUR   one   —

         ge   nǚ   —   háizi
         CL   female —   child

In the doorway was sitting a girl.

(113) zhèi — tiáo xiāngjiāo wǒ chī — bu — xià
      this — CL banana I eat — can't — descend

This banana I can't eat.

(114) māma bu xǐhuān nǐ — de nán — péngyǒu
      mother not like you — GEN male — friend

Mother doesn't like your boyfriend.

(115) tā yǒu yi — ge fāngfǎ zhuàn — qián
      3sg exist one — CL method earn — money

S/He has an idea for making money.

(116) qǐng nǐ bǎ zhèi — xiē píngzi fàng
      please you BA this — PL bottle put

             zài lóushàng
             at upstairs

Please put these bottles upstairs.

(117) ná bèi gěi tā gài — shang
      take blanket to 3sg cover — ascend

Cover him/her with the blanket.

Noun phrases may also be used *nonreferentially*. For example, in sentence (118),

(118) Xīnměi shi gōngchéngshī
      Xinmei be engineer

Xinmei is an engineer.

the noun phrase *gōngchéngshī* 'engineer' is not being used to refer to any particular person. Instead it denotes a quality in terms of which the referential noun phrase *Xīnměi* can be described.

Similarly, the object component of a verb-object compound (see section 3.2.5, chapter 3) is generally nonreferential, as in (119):

(119)	wǒ	bu	huì	chàng	–	<u>gē</u>
	I	not	know:how	sing	–	song

I don't know how to sing.

Here the noun *gē* 'song' is being used, not to refer to any particular song, but rather to name the kind of thing that one sings. In sentence (115) just above, *qián* 'money' is also nonreferential; no particular money is being referred to.

There are other examples of nonreferential noun phrases. For instance, the first noun in a noun-noun compound typically is nonreferential because it functions to provide a description of the second noun in the compound rather than to refer to some particular entity, as in these examples:

(120)	<u>yángmáo</u>-kùzi	'wool-pants'
	<u>yǔ</u>-yī	'rain-coat'
	<u>fēng</u>-chē	'wind-vehicle = windmill'
	<u>fēijī</u>-lúnzi	'airplane-wheel'
	<u>húli</u>-pí	'fox-pelt'

Objects of verbs are often used nonreferentially, as illustrated by the underlined nouns (121):

(121) *a.*	nèi	–	ge	shāngrén	mài	<u>shuǐguǒ</u>
	that	–	CL	merchant	sell	fruit

That merchant sells fruit.

b.	tāmen	tōu	<u>zìxíngchē</u>
	they	steal	bicycle

They steal bicycles.

c.	wǒmen	zhòng	<u>huāshēng</u>
	we	grow	peanut

We grow peanuts.

Similarly, noun phrases within the scope of the negative particle (see chapter 12 for a discussion of the scope of negation) may be used nonreferentially:

(122) *a.*   wǒ   méi   jiàn   −   guo   <u>qíngyú</u>
          I   not   see   −   EXP   whale

     I have never seen a whale.

     b.   tā   bu   xǐhuan   <u>yāzi</u>
          3sg   not   like   duck

     S/He does not like ducks.

     c.   wǒ   méi   yǒu   <u>qiānbǐ</u>
          I   not   exist   pencil

     I don't have a pencil.

Finally, a noun phrase with no classifier phrase occurring either in topic position or after *bǎ* or *bèi* (see chapters 15 and 16) may also be used nonreferentially if it denotes a class of entities rather than any specific member(s) in that class. When they occur in these positions, nonreferential noun phrases denoting a class of entities are sometimes called *generic*. Here is an example of a generic noun phrase in topic position:

(123)   <u>māo</u>   xǐhuān   hē   niú   −   nǎi
        cat   like   drink   cow   −   milk

     Cats like to drink milk.

Only noun phrases that are referential can be definite or indefinite. In other words, the question of definiteness does not arise for nonreferential noun phrases. This situation can be represented as in (124):

(124)

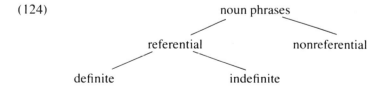

Definite and indefinite noun phrases, then, are both referential. They differ in that a definite noun phrase refers to a.. entity that the speaker believes is known to the hearer, while an indefinite noun phrase refers to an entity about which the speaker believes the hearer does not already know.

How are these distinctions marked in Mandarin grammar? First, as examples (121)–(123) show, nonreferential noun phrases never take classifier phrases. This fact alone cannot serve to identify nonreferential noun phrases, since sometimes a referential noun phrase also occurs with no classifier phrase (such as *bèi* 'blanket' in example [117] above). It does mean, however, that if a noun phrase *has* a classifier phrase, it must be a referential noun phrase. If that classifier phrase includes a demonstrative, then the noun phrase is necessarily definite, since the demonstrative serves to point out known entities. Thus, noun phrases such as the following are always definite:

(125) *a.*   <u>zhèi</u>   —   ge   rén
             this   —   CL   person

             this person

      b.   <u>nèi</u>   —   xiē   yǐzi
             that   —   PL   chair

             those chairs

      c.   <u>zhèi</u>   —   duǒ   huā
             this   —   CL   flower

             this flower

      d.   <u>nèi</u>   —   zhāng   zhǐ
             that   —   CL   paper

             that sheet of paper

If, on the other hand, a classifier phrase includes a numeral but no demonstrative, then it is necessarily indefinite:

(126) *a.*   <u>yi</u>   —   kē   shù
             one   —   CL   tree

             a tree

b.   <u>sān</u>   jiālún   yóu
       three   gallon   oil

three gallons of oil

c.   <u>yi</u>   –   ge   fāngfǎ
      one   –   CL   method

an idea

d.   <u>liǎng</u>   pén   shuǐ
      two   bowl   water

two bowls of water

A referential noun phrase may also occur without a classifier phrase. In such cases, whether the noun phrase is understood as definite or indefinite depends on the context and on the grammar of the rest of the sentence. For example, a subject noun phrase following the existential verb *yǒu* 'exist' is generally indefinite:

(127)   yǒu   <u>rén</u>   gěi   nǐ   dǎ   –   diànhuà
       exist   person   to   you   hit   –   telephone

Someone telephoned you.

As an example of a noun phrase whose definiteness or indefiniteness is strictly a matter of context, consider (128):

(128)   wǒ   mǎi   –   le   shuǐguǒ   le
       I   buy   –   PFV   fruit   CRS

I have bought $\begin{Bmatrix} \text{the fruit} \\ \text{some fruit} \end{Bmatrix}$.

If (128) is uttered in a context in which 'fruit' has already been discussed or is understood by the speaker and hearer, then *shuǐguǒ* 'fruit' is definite. Otherwise, it is indefinite.

Finally, we should point out that Mandarin does not have words that correspond to the English words *the* and *a*. The demonstrative *nèi* 'that', however, is beginning to function as 'the' if it is not stressed, and the numeral *yí* 'one', if it is not stressed, is beginning to function as 'a'. For example:

(129) *a.*

nĭ	rènshi	bu	rènshi	nèi	–	ge	rén ?
you	know	not	know	that	–	CL	person

Do you know { the / that } person?

b.

tā	măi	–	le	yi	–	ge	màozi
3sg	buy	–	PFV	one	–	CL	hat

S/He bought { a / one } hat.

4.2.6 Pronouns

In Mandarin, pronouns constitute a special class of noun phrase in two respects. First, a Mandarin pronoun always refers to an entity whose identity is already established at the time the pronoun is used. In narrative, for instance, the third person pronoun, *tā* 'she/he/it', refers to an entity whose identity is already established by a regular noun phrase that has occurred earlier. In this case, the third person pronoun and the regular noun phrase are said to be *coreferential*—they refer to the same entity in the world—and the noun phrase always precedes the co-referential pronoun, as in this example:

(130)

qù	–	nián	lái	–	le	yi	–	ge	Făguó
last	–	year	come	–	PFV	one	–	CL	France

rén ,	tā	huì
person	3sg	know:how

xiě	Zhōngguó	zì
write	China	character

Last year a French person came. S/He can write Chinese.

In (130), *tā*, the third person pronoun of the second sentence, is coreferential with *yi-ge Făguó rén* 'a French person' of the first sentence. In chapter 24, the role of pronouns in discourse is discussed in detail. What is to be noted here is the inherent referential property of pronouns, which sets them apart from other noun phrases.

The second respect in which Mandarin pronouns constitute a special class of noun phrases is the fact that pronouns do not allow any modifier, whether the modifier is a classifier/measure phrase, an associative phrase, or a modifying phrase. For example, the *b* constructions in (131)−(134) are all ungrammatical:

(i) Classifier/measure phrase:

(131) *a.*   yi   −   ge   rén
             one   −   CL   person

        one person

      b.   *yi   −   ge   tā
             one   −   CL   3sg

(ii) Associative phrase:

(132) *a.*   xuéshú   −   jiè   −   de   rén
             scholarship   −   world   −   ASSOC person

        people in academia

      b.   *xuéshú   −   jiè   −   de   tā
             scholarship   −   world   −   ASSOC 3sg

(iii) Modifying phrase:

(133) *a.*   huài   rén
             bad   person
      b.   *huài   tā
             bad   3sg

(134) *a.* chūmíng   de   rén
           famous   NOM   person

        a famous person

      b. *chūmíng   de   tā
             famous   NOM   3sg

When one is appraising or evaluating oneself, however, it is possible to modify the
first person pronoun:

(135) kělián   de   wǒ
       pitiful   NOM   I
       Poor me!

Since Mandarin does not have inflection, conjugation, or case markers, the
pronominal system is relatively simple:

(136)   wǒ   'I/me'
        nǐ   'you (sg)'
        tā   'he/she/it/him/her'
        wǒmen   'we/us'
        nǐmen   'you (plural)'
        tāmen   'they/them'

The Mandarin pronouns refer primarily to persons. The third person pronouns
are rarely used to refer to animals and even more rarely to refer to inanimate
entities, though such uses do occur because of the influence of English. In general,
a third person pronoun is used to refer to an inanimate entity only when the absence
of a pronoun or other noun phrase would render the construction ungrammatical.
For example, as an answer to the question in (137) a, only b, without the pronoun,
is appropriate; c, with the pronoun, is not. Here the context allows the absence of
the pronoun without impairing the grammaticality of the sentence in b:

(137) a.   nǐ   xǐhuān   nèi   —   běn   shū   ma ?
           you   like   that   —   CL   book   Q

       Do you like that book?

      b.   wǒ   xǐhuān
           I   like

       I like it.

      c. ??wǒ   xǐhuān   tā
           I   like   it

On the other hand, consider (138), in which the pronoun occurs in an associative phrase (see section 4.2.2 of this chapter). For the associative phrase to be grammatical, it must contain a pronoun or a noun phrase preceding the associative particle, -de. The third person singular pronoun, tā, here refers to the inanimate noun phrase Hélán 'Holland' in the preceding sentence.

(138) Hélán dìfang fēicháng xiǎo wǒmen zhīdao tā   —
       Holland place unusually small we   know   3sg —

       de   jīngjì   wèntí   bu   jiǎndān
       ASSOC economy problem   not   simple

Holland is a small country. We know its economic problems are not simple.

Similarly, the bǎ construction requires a noun phrase after bǎ; the third person singular pronoun in (139) refers to the inanimate noun huà 'painting':

(139) guà   huà   —   de   dīngzi diào le ,   wǒ
       hang painting   —   ASSOC   nail   fall   CRS   I

       děi   bǎ   tā   guà   —   hǎo
       must   BA   3sg   hang   —   good

The nail for hanging the painting has fallen out; I have to hang it right.

As a general rule, the third person pronoun, tā, serving as a topic or as a topic that also functions as a subject does not refer to an inanimate entity. Thus, in (140) tā preferably refers to a person; it may refer to an animal, but it cannot refer to an inanimate object, such as, say, a painting:

(140) tā   hěn   hǎo   —   kàn
       3sg   very   good   —   look

S/He is very good-looking.

In the older Beijing dialect, the second person singular pronoun, nǐ, has a polite form, nín. It may be used between people who are not well acquainted. Its usage, however, is not widespread, even in present-day Beijing.

The question words *shéi* 'who', *shénme* 'what', and *năr/năli* 'where' are often called *interrogative pronouns* because they "stand for" an unknown noun phrase in a question. For example:

(141) *a.* <u>shéi</u>   zài   xǐzăo ?
        who   DUR   bathe

      Who is bathing?

    b.   nǐ   mài   <u>shénme</u> ?
        you   sell   what

      What do you sell?

    c.   Zhāngsān   zhù   zài   <u>năr</u> ?
        Zhangsan   live   at   where

      Where does Zhangsan live?

The questions illustrated in (141) are called *question-word questions*; they are discussed in more detail in chapter 18 on questions.

Finally, we should mention that the possessive pronouns in Mandarin are composed simply of the pronouns and the genitive particle, *-de*. In other words, possessive pronouns do not have special independent forms. For example,

(142) *a.*   wŏ   —   de   pídài
         I   —   GEN   belt

      my belt

    b.   tāmen   —   de   shŏubiăo
        they   —   GEN   watch

      their watch

    c.   nǐ   —   de   kùzi
        you   —   GEN   pants

      your pants

4.2.7 Reflexives

The Mandarin reflexive morpheme, roughly meaning 'self', is *zìji*. It can be used in two ways. First, it can function as a reflexive pronoun, in which case it occurs in the verb phrase in any position where a noun phrase could occur and may optionally be preceded by a pronoun that is coreferential with the subject of the sentence:

(i) Direct object:

(143)	Lǐsì	zài	zébèi	(tā)	zìji
	Lisi	DUR	blame	(3sg)	self

Lisi is blaming himself.

(ii) Indirect object:

(144)	tā	gěi	(tā)	zìji	xiě	–	le	yi
	3sg	to	(3sg)	self	write	–	PFV	one

		–	fēng	xìn
		–	CL	letter

S/He wrote himself/herself a letter.

(iii) Coverb object:

(145)	wǒ	gēn	(wǒ)	zìji	shēngqì
	I	with	(I)	self	angry

I'm angry with myself.

(iv) Possessor in a possessive phrase:

(146)	wǒ	chuān	(wǒ)	zìji	–	de	yīfu
	I	wear	(I)	self	–	GEN	clothing

I wear my own clothing.

In sentences like (143)–(146), the (pronoun-plus)-*zìji* sequence functions solely as a reflexive pronoun: that is, it simply signals that its referent is coreferential with that of the subject in the same clause.

The second way in which *ziji* can be used is in an adverblike capacity. In this function it occurs before the verb phrase and serves to contrast oneself with others. Here are two examples:

(147)   wǒ   buzhībujuéde   <u>zìji</u>   yě   zuò   yùndòng   le
         I   unconsciously   self   also   do   exercise   CRS

> I am unconsciously also doing exercises myself (i.e., others were doing it before, and now I too am doing it).

(148)   Zhāngsān   <u>zìji</u>   shāo   cài
         Zhangsan   self   cook   food

> Zhangsan cooks food himself (as opposed to anyone else cooking for him).

In this usage, the subject may be missing if it is understood from the context or from previous mention. For instance, in the following examples, the subject noun phrase can be optionally absent:

(149)   tā   zǒng   juéde   (tā)   <u>zìji</u>   tài   shīyì
         3sg   always   feel   (3sg)   self   too   dissatisfied

> S/He always felt that s/he himself/herself was too dissatisfied (as opposed to the others, who were content).

(150)   (nǐ)   <u>zìji</u>   zuò   gōngkè
         (you)   self   do   homework

> You do the homework yourself (as opposed to anyone doing it for you).

(151)   tā   zhīdao   (tā)   <u>zìji</u>   zuò   cuò   shì   le
         3sg   know   (3sg)   self   do   wrong   affair   CRS

> S/He knew that s/he had done something wrong.

In complex sentences with more than one verb phrase, *ziji* can occur either before the first verb phrase or before the second one. The contrast between self and others which *ziji* expresses is always understood with respect to the verb immediately following *ziji*. Thus, the following sentences convey quite different messages:

(152)   wǒ   ziji   yào   qù
        I   self   want   go

       I myself want to go (i.e., no one else is making me go; it is I who *want* to go).

(153)   wǒ   yào   ziji   qù
        I   want   self   go

       I want to go by myself (i.e., I want myself to be the one to go; no one else should go).

Finally, *ziji* can be used to express a general truth in the form of a proverb. In such cases it means something like 'one' and generally occurs with another *ziji* later in the sentence, with which it is coreferential. The general message is 'If one does X, then that same one can also do Y'. Here is an example:

(154)   ziji   zhuàn   qián   ziji   huā
        self   earn   money   self   spend

       If one earns money, then one can spend it.

Ziji, then, can function either as a reflexive pronoun in a verb phrase to signal coreferentiality with the subject noun phrase of the sentence, or as an adverb to signal a contrast between the 'self' in question and others who could be involved. When *ziji* functions as an adverb, it always occurs after the subject and before the verb phrase.

4.3 The Verb Phrase

The *verb phrase* of a sentence in any language is that part of the simple sentence of which the nucleus is the verb. Verbs describe events, actions, states, processes (change of states), and experiences, and verbs presuppose the presence of noun phrases that refer to the participants in those events. The type and number of participants for each verb are determined to a large extent by the meaning of that verb. In addition, there are a number of grammatical elements denoting certain semantic concepts which tend to appear with the verb in most languages: these are tense, aspect, modals, and negation (Mandarin has aspect but not tense, and Mandarin modals are auxiliary verbs; see chapters 6, 12, and 5 on aspect, negation, and auxiliary verbs, respectively). Aside from the verb, which is the nucleus, a verb phrase includes those grammatical elements that occur with the verb as well as most of the noun phrases that refer to the participants in the event denoted by the verb. What is excluded from the verb phrase is the subject and/or the topic. In the following examples the verb phrases are underlined:

(155)   wǒ   <u>shì</u>   <u>tā</u>   <u>bàba</u>
        I   be   3sg   father

    I am his/her father.

(156)   <u>děng</u>   <u>yíxià</u>
        wait   a:bit

    Wait a minute.

(157)   tā   <u>kàn</u>   —   <u>le</u>   <u>sān</u>   —   <u>běn</u>   <u>shū</u>
        3sg   read   —   PFV   three   —   CL   book

    S/He read three books.

(158)   Zhāngsān   <u>huì</u>   <u>shuō</u>   <u>Zhōngguó</u>   <u>huà</u>
        Zhangsan   can   speak   China   speech

    Zhangsan can speak Chinese.

(159)   wǒ   <u>bu</u>   <u>yào</u>   <u>miànbāo</u>
        I   not   want   bread

    I don't want bread.

(160)   zhèi   —   kē   shù   yèzi   <u>hěn</u>   <u>hǎo</u>   —   <u>kàn</u>
        this   —   CL   tree   leaves   very   good   —   look

    This tree (topic), its leaves are very pretty.

A common term referring to the function of a verb phrase is *predicate*. A predicate, however, is not necessarily a verb phrase. For instance, it can be a noun phrase that has the same function as a verb phrase has. The noun phrase *wŏmen-de láoshī* 'our teacher' in (161) is an example of such a predicate:

(161) Zhāngsān   wŏmen   –   de   láoshī
       Zhangsan   we   –   GEN   teacher

       Zhangsan (is) our teacher.

Thus, the word *predicate* is a functional term in opposition with the functional term *subject*.

In the following presentation we will discuss the different types of verb phrases.

4.3.1 Types of Verb Phrases

Verb phrases are classified according to whether they have no object, one object, or two objects. According to this classification, the types of verb phrases found in Mandarin are by and large the same as those found in other languages:

A. Intransitive (no object)

   1. Adjectival

   2. Copula

   3. Others

B. Transitive (one direct object)

C. Ditransitive (one direct object and one indirect object)

A. Intransitive Verb Phrases

An *intransitive verb phrase* has an intransitive verb as its nucleus. Thus, an intransitive verb phrase may be classified according to whether its nucleus is (1) an adjectival verb, (2) the copula, or (3) neither of these.

A.1. Adjectival Verbs

Adjectives denote qualities or properties that we ascribe to entities.[14] They may be divided into two semantic groups: scalar and absolute. *Scalar* adjectives describe relative qualities, which may be attributed to an entity to a greater or lesser extent, such as *gāo* 'tall', *pàng* 'fat', *ānjìng* 'peaceful and quiet', *měilì* 'beautiful'. *Absolute* adjectives, on the other hand, denote a property that cannot be calibrated in degrees: an entity either has or does not have the property. Some examples of absolute adjectives are *cuò* 'wrong', *kōng* 'empty', *guān-rè* 'boiling hot', *cāngbái* 'pale white', *yuán* 'round', *bīng-liáng* 'ice-cold'. The most important structural difference between the scalar adjectives and the absolute adjectives is that only the former, not the latter, can appear in the comparative construction (see chapter 19 on the comparative construction), as in:

(162) *a.*   Zhāngsān   bǐ   tā   <u>pàng</u>
         Zhangsan   COMP   3sg   fat

       Zhangsan is fatter than s/he is.

     b.   zhèr   bǐ   nàr   <u>ānjìng</u>
         here   COMP   there   quiet

       Here is more quiet than there.

     c.   *zhèi   —   ge   píngzi   bǐ   nèi   —   ge
         this   —   CL   bottle   compare   that   —   CL

            píngzi   <u>kōng</u>
            bottle   empty

     d.   *Zhāngsān   bǐ   Lǐsì   <u>cuò</u>
         Zhangsan   compare   Lisi   wrong

As the term *adjectival verb* suggests, the vast majority of adjectives may function as verbs in Mandarin. That is, they may be the nucleus of a verb phrase, as in (163) and (164), where they are followed by a sentence-final particle:

(163)   Zhāngsān   <u>pàng</u>   le
       Zhangsan   fat   CRS

     Zhangsan has gotten fat.

(164)   jiǔ   —   píng   <u>kōng</u>   le
       wine   —   bottle   empty   CRS

     The wine bottle has become empty.

They can also be negated by the negative particles *bu* or *méi(yǒu)*, just as verbs can be:

(165) Zhāngsān   bu   pàng
        Zhangsan   not   fat

Zhangsan is not fat.

(166) jiǔ   —   píng   méi   kōng
        wine   —   bottle   not   empty

The wine bottle has not become empty.

The scalar adjectives can occur as the sole element of a verb phrase:

(167) tā   pàng
        3sg   fat

S/He is fat.

More often than not, however, a scalar adjective occurring as the sole element of a verb phrase will take on the adverbial modifier *hěn* 'very', as in (168):

(168) *a.*   tā   hěn   pàng
          s/he   very   fat

{ S/He is very fat. }
{ S/He is fat. }

    b.   nèi   —   ge   guójiā   hěn   mínzhǔ
           that   —   CL   country   very   democratic

{ That country is very democratic. }
{ That country is democratic. }

There are two points concerning the usage of *hěn* 'very' that are worth noting. First, if *hěn* is not heavily stressed, its meaning 'very' may be bleached. Thus (168) *a* and *b* are ambiguous. One of the interpretations involves *hěn* with its full-fledged meaning of 'very', while the other involves a semantically bleached *hěn*, which adds no intensive meaning to the sentence. A second point about *hěn* is that it may occur with certain absolute (nonscalar) adjectives also. Thus, although *bīng-liáng* 'ice-cold' and *jiǎ* 'fake' are absolute adjectives that do not occur with *hěn*, the absolute adjectives *duì* 'correct' and *yuán* 'round' can occur with *hěn*:

(169) *a.*

*zhèi	—	bēi	shuǐ	hěn	bīng	—	liáng
this	—	cup	water	very	ice	—	cold

b.

*zhèi	—	jù	huà	hěn	jiǎ
this	—	CL	utterance	very	fake

c.

nèi	—	ge	pénzi	hěn	yuán
that	—	CL	bowl	very	round

That bowl is very round.

d.

tā	shuō	de	hěn	duì
3sg	speak	NOM	very	correct

What s/he says is quite correct.

For the most part, those adjectives that can occur as the sole element of a verb phrase are scalar adjectives; most absolute adjectives do not occur as the sole element of a verb phrase, though there are some exceptions. For example:

(170) *a.*

zhèi	hú	shuǐ	guǎn	—	rè
this	kettle	water	boiling	—	hot

This kettle of water is boiling hot.

b.

jīntiān	tiān	—	sè	cāng	—	bái
today	sky	—	color	pale	—	white

Today, the sky is pale white.

c.

nèi	wǎn	fàn	bīng	—	liáng
that	bowl	rice	ice	—	cold

That bowl of rice is ice-cold.

d.   nǐ   dùi
        you   correct

You are right.

Those absolute adjectives that cannot occur as the sole element of a verb phrase may be nominalized with the particle *de* to occur in the verb phrase of a copula sentence:

(171) *a.*   nèi   —   fēng   xìn   shì   jiǎ   de
              that   —   CL   letter   be   fake   NOM

That letter is fake.

b.   *nèi   —   fēng   xìn   jiǎ
         that   —   CL   letter   fake

In general, the absolute adjectives that cannot occur as the sole element of a verb phrase may also not occur with the sentence-final *le* or with the negative particle:

(172) *a.*   *nèi   —   fēng   xìn   jiǎ   le
               that   —   CL   letter   fake   CRS

b.   *nèi   —   fēng   xìn   bu   jiǎ
         that   —   CL   letter   not   fake

Here are examples of three other adjectives that behave identically: they cannot occur as the sole element in a verb phrase or with a sentence-final particle *le* or a negative particle, but must be nominalized if they are to serve as predicates:

(173) *a.*   zhèi   —   tiáo   kùzi   shì   xiànchéng   de
              this   —   CL   pants   be   ready:made   NOM

This pair of pants is ready-made.

b.   *zhèi   —   tiáo   kùzi   xiànchéng
         this   —   CL   pants   ready:made

c.   *zhèi   —   tiáo   kùzi   xiànchéng   le
         that   —   CL   pants   ready:made   CRS

d.   *zhèi   —   tiáo   kùzi   <u>bu   xiànchéng</u>
     this   —   CL   pants   not   ready:made

(174) *a.*   nèi   —   ge   dàxué   shì   <u>guó   —</u>
     that   —   CL   university   be   nation   —

     <u>lì   de</u>
     establish   NOM

That university is a national university.

b.   *nèi   —   ge   dàxué   <u>guó   —   lì</u>
     that   —   CL   university   nation   —   establish

c.   *nèi   —   ge   dàxué   <u>guó   —   lì   le</u>
     that   —   CL   university   nation   —   establish   CRS

d.   *nèi   —   ge   dàxué   bu   guó   —   lì
     that   —   CL   university   not   nation   —   establish

(175) *a.*   zhèi   —   zhǒng   shāngpǐn   shì   <u>shàngděng   de</u>
     this   —   type   merchandise   be   high:quality   NOM

This type of merchandise is high quality.

b.   *zhèi   —   zhǒng   shāngpǐn   <u>shàngděng</u>
     this   —   type   merchandise   high:quality

c.   *zhèi   —   zhǒng   shāngpǐn   <u>shàngděng   le</u>
     this   —   type   merchandise   high:quality   CRS

d.   *zhèi   —   zhǒng   shāngpǐn   bu   <u>shàngděng</u>
     this   —   type   merchandise   not   high:quality

Certain adjectival verbs can take a clause or a verb phrase as their subject. In the examples in (176), the clause or verb phrase serving as a subject is underlined:

(176) *a.*   <u>nǐ   bu   qù</u>   hǎo
     you   not   go   good

It's fine for you not to go.

b. | zhèi | — | ge | biǎo | huài | le | zhēn | kěxī |
|------|---|-----|-------|--------|-----|------|-------------|
| this | — | CL | watch | broken | CRS | real | regrettable |

It is really regrettable that this watch has broken.

c. | zài | nàli | mǎi | dōngxi | hěn | máfǎn |
|-----|-------|-----|--------|-----|-------------|
| at | there | buy | thing | very | troublesome |

It is a lot of trouble to shop there.

If an adjectival verb allows an abstract noun phrase (one that refers to an abstract rather than a concrete entity in the world) to be its subject, it will also take a clause or a verb phrase as its subject. For instance, all of the adjectival verbs in (176) can also take abstract noun phrases as their subjects:

(177) *a.* | nǐ | — | de | zhǔyì | hěn | hǎo |
|-----|---|-----|-------|-----|------|
| you | — | GEN | idea | very | good |

Your idea is very good.

b. | zhèi | — | jiàn | shì | hěn | kěxī |
|------|---|------|--------|-----|-------------|
| this | — | CL | matter | very | regrettable |

This matter is very regrettable.

c. | nèi | — | ge | shǒuxù | hěn | máfǎn |
|-----|---|-----|-----------|-----|-------------|
| that | — | CL | procedure | very | troublesome |

That procedure is very troublesome.

Since sentences of the type illustrated in (176) involve more than one verb, they are presented and discussed in more detail in chapter 21 on serial verb constructions.

A.2 Copula

The copula verb in Mandarin is *shì* 'be'.[15] It has several characteristics that make it distinct from other verbs.

(i) Unlike other verbs, it does not occur with aspect markers;[16] thus, (178) *b* is ungrammatical:

(178) *a.*

Zhāngsān	shì	yi	—	ge	hùshì
Zhangsan	be	one	—	CL	nurse

Zhangsan $\begin{Bmatrix} \text{is} \\ \text{was} \end{Bmatrix}$ a nurse.

b. *Zhāngsān   <u>shì</u>   — $\begin{Bmatrix} \text{le} \\ \text{guo} \\ \text{zhe} \end{Bmatrix}$ yi   —   ge   hùshì

    Zhangsan   be   — $\begin{Bmatrix} \text{PFV} \\ \text{EXP} \\ \text{DUR} \end{Bmatrix}$ one   —   CL   nurse

(ii) *Shì* can be negated only by *bu*, not by *méi(yǒu)*.

(179) *a.*

wǒ	<u>bu</u>	shì	Zhōngguo	—	rén
I	not	be	China	—	person

I am not a Chinese.

b.

*wǒ	<u>méi</u>	shì	Zhōngguo	—	rén
I	not	be	China	—	person

(iii) Most auxiliary verbs, such as *néng* 'can', *gǎn* 'dare', *yuànyi/kěn* 'be willing to', and *huì* 'will', do not occur with the copula verb *shì* 'be'.

(180)

    *Zhāngsān $\begin{Bmatrix} \text{néng} \\ \text{gǎn} \\ \text{kěn} \\ \text{huì} \end{Bmatrix}$ <u>shì</u>   yi   —   ge   yīshēng

    Zhangsan $\begin{Bmatrix} \text{can} \\ \text{dare} \\ \text{is:willing} \\ \text{will} \end{Bmatrix}$ be   one   —   CL   physician

The auxiliary verbs that can occur with the copula are: *yīnggāi/yīngdāng/gāi* 'should', *děi/bìxū/bìyào/bìděi* 'must'. For example,

(181) *a.*

Zhāngsān	yīnggāi	shì	yi	–	ge	zhéxuéjiā
Zhangsan	should	be	one	–	CL	philosopher

Zhangsan should be a philosopher.

b.

Zhāngsān	bìděi	shì	yi	–	ge	yŭyánxuéjiā
Zhangsan	must	be	one	–	CL	linguist

Zhangsan must be a linguist.

There arc three types of constructions that employ the copula as their verb: (1) simple copula sentences; (2) special affirmative sentences; and (3) presentative sentences.

A.2.1 Simple Copula Sentences

A *simple copula sentence* typically contains a referential subject noun phrase linked to a nonreferential noun phrase by the copula verb. The verb phrase of the sentence is composed of the copula and the nonreferential noun phrase. This nonreferential noun phrase serves to characterize or identify the referent of the subject noun phrase, and the copula verb serves as a link between the two. Thus, the nonreferential noun phrase following the copula is not an object of the copula verb, and the verb phrase of the simple copula sentence is intransitive. Here are some examples:

(182)

tā	shì	wŏ	–	de	hăo	péngyŏu
3sg	be	I	–	GEN	good	friend

S/He is my good friend.

(183)

tā	fùqin	shì	wàijiāo	bùzhăng
3sg	father	be	foreign:affair	minister

His/Her father is the foreign minister.

(184)   wǒ   zuì   xǐhuān   de   shì   Shànghǎi   cài
        I   most   like   NOM   be   Shanghai   dish

What I like the most is Shanghai food.

An interesting phenomenon characterizes the use of *shì* in simple copula sentences: it can occur in sentences that cannot be understood in their literal sense. These have been called "illogical" copula sentences by some Chinese grammarians.[17] For example:

(185)   wǒ   shì   chǎo   —   fàn
        I   be   fry   —   rice

I am (the one with) the fried rice.

(186)   nǐ   bàba   jiù   shì   nǐ   yi   —   ge   érzi
        you   father   just   be   you   one   —   CL   son

Your father is (= has) only you as his son.

(187)   tā   shì   yi   —   piàn   rè   —   xīn
        3sg   be   one   —   expanse   hot   —   heart

S/He is (= can be characterized as having) a lot of enthusiasm.

Sentences like (185)−(187) must be used in appropriate contexts, of course; (185) might be used, for example, in a restaurant if one wanted to remind the waiter what one had ordered. The literal meanings of these sentences are clearly not what the sentences are intended to convey—(185), for example, does not mean 'I am fried rice'. Thus, the Mandarin copula verb allows a very loose linkage or connection between the referential subject noun phrase and the nonreferential noun phrase following the copula. The information in the speech context, then, serves to clarify the precise nature of this linkage. This means that, depending on the context, a sentence like (188) could convey that I voted for Lisi, that I am a member of his group, that he is my favorite of the singers we are discussing, and similar meanings, as well as the literal meaning 'I am Lisi'.

(188)   wǒ   shì   Lǐsì
        I   be   Lisi

A.2.2 The Copula as a Marker of Special Affirmation

The copula *shì* can also be used to mean 'It is true that . . .' or 'It is that . . .'
with respect to a statement already mentioned in the conversation. For example,
consider the following minimal pair:

(189) *a.*   tā   méi   qián
              3sg   not:exist money

       S/He doesn't have any money.

      b.   tā   shì   méi   qián[18]
              3sg   be   not:exist   money

       It's true that s/he doesn't have any money.

As suggested by our translations, (189) *a*, without *shì*, is essentially neutral and
could be used in volunteering information or in answering a question; (189) *b*, with
shì, on the other hand, could be used only to affirm what had been said earlier or
what had been suspected or inferred by the speaker and the hearer. In the construction exemplified by (189) *b*, the *shì* remains a linking verb, as it is in the simple
copula sentence. In this case, though, the copula is not linking the subject noun
phrase and a nonreferential noun phrase: rather, it is linking the subject noun phrase
and a full verb phrase that may include a negative particle, an auxiliary verb, and a
manner adverb. If *shì* in (189) *b* is seen as a linking verb, then (189) *b* must be
regarded as a complex sentence, for it contains more than one verb. Because
constructions such as (189) *b* are essentially copula sentences, however, we choose
to present them in this section of the book.
    Let us examine some examples of discourse in which sentences with the *shì*
signaling special affirmation might occur. Such examples illustrate the important
point that sentences with the *shì* signaling special affirmation always affirm a
statement in the preceding or following discourse.

(190) A: wǒ   xiǎng   tā   hěn   qióng ,   suóyǐ   bu
           I   think   3sg   very   poor   therefore   not

           kěn   shàng   guǎnzi
           willing ascend restaurant

       I think s/he is poor. That's why s/he is not willing to go to restaurants.

B: duì ,   tā   <u>shì</u>   méi   qián ,   kěshi   tā
      right   3sg   be   not:exist   money   but   3sg

        hěn   yǒu   zhìqì
        very   exist   pride

Right, s/he doesn't have any money, but s/he is very proud.

(191) (reluctant child telling on his/her brother in response to mother's suspicion that the brother has not bought any books)

    tā   <u>shì</u>   méi   mǎi   shū
    3sg   be   not   buy   books

(Well,) it's true that he didn't buy books.

(192) (commenting to a friend who wonders why the child is still up at 11:30 P.M. even though s/he is going on an outing the next day)

    tā   míngtiān   <u>shì</u>   dì   —   yi   cì   qù   lǔxíng
    3sg   tomorrow   be   ORD   —   one   time   go   outing

        kěshi   tā   shuì   —   bu   —   zháo   —
        but   3sg   sleep   —   can't   —   succeed   —

        jiào
        sleep

It's true that tomorrow s/he's going on an outing for the first time, but s/he can't get to sleep.

(193) (in a restaurant after some confusion as to who can eat what)

    wǒ   <u>shì</u>   bu   chī   là   de ,   tā   shì
    I   be   not   eat   hot   NOM   3sg   be

        shénme   dōu   kěyi   chī
        what   all   can   eat

It's that I can't eat hot food, and s/he can eat anything.

The usage of the copula to signal special affirmation is not confined to linking a subject noun phrase with a full verb phrase that has been mentioned in earlier discourse. The copula can be placed before an entire sentence referring to some information mentioned earlier in the discourse. In such a case, it conveys the message 'It's that . . .'. The following sentences will illustrate:

(194) (to a friend who is upset because the speaker says s/he can't go out for a snack)

bu	shì	wǒ	bu	yào	lái ,	shì	tā
not	be	I	not	want	come	be	3sg

	bu	ràng	wǒ	lái
	not	let	I	come

It's not that I don't want to come, it's that s/he won't let me come.

(195) (to someone who questions the noise)

shì	wo	zài	nàr	dǎ	gǔ
be	I	at	there	hit	drum

It's that I've been playing drums over there.

With heavy stress on a word (call it X) following the copula shì in sentences such as (194) or (195), the sentences then convey the meaning:

(196) It is X $\left\{ \begin{matrix} \text{that} \\ \text{who} \end{matrix} \right\}$ . . .

For example, with heavy stress on wǒ 'I' of (195), the sentence has the following meaning:

(197) It's I who's been playing drums over there.

On the other hand, if the heavy stress falls on gǔ 'drum', then (195) has the meaning:

(198) It's drums that I've been playing over there.

The copula *shì* itself can also receive heavy stress in sentences (190)−(195). In such a case, the sentence strongly affirms a piece of information in earlier discourse which now follows the *shì*. Thus, when *shì* is stressed in sentences such as (190)−(195), these sentences are generally used in a contentious or argumentative situation. Their meaning can best be described as in (199), with heavy stress on 'true':

(199) It's *true* that . . .

For example, the first part of (193), with heavy stress on *shì*, yields the sentence

(200)	wǒ	**shì**	bu	chī	là	de
	I	be	not	eat	hot	NOM

It's true that I can't eat hot food.

A sentence like this might be used in a dispute about whether the speaker can eat hot food. When heavy stress is applied to the copula, yielding the interpretation given in (199), the construction with the stressed *shì* is often called the *emphatic construction*, roughly equivalent to English emphatic *do* sentences, as in:

(201) *a.* She *did* go to San Francisco.

b. He *does* belong to the country club.

A.2.3 The Copula in Presentative Sentences

There is a type of presentative sentence involving locative and time with the following structure:

(202) $\begin{Bmatrix} \text{locative phrase} \\ \text{time phrase} \end{Bmatrix}$ + shì + noun phrase

For example:

(203)	qiánmiàn	shì	yi	−	ge	miào
	in:front	be	one	−	CL	temple

There is a temple in front.

(204) míngtiān   shì   wǒ   —   de   shēngrì
       tomorrow   be   I   —   GEN   birthday

It is my birthday tomorrow.

(205) dàochù   dōu   shì   yě   huā
      everywhere all   be   wild   flower

There are wild flowers everywhere.

(206) xià   —   ge   yuè   shì   shìjiè   —   yùndòng
       next —   CL   month be   world   —   sport

       —   dà   —   huì
       —   big   —   meeting

It's the Olympics next month.

Presentative sentences are discussed in detail in chapter 17. The contrast between the presentative sentences with the copula, shown in (203)–(206), and their counterparts with the existential verb *yǒu* is discussed in section 17.1 of chapter 17.

A.3. Other Intransitive Verbs

This category of intransitive verbs includes every intransitive verb that is neither an adjectival verb nor the copula. These intransitive verb phrases may contain a coverb phrase (see chapter 9) or an adverbial phrase (see chapter 8). Here are some examples, with the intransitive verb underlined:

(207)   tā   <u>shuì</u>   zài   shāfa   —   shang
        3sg   sleep   at   sofa   —   on

S/He sleeps on the sofa.

(208) wǒmen   měi   —   tiān   qī   —   diǎnzhōng
      we   each —   day   seven —   o'clock

      <u>qǐ   —   lai</u>
      rise   —   come

We get up every day at seven o'clock.

(209)   wǒ   gēn   tā   <u>hé — bu — lái</u>
         I   with   3sg   can't:get:along

I can't get along with him/her.

(210)   Zhāngsān   míng   —   nián   dào   zhèli   <u>lái</u>
         Zhangsan   next   —   year   to   here   come

Next year Zhangsan will come here.

A large number of these intransitive verbs signify motion: for example, *fēi* 'fly',
pá 'crawl', *liú* 'float', *pǎo* 'run', *dǎo* 'collapse', *dòng* 'move', *zǒu* 'walk', *zhuǎn*
'revolve', *dǎdǒu* 'shake, tremble', *shàngqù* 'ascend', *xiàqù* 'descend'.

(211)   niǎor   zài   kōng   —   zhōng   <u>fēi</u>
         bird   at   sky   —   middle   fly

The birds are flying in the sky.

(212)   Zhāngsān   zài   dì   —   shang   <u>pá</u>
         Zhangsan   at   ground   —   on   crawl

Zhangsan is crawling on the ground.

Other members of this third category of intransitive verb include, for instance,
kū 'cry', *xiào* 'laugh', *tiàowǔ* 'dance', *zuò* 'sit', *zhù* 'live', *tǎng* 'lie down', *xiūxi*
'rest', *kāishǐ* 'begin', *chūxiàn* 'appear', *táo* 'escape', *jiào* 'yell', and *wán* 'finish'.
Here are some examples in sentences:

(213)   Zhāngsān   zài   <u>kū</u>
         Zhangsan   DUR   cry

Zhangsan is crying.

(214)   diànyǐng   <u>kāishǐ</u>   le
         movie   begin   CRS

The movie has begun.

(215) nǐ   <u>zhù</u>   zài   nǎr?
       you   live   at   where

Where do you live?

B. Transitive Verb Phrases

When the meaning of a verb requires two participants and one of them is doing something to or directing some behavior at the other one, such a verb is called a *transitive verb*. The participant who is doing something is the *subject*, and the one toward which or whom the behavior is directed is the *direct object*. For example,

(216) tā   chī   —   le   yi   —   ge   yóutiáo
       3sg   eat   —   PFV   one   —   CL   fritter

S/He ate a fritter.

In (216), *chī* 'eat' is a transitive verb, with the subject *tā* 's/he' acting on the direct object *yige yóutiáo* 'a fritter'.

Here are more examples of transitive verb phrases in sentences, with the direct object underlined:

(217) tā   pīpíng   —   le   <u>nèi</u>   —   <u>ge</u>
       3sg   criticize —   PFV   that   —   CL

       <u>nǚ</u>   —   <u>háizi</u>
       female   —   child

S/He criticized that girl.

(218) tā   zài   túshūguǎn   kàn   <u>bào</u>
       3sg   at   library   read   newspaper

S/He's at the library reading the paper.

(219) Zhāngsān   mà   <u>Lǐsì</u>   le   ma ?
       Zhangsan   scold   Lisi   CRS   Q

Did Zhangsan scold Lisi?

(220)	tā	bu	huì	pīn	nǐ	—	de	mingzi
	3sg	not	know:how	spell	you	—	GEN	name

S/He doesn't know how to spell your name.

In most languages of the world, certain transitive verbs may occur without a direct object. In Mandarin, transitive verb phrases without a direct object are particularly common because of zero anaphora: where in English, for instance, an entity in the world is referred to by a pronoun, in Mandarin such an entity is simply understood without the presence of a pronoun (see chapter 24 on pronouns in discourse). The absence of a direct object in a transitive verb phrase, however, does not change the transitive nature of the verb involved. In such a case, the direct object is implied, as here:

(221)	wǒ	chī	—	le
	I	eat	—	PFV

I have eaten (it).

(222)	tā	mǎi	—	le
	3sg	buy	—	PFV

S/He has bought (it).

(223)	wǒ	dǎ	—	le
	I	hit	—	PFV

I have hit (him/her).

Certain verbs, which are not to be confused with transitive verbs whose direct objects are implied, may function either as transitive verbs or intransitive verbs.[19] In the following examples, the *a* sentences are intransitive, and each *b* sentence, which contains the same verb as that of the corresponding *a* sentence, is transitive. The direct object of the transitive verb in each *b* sentence is underlined:

(224) *a.*	bié	xiào
	don't	laugh

Don't laugh.

b. bié   xiào   <u>wǒ</u>
      don't   laugh   <u>I</u>

Don't laugh at me.

(225) *a.*   tā   hěn   tān
             3sg   very   greedy

S/He's very greedy.

b.   tā   hěn   tān   <u>nǐ   —   de   qián-cái</u>
       3sg   very   greedy   <u>you   —   GEN   wealth</u>

S/He's very greedy for your wealth.

(226) *a.*   wǒ   hěn   dāngxīn
             I   very   careful

I am very careful.

b.   wǒ   hěn   dāngxīn   <u>wǒ   —   de   shēntǐ</u>
       I   very   careful   <u>I   —   GEN   body</u>

I am very careful about my health.

B.1 Positions for the Direct Object

In all of the above examples, the direct object occurs immediately after the verb. Depending on the context, however, it can occur in other positions as well: it can be the topic in sentence-initial position, whether or not the subject is expressed; it can occur with the particle *bǎ* before the verb; and it can also occur before the verb without *bǎ*. Let's look at each of these possibilities.

B.1.1 Direct Object as Topic

In our discussion of topic above in section 4.1 of this chapter, we saw several examples of sentences in which the direct object was the topic. For example,

(227)   <u>gǒu</u>   wǒ   bu   xǐhuān
        <u>dog</u>   I   not   like

Dogs, I don't like.

Here are some other examples:

(228) | jīntiān | — | de | bào | nǐ | kàn | — |
       |---------|---|-----|---------|-----|------|---|
       | today | — | GEN | newspaper | you | read | — |

guo	le	ma ?
EXP	CRS	Q

Have you read today's paper yet?

(229) | zhèi | — | běn | shū | tā | yào | sòng | gěi | nǐ |
       |------|---|-----|------|-----|------|---------|-----|-----|
       | this | — | CL | book | 3sg | want | present | to | you |

This book, s/he wants to give you.

When the direct object is the topic, the subject may be unexpressed if it is unimportant, unknown, or understood:

(230) | zhèi | — | běn | shū | bu | néng | suíbiàn | fānyìng |
       |------|---|-----|------|-----|------|---------|-----------|
       | this | — | CL | book | not | can | at:will | reproduce |

This book can't be reproduced at will.

(231) | zhèi | — | jian | shì | děng | yíxià | jiù | gàosu | nǐ |
       |------|---|------|------|------|---------|------|-------|-----|
       | this | — | CL | matter | wait | a:little | then | tell | you |

This matter (I'll) tell you about in a little bit.

B.1.2 Diect Object with *bǎ* before the Verb

In chapter 15 on *bǎ* constructions, the structure and function of the construction is discussed in detail. Here we simply give a few examples:

(232) | qǐng | nǐ | bǎ | zhuōzi | pīn | — | qǐ |
       |-------|-----|-----|--------|------------|---|------|
       | please | you | BA | table | put:together | — | rise |

—	lai
—	come

Please put the tables together.

(233) tā   bǎ   shuǐ   dào   zài   wǒ   shēn   —   shang
       3sg   BA   water   pour   at   I   body   —   on

S/He poured the water on me.

(234) wǒ   yǐjīng   bǎ   nèi   —   suǒ   fángzi   zū
       I   already   BA   that   —   CL   house   rent

       —   chū   —   qu   le
       —   exit   —   go   CRS

I have already rented out that house.

B.1.3 Direct Object without *bǎ* before the Verb

It is often possible to put the direct object before the verb, as in sentences like (235):

(235) tā   gōngkè   yǐjīng   zuò   —   wán   le
       3sg   homework   already   do   —   finish   CRS

S/He's already done his/her homework.

For convenience, we will call the form exemplified by (235) the *SOV form*, where *S* stands for ''subject,'' *O* stands for ''object,'' and *V* stands for ''verb.'' Since the direct object *gōngkè* 'homework' in this example could also just as well be placed after the verb (the *SVO form*), as in (236), one may ask what the communicative difference between the two versions is.

(236) tā   yǐjīng   zuò   —   wán   gōngkè   le
       3sg   already   do   —   finish   homework   CRS

S/He's already finished his/her homework.

In general, the SVO form, as in (236), is essentially neutral: it simply communicates that *tā* 's/he' has done his/her homework. The SOV form, on the other hand, is typically used in a situation in which what is being conveyed is contrary to the expectation expressed by the other person. Thus, the SOV sentence (235), for example, would be a natural thing for one parent to say to another to explain why their child is watching television instead of studying. In this case the second parent's expectation would be that the child should be studying, and the SOV form is used to contradict this expectation.

Let's look at some more examples. Suppose that someone in a group has just proposed that the group go out to eat; one might counter the expectation created by this proposal and say (237), which means that the group should stay home:

(237)	kěshi	Lǐsì	fàn	dōu	zhǔ	–	hǎo	le
	but	Lisi	food	all	cook	–	finish	CRS

But Lisi has already cooked food.

Another example of this type: if one is urged to drop a course in school, s/he can say:

(238)	kěshì	wǒ	shū	yǐjing	mǎi	le
	but	I	book	already	buy	CRS

But I've already bought the books.

If someone wants Zhangsan to drive some people to a party in his car, you might respond with (239):

(239)	Zhāngsān	qìchē	shi	yǒu ,	kěshi	bu
	Zhangsan	car	be	have	but	not

	huì	–	kāi
	know:how	–	drive

Zhangsan has a car all right, but he doesn't know how to drive.

Similarly, if someone asks you what type of sweets you would like for dessert, s/he has expressed the expectation that you want *some* kind of sweets. You can counter this expectation by saying:

(240)	wǒ	tián	de	dōu	bu	xǐhuān
	I	sweet	NOM	all	not	like

I don't like sweet things.

Finally, if there is a discussion of why a certain friend hasn't married, and one person thinks it's due to the friend's lack of money, s/he might say:

(241) tā   fángzi   yě   méi   yǒu ,   chēzi   yě   méi
       3sg   house   also   not   exist   car   also   not

       yǒu ,   zhíyè   yě   méi   yǒu ,   zěnme   huì
       exist   job   also   not   exist   how   likely

       yǒu   rén   yào   jià ?
       exist   person   want   marry

He doesn't have a house, he doesn't have a car, and he hasn't found any work—how could anyone want to marry him?

These examples illustrate that the SOV form is restricted to those situations that are contrary to expectations. Given this pragmatic function of the SOV form, we can see that certain sentences will seem strange in the SOV form because it is hard to imagine a contrary-to-expectation situation in which such sentences could be used. For example, running into a friend can be reported by using the SOV sentence of (242) a, but (242) b is odd because it would be hard to imagine circumstances in which one would want to convey the idea that meeting a friend would be unexpected:

(242) a.   wǒ   pèngjian   péngyou   le
           I   run:into   friend   CRS

I ran into a friend.

      b.   ?wǒ   péngyou   pèngjian   LE
           I   friend   run:into   PFV/CRS

(I ran into a friend.)

In this section we have seen that direct objects, in addition to occurring in "neutral" position after the verb, can occur in three preverbal positions: they can be topics at the beginning of the sentence, they can occur before the verb with bǎ, and they can occur before the verb without bǎ in sentences that counter expectations already existing in the speech context. Not surprisingly, we see that these different word orders are not just ''different ways of saying the same thing,'' but are ways of achieving quite different communicative goals.

B.2 Transitive Verbs Whose Direct Objects are Clauses or Verb Phrases

Certain transitive verbs allow their direct objects to be clauses or verb phrases. Such sentences are examples of serial verb constructions, since they have more than one verb, and will be discussed at greater length in the chapter on serial verbs (chapter 21). A general rule is that if a transitive verb can take an abstract noun as its direct object, it can also take a sentence or a verb phrase as its direct object. Here are some examples in which the direct object of each *a* sentence refers to an abstract notion and the direct object of each *b* sentence is a clause or verb phrase:

(243) *a.*

wǒ	zhīdao	nèi	—	jian	shì
I	know	that	—	CL	matter

I know that affair.

b.

wǒ	zhīdao	nǐ	shì	tā	gēge
I	know	you	be	3sg	older:brother

I know you are his/her older brother.

(244) *a.*

wǒ	pà	chōuxiàng	de	gàiniàn
I	fear	abstract	NOM	concept

I'm afraid of abstract concepts.

b.

wǒ	pà	tā	bu	lái
I	fear	3sg	not	come

I'm afraid s/he won't come.

(245) *a.*

wǒ	méi	xiǎngdào	zhèi	—	ge	fāngfǎ
I	not	realize	this	—	CL	method

I did not think of this method.

b.

wǒ	méi	xiǎngdào	nǐ	zhù	zài	Niǔyuè
I	not	realize	you	live	at	New York

I didn't realize you lived in New York.

B.3 Verb-Object Compounds

Verb-object compounds are presented in detail in chapter 3. What we want to discuss briefly here is a syntactic property of verb-object compounds which is relevant to the types of transitive predicates we have talked about so far. Certain verb-object compounds are fused lexical units. They no longer retain properties of the syntactic structure *verb + object*, and their meanings are also highly idiomatic: for example, (1) *dānxīn* 'worry'; literally, *dān* means 'to bear', and *xīn* means 'heart'; (2) *dézuì* 'offend'; literally, *dé* means 'get', and *zuì* means 'offense'; and (3) *zhùyì* 'pay attention'; literally, *zhù* means 'pour', and *yì* means 'intention'. Certain of these fused verb-object compounds function as transitive verbs, as the sentences below illustrate.

(246) wǒ   hěn   dānxīn   zhè   —   jiàn   shì
      I   very   worry   this   —   CL   matter

I am very worried about this matter.

(247) tā   dézuì   wǒ   le
      3sg   offend   I   CRS

S/He offended me.

(248) wǒ   zhùyì   wǒ   —   de   jiā   —   shì
      I   pay:attenion I   —   GEN   family   —   affair

I pay attention to my family affairs.

There are also fused verb-object compounds that function as intransitive verbs: for example, (1) *kāixīn* 'happy'; literally, *kāi* means 'open', and *xīn* means 'heart'; and (2) *shīwàng* 'be disappointed'; literally, *shī* means 'lose', and *wàng* means 'hope'.

(249) wǒ   hěn   kāixīn
      I   very   happy

I am very happy.

(250) wǒ   hěn   shīwàng
      I   very   disappointed

I am very disappointed.

The fused verb-object compounds present no complication. Each of them is a lexical unit with a meaning that differs from the sum of the meanings of the parts. In other words, each fused verb-object compound is a word. It may be a transitive or intransitive verb, as we have seen from the examples above; it may also be a noun or adverb. The verb-object compounds that do present some complications are the ones that retain some of the syntactic properties of the verb-plus-object construction. In other words, the "object" component of the compound still behaves as an object in many ways, although not completely. For example, consider *chūmíng* 'famous'; literally, *chū* means 'emerge', and *míng* means 'name'. On the one hand, *chūmíng* functions as a lexical unit with an adjectival meaning. For instance, it can be modified by the intensifier, *hěn* 'very', and it can take on the intensifying suffix -*jí* 'extremely':

(251)   tā   hěn   chūmíng
         3sg   very   famous

S/He is very famous.

(252)   tā   chūmíng   —   jí   le
         3sg   famous   —   extremely   CRS

S/He is extremely famous.

On the other hand, the object *míng* can be modified in many ways as if it were a syntactic object of the verb *chū*, and the verb *chū* may take on an aspect marker as if it were an independent verb.

(253)   tā   chū   —   le   dà   míng   le
         3sg   emerge   —   PFV   big   name   CRS

S/He became very famous.

The complication, then, is this: the compound *chūmíng* appears at once both as a lexical unit and as a verb-plus-object construction. Furthermore, different compounds may exhibit the properties of a lexical unit or of a verb-plus-object construction to different degrees. This is one area of Mandarin grammar which requires a great deal of item-by-item memorization.

C. Ditransitive Verb Phrases

Ditransitive verb phrases are those whose verbs have meanings that require two objects, one of which is the direct object and the other the indirect object. In the following examples, the direct object is underlined once and the indirect object twice:

(254) | wǒ | sòng | tā | yi | — | jiàn | lǐwù |
|---|---|---|---|---|---|---|
| I | give | 3sg | one | — | CL | gift |

I gave him/her a gift.

(255) | wǒ | jì | — | le | yi | — | fēng | xìn | gěi | ta |
|---|---|---|---|---|---|---|---|---|---|
| I | mail | — | PFV | one | — | CL | letter | to | 3sg |

I mailed a letter to him/her.

(256) | tā | gěi | wǒ | dǎ | — | diànhuà |
|---|---|---|---|---|---|
| 3sg | to | me | hit | — | telephone |

S/He telephoned me.

These examples illustrate the different forms in which ditransitive sentences can occur. They are described in detail in the chapter on indirect objects (chapter 10).

Notes

1. See Chafe (1976) for a discussion of this point.
2. There are three types of exceptions to this statement. One, pointed out to us by Chauncey Chu, is exemplified by a sentence such as:

(i) | yi | — | ge | rén | jiu | gòu | le |
|---|---|---|---|---|---|---|
| one | — | CL | person | then | enough | CRS |

One person will be enough.

in which the numeral *yi* refers not to some particular indefinite (i.e., unknown) entity, but rather to the abstract quantity (i.e., one) desired. The second type of exception is illustrated by a sentence such as:

(ii) | yi | — | tiáo | tuǐ | duàn | le |
|---|---|---|---|---|---|
| one | — | CL | leg | broken | CRS |

One of its legs is broken.

Here the underlined noun phrase is also not indefinite, but refers to something that is *part of* an entity already known by the hearer. It can therefore be considered a definite noun phrase. A similar example is (iii), cited in Li and Thompson (1975*a*:175):

(iii)	<u>yi</u>	—	ge	nóngfu	shuō ,	"wŏ	xiăng	—
	one	—	CL	peasant	say	I	think	—

	chu	yi	—	ge	bànfǎ	le"
	exit	one	—	CL	way	CRS

One of the peasants said, "I've thought of a way."

The third type of exception occurs when *yi-* is interpreted as 'each', as in:

(iv)	<u>yi</u>	—	ge	rén	chī	yi	—	kŏu
	one	—	CL	person	eat	one	—	mouth

Each person gets one mouthful.

3. Adapted from the discussion in Tsao (1977:86 ff.). See chapter 7 for the use of these particles as sentence-final particles.

4. When a topic is not a noun phrase but a verb phrase, it may be marked by *a, me, ne,* or *ba.* While *a, me,* and *ne* can also occur with noun phrase topics, however, *ba* may occur only with verb phrase topics. Here are some examples:

(i)	hē	jiŭ	{ <u>a</u> / me / <u>ne</u> / <u>ba</u> }	yě	kéyĭ
	drink	wine		also	fine

As for drinking wine, it is also fine.

(ii)	chàng	—	gē	{ <u>a</u> / me / <u>ne</u> / <u>ba</u> }	méi	shénme	xìngqù
	sing	—	song		not	have any	interest

As for singing, (I) don't have any interest.

(iii)	qù	{ <u>a</u> / me / <u>ne</u> / <u>ba</u> }	buhǎoyìsi ;	bu	qù	{ <u>a</u> / me / <u>ne</u> / <u>ba</u> }	yòu	bu	kāixīn
	go		embarrassed	not	go		also	not	happy

As for going, (I) am embarrassed; as for not going, (I) am also unhappy.

5. For a more extensive linguistic discussion of topic and subject in Mandarin, see Li and Thompson (1976) and Tsao (1977).

6. For a more extensive linguistic treatment of double-subject sentences, see Teng (1974*b*).

7. This discussion is adapted from Tsao (1977:chap. 6).

8. For further discussion of classifiers, see Alleton (1973:47−52) and Rygaloff (1973:67−82).

9. There are a few nouns denoting measures of time which do require classifiers: these include *yuè* 'month', *xīngqi* 'week', and *zhōngtou* 'hour'. For instance, 'two months' is *liǎng-ge yuè*, not **liǎng yuè*; 'that week' is *nèi-ge xīngqi*, not **nèi xīngqi*; and 'a few hours' is *jǐ-ge zhōngtou*, not **jǐ zhōngtou*.

10. It is important to note that in order to test whether the particle *-de* of an associative phrase can be omitted, one must place the phrase with the noun it modifies in the direct object position after the verb in a sentence. If the associative phrase is placed in sentence-initial position, it may sound acceptable without the *-de*, but in that case it is structurally a topic and no longer an associative phrase. The sentences in (i) and (ii) illustrate this point:

(i) *a.*

Zhāngsan	nǚ	−	péngyou	hěn	piàoliang
Zhangsan	girl	−	friend	very	beautiful

Zhangsan (topic), (his) girlfriend is very beautiful.

b.

wǒ	xīhuān	Zhāngsān	−	de	nǚ	−	péngyou
I	like	Zhangsan	−	GEN	girl	−	friend

I like Zhangsan's girlfriend.

c.

*wǒ	xīhuān	Zhāngsān	nǚ	−	péngyou
I	like	Zhangsan	girl	−	friend

(ii) *a.*

nǐ	tóufa	hěn	luàn
you	hair	very	messy

You (topic), your hair is very messy.

b.

wǒ	xīhuān	nǐ	−	de	tóufa
I	like	you	−	GEN	hair

I like your hair.

c.

*wǒ	xīhuān	nǐ	tóufa
I	like	you	hair

Sentence (i) *a* is a topic-comment construction in which *Zhāngsān* is the topic and *nǚpéngyou* 'girlfriend' is the subject. Sentence (i) *b* contains an associative phrase modifying the noun *nǚpéngyou* 'girlfriend' in the object position. Sentence (i) *c* differs from (i) *b* only in that the *-de* of the associative phrase is omitted, and we see that it is ungrammatical. Sentences (ii) *a−c* illustrate exactly the same point as (i) does. The conclusion one can draw from (i) and (ii) is that *-de* cannot be deleted from the associative phrases in *nǐ-de tóufa* 'your hair' and *Zhāngsān-de nǚpéngyou* 'Zhangsan's girlfriend'.

11. In this section, we have adapted some ideas from Chao (1968), Alleton (1973:96−100), and Zhu (1956).

12. The difference between these two schemas in terms of the position of the classifier/measure phrase is discussed in chapter 20.

13. For more discussion of definiteness in Mandarin, see Rygaloff (1973:84−91) and Teng (1975*a*:chap. 6).

14. For more discussion of adjectival verbs, see Rygaloff (1973:chap. 9) and Alleton (1973:92 ff.). We have adapted some of our discussion from Paris(1979*a*). The term *stative verb* has been used, especially in the standard textbooks, to refer to what we are calling *adjective* or *adjectival verb*. This is to emphasize the ways in which these forms, in contrast to English adjectives, resemble forms that are uncontroversially verbs in Mandarin. In particular, Mandarin adjectives, unlike English adjectives, (1) are not preceded by the copula *shi* 'be' as predicates:

(i)	*tā	shi	aǐ
	3sg	be	short

and (2) can be negated by the direct addition of *bu*, just as verbs can:

(ii)	tā	<u>bu</u>	xǐhuān	wǒ
	3sg	not	like	I

S/He doesn't like me.

(iii)	ta	<u>bu</u>	aǐ
	3sg	not	short

S/He's not short.

The term *adjective* has the advantage of being the term traditionally used to refer to the class of words denoting a property, so it is the one we will continue to use here.

15. For further discussion of copula predicates, see Rygaloff (1973:chap. 8), Chu (1970), Hashimoto (1969*a*), and Teng (1979*c*).

16. There are a few exceptions to statement (i). Chao(1968:717) gives two examples:

(i) *a*.	wǒ	cónglái	−	méi	shì	−	guo	shéi
	I		never		be		EXP	who

	−	de	rén
	−	GEN	person

I have never been anybody's person.

b.

shì	—	le	jiù	suàn	—	le
be	—	PFV	then	let:go	—	PFV

When it's OK, then let it go.

In the second example, *shì* is functioning more as an adjective meaning 'be OK' than as a copula. The first example is troublesome to most native speakers: it can be understood, but it sounds forced.

17. See especially Chu (1970:129 ff.), as well as Hashimoto (1969*a*) and references that she cites.

18. Our underlining here is meant to draw attention to the morpheme *shì* 'be' and not to indicate special stress. This *shì*, of course, can be stressed (see the discussion below) in certain emphatic situations, but in none of our examples does it have to be.

19. This point is attributable to Huang (1966).

CHAPTER 5

Auxiliary Verbs

The term *auxiliary verb* is widely used in Chinese grammars, and it occurs repeatedly in this book also.[1] What is an auxiliary verb in Mandarin? As a general rule, a set of forms in a language constitutes a grammatical category if it can be shown that those forms share a set of distributional properties not possessed by any other set of forms. Accordingly, we can show that a category "auxiliary verb" can be established for Mandarin on the basis of a set of distributional properties that distinguish its members from verbs and adverbs.

5.1 Auxiliary Verb versus Verb

The term *auxiliary verb* (or *auxiliary*, for short) suggests that the forms to which it refers have some verbal properties and yet are not full-fledged verbs. There are two related properties that auxiliary verbs share with verbs:

(i) An auxiliary verb may occur as the A element in A-not-A questions (see chapter 18):

(1)   tā   néng   bu   néng   chàng   –   gē ?
      3sg   can   not   can   sing   –   song

   Can s/he sing?   { (Does s/he have permission to sing?) }
                     { (Is s/he capable of singing?) }

(ii) An auxiliary verb may be negated:

(2)   tā   <u>bu</u>   <u>néng</u>   chàng   —   gē
        3sg   not   can   sing   —   song

      S/He can't sing.

Auxiliary verbs differ from verbs, however, with respect to the following six properties:

(i) An auxiliary verb must co-occur with a verb (or an "understood" verb). For example, (3) is incomplete and can be used only in a context in which a verb representing what s/he can do is understood:

(3)   tā   <u>néng</u>
        3sg   can

      S/He can.

(ii) An auxiliary verb does not take aspect markers:

(4)   *tā   néng $\left\{\begin{array}{c} \text{-le} \\ \text{-guo} \\ \text{-zhe} \end{array}\right\}$ chàng   —   gē

        3sg   can $\left\{\begin{array}{c} \text{-PFV} \\ \text{-EXP} \\ \text{-DUR} \end{array}\right\}$ sing   —   song

(iii) An auxiliary verb cannot be modified by intensifiers, such as *hěn* 'very' or *gèng* 'even more':[2]

(5)   tā   * $\left\{\begin{array}{c} \text{hěn} \\ \text{gèng} \end{array}\right\}$ néng   chàng   —   gē

        3sg $\left\{\begin{array}{c} \text{very} \\ \text{even:more} \end{array}\right\}$ can   sing   —   song

(iv) An auxiliary verb cannot be nominalized (see chapter 20 on nominalization):

(6)   *tā   <u>shi</u>   <u>néng</u>   <u>de</u>
        3sg   be   can   NOM

(v) An auxiliary verb cannot occur before the subject:

(7)   *néng   tā   chàng   –   gē
        can   3sg   sing   –   song

(vi) An auxiliary verb cannot take a direct object:[3]

(8)   *tā   néng   nèi   –   jian   shì
        3sg   can   that   –   CL   job

Let us now consider some of the candidates for auxiliary verb status which have been included in earlier treatments of auxiliaries.[4] In each case, the form in question can be shown to be a verb and not an auxiliary verb by one of the criteria mentioned above.

First, consider *yào* 'want'. In a sentence such as (9), *yào* is clearly a verb and not an auxiliary verb, since it takes a direct object:

(9)   wǒ   yào   yi   –   ge   píngguǒ
        I   want   one   –   CL   apple

    I want an apple.

In a sentence like (10), however, *yào* occurs with another verb and thus looks like an auxiliary:

(10)   wǒ   yào   xǐzǎo
        I   want   bathe

    I want to bathe.

Even if we assume for the sake of argument that one morpheme can belong to more than one category, a close look at the semantics of *yào* suggests that this would not be the correct analysis of *yào* and that its status as a verb is not challenged by sentences such as (10). The meaning of *yào* requires a participant (the subject) who does the wanting and another participant (the direct object) that signals what is wanted. The only difference between sentences (9) and (10) is a difference in the nature of what is wanted by the subject. In (9), what is wanted is a concrete entity, but in (10), what is wanted is an event. To clarify this point further, observe that (10) exactly parallels (11):

(11)   wǒ   yào   tā   xǐzǎo
        I   want   3sg   bathe

I want him/her to bathe.

The difference between (10) and (11) is that in (10), since the person who will bathe is the same person who 'wants', it is not necessary to restate the subject of 'bathe'. In other words, sentences (9), (10), and (11) all have the same main verb, yào 'want', which, because of its inherent meaning, takes a subject and a direct object. The direct object, though, may vary. In (9), it is a concrete noun, but in (10) and (11) it is an event; in (10), this event may be described as wǒ xǐzǎo 'I bathe', and in (11), this event may be described as tā xǐzǎo 's/he bathes'. In (10) the subject of xǐzǎo is understood, however, because it is identical with the subject of the main verb, yào 'want'.

With an auxiliary verb, on the other hand, it is easy to show that the verb phrase that follows it is *not* an event direct object, since that verb phrase can never have a subject different from the subject of the auxiliary verb itself:

(12)   wǒ   néng   xǐzǎo
        I   can   bathe

I can bathe.

(13)   *wo   néng   ta   xǐzǎo
        I   can   3sg   bathe*

Sentence (10) has another interpretation in which yào has the meaning of 'immediately' or 'in the immediate future'. Given this meaning of yào, sentence (10) can mean 'I am going to bathe.' This meaning of yào, however, is also not sufficient to make it an auxiliary verb. Yào meaning 'in the immediate future' has none of the properties of auxiliary verbs. For example, in A-not-A questions with yào as the A- element, yào can only mean 'want' and not 'in the immediate future':

(14)   nǐ   yào   bu   yào   xǐzǎo   ?
        you   want   not   want   bathe

Do you want to bathe?

*Cf. sentence (11).

Similarly, the abbreviated sentence

(15)   wǒ   yào
        I   want

can only mean 'I want to' but not 'I am going to'. Finally, if we negate a sentence containing *yào*, *yào* again will have the meaning 'want' but not the meaning 'in the immediate future'.

(16)   wǒ   bu   yào   xǐzǎo
        I   not   want   bathe

I don't want to bathe.

In the sense of 'in the immediate future', then, *yào* seems to be functioning like an adverb, since it has no verbal properties at all. (Adverbs are described in chapter 8.)

   There are other verbs that may appear to be auxiliaries but fail to be in the same way as *yào* does. Some examples are *qíngyuàn* 'wish, prefer'; *jìxù* 'continue'; *xūyào* 'need'; *xīwàng* 'hope'; *xiǎng* 'miss'; *biǎoshì* 'express'.

   Notice that *qíngyuàn* 'wish, prefer' and *xīwàng* 'hope' differ from *yào* 'want' in that they *always* require their direct object to be an event. As with *yào*, however, the fact that the event can be an entire clause with its own subject, as illustrated by the *a* sentences in (17) and (18), shows that this event is indeed the direct object of the underlined verb and not the main verb to which the underlined form is an auxiliary:

(17) *a*.   wǒ   <u>qíngyuàn</u>   tā   zuò   zǒngtǒng
            I   prefer   3sg   serve   president

      I prefer him/her to be the president.

    b.   wǒ   <u>qíngyuàn</u>   zuò   zǒngtǒng
            I   prefer   serve   president

      I prefer to be the president.

    c.   *wǒ   <u>qíngyuàn</u>   bīngjilíng
            I   prefer   ice:cream

(18) *a.*   wǒ   xīwàng   tā   qù   Zhōngguó
              I   hope   3sg   go   China

I hope s/he will go to China.

b.   wǒ   xīwàng   qù   Zhōngguó
         I   hope   go   China

I hope to go to China.

c.   *wǒ   xīwàng   Zhōngguó
         I   hope   China

The verb *xiǎng* 'think' looks like it could be an auxiliary verb in a sentence such as this:

(19)   wǒ   xiǎng   hē   jiǔ
         I   think   drink   wine

$\left\{\begin{array}{l}\text{I think I'll drink some wine.}\\ \text{I miss drinking wine.}\end{array}\right\}$

Once again, however, just as with the verbs we have been discussing, *xiǎng* functions as a verb; like *yào*, it can take either a simple direct object or an event as its direct object:

(20)   wǒ   xiǎng   tā
         I   think   3sg

$\left\{\begin{array}{l}\text{I think about him/her.}\\ \text{I miss him/her.}\end{array}\right\}$

(21)   wǒ   xiǎng   tā   hěn   kāixīn
         I   think   3sg   very   happy

I think s/he is very happy.

The difference between *xiǎng* 'think' and *yào* 'want' is simply that when *xiǎng* occurs with a simple direct object or an event direct object whose subject is the same as the subject of *xiǎng* itself, it takes on another possible meaning, that of 'to miss', as illustrated in (19) and (20). This meaning of *xiǎng*, however, is naturally inferred from the basic meaning 'think' according to the type of direct object with which it occurs.

Jìxù 'continue', *xūyào* 'need', and *biǎoshì* 'express' are similar to *xiǎng* 'think'. In the following pairs of sentences, the *a* sentence in each pair has a direct object that is a noun, and the *b* sentence has a direct object that is an event. The verbs in *a* and *b* in each pair of sentences are syntactically and semantically identical:

(22) *a.* wǒmen   jìxù   tā   —   de   gōngzuò
           we   continue 3sg   —   GEN   work

We continue his/her work.

   b. wǒmen   jìxù   gōngzuò
         we   continue work

We continue to work.

(23) *a.* wǒmen   xūyào   fēijī
           We   need   airplane

We need airplanes.

   b. wǒmen   xūyào   jiàshǐ   fēijī
         we   need   pilot   airplane

We need to pilot airplanes.

(24) *a.* wǒmen   biǎoshì   wǒmen   —   de   qínggǎn
           we   express   we   —   GEN   feeling

We express our feelings.

   b. wǒmen   biǎoshì   zàncheng   tā   —   de   yìjiàn
         we   express   approve   3sg   —   GEN   suggestion

We indicated that we approved his/her suggestion.

There is another type of verb that has been mistaken as an auxiliary verb; an example is *kěnéng* 'possible, likely'. Its occurrence in such sentences as (25) is responsible for its being classified as an auxiliary verb:

(25)   tā   <u>kěnéng</u>   qù   Měiguó
           3sg   possible   go   America

           It's likely that s/he'll go to America.

Kěnéng is, however, an adjectival verb similar to *róngyi* 'easy', *nán* 'difficult':

(26)   nèi   –   ge   wènti $\left\{\begin{matrix}\text{róngyi}\\ \text{nán}\end{matrix}\right\}$ jiějué
           that   –   CL   problem $\left\{\begin{matrix}\text{easy}\\ \text{difficult}\end{matrix}\right\}$ solve

           It's $\left\{\begin{matrix}\text{easy}\\ \text{difficult}\end{matrix}\right\}$ to solve that problem.

First of all, notice that since *kěnéng*, *róngyi*, and *nán* are adjectival verbs, they may be modified by the intensifiers *hěn* 'very' and *gèng* 'even more':

(27)   tā   <u>hěn</u>   <u>kěnéng</u>   qù   Měiguó
           3sg   very   likely   go   America

           It is very likely that s/he'll go to America.

(28)   nèi   –   ge   wènti   <u>hěn</u> $\left\{\begin{matrix}\text{róngyi}\\ \text{nán}\end{matrix}\right\}$ jiějué
           that   –   CL   problem   very $\left\{\begin{matrix}\text{easy}\\ \text{difficult}\end{matrix}\right\}$ solve

           It is very $\left\{\begin{matrix}\text{easy}\\ \text{difficult}\end{matrix}\right\}$ to solve that problem.

(29)   tā   <u>gèng</u>   <u>kěnéng</u>   qù   Měiguó
           3sg   even:more   likely   go   America

           It's even more likely that s/he'll go to America.

(30)   nèi   —   ge   wènti   gèng   ⎰róngyi⎱ jiějué
                                            ⎱ nán ⎰

        that   —   CL   problem even:more ⎰ easy ⎱ solve
                                            ⎱difficult⎰

That problem is even   ⎰easier   ⎱   to solve.
                        ⎱more difficult ⎰

As pointed out above, auxiliary verbs cannot be modified by intensifiers such as
hěn 'very' and *gèng* 'further'. For example, (31) and (32) are ungrammatical:

(31)   *wǒ   hěn   néng   lái
         I   very   can   come

(32)   *wǒ   gèng   néng   lai
         I   even:more   can   come

Second, an adjectival verb may be nominalized with *de* to form a noun that can
occur after *shì* 'be', but an auxiliary verb cannot:

(33)   nèi   —   zhǒng chōngtu   shì   kěnéng   de
        that   —   kind conflict be   likely   NOM

That sort of conflict is a likely one.

(34)   *nèi   —   zhǒng chōngtu   shì   néng   de
        that   —   kind conflict be   can   NOM

Finally, some Mandarin speakers find sentences like (35) quite acceptable,
where *kěnéng* occurs in sentence-initial position:

(35)   kěnéng   tā   míngtiān   lái
        likely   3sg   tomorrow   come

It is likely that s/he will come tomorrow.

No auxiliary verb can occur in sentence-initial position as *kěnéng* does in (35). The
correct analysis is to treat *kěnéng* as an adjectival verb that semantically may take a

clause as its subject (see section 21.2.2 of chapter 21). Thus, semantically, (25) specifies that the event *tā qù Měiguó* 's/he will go to America' is 'very likely'. Similarly, the adjectival verbs in (26) are *róngyì* 'easy' and *nán* 'difficult', their semantic subject being the clause *jiějué nèige wèntí* 'solve that problem'.

5.2 Auxiliary Verb versus Adverb

Adverbs occur in prepredicate position, just as auxiliary verbs do:

(36)	tā	dàgài	chī	sān	—	wǎn	fàn
	3sg	approximately	eat	three	—	bowl	rice

S/He eats approximately three bowls of rice.

(37)	tā	yídìng	lái
	3sg	definitely	come

S/He will definitely come.

(38)	tā	kuài(yào)	lái	le
	3sg	soon	come	CRS

S/He will soon come.

Such adverbs differ from auxiliary verbs primarily in that they lack verblike properties. Consider a true auxiliary verb, such as *néng* 'can'. Although it must occur with a full-fledged verb, it may occur along with the subject in a context in which the verb is understood, as we indicated earlier—for instance, in an answer to a yes-no question:

(39) A:	nǐ	néng	lái	ma?
	you	can	come	Q

Can you come?

B:	wǒ	néng
	I	can

I can.

On the other hand, there is no context in which an adverb may occur alone with the subject of a verb:

(40) A: nĭ   yídìng   lái   ma ?
           you   definitely come   Q

     Will you definitely come?

     B: *wŏ   yídìng
           I   definitely

The reason for this distinction is the presence of verbal properties in the auxiliary, which reflects a semantic relationship between the subject of the sentence and the auxiliary. No such semantic relationship exists, though, between the subject of a sentence and an adverb.

Another important distinction between auxiliary verbs and adverbs is the fact that an auxiliary verb possesses the verbal property of being able to serve as the A element in A-not-A questions, as shown by (41):

(41)   nĭ   néng   bu   néng   lái ?
        you   can   not   can   come

     Can you come?

An adverb, on the other hand, does not have this verbal property, as shown in (42):

(42)   *nĭ   yídìng   bu   yídìng   lái ?
        you   definitely not   definitely come

The same principles used in showing *yídìng* to be a false auxiliary verb can be applied to other adverbs as well to show that they are not auxiliary verbs.

5.3 List of Auxiliary Verbs

The criteria we have discussed allow us to designate the following commonly used forms as auxiliary verbs:

(43) yīnggāi, yīngdang, gāi   'ought to, should'
     néng, nénggòu, huì, kĕyi   'be able to'
     néng, kĕyi   'has permission to'

gǎn	'dare'
kěn	'be willing to'
děi, bìxū, bìyào, bìděi	'must, ought to'
huì	'will, know how'

As we pointed out in the beginning of this chapter, in attempting to determine whether a certain grammatical category exists in a given language, it is necessary to show that a group of morphemes possesses a set of properties not shared by any other group of morphemes in the language. Auxiliary verbs occur in the same position within a sentence where certain verbs and adverbs can occur, but they have particular distributional properties not shared by members of either of these two classes.

Notes

1. This chapter incorporates some of the discussion of auxiliaries in Chao (1968:731 ff.).

2. A sentence such as

| (i) | tā | hěn | huì | shuō | — | huà |
| | 3sg | very | know:how | say | — | speech |

S/He is very eloquent.

appears to be a counterexample. In this sentence, however, *huì shuō-huà* is an idiom for 'eloquent', as indicated by the translation. In general, *huì* behaves like all other auxiliary verbs in not allowing *hěn* or *gèng*:

(ii) * tā { hěn / gèng } huì yóuyǒng

3sg { very / even:more } know:how swim

3. On this point, we disagree with Chao (1968:731), who says: "Auxiliary verbs take other verbs or verbal expressions as objects instead of substantives." Note also that this point does not imply that all verbs can take objects. If a verb takes an object, however, we can be sure that it is a full-fledged verb, not an auxiliary verb.

4. For example, see Chao (1968:731 ff.), Teng (1975a:74−78), d'Andrea (1978), and Alleton (1977).

CHAPTER 6

Aspect

The verbal category presented in this chapter expresses what linguists call *aspect*, that is, different ways of viewing a situation. The category of aspect is very different from that of tense: a marker of *tense* relates the time of the occurrence of the situation to the time that situation is brought up in speech. In English, for example, we have past tense, as in

(1) I propos<u>ed</u> a toast.

where the suffix *-ed* signals that the act of proposing took place before the time of speaking. Mandarin has no markers of tense. The language does not use verb affixes to signal the relation between the time of the occurrence of the situation and the time that situation is brought up in speech.

Aspect, on the other hand, refers, not to the time relation between a situation and the moment of its being mentioned in speech, but, rather, to how the situation itself is being viewed with respect to its own internal makeup.[1] To take an example, first let's look at an English sentence:

(2) Rosco <u>was reading</u> when I <u>came in</u>.

Here, two events are expressed in past tense. The first verbal complex, *was reading*, however, differs strikingly from the second verbal complex, *came in*, in terms of the way the two situations are viewed. The second verbal complex presents the totality of the situation referred to (the speaker's coming in) without reference to its internal temporal constituency; the entire situation is viewed as a single, unanalyzable whole. When a language has special verbal forms to indicate this viewing of an event in its entirety, we say that that form expresses *perfective* aspect. In Mandarin, the marker for perfective aspect is *-le*, but perfective aspect can also be expressed by a "perfectivizing expression" (see section 6.1).

The first verbal complex in (2), *was reading*, on the other hand, does not present the situation of Rosco's reading in its entirety, but instead makes explicit reference to the internal makeup of "reading", presenting it as ongoing, referring neither to its beginning nor its end, but to its duration. Verbal markers signaling this ongoing-duration aspect constitute one type of the aspect, referred to as *imperfective*, which we might call *durative*. In Mandarin, the imperfective durative markers are *zài* and *-zhe* (see section 6.2).

In addition to *-le*, *zài*, and *-zhe*, there is a fourth verbal aspect marker in Mandarin, *-guo*, which is an *experiential* aspect, indicating that a situation has been experienced (see section 6.3).

Finally, there is a *delimitative aspect* category that is expressed, not by a particular morpheme, but by the reduplication of the verb (see section 6.4).

The verbal aspects in Mandarin, then, are:

1. Perfective: *-le* and perfectivizing expressions
2. Imperfective (durative): *zài*, *-zhe*
3. Experiential: *-guo*
4. Delimitative: reduplication of verb

Let's look at each of these verbal aspects in more detail.

6.1 The Perfective Aspect

Any description of the verbal aspect marker *-le* must begin with the caveat that it is important to keep the perfective aspect distinct from the sentence-final particle *le* (which is written without the hyphen in this book). The sentence-final particle *le* and sentences containing both *-le* and *le* are described in chapter 7.

6.1.1 Where to Use *-le*: A Bounded Event

We have said that the verbal aspect suffix *-le* expresses perfectivity, that is, it indicates that an event is being viewed in its entirety or as a whole. An event is viewed in its entirety if it is *bounded* temporally, spatially, or conceptually. There are essentially four ways in which an event can be bounded:

A. By being a quantified event
B. By being a definite or specific event

C. By being inherently bounded because of the meaning of the verb

D. By being the first event in a sequence

We will discuss each of these in turn.

A. A Quantified Event

An event can be viewed as bounded when temporal, spatial, or conceptual limits are placed on it. What this means grammatically is that a verb typically will occur with -*le* if the event signaled by the verb is limited by overt phrases naming the extent to which that event occurred, the amount of time it took, or the number of times it happened. For example:

(3)   tā   shuì   —   le   sān   —   ge   zhōngtóu
         3sg   sleep   —   PFV   three   —   CL   hour

S/He slept for three hours.

(4)   wǒ   zài   nàli   zhù   —   le
         I   at   there   live   —   PFV

         liǎng   —   ge   yuè
         two   —   CL   month

I lived there for two months.

(5)   yǐjing   rěn   —   le   zhème   duō
         already   endure   —   PFV   that   many

         nián,   wǒ   huì   zài   rěn   —   xiàqu
         year   I   likely   more   endure   —   continue

I have already tolerated it for so many years, I can go on tolerating it.

(6)   diàn   —   dēng   liàng   —   le   hěn   duō
         electric   —   light   bright   —   PFV   very   much

The electric light got a lot brighter.

(7)   wǒ   bǎ   gǒu   dǎ   —   le   yī   dùn
      I   BA   dog   hit   —   PFV   one   time

I gave the dog a beating.

(8)   wǒ   bǎ   mén   tī   —   le   sān   jiǎo
      I   BA   door   kick   —   PFV   three foot

I gave the door three kicks.

(9)   dírén   wàng   hòu   chètuì   —   le
      enemy   toward   back   retreat   —   PFV

      èr   —   shí   lǐ
      two   —   ten   mile

The enemy fell back twenty miles.

(10) nǐ   gāo   —   le   yìdiǎn
      you   tall   —   PFV   a:little

You've gotten taller.

(11) tā   zuótiān   lái   de   wǎn   —   le   yìdiǎn
      3sg   yesterday   come   NOM   late   —   PFV   a:little

Yesterday s/he came a little late.

(12) jīntiān   gǔpiào   hángshì   dī   —   le   yìdiǎn
      today   stock   market   lower   —   PFV   a:little

The stock market fell slightly today.

Sometimes the quantified event is a state whose limits are set by a phrase expressing the extent to which the subject is in that state. Sentences (13) and (14) illustrate these bounded states:

(13) zhèi   —   ge   dìfang   bu   cuò ,
      this   —   CL   place   not   bad

      jiùshi   chǎo   —   le   yidiǎn
      just   noisy   —   PFV   a:little

This place is not bad, it's just a little noisy.

(14) tā   niánji   bǐ   wǒ   dà   —   le
      3sg   age   COMP   I   great   —   PFV

      jǐ   —   shí   suì
      several —   ten   years

S/He is older than I by a few decades.

The following two examples can each have two interpretations, depending on whether the adjective describes a process or a state:

(15) a. (discussing how a friend has changed since his/her last visit)

      tā   pàng   —   le   yidiǎn
      3sg   fat   —   PFV   a:little

S/He's gotten a little fatter.

      b. (talking about candidates for a volleyball team)

      tā   pàng   —   le   yidiǎn
      3sg   fat   —   PFV   a:little

S/He's a little (too) fat.

(16) a. (talking about a laundry mishap)

      chènshān   xiǎo   —   le   sān   cùn
      shirt   small   —   PFV   three   inch

The shirt got smaller (i.e., shrank) by three inches.

b. (trying on clothes)

chènshān	xiǎo	–	<u>le</u>	sān	cùn
shirt	small	–	PFV	three	inch

The shirt is (too) small by three inches.

Sentence (17) provides a good illustration of the contrast between just naming an event and presenting it as a unified whole by quantifying it:

(17)	Zhāngsān	zài	bówùguǎn	mén	–	kǒu	<u>děng</u>	Lǐsì,
	Zhangsan	at	museum	door	–	mouth	wait	Lisi

<u>děng</u>	–	<u>le</u>	sān	–	<u>shí</u>	<u>fēnzhōng</u>
wait	–	PFV	three	–	ten	minute

Zhangsan waited for Lisi at the entrance to the museum for thirty minutes.

The first mention of *děng* 'wait' is not presented as an event viewed in its entirety but simply names the event; it cannot take *-le*. The second mention of the verb, however, is bounded by a phrase stating the amount of time the 'waiting' took; here *-le* is required.

Similarly, a verb with a specified quantity of the direct object will also typically occur with *-le* because the quantified direct object serves to bound the event signaled by the verb. For illustration, consider sentences (18)–(25):

(18)	tā	shuō	zuìjìn	dàxué	gài	–
	3sg	say	recently	university	build	–

<u>le</u>	bù	shǎo	de	xīn	sùshè
PFV	not	few	NOM	new	dormitory

S/He said that the university had recently built many new dormitories.

(19)	nèi	–	ge	jǐngchá	duì	wǒ	xíng
	that	–	CL	police:officer	to	I	perform

–	<u>le</u>	<u>yī</u>	–	<u>ge</u>	<u>lǐ</u>
–	PFV	one	–	CL	salute

That police officer saluted me.

(20) | tā | jīntiān | mǎi | – | le | hěn | duō | shū |
| --- | --- | --- | --- | --- | --- | --- | --- |
| 3sg | today | buy | – | PFV | very | many | book |

S/He bought a lot of books today.

(21) | tā | zài | miànbāo | – | shang | mǒ | – | le |
| --- | --- | --- | --- | --- | --- | --- | --- |
| 3sg | at | bread | – | on | spread | – | PFV |

yidiǎn	niú	–	you
a:little	cattle	–	oil

S/He spread a little butter on the bread.

(22) | wǒ | fá | – | le | tā | wǔ | kuài | qián |
| --- | --- | --- | --- | --- | --- | --- | --- |
| I | fine | – | PFV | 3sg | five | dollar | money |

I fined him/her five dollars.

(23) | tāmen | fā | – | le | wǔ | – | shí | – |
| --- | --- | --- | --- | --- | --- | --- | --- |
| they | issue | – | PFV | five | – | ten | – |

ge	qǐngtiē
CL	invitation

They sent out fifty invitations.

(24) | zhèi | huí | kǎoshì | wǒ | dé | – | le |
| --- | --- | --- | --- | --- | --- | --- |
| this | time | exam | I | obtain | – | PFV |

bā	–	shí	fēn
eight	–	ten	point

I got eighty points on this exam.

(25) | qiáng | – | shang | guà | – | le |
| --- | --- | --- | --- | --- | --- |
| wall | – | on | hang | – | PFV |

yi	–	fú	huà
one	–	CL	painting

A painting { was hung / had been hung } on the wall.

Sentence (26) is an interesting and typical example with -*le* in which the amount of time spent is expressed grammatically by a quantification of the object component of the verb-object compound *tán-tiān* 'discuss-universe = chat' (see section 3.2.5 of chapter 3 on verb-object compounds):

(26) wŏmen   tán   —   le   yi   yè
      we   discuss —   PFV   one   night

      —   de   tiān
      —   ASSOC   universe

We talked all night.

What these examples show is that it is perfectly normal to use -*le* where the message being communicated has to do with bounding an event by naming a specific quantity of the direct object. It is crucial, however, to notice that *speakers can differ* in their judgment about how much a quantified direct object serves to bound an event. For example, take a sentence such as (27):

(27) tā   jiā   yăng   —   le   yí   —   ge
      3sg   home   raise   —   PFV   one   —   CL

      hěn   kě   —   ài   de   xiăo   māo
      very   can   —   love   NOM   small   cat

His/Her family had a very lovable little cat.

Some native speakers feel that -*le* is not necessary; in other words, they don't feel strongly that the quantified direct object, *yi-ge hěn kě-ài de xiăo māo* 'a very lovable little cat', renders the event bounded. Some native speakers feel that when -*le* is used, (27) represents the beginning of a sequence of utterances about the small cat; in other words, they view the event as bounded, not because of the quantified direct object, but because it is the first in a sequence. Of course, many native speakers feel that sentence (27) is fine as it stands; they view the event as bounded simply because of the presence of the quantified direct object.

A recent experiment makes this point nicely.[2] A story containing sentence (28) was presented to sixty-two native Mandarin speakers. The author of the story had written the sentence with the -le, but only one-third of the subjects thought the -le was necessary:

(28)	hūrán	zǔfù	xū	–	le	yi	kǒu	qì
	suddenly	grandfather	heave	–	PFV	one	mouth	air

Suddenly, grandpa heaved a sigh.

What this example shows is that speakers can have different views about how bounded an event is, and this will determine whether they decide to use -le in certain situations. Those who would use the -le in sentence (28) feel that it is important to the message conveyed by the sentence that what grandpa gave was *one* sigh, while those who wouldn't use -le here feel that the fact that he sighed is more important than the sigh itself.

B. Definite or Specific Event

An event will also often qualify as bounded if the direct object is understood as a definite noun phrase (see section 4.2.5 of chapter 4 for a discussion of definiteness). Once again, the decision to use -le depends on the extent to which the event is judged by the individual speaker to be bounded. Here is an example showing various types of definite direct objects:

(i) Name:

(29)	wǒ	pèng	–	dào	–	le	Lín	Huì
	I	bump	–	arrive	–	PFV	Lin	Hui

I ran into Lin Hui (where the important information in the context is whom I ran into).

(ii) Pronoun:

(30)	nǐ	huǐ	–	le	nǐ	zìji
	you	ruin	–	PFV	you	self

You destroyed yourself.

(iii) Genitive modifier:

(31) tā   ráo   —   le   tā   —   de
      3sg   spare —   PFV   3sg   —   GEN

      dírén   le
      enemy   CRS

S/He spared his/her enemy.

(iv) Demonstrative Modifier:

(32) wǒ   xiǎng   —   chu   —   lai   —   le
      I   think   —   exit   —   come   —   PFV

      nèi   —   ge   zì
      that   —   CL   character

I remembered that character.

(v) Relative clause modifier:

(33) A: nǐ   zěnme   zhīdào   Shànghǎi   yǒu   yi
         you   how   know   Shanghai   exist   one

         —   qıan   —   wàn   rén ?
         —   thousand   —   ten:thousand person

How do you know Shanghai has ten million people?

B: yīnwèi   wǒ   kàn   —   le   xīn
    because   I   see   —   PFV   new

    chūbǎn   de   zīliào
    publish   NOM   material

Because I looked at the newly published figures.

(vi) Noun phrase with *bǎ*:

(34)	tā	bǎ	chē	mài	—	le
	3sg	BA	car	sell	—	PFV

S/He sold the car.

Here is an example from Spanos (1977:45), which shows another way in which *-le* signals the specificity of an event.

(35)	tā	wèn	wǒ	zuótiān	wǎnshang	zuò	(-le)	shénme ?
	3sg	ask	I	yesterday	evening	do	−PFV	what

S/He asked me what I did last night.

In this sentence, out of thirty-nine speakers asked, only seven thought the *-le* should be there, while thirty-two felt it should not. Once again, though, speakers' judgments on this question depend crucially on the nature of the message they imagine the sentence is conveying. With *-le* the event is viewed as bounded and thus as specific; the subject of the sentence, *tā* 's/he', was asking for a specific list of activities in which the speaker of the sentence engaged, as if *tā* were a nurse in charge of making sure the speaker didn't do too much. Since this is a rather unusual speech context, it is no wonder that only seven people out of 39 thought *-le* should be used. Without *-le*, on the other hand, the sentence is quite neutral and implies that *tā* was just making casual conversation. Since this latter case corresponds to a very natural situation, it is reasonable that the majority of speakers would think of this as the most natural context for the sentence and would judge that it should have no *-le*.

As another illustration of the same point, we might contrast (36) *a* and *b*:

(36) *a*.	tā	xiě	—	cuò	—	le	nèi
	3sg	write	—	wrong	—	PFV	that
	—	ge	zì				
	—	CL	character				

S/He wrote that character wrong.

b.	tā	xiě	—	cuò	nèi	—	ge
	3sg	write	—	wrong	that	—	CL

zì	le
character	CRS

S/He has written that character wrong (as I thought s/he would).

Sentence (36) *a*, with *-le*, would be used in a context in which *nèi-ge zì* 'that character' was being singled out, for example, because it is being contrasted with another character that s/he wrote correctly. Sentence (36) *b*, without the perfective *-le*, on the other hand, would be used in a context in which what is important is not *nèi-ge zì* 'that character' as opposed to some other character, but the current relevance of the fact that s/he wrote the character wrong. Our translation suggests one of the possible ways in which this state of affairs might be currently relevant (see chapter 7 for more discussion on current relevance and the sentence-final particle *le*).

The fact that speakers do not agree on matters like this is often frustrating to people trying to learn Mandarin and to linguists trying to analyze Mandarin, who wish that a hard-and-fast "rule" could be stated. It is important to realize, however, that there *is* a rule, but that this rule depends on what the speaker judges to be the significant information the sentence is conveying in the context in which it is used. The reason that speakers disagree when they are presented with sentences in isolation is because they have to imagine what the real conversational situation might be, and they might come to different conclusions on this point. The rule that they actually use in talking to each other is simply this: When the overall conversation makes it important to emphasize the information in the definite direct object, either because one wants to go on to talk about it or because it contrasts with some other possible item that could have been mentioned, *-le* must be used.

C. Verbs with Inherent Bounded Meaning

Some verbs represent specific, bounded events by virtue of their meaning. One such verb is *sǐ* 'die', which has its end point built into its meaning. Another such verb is *wàng* 'forget':

(37)	tā	qù	—	nián	sǐ	—	le
	3sg	last	—	year	die	—	PFV

S/He died last year.

(38)   wǒ   wàng   –   le   tā   –   de   dìzhǐ
        I   forget   –   PFV   3sg   –   GEN   address

I forgot his/her address.

We should notice that the inclusion of the end point in the meaning of such verbs as *sǐ* 'die' and *wàng* 'forget' is an idiosyncrasy of Mandarin Chinese, not a universal feature of all languages of the world. For example, the English verb 'die' does not have the end point of dying included in its meaning, and therefore it is possible to use the verb in a durative aspect, as shown in (39):

(39) S/He is dying.

Because of the inclusion of the end point of dying in the meaning of the Mandarin verb *sǐ* 'die', however, it cannot occur in the durative aspect; thus sentence (40), the Mandarin counterpart of sentence (39), is unacceptable:

(40)   *tá   sǐ   –   zhe
        3sg   die   –   DUR

For the same reasons, the English verb 'forget' may, but its Mandarin counterpart, *wàng*, may not occur in the durative aspect, as shown by the acceptable English sentence (41) and the unacceptable Mandarin sentence (42):

(41) S/He is forgetting his/her French.

(42)   *tā   wàng   –   zhe   tā   –   de   Fǎwén
        3sg   forget   –   DUR   3sg   –   GEN   French

Because they are inherently bounded, then, verbs such as *sǐ* 'die' and *wàng* 'forget' generally occur with the perfective aspect marker *-le*. An exception to this generalization is the use of such verbs to describe a situation that is not part of reality, called the *irrealis mode*. Irrealis mode in English is typically conveyed by the infinitive verb phrase following such verbs as *want, like, prefer, hope, expect*, and so forth; (43) is an example:

(43)   S/He   { wanted }   to die
                { wants }

The Mandarin counterpart of (43) is this:

(44)   tā   yào   sǐ³
        3sg   want   die

        S/He $\begin{Bmatrix} \text{wanted} \\ \text{wants} \end{Bmatrix}$ to die

In (44) *sǐ* is in the irrealis mode. Irrealis verbs in general do not occur with the perfective aspect marker *-le* because they are not describing events viewed in their entirety.

Further examples in which the inherent meaning of the verb specifies its own end point are given in sentences (45)–(49). The verbs in these sentences generally occur with *-le*, except when they are used in the irrealis mode.

(45)   tā   shuì   —   zhǎo   —   le   ma ?
        3sg   sleep   —   succeed   —   PFV   Q

        Did s/he fall asleep?

(46)   huǒ   miè   —   le
        fire   go:out   —   PFV

        The fire went out.

(47)   gàizi   diào   —   le
        lid   fall:off —   PFV

        The lid fell off.

(48)   zhèi   —   ge   yǐzi   huài   —   le
        this   —   CL   chair   broken   —   PFV

        This chair broke.

(49)   zhàdàn   zhà   —   le
        bomb   explode   —   PFV

        The bomb exploded.

D. First Event in a Sequence

Sometimes an event is bounded by being the first event in a sequence, where what is important is that after one event has taken place, another one happens or a new state materializes. In such cases, the first event is of interest as an unanalyzed whole; the speaker signals that its occurrence is *bounded* by the subsequent event. In these instances -*le* is used, and the sentence can often be translated with 'after', 'when', or 'now that' in English.

(50) wǒ   chī   —   wán   —   le   nǐ   chī
      I   eat   —   finish —   PFV   you   eat

After I have finished eating, then you eat.

(51) wǒ   kàn   —   wán   —   le   bào ,
      I   read   —   finish —   PFV   paper

      jiu   shuì
      then   sleep

When I finish reading the paper, I will go to sleep.

(52) tā   shuō   de   hěn   qiǎomiào ,
      3sg   say   CSC   very   skillful

      ràng   rén   tīng   —
      let   person   hear   —

      le   bu   huì   shēngqì
      PFV   not   likely   angry

S/He talks very skillfully so that when people hear him/her they don't get angry.

(53) zěnme   pèng   —   le   bēizi   yě   bu   hē ?
      how   bump   —   PFV   glasses   also   not   drink

How come after you have touched glasses, you still don't drink?

(54) chū   —   le   zhèi   —   ge
      exit   —   PFV   this   —   CL

           jiǎnchá   —   shì,   wàitou   jiu
           examination   —   room   outside   then

           yǒu   yínháng   guìtai
           exist   bank   counter

When you go out of this customs room, just outside there is a bank
counter.

(55) yǒu   —   le   nèi   —   ge
      exist   —   PFV   that   —   CL

           rìguāng   —   dēng,   chúfáng
           sun:light   —   lamp   kitchen

           jiu   liàng   duō   le
           then   bright   much   CRS

Now that (they) have that fluorescent light, the kitchen is much brighter.

(56) tā   kāi   —   le   mén,   nǐ   jiu
      3sg   open   —   PFV   door   you   then

           jìn   —   qu
           enter   —   go

{ When } s/he opens the door, you go in.
{ If }

(57) wǒ   pào   —   le   chá   hē
      I   brew   —   PFV   tea   drink

I made some tea to drink.

(58) wǒ   —   de   yǎnjīng   yǒu   máobìng ,   kàn
      I   —   GEN   eye   exist   trouble   see

      —   duō   —   <u>le</u>   shū ,
      —   much   —   PFV   book

      jiu   bu   shūfu
      then   not   comfortable

I'm having trouble with my eyes; after I've read a lot, they don't feel good.

Sentence (50) nicely illustrates the independence of aspect from tense: both of the actions in (50) may be in the future at the time the sentence is spoken. Sentences (51), (53), and (56) show that the direct object doesn't need to be quantified in order for -le to appear if the event is the first in a sequence. Now, however, this raises an interesting point: there is often something strange and "unfinished" about a sentence containing -le and a simple unquantified direct object noun. Thus, by themselves, sentences like the following seem incomplete and odd:

(59) ?wǒ   lǐ   —   le   fǎ
      I   cut   —   PFV   hair

I had a haircut.

(60) ?wǒ   hē   —   le   chá
      I   drink   —   PFV   tea

I drank tea.

The reason for this is not hard to understand: a simple unquantified direct object noun is usually indefinite and even nonreferential, and normally a simple verb phrase with such a direct object is *not* bounded. That is why such sentences need to be bounded by the addition of either a following clause or a sentence final particle *le* indicating current relevance (see chapter 7 for a discussion of *le*). Thus, for example, (59) becomes perfectly acceptable in contexts where it is followed by another clause, as in (61), or where it occurs with *le*, signaling "currently relevant state", as in (62):

(61)	wǒ	lǐ	—	le	fǎ	jiu	qù	sànbù
	I	cut	—	PFV	hair	then	go	take:walk

I will take a walk as soon as I finish my haircut.

(62)	wǒ	lǐ	—	le	fǎ	le
	I	cut	—	PFV	hair	CRS

I (have) had a haircut.

Sometimes, in the right context, an adverbial expression can serve the function of bounding the event. For example, in a situation in which the issue is *when* s/he got a haircut, sentence (63) could be used; similarly, if it is known that s/he got rich, but the issue is *where*, then sentence (64) would be appropriate:

(63)	tā	zǎoshang	lǐ	—	le	fǎ
	3sg	morning	cut	—	PFV	hair

S/He got a haircut in the morning.

(64)	tā	zài	Jiāzhōu	fā	—	le	cái
	3sg	at	California	issue	—	PFV	wealth

S/He got rich in California.

The important point to be drawn from this discussion is that understanding the grammar of a sentence always involves understanding how that sentence relates to the context in which it occurs, In this case, it is clear that a sentence describing an event never occurs in a vacuum, but is always embedded in some larger conversation or discourse context. Whether a sentence expresses a bounded event depends to a great extent on the nature of the conversation of which that sentence is a part.

So far we have seen that the conditions for the use of *-le* are quite straightforward: *-le* is used when the event described by a sentence is perfective, which means that the event is bounded, and an event is bounded (1) if its temporal or spatial limits are specified, (2) if it signals a specific event and its direct object is definite, (3) if boundedness is inherent in the meaning of the verb of the sentence, or (4) if it is followed by another event.

For a clear understanding of the function of -*le*, it is equally important that we be aware of where -*le* cannot be used. The following section is devoted to this issue.

6.1.2 Where Not to Use -*le*

A. Semantic Conditions for -*le* Not Fulfilled

First, -*le* is never used with verbs expressing states that do not represent bounded events:

(65)	wǒ	xǐhuān	(*-le)	mùguā
	I	like	-PFV	papaya

I like papaya.

(66)	tā	xìng	(*-le)	Wú
	3sg	surname	-PFV	Wu

S/He is named Wu.

(67)	nèi	—	ge	dìfang	hěn	ānjìng	(*-le)
	that	—	CL	place	very	quiet	-PFV

That place is very quiet.

(68)	wǒ	shì	(*-le)	nǐ	—	de	gēge
	I	be	-PFV	you	—	GEN	older:brother

I am your older brother.

For the same reason, -*le* does not occur with verbs denoting ongoing actions:

(69)	tā	shǒu	—	lǐ	ná	—	zhe
	3sg	hand	—	in	hold	—	DUR

(*-le)	shū
-PFV	book

S/He is holding a book in his hand.

(70)   tā   zài   liú   (*-le)   húzi
        3sg   DUR   keep   -PFV   beard

He is growing a beard.

In other words, perfective *-le* is incompatible with the durative aspect markers *zài* and *he* (see section 6.2 of this chapter) because the meanings of perfective (bounded) and durative (unbounded) aspect are incompatible.

Perfective *-le* is also incompatible with habitual or repeated events, since these are not bounded events viewed as a whole. For example, (71) and (72), signaling habitual events, are not acceptable with *-le*:

(71)   tā   tīan   —   tian   huí   —   qu   (*-le)
        3sg   day   —   day   return —   go   -PFV

S/He goes back every day.

(72)   tā   píngcháng   mǎi   (*-le)   hěn   duō   shū
        3sg   usually   buy   -PFV   very   many   book

S/He usually bought a lot of books.

Nor do we find *-le* with "potential" forms of resultative verb compounds (see section 3.2.3 of chapter 3 for discussion of these compounds). Because these forms refer to general states of ability or inability rather than to events viewed in their entirety, *-le* is not compatible with the potential forms. Thus, sentences (73)–(76), which contain resultative verb compounds with a potential infix, are unacceptable with *-le*:

(73)   tā   yā   —   bu   —   zhù   (*-le)   xuéshēng
        3sg   press   —   can't   —   hold:on   -PFV   student

S/He can't suppress the students.

(74)   wǒ   lā   —   bu   —   kāi   (*-le)   mén
        I   pull   —   can't   —   open   -PFV   door

I can't pull the door open.

(75)   nǐ   kàn   —   de   —   jiàn   (*-le)
       you   see   —   can   —   perceive -PFV

               tā   —   de   liǎn   ma ?
               3sg   —   GEN   face   Q

Can you see his/her face?

(76)   wǒ   jiǎng   —   de   —   guò   (*-le)   tā
       I   talk   —   can   —   pass   -PFV   3sg

I can outtalk him/her.

Perfective -le is also incompatible with the experiential aspect suffix -guo (see section 6.3 of this chapter for discussion of this point), as the following sentences show:[4]

(77)   wǒ   chī   —   guo   —   (*-le)   bālà
       I   eat   —   EXP   —   -PFV   guava

I have eaten guava before.

(78)   tā   qù   —   guo   (*-le)   Xiānggǎng
       3sg   go   —   EXP   -PFV   Hong Kong

S/He has been to Hong Kong.

Finally, -le in general does not occur in negative sentences.[5] Compare the a and b forms of the following pairs:

(79) a.   zhǐ   mài   —   guāng   —   le
           paper   sell   —   gone   —   PFV

The paper was sold out.

     b.   zhǐ   méi   mài   —   guāng   (*-le)
           paper   not   sell   —   gone   -PFV

The paper wasn't all sold out.

(80) *a.*   tā   bō   —   cuò   —   <u>le</u>   hàomǎ

         3sg   dial   —   wrong   —   PFV   number

     S/He dialed the wrong number.

     b.   tā   méi   bō   —   cuò   (*-le)   hàomǎ

         3sg   not   dial   —   wrong   -PFV   number

     S/He didn't dial the wrong number.

(81) *a.*   tā   mài   —   <u>le</u>   nèi   sān

         3sg   sell   —   PFV   that   three

               —   zhī   jī

               —   CL   chicken

     S/He sold those three chickens.

     b.   tā   bu   mài   (*-le)   nèi   sān

         3sg   not   sell   -PFV   that   three

               —   zhī   jī

               —   CL   chicken

     S/He wouldn't sell those three chickens.

It is easy to see why *-le* does not occur in negative sentences: the meaning of negative sentences—that some event does not take place or that some state of affairs does not obtain—is incompatible with the meaning of *-le*, which is to signal a bounded event. An event that does not occur, of course, cannot in general be bounded (but see section 6.1.3 of this chapter for *-le* in negative imperatives; also see chapter 12 for further discussion of negation and aspect.)

B. A Perfectivizing Expression Takes the Place of *-le*

Often the conditions for the use of perfective *-le* would appear to be satisfied, and yet no *-le* appears. For example, (82)–(85) are four sentences expressing bounded events viewed in their entirety, yet none has -*le*:

(82)   tā   cóng   fángzi   —   lǐ   zǒu
        3sg   from   house   —   in   walk

           <u>dào</u>   <u>Zhāngsān</u>   <u>nàr</u>
           to   Zhangsan   there

S/He walked from his/her house over to Zhangsan's place.

(83)   wǒ   bǎ   shǒubiǎo   fàng   <u>zài</u>   <u>chōuti</u>   —   <u>lǐ</u>
        I   BA   watch   put   at   drawer   —   in

I put the watch in the drawer.

(84)   wǒ   jì   <u>gěi</u>   <u>tā</u>   yi   —   fēng   xìn
        I   mail   to   3sg   one   —   CL   letter

I sent him/her a letter.

(85)   wǒ   xiào   <u>de</u>   <u>zhàn</u>   —   <u>bu</u>
        I   laugh   CSC   stand   —   can't

          —   <u>qǐ</u>   —   <u>lái</u>
          —   rise   —   come

I laughed so hard that I couldn't stand up.

Why do these sentences have no -*le*? The answer is that each contains *another* element that does the job of "perfectivizing" the verb. That is, each of the underlined morphemes or phrases in the above sentences serves to perform the same function that -*le* does, namely, to signal that the event is to be viewed as a complete whole. In (82)−(84), the perfectivizing expressions are the directional phrase *dào Zhāngsān nàr* 'to Zhangsan's place', the locative phrase *zài chōuti-lǐ* 'in the drawer', and the indirect object phrase *gěi-tā* 'to him/her', which put boundaries on the events of walking, putting, and sending by specifying their spatial limits. In (85) the perfectivizing expression is the complex stative phrase *de zhàn-bu-qǐ-lái* 'so much that I couldn't stand up' (see chapter 22), which bounds the event of laughing by naming the extent to which it happened.

6.1.3 *-le* in Imperatives

Most of the time, imperatives do not have *-le*. The following examples of imperatives, for instance, do not have *-le*:

(86) ná   nǐ   —   de   wàiyī
      take   you   —   GEN   coat

Get your coat!

(87) nǐ   shāo   zhèi   dùn   fàn
      you   cook   this   time   food

You make the meal!

(88) dì   gěi   wǒ   nèi   —   ge   tiáogēng
      hand   to   I   that   —   CL   spoon

Hand me that spoon!

-Le can, however, be used in imperatives when there is some urgency about the action taking place, especially when something is to be disposed of or gotten rid of; (89)−(90) are examples:

(89) yàn   —   le   nèi   —   ge   yào   —
      swallow —   PFV   that   —   CL   medicine —

              wánzi
              pill

Swallow that pill!

(90) hē   —   le   nèi   bēi   yào
      drink   —   PFV   that   cup   medicine

Drink that cup of medicine!

Sometimes *-le* contrasts with the resultative verb ending *-diào* 'off' in an imperative, where *-le* expresses more urgency. For example:

(91) *a.* (neutral)

guān	—	<u>diào</u>	tā
turn:off	—	off	3sg

Turn it off (e.g., the radio).

　　b. (very irritated)

guān	—	<u>le</u>	tā
turn:off	—	PFV	3sg

Get rid of that noise (e.g., on the radio)!

(92) *a.*　　(neutral)

cā	—	<u>diào</u>	tā
erase	—	off	3sg

Erase it.

　　b. (with urgency)

cā	—	<u>le</u>	tā
erase	—	PFV	3sg

Get rid of it (e.g., what's on the blackboard)!

(93) *a.* (neutral)

tuō	—	<u>diào</u>	tā
take:off	—	off	3sg

Take it off (e.g., your ring—I want to try it on).

b. (with intensity)

tuō	—	le	tā
take:off	—	PFV	3sg

Take it off (e.g., your ring—I believe that you should never wear it again)!

(94) *a.* (neutral)

dào	—	diào	tā
pour	—	off	3sg

Pour it out.

b. (with intensity)

dào	—	le	tā
pour	—	PFV	3sg

Pour it out (once and for all and be done with it)!

The *-le* in these examples always correlates with a message in which it is the end point of an action that is important. When an action is to go on for a while, then no *-le* is used, and the verb may be reduplicated (see section 6.4 below):

(95) (taking a picture)

xiào	—	yi	—	xiào	(*-le)
smile	—	one	—	smile	-PFV

Smile a little!

Here is a pair of examples which illustrates this point. If someone wants you to open the door and leave it open, s/he could say:

(96)	kāi	—	kāi	mén
	open	—	open	door

Open the door a little!

If, however, the speaker wants you to get a bottle of soda open once and for all, then s/he might say:

(97)   kāi   —   le   tā
         open   —   PFV   3sg

    Open it!

In negative imperatives, with *bié* 'don't', it is also normal not to find *-le*, as (98)−(100) show:

(98)   bié   guān   mén
         don't   close   door

    Don't close the door.

(99)   bié   jiā   jiàngyóu
         don't   add   soy:sauce

    Don't add   {the}   soy sauce.
                     {any}

(100)   bié   dào   chá
         don't   pour   tea

    Don't pour tea.

There is one type of situation in which *-le* must be used in a negative imperative, though, and that is when the imperative is a *warning* to the listener. Sentences (101)−(103) are examples:

(101)   bié   pèng   —   le   lúzi
         don't   touch   —   PFV   stove

    Don't touch the stove!

(102)   bié   zhuàng   —   le   gǒu
         don't   run:into   —   PFV   dog

    Don't run into the dog!

(103) bié   tūn   —   le   gútou
       don't swallow —   PFV   bone

Don't swallow the bone!

The contrast can be seen clearly if we look at pairs of negative imperatives with and without -le:

(104) a.   bié   qiān   —   míng
            don't sign   —   name

(You) don't (need to) sign your name.

b.   bié   qiān   —   le   míng
      don't sign   —   PFV   name

Don't sign your name (I'm warning you)!

Sentence (104) b means 'Watch it, something bad will happen if you sign your name', but (104) a isn't a warning. The case is similar in this pair:

(105) a.   bié   xuǎn   nèi   —   táng   kè
            don't select that   —   CL   course

Don't take that course (I wouldn't bother if I were you).

b.   bié   xuǎn   —   le   nèi   —   táng   kè
      don't select —   PFV   that   —   CL   course

Don't take that course (you'll be sorry if you do).

Now, why is it that -le has the effect of making the negative imperative into a warning? The reason has to do with the sequencing function of -le, which we discussed above in section D of 6.1. An event in a negative imperative by itself is not a likely candidate for a bounded, or *perfective*, event, since the speaker is actually urging that it *not* happen. Therefore, we should expect never to find -le in negative imperatives. When -le does occur, however, we know that because the event can't be bounded in and of itself, it must be bounded by a following event, which may or may not be expressed. Thus, to take (105) *b*, for example, a possible following clause, which could either be expressed or assumed, is provided in (106):

(106)	bié	xuǎn	–	<u>le</u>	nèi	–	táng	kè,
	don't	select	–	PFV	that	–	CL	course
	nǐ	yòu	gēn	–	bu	–	shàng
	you	again	keep	–	can't	–	ascend

Don't take that course; you won't be able to keep up again.

The same is true for all the other examples of *bié* imperatives with *-le*: they are always incomplete and must be understood in terms of a following clause, either assumed or actually present, giving the adverse consequences if the warning in the *bié* clause is not heeded. In many cases, the negative consequences are obvious enough that they don't need to be mentioned, as in the earlier example (101):

(101)	bié	pèng	–	<u>le</u>	lúzi
	don't	touch	–	PFV	stove

Don't touch the stove!

Here, since the natural setting would be one in which the stove is too hot to touch, it would generally be unnecessary to add in a following clause the information that the hearer would be burned otherwise. The implication is still 'or else . . .', but the hearer can fill in the rest. When it is not as clear why the warning is being given, then the following clause becomes more necessary. For example, if the warning is not to answer the phone, the reasons might not be clear. In such a case, the following clause specifying the consequence is more likely to occur:

(107)	bié	jiē	–	le	diànhuà ,	burán	nǐ
	don't	answer	–	PFV	telephone	otherwise	you
	yòu	yào	shēngqì				
	again	will	angry				

Don't answer the phone; otherwise you'll get angry again.

We see, then, that the use of *-le* in warnings follows naturally from its use to signal the first event in a sequence. The second event that serves to bound the first one is often understood and therefore not explicitly stated in a natural speech context.

6.1.4 -*le* Does Not Mean Past Tense

By now we have seen a number of examples showing that -*le* does not signal past tense. To recapitulate, we find -*le* in such non−past perfective sentences as imperatives:

(108)	hē	−	le	tā
	drink	−	PFV	3sg

Drink it.

(109)	bié	dǎ	−	pò	−	le	bēizi
	don't	hit	−	broken	−	PFV	glass

Don't break the glass.

in sentences indicating simple futures:

(110)	míngtiān	wǒ	jiu	kāichú	−	le	tā
	tomorrow	I	then	expel	−	PFV	3sg

I'll expel him/her tomorrow!

and in future or conditional sequence-of-action sentences:

(111)	wǒ	chī	−	le	fàn	zài	zǒu
	I	eat	−	PFV	rice	then	go

I'll go after I eat.

(112)	tā	kāi	−	le	mén ,	nǐ	jiu
	3sg	open	−	PFV	door	you	then
		jìn	−	qu			
		enter	−	go			

$\left\{ \begin{array}{c} \text{When} \\ \text{If} \end{array} \right\}$ s/he opens the door, you go in.

Furthermore, we know that many sentences expressing past events need not have any *-le*. For example, bounded events with perfectivizing expressions don't take *-le*:

(113)   zuótiān   tā   tiào   <u>zài</u>   <u>chuáng</u>   −   <u>shang</u>
            yesterday   3sg   jump   at   bed   −   on

Yesterday s/he jumped onto the bed.

(114)   tā   bǎ   ròu   qiē   −   <u>chéng</u>   <u>xiǎo</u>   <u>kuài</u>
            3sg   BA   meat   cut   −   become   small   piece

S/He cut the meat into small pieces.

Events that are not explicitly bounded, however, also do not occur with *-le*, even if they refer to past time:

(115)   tāmen   qiántiān   jiào   wǒ   zài   zhèli   děng
            they   day:before:yesterday   tell   I   at   here   wait

The day before yesterday, they told me to wait here.

(116)   zuótiān   ye   −   lǐ   wǒ   mèng
            yesterday   night   −   in   I   dream

                −   jiàn   wǒ   múqīn
                −   perceive   I   mother

Last night I dreamed about my mother.

(117)   nèi   −   běn   shū   shì   wǒ   xiě   de
            that   −   CL   book   be   I   write   NOM

That book was written by me.

(118)   wǒ   zǎo   zhīdào   yǒu   yidiǎn   bu   duì
            I   early   know   exist   a:little   not   right

I knew a long time ago that something was wrong.

(119)	wǒmen	dào	bǎihuògōngsī	qù	mǎi	dōngxi
	we	to	department:store	go	buy	thing

We went to the department store to buy some things.

(120)	tā	wèn	wǒ	nǐ	niánqīng	de	shíhòu
	3sg	ask	I	you	young	NOM	time

	zài	nǎli	niàn	—	shū
	at	where	study	—	book

S/He asked me where you went to school when you were young.

Why is it, then, that sentences with -le so often seem to be referring to past time? The answer is simple: even though -le doesn't *mean* past tense, many perfective events reported in speech are events that occurred prior to the time of speaking. This means that there is a correlation between events in the past and the appearance of -le: ordinarily, unless the context makes it clear that a different time is being referred to, a perfective sentence with -le will be understood to refer to past time. On the other hand, it does not follow from this that past-time events must be perfective; only those past-time events that are bounded will occur with -le.

6.1.5 -le Does Not Mean Completion

It is equally important to recognize that -le cannot be characterized as expressing completion. Typically, of course, an action that is bounded is also complete, but -le need not necessarily signal completed action. For instance, consider sentence (121):

(121)	qiáng	—	shang	guà	—	le	yi	—
	wall	—	on	hang	—	PFV	one	—

	fu	huà
	CL	painting

On the wall hangs a painting.

As it is used in (121), the verb guà 'hang' does not signal an action. Rather, it describes a stative event concerning the painting. The English translation accurately depicts this stative usage of the verb guà 'hang' in (121). The event described by (121) is bounded by the quantifying phrase yi-fu huà 'one painting', and -le is present in (121). There is, however, no sense of completion being conveyed by the sentence.

Let us consider another example clearly showing that *-le* does not mean completion:

| (122) | tā | pǎo | – | le | liǎng | – |
| | 3sg | run | – | PFV | two | – |

| | ge | zhōngtóu | le |
| | CL | hour | CRS |

S/He has run for two hours.

In (122), both the perfective *-le* and the sentence final *le* (see chapter 7) occur. A sentence such as (122), with both the perfective *-le* and the sentence final *le*, conveys the message that the event is bounded (in this case, the time phrase also serves to bound the event), and the starting point of an action, in this case, *pǎo* 'run', occurs before the time of speech, but the end point of the action is left open. In other words, in (122), the action of running might have ended before the time of speech, or it might end at the time of speech, or it might end at some time after the time of speech. Only the total context in which (122) occurs can determine what is the precise end point of the action in time. It is obvious that if *-le* were to signal completed action, sentences such as (122) could not be indeterminate with regard to the end point of the action denoted by the verb.

6.1.6 Summary

We have seen that the function and the use of *-le* are not mysterious once it is understood as a perfective marker and once the notion of perfectivity is made clear. The perfective marker *-le* is used for events that are viewed as bounded because (1) the events are quantified, (2) the events are specific, (3) the verbs have inherently bounded meanings, or (4) there are following events. We have also seen that *-le* can be omitted in the presence of another perfectivizing expression and that in certain instances speakers may be expected to make different decisions as to whether an event is sufficiently bounded to require *-le*.

Learning to control *-le* is one of the most difficult tasks facing a European-language speaker attempting to master Mandarin, partly because European languages have no feature quite like it. This task is further complicated by an equally elusive sentence-final *le* 'CRS' (discussed in chapter 7). If we begin, however, by abandoning any attempt to equate *-le* with a grammatical category such as tense in English, concentrating instead on trying to grasp the semantic notions of perfectivity and boundedness, we will be making a good head start in this challenging task.

Let's turn now to the other aspect markers of Mandarin.

6.2 The Durative Aspect

In the introduction to this chapter, we said that durative markers signal the ongoing, or durative, nature of an event.[6] English uses the verb ending *-ing* together with the copula to express ongoing events, as in (123) and (124):

(123) She *is explaining* the grammar.

(124) He *was holding* the baby.

In Mandarin, there are two aspect markers that signal the durative nature of an event: the word *zài* and the suffix *-zhe*. The usage of the durative markers in a sentence depends on the meaning of the verb. In the following discussion we will correlate the occurrence of the durative markers with various semantic types of verbs.

6.2.1 Semantic Types of Verbs and the Durative Aspect Markers *-zhe, zài*

A. Activity Verbs.

As the name suggests, these verbs signal activity. The most apparent activity is, of course, an action, such as *pǎo* 'run', *dǎ* 'hit'. Action verbs constitute only a subset of activity verbs, however. There are other verbs, such as *xīnshǎng* 'appreciate', *kàn* 'read, look at', *yánjiū* 'research', and *xué* 'learn', which do not name actions but nevertheless represent activities. One way to describe activity verbs is that they generally signal the active participation and involvement of an animate subject in an event. Thus, such verbs as *pàng* 'fat', *yǒu qián* 'have money = rich', *shōudào* 'receive', *zhīdào* 'know', and *tīng-shuō* 'hear-say = hear (about some information)' are not activity verbs because they do not signal the active participation of an animate subject. For example, consider sentence (125):

(125) Zhāngsān shōudào   –   le   yi   –   fēng   xìn
      Zhangsan receive   –   PFV   one   –   CL   letter

     Zhangsan received a letter.

Although *Zhāngsān* is an animate subject of the verb *shōudào* 'receive', the sentence does not convey the message that *Zhāngsān* is actively participating in some sort of activity. In fact, *Zhāngsān* in (125) is simply the passive receiver of a letter. Similarly, in (126):

(126)   Zhāngsān   hěn   pàng
        Zhangsan   very   fat

Zhangsan is very fat.

the subject *Zhāngsān* is merely in a state that is described as "fat"; he is not actively participating in any activity.

Given "activity" as a semantic characterization of a class of verbs, we can state the first rule concerning the use of the durative markers:

(i) Only activity verbs can take *zài* to indicate the durative aspect.

The following sentences illustrate the rule stated in (i). Sentences (127)−(130) contain activity verbs and are well formed; but sentences (131)−(135), with nonactivity verbs, are unacceptable:

(127)   Zhāngsān   zài   dǎ   Lǐsì[7]
        Zhangsan   DUR   hit   Lisi

Zhangsan is hitting Lisi.

(128)   wǒ   zài   xīnshǎng   Bèiduōfēn   −   de   yīnyuè
        I   DUR   appreciate Beethoven   −   ASSOC   music

I am appreciating the music of Beethoven.

(129)   Zhāngsān   zài   liàn   pǎo
        Zhangsan   DUR   practice run

Zhangsan is practicing running.

(130)   Lǐsì   zài   jiěshi   wénfǎ
        Lisi   DUR   explain   grammar

Lisi is explaining the grammar.

(131)   *tā   zài   pàng
        3sg   DUR   fat

(132)　　*wǒ　　zài　　zhīdào　　nèi　　—　　jiàn　　shì
　　　　　I　　　DUR　　know　　　that　　—　　CL　　　matter

(133)　*Zhāngsān　　zài　　yǒu　　qián
　　　　Zhangsan　　DUR　　exist　　money

(134)　*píngzi　　zài　　pò
　　　　bottle　　DUR　　broken

(135)　*tā　　zài　　pèngjian　　péngyou
　　　　3sg　　DUR　　run:into　　friend

There are also dialects of Mandarin which employ -*zhe* . . . *ne* or *zài* . . . -*zhe* . . . (*ne*) to signal the durative aspect for an activity verb: for example,

(136) *a*.　　Zhāngsān　　dǎ　　—　　zhe　　Lìsì　　ne
　　　　　　　Zhangsan　　hit　　—　　DUR　　Lisi　　REx

　　　　Zhangsan is hitting Lisi.

　　　　b.　　Zhāngsān　　zài　　dǎ　　—　　zhe　　Lìsì　　(ne)
　　　　　　　Zhangsan　　DUR　　hit　　—　　DUR　　Lisi　　REx

　　　　Zhangsan is hitting Lisi.

B. Verbs of Posture

In Mandarin there is a class of verbs that denote postures or physical dispositions of an entity at a location, including *zuò* 'sit', *zhàn* 'stand', *dūn* 'squat', *xiē* 'rest', *guì* 'kneel', *tǎng* 'lie', *tíng* 'stop', and *shuì* 'sleep'. These verbs may occur with the durative aspect marker -*zhe* to signal the ongoing posture or physical disposition of an entity at a location. Sentences (137)−(141) will illustrate:

(137)　　tā　　zài　　fángzi　　—　　lǐ　　zuò　　—　　zhe
　　　　　3sg　　at　　house　　—　　in　　sit　　—　　DUR

　　　　S/He is sitting in the house.

(138)　　wǒ　　zài　　qiáng　　—　　shang　　zhàn　　—　　zhe
　　　　　I　　　at　　wall　　—　　on　　　stand　　—　　DUR

　　　　I am standing on the wall.

(139)   Lǐsì   zài   kètīng   —   lǐ   shuì   —   <u>zhe</u>
         Lisi   at   living:room —   in   sleep   —   DUR

Lisi is sleeping in the living room.

(140)   chēzi   zài   wàimian   tíng   —   <u>zhe</u>
         car   at   outside   stop   —   DUR

The car is parked outside.

(141)   tā   zài   chuáng   —   shàng   tǎng   —   <u>zhe</u>
         3sg   at   bed   —   on   lie   —   DUR

S/He is lying on the bed.

C. Activity Verbs Signaling States Associated with Their Activity Meanings.

Consider the verb *ná* 'take'. It names an activity as it occurs in (142), and, as predicted by rule (i), it takes *zài* to express durativity:

(142)   tā   zài   ná   bàozhǐ
         3sg   DUR   take   newspaper

S/He is ⎰taking   ⎱ newspapers.
        ⎱picking up⎰

On the other hand, *ná* could mean a state associated with the activity of 'taking', namely 'holding', as in (143); here durativity is expressed by the suffix *-zhe*:

(143)   tā   ná   —   <u>zhe</u>   liǎng   —   běn   shū
         3sg   take   —   DUR   two   —   CL   book

S/He is holding two books.

Consider another example, *guà* 'hang', which may be an activity verb, as shown in the imperative sentence (144):

(144)   nǐ   bǎ   nèi   —   ge   zhàopiàn   guà   zài   zhèr
         you   BA   that   —   CL   photograph   hang   at   here

Hang that photograph here.

The same verb, however, can also be used to name a state associated with the activity of hanging, as in (145):

(145) | qiáng | – | shang | guà | – | zhe | yi | – |
| wall | – | on | hang | – | DUR | one | – |

| | | ge | zhàopiàn | | | | |
| | | CL | photograph | | | | |

There is a photograph hanging on the wall.

A further example is the verb *chuān*, which can mean either 'put on' or 'be wearing'. With the former meaning, the verb is an activity verb, but with the latter meaning, the verb signals a state associated with the action 'put on'. The pair of sentences in (146) illustrates this semantic contrast:

(146) *a.* | tā | zài | chuān | pí | – | xié |
| 3sg | DUR | put:on | leather | – | shoe |

S/He is putting on his/her leather shoes.

b. | tā | chuān | – | zhe | pí | – | xié |
| 3sg | wear | – | DUR | leather | – | shoe |

S/He is wearing his/her leather shoes.

In (146) *a*, the verb *chuān*, as an activity verb, takes *zài* as the durative aspect marker; in (146) *b*, *chuān* denotes a state and takes -*zhe* as the durative aspect marker.

We can now express a rule with regard to an activity verb that denotes a state associated with its activity meaning:

(ii) An activity verb that signals a state associated with its activity meaning takes -*zhe* as the durative aspect marker.

Here are some further examples of this stative usage of activity verbs:

(147) | zài | mén | – | kǒu | – | de | bōli | – |
| at | door | – | mouth | – | ASSOC | glass | – |

| | shang | xiě | – | zhe | sì | – | ge | zì |
| | on | write | – | DUR | four | – | CL | character |

On the glass in the doorway are written four characters.

(148)   wǒ   wèn   tā   qián   dōu   zài   nǎli   gē   —   <u>zhe</u>
        I   ask   3sg   money all   at   where put   —   DUR

I asked him/her where all his/her money had been put.

With regard to the rule stated in (ii), it should be pointed out that not all activity verbs can be used to denote a state. For example, *tiào* 'jump' is an action and is, therefore, an activity verb, but it cannot be used to describe a state. Thus (149) *a* is acceptable, but (149) *b* is not:

(149) *a*.   Zhāngsān   <u>zài</u>   tiào
             Zhangsan   DUR   jump

        Zhangsan is jumping.

      b.   *Zhāngsān   tiào   —   <u>zhe</u>
             Zhangsan   jump   —   DUR

As is clear from the description in 6.2.1.B and the rule stated in (ii), the verbs that take -*zhe* as the durative aspect marker do not signal activity. On the other hand, not all nonactivity verbs can take the durative aspect marker -*zhe*. In fact, most of the nonactivity verbs cannot take any durative aspect marker. Thus examples (131)−(135) would be equally unacceptable if *zài* were replaced with the verbal suffix -*zhe*, as we can show by replacing *zài* with -*zhe* in (131):

(150)   *tā   pàng   —   <u>zhe</u>
        3sg   fat   —   DUR

D. -*zhe* . . . *ne* as an Intensifier

There is another usage of -*zhe* which is distinct from the durative function of -*zhe* discussed here: it may function as an intensifier together with the sentence-final particle *ne*. For example,

(151)   nèi   —   ge   fángjiān   hēi   —   <u>zhe</u>   <u>ne</u>
        that   —   CL   room   black —   INT   REx

     That room is pretty dark.

The meaning of (151) makes it clear that -*zhe* in such a context does not signal duration. Sentences like (151), however, appear only in certain northern dialects of

Mandarin. In those dialects in which it occurs, *-zhe* as an intensifier may be suffixed to any adjectival verb.

6.2.2 Complex Sentences with the Durative Aspect Marker *-zhe*

Finally, the durative aspect marker *-zhe* can also be used in the first of two clauses to signal that one event provides a durative background for another event. For example, in sentence (152),

(152)	xiǎo	gǒu	yáo	—	zhe	wěiba	pǎo	le
	small	dog	shake	—	DUR	tail	run	CRS

The small dog ran away wagging its tail.

the wagging of the tail is presented as the ongoing background to the running away. The same can be said about these additional examples:

(153)	tā	guāng	—	zhe	jiǎo	shàng	—	kè
	3sg	bare	—	DUR	foot	ascend	—	class

S/He goes to class barefooted.

(154)	tā	kū	—	zhe	pǎo	huí	jiā	qu	le
	3sg	cry	—	DUR	run	return	home	go	CRS

S/He ran home crying.

(155)	nèi	—	zhāng	huà	děi	dēng	—	zhe
	that	—	CL	painting	must	step	—	DUR
		yǐzi	guà					
		chair	hang					

That painting, you have to stand on a chair to hang.

(156)	tā	nào	—	zhe	yào	mǎi	dàyī
	3sg	fuss	—	DUR	want	buy	coat

S/He made a fuss about wanting to buy a coat.

(157) tā   xié   –   zhe   yǎn   xiào   –   zhe
       3sg   slant   –   DUR   eye   smile   –   DUR

               kàn   wǒ
               look   I

Smiling, s/he looked at me out of the corner of his/her eye.

(158) tā   tǎng   –   zhe   kàn   bào
       3sg   lie   –   DUR   look   paper

S/He was lying down reading the newspaper.

In this construction -*zhe* can be used with many different types of verbs, not just those that take it in simple sentences. For example, the verb *tīng* 'listen' would normally take *zài* as its durative marker, since it is an activity verb:

(159) tā   zài   tīng   shōuyīnjī
       3sg   DUR   listen radio

S/He is listening to the radio.

When *tīng* provides the ongoing background for another event, though, it can occur with -*zhe*, as in:

(160) tā   tīng   –   zhe   shōuyīnjī   shuì   –
       3sg   listen –   DUR   radio   sleep   –

               zháo   LE
               achieve   PFV/CRS

S/He fell asleep listening to the radio.

In order for an event to be durative, however, it must extend over a certain period of time. Thus, verbs that describe instantaneous, nonrepeatable activities cannot occur as the durative-background verb:

(161) *tā   sǐ   –   zhe   fā   –   shāo
       3sg   die   –   DUR   put:forth   –   fever

(162) *Xìnměi diào   –   zhe   qián   shēngqì
       Xinmei   lose   –   DUR   money   angry

Since there are two verbs in complex sentences with -*zhe*, we might expect that each could be negated, with the scope properties differing according to which verb the negative occurs with (see section 12.1 of chapter 12 for a discussion of the scope of negation). Indeed, sentences (163) and (164) show that this expectation is justified:

(163)	tā	bu	tăng	—	zhe	kàn	—	bào
	3sg	not	lie	—	DUR	read	—	paper

S/He doesn't read the paper lying down.

(164)	tā	bì	—	zhe	yăn	bu	shuō	—	huà
	3sg	close	—	DUR	eye	not	say	—	speech

S/He had his/her eyes closed, and s/he was not saying a word.

In (163), since the negative particle *bu* precedes the entire verb phrase, that entire verb phrase is what is being negated: the whole activity of reading the paper while lying down is what s/he doesn't do. In (164), on the other hand, it is '*not* saying a word' that is stated against the background of his/her eyes being closed.

Here is a further example of each type of negation:

(165)	wŏ	yixiàng	bu	guāng	—	zhe	jiăo	păo
	I	always	not	bare	—	DUR	foot	run

I never run barefooted.

(166)	tā	kū	—	zhe	bu	chī	—	fàn
	3sg	cry	—	DUR	not	eat	—	food

S/He was crying and not eating.

Auxiliaries, on the other hand, normally occur before the -*zhe* verb in this construction, since it is generally the entire activity with its background which the speaker is claiming that the subject must, should, or is able to do. For example:

(167)	tā	néng	qí	—	zhe	mă	shè	—	jiàn
	3sg	can	ride	—	DUR	horse	shoot	—	arrow

S/He can shoot an arrow while riding a horse.

(168)	tā	yīnggāi	zuò	—	zhe	dǎ	—	zì
	3sg	should	sit	—	DUR	hit	—	word

S/He should type sitting down.

6.3 The Experiential Aspect

The aspect suffix *-guo* means that an event has been *experienced* with respect to some reference time.[8] When the reference time is left unspecified, then *-guo* signals that the event has been experienced at least once at some indefinite time, which is usually the indefinite past:

(169)	wǒ	chī	—	guo	Rìběn	fàn
	I	eat	—	EXP	Japan	food

I've eaten Japanese food (before).

Negating a sentence with *-guo* denies that such an event has ever been experienced, and questioning it asks whether the event has ever been experienced:

(170)	wǒ	méi	chī	—	guo	Rìběn	fàn
	I	not	eat	—	EXP	Japan	food

I have never eaten Japanese food (before).

(171)	nǐ	chī	—	guo	Rìběn	fàn	méiyou ?
	you	eat	—	EXP	Japan	food	not

Have you ever eaten Japanese food (before)?

Here are some further examples:

(172)	wǒ	—	de	yá	yě	téng	—	guo
	I	—	GEN	tooth	also	hurt	—	EXP

My teeth have hurt before, too.

(173)	Zhāngsān	jié	—	guo	hūn	méiyou ?
	Zhangsan	marry	—	EXP	marriage	not

Has Zhangsan ever been married?

(174)	wǒ	shuāi	–	duàn	–	<u>guo</u>	tuǐ
	I	fall	–	break	–	EXP	leg

I fell and broke my leg once.

In other words, the focus of a sentence with -*guo* is not that an event has taken place, but that it has taken place at least once. The contrast between -*le* and -*guo* makes this distinction quite clear: the perfective -*le* signaling a bounded event typically conveys the message that the event took place, while -*guo* signals that an event has been experienced at least once. Consider the following examples as illustrations of this contrast:

(175) *a.*	tā	dédào	–	<u>le</u>	yi	–	ge	hépíng	jiǎngjīn
	3sg	obtain	–	PFV	one	–	CL	peace	prize

S/He won a peace prize.

b.	tā	dédào	–	<u>guo</u>	yi	–	ge	hépíng	jiǎngjīn
	3sg	obtain	–	EXP	one	–	CL	peace	prize

S/He has had the experience of winning a peace prize.

(176) *a.*	nǐ	kàn	–	jian	–	<u>le</u>	wǒ	–
	you	see	–	perceive	–	PFV	I	–

		de	yǎnjìng	ma ?
		GEN	glasses	Q

Have you seen my glasses (recently, around here? I can't find them)?

b.	nǐ	kàn	–	jian	–	<u>guo</u>	wǒ	–
	you	see	–	perceive	–	EXP	I	–

		de	yǎnjìng	ma ?
		GEN	glasses	Q

Have you ever seen my glasses?

(177) *a.*

	tā	zài	Rìběn	zhù	—	le	sì	—
	3sg	at	Japan	live	—	PFV	four	—

	ge	yuè
	CL	month

S/He lived in Japan for four months.

b.

	tā	zài	Rìběn	zhù	—	guo	sì	—
	3sg	at	Japan	live	—	EXP	four	—

	ge	yuè
	CL	month

S/He has had the experience of living in Japan for four months.

In the sentences with -*le*, the focus is on the event being viewed as a whole, which often leads to the inference that the event has already occurred, while in those with -*guo*, the focus is on whether the event has ever been experienced.

All the examples of -*guo* we have looked at so far have involved sentences with no reference time specified, and the translation of these sentences indicated that the event had been experienced at least once in the past, that is, prior to the time of speech. When a reference time is provided, then the focus of the sentence is on the event's having been experienced at least once with respect to that time. If there is no reference time specified or if the specified reference time is in the past, then the focus of the sentence with -*guo* is on the event's having been experienced at least once and *being over now*. The following two sentences convey similar messages, but the focus is different:

(178) *a.*

	tā	qùnián	dào	Zhōngguó	qù	—	le
	3sg	last:year	to	China	go	—	PFV

S/He went to China last year.

b.

	tā	qùnián	dào	Zhōngguó	qù	—	guo
	3sg	last:year	to	China	go	—	EXP

S/He went to China last year.

The focus of sentence (178) *a* is simply on the fact that this event happened. Nothing is said about whether s/he is still there. Sentence (178) *b*, on the other hand, assumes that s/he went to China and claims that this took place at least once during last year and is now over; this is why *b*, but not *a*, implies that s/he is now back from China. The subject's return is not part of the *meaning* of *-guo*, but it is part of the *message* of the *-guo* sentence because we can infer it from the meaning of *-guo*: if something has been experienced, it is over.

The basic distinction helps in understanding a number of similar pairs. For example, consider (179):

(179) *a.* wǒ   jīnnián   xuǎn   —   <u>le</u>   Wú   Jiàoshòu
       I   this:year   select   —   PFV   Wu   professor

               —   de   kè
               —   GEN   class

I $\left\{ \begin{matrix} \text{took} \\ \text{am taking} \end{matrix} \right\}$ Professor Wu's class this year.

  b. wǒ   jīnnián   xuǎn   —   <u>guo</u>   Wú   Jiàoshòu
       I   this:year   select   —   EXP   Wu   professor

               —   de   kè
               —   GEN   class

I have taken Professor Wu's course this year.

The *a* sentence in this pair provides the news that the speaker enrolled in Professor Wu's class, which might still be going on. The *b* sentence, with *-guo*, assumes that the speaker was enrolled in the course and claims that the experience is now over.

Finally, we can see why sentence (180) expresses the message that he no longer loves Miss Huang:

(180)   tā   ài   —   guo   Huáng   Xiǎojiě
       3sg   love   —   EXP   Huang   Miss

He once loved Miss Huang.

Once more we infer that if something has been experienced, it is over.

Now that the experiential meaning of -*guo* and the normal inferences that follow from it are clear, we can easily understand certain restrictions on its use. First, -*guo* makes no sense with verbs naming events that are not repeatable:

(181)   *tā   sǐ   —   guo
         3sg   die   —   EXP

         (*S/He has died before.)

(182)   *tā   lǎo   —   guo
         3sg   old   —   EXP

         (*S/He has been old before.)

Comparing (181) and (182) to (183), we can see that (181) and (182) are unacceptable because 'death' and 'being old' are not repeatable, while (183) is acceptable because 'being fat' is repeatable.

(183)   tā   pàng   —   guo
         3sg   fat   —   EXP

         S/He has been fat before.

Second, because a person cannot be ordered to ''experience'' something (though s/he can certainly be ordered to *do* something), imperatives with -*guo* typically make no sense:

(184)   *hē   —   guo   chá !
         drink   —   EXP   tea

It is conceivable, however, that someone might comment that an event must be experienced *again*, so that we might hear an imperative sentence like:

(185)   zhèi   —   ge   děi   cóng   —   xīn   zuò   —   guo
         this   —   CL   must   from   —   new   do   —   EXP

         This has to be done once again.

Third, -*guo* is not used in a context in which the focus is on the simple fact that an event or a series of events occurred. These are contexts that call for a perfective marker, such as -*le*, or a perfectivizing expression. For example:

(186) zuótiān   Zhāngsān   lái   shuō   tā   xǐhuan   gǒu
       yesterday Zhangsan   come   say   3sg   like   dog

      suǒyǐ   wǒ   jīntiān   sòng   { -le / *-guo }   tā

      therefore   I   today   give   { -PFV / *-EXP }   3sg

      yi   –   tiáo   gǒu
      one   –   CL   dog

Yesterday Zhangsan came to say that he likes dogs, so today I gave him a dog.

(187) wǒ   jiějie   qùnián   jiéhūn ,   jīn   –   nián
      I   elder:sister last:year   marry   this   –   year

      shēng   { -le / *-guo }   yi   –   ge   háizi

      give:birth   { -PFV / *-EXP }   one   –   CL   child

My elder sister got married last year, and this year she gave birth to a child.

(188) wǒ   zuótiān   wǎnshàng   kàn   { -le / *-guo } diànshì , féng { -le / *-guo }

      I   yesterday   evening   watch   { -PFV / *-EXP } TV   sew { -PFV / *-EXP }

      liǎng   –   shuāng   wàzi   jiu   qù   shuì
      two   –   pair   sock   then   go   sleep

      –   jiào
      –   sleep

Last night I watched TV, sewed two pairs of socks, and went to bed.

To sum up, we can say that the aspect marker -*guo* serves to signal that an event has been experienced at least once. Because of this basic meaning, it is not used for events that cannot in principle happen more than once, it is not found in imperatives, nor does it occur in sentences whose focus is the simple fact that an event happened.

6.4 The Delimitative Aspect

The *delimitative aspect* means doing an action "a little bit," or for a short period of time.[9] This aspect is structurally represented by the reduplication of the verb (see section 3.1.1.A of chapter 3); this reduplication may optionally involve the morpheme *yi* 'one' between the verb and the reduplicated syllable, as shown in (189)−(195):

(189)   nǐ   shì   −   (yi-)   shi   kàn
        you   try   −   (one-)   try   see

Try it a little and see.

(190)   zhèi   −   ge   huā   děi   yǎng   −   (yi-)
        this   −   CL   flower   must   cultivate −   (one-)

        yang   cái   huì   kāi
        cultivate only:then   will   open

This flower must be cultivated a little before it will bloom.

(191)   nǐ   xǐhuān   chàng   −   gē ,   nà   nǐ   jiu
        you   like   sing   −   song   then   you   just

        chàng   −   (yi-)   chang   ba !
        sing   −   (one-)   sing   SA

You like to sing, so go ahead and sing a little!

(192)   nǐmen   wèishenme bu   xiān   tǎolùn   −   taolun   zhèi
        you:PL why   not   first   discuss   −   discuss   this

        −   ge   wènti   ne ?
        −   CL   problem REx

Why don't you first discuss this problem a little?

(193)   tā   shuì   —   (yi-)   shuì   jiu   hǎo
         3sg   sleep   —   (one-)   sleep   then   well

S/He will be well after sleeping a little.

(194)   tāmen   tīng   —   (yi-)   tīng   Bèiduōfēn   —   de
         they   listen   —   (one-)   listen   Beethoven   —   ASSOC

         yīnyuè jiù   xǐhuān
         music   then   like

After they listen to the music of Beethoven a little, they'll like it.

(195)   wǒ   wèn   —   (yi-)   wen   zài   juédìng
         I   ask   —   (one-)   ask   then   decide

I'll decide after I inquire a little.

When *yi* 'one' is used in the reduplication, the *yi* plus the reduplicated syllable functions like a quantity adverbial of the type discussed in section 8.5 of chapter 8 on adverbs,[10] as in:

(196)   zhèi   —   běn   xiǎoshuō   wǒ   kàn   —   le   sān   cì
         this   —   CL   novel   I   see   —   PFV   three   time

This novel I've read three times.

One intriguing piece of evidence suggesting that *yi* plus the reduplicated syllable does indeed function grammatically as a quantity adverbial is the fact that the perfective aspect marker *-le* may appear after the first verb in reduplication with *yi*, but not in reduplication without *yi*; for example:

(197) *a.*   tā   shuì   —   le   —   yi   —   shuì
              3sg   sleep   —   PFV   —   one   —   sleep

S/He slept a little.

b.   *tā   shuì   —   le   —   shui
        3sg   sleep   —   PFV   sleep

This difference between (197) *a* and (197) *b* exists because, as we observed in section 6.1.1, the perfective *-le* can occur with a verb whose meaning is bounded by quantified phrase, but does not occur with a verb whose meaning is not bounded at all.

Another piece of evidence in favor of viewing the *yi* plus the reduplicated syllable as an adverbial is that without the *yi*, the reduplicated syllable is normally destressed and receives a neutral tone, but with *yi*, though not shown in (189)−(195), the reduplicated syllable retains its normal stress and its full tone, as seen in (197) *a*. Since quantity adverbials are generally stressed and have their normal tones, this too suggests that the combination of *yi* plus reduplicated syllable is grammatically a quantity adverbial.

If the verb being reduplicated is one signaling an activity leading to a natural end point, such as *cāi* 'guess' or *măi* 'buy', the delimitative aspect may suggest 'trying to (verb)', as in the following example:

(198)	nĭ	cāi	−	yi	−	cāi
	you	guess	−	one	−	guess

You try to guess.

Since the meaning of the delimitative aspect involves doing something "a little bit," several constraints on the types of verbs that may be reduplicated to indicate this aspect follow. First, the verb must be an activity verb. An activity verb may denote an action, as in *dă* 'hit', *zŏu* 'walk', *kàn* 'look', *tiào* 'jump', or it may imply activity of some sort, as in *xiăoxīn* 'be careful'. Thus, nonactivity verbs, such as *pàng* 'fat' and *yŏu* 'exist', cannot be reduplicated to show delimitative aspect:

(199)	*nĭ	pàng	−	pang
	you	fat	−	fat

(200)	*wūzi	−	li	yŏu	−	you	yi	−	ge	hóuzi
	house	−	in	exist	−	exist	one	−	CL	monkey

Second, those activity verbs that can undergo reduplication for the delimitative aspect must be volitional verbs. We will define *volitional verbs* as those that under normal circumstances imply volition on the part of the subject. For example, consider the English verb *hit*. It implies volition under normal circumstances, although one can say, "I didn't intend to hit him; it was an accident," where the lack of volition is made clear. On the other hand, the verbs *forget* and *fall* are not volitional, because under normal circumstances they imply a lack of volition. In other words, a volitional verb normally implies volition if the lack of volition is not explicitly stated, and a nonvolitional verb normally implies the lack of volition if there is no explicit statement to the contrary. Since the delimitative aspect means that the subject does something a little bit, it follows that only volitional verbs, that is, those expressing events over which one has some control, can be reduplicated to show delimitative aspect. Thus (201) is unacceptable because the verb is nonvolitional, whereas (202) is acceptable because the verb is volitional.

(201)	*nǐ	wàng	—	wang	tā
	you	forget	—	forget	he

(202)	nǐ	wén	—	wen	zhèi	—	duo	huā
	you	smell	—	smell	this	—	CL	flower

Smell this flower a little.

Third, a resultative verb compound (see section 3.2.3 of chapter 3) cannot be reduplicated for delimitative aspect. This is because the function of a resultative verb compound is to signal that a given event leads to a certain result. The focus on the result of the event with these compounds is incompatible with the delimitative aspect meaning of doing something for a little while. Hence, the resultative verb compound cannot be reduplicated in the delimitative aspect. Sentence (203) is an illustration:

(203)	*nǐ	<u>dǎ</u>	—	<u>kai</u>	—	<u>dǎ</u>	—	<u>kai</u>
	you	hit	—	open	—	hit	—	open

		nèi	—	ge	mén
		that	—	CL	door

Finally, the delimitative aspect is particularly likely to occur in requests, as in:

(204)	qǐng	nǐ	bǎ	mén	<u>kāi</u>	—	(yi-)	<u>kai</u>
	please	you	BA	door	open	—	(one-)	open

Please open the door.

(205)	nĭ	yào	kàn	—	(yi-)	kan
	you	want	read	—	(one-)	read

	zhèi	—	pian	wénzhāng
	this	—	CL	article

You should read this article.

When one wishes to soften a request so that it will not appear harsh, the delimitative aspect is a perfect device to use, since it reduces the "weight" of the request on the hearer by saying that the action can be done "just a little."

6.5 Summary

The functions of *-le, zài, -guo,* and reduplication have been presented here in terms of the concept of aspect, which signals how an event or situation is to be viewed. We can summarize our findings this way:

1. *-Le:* a bounded event viewed in its entirety.
2. *Zài:* an ongoing activity.
3. *-Zhe:* an ongoing posture or state resulting from an activity.
4. *-Guo:* an event viewed as having been experienced at least once.
5. Reduplication: an event viewed as happening a little bit.

Notes

1. This discussion is adapted from the introduction to Comrie (1976), to which the reader is referred for further discussion of aspect in a number of languages. In writing this chapter, we have also taken examples and descriptions from the following sources: Baron (1970), Teng (1975a), Spanos (1977, 1979), Rohsenow (1978), G.-T. Chen (1979), Kwan-Terry (1979), and Chao (1968), except that we do not agree with Chao's statement (p. 246) that *-le* expresses "completed action." "Perfective," as we will see, is not the same as "completed." We have also benefited from discussion with R. McMillan Thompson, Paul Hopper, and Bernard Comrie.
2. See Spanos (1977, 1979) for extensive discussion of speakers' variation in the use of *-le*. Example (28) is taken up in Spanos (1977:61−64).
3. If *'le'* occurs at the end of this sentence, we have

(i)	tā	yào	sĭ	le
	3sg	want	die	CRS

   S/He wants to die.

   in which the sentence-final *le* signals the current relevance of the sentence in the discourse context. It should be clear that the verb *sĭ* 'die' in (i) is still in the irrealis mode, which is not affected by the presence of *le*.

4. Combinations of *-guo* and *"le"* do occur in sentence-final position, but these instances of *"le"* represent the use of the sentence-final *le*, not the perfective aspect *-le*. Here is a typical example of *-guo* together with the sentence-final *le*:

(i) | zhèi | — | piān | wénzhāng | wǒ | kàn |
|------|---|------|----------|-----|------|
| this | — | CL | article | I | read |

—	guo	le
—	EXP	CRS

I've read this article.

We have two ways of knowing that this *"le"* is the sentence-final CRS *le* and not the perfective aspect *-le*. One is that the sentence becomes unacceptable if the direct object is positioned after the verb:

(ii) | *wǒ | kàn | — | guo | le | zhèi |
|------|-----|---|-----|-----|------|
| I | read | — | EXP | CRS | this |

—	piān	wénzhāng
—	CL	article

If the *"le"* in (i) were the aspect marker *-le*, then sentence (ii) would be just as acceptable as (i). The second piece of evidence is that the *le* in (i) adds precisely the meaning of current relevance to sentence (i) which we expect of the sentence-final *le* (again, see chapter 7 for a full discussion of the meaning of *le*).

5. There is one exception: *-le* can occur in negative imperatives; see section 6.1.3 of this chapter. Note also that, as with *-guo*, *bu* can occur with the sentence-final *le*, as in:

(i) | nà | wǒ | bu | qù | le |
|------|-----|-----|-----|-----|
| in:that:case | I | not | go | CRS |

In that case I'm not going to go.

Again, see chapter 7 for discussion.

6. This section contains a number of ideas inspired by the work of G.-T. Chen (1979), Marney (1977:38−52), Chu (1978), and Teng (1979*b*).

7. In this section, some example sentences are translated into English in the past tense and some in the present tense. It is crucial to remember that Mandarin makes no tense distinction and that any of these examples could be understood either way. For the sake of readability, we will arbitrarily choose either an English present or English past translation and not give both each time.

8. This section has benefited from comments and examples in Ma (1977).

9. This section contains ideas from Chao (1968), from Wang (1947), and from unpublished work of Chui Lim Tsang, to whom the term *delimitative aspect* is also due.

10. As pointed out by Chao (1968:312).

CHAPTER 7

Sentence-Final Particles

Most particles that occur in sentence-final position also occur in other contexts serving different functions. Although this chapter will include a discussion of those other functions of the particles in question, its main thrust concerns the semantic and pragmatic functions of the particles that occur in sentence-final position.

There are six sentence-final particles:

(1) le   'Currently Relevant State'
    ne   'Response to Expectation'
    ba   'Solicit Agreement'
    ou   'Friendly Warning'
    a/ya   'Reduce Forcefulness'
    ma   'Question'

All of them are destressed and have the neutral tone. They typically occur in speech or in writings that reflect or recount conversations. Their semantic and pragmatic functions are elusive, and linguists have had considerable difficulty in arriving at a general characterization of each of them. In the following, we will present these particles one by one, except for *ma*, which is treated in chapter 18 on questions.

7.1 *le*

The sentence-final particle *le* in Mandarin is special for two reasons.[1] First, it can co-occur with certain other particles, such as *a, ou*, and the question particle *ma*, all of which, if they occur, must follow *le*:

(2) A: | Lǎo | Wáng | yě | shì | xuéshēng | ma ? |
|------|------|-----|-----|----------|-------|
| Old | Wang | also | be | student | Q |

Is Lao Wang also a student?

B: | tā | dāngrán | shì | le | a² |
|-----|----------|-----|-----|------|
| 3sg | of:course | be | CRS | RF |

Of course s/he is!

(3) | tā | mǎi | fángzi | le | ma ? |
|-----|-----|--------|-----|-------|
| 3sg | buy | house | CRS | Q |

Did s/he buy a house?

(4) | wǒ | gàosu | tā | nèi | — | jian |
|-----|-------|-----|-----|-----|------|
| I | tell | 3sg | that | — | CL |

shì	le	ou
matter	CRS	FW

I told him/her about that matter.

Second, and more important, *le* is special because it is commonly used in ordinary conversation and at the same time is difficult for the student of Mandarin to master. It seems to appear in a great variety of speech situations with an equally great variety of semantic implications, and no one has yet succeeded in tying these usages of *le* together to arrive at a general statement of its semantic and pragmatic function in the language. We will try to do this here.

In this section, then, we will begin by discussing the communicative function of *le*, showing just what it contributes to messages; then we will show where *le* is not used; finally, we will examine situations where the sentence-final *le* is hard to distinguish from the perfective aspect suffix *-le* in sentence-final position. (Throughout this book we are using the hyphenated form *-le*, glossed 'PFV', to refer to the perfective aspect verbal suffix—see chapter 6—and the unhyphenated form *le*, glossed 'CRS', to refer to the sentence-final particle.)

7.1.1 The Communicative Function of *le*

The basic communicative function of *le* is to signal a 'Currently Relevant State' (abbreviated as *CRS*). What this means is that *le* claims that a *state of affairs has special current relevance with respect to some particular situation*.

Let's look at each part of "Currently Relevant State" in a little more detail, starting with "Currently." The *le* says that some state of affairs is *current* with respect to some particular situation. When no other situation is mentioned, then it is always assumed that the statement signaled by the sentence with the *le* is relevant to *now*, that is, to the situation of the speech context in which the speaker and hearer are engaged. This is by far the most common case.

If another situation is explicitly mentioned, then the statement signaled by the sentence with the *le* is claimed to be relevant to that particular situation. Let's look at some examples. If someone calls Ms. Liao, who is out, the person who answers the phone may say:

(5)	tā	chū	—	qù	mǎi	dōngxi	le
	3sg	exit	—	go	buy	thing	CRS

　　　She's gone shopping.

The *le* says that her having gone shopping is current with respect to some particular situation, and since no situation is explicitly mentioned, it is assumed that her having gone shopping is relevant to the present, that is, that she is out as of the present situation in which the telephone conversation is taking place. On the other hand, suppose two people are discussing whether Ms. Liao made a long-distance telephone call two days ago; in this situation one can say:

(6)	nèi	tiān	tā	chū	—	qu
	that	day	3sg	exit	—	go

	mǎi	dōngxi	le
	buy	thing	CRS

　　　That day she went out shopping.

meaning that the state of her having gone shopping was relevant to the situation of 'that day' in the past. Here are two similar examples:

(7)   qián   yi   —   ge   xīngqi   piào   dōu
      before   one   —   CL   week   ticket   all

      mài   —   guāng   LE³
      sell   —   gone   PFV/CRS

Two weeks ago, the tickets were (i.e., had become) all sold out.

(8)   nèi   —   ge   shíhou   juéde   yǒu
      that   —   CL   time   feel   have

      yidiǎn   è   le
      a:little   hungry   CRS

(We) felt (we had become) hungry at that time.

By the same token, if someone wants to see you next month, but you know that you
will be in Japan at that time, you can say:

(9)   xià   —   ge   yuè   wǒ   jiu
      next   —   CL   month   I   then

      zài   Rìběn   le
      at   Japan   CRS

Next month I'll be in Japan.

Here the state of your being in Japan will be current in the situation specified by
'next month'.

   In fact, the situation can even be hypothetical, and *le* will then relate the
proposition signaled by the sentence to that hypothetical situation. For example, if
you ask a Chinese if s/he is an American, s/he can say:

(10)   wǒ   shi   Měiguó   rén   jiu   bu   huì   shuō
       I   be   America   person   then   not   likely   speak

       zhème   zāo   de   Yīngwén   le
       such   bad   NOM   English   CRS

If I were an American, then I wouldn't be speaking such bad English.

Here, the *le* is claiming that under precisely the hypothetical conditions of the speaker's being an American, the state of his/her not speaking such bad English would hold (see chapter 23 on sentence-linking for a discussion of conditional sentences).

Now let's look at the examples presented so far from the point of view of "Relevance." This is a notion that is very much a matter of the context in which the *le* sentence occurs; *le* claims that some state of affairs signaled by the sentence is *relevant* for the speaker and the hearer, and it is assumed that they can infer from the context in just what ways it is relevant. In the situation we set up for sentence (5):

(5)	tā	chū	—	qu	mǎi	dōngxi	le
	3sg	exit	—	go	buy	thing	CRS

      She's gone shopping.

the state of her having gone shopping is clearly relevant to the caller's desire to talk with her: the caller can't do so, because she isn't here. Similarly, in discussing whether she made a phone call, the state of her having gone shopping in sentence (6) is *relevant* because, in this context, it establishes that she couldn't have made that phone call.

In exactly the same way, in the context of someone wanting to see you next month, sentence (9) is relevant because it claims that the state of your being in Japan will prevent that person from being able to see you, and in (10), the Chinese person's hypothetical statement about his/her bad English is relevant in denying your assumption that s/he is an American.

Here is a minimal pair that shows clearly the difference between a simple statement and the statement plus the information that it is relevant to something going on now. Sentence (11) *a* expresses a simple statement:

(11) *a.*	zhèi	—	ge	guā	hěn	tián
	this	—	CL	melon	very	sweet

      This melon is very sweet.

Sentence (11) *b*, with *le*, however, expresses much more:

b.	zhèi	—	ge	guā	hěn	tián	le
	this	—	CL	melon	very	sweet	CRS

      This melon is very sweet.

Though not conveyed by the English translation, (11) *b* means that the sweetness of the melon is relevant for the current situation. Thus, for example, one could say (11) *b* if one had guessed that the melon would be sweet and found upon eating it that it was indeed sweet, or if, conversely, one had guessed that it wouldn't be sweet, but discovered while tasting it that the guess was wrong. One could even say (11) *b* if one wanted to announce a new "discovery" of the sweetness of the melon or if one wanted the hearer to discover its sweetness.

Finally, one of the most frequently heard questions in the Mandarin-speaking world is:

(12)	nǐ	chī	–	guo	fàn	le	méiyou ?
	you	eat	–	EXP	food	CRS	not

Have you eaten?

Given the cultural concern for being generous to friends, the current relevance of this question in its natural context is obvious. The use of *le*, then, always includes the dimension of relevance.

The third concept contained in the definition of *le* is that of "State." This means that *le* always treats an event signaled by the sentence as a state of affairs and claims that that state is currently relevant to some situation. Let's use (5) once more as an illustration:

(5)	tā	chū	–	qu	mǎi	dōngxi	le
	she	exit	–	go	buy	thing	CRS

She's gone shopping.

The verb phrase *chū-qu mǎi dōngxi* 'go out to buy things' involves an action, but sentence (5), with *le*, is not talking about the *action* of her going out or buying. It concerns, rather, the *state* of her having gone shopping and its relevance to the present situation.

Here is a striking contrast that illustrates this difference: if someone wants to tell you what s/he did simply by describing an action, s/he will use a sentence like (13) *a*:

(13) *a*	wǒ	hē	–	le	sān	bēi	kāfēi
	I	drink	–	PFV	three	cup	coffee

I drank three cups of coffee.

Sentence (13) *b*, with *le*, expresses, on the other hand, something quite different:

b.	wŏ	hē	–	le	sān	bēi	kāfēi	<u>le</u>
	I	drink	–	PFV	three	cup	coffee	CRS

I've drunk three cups of coffee.

Sentence (13) *b* does *not* say simply that s/he drank three cups of coffee; that message is conveyed by (13) *a*. What (13) *b* says is that the state of his/her having drunk three cups of coffee is relevant to the current situation, because, let's say, you want the speaker to have another cup, and s/he's telling you why s/he shouldn't. Or s/he could say (13) *b* to show that s/he likes coffee, if you claim that s/he doesn't. Or s/he could simply be telling you that as of the present time, that is, *relevant to the present moment,* the number of cups of coffee s/he has consumed is three.

We've examined the three parts of the definition of *le*, 'Currently Relevant State'. Every occurrence of *le* expresses this function, but the way in which it does so is not always obvious and therefore must be studied carefully. What we find is that the situations in which *le* expresses CRS can be broadly grouped into five categories: that is, a sentence with *le* can convey CRS if the state of affairs it represents:

A. Is a changed state
B. Corrects a wrong assumption
C. Reports progress so far
D. Determines what will happen next
E. Is the speaker's total contribution to the conversation at that point

Each of these five categories represents a slightly different type of situation in which *le* indicates that a state of affairs signaled by the sentence is relevant. Once these five types of situations are understood, the use of *le* becomes a reasonably straightforward matter. Let's look at each of these five categories of situation in detail.

A. Change of State

One of the most common ways in which a state of affairs is relevant to the present situation is when that state of affairs represents a change from an earlier state.[4] This means that some state of affairs holds *now* which didn't hold before. In each case the relevance of the new state of affairs hinges on the fact that it is a change.

(14) *a.*   tā   zhīdao   nèi   —   ge   xiāoxi
             3sg   know   that   —   CL   news

S/He knows about that piece of news.

b.   tā   zhīdao   nèi   —   ge   xiāoxi   <u>le</u>
        3sg   know   that   —   CL   news   CRS

S/He knows about that piece of news now (s/he didn't before).

(15) *a.* (in response to being asked whether one knows about a meeting)

wǒ   zhīdào
I   know

Yes, I know.

b. The speaker, who went to the wrong room once before, has been reminded which room the meeting will be held in.)

wǒ   zhīdào   <u>le</u>
I   know   CRS

Now I know (i.e., I have learned).

(16) *a.*   tā   táo   —   de   —   chū   —   lái
             3sg   escape —   can   —   exit   —   come

S/He can escape.

b.   tā   táo   —   de   —   chū
        3sg   escape —   can   —   exit

        —   lái   <u>le</u>
        —   come   CRS

S/He can escape now (s/he couldn't before).

(17) *a.* (to a headwaiter who has asked how many people there are)

wǒmen	èr	—	shí	—	sì	—	ge
we	two	—	ten	—	four	—	CL

There are twenty-four of us.

b. (one tour guide to another after the last tourist has finally climbed on the bus)

wǒmen	èr	—	shí	—	sì
we	two	—	ten	—	four

—	ge	le
—	CL	CRS

Now there are twenty-four of us.

(18) *a.*

wǒ	yào	qù
I	will	go

I'm going to go. (a simple statement of intention)

b.

wǒ	yào	qù	le
I	will	go	CRS

I'm going now (i.e., you'd better hurry up if you want to come along).

Here are some further examples:

(19)

yǐjīng	sān	—	diǎn	le
already	three	—	o'clock	CRS

It's already three o'clock.

(20)

xià	yǔ	le
descend	rain	CRS

It's raining (now).

(21) wǒ   lèi   le
      I   tired   CRS

I'm tired (now).

(22) wǒ   dùzi   è   le
      I   stomach   hungry   CRS

I'm hungry (now).

(23) wǒ   yá   téng   le
      I   tooth   hurt   CRS

My tooth aches (now).

(24) tàiyáng   chū   –   lái   le   ma ?
      sun   exit   –   come   CRS   Q

Has the sun come out?

(25) wǒmen   fàngqì   nèi –   zhǒng   shǒuduàn   le
      we   give:up   that –   kind   tactic   CRS

We've given up that kind of tactic by now.

(26) tā   xǐng   –   lái   le
      3sg   awaken   –   come   CRS

S/He's awake (now).

(27) diànbào   fā   le   ma ?
      telegram   issue   CRS   Q

Has the telegram been sent?

(28)   wǒ   –   de   chē   ràng   xuě   mái
         I   –   GEN   vehicle   RANG   snow   cover

         –   qǐ   –   lái   le
         –   rise   –   come   CRS

My car is snowed under.

(29)   zhuāng   –   le   zhèi   –   ge   rìguāng
       install   –   PFV   this   –   CL   fluorescent

         –   dēng   chúfáng   jiu   liàng
         –   light   kitchen   then   bright

        duō   le
       much   CRS

Now that we have installed this fluorescent light, the kitchen is much brighter.

(30) (a three-year-old child upon finishing building a house of blocks)

        fángzi   le
        house   CRS

It's a house (now)!

(31) A: (asking about a certain restaurant)

           nǐ   yǒu   méi   yǒu   tāmen   –   de
          you   exist   not   exist   they   –   GEN

            diànhuà   hàomǎ ?
           telephone   number

Do you have their phone number?

B: (looking through a booklet of phone numbers and finally finding it)

yǒu	le ,	yǒu	le
exist	CRS	exist	CRS

(Now I) have it.

(32) (pointing out an old house near campus)

zhèi	—	dòng	lóu	xiànzài	yǐjīng	bō
this	—	CL	building	now	already	transfer

gěi	wǒmen	xuéxiào	yòng	le
to	we	school	use	CRS

This building has now been transferred to our school to use.

(33)

tiān	hēi	le
sky	black	CRS

It's dark (now).

(34)

nǐ	kǒu	kě	le	me ?
you	mouth	thirsty	CRS	Q

Are you thirsty (now)?

(35)

tā	fā	—	shāo	le
3sg	put:forth	—	fever	CRS

S/He has a fever (now).

(36)

tā	hǎo	le
3sg	good	CRS

S/He's well (now).

(37)

dào	Zhōngshān	Lù	le
arrive	Zhongshan	Road	CRS

Here we are at Zhongshan Road.

(38) (directed at someone serving food or pouring drinks)

gòu   le!
enough   CRS

That's enough (now)!

(39)   wǒ   háizi   yǒu   yi   —   ge
        I   child   exist   one   —   CL

               yá   huódòng   le
               tooth   loose   CRS

My child has a loose tooth.

It will be noticed that many of our examples contain instances of *le* with adjectives (see section 4.3.1 of chapter 4 for a discussion of the category "adjective"). A good general rule is this: whenever one wishes to describe a new, *changed* state, as opposed to a *general* or *habitual* state, with an adjective, *le* should be used to imply that the state is new or newly noticed. In the following examples, the *a* sentences all have adjectival predicates expressing general or habitual states, while the *b* sentences have adjectival predicates expressing new states:

(40) *a.*   tā   hěn   gāo
             3sg   very   tall

     S/He's tall.

     b.   tā   gāo   le
             3sg   tall   CRS

     S/He's gotten tall.

(41) *a.*   zhèi   —   duǒ   huā   hěn   hóng
             this   —   CL   flower   very   red

     This flower is red.

b.	zhèi	—	duǒ	huā	hóng	le
	this	—	CL	flower	red	CRS

This flower is now red (i.e., has turned red).

(42) a.

	zhèi	—	ge	dìfang	hěn	ānjìng
	this	—	CL	place	very	peaceful

This place is very peaceful.

b.

	zhèi	—	ge	dìfang	hěn	ānjìng	le
	this	—	CL	place	very	peaceful	CRS

This place has become very peaceful.

(43) a.

	zhèi	—	ge	guā	hěn	tián
	this	—	CL	melon	very	sweet

This melon is sweet.

b.

	zhèi	—	ge	guā	tián	le
	this	—	CL	melon	sweet	CRS

This melon is sweet now (i.e., it's ready to eat).

When an adjective with an inherent end point as part of its meaning (see section 6.1.1 of chapter 6) is used to convey a change of state, we have a situation in which the "le" is a combination of the perfective -le and the CRS le. We discuss this "le", which we indicate by capital letters (LE), below in section 7.1.3. Here are a few examples:

(44)

bīng	dōu	huà	LE
ice	all	melted	PFV/CRS

The ice all melted.

(45)

zhèi	—	ge	yǐzi	huài	LE
this	—	CL	chair	broken	PFV/CRS

This chair broke.

(46)   wǒ   —   de   bēizi   zhà   LE
        I   —   GEN   cup   cracked   PFV/CRS

My cup cracked.

(47)   tā   huáiyùn   LE
       3sg   pregnant   PFV/CRS

She got pregnant.

(48)   língzi   sī   —   pò   LE
        collar   tear   —   broken   PFV/CRS

The collar tore.

(49)   zhèi   —   ge   zì   xiě   —
        this   —   CL   character   write   —

       cuò   LE
       wrong   PFV/CRS

This character was written wrong.

(50)   píjiǔ   hē   —   guāng   LE
        beer   drink   —   gone   PFV/CRS

The beer got drunk up.

(51)   wǒ   bèi   dòng   —   zhù   LE
        I   BEI   freeze   —   hold:on   PFV/CRS

I got frozen in.

This "change of state" message is very common with negative sentences. Again, when no time reference is named in a negative sentence with *le*, the new, changed situation is assumed to be relevant with respect to the speech context in which the sentence is uttered. First we give some minimal pairs, and then some further illustrative examples:

(52)   (waiter after having been asked whether the restaurant has any
        guōtiě 'pot stickers')

    a.   méi   yǒu
               not   exist

        No.

    b.   méi   yǒu   <u>le</u>
               not   exist   CRS

        Not anymore (i.e., we've run out).

(53)   (to person serving food)

    a.   wǒ   bu   chī
               I   not   eat

        I'm not going to eat.

    b.   wǒ   bu   chī   <u>le</u>
               I   not   eat   CRS

        I'm not going to eat anymore (either I've had enough food, or I've
        changed my mind regarding whether I'll eat—i.e., my not eating is a
        new situation).

(54) *a.*   tā   kàn   —   bu   —   jiàn   rén
          3sg   look   —   can't   —   perceive person

        S/He can't see people.

    b.   tā   kàn   —   bu   —   jiàn   rén   <u>le</u>
          3sg   see   —   can't   —   perceive person CRS

        S/He can't see people anymore.

(55) *a.*   wǒ   bu   zhèi   —   yàng   shuō   —   huà
          I   not   this   —   way   talk   —   speech

        I don't talk this way.

b. wǒ   bu   zhèi   —   yàng   shuō
    I   not   this   —   way   talk

    —   huà   le
    —   speech   CRS

    I don't talk this way anymore.

(56) *a.* xìnfēng   —   lǐ   zhuāng   —   bu   —
    envelope   —   in   fit   —   can't   —

    xià   zhèi   —   xiē   zhàopiàn
    descend   this   —   PL   photo

    These photos won't fit in this envelope.

b. xìnfēng   —   lǐ   zhuāng   —   bu   —   xià
    envelope   —   in   fit   —   can't   —   descend

    zhèi   —   xiē   zhàopiàn   le
    this   —   PL   photo   CRS

    There's no more room in this envelope into which to fit these photos.

(57) shíhou   bu   zǎo   le
    time   not   early   CRS

    It's not early anymore (i.e., it's getting late).

(58) wǒ   shízài   huó   —   bu   —   xiàqù   le
    I   really   live   —   can't   —   continue   CRS

    I can't go on living anymore.

(59) kěxi   tā   bu   zài   cūn   —   lǐ   le
    pity   3sg   not   at   village   —   in   CRS

    It's a pity that s/he's no longer in the village.

(60) (after some discussion as to whether addressee should go to America)

ou	yuánlái	nǐ	fùqin	yào	nǐ	qù ,
Oh	it:turns:out	your	father	want	you	go

nà	wǒmen	bu	bì	tǎolùn	zhèi
in:that:case	we	not	need	discuss	this

—	jiàn	shì	le
—	CL	matter	CRS

Oh, it turns out your father wants you to go—in that case, we don't need to discuss this matter anymore.

(61)

tā	jìnshi	de	lián	tā	tàitai
3sg	near:sighted	CSC	even	3sg	wife

dōu	rèn	—	bu	—
all	recognize	—	can't	—

chū	—	lái	le
exit	—	come	CRS

He's so nearsighted he can't even recognize his wife, anymore.

(62)

bié	míhuò	tā	le
don't	bewitch	3sg	CRS

Don't bewitch him/her anymore.

(63)

bié	mí	—	lù	le
don't	lose	—	road	CRS

Don't lose your way (this time).

All the examples we've seen so far illustrate the change of state in terms of the present time, the time of speaking. As we mentioned earlier, however, if the sentence refers to another time, say, general time, as in (64)–(66), or future, as in (67)–(69), then the change of state is relevant to that general or future time. The relationship between the general or future time mentioned in the sentence and the changed situation is typically marked by *jiu*, as the examples illustrate:

(64) wèidao   wǒ   dǒng   kěshi   shuō   yíngyǎng ,
      flavor   I   understand but   talk   nutrition

            wǒ   jiu   wàiháng   le
            I   then   be:layperson   CRS

About flavor, I'm knowledgeable, but when we talk about nutrition,
then (things change, and) I'm just a layperson.

(65) A: Gōngguǎn   zěnme   qù ?
            Gongguan   how   go

      How do you get to Gongguan?

      B: nǐ   dā   sān   —   hào   chē   zài   Gōngguǎn
           you   take   three   —   number   vehicle at   Gongguan

               zhàn   xià   —   chē   jiu   kěyi   le
               stop   descend —   vehicle then   OK   CRS

      You take the number three bus, get off at the Gongguan stop, and
      then (under those conditions) you'll be there.

(66) guò   —   le   shàng   —   xià   —   bān
      cross   —   PFV   ascend   —   descend —   work

            de   shíhou   huǒche   jiu   kōng   le
            NOM   time   train   then   empty   CRS

Once rush hour is over, the train becomes empty.

(67) shōuyīnjī   guǎngbō   bu   jiǔ   jiānglái   huòwù   jiu
      radio   broadcast not   long   future   merchandise then

               yào   guì   yidiǎn   le
               will   expensive   a:bit   CRS

They say on the radio that in the near future things will be (i.e., have
become) more expensive.

(68) tāmen   —   de   xuéxiào míngnián <u>jiu</u>   yào
      they   —   GEN   school   next:year then   will

      zhāo   nǔshēng   <u>le</u>
      recruit woman:student CRS

Next year (the changed state will be that) their school will be open to women students.

(69) nǐ   bǎ   zhèi   liǎng   —   ge   jùzi   huàn
      you   BA   this   two   —   CL   sentence change

      yixià   yìsi   <u>jiu</u>   qīngchǔ duō   <u>le</u>
      once   meaning then   clear   much   CRS

If you reverse these two sentences, (the changed situation will be that) the meaning will then be much clearer.

The changed situation can also be in the past; for example:

(70) (describing an afternoon of walking)

      wǒmen   zǒu   de   hěn   lèi   <u>le</u>
      we   walk   CSC   very   tired CRS

We had walked so much that we'd gotten very tired.

(71) tā   shēngmíng   tā   tuìchū   nèi   —   ge
      3sg   announce   3sg   withdraw that —   CL

      zǔzhí   <u>le</u>
      organization   CRS

S/He announced that s/he had withdrawn from that organization.

The same is true of negative sentences, in which *le* can refer to a changed situation at a general time, as in (72)−(74), or to a future time, as in (75) and (76).

Again, *jiu* is typically found connecting the general- or future-time reference to the changed situation:

(72) jiéhūn   —   le   yǐhòu   shēnghuo   jiu   gēn
      marry   —   PFV   after   life   then   and

      yǐqián   wánquán   bu   yíyàng   le
      before   complete   not   same   CRS

After one marries, life is simply not the same as before.

(73)   nà   wǒ   jiu   bu   zǒu   le
      in:that:case   I   then   not   go   CRS

In that case, then, I won't go (i.e., I've just decided not to go).

(74) yàoshi   méi   dài   xuéshēng   —   zhèng   jiu
      if   not   carry   student   —   card   then

      bu   néng   mǎi   xuéshēng   piào   le
      not   can   buy   student   ticket   CRS

If you didn't bring your student I.D., then (the changed situation will be that) we won't be able to buy student tickets.

(75) wǒmen   duō   tán   —   tán ,   huí   —   jiā
      we   more   chat   —   chat   return   —   home

      le   jiu   méi   shíjiān   tán   le
      CRS   then   not   time   chat   CRS

Let's chat some more; after (we) return home (the changed situation will be that) there won't be time to chat.

(76) nǐ   dǎ   —   diànhuà   gěi   tā   wǒ   jiu
      you   hit   —   telephone to   3sg   I   then

      bu   yòng   xiě   xìn   le
      not   need   write   letter   CRS

If you phone him/her, I won't need to write a letter (i.e., I would need to otherwise).

Furthermore, as we would expect, with negatives, just as with affirmative sentences, the changed situation can be in the past:

(77) qùnián   fēijī   chūshì   zài   qǐfēi   —   de
      last:year airplane have:accident   at   take:off   —   ASSOC

      bàn   —   ge   zhōngtóu   yǐnèi   hái   yǒu
      half   —   CL   hour   within   still   exist

      diànhuà ,   yǐhòu   jiu   méi   liánluò   le
      telephone   after   then   not   contact   CRS

> In last year's plane accident, for a half hour after takeoff there was still telephone contact, then (the changed situation was that) there was no more contact.

Sometimes the change is simply a realization on the part of the speaker, though not necessarily a change in the objective situation. Chao (1968:798), for example, points out that a sentence like

(78) xià   yǔ   le
      descend   rain   CRS

> It's raining.

can be used not only when it has just begun to rain but also when the speaker has just discovered that it is raining. Similarly, children often use *le* in commenting on something that has just come to their attention, as in (79):

(79) (a three-year-old child who has just noticed the parrot in the zoo)

      zhèi   shì   yīngwǔ   le!
      this   be   parrot   CRS

> This is a parrot!

Here are some further illustrations of the use of *le* for situations that are newly realized by the speaker:

(80) (Two friends haven't seen each other for a long time; one asks the
      other where s/he has been.)

A:	wǒ	dào	nánbù	qù	—	le	yi	tàng
	I	to	south	go	—	PFV	one	time

I took a trip to the south.

B:	ou	yuánlái	nǐ	dào	nánbù	qù	—	le ,
	Oh	it:turns:out	you	to	south	go	—	PFV

	nánguài	hǎo	jiǔ	méi	kàn	—	jian
	no:wonder	very	long	not	see	—	perceive

	nǐ	le
	you	CRS

Oh, so you went to the south; no wonder I haven't seen you for a long time.

(81) (concluding a lengthy discussion about whether the speaker would con-
      sent to give a speech to a group)

nǐ	zhēn	gěi	wǒ	yi	—	ge
you	really	give	I	one	—	CL

	nántí	le
	knotty:problem	CRS

You've really given me a knotty problem!

(82) (to a roommate who has just returned from class)

nǐ	huí	—	lái	le
you	return	—	come	CRS

You've come back.

(83) nǐ   yào   qù   <u>le</u> !
      you   will   go   CRS

(I see, so) you're going after all (I'd thought you were still hanging around)!

(84) (salesperson returning from looking for a smaller skirt)

duìbuqǐ , zhèi   shi   zuì   xiǎo   de   <u>le</u>
sorry   this   be   most   small   NOM   CRS

Sorry, (I find that) this is the smallest (we have).

It is easy to see that the realization may be expressing some annoyance or irritation if it has been hard to arrive at. Here is a minimal pair that makes the point:

(85) *a*. (bus-ticket salesperson in answer to a question about whether s/he has tickets selling for ninety dollars)

yě   yǒu   de
also   have   NOM

(We) also have (them).

b. (annoyed bus-ticket salesperson to a customer who is not making himself/herself clear in asking about the availability of the ninety-dollar tickets)

yě   yǒu   de   <u>le</u>!
also   have   NOM   CRS

Oh yes, (we) also have those (why didn't you make yourself clear?)!

Note that explicit requests to be brought up to date about a certain person will typically elicit announcements of information new to the person making the request, and these, of course, always take *le*:

(86) A.   Zhāng   Měiyīng   zěnme   yàng ?
            Zhang   Meiying   how   way

How is Zhang Meiying?

B: *a.*

tā	zuò	jiàoshòu	le
3sg	be	professor	CRS

She's become a professor.

b.

tā	bèi	kāichú	le
3sg	BEI	expelled	CRS

She's been expelled (from school).

c.

tā	huí	—	guó	le
3sg	return	—	country	CRS

She's gone back to her country.

d.

tā	jiéhūn	le
3sg	marry	CRS

She's gotten married.

e.

tā	huáiyùn	le
3sg	pregnant	CRS

She's gotten pregnant.

f.

tā	cízhí	le
3sg	quit	CRS

She's quit.

g.

tā	shēnqíng	—	bu	—	dào
3sg	apply	—	can't	—	arrive

dàxué	suǒyǐ	jiu	qù	zuò	—
university	so	then	go	do	—

shì	le
work	CRS

She didn't get into the university, so she's taken a job.

h.	wǒ	zhěng	yi	nián	méi	kàn	–
	I	whole	one	year	not	see	–

	jian	tā	le
	perceive	3sg	CRS

I haven't seen her for a whole year.

What we can conclude from all these examples is that one set of circumstances under which *le* can signal a Currently Relevant State is when that state is *new* or *changed* either from the way it was before or from the way the speaker thought it was before.

B. Correcting a Wrong Assumption

Another common way in which a state of affairs becomes relevant to a particular situation is when that state of affairs is different from what the *hearer* has been assuming.

Consider, for example, a speech context in which A has told B that C made a phone call at a certain time, and B responds by saying:

(87)	nèi	–	ge	shíhou	tā	chū	–	mén	le
	that	–	CL	time	3sg	exit	–	door	CRS

At that time s/he had gone out.

which is relevant in denying A's belief that C had made the call. Here is a minimal pair of sentences illustrating this point:

(88) *a.* (child pointing to soda)

	wǒ	yào	hē
	I	want	drink

I want to drink it. (neutral)

b. (child to mother, who does not think the child wants his/her soda)

	wǒ	yào	hē	le
	I	want	drink	CRS

(But) I want to drink it. (contradicting the mother's belief)

The following are some further examples:

(89) (exasperated mother to her child, who has refused what s/he was given to drink and wants what the adults are drinking)

yíyàng	de	le
same	NOM	CRS

It's the same (i.e., you're wrong in thinking that what you have is different)!

(90) (to a friend who has just asked if the speaker has seen a certain movie)

wǒ	yǒu	yi	–	ge	yuè	méi	kàn	diànyǐng	le
I	exist	one	–	CL	month	not	look	movie	CRS

I haven't seen a movie for a month (i.e., you're wrong in assuming that I've been keeping up with the latest films).

(91) (telling someone about a meeting)

dìdiǎn	zài	qī	–	hào	jiàoshì,	jiàoshì
place	at	seven	–	number	classroom	classroom

	wàibiān	yǐjīng	yǒu	yi	–	ge
	outside	already	exist	one	–	CL

bùgào	le
announcement	CRS

The place is classroom number seven. Outside the classroom there is already an announcement (and you should have known that).

(92) (to the accusation that the speaker has spent the afternoon sleeping)

wǒ	kàn	–	le	sān	–	běn	shū	le!
I	look	–	PFV	three	–	CL	book	CRS

(What do you mean?!) I have read three books!

(93) (talking about a certain author)

A:
nǐ	yīnggāi	kàn ,	tā	shū	xiě	de	hǎo
you	should	look	3sg	book	write	CSC	good

You should take a look; s/he writes well.

B:
wǒ	kàn	—	guo	tā	hǎo	jǐ	—
I	look	—	EXP	3sg	very	several	—

běn	shū	le
CL	book	CRS

(But) I have read quite a few of his/her books (i.e., you're wrong to think I haven't).

(94) (consoling a friend who can't forget her ex-boyfriend)

tā	wàngjì	nǐ	le !
3sg	forget	you	CRS

(Please realize that) he's forgotten you (so quit thinking about it and get on with new things)!

(95) (to friends who want the speaker to go out for a late-night snack)

wǒ	yào	xiě	wǒ	—	de	bàogào	le
I	want	write	I	—	GEN	report	CRS

(But) I have to write my report (i.e., you are wrong in assuming I am free).

(96) (to a friend who has asked whether the speaker needs more money to pay the salesperson)

wǒ	yǐjīng	gěi	tā	liǎng	—	bǎi	kuài
I	already	give	3sg	two	—	hundred	dollar

qián	le
money	CRS

(But) I already gave him/her $200 (i.e., you were wrong in thinking that I hadn't paid enough).

(97) (to a friend who has inquired solicitously whether the speaker wants
anything to eat)

wǒ	chī	—	guo	le
I	eat	—	EXP	CRS

(The new situation that you don't realize yet is that) I've already eaten
(so no thanks).

(98) (protesting to someone who doesn't believe that the speaker has had
enough to drink)

wǒ	hē	—	le	sān	bēi	le
I	drink	—	PFV	three	glass	CRS

(Look—I tell you) I've drunk three glasses!

(99) (to the bus conductor, who has just urged the speaker to move away
from the door)

zài	guò	liǎng	zhàn	wǒ	jiu	yào	xià
further	cross	two	stop	I	then	will	descend

—	chē	le
—	vehicle	CRS

After two more stops, I'm going to get off (so I'm not going to move
away from the door).

(100) (a busy waiter in a Taipei restaurant who has been asked repeatedly to
bring more rice)

hǎo ,	hǎo ,	fàn	jiu	mǎshàng	le !
good	good	rice	then	immediately	CRS

OK! OK! Rice will be coming up right away (already)!

(101) A:	wǒ	xiǎng	zhǎo	fángzi	bān	—	jiā
	I	think	look:for	house	move	—	home

I think I'm going to find a new place to live.

B:	nǐ	bu	shì	mǎshàng	jiu	yào	huí
	you	not	be	immediately	then	will	return

	Rìběn	le	ma ?
	Japan	CRS	Q

(But) aren't you going back to Japan right away?

(102) (son to mother who has been urging him to write to his aunt)

	wǒ	míngtiān	jiu	xiě	le
	I	tomorrow	then	write	CRS

(OK, OK,) I'll write tomorrow (i.e., you're wrong to think I'm never going to do it).

Finally, here are two conversations that nicely illustrate the use of *le* in signaling the relevance of a state of affairs to correct a wrong impression.

(103) (father to three-year-old daughter)

F:	yào	bu	yào	bàba	xǐ ?
	want	not	want	daddy	wash

Do you want Daddy to wash (you)?

D:	bu	yào
	not	want

No.

F:	yào	shéi ?
	want	who

Whom do you want?

D:	māma
	Mommy.

F:	māma	bu	xǐ	le
	Mommy	not	wash	CRS

Mommy isn't going to wash you (though you thought she was).

(104) (in a cartoon, Quacky the duck to the dog Scamp, who has asked why
       Quacky is sitting in the pond when he should be migrating south)

bu	xíng ,	wǒ	bèi	dòng	–	zhù	le
not	OK	I	BEI	freeze	–	hold:on	CRS

I can't, I'm frozen in!

All the examples we have presented so far illustrate *le* sentences that are relevant
to the current situation because they contradict an assumption that has been
explicitly brought out in the preceding conversation. Sometimes, though, a *le*
sentence can be relevant because it contradicts an assumption that has not been
mentioned at all but that the speaker knows the hearer holds. Here is a particularly
nice example from another newspaper cartoon:

(105) (the dog Scamp calls out to his friend, Quacky the duck, who is flying
       past him supposedly migrating south)

hāi ,	Guā	–	guā !	nǐ	wàng	běifang	qù	le !
hey	Quack	–	quack	you	toward	north	go	CRS

Hey, Quacky! You're going *north* (and not south, as you obviously are
assuming)!

In the next example, also from a comic strip, Glorie Bee is contradicting a normal
assumption between her and Goofy:

(106)	nǐ	zuì	hǎo	bu	yào	lái	kàn	diànshì
	you	must	good	not	will	come	look	TV

	le ,	wǒ	dé	–	le	zhòng	shāngfēng
	CRS	I	get	–	PFV	heavy	cold

(Contrary to our usual practice,) you'd better not come over to watch TV
(this time)—I caught a terrible cold.

Often, in reporting something unusual which has just happened, the speaker uses
le because the state of affairs contradicts our normal expectations. For example,
(107) is what a neighbor tells Zengshen's mother as s/he runs toward her:

(107) Zēngshēn   shā   rén   le !
       Zengshen   kill   person CRS

Zengshen has killed someone!

Here are some other, equally illustrative examples:

(108)   wǒ   zuótiān   zuò   —   le   yi   —   jiàn
        I   yesterday do   —   PFV   one   —   CL

        huài   shì   le
        bad   matter CRS

(I must tell you that) I did a bad thing yesterday (which you wouldn't
expect).

(109) (Two friends exchange pleasantries; A says s/he is fine but busy, and B
       responds.)

        wǒ   yěshi   máng   de   yào   sǐ ,   duì   —
        I   also   busy   CSC   want die   right —

        le ,   wǒ   yào   gàosu   nǐ   wǒmen jiùyào
        PFV   I   want   tell   you   we   soon

        bān   —   jiā   le
        move   —   home   CRS

I am also terribly busy—say, I want to tell you that we're moving soon.

(110) tā   bǎ   wǒ   —   de   biǎo   ná   —   zǒu   le
       3sg   BA   I   —   GEN   watch   take —   away CRS

(Hey!) S/He took my watch!

(111) (to friends as they are watching a television show)

        tāmen   yào   zhuā   tā   le !
        they   will grab   3sg   CRS

(Watch—you might not believe it, but the new situation is that) they're
going to grab him/her.

This second set of examples snows how *le* is used to express a state that is currently relevant for the purpose of correcting a wrong assumption on the part of the hearer. As we have seen, this wrong assumption may be explicitly brought out in the conversation, it may be an assumption that the speaker simply knows the hearer holds, or it may be a normal assumption that people hold unless told differently. No matter which of these three types of mistaken assumptions is playing a role in the conversation, *le* will appear with the sentence whose current relevance is to correct the wrong assumption.

C. Progress So Far

Sometimes a state of affairs is relevant to the current situation because it brings the hearer up to date on the progress made so far in a more extensive project or venture about which both speaker and hearer know. Thus, if A knows, for example, that B is studying Tang dynasty poetry, B can say:

(112)	Táng	shī	sān	—	bǎi	—	shou	wǒ
	Tang	poem	three	—	hundred	—	CL	I

	bèi	—	chu	—	lái	—	le
	memorize	—	exit	—	come	—	PFV

	yi	—	bàn	le
	one	—	half	CRS

I've memorized half of the 300 Tang poems now (so far).

Note that this example contains both a perfective suffix *-le* and a CRS particle *le*. Since the event that represents the progress made so far is typically a bounded and, therefore, perfective event (in this case, memorizing 150 poems), many sentences that illustrate the use of *le* in signaling current relevance by giving the progress to date in an extensive project turn out to have both the perfective *-le* and the CRS *le*.[5] Here are some other examples:

(113) (talking about the "project" of my living arrangements)

	wǒ	zài	nàli	zhù	—	le	liǎng	—
	I	at	there	live	—	PFV	two	—

	ge	yuè	le
	CL	month	CRS

I've lived there for two months (now).

(114)	nèi	–	wei	nǚshì	huái	–	<u>le</u>
	that	–	CL	woman	conceive	–	PFV

	bā	–	ge	yuè	yùn	<u>le</u>
	eight	–	CL	month	pregnancy	CRS

That woman is eight months pregnant.

(115) (to a friend who is waiting to go to the movies with the speaker)

	wǒ	xǐ	–	hǎo	–	<u>le</u>	yīfu	<u>le</u>
	I	wash	–	finish	–	PFV	clothes	CRS

I've finished (the project of) clothes washing (which you knew I had
to do).

(116)	fēijī	chū	–	<u>le</u>	máobìng	<u>le</u>
	airplane	exit	–	PFV	trouble	CRS

The airplane has developed some trouble. (the progress report with
respect to our plane trip getting under way)

Progress to date can also be expressed, however, by nonperfective sentences.
For instance, a visitor in China trying to have as many Chinese experiences as
possible may say to his/her host:

(117)	wǒ	jīntiān	zǎochen	chī	yóutiáo	<u>le</u> !
	I	today	morning	eat	fritter	CRS

I had a yóutiáo this morning! (Yóutiáo is a common Chinese breakfast
item.)

Similarly, if A knows that B has been planning to go to the Zhangs' for dinner or
that B has been hoping to get an invitation, then B can use sentence (118) to tell A
what s/he has achieved with that project:

(118)	wǒ	zuótiān	dào	Zhāng	–	jiā	chī	–
	I	yesterday	to	Zhang	–	home	eat	–

	fàn	<u>le</u>
	food	CRS

(Well,) I (finally) went yesterday to have dinner at the Zhangs'.

Another example:

(119) (with reference to the speaker's project of having a dress made)

cáiféng	bǎ	xiùzi	jiǎn	—	duǎn	le
dressmaker	BA	sleeve	cut	—	short	CRS

The dressmaker cut the sleeves short (i.e., either s/he cut them too short, or s/he cut short sleeves when I wanted long ones).

Finally, here is a minimal pair that nicely illustrates this particular use of *le*:

(120) *a.* (discussing the personality of a character in a play, independent of the larger setting)

tā	tài	zìsī
3sg	too	selfish

S/He's too selfish.

b. (discussing a specific action of a character in relation to a series of ongoing events in a play)

tā	tài	zìsī	le !
3sg	too	selfish	CRS

S/He's being too selfish.

Sentences with *yòu* 'again' typically relate an event to another event and can be seen as expressing progress in an extensive project encompassing both events. Thus, sentences with *yòu* 'again' typically occur with *le*. For example, if one knows that a friend has been trying to quit smoking, one could report his/her backsliding with:

(121)	tā	yòu	chōu	—	yān	le
	3sg	again	extract	—	smoke	CRS

S/He's started to smoke again.

Or, if one cooperates with others in a regular project of doing laundry, one might say:

(122) jīntiān yòu gāi nǐ xǐ yīfu le
today again be:one's:turn you wash clothes **CRS**

Today it's your turn again to do the laundry.

Or, if the hearer knows that the overall issue is that the speaker has something to tell Zhangsan, the speaker can say (123) to the hearer:

(123) wǒ yòu wàngji gàosu tā le
I again forget tell 3sg **CRS**

I forgot to tell him again.

Finally, to the child who continues to get his/her hands dirty, one can say:

(124) bić yòu nòng — zāng le
don't again make — dirty **CRS**

Don't get (them) dirty again.

One interesting situation in which *le* signals progress so far is with questions or suggestions between people who know something about each other or who are involved with each other. In such a situation the speaker is typically concerned with the hearer's progress as s/he moves through life, for example, or through the day's activities. Here are two striking minimal pairs illustrating this use of *le*:

(125) *a.* (neutral question, such as a bookstore clerk might pose to an unfamiliar student)

nǐ niàn gāo — zhōng ma ?
you study upper — middle Q

Are you in upper middle school?

    b. (to a student whom one has known for a long time)

nǐ	niàn	gāo	—	zhōng	le	ma ?
you	study	upper	—	middle	CRS	Q

Are you in upper middle school?

(126) *a*. (school official registering children)

nǐ	jǐ	suì ?
you	how:many	year

How old are you?

    b. (to friend's child at home)

nǐ	jǐ	suì	le ?
you	how:many	year	CRS

How old are you?

Because inquiries between people who know each other well typically reflect the speaker's concern with the hearer's progress, questions with *le* always seem more friendly, more involved, and more concerned than the same utterances without *le*, which seem relatively formal, cold, and indifferent. Here are some further examples:

(127) *a*. (random neutral question)

nǐ	zuótiān	wǎnshang	tīng	—	dào	léi
you	yesterday	evening	hear	—	arrive	thunder

	—	shēng	ma ?
	—	sound	Q

(Say,) did you (happen to) hear the thunder last night?

b. (to someone with whom the speaker has been discussing thunder)

nǐ	zuótiān	wǎnshang	tīng	—	dào	léi
you	yesterday	evening	hear	—	arrive	thunder

	—	shēng	le	ma ?
	—	sound	CRS	Q

(Well,) did you hear the thunder last night?

(128) *a.* (one business associate of Miss Hua's to another)

Huá	Xiǎojiě	xià	—	ge	yuè	yào
Hua	Miss	next	—	CL	month	will

xiūjià	ma ?
take:vacation	Q

Will Miss Hua take a vacation next month?

b. (one close friend of Miss Hua's to another)

Huá	Lìzhēn	xià	—	ge	yuè	yào
Hua	Lizhen	next	—	CL	month	will

xiūjià	le	ma ?
take:vacation	CRS	Q

Will Hua Lizhen (be able to) take her vacation next month (i.e., I know she was planning one, and I'm concerned to know whether she can go or not)?

Suggestions work in an analogous way: when the speaker is concerned with the progress to that point of the set of activities in which the hearer is engaged, *le* will be used.

(129) *a*. (making casual conversation with a taxi driver about a political
leader)

tā	niánji	duō	dà ?
3sg	age	how	big

How old is s/he?

b. (in discussion about the ongoing career of a political leader)

tā	niánji	duō	dà	le ?
3sg	age	how	big	CRS

How old is s/he (at this point)?

Here are some further examples:

(130) *a*. (cold, almost as a command)

nǐ	lèi	le ,	nǐ	kěyǐ	qù	shuì
you	tired	CRS	you	can	go	sleep

You're tired (now), you can go to bed (i.e., you can be excused).

b. (solicitously, to a friend who seems sleepy)

nǐ	lèi	le ,	nǐ	kěyǐ	qù	shuì	le
you	tired	CRS	you	can	go	sleep	CRS

You're tired (now, if you want) you can go to bed (i.e., it's been a
long day).

(131) *a*. (to a teammate in a basketball game or a teacher to a student)

Xiǎo	Lǐ ,	gāi	nǐ
Little	Li	be:one's:turn	you

Little Li, it's your turn. (no "bigger project")

b. (to a friend, as people are introducing themselves, or taking turns reading)

Xiǎo	Lǐ ,	gāi	nǐ	le
Little	Li	be:one's:turn	you	CRS

Little Li, it's your turn (now).

(132) *a.* (one business associate to another after scheduling a time to meet on the following day)

nà	wǒmen	míngtiān	zài	jiàn
in:that:case	we	tomorrow	again	perceive

Then we'll meet again tomorrow.

b. (to a good friend or a lover)

nà	wǒmen	míngtiān	zài	jiàn	le
in:that:case	we	tomorrow	again	perceive	CRS

Then we'll meet again tomorrow (i.e., that's the situation at the moment with regard to our ongoing relationship).

(133) *a.* (complaining to a companion as if the matter is very grave)

jìrán	tāmen	zhǐ	mài	qìshuǐ	wǒmen	jiu
since	they	only	sell	soft:drink	we	then

hē	qìshuǐ
drink	soft:drink

Since they sell only soft drinks, we will drink soft drinks.

b. (advising a companion about how to make the best of the situation)

jìrán	tāmen	zhǐ	mài	qìshuǐ	wǒmen
since	they	only	sell	soft:drink	we

	jiu	hē	qìshuǐ	le
	then	drink	soft:drink	CRS

Since they sell only soft drinks, (our best move at this point in our activities is just to) have soft drinks.

The use of *le* in sentences giving progress so far in a larger venture, project, or ongoing concern is another clear illustration of a state of affairs as being currently relevant: it is relevant in assessing how far we have come in the larger venture.

D. What Happens Next

Another class of contexts in which a state of affairs is relevant includes those in which that state of affairs *determines* what happens next. We considered sentence (115) earlier in a context in which the hearer had known that there was a clothes-washing project under way:

(115)	wǒ	xǐ	—	hǎo	—	le	yīfu	le
	I	wash	—	finish	—	PFV	clothes	CRS

I've finished washing the clothes.

That sentence, however, could just as well be currently relevant as a signal to the hearer that something else can happen now:

(134)	wǒ	xǐ	—	hǎo	—	le	yīfu	le
	I	wash	—	finish	—	PFV	clothes	CRS

I've finished washing the clothes ⎰(so now: we can go to the movies

⎱ you can do your yoga in the laundry room

I'm free to play chess with you

etc.).

Example (98), which we looked at earlier, can be viewed in the same way:

(98)	wǒ	hē	—	le	sān	bēi	<u>le</u> !
	I	drink	—	PFV	three	glass	CRS

(Look—I tell you) I've drunk three glasses ⎧(so: don't pour me any⎫
more
quit saying <u>gānbēi</u>
'bottoms up' to me
let's just talk now
etc.)!

That is, the new situation announced in (98) can serve both to correct the false impression that the speaker needs more to drink and at the same time to make it clear that the state of affairs is relevant because it has some consequences for what the hearer should do next.

Here are three examples that demonstrate this double function very clearly:

(135) *a.*	wǒ	chī	—	guo	mùguā
	I	eat	—	EXP	papaya

I've eaten papaya (i.e., I've had the experience).

b.	wǒ	chī	—	guo	mùguā	<u>le</u>
	I	eat	—	EXP	papaya	CRS

I've had (my) papaya (so please don't keep asking me to have more papaya now).

(136) *a.*	wǒmen	qù	—	guo	Disneyland
	we	go	—	EXP	Disneyland

We've been to Disneyland (i.e., we've had the experience).

b.	wǒmen	qù	—	guo	Disneyland	<u>le</u>
	we	go	—	EXP	Disneyland	CRS

We've been to Disneyland (and that's why we don't want to go there with you this afternoon).

(137) (to friends getting out of a taxi, as they all reach for their wallets)

wǒ	yǒu	le
I	exist	CRS

I have it (i.e., the money, so I'll pay—you don't have to).

Often a *le* sentence is used to announce that a new state of affairs is just about to be realized, and the hearer is expected to make an appropriate response.[6] A minimal pair illustrates this point:

(138) *a.*

Xiǎo	Huáng	jiù	yào	lái
Little	Huang	soon	will	come

Little Huang will be here soon. (a simple neutral comment or an answer to a question)

b.

Xiǎo	Huáng	jiù	yào	lái	le
Little	Huang	soon	will	come	CRS

(Hurry!) Little Huang is about to arrive (so: hide the gifts / put your pants on / get ready to holler "Surprise" / etc.)!

Another very familiar example is this one:

(139) (coming to answer the door)

lái	le ,	lái	le
come	CRS	come	CRS

I'm coming, I'm coming (so don't be impatient)!

Here are some additional examples:

(140) wŏmen   gāi   zŏu   <u>le</u>
      we   should   leave   CRS

We should go now $\left\{\begin{array}{l}\text{(so: get your coat}\\ \text{get ready to say good-bye}\\ \text{etc.).}\end{array}\right.$

(141) (in a children's story, wolf to Mr. Dongguo)

lièrén   zhuī   —   lái   <u>le</u> ,   ràng   wŏ   zài
hunter   chase   —   come   CRS   let   I   at

nĭ   —   de   kŏudài   —   lĭ   duŏ
you   —   GEN   pocket   —   in   hide

yihuĭr   ba
awhile   SA

The hunter is chasing me, so let me hide in your pocket for a while, OK?

(142) kuài   yào   xià   yŭ   <u>le</u>
      fast   will   descend   rain   CRS

It's about to rain $\left\{\begin{array}{l}\text{(so: what are we going to do?}\\ \text{take your umbrella}\\ \text{we can't go for our walk}\\ \text{etc.).}\end{array}\right.$

(143) (pointing at the alarm clock)

kuài   xiǎng   <u>le</u>
fast   sound   CRS

It's about to ring $\left\{\begin{array}{l}\text{(so: shut it off}\\ \text{let's get up}\\ \text{etc.).}\end{array}\right.$

(144)　fàn　　kuài　pū　　—　　chū　　—　　lái　　le
　　　　food　　fast　spread　—　　exit　　—　　come　CRS

> (Hurry!) The rice is about to boil over ⎰(so: take it off the fire
> ⎱　　　take the lid off
> ⎰　　　turn the fire down
> ⎱　　　etc.)!

(145)　huǒchē　kuài　yào　kāi　　le
　　　　train　　fast　will　operate　CRS

> The train's about to leave ⎰(so: you'd better get on
> ⎱　　　here's your lunch
> ⎰　　　kiss me good-bye
> ⎱　　　etc.).

Finally, here is an example from the first-person short story "Jing-jing de shēngri" [Jing-jing's birthday] by Chen Ruoxi (1976:4):

(146)　jìde　　　shì　nèi　　—　　nián　jiǔ　　—
　　　　remember　be　that　—　　year　nine　—

　　　　yuè　　—　chū ,　　　wàizi　　cóng　Sū
　　　　month　—　beginning　husband　from　Jiangsu

　　　　—　běi　　lái　　xìn ,　shuō　tāmen
　　　　—　north　arrive　letter　say　　they

　　　　láodòng　kuài　jiéshù　le
　　　　labor　　fast　finish　CRS

> I remember it was at the beginning of September of that year, and my husband sent a letter from northern Jiangsu saying that their (period of) labor would soon be over.

Again, the relevance of this state of affairs in this story was that the husband would soon be able to come home.

It is appropriate to use *le*, then, whenever the state of affairs is relevant in determining what happens next.

E. Closing a Statement

An interesting use of *le* in signaling the current relevance of a state of affairs is its function as a mark of *finality*. That is, for many *le* sentences in conversations, the *le* "completes" the sentence; without it, the sentence sounds incomplete, as if the speaker intends to say more. It is almost as though the *le* were functioning as a sentence-final punctuation marker.

Many sentences in conversation, however, do not have this marker. Why, then, do some sentences seem to need it in order to sound complete to speakers? The answer is that when a person tells about something that happened or mentions a state of affairs as his/her contribution to the conversation and not as a response to some question or comment from another person, s/he is required to use *le* to tell the hearer why the proposition has been introduced. The speaker using *le* in this way signals, "This is my contribution to the conversation." Without *le*, the proposition would elicit an "And what about it?" response; it would need another clause, such as one beginning with 'so','because', or 'but', which would "validate" it by explicitly stating the purpose for which the speaker brought it up. In other words, *le* is required to tell the hearer that the proposition is relevant to the speech situation by being "newsworthy" in and of itself; it brings a statement into the current situation by tagging it as the speaker's total contribution as of that moment.

Here are two examples, one with *le* and one without, to illustrate:

(147) A: (to child)

nǐ	wèishénme	dùzi	zhème	dà ?
you	why	abdomen	this	big

Why are you so big in the abdomen?

B:	wǒ	chī	de	tài	bǎo
	I	eat	CSC	too	full

I am too full from eating.

(148) (to a friend, as an afterthought after a banquet)

wǒ	chī	de	tài	bǎo	le
I	eat	CSC	too	full	CRS

Let me tell you, I am too full from eating.

The contrast here is clear: as a response to a question, the relevance of the child's remark (147) is clear and needs no *le* to mark it, while the same utterance made in a context where it serves as an unsolicited comment, as in (148), must have the *le* to signal that the volunteered information is all the speaker has to contribute at the moment. Here is a precisely parallel example:

(149) *a.* (to a friend who has asked why the speaker didn't choose a certain university)

yīnwei	nàli	xuéfèi	tài	guì
because	there	tuition	too	expensive

The tuition is too high there. (neutral response)

   b. (one student to another, standing in line to pay fees)

xuéfèi	tài	guì	le !
tuition	too	expensive	CRS

(I tell you,) the tuition is (really) too high!

We can look at this function of *le* from a slightly different point of view. As we have seen, a sentence that answers a particular question may not need *le* because its relevance is perfectly obvious (unless, of course, *le* is required for expressing one of the other types of relevance we have considered). The same sentence functioning as a piece of volunteered information, on the other hand, may need *le* to "finish" it and to signal that it is the speaker's total contribution at the moment. In addition to answering a question, the sentence without the *le* can also function as background to some further information. For example, compare sentences (150) *a* and *b*:

(150) (commenting on a mutual friend)

	tā	yǐjing	líkai	Měiguó	le
a.	3sg	already	leave	America	CRS

S/He's already left America.

b.   tā   yǐjing   líkai   Měiguó ,
   3sg   already   leave   America

$\Big\{$(i)   suǒyǐ   tā   bu   −   bì   jiāo   shuì $\Big\}$
   therefore 3sg   not −   need   hand:over   tax

$\Big\{$(ii) xiànzài   zài   Zhōngguo   jiāo   −   shū $\Big\}$
   now   at   China   teach −   book

S/He has already left America, $\Big\{$ (i) so s/he doesn't have to pay taxes.

(ii) and (s/he is now teaching in China. $\Big\}$

It is easy to see that (150) *a* is an example exactly like (148) and (149) *b*, and it ends with *le*, just as we would expect, since it completes the presentation of a state of affairs to the hearer. The very same sentence occurs in (150) *b*, but without the *le*; in this case it must be followed by another clause—it becomes the background to another piece of news.

Let us look at another example containing two contrasting sentences:

(151) *a.*   wǒ   zài   nàli   zhù   −   le   liǎng
     I   at   there   live   −   PFV   two

            −   ge   yuè   <u>le</u>
            −   CL   month CRS

I've lived there for two months.

b.   wǒ   zài   nàli   zhù   −   le   liǎng   −
   I   at   there   live   −   CL   two   −

     ge   yuè ,   kěshi   hái   bu   tài   xíguàn
     CL   month   but   still   not   too   used:to

I have lived there for two months, but I'm still not very used to it.

Similarly, the difference between *hǎo* 'good' and *hǎo le* 'good CRS' illustrates just this point. While *hǎo le* is an announcement of a new situation, *hǎo* can serve only as a response to a question or as background to another utterance:

(152) (to friends who are arguing or announcing that something is over and done)

      hǎo   le !
      good   CRS

$$\left\{ \begin{array}{l} \text{That's it!} \\ \text{Stop it!} \\ \text{That's enough!} \\ \text{It's done!} \\ \text{It's over!} \end{array} \right\}$$

(153) A: nǐ   hǎo   ma ?
          you   good   Q

      How are you?

    B: hǎo
         good

    OK.

(154) A: wǒmen   qù   hē   yi   bēi   kāfēi   ba
        we   go   drink   one glass coffee   SA

      Let's go get some coffee.

    B: hǎo
         good

    OK.

(155) hǎo ,
       good

	(i)	míngtiān	jiàn
		tomorrow	see
	(ii) wǒmen	zǒu	ba
		we	leave	SA
	(iii)	nǐ	shuō
		you	say
		etc.	

Good, (i) see you tomorrow
       (ii) let's go
       (iii) you decide
            etc.

This usage of *le* can even be seen to function in "wrapping up" a story; here it signals the current relevance of the state of affairs represented by the last line in the story by signaling that the story is now over. The following example shows the end of a story:

(156) | jiéguǒ | wǒmen | jiù | bān |
       |---|---|---|---|
       | in:the:end | we | then | move |

huí	Zhōngguó	le
return	China	CRS

In the end, we moved back to China.

There are three reasons why the use of *le* in conveying the speaker's feeling that the statement s/he has made is his/her contribution to the conversation is particularly important for the language learner to internalize and be conscious of. First, it is easy to miss this use of *le* as an instance of Currently Relevant State. That is, it is quite straightforward to view situations such as those involving change of state, correcting mistaken assumptions, progress to date, and determining what happens next as instances of Currently Relevant States, but it is somewhat more difficult to recognize the examples involving *le* signaling the end of the speaker's contribution as currently relevant. Their relevance to the current situation is, however, just as strong; as we shall see in a moment, *le* in these cases signals to the hearer that the speaker is through with what s/he wanted to say, so that the hearer *can now say something* if s/he wants to. This kind of signal is obviously quite relevant to the flow of the conversation between two people.

The second reason why it is important to internalize this function of *le* is that as language learners, we frequently ask our teachers and friends how to say something. Very often the response contains a *le* because, unless the sentence denotes a general truth or a perfective event, it simply *isn't complete* with the *le*. For example, if you ask your Mandarin-speaking friend how to say 'S/He took off his/her coat', the answer is likely to be:

(157)   tā   bǎ   dàyī   tuō   —   xia
         3sg   BA   coat   remove —   descend

         —   lai   le
         —   come   CRS

S/He took off her/his coat.

As a language learner, you may wonder what that *le* is doing there, without realizing that to a Mandarin speaker, the sentence without the *le* sounds incomplete, as if more is going to be said, whereas with it the sentence sounds like a complete contribution to the conversation.

The third reason why it is important to internalize this use of *le* is that omitting it is probably the most common error made by nonnative speakers. Chinese people consistently comment that nonnative speakers do not use *le* where they should, and it is generally this finality *le* that is missing. This is perfectly natural, of course, since Western languages do not have any element that functions similarly in conversations, but it does mean that nonnative speakers must put some extra effort into becoming accustomed to hearing and using *le* to signal the end of one's contribution to a conversation.

One more important point: It is not that the sentences we have been considering in this subsection would be *ungrammatical* without *le*. Failing to use *le* in these contexts may cause uneasiness in our Mandarin-speaking conversational partners, but not of the type that English speakers feel when they hear someone say something like:

(158) *I am living in Chicago three years.

Rather, such sentences as (147) *b* and (149) *a*, if they are not answering a question, are simply incomplete in that the hearer senses that the speaker has not yet finished talking. The sentence is felt to have been left "hanging in mid air," and the hearer is uncomfortable because, strictly speaking, it isn't his/her turn to talk.

F. More Than One Use of *le*

Sometimes a sentence with *le* can be understood to be currently relevant in more than one of the five ways described above, depending on the context. For example, the sentence

(159)	tā	jìn	—	lái	le
	3sg	enter	—	come	CRS

can be understood to be relevant to the current situation as a changed state, as in:

(i) S/He has come in.

or as an imminent state to which the hearer is supposed to respond in some way:

(ii) S/He's coming in.

or as a correction of someone's mistaken assumption that s/he isn't coming in:

(iii) S/He *is* coming in.

Similarly,

(160)	tā	hūn	—	dǎo	le
	3sg	faint	—	overturn	CRS

can be understood as relevant to the current situation in several ways. For example, if the speaker is reporting an earlier event as a piece of news, then *le* signals the end of that contribution, and the sentence would mean simply

(i) S/He fainted.

On the other hand, (160) could be used to describe a changed state as of the present moment, in which case it would mean

(ii) S/He has fainted.

The fact that such sentences, when looked at in isolation, can be understood in more than one way is not surprising, of course. The way *le* functions to signal CRS varies according to the conversation of which it is a part; which of the five types of CRS situations is being conveyed at any one time can always be determined from the context.

G. Summary

What we have seen so far, then, is the various ways in which *le* can be used to signal a Currently Relevant State: (1) talking about a state that involves a change, (2) correcting a wrong assumption, (3) reporting progress so far, (4) alerting the hearer about what will happen next, and (5) tagging a comment to signal the end of a narrative or the end of the speaker's current contribution to the conversation. In each case *le* says that the *state* of affairs represented by the sentence to which it is attached is *currently relevant*, the exact ways in which it is relevant being a matter for the hearer to decide on the basis of his/her knowledge of the relationship between him/her and the speaker, of the situation in which they are interacting, and of the world at large.

7.1.2 Where Not to Use *le*

Before we move on to discuss cases in which it is difficult to distinguish the perfective -*le* from the CRS *le*, we would like to complement our discussion of the contexts in which *le* is used with a survey of contexts in which *le* is *not* used. We hope in this way to help the reader understand as thoroughly as possible the five types of situations in which *le* should be used.

We have emphasized the current relevance property of the meaning of *le*. A review of the five types of situations in which a state of affairs is claimed to be relevant to a given time frame shows very quickly that they are heavily *conversational* situations. The time frame, as we have seen, may be present, past, or future, but the need to tag a state of affairs as relevant to that time frame typically arises only in conversation.

This means that *le* is generally not used in written expository or descriptive prose, and it is rare in formal spoken-language situations such as news reports, speeches, lectures, and proclamations. For example, in seven news stories randomly chosen from the pages of the February 23, 1979, issue of the *Southern California Chinese News Dispatch*, which is published by the Southern California Chinese Service Association, *le* does not occur once. In ''A Twelve Point Proclamation by the Non-Nationalist Politicians in Taiwan'' (1978), there isn't a single occurrence of *le*. Following the United States' recognition of the People's Republic of China, the same group of politicians issued another proclamation. Again, it does not contain any occurrence of *le*. In the Chinese news dispatch of the joint communiqué by President Jimmy Carter and Vice-Premier Deng Xiaoping on February 1, 1979, not one occurrence of *le* can be found.

Similarly, descriptive writing contains few, if any, occurrences of *le*. As an example, we randomly selected twenty pages from *Zhōngguó Lìshǐ Gàiyào* [Outline of Chinese history] by B. Z. Jian et al. (Beijing: Renming Chubanshi, 1956, pp. 1-5, 34-45, 51-55, and 84-86) for survey and found only one occurrence of *le*.

The low incidence of *le* in these types of discourse is easy to explain if one understands the function of *le* to be to signal that a given state of affairs is relevant to a particular time frame.

Of course, *le* can be found in written narratives and stories, where it serves to relate a state of affairs to the time at which the story took place, just as in conversational stories, as we saw above in (77). Here is another example from the first-person short story "Jīng-jing de shēngrì" [Jing-jing's birthday] by Chen Ruoxi (1976:2):

(161) nèi   shí,   wǒ   zhèng   huái   —
       that   time   I   precisely bear   —

       zhe   lǎo   —   èr,   yǐjīng
       DUR   number —   two   already

       bā   —   ge   yuè   le
       eight —   CL   month CRS

At that time, I was pregnant with my second child and was already eight months into the pregnancy.

Even within conversational language, however, there are several types of situations in which *le* is not used.

First, *le* is not used when the speaker is simply asserting a general truth in an ordinary conversation where no change is involved:

(162) Zhōngguó   rén   dōng,   nán,   xī,   běi   —   de
      China   person   east   south   west   north   —   ASSOC

      kǒuwèi   dōu   bu   yíyàng
      taste   all   not   same

The tastes of Chinese people in the north, south, east, and west are all different.

(163)   tāmen   zhǐ   pīfā ,   bu   língmài
        they   only   sell:wholesale   not   sell:retail

They only sell wholesale, not retail.

(164)   tā   tàitai   —   de   xìngqíng   hěn   wēnróu
        3sg   wife   —   GEN   disposition   very   gentle

His wife has a gentle disposition.

(165)   wǒ   měi   —   tiān   zǎoshang   chī   xīfàn
        I   every   —   day   morning   eat   rice:porridge

I eat rice porridge every morning.

(166)   tā   chàng   —   gē   chàng   de   bu   cuò
        3sg   sing   —   song   sing   CSC   not   wrong

S/He sings not badly.

(167)   wǒ   chángchang   gēn   tā   xué   quán
        I   often   with   3sg   learn   boxing

I often study boxing with him/her.

Similarly, general states or ongoing situations involving no change are generally not described with *le*. For example:

(168)   gōngsī   —   de   zhàngmù   hěn   qīngchu
        company   —   ASSOC   account   very   clear

The company's accounts were in good order.

(169)   tā   shuō   de   gēn   nǐ   shuō
        3sg   say   NOM   and   you   say

                   de   bu   yiyàng
                 NOM   not   same

What he says and what you say are different.

(170)   nǐ   —   de   nóngchǎng   yǒu   duōshǎo   yīngmǔ ?
         you   —   GEN   farm   exist   how:many   acre

How many acres does your farm have?

(171)   nèi   —   tiáo   mǎlù   shi   wéi   —   zhe
         that   —   CL   road   be   surround —   DUR

                hú   —   biān   zǒu
                lake —   side   go

The road goes around the lake.

(172)   tā   niē   —   zhe   yidiǎn   yán
         3sg   hold:between:fingers —   DUR   a:little   salt

S/He was holding a pinch of salt between his/her fingers.

(173)   tā   zài   shuì   —   jiào
         3sg   DUR   sleep   —   sleep

S/He's sleeping.

Another type of situation in which *le* is not found is a simple assertion of an event that happened in the past. Here the perfective verbal suffix *-le* would be used if the event named were a perfective one (see section 6.1 of chapter 6), but the CRS *le* would not be called for:

(174)   wǒ   shuō   kěyi
         I   say   can

I said it was OK.

(175)   wǒ   zuótiān   kǎo   —   le   liǎng
         I   yesterday   take:test —   PFV   two

                —   táng   shì
                —   class   exam

I had two exams yesterday.

(176)   tā   shōuxià   —   le   wǒ   gěi
         3sg   accept   —   PFV   I   give

         tā   de   qián
         3sg   NOM   money

S/He accepted the money I gave him/her.

(177)   wēndù   jiàng   de   hěn   kuài
         temperature   drop   CSC   very   fast

The temperature dropped very quickly.

(178)   wǒ   yi   xià   chē ,   jiu   guò   —   lái
         I   once   descend   car   then   cross   —   come

         —   le   yi   —   ge   jǐngchá
         —   PFV   one   —   CL   police:officer

As soon as I got out of the car, a police officer came over.

Normally, sentences expressing an event or situation in the future, requests, suggestions, and commands also occur without *le*:

(179)   wǒ   suǒ   zhīdào   de   dōu   gàosu   nǐ
         I   all   know   NOM   all   tell   you

I'll tell you what I know about it.

(180)   wǒ   míngtiān   huí   —   lái
         I   tomorrow   return —   come

I'll be back tomorrow.

(181)   nǐ   kàn   huì   xià   yǔ   ma ?
         you   see   likely   descend rain   Q

Do you think it'll rain?

(182)   wǒmen   guò   tiān   —   qiáo   ba
          we   cross   sky   —   bridge   SA

Let's cross the overhead bridge.

(183)   wǒ   yídìng   jìnliàng   zǎo   yidiǎn
         I   certainly   try   early   a:little

         zuò   —   wán
         do   —   finish

I'll certainly try to finish a little sooner.

(184)   zhèi   —   ge   yá   yào   bá
         this   —   CL   tooth   want   pull

This tooth needs to be pulled.

(185)   wǒmen   yào   yi   —   pán   pàocài
         we   want   one   —   plate   pickled:vegetable

We want a plate of pickled vegetables.

(186)   bǎ   cài   —   dān   dì   gěi   wǒ
         BA   dish   —   list   hand   to   I

Hand me the menu.

Thus, in the contexts we've given for these sentences, that is, in talking about simple general truths, ongoing states, past and future events, and commands, suggestions, and requests, *where no Currently Relevant State is involved, le* will not be used. This doesn't mean, of course, that *le* can't be used with any of the sentences that we've used as examples (162)−(186); it can be if one can imagine an appropriate context, but then it will always imply current relevance in one of the five ways discussed under section 7.1.1 above.

7.1.3 Perfective -le versus CRS le

As long as "*le*" occurs at the end of a sentence after any word other than a verb, it is easy to be sure that it is the CRS *le*, as in (187):

(187) tāmen   yào   zhuā   <u>tā</u>   <u>le</u>
       they   will   grab   3sg   CRS

They're going to grab him/her.

Sometimes, however, when a "*le*" comes after a verb at the end of a sentence, it is difficult to determine whether it is the perfective verb suffix -*le* (see section 6.1 of chapter 6) or the CRS sentence-final particle *le*. Here we will try to show how the context helps us to know which "*le*" is which.

The first step in sorting out which "*le*" is involved is to see what the possibilities are. In any given sentence with a postverbal "*le*" at the end of the sentence, there are exactly three possibilities:

(i) It could be *le*, in which case the sentences must have a *current relevance* meaning.

(ii) It could be -*le*, in which case the sentence must have a *perfective* meaning.

(iii) Since the combination -*le le* never occurs phonologically, "*le*" could have the function of both -*le* and *le*, in which case the sentence must have the meaning of a *perfective* event that is a *Currently Relevant State*.

Let's look at each of these possibilities one at a time. In case (i), the *le* is simply the CRS *le*, where there is no perfective meaning possible. To illustrate this situation we must find examples of states that are not perfective, that is, not bounded, and that are claimed to be currently relevant. Sentences expressing imminent states to which some reaction is expected (see section 7.1.1 above) provide good illustrations:

(188) Xiǎo   Huáng   kuài   yào   lái   <u>le</u> !
       Little   Huang   fast   will   come   CRS

Little Huang is coming!

(189) huǒchē   mǎshang   jiù   kāi   <u>le</u>
       train   immediately   soon   leave   CRS

The train is leaving immediately.

Another illustration is provided by sentence (190):

(190) wǒ   bu   jìn   —   lái   le
       I   not   enter —   come   CRS

I'm not coming in.

Sentence (190), being a negative sentence, does not represent a bounded event, but it would represent a currently relevant state if it were used, say, to correct your mistaken assumption that I was coming in (see section 7.1.1.B above). Finally, sentence (191) illustrates the currently relevant state of a nonperfective but changed state:

(191) guò   —   le   shàng   —   xià   —   bān
       cross —   PFV   ascend —   descend —   work

       de   shíhou   gōnggòng   —   qìchē   jiu
       NOM   time   public   —   car   then

       kōng   le
       empty CRS

Once rush hour is over, the buses will be empty.

Finally, sentences such as the following are also good examples of sentence-final "*le*" that is purely the CRS *le*:

(192) wǒ   xǐng   —   guo   —   lái   le
       I   wake   —   cross   —   come   CRS

I woke up.

(193) tā   bǎ   huà   sī   —   diào   le
       3sg   BA   painting tear   —   off   CRS

S/He tore up the painting.

(194) tā   bǎ   xìn   chāi   —   kāi   le
       3sg   BA   letter open   —   open   CRS

S/He opened the letter.

Each of the preceding three sentences is an example of the situation we discussed above in section 7.1.1.E, where *le* is needed to close out the remark and signal current relevance by tagging it as the speaker's whole contribution to the conversation. In each of these, and in similar sentences, omitting the *le* would be possible only if something more were going to be said.

In sentences expressing Currently Relevant States which are not bounded in any way, then, a postverbal sentence-final "*le*" is always the CRS *le*.

Turning next to case (ii), we want to consider instances in which a sentence-final "*le*" can be only the perfective *-le*. Since perfective *-le* is used for signaling *bounded* events, a sentence-final "*le*" can be just the perfective *-le* only with verbs that have an end point as part of their inherent meaning, such as *miè* 'extinguish' and *sǐ* 'die' (see section 6.1.1.C of chapter 6 for a discussion of these cases). In each of these examples, we are assuming a context in which the speaker is not claiming current relevance (if s/he is, then we have an instance of case [iii], which we will discuss next).

(195)   zhàdàn   bào   —   le
         bomb   explode   —   PFV

The bomb exploded.

(196)   huǒ   zuótiān   wǎnshang   miè   —   le
         fire   yesterday   evening   go:out   —   PFV

The fire went out last night.

(197)   tā   1969   sǐ   —   le
         3sg   1969   die   —   PFV

S/He died in 1969.

When the verb at the end of the sentence has an end point as part of its inherent meaning, the event is bounded, and if the sentence is not being used to convey a Currently Relevant State, the sentence-final "*le*" is quite clearly the perfective *-le*.

Let us look now at case (iii), the case in which a sentence-final "*le*" is actually *both* the perfective *-le* and the CRS *le*. In these cases the capital-letter form *LE* is used to signal that it has the function of both *-le* and *le*. In other words, phonologically *-le le* is always manifested by the syllable "*le*," as pointed out by Chao (1968:247), and we will represent it by *LE* in order to distinguish it functionally from *-le* and from *le*.

To find examples of this phenomenon, all we have to do is take the perfective examples of case (ii) and use them in situations in which current relevance is implied.

For example, let's consider (195) in a context in which the speaker is signaling that this is his/her contribution to the conversation. Then both current relevance and perfectivity are implied, and we have (198):

(198)   zhàdàn   bào   <u>LE</u>
           bomb   explode   PFV/CRS

      The bomb exploded (and that is what I have to say).

If we add a specific time phrase to (195), the perfective meaning of "*le*" will be more prominent, as in (199):

(199)   zhàdàn   jiǔ − diǎnzhōng   bào   −   <u>le</u>
           bomb   nine−o'clock   explode   −   PFV

      The bomb exploded at nine o'clock.

On the other hand, we could make "*le*" have only the CRS function by adding the word *yǐjing* 'already', which is typically used in the description of states:

(200)   zhàdàn   yǐjing   bào   <u>le</u>
           bomb   already   explode   CRS

      The bomb has already exploded.

Exactly the same point can be made with the sentence:

(201)   huǒ   miè   "<u>le</u>"
           fire   extinguish

In its simple perfective interpretation, "*le*" is *-le*, and the sentence means:
     (i) The fire went out.

A time phrase makes this interpretation stronger, as in (196) above:

(196)   huǒ   zuótiān   wǎnshang   miè   −   <u>le</u>
           fire   yesterday   evening   extinguish   −   PFV

      The fire went out last night.

In its most natural CRS interpretation, *"le"* is the particle *le* signaling that the extinction of the fire is relevant to the current speech situation, and sentence (201) means:

(ii) The fire has gone out.

Again, *yǐjīng* 'already' brings out this interpretation more clearly:

(202) huǒ   yǐjīng   miè   le
        fire   already   extinguish   CRS

The fire has already gone out.

Finally, (201) may also express both Currently Relevant State and perfectivity simultaneously. In that case, *"le"* is *LE*, and (196) has the meaning:

(iii) The fire went out, and that's what I am telling you.

What we have seen, then, is that sentences with a verb at the end followed by a *"le"* can be analyzed in at least one of the following three ways:

(i) When the sentence expresses Currently Relevant State alone, it can be interpreted as *le*.

(ii) When the sentence expresses perfectivity alone, it can be interpreted as *-le*.

(iii) When the sentence expresses *both* Currently Relevant State and perfectivity, it can be interpreted as *LE* (i.e., *-le le*). The fact that the perfective suffix *-le* and the CRS *le* are pronounced the same way and the fact that a single *LE* is actually the way *-le le* is pronounced initially makes such sentences difficult to analyze. In most instances, though, a clear understanding of the different functions of the perfective suffix *-le* and the CRS particle *le* allows us to sort out which is which when they occur at the end of the sentence.

7.2 *ne*

7.2.1 *ne* as 'Response to Expectation'

As the final particle of a declarative sentence, *ne* has the semantic function of pointing out to the hearer that the information conveyed by the sentence is the speaker's response to some claim, expectation, or belief on the part of the hearer. We will gloss it as 'Response to Expectation', or REx. On the basis of its semantic function, this particle has the effect of calling on the hearer to pay particular attention to the information conveyed by the sentence because it is a response to the hearer's claim, expectation, or belief. Let us examine a contrastive pair of declarative sentences with and without the sentence-final particle *ne*.

(203) *a.*

tāmen	yǒu	sān	—	tiáo	niú
they	exist	three	—	CL	cattle

They have three cattle.

b.

tāmen	yǒu	sān	—	tiáo	niú	ne
they	exist	three	—	CL	cattle	REx

They have three cattle.

The complete information conveyed by the *b* sentence can be paraphrased as in (204):

(204) Listen, they have three cattle.

That is to say, the presence of *ne* in (203) *b* calls the hearer's attention to the information in the sentence by telling him/her that this is what the speaker wishes to say in connection with the hearer's previous claim. On the other hand, sentence (203) *a* is completely neutral in terms of the pragmatic function of the sentence. It merely states the fact that 'they have three cattle'. Thus, one would imagine sentence (203) *a* but not (203) *b* to be appropriate in an official report, whereas one can imagine a variety of speech contexts in which (203) *b* would be appropriate and (203) *a*, while perhaps not inappropriate, would not convey the additional semantic nuance that (203) *b* does. For example, one context for which (203) *b* would be a perfect response would be one in which A has just stated that 'they' don't have any money and are very poor, and B then challenges A's claim, ending the challenge with (203) *b*. In such a context, (203) *a*, though acceptable, would not be as effective in concluding the challenge as (203) *b* would. Thus, the information conveyed by (203) *b* is significant in connection with what the hearer has just said in that it contradicts the hearer's expectation. Of course, a contradiction is not the only situation in which the information conveyed by (203) *b* would be significant in connection with the hearer's claim or expectation. For example, another speech context for (203) *b* could be that A had been describing how rich these people are; B could then utter (203) *b* in support of A's claim. In this context, (203) *b* would be more appropriate if the adverb *hái* 'even, still, also' were placed in front of the verb *yǒu* 'exist' so that the complete meaning of the sentence would be: 'You know, they even have three cattle.'

Let us examine the four semantic functions attributed by Chao (1968:802–804) to *ne*. First, Chao claims that *ne* describes "continued state," as in (205):

(205)	Zhāngsān	shuō	–	zhe	huà	ne
	Zhangsan	speak	–	DUR	utterance	REx

Zhangsan is speaking (to someone).

The second meaning of *ne*, according to Chao, is 'as much as', which he calls "assertion of an equaling degree."

(206)	yǒu	yi	bǎi	chǐ	ne
	exist	one	hundred	feet	REx

It's as much as one hundred feet.

Third, according to Chao, *ne* depicts "interest in additional information," as in:

(207)	tāmen	hái	mài	gǔ	qín	ne
	they	also	sell	ancient	zither	REx

They also sell ancient zithers.

Finally, Chao claims that *ne* has the meaning of 'mind you', that is, it provides a mild warning, as in:

(208)	zhèi	dào	hěn	wéixiǎn	ne
	this	actually	very	dangerous	REx

This is rather dangerous, mind you.

Chao's observation that the particle *ne* in (206) "strengthens" the assertion of equaling degree is in accord with the semantic function we ascribe to *ne*. The meaning Chao gives for *ne* in sentence (208), 'mind you', also corresponds closely to what we have suggested is the function of *ne*, namely, to call the hearer's attention to the relevance of the information conveyed by the sentence in connection with the hearer's claim or expectation. The continued-state meaning of (205) is conveyed, however, not by *ne*, but by the durative aspect marker -*zhe* (see section 6.2 of chapter 6). In order to understand the semantic function of *ne* in (205), let's consider a context in which it would be likely to be uttered. Suppose that someone wishes to go into Zhangsan's office to see him and is presented with sentence (205) in response to his/her request. The *ne* in (205) is then calling to the visitor's attention that, contrary to his/her expectation, Zhangsan is unable to see him/her.

The total message conveyed by (207) can be described as:

(209) You will be interested in knowing that they also sell ancient zithers.

Let's think of an appropriate context for (207): Suppose the speaker and his/her friends are visiting a musical instrument shop. One friend makes the discovery that the shop carries some exotic instruments, at which point the speaker responds with (207). Again, *ne* in (207) indicates that in response to the friend's discovery, the speaker is calling the friend's attention to the message conveyed by the sentence. Let's contrast (207) with (210), which does not contain *ne*:

(210) tāmén hái mài gǔ qín
      they also sell ancient zither

    They also sell ancient zithers.

The difference between (210) and (207) is that (207), with *ne*, can be uttered only as a *response* to an earlier comment, while (210) could be a neutral piece of information offered, say, as a continuation of something the speaker himself/ herself has just said.

Since any declarative sentence may serve the purpose of conveying significant information in connection with the hearer's claim or expectation, as long as the speech context is appropriate, *ne* can occur with any declarative sentence. The following sentences will illustrate:

(211) (in response to a person's remark that the speaker doesn't have anything to worry about anymore)

    wǒ hái děi xiě yi — piān lùnwén ne
    I still must write one — CL dissertation REx

    I still have to write a dissertation.

(212) (in response to a person's observation that a friend does not appear to be too disturbed by an accident)

tā	hěn	kāixīn	<u>ne</u>
3sg	very	happy	<u>REx</u>

S/He is very happy.

(213) (in response to someone's remark that the speaker should engage in physical exercise)

wǒmen	yào	dǎ	wǎngqiú	<u>ne</u>
we	want	hit	tennis	<u>REx</u>

We want to play tennis.

(214) (in a discussion about the fact that Zhangsan is a frequent traveler)

Zhāngsān	mǎi	fēijī	piào	qù	Zhōngguó	<u>ne</u>
Zhangsan	buy	airplane	ticket	go	China	<u>REx</u>

Zhangsan bought a plane ticket to go to China.

(215) (in response to a relative's complaint that the boy or girl is not making money)

tā	háishi	yi	—	ge	xiǎo	—	háizi	<u>ne</u>
3sg	still	one	—	CL	small	—	child	<u>REx</u>

S/He is still a kid.

When we speak of the hearer's claim, expectation, or belief, we should be aware that a speaker can assume unilaterally that a hearer has a claim, an expectation, or a belief. For example, consider (207) again. Someone could utter (207) in a musical instruments shop even though none of his/her companions has said anything if s/he unilaterally assumes that the companions believe the shop doesn't carry anything exotic.

Given the function of *ne*, it follows that it will not occur with declarative sentences that are not being used in a speech situation. In other words, *ne* is a strictly conversational particle that requires at least two conversationalists, since the function of *ne* is to bring the hearer's attention to the significance of the information conveyed by the sentence in connection with the hearer's claim, expectation, or belief. Thus, we don't find *ne* in scientific reports or in expository writings. Similarly, *ne* normally does not occur in a presentative sentence, which typically serves to initiate a conversation. For instance, (216) is odd when it is used as a presentative sentence initiating a conversation:

(216)	?yǒu	yi	—	ge	rén	yào	jìn	—
	exist	one	—	CL	person	want	enter	—

	lai	ne
	come	REx

There is a person who wants to come in.

7.2.2 *ne* as a Question Particle

Unlike *ma* (see chapter 18), *ne* cannot by itself turn a declarative sentence into a question, as is illustrated by the sentences in (217):

(217) *a.*	nǐ	hǎo	ma ?
	you	well	Q

Are you well?

b.	*nǐ	hǎo	ne ?
	you	well	REx

Instead, *ne* as a question particle occurs with A-not-A questions, question-word questions, and truncated questions consisting of only one noun. Let us illustrate each of the three contexts with examples.

(218)	nǐ	xǐhuan	bu	xǐhuan	tā	ne ?
	you	like	not	like	3sg	REx

(In that case,) do you like him/her?

(219)	tā	yào	chī	shénme	ne ?
	3sg	want	eat	what	REx

(In that case,) what does s/he want to eat?

(220) A: tā   míngtiān   qù   xuéxiào
              3sg   tomorrow   go   school

        Tomorrow s/he'll go to school.

       B: nǐ   ne ?
              you   REx

        And how about you?

The semantic function of *ne* in the declarative sentence is carried over here to its use in the questions. That is, *ne* remains a particle with the meaning 'This is what I say in connection with your previous claim, expectation, or belief'. Of course, in the case of questions, the precise meaning of *ne* will be: 'In connection with your claim or expectation, let me find out . . .'. Thus, the English translations for questions (218) and (219) contain the preamble 'in that case', meaning 'with respect to what you have just said, let me ask you . . .'.

The message described by such a preamble is clearly shown by the truncated question ending in *ne* illustrated by (220). In (220), when B says 'And how about you?', it is clearly in reference to what A has just said: 'Tomorrow s/he'll go to school'.

Again, like declarative sentences with *ne*, questions with *ne* are not used to initiate discourse unless the hearer's claim, expectation, or belief is assumed or already in the air. Similarly, questions with *ne* are like declarative sentences with *ne* in that they are unlikely to be found in scientific reports or expository writings, because of the conversational nature of the function of *ne*.

Ne and *ma* are in complementary distribution as sentence-final particles for questions. *Ma*, unlike *ne*, is a plain question marker and does not occur with A-not-A questions, question-word questions, and truncated questions, as shown in sentences (221)−(223):

(221)   *nǐ   xǐhuan   bu   xǐhuan   tā   ma ?
          you   like   not   like   3sg   Q

(222)   *tā   yào   chī   shénme   ma ?
          3sg   want   eat   what   Q

(223) A: tā   míngtiān   qù   xuéxiào
              3sg   tomorrow   go   school

        Tomorrow s/he'll go to school.

B: *nǐ <u>ma</u>?
  you Q

On the other hand, in *ma* questions, *ne* cannot be substituted for *ma*, as shown in (217) *a* and *b* above and in (224) *a* and *b*:

(224) *a.* nǐ kāixīn <u>ma</u>?
    you happy Q

   Are you happy?

 b. *nǐ kāixīn <u>ne</u>?
    you happy REx

   (Are you happy?)

The reason that *ma* does not occur with A-not-A questions or question-word questions is obvious. Both types of questions already contain the information that the construction is a question. Thus, there is no need for the presence of *ma*, whose sole function is to mark an utterance as a question. As for the truncated questions, they must take *ne*, not *ma*, because they are always uttered only in response to what the hearer believes or has just said.

7.3 *ba*

The semantic function of *ba* can be best described as equivalent to that of the "Don't you think so?" or "Wouldn't you agree?" type of question that is tagged onto a statement in English. Thus, *ba* has the effect of soliciting the approval or agreement of the hearer with respect to the statement to which *ba* is attached; we gloss it 'Solicit Agreement' (*SA*). This is why *ba* often occurs as the marker for first person plural commands (see chapter 14 on imperatives). For example:

(225) wǒmen zǒu <u>ba</u>
    we go SA

   Let's go!

(226) qǐ — lái ba
    rise — come SA

   Let's get up!

When the subject of a command is the inclusive "we" (i.e., including the speaker), and the sentence-final particle *ba* signals the speaker's desire to solicit approval or agreement with respect to the information conveyed by the sentence, the 'let's . . .' meaning follows naturally.

The semantic function of *ba* also explains why *ba* is described as an "advisative" particle by Chao (1968:807). When the subject of a sentence is the second person and *ba* occurs as the sentence-final particle, signaling a solicitation of approval/agreement from the hearer with regard to the information contained in the sentence, it follows that the total effect of the sentence is one of advice. For example:

(227)   nǐ   hē   shuǐ   ba
         you   drink   water   SA

    Why don't you drink some water?

(228)   nǐ   xiǎng   —   yi   —   xiǎng   ba
         you   think   —   one   —   think   SA

    Why don't you think about it a little?

When the subject of a sentence is the first person, it is easy to see the semantic function of *ba* by contrasting a sentence ending in *ba* and the same sentence without the *ba*. For example:

(229) *a.*   wǒ   hē   bàn   bēi
              I   drink   half   glass

    I'll drink half a glass.

    b.   wǒ   hē   bàn   bēi   ba
             I   drink   half   glass   SA

    I'll drink half a glass, OK?

Sentence (229) *a* functions as a neutral statement. For instance, it can be an answer to a question such as:

(230) nǐ   hē   duōshǎo ?
       you   drink how:much

How much do you want to drink?

Sentence (229) *b*, on the other hand, would be used only in a context in which the speaker had some reason to request the hearer to agree that half a glass would be an acceptable amount to drink. For example, if the speaker was being repeatedly toasted at a banquet, s/he could utter (229) *b* as a plea to be given only half a glass to down this time.

Consider another contrasting pair:

(231) *a.* tā   bu   huì   zuò   zhè   —   yàng   —
            3sg   not   will   do   this   —   manner   —

            de   shì
            ASSOC   thing

S/He wouldn't do such things.

b. tā   bu   huì   zuò   zhè   —   yàng   —
      3sg   not   will   do   this   —   manner   —

      de   shì   <u>ba</u>
      ASSOC   thing   SA

S/He wouldn't do such things, don't you agree?

Here we might imagine a context in which two people are discussing whether Zhangsan has done something he shouldn't have done. If the person who is defending Zhangsan is angry, then only (231) *a* is an appropriate form for his/her defense to take. Under these circumstances, (231) *b*, which attempts to solicit agreement from the hearer, would not be used: its accommodating and conciliatory tone would be incompatible with the anger of the person defending Zhangsan.

The function of soliciting agreement which we have described for *ba* is clearly comparable to the function of a tag question, which seeks confirmation of a statement (see chapter 18, section 18.4). Thus (232) *a* and *b* convey similar messages:

(232) *a.* | tā | hěn | hǎo | – | kàn | <u>ba</u> |
|------|------|------|----|------|------|
| 3sg | very | good | – | look | SA |

S/He is very good looking, don't you agree?

b. | tā | hěn | hǎo | – | kàn, | duì | bu | duì ? |
|------|------|------|----|------|-------|-----|-------|
| 3sg | very | good | – | look | right | not | right |

S/He is very good looking, isn't s/he?

It is not surprising, then, that in general *ba* cannot be added to an utterance that is already marked as a question, as shown by the unacceptability of the sentences in (233):

(233) *a.* | *<u>tā</u> | hǎo | – | kàn | bu | hǎo | – | kàn | ba ? |
|------|------|----|------|-----|------|----|------|------|
| 3sg | good | – | look | not | good | – | look | SA |

b. | *<u>shéi</u> | hē | jiǔ | <u>ba</u> ? |
|------|-------|------|------|
| who | drink | wine | SA |

c. | *nǐ | hǎo | <u>ma</u> | <u>ba</u> ? |
|------|------|------|------|
| you | good | Q | SA |

The reason that *ba* cannot occur with question-word questions, A-not-A questions, and *ma* questions is straightforward: since these types of questions are already marked as questions whose function is to request certain types of information, in general they cannot be converted into a sentence type that requests the hearer to agree to some statement. Chao (1968:807) gives an interesting counterexample: (234) is a question-word question with *ba*:

(234) | nǐ | dàodǐ | yào | <u>shénme</u> | <u>ba</u> ? |
|------|------------|------|------|------|
| you | ultimately | want | what | SA |

Tell me, what do you want?

Let us first contrast (234) with (235). Whereas (234) is acceptable, (235) appears unacceptable:

(235)   *tā   yào   <u>shénme</u>   <u>ba</u> ?
        3sg   want   what   SA

The difference between (234) and (235) is, first, that the subject in (234) is *nǐ* 'you', while in (235) it is *tā* 's/he'; and, second, that the adverb *dàodǐ* 'ultimately' is present in (234) but not in (235). Both of these points have to do with the context in which (234) might be used. The most natural context in which this sentence might occur is one in which two people are quarreling, and one finally says (234) in exasperation; the translation given in (236) gives an idea of the full message conveyed by (234):

(236) OK, don't you think you should let me know what in the world you want?

which clearly makes use of the function of *ba*, namely, soliciting agreement from the hearer that s/he should make his/her wishes clear. When the subject of the question is *tā* 's/he', however, as in (235), it is much more difficult to think of an analogous context in which the speaker requests the hearer to agree that *someone else* should make his/her wishes clear, as suggested in (237):

(237) OK, don't you think you should let me know what in the world s/he wants?

7.4 *ou*

The semantic function of *ou* can best be described as that of a friendly warning showing concern and caring on the part of the speaker. It signals the message 'Let me warn you or tell you in a friendly way'; we gloss it 'Friendly Warning', or *FW*. Chao (1968) correctly characterizes *ou* as a ''warning reminder''; but it also has the connotation of friendliness, showing that the speaker is concerned. Thus, it is often used to soften a command, in which situation it converts the command into a concerned warning, as in sentences (238)−(240):

(238) xiǎoxīn   <u>ou</u>
      careful   FW

      Be careful, OK?

(239)   yào   zuò   gōngkè   ou
         must   do   homework   FW

Listen, you'd better do your homework.

(240)   bié   shēngqì   ou
         don't   angry   FW

Say, don't get angry, OK!

Another type of sentence that often can serve as a warning is the conditional sentence (see section 23.1.3 of chapter 23). Thus *ou* often occurs with conditionals. For example:

(241)   nǐ   bu   lái   tā   jiu   shāng   —   xīn   ou
         you   not   come   3sg   then   wound   —   heart   FW

Let me tell you, if you don't come, s/he'll be hurt.

(242)   rúguo   tā   qù   Měiguó   wǒ   jiu   mà   tā   ou
         if   3sg   go   America   I   then   scold   3sg   FW

Let me tell you, if s/he goes to America, I'll scold him/her.

(243)   nǐ   chī   duō   le   jiu   dùzi   téng   ou
         you   eat   much   CRS   then   abdomen   hurt   FW

Let me tell you, if you eat too much, you'll have a stomachache.

Because of the semantic nature of *ou*, it is commonly found in the speech of an adult addressing a child. Similarly, because of the implication of concern and care on the part of the speaker, *ou* will not occur in the speech of an adversary or in impersonal speech or writing. Thus, for instance, it is perfectly imaginable for a parent to warn a naughty child by saying:

(244)   wǒ   yào   dǎ   nǐ   ou
         I   will   hit   you   FW

Let me tell you, (if you do this,) I will hit you.

On the other hand, though, it would be unimaginable or comical for one fighter to say (244) to another in a boxing ring or in a gang fight, because in these types of situations there is a lack of care and concern.

7.5 *a/ya*

A/ya performs the function of reducing the forcefulness of the message conveyed by the sentence; it is glossed as 'Reduced Forcefulness', or *RF*. Thus when *a/ya* is placed after an A-not-A question or a question-word question, it has the semantic effect of softening the query, in much the same way that the English preambles 'excuse me', 'by the way', and 'to change the subject' do, as observed by Chao (1968:804). The following examples illustrate A-not-A questions and question-word questions with the particle *a/ya*:[7]

(245)　　shéi　　a/ya ?
　　　　　who　　 RF

　　　Who is it?

(246)　　nǐ　　 qù　　 nǎr　　a/ya ?
　　　　　you　　go　　where　 RF

　　　Where are you going?

(247)　　nǐ　　xǐhuan　bu　　xǐhuan　zhèi　　—　　ge　　chēzi　a/ya ?
　　　　　you　　like　　not　　like　　this　　—　　CL　　car　　RF

　　　Do you like this car?

(248)　　nǐ　　xiǎng　bu　　xiǎng　tā　　a/ya ?
　　　　　you　　think　not　　think　3sg　　RF

　　　Do you miss her/him?

When one contrasts the questions (245)−(248) and the same questions without the final particle *a/ya*, the first impression one has is that the questions with the particle are much softer and thus tend to suggest kindness on the part of the speaker. This effect, of course, is derived from the meaning of *a/ya*, which reduces the forcefulness of the message conveyed by the utterance.

Chao (1968) gives ten different meanings of *a/ya*, only some of which concern *a/ya* as sentence-final particle; here we will deal exclusively with *a/ya* as a sentence-final particle. Closer examination shows that most of those meanings can be understood on the basis of the meaning of the sentence to which *a/ya* is attached. In other words, most of those various meanings should not be attributed to *a/ya*. We have considered questions. Let us now examine the other meanings Chao attributes to *a/ya*.

(i) "Confirmation question": In Mandarin one can seek confirmation simply by using a question intonation. Thus, if A thinks B has said that s/he will come here, and wishes to get a confirmation, A can ask either (249), which is a declarative sentence with rising intonation, or (250), which uses the sentence-final particle *a/ya*:

(249)   nǐ   lái ?
            you   come

Are you coming?

(250)   nǐ   lái   a̲ ?
            you   come   RF

Are you coming?

Both (249) and (250) are confirmation questions in the context given for them. Contrasting them reveals that (250) is less forceful and more endearing or more polite than (249). Hence, *a* in (250) performs the function of reducing the force of the question, but it does not by itself signal that the question is a confirmation question.

(ii) "Vocative particle": Chao has correctly observed that uttering a name with the particle *a/ya* has a less blunt effect than a direct address without any particle. "Vocative" is not, however, the function or the meaning of *a/ya*. Both (251) *a* and (251) *b* are vocative because they directly address the hearer; the difference is that (251) *b* is less blunt or more friendly.

(251) *a.*   Zhāngsān!

     b.   Zhāngsān a̲/ya̲!

(iii) "Commands": *A/ya* occurs with commands. Again, however, it is not the function of *a/ya* to signal that the utterance is a command. Rather, the utterance itself signals that it is a command, and *a/ya* has the usual function of reducing the forcefulness of the command. For example, if we take the utterance in (249) and change the intonation from a question intonation (rising) to a command intonation (falling), we have the command:

(252) nǐ   lái !
      you   come

    You come here!

If the particle *a/ya* is added to (252) to form (253),

(253) nǐ   lái   a/ya
      you   come   RF

    You come here.

then sentence (253) conveys the message that it is more of a suggestion or an encouragement than a command. This is because *a/ya* has the function of reducing the forcefulness of the utterance.

Another pair of examples is:

(254) *a.* chī   —   fàn !
         eat   —   food

    Eat!

    b. chī   —   fàn   a/ya
         eat   —   food   RF

    Eat, OK?!

Sentence (254) *b* is a much more friendly comand than (254) *a*. One can imagine (254) *a* being used by a marine sergeant addressing the recruits in a mess hall. In such a context, it would be strange for the marine sergeant to use (254) *b*, as marine sergeants are notorious for being harsh martinets. On the other hand, one can imagine a context in which a concerned parent is urging his/her child to eat. Such a context would be perfect for (254) *b* but inappropriate for (254) *a*.

   (iv) ''Impatient statement'': *A/ya* may occur with an utterance that signals impatience. Once again, however, it is not *a/ya* but the utterance itself that conveys the message that the speaker is impatient. *A/ya* functions merely to reduce the force of the message, as can be illustrated by the following pair of sentences. Sentence (255) is an example of Chao's (1968:805); let's contrast it with (256):

(255)	wǒ	bìng	méi	zuò	—	cuò	a/ya
	I	on:the:contrary	not	do	—	wrong	RF

On the contrary, I didn't do wrong.

(256)	wǒ	bìng	méi	zuò	—	cuò
	I	on:the:contrary	not	do	—	wrong

On the contrary, I didn't do wrong.

Both (255) and (256) can be used to convey the message that the speaker is impatient. What suggests impatience in these sentences is the negative meaning of each statement and the use of the adverb *bìng* 'on the contrary'.

There is also, however, a difference between the total message conveyed by (255) and that conveyed by (256): (255) is the more conciliatory, less belligerent statement. One can imagine (255) being uttered in a dispute between two friends or relatives. An appropriate situation for the use of (256), on the other hand, would be one in which two people are arguing in a courtroom; for example, (256), but not (255), could be said by an unfriendly witness to the lawyer.

(v) "Warning": *A/ya* may occur in a sentence that serves as a warning. Again, *a/ya* does not make an utterance into a warning. Consider this example provided by Chao (1968:805):

(257)	zhèi	—	ge	rén	—	de	huà	shì
	this	—	CL	person	—	GEN	speech	be

	kào	—	bu	—	zhù	de	a
	rely	—	can't	—	hold:on	NOM	RF

This person's words are unreliable.

The warning message of (257) is inferred from the literal meaning of the sentence, namely, 'This person's words are unreliable'. Let us contrast (257) with (258), in which *a* is not used:

(258)	zhèi	—	ge	rén	—	de	huà	shì
	this	—	CL	person	—	GEN	speech	be

	kào	—	bu	—	zhù	de
	rely	—	can't	—	hold:on	NOM

This person's words are unreliable.

Both (257) and (258) are warnings because both have the same basic meaning; but (258), without the sentence-final particle *a/ya*, is more urgent, more official, and more detached than (257). If a military intelligence chief is briefing subordinates about a certain informant, (258) will be appropriate, but (257), with *a/ya*, will be awkward. On the other hand, (257) would be appropriate as avuncular advice warning a young person not to trust 'this person's words'. Thus, *a/ya* again has the function that was described at the beginning of this section: to reduce the forcefulness of the message conveyed by the utterance.

7.6 Conclusion

Traditional Chinese grammar refers to the sentence-final particles as *yŭqì cí* 'mood words'; this term aptly suggests that the function of these sentence-final particles is to relate to the conversational context in various ways the utterance to which they are attached and to indicate how this utterance is to be taken by the hearer.

Notes

1. Discussions with the following people have helped to shape the presentation in this section: Dale Elliott, Mary Erbaugh, Huang Shuan-fan, Robert McCoard, Claudia Ross, George Spanos, and R. McMillan Thompson. We have also adapted some ideas from Chao (1968) and Spanos (1977, 1979). Nearly all the examples in this chapter have been taken from actual conversations. For a more technical discussion of the ideas presented here, see Li, Thompson, and Thompson (forthcoming).

2. In speech *le* and *a* typically merge into *la*.

3. In sentences that end with a verb plus a ''*le*,'' it is sometimes difficult to tell whether this ''*le*'' is the perfective verbal suffix *-le* (see chapter 6) or the CRS sentence-final particle *le*. We consider the ''*le*'' in sentence (7) to be a combination of the two forms of ''*le*,'' which we will write as *LE*. This combination of the two forms is discussed in section 7.1.3 of this chapter.

4. In fact, this change-of-state meaning, which is actually just one of the functions of *le*, has been taken as its only meaning by most grammarians, who ignore its other functions altogether; Chao (1968) and Spanos (1977, 1979) are exceptions.

5. See section 6.1 of chapter 6 for discussion of the perfective -le. In the context given for (112), it implies that more poems are to be memorized, but, of course, this is not a necessary implication of such "double LE" sentences, as example (108) above clearly shows.

6. This is the class of le examples which is sometimes referred to as expressing *imminent action*. This is not a very helpful term, unfortunately, since many sentences that express imminent actions do not have to take le simply because they do not involve announcement of a new situation, such as:

(i)	wǒ	qù	huàn	yixiē	qián
	I	go	change	some	money

I'm going to go change some money.

(ii)	wǒ	qù	pào	yixiē	chá
	I	go	brew	some	tea

I'm going to go make some tea.

(iii)	wǒ	hē	yi	bēi	kāfēi
	I	drink	one	glass	coffee

I'll have a cup of coffee.

7. The distinction between *a* and *ya* is a matter of which dialect of Mandarin one speaks.

CHAPTER 8

Adverbs

Adverbs in Mandarin typically occur after the subject or after the topic if there is no subject (see section 4.1 of chapter 4 for a discussion of topic and subject).[1] For example:

(1) Zhāngsān   <u>gāng</u>   lái
     Zhangsan   just   come

Zhangsan has just arrived.

(2) Zhāngsān   <u>tài</u>   gāo
     Zhangsan   too   tall

Zhangsan is too tall.

(3) Zhāngsān   <u>zhēn</u>   cōngming
     Zhangsan   truly   smart

Zhangsan is really smart.

(4) Zhāngsān   <u>cháng(chang)</u>   tiàowǔ
     Zhangsan   frequently   dance

Zhangsan dances frequently.

(5) píngguǒ Zhāngsān zhǐ   mǎi   —   le   yi   —   ge
    apple Zhangsan only   buy   —   PFV   one —   CL

Apples, Zhangsan bought only one.

When a sentence contains both an adverb and an auxiliary verb, the adverb always precedes the auxiliary verb. In other words, the adverb remains immediately after the subject, as here:

(6) Zhāngsān yídìng   néng   tiàowǔ
    Zhangsan definitely can   dance

Zhangsan definitely can dance.

In this chapter, we will discuss several types of adverbs, which can be classified as follows:
1. Movable adverbs, which occur either at the beginning of the sentence or after the topic or subject, and modify the entire sentence
   a. time adverbs
   b. attitude adverbs
2. Nonmovable adverbs, which occur only after the topic or subject
   a. manner adverbs
   b. nonmanner adverbs
3. Postverbal adverbials, which occur only after the verb and signal frequency or duration

8.1 Movable Adverbs

Certain adverbs may occur not only after the topic of a sentence but also in sentence-initial position, that is, preceding the topic. These adverbs are often called *movable adverbs*, meaning that they may occur either before or after the topic or subject of a sentence. One of the major functional characteristics of the movable adverbs is that they are *sentential* adverbs, in the sense that they provide a semantic frame within which the event described by the sentence occurs. The frame may be time related, as signaled by such adverbs as *míngtiān* 'tomorrow', or attitudinal, as signaled by such adverbs as *xiǎnrán* 'obviously'.

8.1.1 Movable Adverbs of Time

The first subgroup of movable adverbs is the set of *time adverbs*, including *jīntiān* 'today', *qùnián* 'last year', *jiānglái* '(in the) future', *jìnlái* 'recently', *xiànzài* 'now', *xiàwŭ* '(in the) afternoon', *zhànshí* 'temporarily', *sān-diănzhōng* '(at) three o'clock', *gāng(gang)* 'just now'. For example:

(7) *a.*

jīntiān	wŏ	bu	shūfu
today	I	not	comfortable

Today I don't feel well.

b.

wŏ	jīntiān	bu	shūfu
I	today	not	comfortable

Today I don't feel well.

(8) *a.*

zhànshí	wŏ	zhù	zài	zhèr
temporarily	I	live	at	here

Temporarily I live here.

b.

wŏ	zhànshí	zhù	zài	zhèr
I	temporarily	live	at	here

Temporarily I live here.

These time adverbs clearly function as sentential adverbs; they typically signal the time at which or during which the entire event described by the sentence occurs. In this respect they contrast with a semantically similar set of adverbs, such as *yĭjing* 'already' or *chángcháng* 'frequently', which are associated with the verb rather than with the entire sentence.

8.1.2 Movable Adverbs of Attitude

The other subset of movable adverbs are *attitude adverbs*, those that denote the speaker's attitude toward or evaluation of the event expressed by the sentence. For example, consider the adverb *xiănrán* 'obviously' in (9):

(9) *a.*

xiănrán	Zhāngsān	bu	gāoxing
obviously	Zhangsan	not	happy

Obviously, Zhangsan is not happy.

    b.   Zhāngsān   <u>xiǎnrán</u>   bu   gāoxing
         Zhangsan   obviously   not   happy

    Obviously, Zhangsan is not happy.

What (9) *a* and *b* express is that it is obvious *to the speaker* of the sentence that Zhangsan is not happy. Thus the adverb *xiǎnrán* 'obvious' in (9) conveys information concerning the attitude of the *speaker* of the sentence. In contrast, consider the nonmovable manner adverb *jìng-jìng-de* 'quietly' in (10):

(10)   tā   <u>jìng-jìng-de</u>   zuò   zài   nàr
        3sg   quietly   sit   at   there

    Quietly, s/he sat there.

As (10) shows, *jìng-jìng-de* 'quietly' has nothing to do with the evaluation of the *speaker*, but rather describes the manner in which the subject, *tā* 's/he', behaved. Other attitude adverbs include: *yěxǔ* 'perhaps', *dàgài (dàyue)* 'more or less', *xìngkuī* 'fortunately', *nándào* 'Is it conceivable . . . ?', *jiùjing* 'after all, in the end', *dāngrán* 'of course', *tūrán (hūrán)* 'suddenly', *yuánlai (běnlai)* 'originally', *qíshi* 'in fact', and *fǎnzhèng (héngshù, hǎodǎi)* 'in any case', as well as some of the sentence-linking adverbs discussed in chapter 23.

8.2 Nonmovable Adverbs

As we have indicated above, the vast majority of adverbs in Mandarin are *nonmovable adverbs*: that is, they occur only in the position immediately following the subject or topic and before the verb. Two main groups of nonmovable adverbs may be established: manner adverbs and nonmanner adverbs. We will discuss them separately in this section.

8.2.1 Manner Adverbs

Manner adverbs, as the name indicates, modify the verb phrase by signaling the manner in which the action of the verb phrase is carried out. With a few exceptions, such as *gùyi* 'on purpose', manner adverbs are derived from adjectives. The process by which an adjective becomes an adverb involves the addition of the suffix *-de* and, for many adjectives, reduplication as well. For example, the adjective *kuài* 'quick' can be transformed into an adverb, as in (11), through reduplication and the addition of the suffix *-de*:

(11)   tā   <u>kuài-kuài-de</u>   zǒu
         3sg   quickly   walk

        S/He walked quickly.

When the adjective is disyllabic, the strategy of reduplication is to reduplicate each syllable independently, as in *kuài-kuài-lè-lè-de* 'happily' from *kuàilè* 'happy', *shū-shū-fú-fú-de* 'comfortably' from *shūfu* 'comfortable'. (For further discussion on reduplication, see section 3.1.1. of chapter 3.)²

Many currently used manner adverbs are derived from adjectives that have recently come into Mandarin as a result of the influence of Indo-European languages. Most of these adjectives can be made into adverbs simply by the addition of the suffix *-de* without reduplication, as in *xīngfèn* 'excited': *xīngfèn-de* 'excitedly'; *zǐxì* 'meticulous': *zǐxì-de* 'meticulously'; *kuàilè* 'happy': *kuàilè-de* 'happily'; *jiǎndān* 'simple': *jiǎndān-de* 'simply'; *zhèndìng* 'calm': *zhèndìng-de* 'calmly'.

Semantically, manner adverbs in general describe the manner in which the subject carries out an activity. Here are some examples:

(12)   tā   <u>xīngfèn-de</u>   pǎo   −   jìn   −   lai
         3sg   excitedly   run   −   enter   −   come

        S/He excitedly ran in.

(13)   tā   <u>jìng-jìng-de</u>   tǎng   zài   cǎo   −   shang
         3sg   quietly   lie   at   grass   −   on

        S/He quietly lay on the grass.

(14)   wǒ   <u>yánli-de</u>   zébèi   tā   le
         I   sternly   reproach   3sg   CRS

        I sternly reproached him/her.

A special problem arises, however, when manner adverbs occur in *bèi* sentences (see chapter 16).[3] Let us briefly describe the *bèi* construction here:

(15)   noun phrase$_1$ bèi   noun phrase$_2$ verb

In this schema, the first noun phrase, in sentence-initial position, is typically the direct object, *bèi* or one of its variants is the passive marker, and the second noun phrase is the agent, as in:

(16)   Zhāngsān   bèi   Lǐsì   pīping   LE
       Zhangsan   BEI   Lisi   criticize PFV/CRS

       Zhangsan was criticized by Lisi.

For convenience, we will refer to the first noun phrase as NP_1 and to the second noun phrase, the *bèi* noun phrase, as NP_2. Since adverbs normally occur immediately after the first noun phrase, which is usually the subject, we expect them to be placed immediately after NP_1 in the passive construction. This is indeed true with most adverbs, as in (17) and (18):

(17) Zhāngsān <u>yǐjīng</u>   bèi   Lǐsì   pīping   LE
     Zhangsan already   BEI   Lisi   criticize PFV/CRS

     Zhangsan has already been criticized by Lisi.

(18) Zhāngsān <u>zuótiān</u>   bèi   Lǐsì   pīping   LE
     Zhangsan yesterday BEI   Lisi   criticize PFV/CRS

     Yesterday, Zhangsan was criticized by Lisi.

Many manner adverbs, however, have meanings that can modify an action only with regard to the *agent*. We call these manner adverbs *agent-oriented adverbs*. Some examples of agent-oriented adverbs are: *gōngpíng-de* 'fairly, justly', *yánlì-de* 'sternly', *jiāoào-de* 'arrogantly', *yǒu-lǐmào-de* 'politely', *zhèndìng-de* 'calmly', *cánrěn-de* 'cruelly', *yěmán-de* 'savagely'. These agent-oriented manner adverbs cannot be placed immediately after NP_1, the regular adverbial position, in a passive sentence; for example, (19) is unacceptable:

(19) *Zhāngsān <u>gōngpíng-de</u>   bèi   Lǐsì   pīping   LE
       Zhangsan   justly   BEI   Lisi   criticize PFV/CRS

Instead, the agent-oriented adverb must be placed immediately after NP$_2$, the agent, as in:

(20) Zhāngsān   bèi   Lǐsì   <u>gōngpíng-de</u> pīping   LE
       Zhangsan   BEI   Lisi   justly   criticize PFV/CRS

      Zhangsan was justly criticized by Lisi.

The reason for this distributional property of agent-oriented adverbs is straight-forward: since the agent-oriented adverb comments on the agent, not the direct object, it should follow the agent instead of the direct object.

Manner adverbs whose meanings do not necessarily comment on the agent, on the other hand, may occur either immediately after NP$_1$ or after NP$_2$ in the *bèi* construction. As we might expect, though, there is a meaning difference: the manner adverb that is not expressly agent oriented describes whichever noun phrase it immediately follows. As an example, consider the adverb *gāo-gāo-xìng-xìng-de* 'happily', as in (21):

(21) *a.* Zhāngsān   <u>gāo-gāo-xìng-xìng-de</u>   bèi   Lǐsì   kuājiǎng
            Zhangsan   happily   BEI   Lisi   praise

                   —   le   yi   dùn
                   —   PFV   one   time

      Zhangsan was happy in being praised by Lisi.

      b. Zhāngsān   bèi   Lǐsì   <u>gāo-gāo-xìng-xìng-de</u> kuājiǎng
            Zhangsan   BEI   Lisi   happily   praise

                   —   le   yi   dùn
                   —   PFV   one   time

      Zhangsan was praised in a happy way by Lisi.

As our English translations suggest (though somewhat inadequately), in (21) *a*, 'happily' refers to Zhangsan, whereas in (21) *b*, 'happily' refers to Lisi. Anot^er such example is *kōng-shǒu* 'empty-handed':

(22) *a.* Zhāngsān kōng — shǒu bèi Lìsì zhìfú LE
        Zhangsan empty — hand BEI Lisi subdued PFV/CRS

    Zhangsan, empty-handed, was subdued by Lisi.

   b. Zhāngsān bèi Lìsì kōng — shǒu zhìfú LE
        Zhangsan BEI Lisi empty — hand subdue PFV/CRS

    Zhangsan was subdued by Lisi empty-handedly.

Again, the understanding of precisely who is empty-handed changes according to the position of the manner adverb *kōng-shǒu*, which is not agent oriented. Other examples of non-agent-oriented manner adverbs are: *mǎn-tóu-dà-hàn-de* literally 'full-head-big-sweat', meaning 'covered with perspiration'; *zìyóu-zìzài-de* 'nonchalantly'; *xiū-xiū-de* 'bashfully'; *hūn-tóu-hūn-nǎo-de* literally 'faint-head-faint-brain', meaning 'muddleheadedly'; *jiāojí-de* 'anxiously'; and *mè-mè-de* 'quietly'.

Similarly, adverbial clauses formed with the durative aspect marker *-zhe* (see section 6.2.2 of chapter 6) behave in exactly the same way in passives as do agent-oriented adverbs: which noun they refer to depends on their position. The meaning contrast is quite clear here:

(23) *a.* Zhāngsān guāng — zhe jiǎo bèi Lìsì tī
        Zhangsan bare — DUR foot BEI Lisi kick

        — shāng LE
        — injure PFV/CRS

    Zhangsan, barefooted, was kicked to the point of injury by Lisi.

   b. Zhāngsān bèi Lìsì guāng — zhe jiǎo
        Zhangsan BEI Lisi bare — DUR foot

        tī — shāng LE
        kick — injure PFV/CRS

    Zhangsan was kicked to the point of injury by Lisi, who was barefooted.

There are, however, certain other manner adverbs that may occur either after NP₁, the direct object, or after NP₂, the agent, but that *always* comment on NP₁, the *direct object*. These adverbs include, for example, *bu-zhī-bu-jué-de* 'unknowingly', *bàn-shēng-bàn-sǐ-de* 'half-dead', *huó-shēng-shēng-de* 'alive':

(24) *a.*

Zhāngsān	bu-zhī-bu-jué-de	bèi	Lǐsì	gǎn	—
Zhangsan	unknowingly	BEI	Lisi	chase	—

shàng	—	qù	LE
ascend	—	go	PFV/CRS

Zhangsan, unknowingly, was surpassed by Lisi.

b.

Zhāngsān	bèi	Lǐsì	bu-zhī-bu-jué-de	gǎn	—
Zhangsan	BEI	Lisi	unknowingly	chase	—

shàng	—	qù	LE
ascend	—	go	PFV/CRS

Zhangsan, unknowingly, was surpassed by Lisi.

In both (24) *a* and (24) *b*, the adverb *bu-zhī-bu-jué-de* 'unknowingly' describes the direct object, *Zhāngsān*, but cannot describe the agent, *Lǐsì*. The reason for this is simply that in the "real" world on which language comments, it is much more likely that if one person is doing something to another, the one who can be unknowing is the direct object rather than the agent.

In passive sentences, then, the meaning of the manner adverb determines both what position it can take and whether it can be understood to describe the agent or the direct object.

In present-day Mandarin, again because of the influence of Indo-European languages, particularly English, certain manner adverbs can also be derived from abstract nouns—for example, *kēxué-de* 'scientifically' from *kēxué* 'science', *chuàngzào-xìng-de* 'creatively' from *chuàngzào-xìng* 'creativity', *juédìng-xìng-de* 'decisively' from *juédìng-xìng* 'decisiveness':

(25)

wǒmen	kēxué-de	yánjiū	nèi	—	ge	wèntí
we	scientifically	research	that	—	CL	problem

We will research that problem scientifically.

(26) wŏmen chuàngzào-xìng-de jiějué nèi — ge wèntí
      we   creatively   solve   that — CL problem

We will solve that problem creatively.

Onomatopoeic adverbs constitute another class of manner adverbs. They are formed in imitation of the natural sounds associated with various actions.

(27) nèi   — ge zhōng dīngdāng-dīngdāng-de xiǎng
      that — CL bell   make:noise

That bell makes noise in a dingdong-dingdong manner.

As a general rule, onomatopoeic manner adverbs take the suffix -de. Occasionally, though, -de may be optionally deleted, as in this example:

(28) tā   pècā diē — le   yi jiāo
      3sg   fall — PFV a   fall

S/He fell down with a thud.

8.2.2 Nonmanner Adverbs

The class of nonmovable *nonmanner adverbs* includes such forms as *yǐjīng* 'already', *yìzhí* 'straight', *cháng* 'often', and *zǎo* 'early', as in:

(29) tā   yǐjīng   zǒu   le
      3sg already leave CRS

S/He's already left.

Because of certain interesting semantic properties, we have chosen to discuss the following members of this class in slightly greater detail: *yě* 'also', *zài* 'again', *jiù* 'only', immediately, emphatic, thereupon (then)', *zhǐ* 'only', *hěn* 'very', *cái* 'just now, only then', *dōu* 'all', *hái* 'still', and *yòu* 'again'.[4]

A. *yòu* and *zài*

Zài 'again' refers to events that have not yet happened, whereas *yòu* 'again' applies either to past or to present events. The following sample sentences will illustrate:

(30) *a.*

tā	yòu	chī	le
3sg	again	eat	CRS

S/He is eating again.

b.

tā	zuótiān	yòu	chī	le
3sg	yesterday	again	eat	CRS

S/He ate again yesterday.

c.

*tā	míngtiān	yòu	chī	le
3sg	tomorrow	again	eat	CRS

Sentence (30) *c* is ungrammatical because the presence of *míngtiān* 'tomorrow' indicates an event that has not yet occurred. On the other hand, *zài* 'again' can never be used to refer to events that have occurred or are occurring. Thus, (31) *a* is unacceptable:

(31) *a.*

*tā	zuótiān	zài	chī
3sg	yesterday	again	eat

b.

tā	míngtiān	zài	chī
3sg	tomorrow	again	eat

S/He'll eat again tomorrow.

Zài 'again' can occur in commands (the imperative construction), where the action is in the future with respect to the time of the utterance:

(32)

(nǐ)	zài	chī !
(you)	again	eat

(You) eat again!

Zài 'again' can also occur with events that have *not yet* happened *again*, as in:

(33) Lăo   Zhāng   líkāi   —   le   zhèr   yǐhòu ,   tā
      Old   Zhang   depart   —   PFV   here   after   3sg

      jiu   méiyou   zài   huí   —   lái   —
      then   not   again   return   —   come   —

      guo
      EXP

After Old Zhang left here, he has never come back.

The semantic difference between *yòu* and *zài* can be nicely illustrated by the following pair of sentences:

(34) *a.*   tā   míngtiān   yòu   yào   chī   le
            3sg   tomorrow   again   want   eat   CRS

S/He again wants to eat tomorrow.

b.   tā   míngtiān   yào   zài   chī
       3sg   tomorrow   want   again   eat

S/He wants to eat again tomorrow.

In (34) *a*, *yòu* 'again' is used to convey that s/he 'again *wants*', a present event, while in (34) *b*, *zài* is used to say that s/he'll 'again *eat*', an event that has not yet happened.

In certain contexts, *yòu* has the meaning 'also' rather than 'again'. For example, consider sentence (35):

(35) tā   dài   —   le   yi   —   zhi   māo ,
      3sg   bring   —   PFV   one   —   CL   cat

      yòu   măi   —   le   yi   —   tiáo
      also   buy   —   PFV   one   —   CL

      gŏu
      dog

S/He brought a cat and also purchased a dog.

Whether the adverb *yòu* means 'again' or 'also' depends completely on the discourse context.

B. *jiù*

A very common use of *jiù* is as a sentence-linking element meaning 'then, thereupon' (see chapter 23 on sentence linking). In this usage, it normally has a neutral tone, as in (36):

(36)	wǒ	lái	–	le	yǐhou ,	tā	jiù	bu	gāoxìng
	I	come	–	PFV	after	3sg	then	not	happy

After I came, s/he became unhappy.

Jiù can also be used in a simple sentence to mean 'immediately' or 'soon with respect to the time of utterance'. With this meaning, of course, it can never describe events in the past. Sentence (37) illustrates this point:

(37) *a.*	wǒ	jiù	qù
	I	soon	go

I'll soon go.

b.	*wǒ	zuótiān	jiù	qù
	I	yesterday	soon	go

When *jiù* is used as an emphatic particle, it receives special stress and optionally takes the destressed copula verb *shi* 'be' with a neutral tone:

(38)	tā	jiù	(shi)	zuò	zài	nàr
	3sg	emphatic	(be)	sit	at	there

S/He simply sat there.

Jiù may also mean 'only':

(39)	tā	jiù	xǐhuān	Zhāngsān
	3sg	only	like	Zhangsan

S/He likes only Zhangsan.

Again, the precise meaning of *jiù* in a sentence must be determined on the basis of contextual factors.

C. *zhǐ*

Zhǐ unambiguously means 'only'. Since it is a predicate-modifying adverb in Mandarin, it modifies solely the entire predicate phrase, as does *jiù* 'only'; for example:

(40) wǒmen   zhǐ   yào   kāfēi
      we   only   want   coffee

We only want coffee.

That is, it can never modify a noun phrase alone, as 'only' can in English. Thus, while sentence (41) *a* is acceptable English, its Mandarin equivalent, (41) *b*, is not acceptable:

(41) *a*. Only passengers can board the ship.

   b.   *zhǐ   zuò   chuán   de   kěyǐ   shàng   chuán
        only   ride   boat   NOM   can   ascend   boat

D. *cái*

Cái basically has two meanings: 'just now' and 'only then'. In the first meaning, 'just now', it is synonymous with the adverb *gāng*:

(42)   wǒ   cái   dào
       I   just   arrive

I've just arrived.

In the second meaning of *cái*, 'only then', it must refer back to some element specifying a time or a set of conditions under which the predicate with *cái* holds true. This element can be a word or a phrase earlier in the same clause, as in:

(43)   wǒ   míngtiān   cái   zǒu   ne
    I   tomorrow   only:then leave   REx

I'm not leaving until tomorrow.

(44) | zuì | yǒu | qián | de | rén | cái | néng |
|-----|-----|------|-----|-----|-----|------|
| most | exist | money | NOM | person | only:then | can |

	mǎi	zhèi	—	zhǒng	cíqì
	buy	this	—	kind	porcelain

Only the most wealthy can buy this kind of porcelain.

The element specifying the time or conditions under which the predicate holds can also be located in a previous clause. For example:

(45) | wǒ | zuótian | lái | kàn | nǐ , | tā | cái |
|-----|---------|-----|-----|------|-----|-----|
| I | yesterday | come | see | you | 3sg | only:then |

	bu	gāoxing
	not	happy

I came to see you yesterday; only then did s/he become unhappy.

(46) | wǒ | dào | — | le | nàr | cái | niàn |
|-----|-----|---|-----|-----|-----|------|
| I | arrive | — | PFV | there | only:then | study |

	—	shū
	—	book

I studied only after I arrived there.

(47) | yǒu | liǎng | — | ge | rén | cái | bān |
|-----|-------|---|-----|-----|-----|------|
| exist | two | — | CL | person | only:then | move |

	—	de	—	dòng
	—	can	move

Only if we have two people can we move it.

E. *hái, yě*

Hái has three meanings: 'still/even', 'also', and 'moderately'. Sentences (48)—
(50) illustrate *hái* meaning 'still':

(48) wǒmen   hái   bu   zhīdào
      we   still   not   know

We still don't know.

(49) tāmen   bǐ   wǒmen   hái   qióng
      they   COMP   we   still   poor

They are even poorer than we are.

(50) nǐmen   hái   yào   qù   ma ?
      you:PL   still   want   go   Q

Do you still want to go?

In this meaning, *hái* may optionally take on the copula verb:

(51)   tā   hái   (-shi)   xǐhuan   Lǐsì
        3sg   still   (-be)   like   Lisi

S/He still likes Lisi.

An important distinction must be made between *hái* meaning 'also' and *yě*
meaning 'also'. In the case of *hái*, the meaning 'also' is applied to the predicate,
not the subject, whereas in the case of *yě*, the meaning 'also' is applied to the
subject, not the predicate. For example:

(52) tā   hái   mǎi   —   le   yi   —   ge   huāpíng
      3sg   also   buy   —   PFV   one   —   CL   vase

S/He also bought a vase (in addition to buying some other things).

(53) tā   yě   mǎi   —   le   yi   —   ge   huāpíng
      3sg   also   buy   —   PFV   one   —   CL   vase

S/He (in addition to some other people) also bought a vase.

Other examples of *hái* meaning 'also' are these:

(54) zhèibiān   <u>hái</u>   yǒu   méiguì
  here   also exist rose

  There are also some roses over here.

(55) nǐ <u>hái</u> yǒu duōshǎo qián ?
   you also exist how:much money

  How much more money do you have?

Examples of *hái* meaning 'moderately' include:

(56) zhèi — gc bànfǎ <u>hái</u> kěyǐ
   this — CL method moderately OK

  This method is fairly good.

(57) A: nǐ zhù de dìfang zěnme — yàng ?
    you live NOM place how — way

  How is the place (where) you're living?

  B: <u>hái</u> hǎo
    moderately good

  It's not bad.

(58) tā <u>hái</u> nénggàn
   3sg moderately talented

  S/He is moderately talented.

F. *dōu, lián . . . dōu/yě*

Dōu 'all' is unique among the adverbs in Mandarin: it can refer only to a *preceding* noun phrase, and this noun phrase is generally the topic or the subject.[5]

In (59) *dōu* 'all' refers to the topic, and in (60) it refers to the subject:

(59)   zhèi   —   xie   háizi   wǒ   dōu   xīhuān
         this   —   PL   child   I   all   like

       I like all these children.

(60)   zhèi   —   ge   háizi   wǒmen   dōu   xīhuān
         this   —   CL   child   we   all   like

       We all like this child.

That is, in (59) it is *all of the children* whom I like, while in (60), it is *all of us* who like the child. In each of these sentences, since *dōu* 'all' can refer only to a preceding plural noun phrase, the interpretation given is the only one possible. If both the topic and the subject were plural, then we would predict that the *dōu* could refer to either one, and this is indeed true—such sentences have three interpretations:

(61)   zhèi   —   xie   háizi   wǒmen   dōu   xīhuān
         this   —   PL   child   we   all   like

     (i)   Dōu refers to the topic: 'We like all these children'.
    (ii)   Dōu refers to the subject: 'We all like these children'.
   (iii)   Dōu refers to both: 'We all like all these children'.

Sentences (59)−(61) illustrate that *dōu* can refer to any semantically eligible *preceding* noun phrase. What *dōu* cannot do is refer to a noun phrase *after* it:

(62) *a*.   wǒ   xīhuān   zhèi   —   xiē   háizi
         I   like   this   —   PL   child

       I like these children.

    b.   *wǒ   dōu   xīhuān   zhèi   —   xiē   háizi
         I   all   like   this   —   PL   child

       (I like all these children.)*

*Cf. example (59).

If the noun phrase referred to by *dōu* denotes two referents, then *dōu* can be translated as 'both':

(63)

zhèi	—	zhí	niǎo	gēn	nèi	—	zhi
this	—	CL	bird	and	that	—	CL

niǎo	dōu	shi	wǒ	—	de
bird	all	be	I	—	GEN

This bird and that bird are both mine.

Of course, *dōu* 'all' can also be used to refer to all of one thing or to a mass noun:

(64)

jīntian	—	de	bàozhi	wǒ	dōu	kàn	le
today	—	ASSOC	paper	I	all	read	CRS

I have read all of today's paper.

(65)

píjiǔ	dōu	hē	—	guāng	le
beer	all	drink	—	gone	CRS

The beer has all been drunk up.

In our definition of nonmovable adverbs, we said that they must occur after the subject (if there is one) or after the topic (if there is no subject) and before the verb. This means that in most sentences there will be just one position in which the *dōu* will occur. In sentences with certain kinds of coverb phrases (see chapter 9), however, which also occur after the subject or topic and before the verb, *dōu* could come either before or after the coverb phrase. When this happens, there is a meaning difference: *dōu* refers to the plural noun phrase *immediately* preceding it. Here are two examples:

(66)

wǒmen	bǎ	zhèi	—	xie	shū	dōu	sòng
we	BA	this	—	PL	book	all	give

gěi	wǒmen	—	de	péngyǒu
to	we	—	GEN	friend

We gave all the books to our friend.

(67) wǒmen   dōu   bǎ   zhèi   —   běn   shū   sòng
      we   all   BA   this   —   CL   book   give

      gěi   lǎoshī
      to   teacher

We all gave this book to the teacher.

The *lián . . . dōu/yě* construction singles out one part of the sentence with the meaning 'even'. It is formed by putting the particle *lián* before the element being singled out. This element must occur at some point in the sentence before *dōu* (or *yě*, which is interchangeable with *dōu*), but not necessarily immediately before it. For example,

(68) lián   tā   dōu   shēngqì
      even   3sg   all   angry

Even s/he is angry.

(69) *a*.   wǒ   lián   tā   dōu   bu   xǐhuan
            I   even   3sg   all   not   like

I don't even like him/her.

    b.   lián   tā   wǒ   dōu   bu   xǐhuan
            even   3sg   I   all   not   like

I don't even like him/her.

In (69) *a lián tā* 'even him/her' occurs after the subject, and in (69) *b* it occurs before the subject; the meanings are the same.

The element being singled out by *lián* can be a verb phrase or a coverb phrase:

(70) tā   lián   dǎ   —   zì   dōu   bu   huì
      3sg   even   hit   —   character   all   not   know:how

S/He doesn't even know how to type.

(71) tā   lián   gēn   tā   nǚér   dōu   bu   shuō
      3sg even   with 3sg   daughter all   not speak

      —   huà
      —   speech

S/He doesn't even speak to his/her daughter.

G. *hěn*

The adverb *hěn* 'very' is most frequently found preceding an adjectival verb, as in:

(72) tā   hěn   gāo
      3sg very tall

S/He is very tall.

Certain verb-object compounds are adjectival because of their idiomatic meaning. Such compounds can be modified by *hěn* as long as they function as adjectival verbs, as in these examples:

(73) *a.* tā   hěn   yǒu   —   qián
           3sg very exist —   money

S/He is very rich.

b. nèi — jiàn gǔdǒng hěn   yǒu   —   jiàzhi
      that — CL   antique very exist —   value

That antique piece is very valuable.

c. zhèi — ge   rén   hěn   yǒu   —   quán
      this — CL   person very exist —   power

This person is very powerful.

Other than adjectival verbs, certain experiential verbs are the only ones that can take the adverbial modifier *hěn*. These experiential verbs constitute a semantic class of verbs whose function it is to signal the mental disposition of an animate being. Here are some examples:

(74)   tā   hěn   xiǎng   wǒ
         3sg   very   miss   I

S/He misses me a lot.

(75)   wǒ   hěn   pà   gǒu
         I   very   afraid   dog

I am very afraid of dogs.

(76)   wǒmen   hěn   zhùzhòng   cáigàn
         we   very   emphasize competence

We put a lot of emphasis on competence.

In spoken Mandarin, the adverb *hěn* occurring with an adjectival verb usually loses its semantic content when it is destressed. In such a case, we say its meaning is *bleached*. Thus, for example, (72) can simply mean:

(77) S/He is tall.

8.3 Negation and Adverbs

Although negation is discussed in depth in chapter 12, it should be noted here that the negative particles *bu* and *méi(yǒu)* typically occur immediately after the topic or subject of a sentence and are themselves adverbs. In this section, we will confine our discussion of negation to its interaction with other adverbs.

8.3.1 Negation and Movable Adverbs

In languages of the world, the *scope* of an element such as a negative particle or an adverb is that portion of the sentence which is semantically *affected* by that element. We can say that the material that is semantically affected by a certain element is in the semantic *domain* of that element. In general, the material in the scope of a given element is the material *following* that element. Thus, the scope of the negative particle is typically the predicate, which is that portion of the sentence following it:

(78) Zhāngsān   <u>bu</u>   xǐhuan   Lǐsì
     Zhangsan   not   like   Lisi

Zhangsan does not like Lisi.

In other words, in (78) *bu* 'not' serves to negate *xǐhuan Lǐsì* 'like Lisi'; it does not negate *Zhāngsān*.

Now, since movable adverbs are sentential adverbs in the sense that they provide a semantic frame for the sentence, we do not expect negation to include the movable adverb in its scope. In fact, since negation typically negates the predicate, we should expect to find the entire negative sentence or predicate in the scope of the movable adverb. Since the movable adverb does not fall in the scope of the negative particle, it is natural, then, that the *movable adverb should precede, not follow, the negative particle*. This is confirmed by the fact that (79) *a* and *b* are acceptable, but (79) *c* is not. The movable adverb is *yǒu-(de)-shíhou* 'sometimes':

(79) *a*.   <u>yǒu</u>   —   (de)   —   shíhou   Zhāngsān   <u>bu</u>
       exist   —   (NOM)   —   time   Zhangsan   not

       xǐhuan   Lǐsì
       like   Lisi

Sometimes Zhangsan does not like Lisi.

   b.   Zhāngsān   <u>yǒu</u>   —   (de)   —   shíhou   <u>bu</u>   xǐhuan   Lǐsí
      Zhangsan   exist   —   (NOM)   —   time   not   like   Lisi

Zhangsan sometimes does not like Lisi.

   c.   *Zhāngsān   <u>bu</u>   <u>yǒu</u>   —   (de)   —   shíhou
      Zhangsan   not   exist   —   (NOM)   —   time

      xǐhuan   Lǐsì
      like   Lisi

Examples (80) and (81) also show that a movable (i.e., sentence) adverb cannot be in the scope of the negative, but must have the entire negative sentence or predicate in its scope:

(80) *a.*

yĭqián	wŏ	bu	chōu	—	yān
formerly	I	not	extract	—	smoke

Formerly I didn't smoke.

b.

wŏ	yĭqián	bu	chōu	—	yān
I	formerly	not	extract	—	smoke

Formerly I didn't smoke.

c.

*wŏ	bu	yĭqián	chōu	—	yān
I	not	formerly	extract	—	smoke

(81) *a.*

xiàwŭ	wŏ	bu	zuò	—	shì
afternoon	I	not	do	—	work

I don't work in the afternoon.

b.

wŏ	xiàwŭ	bu	zuò	—	shì
I	afternoon	not	do	—	work

I don't work in the afternoon.

c.

*wŏ	bu	xiàwŭ	zuò	—	shì
I	not	afternoon	do	—	work

8.3.2 Negation and Nonmovable Adverbs

The interaction between negation and nonmovable adverbs, as we might expect, has to do with the meaning of the adverb in question and the scope of the adverb and the negative particle. The general rule is that when the negative has the adverb in its scope, then the order is:

(82) . . . Negative Adverb . . .

and when the adverb has the negative in its scope, then the order is:

(83) . . . Adverb Negative . . .

In other words, whichever element includes the other in its scope comes first. For example, consider (84):

(84) *a.*

tā	zīxì-de	zuò	—	shì
3sg	meticulously	do	—	work

S/He works meticulously.

b.

tā	bu	zīxì-de	zuò	—	shì
3sg	not	meticulously	do	—	work

S/He does not work meticulously.

c.

*tā	zīxì-de	bu	zuò	—	shì
3sg	meticulously	not	do	—	work

The meaning of *zīxì-de* 'meticulously' allows us to express the idea of 'doing an action but not in a meticulous way'. This is what (84) *b* means, and it is a perfectly acceptable sentence. We can think of the sentence as expressing the idea 'It is not meticulously that s/he works'. The meaning of *zīxì-de* does not, however, allow the possibility that one can be meticulous about *not* doing something. One can be *cautious* or *careful* not to do something, but not *meticulous*. *Zīxì-de* can describe only how an action is performed. This is why (84) *c* is not an acceptable sentence. What we have just said is simply another way of stating this general principle: Because of its meaning, *zīxì-de* 'meticulously' can be in the scope of *bu*, but it cannot have *bu* in its scope.

Most agent-oriented adverbs behave as does *zīxì-de* 'meticulously'. If they allow the negative particle at all, it must precede the adverb:

(85) *a.*

wǒmen	cánrěn-de	kǎowèn	tā
we	cruelly	interrogate	3sg

We interrogated him/her cruelly.

b.

wǒmen	bu	cánren-de	kǎowèn	tā[6]
we	not	cruelly	interrogate	3sg

We do not interrogate him/her cruelly.

    c. *wŏmen   cánrĕn-de   <u>bu</u>   kăowèn   tā
        we   cruelly   not   interrogate   3sg

(86) a. wŏmen   <u>yĕmán-de</u>   duìdài   tā
        we   savagely   treat   3sg

       We treated him/her savagely.

    b. wŏmen   <u>bu</u>   <u>yĕmán-de</u>   duìdài   tā[7]
        we   not   savagely   treat   3sg

       We did not treat him/her savagely.

    c. *wŏmen   <u>yĕmán-de</u>   <u>bu</u>   duìdài   tā
        we   savagely   not   treat   3sg

The reason for the unacceptability of (85) c and (86) c is the same as we gave above for (84) c: it is not possible to be *cruel* or *savage* about *not* doing something, about an action that does *not* take place.[8]

Onomatopoeic adverbs obey exactly the same principle. Onomatopoeic adverbs, as we said above, imitate the natural sound associated with the action named by the predicate. For instance,

(87) dà   yŭ   <u>huālālā-de</u>   dào   —   xià   —   lái
      big   rain   pour   —   descend   —   come

     Heavy rain poured down with the sound ''hualala.''

Since the onomatopoeic adverb denotes the sound associated with the action predicate, we do not expect to negate the predicate without including the adverb in the scope of negation. That is, we can talk about the rain falling without making a ''hualala'' sound:

(88) dà   yŭ   <u>méiyou</u>   <u>huālālā-de</u>   dào   —
      big   rain   not   pour   —

              xià   —   lái
              descend —   come

     The heavy rain did not pour down with the sound ''hualala.''

but it does not make sense to talk about the rain making such a sound if it did not fall at all!

| (89) | *dà | yǔ | huālālā-de | méiyou | dào | – |
| | big | rain | | not | pour | – |

| | xià | – | lái | |
| | descend | – | come | |

Now let's look at an example of exactly the opposite type. The negative particle must follow the adverb *hái* 'still':

| (90) *a.* | tā | hái | xǐhuan | Zhōngguó | cài |
| | 3sg | still | like | China | dish |

S/He still likes Chinese dishes.

| *b.* | *tā | bu | hái | xǐhuan | Zhōngguó | cài |
| | 3sg | not | still | like | China | dish |

| *c.* | tā | hái | bu | xǐhuan | Zhōngguó | cài |
| | 3sg | still | not | like | China | dish |

S/He still does not like Chinese dishes.

Here the meaning of the adverb *hái* 'still' is that some state of affairs which is true at the present time also used to be true previously; that state of affairs can be either affirmative, as in (90) *a*, or negative, as in (90) *c*. The message conveyed by (90) *c* is 'It is still the case that s/he does not like Chinese dishes'. It does not make any sense, however, for it to be 'not still' that s/he likes Chinese dishes, so (90) *b* is not acceptable. Hence, *hái* can have *bu* in its scope, but *bu* cannot have *hái* in its scope.

The nonmovable adverbs expressing time-related meanings which we discussed in section 8.2.2 above behave in exactly the same way as *hái*. These adverbs include *gāngang* 'just now', *yǐjīng* 'already', *jiù* 'then, thereupon', *cái* 'just now, only then'. For example:

| (91) *a.* | tā | gānggang | bu | shuō | – | huà |
| | 3sg | just:now | not | speak | – | speech |

S/He has shut up just now.

b.	*tā	<u>bu</u>	<u>gānggang</u>	shuō	—	huà
	3sg	not	just:now	speak	—	speech

(92) a.

tā	<u>yǐjīng</u>	<u>bu</u>	zuò	huài	shì	le
3sg	already	not	do	bad	deed	CRS

S/He has already stopped doing bad deeds.

b.

*tā	<u>bu</u>	<u>yǐjīng</u>	zuò	huài	shì	le
3sg	not	already	do	bad	deed	CRS

(93) a.

wǒ	<u>jiù</u>	<u>bu</u>	zǒu	le
I	then	not	leave	CRS

Then I won't go.

b.

*wǒ	<u>bu</u>	<u>jiù</u>	zǒu	le
I	not	then	leave	CRS

Each of these adverbs includes as part of its meaning the idea of 'as of a certain time': *gānggang* means 'as of a moment ago', *yǐjīng* means 'as of the present (unexpectedly)', and *jiù* means 'as of some previous event (mentioned in the discourse)'. While it makes sense, just as we suggested for *hái* 'still', to talk of some event or state being true or not being true as of a certain time, it doesn't make sense to talk about an event being true but not as of a certain time. The idea of 'as of a certain time' must have the entire rest of the sentence in its scope.

Some nonmovable adverbs allow both possibilities: that is, they both precede and follow the negative particle. For example, consider (94):

(94) a.

tā	<u>chángchang</u>	hē	jiǔ
3sg	frequently	drink	wine

S/He frequently drinks wine.

b.

tā	<u>bu</u>	<u>chángchang</u>	hē	jiǔ
3sg	not	frequently	drink	wine

S/He does not frequently drink wine.

c. tā   chángchang   bu   hē   jiŭ
    3sg   frequently   not   drink   wine

S/He frequently does not drink.

In (94) *b*, the adverb *chángchang* is in the scope of the negative particle *bu*, whereas in *c*, the negative particle *bu* is in the scope of the adverb *chángchang*. It just happens that 'not frequently drink wine' is essentially equivalent to 'frequently not drink wine'. We can demonstrate the difference in meaning between the two orders, *negative + nonmovable adverb* and *nonmovable adverb + negative*, more clearly by citing another example, *gùyì* 'deliberately', as in:

95 *a.*   tā   gùyì   hē   jiŭ
            3sg   deliberately   drink   wine

S/He drinks wine deliberately.

b.   tā   bu   gùyì   hē   jiŭ
        3sg   not   deliberately   drink   wine

S/He does not deliberately drink wine.

c.   tā   gùyì   bu   hē   jiŭ
        3sg   deliberately   not   drink   wine

S/He deliberately doesn't drink wine.

The difference in meaning between (95) *b* and (95) *c* is clear: in *b*, s/he drinks but *not deliberately*, whereas in *c*, s/he is deliberate in *not drinking*. The difference in position correlates precisely with the difference in scope.

Many other nonmovable manner adverbs (with some exceptions to be discussed later) behave in the same way as *gùyì* 'deliberately': they allow the negative particle to occur either before them or after them, with a concomitant meaning difference. Another example is *gānxīn-qíngyuàn-de* 'willingly', as in:

(96) *a.*   tā   bu   gānxīn-qíngyuàn-de   chàng   —   gē
            3sg   not   willingly   sing   —   song

S/He does not willingly sing.

b.	tā	gānxīn-qíngyuàn-de	bu	chàng	–	gē
	3sg	willingly	not	sing	–	song

S/He is willingly not singing.

Just as we pointed out above for *gùyì* 'deliberately', either the *bu* or the adverb can have the other in its scope. In (96) *a*, s/he sings, but *not willingly,* while in (96) *b*, s/he is willing *not to sing.*

The generalizations we have given about the order of adverbs and the negative particles *bu* and *méi (you)* can clearly be seen to be direct manifestations of the idea of semantic scope: when the meaning of the adverb is such that an event can occur, but not in the way designated by the adverb, then this means that the adverb can be in the scope of the negative and can occur after the negative, as with *zǐxì-de* 'meticulously'. When the meaning of the adverb is such that it provides a frame within which some event is or is not true, however, then the affirmative or negative predicate must be within the scope of the adverb and must follow it.

These generalizations are accurate for ordinary neutral conversational situations. Negative sentences are often used in special nonneutral conversational situations, though. For example, if we are contrasting an affirmative and a negative proposition, or if we are emphatically denying what someone else has said, we may use *bu shì* 'it is not the case that . . .', which may always precede the predicate, including any adverbs:

(97)	tā	bu	shì	hái	zài	hǎi	–	biān ,
	3sg	not	be	still	at	sea	–	side

	tā	shì	hái	zài	xuéxiào
	3sg	be	still	at	school

It's not the case that s/he's still at the beach, it's that s/he's still at school.

Another example of a nonneutral conversational situation is one in which the speaker is asking a rhetorical question, a question to which s/he expects no answer. Here the negative can sometimes precede the adverb, even when it ordinarily would not be allowed to:

(98)	tā	bu	jiù	lái	ma ?
	3sg	not	immediately	come	Q

Isn't it true that s/he will come immediately?

(99)   nǐ   bu   hái   zuò   —   shì   ma?
       you   not   still   do   —   work   Q

   Isn't it true that you still work?

8.4 Adverbs and the *bǎ* Construction

The *bǎ* construction (see chapter 15) has the following structure:

   (100)   noun phrase   bǎ   noun phrase   verb

In the *bǎ* construction, the direct-object noun phrase is marked by the coverb *bǎ* and precedes the verb. Let's examine the behavior of adverbs in the *bǎ* construction. Movable adverbs, whether they are time adverbs or attitude adverbs, as we would expect, occur in sentence-initial position or in postsubject/topic position in the *bǎ* construction, just as they do in other sentences. Time adverbs, however, unlike attitude adverbs, can also occur *after* the *bǎ* phrase; so (101) *c* is acceptable, but (102) *c* is not:

(101) *a.*   zuótiān   wǒ   bǎ   chēzi   mài   le
             yesterday   I   BA   car   sell   CRS

   I sold the car yesterday.

   b.   wǒ   zuótiān   bǎ   chēzi   mài   le
          I   yesterday   BA   car   sell   CRS

   I sold the car yesterday.

   c.   wǒ   bǎ   chēzi   zuótiān   mài   le
          I   BA   car   yesterday   sell   CRS

   I sold the car yesterday.

(102) *a.*   xiǎnrán   tā   bǎ   Lǐsì   gǎn   —   chū
             evidently   3sg   BA   Lisi   chase   —   exit

                           —   qu   le
                           —   go   CRS

   S/He evidently chased Lisi out.

b.

tā	xiǎnrán	bǎ	Lǐsì	gǎn	–	chū
3sg	evidently	BA	Lisi	chase	–	exit

| | – | qu | le |
| | – | go | CRS |

S/He evidently chased Lisi out.

c.

*tā	bǎ	Lǐsì	xiǎnrán	gǎn	–	chū
3sg	BA	Lisi	evidently	chase	–	exit

| | – | qu | le |
| | – | go | CRS |

Nonmovable adverbs were defined above as those occurring after the subject and before the verb. In a *bǎ* construction, though, there are *two* positions that are after the subject and before the verb, namely, before the *bǎ* phrase and after it, as indicated in the following schema:

(103)   noun phrase _____ <u>bǎ</u> noun phrase _____ verb

It should follow, then, that nonmovable adverbs, which may not occur in sentence-initial position, can occur in either of the two preverbal positions in a *bǎ* sentence with no change in meaning, and this is indeed true. Here are some examples:

(i) Agent-oriented manner adverb:

(104) *a.*

wǒ	bǎ	tā	yánlì-de	mà	–
I	BA	3sg	sternly	scold	–

| le | yi | dùn |
| PFV | one | time |

I sternly scolded him/her once.

b.

wǒ	yánlì-de	bǎ	tā	mà	–
I	sternly	BA	3sg	scold	–

| le | yi | dùn |
| PFV | one | time |

I sternly scolded him/her once.

(ii) Non-agent-oriented manner adverb:

(105) *a.*

wǒ	bǎ	tā	cánkuì-de	mà	—	le	yi	dùn
I	BA	3sg	ashamedly	scold	—	PFV	one	time

I "ashamedly" scolded him/her once.

b.

wǒ	cánkuì-de	bǎ	tā	mà	—
I	ashamedly	BA	3sg	scold	—

le	yi	dùn
PFV	one	time

I "ashamedly" scolded him/her once.

(106) *a.*

wǒ	bǎ	nèi	—	běn
I	BA	that	—	CL

shū	gānxīn-qíngyuàn-de	mài	le
book	willingly	sell	CRS

I willingly sold that book.

b.

wǒ	gānxīn-qíngyuàn-de	bǎ	nèi	—
I	willingly	BA	that	—

běn	shū	mài	le
CL	book	sell	CRS

I willingly sold that book.

(iii) Nonmovable nonmanner adverb:

(107) *a.*

wǒ	zài	bǎ	tā	mà	yi	dùn
I	again	BA	3sg	scold	one	time

I will scold him/her once again.

b.

wǒ	bǎ	tā	zài	mà	yi	dùn
I	BA	3sg	again	scold	one	time

I will scold him/her once again.

(iv) Onomatopoeic adverb:

(108) *a.* wǒ   pàde   bǎ   tā   dǎ   —   le   yi   zhǎng
      I   BA   3sg   hit   —   PFV   one   palm

I hit him/her with my hand with a sound "pade."

b. wǒ   bǎ   tā   pàde   dǎ   —   le   yi   zhǎng
      I   BA   3sg   hit   —   PFV   one   palm

I hit him/her with my hand with a sound "pade."

On the other hand, there are adverbs that are not manner adverbs but may change the meaning of the *bǎ* sentence, depending on the position of the adverb. For instance, *yě* 'also', because of its meaning, is an adverb of this type.

(109) *a.* wǒ   yě   bǎ   tā   qǐng   —   lái   le
      I   also   BA   3sg   invite   —   come   CRS

I also invited him/her to come.

b. wǒ   bǎ   tā   yě   qǐng   —   lái   le
      I   BA   3sg   also   invite   —   come   CRS

I invited him/her to come also.

In (109) *a*, the implication is that someone else invited him/her as I did, whereas in *b*, the implication is that I invited someone else in addition to him/her.

In *bǎ* sentences, then, with the exception of certain adverbs, such as *yě* 'also', a nonmovable adverb can occur either before or after the *bǎ* phrase with no change in meaning.

8.5 Quantity Adverbial Phrases

Quantity adverbial phrases are made up of more than one word, which is why they are called adverbial phrases rather than adverbs. These phrases specify the extent or duration of an activity and must occur after the verb. They consist of a number, a classifier (if one is required),[9] and a noun. Here are some examples:

(110) tā   zǒu   –   le   shí   fēnzhōng   le
       3sg   leave   –   PFV   ten   minute   CRS

S/He's been gone ten minutes.

(111) tā   shuì   –   le   sān   –   ge
       3sg   sleep   –   PFV   three   –   CL

       zhōngtóu   le
       hour   CRS

S/He has slept for three hours.

(112) tā   zhǎo   –   le   liǎng   cì   le
       3sg   search –   PFV   two   time   CRS

S/He has already searched twice.

The underlined forms in these three examples are obvious cases of quantity adverbial phrases, specifying the number of times some action was done or the length of time some event took place. The underlined phrases in the following examples may not appear to be adverbial phrases in the same way, but, upon inspection, it is obvious that in both form and function they are identical to (110)–(112):

(113) tā   bǎ   wǒ   tī   –   le   yi   jiǎo
       3sg   BA   I   kick   –   PFV   one   foot

S/He kicked me once.

(114) tā   bǎ   wǒ   yǎo   –   le   yi   kǒu
       3sg   BA   I   bite   –   PFV   one   mouth

S/He bit me once.

(115) wǒ   bǎ   tā   dǎ   –   le   sān   quán
       I   BA   3sg   hit   –   PFV   three   punch

I hit him/her with three punches.

(116)	nèi	–	ge	dìfang	wǒ	yǐjīng	pǎo	–
	that	–	CL	place	I	already	run	–

le	<u>hǎo</u>	<u>jǐ</u>	<u>tàng</u>	le
PFV	good	several	time	CRS

I've already made quite a few trips to that place.

There are two unusual features characterizing the underlined phrases in (113)–(116): first, they involve meanings that are idiomatic and therefore must be learned individually (*yi jiǎo* 'one foot', for example, does not go with any verb except *tī* 'kick'); second, nouns such as *jiǎo* 'foot' and *kǒu* 'mouth' are typically used with classifiers, but in these expressions they occur without classifiers. Because of these two properties, Chao (1968:313) calls them "cognate objects." Functionally, however, they are not objects; in (114), for instance, what was bitten was not *yi kǒu* 'one mouth', but rather *wǒ* 'I', so the direct object in (114) is *wǒ* 'I'. Instead, these forms specify the extent or duration of an activity and function as adverbial phrases, just as those in (110)–(112) do, and should be classified that way.

Notes

1. Tai (1973) gives a broad discussion of various types of adverbial elements, including prepositional phrases, and their interactions with each other and with various parts of the verb phrase. We have also taken some ideas from Mei (1972).
2. Manner adverbs derived from monosyllabic adjectives, such as *kuài* 'quick', *màn* 'slow', and *hǎo* 'good', may optionally appear unreduplicated and/or without the suffix *-de* in imperatives (see chapter 14), as in:

(i)	<u>kuài</u>	–	<u>kuài</u>	chī
	quick	–	quick	eat

Eat quickly.

(ii)	<u>màn</u>	zǒu
	slow	leave

Leave slowly. (a formal leave-taking expression)

Not all adverbs composed of reduplicated syllables are derived from adjectives. A number of monosyllabic adverbs may themselves optionally appear in a reduplicated form without any change in meaning, such as *cháng/cháng-chang* 'frequently', *piān/piānpian* 'deliberately', *gāng/gānggang* 'just now'. These adverbs are different from those derived from adjectives in that they do not take the suffix *-de*.

3. This discussion owes much to Hashimoto (1971*b*).

4. Of these, the following seven are described in detail in Alleton (1972): *dōu, yĕ, yòu, zài, hái, cái,* and *jiù.*

5. Our description of *dōu* 'all' has taken several points from Alleton (1972:51 ff.); on the *lián . . . dōu/yĕ* 'even' construction, see Paris (1979*b*).

6. Since many of the agent-oriented manner adverbs are modern innovations, their acceptance by native speakers as part of their natural speech varies from case to case and from speaker to speaker; by and large, native speakers know that these adverbs occur in journalistic writing, and they tend to accept them and use them in their speech, although some conservative speakers may find them odd.

7. See n. 6.

8. One can, of course, cruelly *refuse* to do something, but that would require the use of a verb explicitly meaning 'refuse'.

9. Some time nouns, such as *nián* 'year' and *tiān* 'day', as well as certain other nouns found in quantity adverbial phrases, do not take classifiers (see chapter 4, section 4.2.1).

CHAPTER 9

Coverbs/Prepositions

9.1 The Function of Coverbs

The term coverb refers to a class of morphemes in Mandarin which includes such words as *gēn* 'with', *cóng* 'from', *cháo* 'facing', *yán* 'along', *lí* 'be apart from', and the like, as well as forms that figure prominently in certain grammatical constructions, such as *zài* 'at', used in locative constructions (see chapter 11), *bǎ*, the marker of the *bǎ* construction (see chapter 15), *bǐ*, the comparative morpheme (see chapter 19), *bèi*, the marker of the passive construction (see chapter 16), and certain uses of *gěi*, the marker of benefactive and indirect object constructions (see chapter 10).[1] A more complete list can be found in table 9.1 at the end of this chapter.

The coverb introduces a noun phrase,[2] and the phrase formed by the coverb plus the noun phrase generally precedes the main verb and follows the subject or topic:

(1) $\begin{Bmatrix} \text{subject} \\ \text{topic} \end{Bmatrix}$ <u>coverb + noun phrase</u>   verb   (noun phrase)

The following are examples:

(2)   wǒ   yào   <u>gēn   tā</u>   shuō   —   huà
        I   want   with   3sg   talk   —   speech

I want to talk with him/her.

(3) nǐ cóng nǎr lái ?
    you from where come

Where have you come from?

(4) tā cháo dōng zhàn — zhe
    3sg face east stand — DUR

S/He is standing facing east.

(5) wǒ jiā lí gōngyuán bu yuǎn
    I home apart:from park not far

My home is not far from the park.

(6) wǒmen àn tā — de yìsi bàn
    we according:to 3sg — GEN idea do

We'll do it according to his/her ideas.

(7) wàng nán kàn
    toward south look

Look toward the south.

(8) nǐ tì wǒ mǎi piào ba
    you instead:of I buy ticket SA

You buy the tickets instead of me, OK?

(9) rénmín dàibiǎo yīnggāi yóu
    people representative should be:up:to

                rénmín lái xuǎn
                people come elect

It should be up to the people to elect their own representatives.

(10)   wǒ   duì(yu)   zhèi   —   jiàn   shì
        I   toward   this   —   CL   matter

            méi   yǒu   yìjian
            not   exist   opinion

I have no opinion about this matter.

(11)   tā   zài   hòu   —   yuán   —   lǐ
        3sg   at   back   —   yard   —   in

            niàn   —   shū
            study   —   book

S/He's studying in the backyard.

(12)   tā   bǎ   shū   fàng   —   xia
        3sg   BA   book   put   —   descend

            —   lái   le
            —   come   CRS

S/He put the books down.

(13)   wǒ   bèi   tā   zhuī   —   le   sān   tiān
        I   BEI   3sg   chase   —   PFV   three   days

I was chased by him/her for three days.

(14)   māma   gěi   wǒ   zuò   jiǎozi
        mother   for   I   make   dumpling

Mother made dumplings for me.

There are certain coverbs that need not precede the main verb; the most important of these are *zài* 'at' and *dào* 'to', which are discussed in chapter 11 on locative and directional phrases, and *gěi* 'to', which is discussed in chapter 10 on indirect objects and benefactives. As is pointed out in those chapters, under certain conditions each of these three coverbs can occur after the verb:

(15)   wǒ   zhù   <u>zài</u>   Qīngdǎo

          I   live   at   Qingdao

I live in Qingdao.

(16)   niàn   <u>dào</u>   dì   —   wǔ   <u>háng</u>

          read   to   ORD   —   five   line

Read to the fifth line.

(17)   bǎ   nèi   —   ge   bēi   dì   <u>gěi</u>   wǒ

          BA   that   —   CL   cup   hand   to   I

Hand me that cup!

There are also a few coverbs that may occur with their nouns in sentence-initial position. For example:

(18)   <u>guānyu</u>   guó   —   wài   —   de

          as to   country   —   outside   —   ASSOC

          qíngxing   tā   yidiàn   dōu

          situation   3sg   a:little   all

          bu   shúxi

          not   familiar

As to conditions abroad, s/he really knows nothing.

(19)   <u>zhìyu</u>   kè   —   wài   —   de

          as to   class   —   outside   —   ASSOC

          huódòng   tāmen   bu   guǎn

          activity   they   not   concerned

As to extracurricular activities, they are not concerned with them.

An atypical coverb is *chúle . . . (yǐwài)* 'except'. It is atypical because it involves an optional part, *yǐwài*, that comes at the end of the noun phrase introduced by the first part of the coverb *chúle*. Sentence (20) is an example:

(20)	chúle	tā	(yǐwài) ,	nǐmen	dōu	zhàn
	except	3sg		you	all	stand
	–	qǐ	–	lái		
	–	rise	–	come		

Except for him/her, all of you stand up!

Coverbs function as *prepositions*: a coverb and its noun form a phrase that modifies the verb of the sentence. A coverb phrase, therefore, must always occur in a sentence with a verb. If the Mandarin coverbs are essentially prepositions, why, then, are they called coverbs rather than prepositions? The answer is simply that the class of coverbs contains words that are partly like verbs and partly like prepositions; the traditional term *coverb* was coined to avoid labeling them either verbs or prepositions.[4] They have this mixed status because most of these present-day coverbs used to be verbs at earlier stages of the language, and many of them still have characteristics of verbs and can be used as verbs that have similar meanings. For example, the coverb *bǎ* was once a verb meaning 'hold, take'; *duì* 'to, toward' was once a verb meaning 'face'; and *gēn* 'with' was once a verb meaning 'follow'.

Their verbal origin accounts for a number of properties of the present-day coverbs. In particular, some of them are more like verbs, and some are more like prepositions, because in their historical transition from verbs to prepositions, some of these morphemes have progressed farther than others.

Let us consider two properties that show the verbal nature of coverbs.

9.1.1 Occurrence with Aspect Markers

That some coverbs can occur with verbal aspect markers (see chapter 6) is explained by the fact that they used to be verbs: a coverb that can take an aspect marker has progressed less far along the historical route from verb to preposition than one that cannot.

A. *-zhe*

A number of coverbs can optionally occur with the durative verbal suffix *-zhe* (see section 6.2 of chapter 6 for further discussion of the durative aspect).[3] Some of these are given below:

(21) àn   'according to'   nì   'against'

      chòng   'facing'   píng   'according to'

      cháo   'facing'   shùn   'along'

      duì   'toward'   xiàng   'facing'

      wàng   'toward'   wèi   'for the sake of'

      yán   'along'   āi   'adjacent to'

As an illustration, consider the following sentences. For many speakers, the coverb may occur either with or without *-zhe*, with no change in meaning:

(22) wǒmen   děi   àn   (-zhe)   fǎlü   bàn
      we   must   according:to   (-DUR)   law   do

We must do it according to the law.

(23) tāmen   wàng   (-zhe)   chuán   —   shang
      they   toward (-DUR)   boat   —   on

              fàng   —   qiāng
              fire   —   gun

They fired at the boat.

In fact, according to Chao (1968:763), some coverbs, such as *yán* 'along', must carry the *-zhe* suffix, except for certain fused phrases in which it is optional, such as *yán hǎi* 'along the sea (coast)' and *yán jiāng* 'along the river'. An example of this coverb occurring with *-zhe* is:

(24) qiānshuǐtǐng   yán   —   zhe   hǎi
      submarine   along   —   DUR   sea

                     —   àn   màn-màn-de   zǒu
                     —   coast   slowly   go

The submarine coasted along the shore.

Many coverbs, on the other hand, cannot take -zhe:

(25)	*wǒ	cóng	–	zhe	nàr	zǒu		
	I	from	–	DUR	there	leave		

(26)	*tā	zài	–	zhe	jiā	shuì	–	jiào
	3sg	at	–	DUR	home	sleep	–	sleep

(27)	*wǒ	gěi	–	zhe	tā	xiě	xìn	
	I	to	–	DUR	3sg	write	letter	

There are two differences between the use of -zhe with true verbs and its occurrence with coverbs. First, the list of coverbs that can take -zhe must be memorized; -zhe cannot be added freely to just any coverb. Second, -zhe, when it occurs with these coverbs, has no durative meaning, as it has when it occurs as an aspect marker with a true verb. That is why some coverbs may occur either with or without -zhe, with no change in meaning, as in (22) and (23).

B. -le

A few coverbs can occur with -le, including wèi 'for':

(28)	wǒ	wèi	–	le	nǐ	yi	yè
	I	for	–	PFV	you	one	night

		méi	shuì	–	jiào	
		not	sleep	–	sleep	

For you I stayed awake a whole night.

The second syllable le in the atypical coverb chúle . . . (yǐwài) 'except' is also originally the perfective aspect marker. Its presence in chúle, though, is obligatory, and it is no longer clear for either wèile or chúle that the second syllable still bears the function of the perfective aspect.

9.1.2 Coverbs That Can Also Function as Verbs

A second respect in which coverbs form a mixed class is that many of them can also be used as verbs in the present-day language. In a small number of cases, the coverb has a different meaning when it is used as a verb. Consider the following examples. In the *a* sentences, the coverb functions as a coverb, and in the *b* sentences, as a verb.

(i) Coverb has the same meaning when used as a verb:

(29) *a.*
tā	cháo	nán	bài
3sg	facing	south	worship

S/He worships facing south.

b.
tā	—	de	wūzi	cháo	hǎi
3sg	—	GEN	room	face	sea

His/Her room faces the sea.

(30) *a.*
wǒmen	cháng	dào	Niǔyuē	qù
we	often	go	New York	go

We often go to New York.

b.
wǒmen	jǐ	—	diǎnzhōng	dào	Niǔyuē ?
we	how:many	—	o'clock	arrive	New York

What time do we arrive in New York?

(ii) Coverb has a different meaning when used as a verb:

(31) *a.*
women	àn	tā	—	de	yìsi	bàn	ba !
we	according:to	3sg	—	GEN	idea	do	SA

Let's do it according to his/her ideas.

b.
yǒu	rén	àn	mén	—	líng
exist	person	press	door	—	bell

Someone is ringing the doorbell.

(32) *a.*
tā	yòu	gēn	wǒ	jiè	qián
3sg	again	with	I	borrow	money

S/He again borrowed money from me.

b.	jǐngchá	gēn	—	le	tā	sān	tiān	le
	police	follow	—	PFV	3sg	three	day	CRS

The police have followed him/her for three days.

(iii) Coverb has no verbal use:

(33) a.	nǐ	děi	cóng	gè	fāngmiàn	kàn
	you	must	from	every	angle	look

You must look at it from every angle.

b.	*nǐ	děi	cóng	zhèr
	you	must	from	here

(34) a.	bié	hé	wǒ	kāiwánxiào
	don't	with	I	joke

Don't joke with me.

b.	*bié	hé	wǒ
	don't	with	I

Once again, the difference among these three types of coverbs with regard to whether they have verbal uses is to be expected, given that some coverbs have become more like prepositions than others. In this case, we see that certain coverbs have not diverged far from their verbal origins, in that they can still be employed as verbs as well. Other coverbs have become more independent: they cannot be used as verbs (except in some cases in a compound; for example, corresponding to the coverb *cóng* 'from', there is the verb *suícóng* 'to follow').

The question that now arises is this: Given that many coverbs can be used as verbs, and given that it is common for verbs to occur together in the same sentence (see chapter 21 on serial verb constructions), how can we be sure, when we see a verblike item in a sentence with another verb, whether it is actually a verb or a coverb?

The answer to this question is that an element is considered to be a coverb if it occurs in at least some contexts where it could not be a verb. Let's consider some examples.

To begin, we might look at a coverb that fits the criterion absolutely: *bèi*, which cannot be a verb in *any* context. The marker of an agent in a passive sentence (see chapter 16), *bèi* can occur in a sentence such as:

(35)   wǒ   <u>bèi</u>   māma   pīping   LE
       I   BEI   mother criticize PFV/CRS

   I was criticized by mother.

Bèi must be a coverb because it can never be a verb. In particular, it cannot occur in a sentence with no other verb:

(36)   *wǒ   bèi   māma
        I   BEI   mother

Bèi and other coverbs such as *bǎ* and *cóng* 'from', which can never be used as verbs, are easy to identify as coverbs. They are the most prepositionlike members of the coverb class.

Now, though, consider such forms as *zài* 'at', *gěi* 'to, for', and *dào* 'to'. These coverbs *can* function as verbs, as the following sentences show:

(37)   Lǐsì   <u>zài</u>   hǎi   —   biān
       Lisi   at   ocean —   side

   Lisi is by the ocean.

(38)   bàba   <u>gěi</u>   wǒ   qián
       papa   give   I   money

   Papa gives me money.

(39)   wǒmen   <u>dào</u>   —   le   Xiānggǎng
       we   arrive   —   PFV   Hong Kong

   We have arrived in Hong Kong.

They also qualify as coverbs, however, because they can each be used in sentences in which they need not have their verbal meanings. For example, consider *zài* 'at' in sentence (40):

(40)	tā	zài	guō	—	li	fàng	shuǐ
	3sg	at	pot	—	in	put	water

S/He put water in the pot.

In this interpretation of (40), *zài* is not a verb, because it does not have the verbal meaning of 'be in'. That is, this interpretation of (40) does not involve *tā* 's/he' being in the pot. It is possible for *zài* in (40) to be a verb; in that case the sentence would be an example of a serial verb construction, with the somewhat unnatural interpretation 'S/He was in the pot and was putting water (somewhere)'. The point is that *zài* qualifies as a coverb precisely because there are sentences like (40) in which it need not have its verbal meaning.

Similarly, *gěi* in (41) can't be a verb, because here it has the meaning 'for' and not its verbal meaning 'give':

(41)	wǒ	gěi	nǐ	dào	chá
	I	for	you	pour	tea

I'll pour you some tea.

Dào in (42) is also not a verb, because it does not have its verbal meaning 'arrive':

(42)	tā	dào	Lúndūn	qù	le
	3sg	to	London	go	CRS

S/He has gone to London.

As with *zài* in (40), it is possible for *dào* in (42) to have its verbal meaning 'arrive'; in this case the sentence would also be a serial verb construction with the meaning 'S/He arrived in London and went (somewhere)'.

To be a coverb, then, an element must occur in at least some contexts in which it cannot have its verbal meaning, where it must be counted as having a nonverbal (that is, prepositional) function. The examples in (40)–(42) illustrate three forms that can be proved to be coverbs by this criterion. To round out the picture, let's examine one case that the criterion clearly indicates does *not* have coverb status. Consider *yòng* 'use': *yòng* obviously has a verbal function, since it can be used as the only verb in a sentence:

(43) tāmen   bu   huì   yòng   kuàizi
      they   not   know:how   use   chopstick

They don't know how to use chopsticks.

When it appears with another verb, though, speakers of English might think it has a coverb function, since it *could* be translated into English with the preposition 'with':

(44) wǒ   yòng   máobǐ   xiě   zì
      I   use   brush   write   character

{I use a brush to write characters.}
{I write characters with a brush.}

Here, however, even though *yòng* in (44) could be translated into English with the preposition 'with', in Mandarin there exists essentially no difference in the interpretation of the verb *yòng* in (43) and in (44). There is, therefore, by our criterion, no reason to consider it anything but a verb.

The criterion, then, does provide a clear distinction between coverbs and verbs: a coverb must occur in some contexts where it cannot be interpreted as a verb. Thus *bèi*, *bǎ*, and *cóng* 'from', which can never be interpreted as verbs, as well as *zài* 'at', *gěi* 'to, for', and *dào* 'to', which sometimes cannot be interpreted as verbs, can be considered to be coverbs. On the other hand, *yòng* 'use' is always interpretable with its verbal meaning and so does not qualify as a coverb.

9.2 A List of Coverbs

Table 9.1 lists some of the more commonly used coverbs in Mandarin as well as their corresponding glosses.

TABLE 9.1
Representative List of Coverbs

Preposition	Rough Gloss	Gloss of Present-day Use as Verb	Gloss of Older Verbal Ancestor (If Different from Present-day Verb)
āi	next to	be next to	
àn	according to	press	
bǎ	(direct object marker)		take, hold
bèi	(agent marker)		receive
bèn	toward	go to	
bǐ	compare	compare	
bùjí	not as	ji = reach	
bùrú	not as	ru = follow	
cháo	facing	face	have audience with the emperor
chèn	take advantage of		ride
chéng	by (e.g., the dozen)	form	
chéng	take advantage of	ride on	
chòng	facing	face	
chúle	except, besides	remove	
cóng	from		follow
dǎ	from	hit	
dàiti	in place of	take the place of	
dāng	in front of	serve as	
dào	to (a place)	arrive	
duì	to	face	
duì (yu)	concerning, with regard to	face	face toward
gěi	for, by	give	
gēn	with	follow	
gēn	at	be at	
guǎn	call (used with jiào)	control, manage	
guānyu	concerning, with regard to		
guī	(agent marker)	put away	
hàn	with		mix
hé	with		mix
jiāng	(= bǎ [literary])	checkmate	
jiào	(agent marker)	call	
jiě	from	untie, relieve	
jǐn	take first, limit oneself to	let someone go first	
jiù	take advantage of		go
jiù	with (food or drink)	go with (food or drink)	
(gēn) jù	according to		
kào	depend on	lean against	
lí	separated from		keep distance

TABLE 9.1 (Continued)
REPRESENTATIVE LIST OF COVERBS

PREPOSITION	ROUGH GLOSS	GLOSS OF PRESENT-DAY USE AS VERB	GLOSS OF OLDER VERBAL ANCESTOR (IF DIFFERENT FROM PRESENT-DAY VERB)
lùn	by (some unit measure)		evaluate
nì	against	be opposed to	meet, welcome
píng	depend on, according to	depend on	
qǐ	from (a time, place)	rise	
shǐ	use, with	cause	
shòu	(agent marker)	receive	
shùn	along	follow	
tì	in place of	substitute for	
tóng	with	be the same	
wàng	facing	face	
wǎng	toward		go
wèi	for	be for the sake of	
xiàng	like	be like	
xiàng	facing	face	
yán	along	follow along	
yī	according to	agree with	
(yī) zhào	according to	zhào = reflect	
yóu	from, be up to		follow
yú	to, for		be at
zhìyu	concerning, with regard to		

Notes

1. This chapter is adapted from our papers, Li and Thompson (1974*a*, 1974*b*, 1974*d*), where the documentation for some of the points we make is given, and from Chao (1968), Cartier (1970), Huang (1974*a*, 1978), and Chang (1977). For a very detailed discussion of prepositions in Chinese as well as in other languages, the reader is referred to Hagège (1975).

2. The only coverb that may occur without a following noun phrase is *bèi*, the marker of the passive (see chapter 16 for discussion).

3. See Simon (1958) and Huang (1974*a*) for further discussion of this point.

4. The traditional Chinese term is *fù dòngcí* 'subordinate verb', introduced in Wang (1947).

CHAPTER 10

Indirect Objects and Benefactives

A number of verbs can take two objects, a direct object and an indirect object.[1] In the discussion of types of verb phrases in section 4.3.1 of chapter 4, we refer to such verbs as ditransitive. As the names *direct object* and *indirect object* suggest, the semantic relationship between a verb and its direct object is more direct, tighter, and closer than the semantic relationship between a verb and its indirect object. Thus, if the verb is an action verb taking both a direct object and an indirect object, the direct object generally represents what is being transferred as a result of the action, and the indirect object denotes who is being affected by the action. For example:

				D.O.				I.O.
(1)	wǒ	rēng	–	le	nèi	kuài	ròu	gěi	tā
	I	toss	–	PFV	that	piece	meat	to	3sg

I tossed that piece of meat to him/her.

In (1), the direct object (= D.O.) is *nèi kuài ròu* 'that piece of meat', and the indirect object (= I.O.) is *tā* 's/he'. The tighter semantic bond between *nèi kuài ròu* 'that piece of meat' and the verb *rēng* 'throw, toss' should be apparent. A useful diagnostic aid for distinguishing the direct object from the indirect object of a transitive action verb is the *bǎ* construction (see chapter 15). Only the direct object but not the indirect object of a transitive action verb may serve as the noun phrase introduced by the coverb *bǎ*. Using sentence (1) as our point of reference, we would expect that the direct object *nèi kuài ròu* 'that piece of meat' but not the indirect object *tā* 's/he' can be the *bǎ* noun phrase. Sentences (2) and (3) confirm our expectation.

(2)	wǒ	bǎ	nèi	kuài	ròu	rēng	gěi	tā
	I	BA	that	piece	meat	toss	to	3sg

I tossed that piece of meat to him/her.

(3)	*wǒ	bǎ	tā	rēng	—	le	nèi	kuài	ròu
	I	BA	3sg	toss	—	PFV	that	piece	meat

An important characteristic of the indirect object is that it is always either an animate noun denoting a human being or an animal, or the name of a societal institution, such as *yīyuàn* 'hospital'. Although there is no such constraint on the direct object in terms of semantic types of nouns, when a direct object and an indirect object cooccur, it is typically the case that the direct object is *inanimate* and the indirect object is *animate*. There are in general two orders in which the direct object and the indirect object can occur. Observe that in sentence (1), repeated here, the direct object, *nèi kuài ròu* 'that piece of meat', precedes the indirect object, *tā* 's/he', and, furthermore, the indirect object *tā* 's/he' is marked by the preceding coverb *gěi* 'to'.

				D.O.			I.O.	
(1)	wǒ	rēng	—	le	nèi	kuài	ròu	gěi	tā
	I	toss	—	PFV	that	piece	meat	to	3sg

I tossed that piece of meat to him/her.

Sentence (1) has an alternative form, shown in (4):

			I.O.		D.O.		
(4)	wǒ	rēng	gěi	tā	nèi	kuài	ròu[2]
	I	toss	to	3sg	that	piece	meat

I tossed that piece of meat to him/her.

In (4), the indirect object marked by *gěi* 'to' precedes the direct object.

Thus, sentences (1) and (4) show that the positions of the direct object and indirect objects can be reversed. Two significant points may be made about this reversal. First, there is a slight functional difference between sentences in which the direct object precedes the indirect object, *direct object + indirect object*, and those in which the direct object follows the indirect object, *indirect object + direct object*, in the sense that they are used in different speech contexts. If the speech context is such that the direct object but not the indirect object is a piece of information that has already been mentioned, then the order *direct object + indirect object* is used. On the other hand, if in the speech context the indirect object but not the direct object is a piece of information that has already been mentioned, then the order *indirect object + direct object* is used.[3] Let us consider an example. Suppose Zhangsan stated that he had had a piece of meat and a cake in the kitchen, and he demanded of Lisi what had happened to them. In this speech context, sentence (5) *a* but not (5) *b* would be appropriate as Lisi's response.

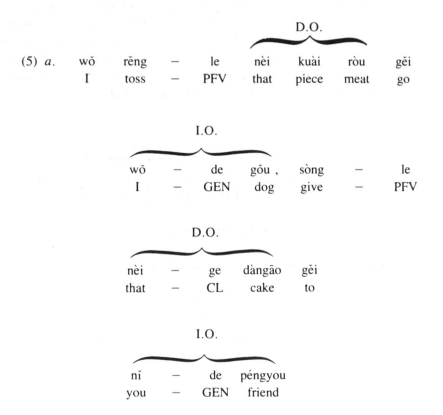

					D.O.		
(5) *a*.	wǒ	rēng	—	le	nèi	kuài	ròu	gěi
	I	toss	—	PFV	that	piece	meat	go

		I.O.					
	wǒ	—	de	gǒu ,	sòng	—	le
	I	—	GEN	dog	give	—	PFV

		D.O.				
	nèi	—	ge	dàngāo	gěi	
	that	—	CL	cake	to	

		I.O.		
	nǐ	—	de	péngyou
	you	—	GEN	friend

I threw that piece of meat to my dog and gave that cake to your friend.

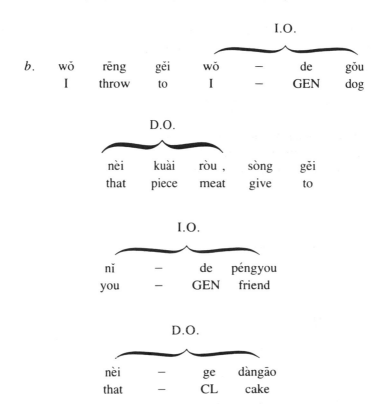

	I.O.					
b.	wǒ	rēng	gěi	wǒ	—	de	gǒu
	I	throw	to	I	—	GEN	dog

	D.O.				
nèi	kuài	ròu ,	sòng	gěi
that	piece	meat	give	to

	I.O.		
nǐ	—	de	péngyou
you	—	GEN	friend

	D.O.		
nèi	—	ge	dàngāo
that	—	CL	cake

I threw that piece of meat to my dog and gave that cake to your friend.

On the other hand, if we had a different speech context in which Zhangsan asked Lisi what had been done about the hungry dog and the hungry friend, sentence (5) *b* but not (5) *a* would be an appropriate response from Lisi.

The second point to be noted about the variation in the order of the indirect object and direct object is that when the indirect object comes after the direct object, as in (1), the particle *gěi* 'to' must be used. Compare (1) to (6), which is unacceptable.

(1)	wǒ	rēng	—	le	nèi	kuài	ròu	gěi	tā
	I	toss	—	PFV	that	piece	meat	to	3sg

I tossed that piece of meat to him/her.

(6)	*wǒ	rēng	—	le	nèi	kuài	ròu	tā
	I	toss	—	PFV	that	piece	meat	3sg

Sentence (6) is unacceptable because, just as in English, if the indirect object is not immediately following the verb, it must be marked as an indirect object by a preposition/coverb:

(7) *I tossed that piece of meat him.

On the other hand, when the indirect object precedes the direct object, some verbs require the presence of *gěi* 'to', some verbs allow it optionally, and other verbs cannot have *gěi* at all.[4] Let's consider each of these three classes of verbs in turn.

10.1 *gěi* Obligatory

Some of the verbs that require *gěi* before an indirect object are:

(8) dì   'bring to'   xiě   'write'
    fēn   'allocate'   zū   'rent to'
    ná, dài   'bring to'   liú   'keep, save'
    jì   'mail'   dǎ (diànhua) 'telephone'
    jiāo   'deliver, hand in' tī   'kick'
    mài   'sell'   bān   'move'
    diū, rēng   'toss, throw'   tuī   'push'
    shū   'lose'

The following sentences are illustrations:

(9) *a*. tā   dài   —   le   yi   bāo   táng
          3sg   bring —   PFV   one   bag   candy

          gěi   Zhāngsān
          to   Zhangsan

    S/He brought a bag of candy to Zhangsan.

    b. tā   dài   gěi   Zhāngsān   yi   bāo   táng
          3sg   bring to   Zhangsan   one   bag   candy

    S/He brought a bag of candy to Zhangsan.

    c. *tā   dài   —   le   Zhāngsān   yi   bāo   táng
          3sg   bring —   PFV   Zhangsan   one   bag   candy

(10) *a.*

wǒ	shū	—	le	yi	kuài	qián	<u>gěi</u>	<u>tā</u>
I	lose	—	PFV	one	dollar	money	to	3sg

I lost a dollar to him/her.

b.

wǒ	shū	<u>gěi</u>	<u>tā</u>	yi	kuài	qián
I	lose	to	3sg	one	dollar	money

I lost one dollar to him/her.

c.

*wǒ	shū	—	le	<u>tā</u>	yi	kuài	qián
I	lose	—	PFV	3sg	one	dollar	money

(11) *a.*

wǒ	bān	—	le	yi	—	ge	zhuōzi
I	move	—	PFV	one	—	CL	table

<u>gěi</u>	<u>tā</u>
to	3sg

I moved a table over to him/her.

b.

wǒ	bān	<u>gěi</u>	<u>tā</u>	yi	—	ge	zhuōzi
I	move	to	3sg	one	—	CL	table

I moved a table over to him/her.

c.

*wǒ	bān	—	le	<u>tā</u>	yi	—	ge	zhuōzi
I	move	—	PFV	3sg	one	—	CL	table

In (9)−(11), the *c* sentences are ungrammatical because the coverb *gěi* is absent before the indirect object.

10.2 *gěi* Optional

Examples of verbs with which one may but is not required to use *gěi* before an indirect object are:

(12)

<u>sòng, zèng</u>	'give'	huán	'return'
<u>jiāo</u>	'teach'	<u>péi</u>	'compensate, pay back'
<u>shǎng, cì</u>	'bestow'	<u>fù</u>	'pay'
<u>jiā</u>	'add on'	<u>xǔ</u>	'promise to give'
<u>chuán</u>	'pass'	<u>jiè</u>	'lend'

The following sentences illustrate the characteristics of sentences with these verbs:

(13) *a.*

wǒ	sòng	—	le	yi	pîng	jiǔ	<u>gěi</u>	<u>tā</u>
I	give	—	PFV	one	bottle	wine	to	3sg

I gave a bottle of wine to him/her.

b.

wǒ	sòng	<u>gěi</u>	<u>tā</u>	yi	píng	jiǔ
I	give	to	3sg	one	bottle	wine

I gave a bottle of wine to him/her.

c.

wǒ	sòng	—	le	<u>tā</u>	yi	píng	jiǔ
I	give	—	PFV	3sg	one	bottle	wine

I gave a bottle of wine to him/her.

(14) *a.*

tā	huán	—	le	yi	wǎn	ròu
3sg	return	—	PFV	one	bowl	meat

<u>gěi</u>	<u>nǐ</u>
to	you

S/He returned a bowl of meat to you.

b.

tā	huán	<u>gěi</u>	<u>nǐ</u>	yi	wǎn	ròu
3sg	return	to	you	one	bowl	meat

S/He returned a bowl of meat to you.

c.

tā	huán	—	le	<u>nǐ</u>	yi	wǎn	ròu
3sg	return	—	PFV	you	one	bowl	meat

S/He returned a bowl of meat to you.

(15) *a.*

wǒ	fù	—	le	liǎng	—	bǎi
I	pay	—	PFV	two	—	hundred

kuài	qián	<u>gěi</u>	<u>tā</u>
dollar	money	to	3sg

I paid $200 to him/her.

b.	wǒ	fù	<u>gěi</u>	tā	liǎng	—	bǎi
	I	pay	to	3sg	two	—	hundred

	kuài	qián
	dollar	money

I paid $200 to him/her.

c.	wǒ	fù	—	le	tā	liǎng	—
	I	pay	—	PFV	3sg	two	—

	bǎi	kuài	qián
	hundred	dollar	money

I paid $200 to him/her.

(16) *a.*	wǒ	jiè	—	le	yi	liǎng	yínzi
	I	lend	—	PFV	one	ounce	silver

	<u>gěi</u>	tā
	to	3sg

I lent one ounce of silver to him/her.

b.	wǒ	jiè	<u>gěi</u>	tā	yi	liǎng	yínzi
	I	lend	to	3sg	one	ounce	silver

I lent one ounce of silver to him/her.

c.	wǒ	jiè	—	le	tā	yi	liǎng	yínzi
	I	lend	—	PFV	3sg	one	ounce	silver

I lent one ounce of silver to him/her.

The above examples clearly show the optional nature of *gěi* with this class of verbs.

10.3 *géi* Forbidden

The class of verbs that may not take *gěi* before an indirect object differs from the first two classes in two ways. Verbs in this class not only cannot have the particle *gĕi*, but they also require the indirect object to precede the direct object.[5] Here are some such verbs:

(17)
gĕi	'give'	tōu	'steal'
gàosu	'tell'	qīngjiào	'ask for enlightenment'
dāyìng	'promise'	yíng	'win'
huídá	'answer'	qiǎng	'rob'
wèn	'ask'	duó	'snatch'

The following examples serve to illustrate the characteristics of sentences containing verbs of this class:

(18) *a.*

*wǒ	wèn	—	le	jǐ	—	ge
I	ask	—	PFV	several	—	CL

wènti	gĕi	tā
problem	to	3sg

b.

*wǒ	wèn	gĕi	tā	jǐ	—	ge	wènti
I	ask	to	3sg	several	—	CL	problem

c.

wǒ	wèn	—	le	tā	jǐ	—
I	ask	—	PFV	3sg	several	—

ge	wènti
CL	problem

I asked him/her several questions.

(19) *a.*

*tā	qiǎng	—	le	liǎng	—
3sg	rob	—	PFV	two	—

wàn	kuài	qián	gĕi	yínháng[6]
ten:thousand	dollar	money	to	bank

b.

*tā	qiǎng	gĕi	yínháng	liǎng	—
3sg	rob	to	bank	two	—

wàn	kuài	qián
ten:thousand	dollar	money

c.	tā	qiǎng	—		le	yínháng	liǎng
	3sg	rob	—		PFV	bank	two

		—	wàn	kuài	qián
		—	ten:thousand	dollar	money

S/He robbed $20,000 from the bank.

In certain Mandarin dialects, the verbs *chī* 'eat' and *hē* 'drink' can be used in the sense of 'eat off of' and 'drink off of', in which cases they take both a direct and an indirect object. For example:

(20)	wǒ	chī	—	le	tā	sān	—	ge
	I	eat	—	PFV	3sg	three	—	CL

		yuè	—	de	fàn
		month	—	ASSOC	food

I ate off of him/her for three months (i.e., at his/her expense).

(21)	tā	hē	—	le	nǐ	wǔ	píng	jiǔ
	3sg	drink	—	PFV	you	five	bottle	wine

S/He drank five bottles of wine off of you (i.e., at your expense).

In the usage exemplified in (20) and (21), *chī* 'eat off of' and *hē* 'drink off of' belong to this third class of verbs that take both a direct object and an indirect object with no *gěi*.

10.4 Apparent Indirect Objects

Not all verbs that appear to be followed by two objects are actually examples of indirect object verbs. Let us look at two such examples. The verbs *fá* 'fine, penalize, punish' and *piàn* 'swindle, cheat' might be thought to be included in this category of verbs that require the indirect object to precede the direct object and that cannot take the particle *gěi*. Sentences such as (22) and (23) seem to provide evidence for this classification:

(22) tā   fá   —   le   Zhāngsān   sì   —
      3sg   fine   —   PFV   Zhangsan   four   —

      shí   kuài   qián
      ten   dollar money

S/He fined Zhangsan $40.

(23) tā   piàn   —   le   Zhāngsān   sì   —
      3sg   cheat   —   PFV   Zhangsan   four   —

      shí   kuài   qián
      ten   dollar money

S/He cheated Zhangsan out of $40.

On the other hand, it is far from clear that the noun phrase *Zhāngsān* in (22) and (23) is an indirect object. In fact, there is evidence suggesting that it is the *direct* object of the verbs *fá* 'fine' and *piàn* 'cheat'. Let us look at the facts. First, all the verbs in the three classes we have discussed so far allow the direct object to occur alone with them. For example:

(24) wǒ   shū   —   le   yi   kuài   qián
      I   lose   —   PFV   one   dollar money

I lost a dollar.

(25) tā   huán   —   le   yi   wǎn   ròu
      3sg   return —   PFV   one   bowl   meat

S/He returned a bowl of meat.

(26) wǒ   huída   —   le   jǐ   —   ge   wèntí
      I   answer —   PFV   several —   CL   question

I answered several questions.

With *fá* 'fine' in (27) and *piàn* 'cheat' in (28), however, we find that only *Zhāngsān* but not *sìshí kuài qián* 'forty dollars' may occur alone:

(27) *a.* tā   fá   —   le   <u>Zhāngsān</u> le
          3sg   fine   —   PFV   Zhangsan   CRS

    S/He fined Zhangsan.

    b. *tā   fá   —   le   <u>sì   —   shí</u>
          3sg   fine   —   PFV   four   —   ten

             <u>kuài   qián</u>   le
                  dollar   money   CRS

(28) *a.* tā   piàn   —   le   <u>Zhāngsān</u> le
          3sg   cheat   —   PFV   Zhangsan   CRS

    S/He cheated Zhangsan.

    b. *tā   piàn   —   le   <u>sì   —   shí</u>
          3sg   cheat   —   PFV   four   —   ten

             <u>kuài   qián</u>   le[7]
                  dollar   money   CRS

Second, of all the verbs that take a direct object and indirect object, some may occur in the *bǎ* construction with the direct object as the *bǎ* noun phrase, and some may not occur in the *bǎ* construction, but, as mentioned at the beginning of this chapter, none may occur in the *bǎ* construction with the *indirect* object as the *bǎ* noun phrase:

(29) *wǒ   bǎ   <u>tā</u>   shū   —   le   yi
       I   BA   3sg   lose   —   PFV   one

             kuài   qián
                  dollar   money

(30) *tā   bǎ   <u>nǐ</u>   liú   —   le   yi
       3sg   BA   you   keep   —   PFV   one

             wǎn   ròu
                  bowl   meat

(31)　*wō　　bǎ　　tā　　huída　　—　　le　　jǐ
　　　　 I　　 BA　　3sg　 answer　　—　 PFV　 several

　　　　　　　　—　　ge　　wèntí
　　　　　　　　—　　CL　　question

Again, the verbs *fá* 'fine, penalize' and *piàn* 'cheat' are exceptions. Taking (22) and (23) as a reference point, we see that *Zhāngsān* but not *sìshí kuài qián* 'forty dollars' may occur as the *bǎ* noun phrase.

(32) *a.*　tā　　　bǎ　　 Zhāngsān　 fá　　 —　　 le
　　　　　 3sg　　 BA　　 Zhangsan　 fine　 —　　 PFV

　　　　　　　　 (sì　　　—　　 shí　　 kuài　 qián)
　　　　　　　　 (four　　—　　 ten　　 dollar　 money)

　　　S/He fined Zhangsan ($40).

　　b.　*tā　　 bǎ　　 sì　　 —　　 shí　　 kuài　 qián
　　　　　 3sg　 BA　　 four　 —　　 ten　　 dollar　 money

　　　　　　　 fá　　 —　　 le　　 Zhāngsān
　　　　　　　 fine　 —　　 PFV　 Zhangsan

(33) *a.*　tā　　 bǎ　　 Zhāngsān　 piàn　 —　 le
　　　　　 3sg　 BA　　 Zhangsan　 cheat　—　 PFV

　　　　　　　　 (sì　　　—　　 shí　　 kuài　 qián)
　　　　　　　　 (four　　—　　 ten　　 dollar　 money)

　　　S/He cheated Zhangsan (out of $40).

　　b.　*tā　　 bǎ　　 sì　　 —　　 shí　　 kuài　 qián
　　　　　 3sg　 BA　　 four　 —　　 ten　　 dollar　 money

　　　　　　　 piàn　 —　　 le　　 Zhāngsān
　　　　　　　 cheat　 —　　 PFV　 Zhangsan

Thus the claim that verbs such as *fá* 'fine, penalize, punish' in (22), and *piàn* 'cheat' in (23) take an indirect object is suspect. In fact, the structures of sentences (22) and (23) appear to parallel that of sentence (34):

(34)	tā	tī	—	le	Zhāngsān	liǎng	jiǎo
	3sg	kick	—	PFV	Zhangsan	two	foot

S/He dealt Zhangsan two kicks.

If our analysis of (22) and (23) is correct, then *Zhāngsān* is the *direct* object of the verbs *fá* 'fine' and *piàn* 'cheat', and *sìshí kuài qián* 'forty dollars' functions as a quantity adverbial denoting the *extent* of the actions of fining and cheating, just as *liǎng jiǎo* 'two kicks' denotes the extent of the action *tī* 'kick' in (34) (see section 8.5 of chapter 8 for a discussion of such quantity adverbials). *Fá* 'fine' and *piàn* 'cheat', then, although they look like verbs that take an indirect object, can be shown to be ordinary transitive verbs taking a direct object and a quantity adverbial phrase.

10.5 Explanation for the Indirect Object Facts

We have seen that verbs taking both a direct object and an indirect object fall into three classes according to the presence of *gěi* when the indirect object precedes the direct object. In this section, we will try to explain the reasons for this classification.

First, the meaning of *gěi* plays a crucial role in the behavior of the verbs that take both a direct object and an indirect object. As a verb, *gěi* means 'give'. Let us analyze the meaning 'give' by examining this English sentence:

(35) Mary gave John a book.

The verb 'give' signals a *transaction*. It requires a *source* from which the transaction originates, a *goal* at which the transaction terminates, and an *entity* that is transferred. In (35) the subject of the sentence, *Mary*, is the source, the indirect object, *John*, is the goal, and the direct object, *a book*, is the entity being transferred. Now, the meaning of the coverb *gěi* 'to' is closely related to the meaning of the verb *gěi* 'give'. Thus coverb *gěi* 'to' must occur with a verb denoting some sort of transaction. This transaction may be concrete, as in *rēng* 'throw, toss', or abstract, as in *jiāo* 'teach'. The semantic function of the coverb *gěi* is to mark the goal of the transaction named by the verb.

With this fact about *gěi* in mind, let us examine the verbs with obligatory *gěi* (section 10.1) and with optional *gěi* (section 10.2). Both of these classes of verbs involve transactions in which the subject is the source and the indirect object the goal. From this semantic fact we can predict the presence of *gěi* to mark the indirect object as the goal of the transaction. The only question, then, is why it is that the verbs in the first group obligatorily require *gěi*, while the verbs in the second group may dispense with *gěi* when the indirect object precedes the direct object. Unfortunately, to this question there is at present no satisfactory answer. Which verbs require *gěi* and which verbs allow it optionally is something that simply has to be learned for each verb.

When we examine the third class of verbs, those that do *not* allow the presence of *gěi* and that require the indirect object to precede the direct object (section 10.3), however, we find that these verbs fall into three groups, and for each group there is a reason why *gěi* is disallowed. The first group consists simply of the verb *gěi* 'give' itself. It seems reasonable to suggest that the reason *gěi* 'give' does not allow the coverb *gěi* is partially a historical one: the coverb *gěi* is historically derived from the verb *gěi,* so there is no historical basis for the two to co-occur. The second group of verbs in this class consists of *gàosu* 'tell', *dāyìng* 'promise', *huídá* 'answer', *wèn* 'ask'. All these are verbs of linguistic communication—words are being spoken, but, in a strict sense, there is no transaction taking place. This explains why they do not occur with *gěi,* whose literal function is to mark goals in transactions. The last group of verbs in this class includes the following verbs:

(36) tōu   'steal'
      qǐngjiào   'ask for enlightenment'
      yíng   'win'
      qiǎng   'rob'
      duó   'snatch'

It is easy to see that all of these verbs involve, not transacting *to*, but deprivation *from* the indirect object. Another way of stating this is to say that the *subject* rather than the indirect object of the sentence is the *goal*, and the *indirect object*, from whom or which something is being taken, is the *source*. Since nothing is transferred to the indirect object in the transaction, it is clear why indirect objects with these verbs may not be preceded by *gěi*.

We mentioned above another requirement of this third class of verbs: the indirect object must immediately follow the verb. That is, sentence (6), which is repeated here, is not acceptable.

(6)	*wǒ	rēng	—	le	nèi	kuài	ròu	tā
	I	toss	—	PFV	that	piece	meat	3sg

Why does the indirect object have to follow the verb immediately if it is a member of this third class of verbs taking indirect objects? The answer has to do with the fact that these indirect objects are not preceded by the coverb *gěi*. As we saw above, if an indirect object does not immediately follow the verb, it must be preceded by *gěi*; but since these verbs never occur with *gěi*, the indirect object may never appear in any position other than immediately after the verb.

10.6 Benefactive Noun Phrases and Preverbal Indirect Objects

A benefactive noun phrase in a sentence typically refers to the one indirectly affected by the activity signaled by the verb of the sentence. In Mandarin, a benefactive noun phrase is marked with either *wèi* or *gěi*, both of which may be translated as 'for'; *wèi*, the more archaic form, is unrestricted in its usage, while *gěi*, the more innovative form, is restricted to certain verbs only. Marked with one of these two coverbs, the benefactive noun phrase precedes the verb. For example:

(37)	ta	gěi	wǒ	zào	—	le	yi	—
	3sg	for	I	build	—	PFV	one	—

	dòng	fángzi
	CL	house

S/He built a house for me.

(38)	tā	wèi	wǒ	niàn	—	shū
	3sg	for	I	study	—	book

S/He studies for me.

(39)	tā	gěi	wǒ	tiāo	—	le	liù	—
	3sg	for	me	select	—	PFV	six	—

	jiàn	dàyī
	CL	coat

S/He chose six coats for me.

(40)	tā	wèi	wǒ	chàng	—	gē
	3sg	for	me	sing	—	song

S/He sang for me.

(41)   tā   gěi   xuésheng   jiěshi   wénfǎ
        3sg   for   student   explain   grammar

S/He explained the grammar for the students.

(42)   tā   gěi   wǒ   zhào   –   le   bu
        3sg   for   me   make   –   PFV   not

        shǎo   máfan
        little trouble

$\begin{cases} \text{S/He made a lot of trouble for me.} \\ \text{S/He gave me a lot of trouble.} \end{cases}$

(43)   tā   gěi   Lǐsì   hèxǐ
        3sg   for   Lisi   congratulate

S/He congratulated Lisi.

(44)   Zhāng   yīshēng   gěi   Lǐsì   kàn   –   bìng
        Zhang   doctor   for   Lisi   see   –   illness

Doctor Zhang is treating Lisi.

(45)   wǒ   gěi   nǐ   dàoqiàn
        I   for   you   apologize

I apologize to you.

Now, since the benefactive noun phrase precedes the verb and the indirect object follows the verb in a sentence, they should be easily distinguishable, although *gěi* may be involved in both cases. This is, however, not exactly the case in modern Mandarin: the indirect object marked by *gěi* has begun to appear in the preverbal position. This is a manifestation of the general structural change that is pushing the language toward the verb-final type, discussed in section 2.4.2 of chapter 2, for more than a millennium, Mandarin has been moving toward a preferred word order in which noun phrases occur before rather than after the verb. The appearance of the indirect object in the preverbal position, however, is confined to only a few verbs, such as *xiě* 'write', *mǎi* 'buy', *liú* 'keep, save', *dǎ (diànhua)* 'telephone', *sòng* 'give', *jiā* 'add on', all belonging to the first two groups of verbs discussed above in 10.1 and 10.2, that is, to those groups for which *gěi* is either obligatory or optional. Hence, sentence (46) *a* can also be expressed as (46) *b* with no change in meaning:

(46) *a.*	wǒ	sòng	—	le	yi	—	běn
	I	give	—	PFV	one	—	CL

		shū	gěi	tā
		book	to	3sg

I gave a book to him/her.

b.	wǒ	gěi	tā	sòng	—	le	yi
	I	to	3sg	give	—	PFV	one

		—	běn	shū
		—	CL	book

I gave him/her a book.

For (46) *a*, a benefactive interpretation is possible but not preferable ('I gave a book [to someone] for him'), but with some verbs, sentences with preverbal *gěi* phrases are quite natural with either an indirect object or a benefactive interpretation. For example,

(47)	wǒ	gěi	tā	xiě	—	le	yi	—
	I	{ to / for }	3sg	write	—	PFV	one	—

		fēng	xìn
		CL	letter

I wrote a letter { to / for } him/her.

For those verbs that do not yet allow the indirect object in the preverbal position, such as *jì* 'mail', the semantic contrast between the benefactive preverbal *gěi* phrase and the indirect object postverbal *gěi* phrase is clear:

(48) *a.* (benefactive)

wǒ	gěi	tā	jì	–	le	yi	–
I	for	3sg	mail	–	PFV	one	–

fēng	xìn
CL	letter

I mailed a letter <u>for him/her</u>.

b. (indirect object)

wǒ	jì	–	le	yi	–	fēng	xìn
I	mail	–	PFV	one	–	CL	letter

gěi	tā
to	3sg

I mailed a letter <u>to him/her</u>.

10.7 Other Functions of *gěi*

In this section, we will briefly mention those usages of *gěi* in which it introduces neither an indirect object nor a benefactive noun phrase.

The first construction involving a preverbal *gěi* phrase whose noun phrase is neither an indirect object nor a benefactive involves the verbs *kàn* 'see' and *tīng* 'hear', usages in which it conveys a special meaning of 'allow to see' and 'allow to hear'. For example:

(49)	qǐng	nǐ	gěi	wǒ	kàn	nèi	–
	please	you	to	I	look	that	–

běn	shū
CL	book

Please let me look at that book.

(50) wǒ   chàng   –   gē   gěi   nǐ   tīng
      I   sing   –   song   to   you   hear

I'll sing for you to hear.

The second *gěi* construction that is neither an indirect object nor a benefactive construction is found in sentences where *gěi* functions as a passive marker, like *bèi*, as in (51). This function is discussed further in chapter 16.

(51) wǒ   gěi   tā   piàn   –   le
      I   3sg   cheat   –   PFV

I was cheated by him/her.

Notes

1. For this chapter, we have taken some ideas from Mei (1972:144–148) and Teng (1975a:149–154).

2. The reason why the perfective *-le* appears in sentence (1) but not in sentences (2) and (4) is that the *gěi* phrase acts as a perfectivizing expression (see chapter 6, section 6.1.2.B).

3. For a general cross-linguistic discussion of this principle, see Givón (1979a:chap. 4).

4. This insight is due to Chao (1968:317–319), though we disagree with him slightly on the categorization of certain verbs; see section 10.4.

5. One may pose the question: How do you use the verbs in this class if the speech context is one in which the direct object but not the indirect object has just been mentioned, since the direct object of these verbs cannot precede the indirect object? The answer is that you make the direct object into the topic of the sentence, as in:

(i)   D.O.
      nèi   kuài   ròu   wǒ   gěi   –   le   wǒ
      that   piece   meat   I   give   –   PFV   I

             –   de   gǒu
             –   GEN   dog

That piece of meat (topic) I gave to my dog.

6. It should be noted that (19) *a* is acceptable if *gěi* is interpreted as the verb 'to give'; the sentence, then, becomes a serial verb construction (see chapter 21). As a serial verb construction, (19) *a* has the meaning 'S/He stole $20,000 to give to the bank'.

7. To some native speakers of Mandarin, this sentence is acceptable with the meaning 'He got $40 by cheating'.

CHAPTER 11

Locative and Directional Phrases

11.1 Locative Phrases

In this section on locative phrases, we will first examine the internal structure of the locative phrase and then discuss the semantic implications of the position of the locative phrase in the sentence.[1]

11.1.1 The Structure of the Locative Phrase

The locative phrase has the following structure:

(1)   <u>zài</u>   noun phrase − (locative particle)
      'at'

The underlined portions of (2) and (3) give examples of locative phrases:

(2)	tāmen	<u>zài</u>	<u>fángzi</u>	−	<u>hòumian</u>	xiūli	diànshìjī
	they	at	house	−	behind	repair	television

They repair televisions behind their house.

(3)	wǒ	bǎ	qiānbǐ	chā	<u>zài</u>	<u>píngzi</u>	−	<u>lǐtou</u>
	I	BA	pencil	insert	at	vase	−	in

I put the pencils in the vase.

A. The Locative Particle

The locative particle that follows the noun phrase, as illustrated in examples (2) and (3), specifies a spatial relationship. Table 11.1 shows the forms of the various locative particles. The locative particles *wài* 'outside', *qián* 'in front of', *hòu* 'in back of', and *páng* 'beside' are rarely used by themselves, but normally occur with one of the suffixes *-bian*, *-mian*, *-tou*, as shown in (4)–(7):

(4) *a.*   zài   huāyuán   –   qiánmian
            at   garden   –   front

       in front of the garden

    b.   *zài   huāyuan   –   qián
            at   garden   –   front

(5) *a.*   zài   xuéxiào   –   wàibian
            at   school   –   outside

       outside of school

TABLE 11.1
LOCATIVE PARTICLES

LOCATIVE PARTICLES				GLOSS
shàng	*shàngbian*	*shàngmian*	*shàngtou*	'on top of, above'
xià/dǐxia	*xiàbian*	*xiàmian*	*xiàtou*	'under, below'
lǐ	*lǐbian*	*lǐmian*	*lǐtou*	'in, inside'
wài	*wàibian*	*wàimian*	*wàitou*	'outside'
qián	*qiánbian*	*qiánmian*	*qiántou*	'in front of'
hòu	*hòubian*	*hòumian*	*hòutou*	'in back of, behind'
páng	*pángbian*			'beside'
zhōngjian/dāngzhong				'in the center of'
	zuǒbian	*zuǒmian*		'left of'
	yòubian	*yòumian*		'right of'
dōngbu	*dōngbian*			'east of'
nánbu	*nánbian*			'south of'
xību	*xībian*			'west of'
běibu	*běibian*			'north of'
zhèr/zhèli	*zhèbian*	*zhèmian*		'this side of'
nàr/nàli	*nàbian*	*nàmian*		'that side of'

b.	*zài	xuéxiào	—	wài
	at	school	—	outside

(6) *a.*	zài	shùlín	—	hòumian
	at	forest	—	behind

behind the forest

b.	*zài	shùlín	—	hòu
	at	forest	—	behind

(7) *a.*	zài	fángzi	—	pángbian
	at	house	—	beside

beside the house

b.	*zài	fángzi	—	páng
	at	house	—	beside

To account for the unacceptability of the *b* phrases, we note that in chapter 2, it was pointed out that modern Mandarin has been moving away from the monosyllabic characteristics of classical Chinese; in other words, morphemes in modern Mandarin words tend to be disyllabic. For those nouns that have both a monosyllabic and a disyllabic form in modern Mandarin, it is often the case that the *monosyllabic* form may take the *monosyllabic* locative particle, *wài, qián, hòu,* or *páng,* but the *disyllabic* form must take the *disyllabic* locative particle, which is composed of the locative morpheme with one of the suffixes *-bian, -mian,* or *-tou,* as can be seen in (8) and (9) below. The monosyllabic forms *chéng* 'city' and *shān* 'hill' can occur with both the monosyllabic and the disyllabic locative particles, as shown in the *a* and *b* examples of (8) and (9), but the disyllabic forms *chéngzi* 'city' and *shānzi* 'hill' can occur only with the disyllabic locative particles, as shown in the *c* and *d* examples of (8) and (9) which parallel (4)–(7) above.

(8) *a.*	zài	chéng	—	wài
	at	city	—	outside

outside the city

b.	zài	chéng	—	wàibian
	at	city	—	outside

outside the city

c.	*zài	chéngzi	–	wài
	at	city	–	outside

d.	zài	chéngzi	–	wàibian
	at	city	–	outside

outside the city

(9) a.

zài	shān	–	hòu
at	hill	–	back

behind the hill

b.

zài	shān	–	hòubian
at	hill	–	back

behind the hill

c.

*zài	shānzi	–	hòu
at	hill	–	back

d.

zài	shānzi	–	hòubian
at	hill	–	back

behind the hill

The direction words *dōng* 'east', *nán* 'south', *xī* 'west', and *běi* 'north', which, together with the suffix *-bian*, occur as locative particles, may be combined to form *dōng-nán* 'east-south = southeast', *dōng-běi* 'east-north = northeast', *xī-nán* 'west-south = southwest' and *xī-běi* 'west-north = northwest'. Note that in these combinations *dōng* 'east' and *xī* 'west' always precede *nán* 'south' and *běi* 'north'. The reverse order will be unacceptable: **nán-xī* 'south-west', **běi-dōng* 'north-east'.

The locative particle is not used when the noun phrase in the locative phrase is a place name, as in *Sānfānshì* 'city of San Francisco', *Hélán* 'Holland' and *Běijīng* 'Beijing', as illustrated in (10):

(10)

tā	zhù	zài	Zhōngshān	lù
3sg	live	at	Zhongshan	Road

S/He lives on Zhongshan Road

When the locative phrase occurs before the verb, certain nouns need no locative particle. These nouns usually refer to familiar places, including rooms, buildings, organizations, and institutions, such as *xuéxiào* 'school', *fànguar* 'restaurant', *jiā* 'home', *chúfang* 'kitchen', *fànting* 'dining room', *shūfang* 'study', *jiàotang* 'church', *yóuzhèngjú* 'post office', *yīyuàn* 'hospital', *jǐngchájú* 'police station', *chēzhàn* 'station', and *fēijīchǎng* 'airport'. The phrases in (11)–(12) show that nouns of this type may occur in a locative phrase without a locative particle only if the locative phrase precedes the verb. If the locative phrase follows the verb, these nouns must take the locative particle:

(11) *a.*

zài	jiàotang	–	li	guì	–	zhe
at	church	–	in	kneel	–	DUR

   kneeling in the church

b.

zài	jiàotang	guì	–	zhe
at	church	kneel	–	DUR

   kneeling in the church

c.

*guì	zài	jiàotang	.
kneel	at	church	

d.

guì	zài	jiàotang	–	li
kneel	at	church	–	in

   kneeling in the church

(12) *a.*

zài	jǐngchájú	–	li	shuì
at	police:station	–	in	sleep

   sleep in the police station

b.

zài	jǐngchájú	shuì
at	police:station	sleep

   sleep in the police station

c.

*shuì	zài	jǐngchájú
sleep	at	police:station

d.   shuì   zài   jǐngchájú   –   li
       sleep   at   police:station   –   in

sleep in the police station

A few nouns other than place names which do not take the locative particle are *biéchu* 'elsewhere', *dàochu/gèchu* 'everywhere', *jìnchu* 'nearby place', *yuǎnchu* 'distant place'. These few nouns all end in the bound morpheme *-chu*, which means 'place, locality'. For example:

(13)   tā   zhù   zài   biéchu
         3sg   live   at   elsewhere

S/He lives somewhere else.

Finally, we note that all the locative particles, except the monosyllabic ones, may occur without a preceding noun phrase. In such cases, the noun phrase is understood from context. For example, if one says

(14)   wàimian   hǎo   lěng   a
        outside   very   cold   RF

It's really cold outside.

it is assumed that *wàimian* 'outside' refers to outside of wherever the speaker is. Similarly, with the sentence

(15)   pángbian   dōu   zāng   le
        side   all   dirty   CRS

The side is all dirty.

what it is whose side is dirty would be clear from context. And for a sentence such as

(16)   nánbu   xiàtiān   hěn   mèn
        south   summer   very   muggy

In the south, it's very muggy in the summer.

the context would make it clear what place *nánbu* is to the south of.

B. The Locative Coverb

The coverb *zài* 'at' introduces the locative phrase (see chapter 9 on coverbs). It is obligatory except in those presentative constructions (see chapter 17) where a locative phrase is in sentence-initial position; in presentative sentences, *zài* 'at' is in general optional, as (17)−(19) illustrate:

(17)	(zài)	wūzi	—	li	yǒu	sān
	(at)	house	—	in	exist	three

	—	ge	rén
	—	CL	person

In the house, there are three people.

(18)	(zài)	qiáng	—	shang	guà	—	zhe
	(at)	wall	—	on	hang	—	DUR

	yi	—	fu	huà
	one	—	CL	painting

On the wall hangs a painting.

(19)	(zài)	shān	—	shang	xià	—
	(at)	mountain	—	on	descend	—

	zhe	dà	yǔ	ne
	DUR	big	rain	REx

It's raining hard on the mountain.

If, however, the presentative sentence contains an activity verb understood in a stative sense, as in (20)

(20)	zhuōzi	—	shàng	duī	—	le
	table	—	on	pile	—	PFV

	hěn	duō	shū
	very	many	book

A lot of books are piled on the table.

the occurrence of the coverb *zài* 'at' at the beginning of the locative phrase changes the meaning: the sentence is no longer serving a presentative function, and the activity verb is no longer understood in a stative sense. Sentence (21) illustrates these points:

(21)	<u>zāi</u>	zhuōzi	—	shàng	duī	—	le
	at	table	—	on	pile	—	PFV

	hěn	duō	shū
	very	many	book

(Someone) piled a lot of books on the table.

As indicated by the translation, (21) functions to name an activity, where the agent of the activity is understood from the context, whereas (20) describes a state and has the function of presenting the noun phrase 'a lot of books' into the discourse.

If a locative phrase follows a verb, on the other hand, it must be introduced by *zài* 'at',[2] as shown in (22):

(22)	wǒ	bǎ	tā	—	de	míngzi
	I	BA	3sg	—	GEN	name

	xiě	*(zài)	xìnfēng	—	shang
	write	at	envelope	—	on

I wrote his/her name on the envelope.

11.1.2 The Position of the Locative Phrase in the Sentence

As we have seen, the locative phrase either precedes or follows the verb in a sentence. We can represent the two orderings thus:

(23) *a.* <u>(zài) noun phrase — locative particle</u> verb

b. verb <u>zài noun phrase — locative particle</u>

For example,

(24)	tā	zài	kètīng	—	li	tiàowǔ
	3sg	at	living:room	—	in	dance

S/He is dancing in the living room.

(25)	qìchē	tíng	<u>zài</u>	<u>lù</u>	—	<u>zhōngjiān</u>
	car	stop	at	road	—	center

The car stopped in the middle of the road.

The single factor that determines whether the locative phrase occurs before or after the verb is the meaning of the verb. The generalization for preverbal locative phrases can be stated as in (i):

(i) Preverbal locative phrases: Any verb naming an event or state that can occur at some location can take a preverbal locative phrase specifying the general location at which that event or state occurs. Sentences (26) and (27) are good examples of preverbal locative phrases naming the general location of the event or state:

(26)	tā	<u>zài</u>	<u>Xīzàng</u>	xùmù
	3sg	at	Tibet	do:animal:husbandry

S/He does (i.e., is engaged in) animal husbandry in Tibet.

(27)	tā	<u>zài</u>	<u>chuáng</u>	—	<u>shang</u>	shuì
	3sg	at	bed	—	on	sleep

S/He sleeps on the bed.

Since nearly any event or state can have a location, most verbs allow a preverbal locative phrase. Relatively few verbs, however, allow a postverbal locative phrase. In fact, there are just four classes of verbs that do. We will discuss each of these four classes in turn.

A. Verbs of Displacement

A *verb of displacement* (Vdi) is an action verb whose meaning includes the *local* displacement of either the subject (in the case of an intransitive verb) or the direct object (in the case of a transitive verb). Verbs of the class Vdi include:

(28)	<u>tiào</u>	'jump'	<u>dǎo</u>	'fall'
	<u>rēng</u>	'toss'	<u>xià</u>	'drop'
	<u>tuī</u>	'push'	<u>dié</u>	'fall'
	<u>diào</u>	'drop, fall'	<u>liú</u>	'flow'
	<u>bō</u>	'sprinkle'	<u>pá</u>	'crawl'
	<u>shuāi</u>	'fall, trip'	<u>mǒ</u>	'spread, smear'

Any resultative verb compound whose second element is *dǎo*, such as *tī-dǎo* 'kick-fall'.

Verbs of displacement allow both preverbal and postverbal locative phrases, but there is a meaning difference correlating with this positional difference: the preverbal locative phrase signals the general location where the action takes place, as predicted by generalization (i), while the postverbal locative phrase specifies the location of the subject (in the case of an intransitive verb) or the direct object (in the case of a transitive verb) *as a result* of the displacement.

Consider the following examples, which illustrate the contrast between the postverbal locative phrase and the preverbal locative phrase when the verb belongs to the category Vdi:

(29) *a.*

tā	zài	zhuōzi	—	shang	tiào
3sg	at	table	—	on	jump

S/He is on the table jumping.

b.

tā	tiào	zài	zhuōzi	—	shang
3sg	jump	at	table	—	on

S/He jumped onto the table.

In (29) *a*, the locative phrase, occurring before the verb, denotes the general location of the action 'jump'; that is, (29) *a* means that s/he is jumping up and down on the top of the table. In (29) *b*, on the other hand, the locative phrase occurs after the verb *tiào* 'jump'. Since 'jump' is an action that may result in locally displacing the subject, the postverbal locative phrase names the location of the subject as a *result* of the action. Sentences (30) *a* and *b* are another pair of contrasting sentences with a verb from the category Vdi which illustrates the distinct semantic functions of the preverbal and postverbal locative phrases. In this pair of sentences, the verb is transitive (a resultative verb compound), so this time it is the *direct object* of the verb which is displaced within the immediate vicinity of the action:

(30) *a.*

wǒ	zài	shāfa	—	shang	bǎ	tā
I	at	sofa	—	on	BA	3sg

	tuī	—	dǎo	LE
	push	—	fall	PFV/CRS

On the sofa, I pushed him/her down.

b.	wǒ	bǎ	tā	tuī	—	dǎo	<u>zài</u>
	I	BA	3sg	push	—	fall	at

<u>shāfa</u>	—	<u>shang</u>
sofa	—	on

I pushed him/her onto the sofa.

Again, (30) *a*, with a preverbal locative phrase, means simply that the general location of the action of pushing him/her down was 'on the sofa'. That is, both *wǒ* 'I' and *tā* 's/he' were on the sofa when the 'pushing down' happened. Sentence (30) *b*, however, has a postverbal locative phrase and thus conforms to the generalization for the category Vdi: the locative phrase specifies that s/he ended up on the sofa as a result of the pushing down.

The importance of the condition specifying that the subject or direct object must be *locally* displaced is demonstrated by the fact that verbs whose actions result, not in locally displacing, but in *transporting* the subject or the direct object to a new location cannot take a locative phrase in postverbal position. Such action verbs include, for example, *fēi* 'fly', *pǎo* 'run', and *gǎn* 'herd'. They take a postverbal phrase that is introduced by the morpheme *dào* 'to', which is called a *directional phrase*, and will be discussed in section 11.2.

(31) *a*.	*tā	fēi	<u>zài</u>	<u>Jiā</u>	—	<u>zhōu</u>	le
	3sg	fly	at	California	—	state	CRS

b.	tā	fēi	<u>dào</u>	<u>Jiā</u>	—	<u>zhōu</u>	le
	3sg	fly	to	California	—	state	CRS

S/He flew to California.

(32) *a*.	*wǒ	bǎ	yáng	gǎn	<u>zài</u>	<u>hòu</u>
	I	BA	sheep	herd	at	back

—	yuán	—	<u>li</u>
—	yard	—	in

b.	wǒ	bǎ	yáng	gǎn	<u>dào</u>
	I	BA	sheep	herd	to

<u>hòu</u>	—	<u>yuán</u>	—	<u>li</u>
back	—	yard	—	in

I herded the sheep into the backyard.

So far we have seen that for action verbs of type Vdi, where a subject or a direct object is locally displaced, postverbal locative phrases express the new location of the subject or the direct object as a result of the local displacement.

B. Verbs of Posture

Verbs of posture (Vpo) depict the posture of an entity, which is typically an animate being. This class includes such verbs as:

(33)

zhàn	'stand'	zuò	'sit'
shuì	'sleep'	tǎng	'lie down'
pā	'crouch'	guì	'kneel'
dūn	'squat'	yǐ	'lean on'
fó	'float'	zhù	'have residence'
tíng	'stop'	piāo	'float'

With verbs of posture, both preverbal and postverbal locative phrases can be used. Since in the case of these verbs there is no difference between naming the general location where the event occurs (which is the function of a preverbal locative phrase, as we saw in the generalization stated in [i]) and naming the place where the subject assumes a certain posture (which is what the postverbal locative phrase does when it occurs with these verbs), there is essentially no difference between the meanings of the preverbal and the postverbal locative phrases with verbs of this class. Thus, the *a* and *b* forms of (34)–(37) are synonymous:

(34) *a.*

tā	zài	wū	—	yán	—	xià
3sg	at	house	—	eaves	—	under

zhàn	—	zhe
stand	—	DUR

S/He is standing under the eaves.

b.

tā	zhàn	zài	wū	—	yán	—	xià
3sg	stand	at	house	—	eaves	—	under

S/He is standing under the eaves.

(35) *a.*

tā	zài	chuáng	—	shang	shuì
3sg	at	bed	—	on	sleep

S/He sleeps on the bed.

b.	tā	shuì	zài	chuáng	—	shang
	3sg	sleep	at	bed	—	on

S/He sleeps on the bed.

(36) a.	tā	zài	dì	—	shang	guì	—	zhe
	3sg	at	ground	—	on	kneel	—	DUR

S/He is kneeling on the ground.

b.	tā	guì	zài	dì	—	shang
	3sg	kneel	at	ground	—	on

S/He is kneeling on the ground.

(37) a.	tā	zài	zhuōzi	—	shang	pā	—	zhe
	3sg	at	table	—	on	crouch	—	DUR

S/He is crouching on the table.

b.	tā	pā	zài	zhuōzi	—	shang
	3sg	crouch	at	table	—	on

S/He is crouching on the table.

Verbs of this class also share the property of taking -zhe as the durative aspect marker (see section 6.2.1 of chapter 6 on aspect), as illustrated by the a sentences of (34)–(37).

Among all of the verbs of posture, only the verb tíng 'stop, park' usually takes an inanimate subject, as in:

(38)	chēzi	tíng	zài	mén	—	wài
	car	stop	at	door	—	out

The car is parked outside of the door.

Thus tíng as a member of the class Vpo depicts posture in a metaphorical sense. Similarly, zhù 'live, reside' is a verb of posture in the metaphorical sense. Zhù is a posture only with regard to the overall disposition of the person(s) to whom the subject noun phrase refers.

C. Verbs of Appearing

The verbs in this class behave identically to those in class Vpo. The difference between them is simply that *verbs of appearing* (Vap) signal an appearing or disappearing of the subject. Examples of verbs of this type include:

(39) fāshēng   'happen, occur'
      chūxian   'appear'
      (chū)shēng   'be born'
      shēngzhǎng   'grow up'
      zhǎngdà   'grow up'
      chǎnshēng   'occur'
      sǐ   'die'
      xiāoshī   'disappear'

As with verbs of posture, since there is no difference between naming the general location where the event occurs and the location of the appearance or disappearance of the subject, sentences with verbs of appearing have the same meaning with preverbal locative phrases as they do with postverbal locative phrases, as seen in the following examples:

(40) *a.* nèi — zhǒng shì kěnéng zài Shànghǎi fāshēng
           that — sort event possible at Shanghai happen

That sort of event may happen in Shanghai.

     b. nèi — zhǒng shì kěnéng fāshēng zài Shànghǎi
            that — sort event possible happen at Shanghai

That sort of event may happen in Shanghai.

(41) *a.* Zhāngsān zì — yòu zài Běijīng shēngzhǎng
           Zhangsan since — youth at Beijing grow:up

Zhangsan grew up in Beijing from the time he was young.

     b. Zhāngsān zì — yòu shēngzhǎng zài Běijīng
            Zhangsan since — youth grow:up at Beijing

Zhangsan grew up in Beijing from the time he was young.

(42) *a.*

tā	qíngyuàn	zài	yīyuàn	–	li	sĭ
3sg	willing	at	hospital	–	in	die

S/He is willing to die in the hospital.

b.

tā	qíngyuàn	sĭ	zài	yīyuàn	–	li
3sg	willing	die	at	hospital	–	in

S/He is willing to die in the hospital.

So far, we have seen that while nearly any verb allows a preverbal locative phrase specifying where the event or state it names takes place, only certain classes of verbs allow postverbal locative phrases. The last class of verbs to be considered is exceptional in an interesting way.

D. Verbs of Placement

Verbs of placement (Vpl) name actions that place the direct object in a certain location. The verbs in this class differ in a subtle but important way from those in class Vdi: sentences using verbs of displacement involve *movement*, or *displacement*, from one location to another, whereas sentences employing verbs of placement involve the subject placing the direct object somewhere *but do not specify where it started out*. Examples of verbs in the class Vpl include:

(43)

fàng	'put, place'	cáng	'hide'
zhòng	'plant'	xiĕ	'write'
huà	'draw, paint'	chāo	'copy'
tŭ	'expectorate'	yìn	'print'
kè	'carve, sculpt'	jiànlì	'establish'
să	'spill'		

Class Vpl is an exception to the pattern exhibited by all the other verb classes we have considered: with verbs of placement, *both* the preverbal locative phrase and the postverbal locative phrase can specify the location where the direct object is placed. Hence the *a* and *b* sentences of (44)–(46) are semantically equivalent:

(44) *a.*

wǒ	zài	shūjià	–	shang	fàng	zázhì
I	at	bookcase	–	on	place	magazine

I put the magazine on the bookcase.

b. | wǒ | bǎ | zázhì | fàng | <u>zài</u> | shūjià | – | <u>shang</u> |
|------|------|-------|------|------|--------|------|------|
| I | BA | magazine | place | at | bookcase | – | on |

I put the magazine on the bookcase.

(45) *a.* | wǒ | <u>zài</u> | guìzi | – | li | cáng | jiǔ |
|------|------|-------|------|------|------|------|
| I | at | cabinet | – | in | hide | liquor |

I hid the liquor in the cabinet.

b. | wǒ | bǎ | jiǔ | cáng | <u>zài</u> | guìzi | – | li |
|------|------|------|------|------|-------|------|------|
| I | BA | liquor | hide | at | cabinet | – | in |

I hid the liquor in the cabinet.

(46) *a.* | wǒ | <u>zài</u> | wǒ | – | de | běnzi | – | <u>shang</u> |
|------|------|------|------|------|--------|------|------|
| I | at | I | – | GEN | notebook | – | on |

huà	yi	–	ge	lǎohǔ
draw	one	–	CL	tiger

I drew a tiger in my notebook.

b. | wǒ | bǎ | yi | – | ge | lǎohǔ | huà | <u>zài</u> |
|------|------|------|------|------|--------|------|------|
| I | BA | one | – | CL | tiger | draw | at |

wǒ	–	de	běnzi	–	<u>shang</u>
I	–	GEN	notebook	–	on

I drew a tiger in my notebook.

(For the reason why the *b* sentences of (44)–(46) are expressed with *bǎ*, see the discussion of rule (ii) in section 11.1.2.E just below.)

What we see, then, is that the Vpl class is the only class of verbs with which a preverbal locative phrase does *not* have to convey the general location where the event occurs, but can instead name the place where the direct object ends up as a result of the action of the verb. A verb of placement, of course, *may* take a preverbal locative phrase specifying the general location of the action, as in (47); the point is that it does not have to.

(47) wǒ zài shū — fáng — li bǎ

    I   at   study — room — in BA

       yi   — ge lǎohǔ huà

       one — CL tiger draw

       zài wǒ — de běnzi

       at   I   — GEN notebook

       — shang

       — on

In the study, I drew a tiger in my notebook.

If we compare (46) *a* with (47), it is clear that in the former, the preverbal locative phrase specifies the location where the direct object *lǎohǔ* 'tiger' is placed as a result of drawing, while in the latter, the preverbal locative phrase simply specifies the place where the drawing is happening, according to the generalization stated in (i).

We have seen that, while most verbs take preverbal locative phrases, only certain verbs allow postverbal locative phrases. With verbs of local displacement, a postverbal locative phrase signals the place to which the actor or direct object is displaced. With verbs of posture and appearance, however, because of their "stationary" meanings, both preverbal and postverbal locative phrases may be used for the location of the posture or appearance, and there is no difference in meaning between them. Finally, with verbs of placement, both preverbal and postverbal locative phrases may also be used, but for this class of verbs alone, the preverbal locative phrase can signal either the general location of the action or the location where the direct object is placed.

E. The Postverbal Locative Phrase Must Immediately Follow the Verb

In addition to the restrictions relating to classes of verbs, however, there exists another interesting condition on the postverbal locative phrase, which we can express as (ii):

(ii) The postverbal locative phrase must *immediately* follow the verb. Condition (ii) accounts for the fact that (48) is unacceptable:

(48) *wǒ   cáng   bǎo   —   shí   zài
       I   hide   precious —   stone   at

       xiāngzi   —   li
       chest   —   in

Here, since the direct object comes right after the verb, separating the verb from its postverbal locative phrase, the sentence is ungrammatical. In order to ensure that the postverbal locative phrase immediately follows the verb, either the *bǎ* structure (see chapter 15), which places the direct object before the verb, must be employed, or the verb must appear twice (see chapter 13 on verb copying):

(49) wǒ   bǎ   bǎo   —   shí   cáng
       I   BA   precious —   stone   hide

       zài   xiāngzi   —   li
       at   chest   —   in

I hide the precious stone in a chest.

(50) wǒ   cáng   bǎo   —   shí   cáng
       I   hide   precious —   stone   hide

       zài   xiāngzi   —   li
       at   chest   —   in

I hide the precious stone in a chest.

According to rule (ii), then, the following sequence of elements is ungrammatical:

(51) *noun phrase verb noun phrase zài noun phrase — locative particle
      subject   object   locative phrase

Rule (ii) explains why the *b* sentences in examples (30) and (44)–(46) above had to be in the form of a *bǎ* construction. In fact, however, generalization (ii) extends beyond rendering sentences having the form of (51) ungrammatical. If a verb is a compound composed of a verb and an object *morphologically* (see section 3.2.3 of chapter 3), the locative phrase cannot even occur after the verb compound. A good example illustrating this extended constraint involves the verb-object compound *shuì-jiao* 'sleep', as opposed to the noncompound verb *shuì* 'sleep'. The two verbs are semantically equivalent, but only the noncompound verb, *shuì*, not the verb-object compound, can take a postverbal locative phrase:

(52) *a*.

tā	shuì	zài	chuáng	—	shang
3sg	sleep	at	bed	—	on

S/He sleeps in bed.

b.

*tā	shuì	—	jiao	zài	chuáng	—	shang
3sg	sleep	—	sleep	at	bed	—	on

Consider another example, the compound *dǎ-zuò* 'sit in meditation': *dǎ-zuò* is a lexical compound whose meaning is idiomatic, that is, not the amalgamation of the meanings of the two component parts. This compound, however, has the morphological composition of *verb + object*. According to its meaning, *dǎ-zuò* should belong to the category of verbs of posture, which allow a postverbal locative phrase. It does not take a postverbal locative phrase, though, because of its internal syntactic composition, *verb + object*.

(53)

*tā	dǎ — zuò
3sg	sit:in:meditation

zài	dì	—	shang
at	ground	—	on

It is easy to show that what is wrong with (52) *b* and (53) is not that their verbs are disyllabic verbs. *Jiànli* 'establish', for example, is a disyllabic verb that belongs to the class Vpl. Sentence (54) shows that it takes a postverbal locative phrase:

(54)

tāmen	bǎ	shóudū	jiànli	zài	běibian
they	BA	capital	establish	at	north

They established the capital in the north.

As we would expect from generalization (ii), the locative phrase must immediately follow the verb *jiànli* 'establish'. Sentence (55) is ungrammatical because rule (ii) is not satisfied:

(55)   *tāmen   jiànli   shǒudū   <u>zài</u>   <u>běibian</u>
        they   establish   capital   at   north

Generalization (ii), then, forbids the occurrence of a locative phrase after any direct object, even when that direct object is part of a verb-object compound. Postverbal locative phrases must directly follow the verb itself.[3]

In conclusion, we observe that the locative phrase may occur in either the preverbal position or the postverbal position. In the preverbal position, it has a general locational meaning and is essentially unconstrained with respect to the verbs with which it can occur; accordingly, the preverbal locative phrase is called *zhuàngyǔ* 'adverbial' by Chinese grammarians.

Postverbal locative phrases, on the other hand, are restricted to certain types of verbs, just as direct objects are, and are designated by the term *bǔyǔ*, 'complement', which is also used for objects, in traditional Chinese grammar. This distinction between these two grammatical terms captures the difference between the relatively free preverbal locative phrase and the more tightly restricted postverbal locative phrase in terms of semantic "intimacy." The four classes of verbs allowing a postverbal locative are: (1) the displacement verbs, which result in locally displacing the subject (in the case of an intransitive verb) or the direct object (in the case of a transitive verb); (2) the verbs of posture; (3) the verbs of appearance; and (4) the placement verbs. In addition, the postverbal locative phrase must occur immediately after the verb; in other words, if a verb takes a postverbal locative phrase, there must be no intervening element, not even the object noun in a verb-object compound, between the verb and the postverbal locative phrase. Locative phrases thus provide a good example of the interaction between the position of an expression vis-à-vis the verb and its semantic interpretation.

11.2 Directional Phrases with *dào* 'to'

Direction toward which a motion is aimed can be expressed by phrases beginning with any of the coverbs *xiàng, wǎng/wàng*, or *dào*, all meaning roughly 'to, toward'. Because *xiàng* and *wǎng/wàng* behave like ordinary coverbs and generally occur only preverbally, they are included in chapter 9 on coverbs. *Dào*, on the other hand, parallels *zài* in certain respects. Hence it is presented here in this chapter.

We will define a *directional phrase* as consisting of the coverb *dào* 'to', a noun phrase, and an optional locative particle, as schematized in (58):

(56)   <u>dào</u>   noun phrase   —   (locative particle)
        'to'

The conditions for the occurrence of the locative particle at the end of the directional phrase are exactly the same as those for the occurrence of locative phrases: the locative particle is usually omitted with place names and with nouns referring to familiar places.

Like locative phrases, directional phrases can also occur both preverbally and postverbally. Furthermore, as with *zài* phrases, the *dào* phrase in preverbal position is essentially unconstrained. For most verbs, a directional phrase in preverbal position means simply that the subject moves to a destination where the event named by the verb takes place. For example:

(57)   tāmen   <u>dào</u>   <u>gōngyuán</u>   niàn   —   shū
       they   to   park   read   —   book

    They went to the park {and studied.}
                      {to study. }

(58)   tā   měi   —   tiān   <u>dào</u>   <u>cǎochǎng</u>   pǎo
    3sg   each   —   day   to   field   run

    Every day s/he goes to the field {and runs.}
                              {to run. }

In postverbal position, however, the directional phrase is tightly constrained by the meaning of the verb: it can occur only with verbs involving destination, and it signals that the action named by the verb is carried out to the destination named by the directional phrase. Here are some examples:

(59)   nǐ   xiān   niàn   <u>dào</u>   <u>dì</u>   —   <u>sān</u>   <u>háng</u>
    you   first   read   to   ORD   —   three   line

    First read up to the third line.

(60)   wǒmen   fēi   <u>dào</u>   <u>Shànghǎi</u>   le
    we   fly   to   Shanghai   CRS

    We flew to Shanghai.

(61)   tā   pǎo   <u>dào</u>   <u>cǎochǎng</u>   le
    3sg   run   to   field   CRS

    S/He ran to the field.

(62) bǎ   qìchē   kāi   dào   hòumian   qu
      BA   car   drive to   back   go

Drive the car around to the back.

Directional phrases are subject to generalization (ii) just as locative phrases are: both directional and locative phrases, if postverbal, must immediately follow the verb. Thus sentence (59) above, for example, could not be expressed with the directional phrase after a direct object, as (63) shows:

(63) *nǐ   xiān   niàn   wǒ   —   de   xìn
      you   first   read   I   —   GEN   letter

      dào   dì   —   sān   háng
      to   ORD   —   three   line

On the other hand, (64) appears to be a counterexample to our claim that a directional phrase must immediately follow the verb.

(64) wǒmen   kāi   qìchē   dào   Xiānggǎng
      we   drive   car   to   Hong Kong

We drove a car to Hong Kong.

In (64), however, *dào* is serving as a verb with the meaning 'arrive', and (64) is a serial verb construction. To show that *dào* is a verb in (64), we cite sentence (65), in which *dào* occurs with the perfective aspect marker *-le*, signaling that *dào* 'arrive' is to be viewed in the perfective aspect:

(65) wǒmen   kāi   qìche   dào   —   le   Xiānggǎng
      we   drive   car   arrive   —   PFV   Hong Kong

      yǐhòu   jiù   xiūxi
      after   then   rest

We will rest after we arrive in Hong Kong by car.

As a coverb introducing a directional phrase, *dào* cannot take an aspect marker of any kind. The conclusion, then, is that directional phrases, which are introduced by the *coverb dào*, obey generalization (ii) and must directly follow the verb. A *dào* that follows a direct object is not the coverb *dào*, but the *verb dào* in a serial verb construction (see chapter 9 on coverbs for further discussion of this point).

There are two motion verbs that behave in a special way with respect to directional phrases. These two verbs are *lái* 'come' and *qù* 'go', whose meanings include the idea of a destination point.[4] That is, unlike the cases of *fēi* 'fly' or *pá* 'crawl', where the flying or the crawling can occur without a destination being reached, *lái* and *qù* can be used only when reaching a destination is implied.

As in English, *lái* is used when the arrival point is where the speaker is, and *qù* is used when the arrival point is away from the speaker.[5] When *lái* is used without naming the arrival point, it is always assumed to be simply where the speaker is:

(66)   Zhāngsān   lái   le
        Zhangsan   come   CRS

    Zhangsan is coming here.

The first unusual fact about *lái* and *qù* with directional phrases is that these two motion verbs can generally be added at the end of any sentence with a directional phrase in it to specify whether the destination is away from or toward the speaker. Sentences (60) and (61), then, repeated here as (67) *a* and (68) *a*, could just as well be said with *lái* or *qù* ([67] *b* and [68] *b*):

(67) *a.*   wǒmen   fēi   dào   Shànghǎi   le
          we   fly   to   Shanghai   CRS

    We flew to Shanghai.

   b.   wǒmen   fēi   dào   Shànghǎi $\begin{Bmatrix} qù \\ lái \end{Bmatrix}$ le

        we   fly   to   Shanghai $\begin{Bmatrix} go \\ come \end{Bmatrix}$ CRS

    We flew to Shanghai $\begin{Bmatrix} \text{(away from speaker).} \\ \text{(toward speaker).} \end{Bmatrix}$

(68) *a.*   tā   pǎo   dào   cǎochǎng   le
         3sg   run   arrive   field   CRS

    S/He ran to the field.

b.   tā   pǎo   dào   cǎochǎng $\begin{Bmatrix} qù \\ lái \end{Bmatrix}$ le

     3sg   run   to   field $\begin{Bmatrix} go \\ come \end{Bmatrix}$ CRS

     S/He ran to the field $\begin{Bmatrix} \text{(away from speaker).} \\ \text{(toward speaker).} \end{Bmatrix}$

The second compelling fact about *lái* 'come' and *qù* 'go' with directional phrases is that a directional phrase used with one of these verbs as the only verb in the sentence will always be understood to refer to the destination, whether it occurs preverbally or postverbally:

(69) *a.*   tāmen   <u>dào   wàibian</u>   qù   –   le
         they   to   outside   go   –   PFV

They went outside.

     b.   tāmen   qù   <u>dào</u>   wàibian[6]
         they   go   to   outside

They went outside.

(70) *a.*   tā   <u>dào   wǒmen   xuéxiào</u>   lái   –   le
         3sg   arrive   we   school   come   –   PFV

S/He came to our school.

     b.   tā   lái   <u>dào   wǒmen   xuéxiào</u>
         3sg   come   arrive   we   school

S/He came to our school.

Directional phrases, in sum, are similar to locative phrases in most respects: both directional and locative phrases are relatively unconstrained in their interpretation when they occur preverbally and are more restricted by the meaning of the verb when they occur postverbally. Directional phrases differ from locative phrases in their behavior with *lái* 'come' and *qù* 'go', however, because of the destination component in the meanings of these two verbs.

Notes

1. This chapter draws on some of the ideas found in Chao (1968). Tai (1973). Teng (1975*b*), Peyraube (1977), and Huang (1978), as well as in unpublished work by Charles A. Liu.

2. There is one exception to this generalization: when one location is being contrasted with another, *zài* 'at' may be omitted for verbs of posture (see section 11.1.2.B of this chapter), such as *shuì*, as in:

(i)	wǒ	shuì	shāfa	–	nǐ	shuì	dìbǎn
	I	sleep	sofa	–	you	sleep	floor

I'll sleep on the sofa, and you sleep on the floor.

3. A sentence such as the following might be considered a counterexample:

(i)	Qīng	–	cháo	jiàn	–	dū	zài	Běijīng
	Qing	–	dynasty	establish	–	capital	at	Beijing

The Qing dynasty established its capital at Beijing.

This sentence appears to be a counterexample because the verb *jiàn-dū* 'establish capital' belongs to the class Vpl, which allows a postverbal locative phrase, and *dū* 'capital' is an object following the verb *jiàn* 'establish'. Sentence (i) is not, however, a real counterexample to generalization (ii); rather, it reflects the classical Chinese syntax in which a locative phrase typically does follow the object of a transitive verb. What makes it appear as a counterexample to generalization (ii) is the use of the modern Chinese morpheme *zài* instead of its classical Chinese counterpart, *yù*.

4. For further discussion of *lái* and *qù*, see Lin (1977).

5. Unlike the English *go*, however, *qù* always implies an arrival point, so that messages such as 'we're going' or 'he went' must be communicated with the verb *zǒu* 'leave, go' in Mandarin.

6. For the omission of the PFV aspect marker with locative and directional phrases, see section 6.1.2.B of chapter 6 on aspect.

CHAPTER 12

Negation

There are four negative forms in common use in Mandarin: *bu*, *bié*, *méi*, and *méi(yǒu)*.[1] The most general and neutral form of negation is *bu*, as in:

(1) tā   <u>bu</u>   shì   Zhōngguó   rén
      3sg   not   be   China   person

      S/He is not Chinese.

(2) wǒ   <u>bu</u>   jìde   tā
      I   not   remember   3sg

      I don't remember him/her.

(3) nǐ   <u>bu</u>   gēn   wǒ   zǒu   ba ?
      you   not   with   I   go   SA

      You're not going with me, right?

The negative marker used in imperatives is *bié* 'don't' (see chapter 14 on imperatives):

(4) <u>bié</u>   guān   mén !
      don't   close   door

      Don't close the door.

(5)   *bu   guān   mén !
        not   close   door

(unacceptable as a command)

When the verb of a sentence is *yǒu* (see chapter 17 on existential sentences), the form of the negative must be *méi*, and *yǒu* can be optionally deleted, as in (6) and (8):

(6)   méi   (yǒu)   rén   zài   wàimian
        not   exist   person   at   outside

There's no one outside.

(7)   *bu   yǒu   rén   zài   wàimian
        not   exist   person   at   outside

(8)   wǒ   méi   (yǒu)   qián
        I   not   exist   money

I don't have any money.

(9)   *wǒ   bu   yǒu   qián
        I   not   exist   money

Yǒu can also occur as part of an adjective, as in *yǒu-yìsi* 'interesting' (literally 'exist-idea'). In such a case, the negative remains *méi*, and *yǒu* may be optionally deleted:

(10)   zhèi   —   ge   gùshi   hěn   méi   (yǒu)   —   yìsi
        this   —   CL   story   very   not   exist   —   idea

This story is not very interesting.

Since *yǒu* can be omitted in (6), (8), and (10), the negative form *méi* itself must be able to carry both the meaning of negation and the meaning of the existential *yǒu* in those sentences. This is an unusual characteristic of *méi* as a negative form.

    The form *méi(yǒu)* also appears in sentences expressing comparison of "inferiority" (see chapter 19), as in:

(11) wǒ <u>méi(yǒu)</u> tā nème pàng
    I   not   3sg   that   fat

I'm not as fat as s/he is.

Méi yǒu in the sense of 'not exist' can be used in some dialects to deny what someone else has stated or implied. For example, if A and B are discussing A's cooking lessons, B can say:

(12) nà nǐ xiànzài hěn huì zuò fàn ba ?
   in:that:case you now very know:how make food SA

In that case, now you must really know how to cook, right?

To deny the claim implicit in B's comment, A could say:

(13) méi yǒu
   not exist

Besides appearing in sentences expressing comparison of "inferiority," the negative particle *méi(yǒu)*, that is, *méi* with or without *yǒu*, negates the completion of an event. An example is (14); we shall have more to say about this form in section 12.2 below.

(14) wǒ <u>méi(yǒu)</u> kànjian nǐ
    I   not   see   you

I didn't see you.

We will refer to *bu*, *bié*, *méi*, and *méi(yǒu)* as *negative particles*; since *bié* is discussed in chapter 14, in the rest of this chapter we shall be concerned primarily with *bu*, *méi*, and *méi(yǒu)*.

12.1 The Position and Scope of Negative Particles

In general, negative particles follow the subject and precede the verb phrase:

(15) tā <u>bu</u> niàn — shū
   3sg not study — book

S/He does not study.

(16)   tā   <u>méi(yǒu)</u>   kāi   mén
        3sg   not   open   door

S/He didn't open the door.

If a subject occurs in the first position of a sentence, the negative can be said to occur in the second position. The negative, therefore, generally precedes the verb phrase no matter what the verb phrase is composed of. The following examples provide verb phrases containing a manner adverb (chapter 8, section 8.2.1), an auxiliary verb (chapter 5), and a coverb phrase (chapter 9):

(17)   tā   <u>bu</u>   <u>màn-màn-de</u>   qí   jiǎotāchē
        3sg   not   slowly   ride   bicycle

S/He does not ride a bike slowly.

(18)   tā   <u>bu</u>   <u>kěn</u>   zuò   —   xià   —   lai
        3sg   not   willing   sit   —   descend   —   come

S/He is not willing to sit down.

(19)   wǒmen   <u>bu</u>   xiàng   xībiar   fēi
        we   not   toward   west   fly

We don't fly to the west.

Conversely, the subject may be complex; but the negative always follows the subject. For example, the subject may be a clause (see section 21.2.1 of chapter 21):

(20)   <u>wǒmen   zài   zhèr   zuò   shēngyi</u>   <u>bu</u>   róngyi
        we   at   here   do   business   not   easy

It is not easy for us to do business here.

The semantic effect of the general rule that the negative particle follows the subject and precedes the verb phrase is that the verb phrase is in the *scope* of the negative. In other words, the verb phrase, the part of the sentence which *follows* the negative particle, is what is being denied by the negative particle.

When the sentence contains an adverb, however, whether the negative precedes the adverb or the adverb precedes the negative depends entirely on scope. If the adverb has the negative in its scope, then it precedes the negative; if the negative has the adverb in its scope, then it precedes the adverb. This generalization is discussed and illustrated in detail in chapter 8; here we will just give a few examples.

(i) Adverb precedes the negative:

(21) | tā | <u>míngtiān</u> | <u>bu</u> | shàng | — | xué |
|---|---|---|---|---|---|
| 3sg | tomorrow | not | ascend | — | school |

Tomorrow s/he won't attend school.

(22) | tā | <u>yěxǔ</u> | <u>bu</u> | xūyào | bǎobiāo |
|---|---|---|---|---|
| 3sg | perhaps | not | need | bodyguard |

Perhaps s/he does not need bodyguards.

(ii) Adverb follows the negative:

(23) | tā | <u>bu</u> | <u>màn-màn-de</u> | qí | jiǎotāchē |
|---|---|---|---|---|
| 3sg | not | slowly | ride | bicycle |

S/He doesn't ride a bike slowly.

(24) | tā | <u>bu</u> | <u>zǐxì-de</u> | zuò | — | shì |
|---|---|---|---|---|---|
| 3sg | not | meticulously | do | — | work |

S/He does not work meticulously.

(iii) Either order possible, depending on scope:

(25) *a.* | tā | <u>hūn-tóu-hūn-nǎo-de</u> | <u>méi</u> | yòng | máobǐ |
|---|---|---|---|---|
| 3sg | muddleheadedly | not | use | brush |
| | xiě | zì | | |
| | write | character | | |

S/He muddleheadedly failed to use a brush to write the characters.

b.	tā	bu	hūn-tóu-hūn-nǎo-de	zuò	—	shì
	3sg	not	muddleheadedly	do	—	work

S/He does not work in a muddleheaded manner.

(26) *a.*

	tā	gùyì	bu	shuō	—	huà
	3sg	deliberately	not	talk	—	word

S/He is deliberately not talking.

b.

	tā	bu	gùyì	zuò	huài	shì
	3sg	not	deliberately	do	bad	deed

S/He does not deliberately do bad things.

(27) *a.*

	tā	yīdìng	bu	lái
	3sg	definitely	not	come

S/He is definitely not coming.

b.

	tā	bu	yīdìng	lái
	3sg	not	definitely	come

S/He is not definitely coming.

(28) *a.*

	tā	tiāntiān	bu	xǐzǎo
	3sg	daily	not	bathe

Every day s/he does not bathe.

b.

	tā	bu	tiāntiān	xǐzǎo
	3sg	not	daily	bathe

S/He does not bathe every day.

Similarly, with certain auxiliary verbs (see chapter 5) either the negative could be in the scope of the auxiliary or vice versa; consider the two possibilities with the negative particle and the auxiliary *néng* 'can'. The more usual situation is for the negative particle to include the auxiliary in the scope of what is being negated, as in (18) above and (29):

(29) wǒ   bu   néng   qù
      I   not   can   go

I cannot go.

If 'not go' is what the subject can do, however, then the other order is appropriate:

(30) wǒ   néng   bu   qu
      I   can   not   go

I'm capable of not going.

In fact, with auxiliary verbs, it is even possible to negate both the auxiliary and the main verb, as in (31):

(31) wǒ   bu   néng   bu   qù
      I   not   can   not   go

I am not capable of not going.

We see, then, that the general position of a negative particle is before the verb phrase and that the variations in the position of the negative particle can be explained entirely in terms of the scope of the negative particle with respect to certain adverbs and auxiliary verbs.

12.2 The Functions of *bu* and *méi(yǒu)*

The difference between *bu* and *méi(yǒu)* is a purely functional one: *bu* provides a neutral negation, and *méi(yǒu)* negates the completion of an event. A number of provocative facts can be explained in terms of this difference.

12.2.1 Variation in the Meanings of Sentences with *bu*

If the central difference between *bu* and *méi(yǒu)* is, as we have stated, whether completion is involved, then it stands to reason that there might be different ways in which *bu* can express negation of an event without denying that the event is completed, depending on the meaning of the verb.

The most straightforward cases are those involving stative verbs and adjectives, where *bu* simply denies the existence of the state.

(32)   tā   bu   cōngmíng
        3sg   not   intelligent

S/He { is } not intelligent.[2]
      { was }

(33)   wǒmen   bu   zhīdào   tā   zài   nǎr
        we   not   know   3sg   at   where

{ We don't know where s/he is.   }
{ We didn't know where s/he was. }

(34)   tā   bu   shì   xiào   —   zhǎng
        3sg   not   be   school —   chief

S/He { is } not the principal.
      { was }

With such verbs, *méi(yǒu)* is not possible:

(35)   *tā   méi(yǒu)   cōngmíng
        3sg   not   intelligent

(36)   *wǒmén méi(yǒu)   zhīdào   tā   zài   nǎr
        we   not   know   3sg   at   where

(37)   *tā   méi(yǒu)   shì   xiào   —   zhǎng
        3sg   nŏt   be   school —   chief

Similarly, auxiliary verbs, which are always stative, are negated with *bu* and not by *méi(yǒu)*:

(38) *a*.   tā   bu   huì   yóuyǒng
             3sg   not   know:how   swim

S/He doesn't know how to swim.

     b.   *tā   méi(yǒu)   huì   yóuyǒng
             3sg   not   know:how   swim

Now, however, let's consider activity predicates over which the subject has some control, as in (39):

(39)	tā	hē	jiŭ
	3sg	drink	wine

S/He drinks wine.

The negative version, (40), with *bu*,

(40)	tā	bu	hē	jiŭ
	3sg	not	drink	wine

$\begin{cases} \text{S/He does not drink wine.} \\ \text{S/He refuses to drink wine.} \\ \text{S/He refused to drink wine.} \end{cases}$

cannot mean that s/he *didn't* drink wine, since if that were the intended meaning, *méi(yŏu)* instead of *bu* would have to have been used. Therefore, (40) can only mean that s/he *doesn't* drink wine. The extended idea of 'refusing to' is the natural inference from the fact that if someone does not do something over which s/he has control, s/he is generally unwilling to do it. Here are some similar examples:

(41)	tā	bu	chī	—	fàn
	3sg	not	eat	—	food

$\begin{cases} \text{S/He won't eat.} \\ \text{S/He wouldn't eat.} \end{cases}$

(42)	wŏ	bu	mài	nèi	—	ge	píngzi
	I	not	sell	that	—	CL	vase

$\begin{cases} \text{I'm not selling that vase.} \\ \text{I won't sell that vase.} \\ \text{I wouldn't sell that vase.} \end{cases}$

(43)	tā	bu	gēn	wŏ	jiăng	—	huà
	3sg	not	with	I	speak	—	speech

$\begin{cases} \text{S/He won't talk to me.} \\ \text{S/He wouldn't talk to me.} \end{cases}$

Some of the preceding examples point to another fact concerning the function of *bu*: it can negate verb phrases that refer to events in the past as easily as it can those referring to events in the present. This means that, in the appropriate contexts, sentences (32)−(34) and (40)−(43) could be translated into English with a past tense, as indicated by the two translations given. For example, if one wishes to deny that at some period in the past a certain person was not the principal, (34), which is repeated here, would be the form to use:

(34)	tā	bu	shì	xiào	−	zhǎng
	3sg	not	be	school	−	chief

S/He was not the principal.

The other examples in (32)−(34) and (40)−(43) are entirely analogous.

Thus, the fact that sentences with *bu* sometimes mean simple denial (for states) and sometimes mean refusal, referring to either past time or present time, follows directly from the fact that the basic function of *bu* is negation that does *not* involve completion, regardless of the time frame.

12.2.2 Types of Verb Phrases

Given that *méi(yǒu)*, but not *bu*, is used to deny the completion of an event, we would expect that some verbs could take only one of the two and some could take either one of the two. This is indeed true. Just above, in examples (35)−(37), we saw some verbs that could not be used with *méi(yǒu)*, since their meanings involve no notion of completion.

There are, however, no verbs that cannot be used with *bu*. It has been claimed[3] that process verbs, verbs whose meanings signal processes or change of states, cannot take *bu*. The fact is that sentences such as (44) *b* and (45) *b*, which involve *bu* and process verbs, are appropriate only in unusual circumstances, and because it is difficult to think of such circumstances, they have been regarded as unacceptable sentences. A context in which (44) *b* would be perfectly natural could be, for example, if the speaker has been shooting at a person repeatedly but the victim remains alive; (44) *b* then has the effect of saying, 'S/He refuses to die', just as in (40)−(43), where the meaning 'refuse to' is inferred. Similarly, an appropriate context for (45) *b* could be one in which the speaker has been trying to sink the boat to no avail and finally utters this line in exasperation.

(44) *a.*

tā	méi(yǒu)	sǐ
3sg	not	die

$\begin{Bmatrix} \text{S/He hasn't died.} \\ \text{S/He didn't die.} \end{Bmatrix}$

b.

tā	bu	sǐ
3sg	not	die

S/He $\begin{Bmatrix} \text{refuses} \\ \text{won't} \end{Bmatrix}$ die.

(45) *a.*

nèi	–	ge	chuán	méi(yǒu)	chén
that	–	CL	boat	not	sink

$\begin{Bmatrix} \text{That boat hasn't sunk.} \\ \text{That boat didn't sink.} \end{Bmatrix}$

b.

nèi	–	ge	chuán	bu	chén
that	–	CL	boat	not	sink

That boat won't sink.

Here are some further examples of verbs that can be negated either way, with a predictable meaning difference:

(46) *a.*

wǒ	bu	pàng
I	not	fat

I am not fat.

b.

wǒ	méi(yǒu)	pàng
I	not	fat

I have not gotten fat.

(47) *a.*

tā	bu	mài	nèi	–	ge	píngzi
3sg	not	sell	that	–	CL	vase

S/He refused to sell that vase.

b.   tā   méi(yǒu)   mài   nèi   —   ge   píngzi
          3sg   not   sell   that   —   CL   vase

S/He didn't sell that vase.

(48) *a.*   tā   bu   xiào
              3sg   not   smile

S/He won't smile.

b.   tā   méi(yǒu)   xiào
            3sg   not   smile

S/He didn't smile.

(49) *a.*   tāmen   bu   guān   chuānghu
            they   not   close   window

They won't close the window.

b.   tāmen   méi(yǒu)   guān   chuānghu
          they   not   close   window

They didn't close the window.

Which verbs are negated with *bu*, which with *méi(yǒu)*, and which with both is, as we have come to expect, entirely a matter of the compatibility between the meanings of those verbs and the specific functions of *bu* and *méi(yǒu)*.

12.2.3 Resultative Verb Compounds

Resultative verb compounds are discussed in detail in chapter 3.[4] In very general terms, a verb in this class consists of two verbs together, one referring to an action, the other to a result, as in:

(50)   wǒ   bǎ   bàogào   xiě   —   wán   LE
         I   BA   report   write   —   finish   PFV/CRS

I finished writing the report.

One of the defining characteristics of this type of compound is that it can occur in the *potential form*, that is, it can occur with either a *-de-* 'can' or a *-bu-* 'can't' between the two parts of the compound, as in:

(51) *a.* tā   tiào   —   de   —   guò   —   qu
           3sg   jump   —   can   —   cross —   go

        S/He can jump across.

    b. tā   tiào   —   bu   —   guò   —   qu
           3sg   jump   —   can't   —   cross —   go

        S/He cannot jump across.

What this means for our discussion of negation is that resultative verb compounds have two ways of being negated, depending on whether or not the completion of the action is being denied. If the completion of the action is being denied, that is, if the event did not occur, then *méi(yǒu)* must be used:

(52) tā   méi(yǒu)   tiào   —   guò   —   qu
      3sg   not   jump   —   cross —   go

        S/He didn't jump across.

In the negative potential form, (51) *b*, however, the *-bu-* simply denies the existence of the resulting state, in this case the state of being 'across'. It is important to emphasize that the contrast between the functions of *bu* and *méi(yǒu)* here is exactly the same as it is in all the other sentences we have considered. The 'can't' interpretation of the *-bu-* form in resultative verb compounds is again an inference, the most natural inference from the juxtaposition of an action verb that is carried out and the denial of the result: if someone carries out an action, but the intended resulting state does not exist, then we naturally infer that s/he *cannot* accomplish that result. To see this distinction even more clearly, let's look at another pair:

(53) *a.* wǒ   méi(yǒu)   kàn   —   jian   ni
           I   not   look   —   perceive you

        I didn't see you.

b.	wǒ	kàn	—	<u>bu</u>	—	jian	nǐ
	I	look	—	not	—	perceive	you

I can't see you.

As our translations suggest, sentence (53) *a*, with *méi(yǒu)*, denies the completion of 'looking to perception', while (53) *b*, with *-bu-*, denies the state of perceiving, though the looking may be going on; clearly, 'looking' without 'perceiving' is 'not being able to see'.

We see, then, that the two ways in which resultative verb compounds are negated can be understood in terms of the function of *bu* as the general negative marker and the function of *méi(yǒu)* as the denial of completion.

We have considered the position of the negative particles, their scope, and the basic functional difference between *bu* and *méi(yǒu)*. Now we take up three other facts about negation.

12.3 *méi(yǒu)* Is Not a Past Tense Negative Particle

We have seen that *méi(yǒu)* means noncompletion. Now, the most frequent situation involving noncompletion of an event or an action is one that occurs in the past, which accounts for the prevalent use of the past tense in the English translation of Mandarin sentences containing *méi(yǒu)*, as in (54):

(54)	wǒ	<u>méi(yǒu)</u>	xǐzǎo
	I	not	bathe

I didn't bathe.

It is important to observe, however, that "noncompletion" is not the semantic equivalent of "past-tense negation." To demonstrate conclusively that *méi(yǒu)* is not past-tense negation, we cite sentences (55) *a* and *b*, which involve the past and a negative state: (55) *a* employs the negative particle *bu*, and the sentence is well formed; (55) *b* employs *méi (yǒu)*, and it is ill formed:

(55) *a.*	yǐqián	zhèi	—	ge	dìfang	<u>bu</u>	qióng
	in:the:past	this	—	CL	place	not	poor

In the past, this place was not poor.

b.	*yǐqián	zhèi	—	ge	dìfang	<u>méi</u>	qióng
	in:the:past	this	—	CL	place	not	poor

Sentence (55) *a* shows that *bu* can be used in a sentence expressing a state in the past. We can also show *méi(yǒu)* functioning to express noncompletion of an action in future time, as in (56) and (57):

(56) míngnián   zhèi   —   ge   shíhou   nǐ
      next:year   this   —   CL   time   you

      hái   méi(yǒu)   bìyè   ne
      still   not   graduate   REx

By this time next year, you still won't have graduated.

(57) nǐ   xiǎng   —   yi   —   xiǎng ,   dào   míngnián
      you think   —   one   —   think   arrive   next:year

      zhèi   —   ge   shíhou   wǒ   hái   méi(yǒu)
      this   —   CL   time   I   still   not

      chī   —   guo   píngguǒ   ne
      eat   —   EXP   apple   REx

Think about it a minute; by this time next year, I still won't have eaten apples.

There is, however, one restricted case of *méi(yǒu)* being used to indicate what appears to be past tense; this is the occurrence of *méi(yǒu)* with the durative *-zhe*, as in (58):[5]

(58) tā   méi(yǒu)   ná   —   zhe   shū   ne
      3sg   not   hold   —   DUR   book   REx

S/He wasn't holding books.

where the more normal negation would be with *bú shì* 'it isn't/wasn't the case that' (see section 12.5 below):

(59) tā   bu   shì   ná   —   zhe   shū   ne
      3sg   not   be   hold   —   DUR   book   REx

It's not true that s/he was holding books.

Since *méi(yǒu)* in (58) does not seem to have anything to do with completion and would be used by a speaker only in a sentence referring to a situation in the past, it does appear that this instance qualifies as an extension of the typical use of *méi(yǒu)* marking noncompletion to negation of past events. This usage, however, at least for the time being, remains exceptional.

Thus we see that although sentences with *méi(yǒu)* are often translated as past-tense forms in English, this is simply because most of the time a completed event involves completion before the time of speaking. The examples in this section, though, show clearly that *méi(yǒu)* is not a past-time negative particle, because (1) *bu* can be used to express past-time negation, and (2) *méi(yǒu)* can be used to express non-past-time negation. The difference is, rather, one of completion versus noncompletion.

12.4 Negation and Aspect

In chapter 6 on aspect, we point out that the perfective aspect marker *-le* cannot occur in negative sentences. Here we examine the interaction between negation and aspect in more detail.[6]

First, as we just mentioned, a verb with the perfective *-le* cannot be negated with either *bu* or *méi(yǒu)*.[7] The reason is clear: *-le* signals a *bounded* event, and an event that does not occur cannot be bounded.

(60)	*tā	bu	chī	—	le	nèi	kuài	dàngāo
	3sg	not	eat	—	PFV	that	piece	cake

(61)	*wǒ	méi	xiě	—	cuò	—	le
	I	not	write	—	wrong	—	PFV
		nèi	—	ge	zì
		that	—	CL	character

What this means is that an affirmative *-le* sentence and its negative counterpart have quite different forms. Consider (62)−(63):

(62)	wǒ	xiě	—	cuò	—	le	nèi
	I	write	—	wrong	—	PFV	that
		—	ge	zì
		—	CL	character

I wrote that character wrong.

(63)	wǒ	méi(yǒu)	xiě	—	cuò	nèi	—
	I	not	write	—	wrong	that	—

ge	zì
CL	character

I didn't write that character wrong.

Whereas sentence (62) has a perfective suffix *-le*, sentence (63) has the negative of completion *méi(yǒu)* before the verb.

Now, this difference in form exemplified by (62) and (63) has some interesting consequences. For example, if we wish to question a *-le* sentence, the standard way to do so in the A-not-A form, of course, is to juxtapose the affirmative and the negative forms of the verb phrases (see chapter 18 on questions for further discussion of this point), as in:

(64)

A

wǒ	xiě	—	cuò	—	le	nèi	—	ge	zì
I	write	—	wrong	—	PFV	that	—	CL	character

not A

méi(yǒu) ?
not

Did I write that character wrong?

And the affirmative answer to such a question would be:

(65)	(nǐ)	xiě	—	cuò	—	le
	(you)	write	—	wrong	—	PFV

(You) wrote (it) wrong.

In certain of the southern Chinese dialects, however, including those in the Yue group, such as Cantonese, and in the Min group, such as Chaozhou and Taiwanese, the perfective aspect marker itself is the word that corresponds to *yǒu*, which occurs in preverbal position. Here are examples from Cantonese and Taiwanese to illustrate:

(66) (Cantonese)

keuih	yauh	sihk	faahn
3sg	PFV	eat	food

S/He ate.

(67) (Taiwanese)

i	u	chia	peng
3sg	PFV	eat	food

S/He ate.

What this means is that when speakers of these southern languages speak Mandarin, they are likely to use *yǒu* in questions and answers as if it were also the perfective aspect marker in Mandarin. Instead of (64), then, a southern speaker is likely to say in Mandarin:

(68)

	A	not A			
wǒ	yǒu	méiyǒu	xiě	—	cuò
I		not	write	—	wrong

	nèi	—	ge	zì ?	
	that	—	CL	character	

Did I write that character wrong?

with *yǒu* being treated as the first element in the verb phrase; or they may even say it this way:

(69)

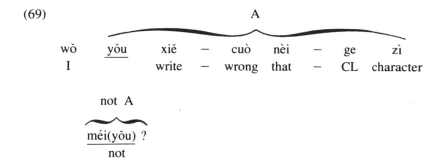

wǒ	yǒu	xiě	—	cuò	nèi	—	ge	zì
I		write	—	wrong	that	—	CL	character

not A

méi(yǒu) ?
not

Did I write that character wrong?

which treats *yǒu xiě-cuò nèige zì* 'wrote that character wrong' as the A part of the question and *méiyǒu* as the not-A part. In fact, for these speakers, a possible affirmative answer to these questions is:

(70) (nǐ)   yǒu   xiě   —   cuò
      (you)   write — wrong

(You) wrote (it) wrong.

The point here is that for southern speakers of Mandarin, the use of *méiyǒu* as the negative of a verb with *-le* has extended to using *yǒu* as the *affirmative* of *méiyǒu* in questions and answers to questions,[8] because that is the way it is said in the southern Chinese dialects.

   The significance of the way southerners speak Mandarin is that, for reasons having to do with recent political developments in China, many southerners nowadays speak Mandarin with northerners, and this means that even northerners are changing their speech under the influence of these southern speakers. This is most strikingly obvious in Taiwan and Singapore, but it is also true of southern China and Hong Kong as well. If we consider only Mandarin speakers of the north, then, the question form

(71) subject   verb   —   le   méiyǒu ?

(as exemplified in [64] above) is the only possible form for a perfective sentence, and all the other sentences in which *yǒu* appears as a perfective marker will sound strange. Among speakers who are influenced by the Mandarin of southern Chinese, though, sentences with *yǒu* as the perfective marker are coming to be used more and more.

Because the negation of a sentence with the perfective aspect *-le* seems to involve the presence of *méi(yǒu)* and the absence of *-le*, as illustrated by (72) *a* and *b*, many grammarians have assumed that *méi(yǒu)* is the negative form of the perfective aspect marker *-le*:[9]

(72) *a.*

háizi	sī	—	pò	—	le	nèi
child	tear	—	broken	—	PFV	that

—	běn	zázhì
—	CL	magazine

The child tore up that magazine.

b.

háizi	méi(yǒu)	sī	—	pò	nèi	—
child	not	tear	—	broken	that	—

běn	zázhì
CL	magazine

The child didn't tear up that magazine.

Rather than saying that *méi(yǒu)* in such sentences as (72) *b* is the negative form of *-le*, though, it makes sense for us to say that since *méi(yǒu)* is the denial of completion, and since *-le* signals a bounded event, they are simply semantically incompatible and cannot co-occur.

There are several reasons for not viewing *méi(yǒu)* as the negative version of *-le*. First, *-le* cannot co-occur with the experiential aspect marker *-guo*, as discussed in chapter 6. *Méi(yǒu)* can, however, occur with *-guo*:

(73)

tā	méi(yǒu)	qù	—	guo	Zhōngguó
3sg	not	go	—	EXP	China

S/He hasn't been to China.

If *méi(yǒu)* were the negative form of *-le*, then there would be no way to explain why *méi(yǒu)* can occur in sentences in which *-le* cannot occur.

A second reason for not considering *méi(yǒu)* to be the negative form of *-le* is that with certain predicates, when *-le* signals that an event is bounded by a following event, as in (74)

(74)

tā	hē	—	le	jiŭ	yǐhou ,	wǒ	jiu
3sg	drink	—	PFV	wine	after	I	then

gēn	tā	shuō	—	huà
with	3sg	talk	—	speech

After s/he drinks, I'll talk to him/her.

we negate the clause with *-le*, not by the particle *méi(yŏu)*, but by the particle *bu*. The unacceptability of sentence (75) *a* and the acceptability of sentence (75) *b* illustrate this point:

(75) *a.*

*tā	méi(yŏu)	hē	jiŭ	yǐhòu ,	wǒ	jiu
3sg	not	drink	wine	after	I	then

gēn	tā	shuō	—	huà
with	3sg	talk	—	speech

b.

tā	bu	hē	jiŭ	yǐhòu ,	wǒ	jiu
3sg	not	drink	wine	after	I	then

gēn	tā	shuō	—	huà
with	3sg	talk	—	speech

After s/he stops drinking, I'll talk to him/her.

Third, there are a number of verbs that do not occur with *-le* because they do not signal bounded events. Here are two examples:

(76)

wǒ	tīngshuō	(*-le)	tā	líhūn	LE
I	hear	(*-PFV)	3sg	divorce	PFV/CRS

I hear that s/he got divorced.

(77)

wǒ	zhŭzhāng	(*-le)	nímen	jīntian	wănshang	xiūxi
I	advocate	(*-PFV)	you:PL	today	evening	rest

I suggest that you all rest this evening.

Both of these verbs can be negated with *méi(yǒu)*, however:

(78)	wǒ	méi(yǒu)	tīngshuō	tā	líhūn	LE
	I	not	hear	3sg	divorce	PFV/CRS

I didn't hear that s/he got divorced.

(79)	wǒ	méi(yǒu)	zhǔzhāng	nǐmen	jīntiān	wǎnshang	xiūxi
	I	not	advocate	you:PL	today	evening	rest

I didn't suggest that you all rest this evening.

If *méi(yǒu)* could occur only as the negative of the perfective *-le*, then it would be difficult to explain how sentences such as (78) and (79) could occur, since there are no corresponding affirmative versions with *-le*.

Rather than being the negative form of the perfective *-le*, then, *méi(yǒu)*, it seems clear, is simply the negation of completion of an event. It cannot be used to negate the completion of an event whose *boundedness* is asserted by the perfective *-le*, and this is why it never co-occurs with *-le*.

The experiential aspect marker *-guo*, on the other hand, has nothing to do with bounding and so is not incompatible with *méi(yǒu)*:

(80)	wǒ	méi(yǒu)	zuò	—	guo	fēijī
	I	not	sit	—	EXP	airplane

I haven't been on an airplane yet.

Sentence (80) simply asserts that the event of my having had the experience of traveling in an airplane has not been completed. A *-guo* sentence is not compatible with *bu*, though: the only way to deny that one has had a certain experience is to say that that experience *has not taken place*, that is, with *méi(yǒu)*. Hence, (81) is unacceptable:

(81)	*wǒ	bu	zuò	—	guo	fēijī
	I	not	sit	—	EXP	airplane

The durative-action aspect marker *zai* is compatible with *bu*, but not with *méi(yǒu)*:

(82) *a.*   tā   <u>bu</u>   <u>zài</u>   shuì   —   jiào
              3sg   not   at   sleep   —   sleep

     S/He isn't sleeping.

    b.   *tā   <u>méi(yǒu)</u>   <u>zài</u>   shuì   —   jiào
              3sg   not   DUR   sleep   —   sleep

Again, the reason is semantic: if an activity is ongoing, then there is no question of its having been completed, so *méi(yǒu)* is impossible to use. The only way to negate an ongoing activity is to use *bu*, the neutral negative marker.

The durative-state aspect marker *-zhe* marks a state associated with some activity:

(83)   tā   hái   liú   —   <u>zhe</u>   húzi   ne
         3sg   still   grow   —   DUR   beard   REx

    He still has a beard.

(84)   qiáng   —   shang   guà   —   <u>zhe</u>   yí   —
         wall   —   on   hang   —   DUR   one   —

               fu   huà
               CL   painting

    There's a painting hanging on the wall.

Now the most obvious way to express the denial of a state is to negate the existence of that state, which is simply done by negating the existential verb *yǒu* 'exist' with *méi*. Thus, (85) and (86) are the natural negative versions of (83) and (84), respectively:

(85)   tā   <u>méi</u>   <u>yǒu</u>   liú   húzi
         3sg   not   exist   grow   beard

    He doesn't have a beard.

(86)   qiáng   —   shang   <u>méi</u>   <u>yǒu</u>   guà   huà
         wall   —   on   not   exist   hang   painting

    There isn't any painting on the wall.

To summarize, we find that the following affirmative-negative correspondences hold for sentences containing one of the four aspect markers:

(87)   (affirmative)   (negative)

a.	verb —	<u>le</u> PFV	<u>méi(yǒu)</u> not	verb	
b.	<u>zài</u> DUR	verb	<u>bu</u> not	<u>zài</u> DUR	verb
c.	verb —	<u>zhe</u> DUR	<u>méi</u> not	<u>yǒu</u> exist	
d.	verb —	<u>guo</u> EXP	<u>méi(yǒu)</u> not	verb —	<u>guo</u> EXP

12.5 Negating Some Element other than a Simple Verb Phrase

For negating an ordinary verb phrase, one of the four negative particles we have considered in this chapter will be used. Sometimes, however, we want to express denial of what someone else has said or implied. For these purposes, *bu* plus *shi* 'be' is used, the effect being to say, 'It is not the case that . . .' (see chapter 4 for a discussion of *shi* 'it is the case that').

Here are some examples; in each case the sentence suggests a denial or contradiction of what someone else has said or implied.

(88)   tā   <u>bú</u>   <u>shì</u>   guāng   —   zhe   jiǎo   shàng
         3sg   not   be   bare   —   DUR   foot   ascend

                 —   kè
                 —   class

It's not the case that s/he goes to class barefooted.

(89)   wǒ   <u>bú</u>   <u>shì</u>   yě   mǎi   xīn   fángzi
         I   not   be   also   buy   new   house

It's not true that I am also buying a new house.

(90)
qiáng	—	shang	bú	shì	guà	—	zhe
wall	—	on	not	be	hang	—	DUR

yi	—	fu	huà
one	—	CL	painting

It is not true that there is a painting hanging on the wall.

(91)
tā	bú	shì	bǎ	Zhāngsān	dài	—
3sg	not	be	BA	Zhangsan	bring	—

jìn	—	lái
enter	—	come

It is not true that s/he brought in Zhangsan.

(92)
tā	bú	shì	bèi	Wángèr	mà
3sg	not	be	BEI	Wanger	scold

It is not true that s/he was scolded by Wanger.

(93)
tā	bú	shì	yǒu	yi	—	ge
3sg	not	be	exist	one	—	CL

mèimei	hěn	xǐhuan	Lǐsì
younger:sister	very	like	Lisi

It is not true that s/he has a younger sister who happens to like Lisi.

Because the function of *bú shì* is to express denial, it is usually stressed, whereas *bu* in other negative sentences tends to be unstressed. We should note that since any statement can be denied, all declarative constructions, regardless of their syntactic structure, may take on *bú shì* to serve as a denial. This point is illustrated by the above examples.

Another usage of *bú shì* is to negate a noun phrase. In such a case, it is the negative counterpart of an affirmative construction that has the noun phrase marked by the affirmative *shì* (again, see chapter 4 on this use of *shì*). Let us illustrate with the following examples:

(94) *a.*

<u>shì</u>	tā	gĕi	wŏ	táng	chī
be	3sg	give	I	candy	eat

It is s/he who gives me candy to eat!

b.

<u>bú</u>	<u>shì</u>	tā	gĕi	wŏ	táng	chī
not	be	3sg	give	I	candy	eat

It isn't s/he who gives me candy to eat!

(95)

<u>bú</u>	<u>shì</u>	Zhāngsān	wŏ	bu	xĭhuan ,	<u>shì</u>	Lĭsì
not	be	Zhangsan	I	not	like	be	Lisi

It is not Zhangsan whom I don't like, it is Lisi!

It is clear in (94) *a* that it is already assumed that someone gives the speaker candy to eat. The information conveyed by (94) *a* is that, given this presupposition, *tā* 's/he' is the culprit. Thus, in (94) *b*, it is assumed that someone gives the speaker candy to eat, but *tā* 's/he' is *not* the one. In (95), the direct object noun phrase *Zhāngsān* is negated with *bú shì* to contrast it with the direct object noun phrase marked with the affirmative *shì, Lĭsì*.

12.6 Summary

There are four negative particles in Mandarin, and their meanings can be represented as follows:

1. *Bu*: negation
2. *Méi(yŏu)*: noncompletion
3. *Bié*: negative imperative
4. *Méi*: negative of *yŏu*

We have seen that the position of the negative particle in the sentence depends on what is in its scope and that the functional difference between *bu* and *méi(yŏu)* explains a number of facts about their occurrence with various types of verbs and aspects. In addition, explicit denial is conveyed by the expression *bú shì* 'not be = it is not true that . . .', and *bú shì* also functions as the negation of a noun marked by *shì*.

Notes

1. In this chapter, we have drawn on some ideas in Shih (1966), Rygaloff (1973:111–114), and Teng (1973, 1974c).

2. The past-tense translation will be discussed immediately below.

3. See Teng (1974a, 1975a).

4. This section adapts some points from Light (1977).

5. Not all native speakers of Mandarin feel comfortable with this sentence. The origin of such a type of construction may be the interaction of Mandarin with other Chinese dialects.

6. For this section, we have drawn on Teng (1973).

7. If the sentence containing the perfective aspect marker -le has as its main verb the affirmative shi 'be' (see section 4.3.1 of chapter 4), then, as in (i), that shi can be negated with bu (see section 12.5 below); our point is that a perfective verb itself cannot be negated.

(i)	tā	bu	shi	mài	—	le	tā	—
	3sg	not	be	sell	—	PFV	3sg	—

	de	chē
	GEN	vehicle

It's not the case that s/he sold his/her car. (an explicit refutation of the claim tā mài-le tā-de chē 's/he sold his/her car')

8. This southern usage extends even to other nonassertive environments besides questions and their answers, as pointed out to us by J. Edmonson. Thus southern speakers can say

(i)	jiǎru	tā	yǒu	chī ,	tā	jiu
	if	3sg		eat	3sg	then

	bu	huì	shēng	—	bìng
	not	likely	put:forth	—	sickness

If s/he'd eaten, s/he wouldn't have gotten sick.

while northerners would say

(ii)	jiǎrú	tā	chī	—	le ,	. . .
	if	3sg	eat	—	PFV	

If s/he had eaten, . . .

9. See, for example, Wang (1965) and Chao (1968:439).

CHAPTER 13

Verb Copying

13.1 Where Verb Copying Occurs

Verb copying refers to a grammatical process in which a verb is "copied" after its direct object when in the presence of certain adverbial elements. Thus, instead of an unacceptable construction such as

(1)   *(subject)   <u><u>verb</u></u>   direct object   <u>adverbial element</u>

we have a construction of the following form:

(2)   (subject)   <u><u>verb</u></u>   direct object   <u><u>verb</u></u>   <u>adverbial element</u>

The term *adverbial element* is meant to be a cover term for four different types of adverbial expressions, to be enumerated below. What is labeled direct object can be either an actual direct object or the object component of a verb-object compound (see section 3.2.5 of chapter 3 on verb-object compounds). In each of the following examples, we present the unacceptable version of the sentence, without verb copying, and then the acceptable version, with verb copying. As in (2) above, the verb and its copy are underlined twice, and the adverbial phrase is underlined once.

(i) Quantity adverbial phrase (see section 8.5 of chapter 8):

(3) *a.*	*wǒ	<u><u>shuì</u></u>	—	le	—	jiào	<u>wǔ</u>
	I	sleep	—	PFV	—	sleep	five

—	ge	<u>zhōngtóu</u>
—	CL	hour

b.

wǒ	shuì	—	jiào	shuì	—	le
I	sleep	—	sleep	sleep	—	PFV

wǔ	—	ge	zhōngtóu
five	—	CL	hour

I slept for five hours.

(4) *a.*

*wǒ	pāi	—	le	—	shǒu	liǎng	cì
I	clap	—	PFV	—	hand	two	time

b.

wǒ	pāi	—	shǒu	pāi	—	le
I	clap	—	hand	clap	—	PFV

liǎng	cì
two	time

I clapped (my) hands twice.

(ii) Complex stative construction (see chapter 22):

(5) *a.*

*tā	niàn	—	shū	de	hěn	kuài
3sg	read	—	book	CSC	very	fast

b.

tā	niàn	—	shū	niàn	de	hěn	kuài
3sg	read	—	book	read	CSC	very	fast

S/He reads very quickly.

(6) *a.*

*tā	jiǎng	gùshi	de	wǒmen
3sg	tell	story	CSC	we

dōu	mèn	le
all	bored	CRS

b.

tā	jiǎng	gùshi	jiǎng	de	wǒmen
3sg	tell	story	tell	CSC	we

dōu	mèn	le
all	bored	CRS

S/He told stories until we were all bored.

(iii) Locative Phrase (see section 11.1 of chapter 11):

(7) *a.*   *bàba   guà   màozi   zai   yī
          papa   hang   hat   at   clothes

          —   jiàzi   —   shang
          —   rack   —   on

   b.   bàba   guà   màozi   guà   zai   yī
          papa   hang   hat   hang   at   clothes

          —   jiàzi   —   shang
          —   rack   —   on

       Papa hangs hats on the clothes rack.

(iv) Directional phrase (see section 11.2 of chapter 11):

(8) *a.*   *wǒmen   zǒu   —   lù   dào   shìchǎng   le
          we   walk   —   road   to   market   CRS

   b.   wǒmen   zǒu   —   lù   zǒu   dào   shìchǎng   le
          we   walk   —   road   walk   to   market   CRS

       We walked to the market.

There are two constraints on verb copying. First, with the last three types of
adverbial elements exemplified just above—the complex stative construction, the
locative phrase, and the directional phrase—verb copying is obligatory. With the
first type, the quantity adverbial phrase, however, as in (3) and (4), verb copying is
generally not used when the direct object is referential (see section 4.2.5 of chapter
4) and animate or definite. Therefore, while (3) *a* above, repeated here, and (9) *a*
below are unacceptable, sentence 9 *b*, whose direct object is the animate pronoun
tā 's/he', is fine:

(3) *a.*   *wǒ   shuì   —   le   —   jiào   wǔ
          I   sleep   —   PFV   —   sleep   five

          —   ge   zhōngtóu
          —   CL   hour

(9) *a.*

*wǒ	kàn	—	le	yi	—	ge
I	see	—	PFV	one	—	CL

diànyǐng	wǔ	—	ge	zhōngtóu
movie	five	—	CL	hour

(I saw a movie for five hours.)

b.

wǒ	kàn	—	le	tā	wǔ
I	see	—	PFV	3sg	five

—	ge	zhōngtóu
—	CL	hour

I saw (i.e., visited) him/her for five hours.

In (3) *a* the verb *shuì-jiào* 'sleep' is a verb-object compound. The object component of this compound, *jiào*, is nonreferential. In (9) *a* the direct object of the verb, *yi-ge diànyǐng* 'a movie', is referential but neither animate nor definite. Hence, without verb copying, (3) *a* and (9) *a* are unacceptable.

Consider another contrasting pair of sentences. Here the quantity adverbial phrase signals frequency:

(10) *a.*

*wǒ	tīng	—	le	yīnyuè	liǎng	cì
I	hear	—	PFV	music	two	time

(I heard music twice.)

b.

wǒ	tīng	—	le	Zhāngsān	liǎng	cì
I	hear	—	PFV	Zhangsan	two	time

I heard Zhangsan twice.

Sentence (10) *a*, again, is unacceptable because the direct object is nonreferential and there is no verb copying. Sentence 10 *b*, on the other hand, does not need verb copying because the direct object is referential, animate, and definite.

Finally, let's contrast a pair of examples in which the direct object is animate, but in one case the animate direct object is nonreferential, and in the other case the animate direct object is referential. In the former case, but not in the latter case, verb copying is necessary:

(11) *a.*

*tā	dǎ	—	le	rén	liǎng	cì
3sg	hit	—	PFV	person	two	time

b.

tā	dǎ	—	le	yi	—	ge
3sg	hit	—	PFV	one	—	CL

rén	liǎng	cì
person	two	time

S/He hit a person twice.

In (11) *a*, the direct object of the verb is the nonreferential *rén* 'person'. In (11) *b*, however, the direct object, *yi-ge rén* 'one-CL person', is referential, denoting as it does a certain person.

The above examples show that if the direct object is referential and if, furthermore, it is either animate or definite, verb copying is not needed.

The second constraint on verb copying is that it is used only when one of the above types of adverbial phrases follows the direct object. Other types of elements can follow the direct object without occasioning this verb-copying process. For example, in a serial verb construction (see chapter 21), many different types of predicates can follow a verb and its direct object without giving rise to verb copying. In sentence (12), for instance, the first clause, *tā zǒu-lù* 's/he walks', is the subject of the verb phrase *hěn kuài* 'very fast'; here *zǒu* 'walk' is not copied:

(12)

tā	zǒu	—	lù	hěn	kuài
3sg	walk	—	road	very	fast

S/He walks very fast.

The following examples are all serial verb constructions. In each case the second verb phrase, which follows the first verb and its direct object, is underlined; in none of them is there any verb copying of the first verb.

(13)

zài	zhèr	tíng	chē	fàn	fǎ
at	here	stop	vehicle	violate	law

It is against the law to park here.

(14)　　tā　　zhǎo　　rén　　<u>bāng</u>　　<u>tā</u>
　　　　　3sg　　seek　　person　　help　　3sg

S/He is looking for someone to help him/her.

(15)　　wǒ　　yào　　Zhāngsān　　<u>qù</u>　　<u>kàn</u>　　<u>yīshēng</u>
　　　　　I　　want　　Zhangsan　　go　　see　　doctor

I want Zhangsan to see a doctor.

(16)　　tāmen　　gǎo　　gémìng　　<u>jiù</u>　　<u>guó</u>
　　　　　they　　make　　revolution　　save　　country

They make revolution in order to save their country.

13.2 Grammatical Properties of the Verb-Copying Construction

The verb-copying construction schematized previously

(2) (subject)　<u>verb</u>　direct object　<u>verb</u>　<u>adverbial element</u>

has several grammatical properties.

First, as we have mentioned above, verb copying is usually not needed when the direct object is referential and animate or definite. Conversely, when verb copying occurs, the direct object is typically, though not necessarily, nonreferential. Thus, the direct objects of the *b* sentences in examples (3)–(7) are all nonreferential. Let us recall (7) *b*:

(7) *b*.　bāba　<u>guà</u>　màozi　<u>guà</u>　<u>zài</u>　<u>yī</u>
　　　　papa　hang　hat　hang　at　clothes

　　　　　　—　jiàzi　—　shang
　　　　　　—　rack　—　on

Papa hangs hats on the clothes rack.

In (7) *b*, *màozi* 'hat' is nonreferential: the sentence can be describing only what

Papa does with hats in general. To refer to a specific hat, the *bǎ* construction would have to be used (see chapter 15):

(17)	bàba	bǎ	màozi	guà	zài	yī
	papa	BA	hat	hang	at	clothes

	—	jiàzi	—	shang
	—	rack	—	on

Papa hangs his hat on the clothes rack.

Second, the first occurrence of the verb in (2) typically does not take any aspect marker. For example, if the perfective *-le* or the experiential *-guo* is added to the first verb in (3) *b* and (4) *b*, the results are unacceptable:

(18)	*wǒ	shuì	—	le	—	jiào	shuì	—
	I	sleep	—	PFV	—	sleep	sleep	—

	le	wǔ	—	ge	zhōngtóu
	PFV	five	—	CL	hour

(19)	*wǒ	pāi	—	guo	—	shǒu	pāi	—
	I	clap	—	EXP	—	hand	clap	—

	le	liǎng	cì
	PFV	two	time

Third, the negative of schema (2) involves placing the negative particle before the second verb, not before the first verb:

(20)	(subject)	<u>verb</u>	direct object	<u>neg</u>	<u>verb</u>	adverbial element

For instance, the negative of (4) *b* is (21) *a*, not (21) *b*:

(21) *a.*	wǒ	pāi	—	shǒu	méi	pāi	liǎng	cì
	I	clap	—	hand	not	clap	two	time

I didn't clap (my) hands twice.

b.	*wǒ	méi	pāi	—	shǒu	pāi	liǎng	cì
	I	not	clap	—	hand	clap	two	time

Similarly, the negative of (7) *b* is (22) *a*, not (22) *b*:

(22) *a.*	bàba	guà	màozi	bu	guà	zài
	papa	hang	hat	not	hang	at

	yī	—	jiàzi	—	shang
	clothes	—	rack	—	on

Papa does not hang hats on the clothes rack.

b.	*bàba	bu	guà	màozi	guà	zài
	papa	not	hang	hat	hang	at

	yī	—	jiàzi	—	shang
	clothes	—	rack	—	on

Fourth, certain adverbs, such as *zhǐ* 'only', *hái* 'still', also, moderately', and *yě* 'also', can occur only before the second occurrence and not before the first occurrence of the verb in (2). For example:

(23) *a.*	wǒ	qí	mǎ	zhǐ	qí	—	le
	I	ride	horse	only	ride	—	PFV

	bàn	—	ge	zhōngtóu
	half	—	CL	hour

I rode horses for only half an hour.

b.	*wǒ	zhǐ	qí	mǎ	qí	—	le
	I	only	ride	horse	ride	—	PFV

	bàn	—	ge	zhōngtóu
	half	—	CL	hour

(24) *a.*

tā	xiě	xiǎoshuō	<u>hái</u>	xiě
3sg	write	novel	moderately	write

de	bu	—	cuò
CSC	not	—	bad

S/He is not bad at writing novels.

b.

*tā	<u>hái</u>	xiě	xiǎoshuō	xiě
3sg	moderately	write	novel	write

de	bu	—	cuò
CSC	not	—	bad

(25) *a.*

wǒ	hē	jiǔ	<u>yě</u>	hē	—
I	drink	wine	also	drink	—

le	sān	bēi
PFV	three	glass

I also drank three glasses of wine.

b.

*wǒ	<u>yě</u>	hē	jiǔ	hē	—
I	also	drink	wine	drink	—

le	sān	bēi
PFV	three	glass

All of the grammatical properties of the verb-copying construction described above suggest that the constituent consisting of the first verb plus the direct object behaves as a "frozen" unit in the sense that it is not subject to any grammatical modification. Thus, the direct object is typically nonreferential; the verb does not take any aspect markers; and the entire unit must be outside of the scope of negation and certain adverbial elements. (For the notion of scope, see chapter 12 on negation.)

CHAPTER 14

The Imperative

The grammatical term *imperative* generally refers to the form of a sentence expressing a command.[1] The dividing line between commands and noncommands, however, is not a clear one. For one thing, in normal social interaction, it is often desirable to avoid giving direct orders. Hence all languages have ways of softening commands to make them more like requests or suggestions. Furthermore, because commands involve judgments about what people should and shouldn't do, we find that the grammatical elements occurring in imperatives addressed to the listener also occur in sentences with first person (I, we) and third person (he, she, they) subjects as well. Let us look at some of the properties of imperative sentences in more detail.

We will begin with commands addressed to the listener. To get our listener to do something, in Mandarin, as in any other language, we can say just a verb phrase, or we can use a sentence with a *nǐ* or *nǐmen* 'you' or 'you (plural)' subject:

(1)　chī
　　　eat

　　Eat!

(2)　guāi
　　　good

　　Be good! (referring to the behavior of children)

(3) kuài   yidiǎn
     fast   a:little

     A little faster!

(4) guò   —   lái
     cross   —   come

     Come here!

(5) ná   wǒ   —   de   qiānbǐ   lái
     take   I   —   GEN   pencil   come

     Bring my pencil!

(6) màn-man-de   kāi
          slowly   drive

     Drive slowly!

(7) nǐ   zuò   zhèli
     you   sit   here

     Sit here!

(8) nǐmen   kuài   qu   shuì   —   jiào
     you:PL   fast   go   sleep   —   sleep

     Go to bed quickly (all of you)!

We can also say just a noun phrase in the right context, and it will have the force of a command. Typically, the context for such a command, as noted by Chao (1968), is one in which the noun phrase represents the thing or things desired by the speaker:

(9) yi   bēi   chá
     one   glass   tea

     A glass of tea.

(10)	nèi	liǎng	—	bǎ	dāo
	that	two	—	CL	knife

Those two knives.

To soften a command, one of the verbs *qǐng* 'invite', *láojià* 'trouble you', or *máfan* 'to trouble' is often used with the force of 'please' at the beginning of the sentence. For example:

(11)	láojià	nǐ	bǎ	zhèi	—	fu	huà
	please	you	BA	this	—	CL	painting

	guà	zài	wòfáng	—	lǐ
	hang	at	bedroom	—	in

Please hang this painting in the bedroom.

(12)	qǐng	shàng	—	zuò
	please	ascend	—	seat

Please take your seat.

(13)	máfan	nǐ	lái	chá
	please	you	come	tea

Please bring tea.

(14)	qǐng	nǐ	yòng	cài
	please	you	use	food

Please eat.

In softening a command, *qǐng* is the most commonly used of these verbs. There is no constraint on its usage in a command, and the second person pronoun, *nǐ* 'you' or *nǐmen* 'you (plural)', in a command beginning with *qǐng* remains optional, as in a regular command without *qǐng*. The uses of *láojià* and *máfan* are more constrained than that of *qǐng*. They are typically used to soften a command requesting the addressee to do something that benefits someone other than the addressee himself/herself. Thus, (15) is odd because under normal circumstances eating benefits only the eater, that is, the addressee:

(15) $\left\{ \begin{array}{l} \text{?láojià} \\ \text{?máfan} \end{array} \right\}$ nǐ   yòng   cài

         please   you   use   food

       Please eat.

Under normal circumstances, in fact, (15) would sound facetious or sarcastic.

   Another feature of *máfan* is that it requires the presence of the second person pronoun, *nǐ/nǐmen* 'you/you (plural)', denoting the addressee. For example, if the addressee pronoun in (13) is left out, the resulting sentence is unacceptable:

(16) *máfan   lái   chá
       please   come   tea

The reason for this property of *máfan* is that it has not completely acquired the meaning of 'please', as *qǐng* has. *Máfan* functions in imperative sentences as it does in declarative sentences: it is a pivotal verb meaning 'to trouble'. A pivotal verb cannot exist without its direct object, which also serves as the subject of the following verb (see section 21.2 of chapter 21 for pivotal constructions).

   Qǐng signaling 'please' in a command also differs from *máfan* and *láojià* in that it may occur before as well as after the addressee *nǐ/nǐmen* 'you/you (plural)'. For example:

(17) nǐ   qǐng   zuò
       you   please   sit

       Please sit down.

(18) nǐ   qǐng   hē   jiǔ
       you   please   drink   wine

       Please drink some wine.

(19) nǐ   qǐng   xiān   zǒu
       you   please   first   go

       Please go first.

This positioning of *qǐng* after the addressee in (17)–(19) is another sign of the semantic shift of *qǐng* away from the pivotal verb meaning 'to invite' toward the polite imperative marker 'please' in imperative constructions.

Negative imperatives are expressed with the negative particle *bié* 'don't', which functions exclusively as a negative imperative particle. In other words, it is used only in imperative constructions. Like the other negative particles, *bu* and *méi(yǒu)*, the negative imperative particle occurs after the subject and before the verb. For example:

(20)   <u>bié</u>   dòng
         don't   move

Don't move!

(21)   nǐ   <u>bié</u>   dǎ   rén
         you   don't   hit   person

Don't hit anyone!

(22)   *tā   bié   dǔ   —   qián
         3sg   don't   gamble   —   money

Sentence (22) is unacceptable because it has a third person subject and is therefore not a command. Thus, it is incompatible with the occurrence of *bié*.[2]

If the negative imperative particle is used in a sentence with a first person plural pronoun as the subject, then the command is of the form 'Let's not . . .'. For example:

(23)   wǒmen   bié   shuō   —   huà
         we   don't   talk   —   speech

Let's not talk!

Negative imperatives can also be expressed with such constructions as *bu-yào* 'don't', *bu-bì* 'not necessary', and *bu-yòng* 'not use', all of which involve the negative particle *bu* 'not'. *Bu-yào* literally means 'not-want'. When used in a command, *bu-yào* 'not-want' has the force of 'don't', as shown in (24):

(24)   nǐ   <u>bu   —   yào</u>   zhèi   —   yang   jiào
         you   not   —   want   this   —   manner   shout

Don't shout like this.

The following sentences are some examples with *bu-bì* and *bu-yòng*:

(25)   nĭ   <u>bu   —   bì</u>   tiàowŭ
        you   not   —   necessary   dance

You don't need to dance.

(26)   <u>bu   —   bì</u>   tuō   xié   le
        not   —   necessary   remove   shoe   CRS

(You) don't need to take off (your) shoes.

(27)   nĭ   <u>bu   —   yòng</u>   kèqi
        you   not   —   use   polite

You don't need to be polite.

(28)   <u>bu   —   yòng</u>   shēnqĭng
        not   —   use   apply

(You) don't need to apply.

In certain northern Mandarin dialects, *bu-yòng* may be contracted to *bèng*:

(29)   nĭ   <u>bèng</u>   rèn   —   shū
        you   not:use   concede   —   defeat

You don't need to concede defeat.

An important distinction between *bié* on the one hand and *bu-yòng*/*bu-bì* on the other is that the former is only a negative imperative particle, whereas the latter are compounds composed of the negative particle *bu* and either the verb *yòng* 'use', or the bound adjective *bì* 'necessary'. Thus, *bu-yòng* and *bu-bì* but not *bié* may occur in declarative sentences or questions. For example:

(30)   tā   <u>bu   —   yòng</u>   shàngbān   ma?
        3sg   not   —   use   work   Q

Doesn't s/he need to go to work?

(31)

tā	bu	–	bì	piàn	rén
3sg	not	–	necessary	deceive	people

S/He need not deceive people.

Correlated with this distinction between *bié* and *bu-yòng/bu-bì* is the fact that only *bié* but not *bu-yòng/bu-bì* may co-occur with the polite imperative marker *qǐng*'please'. Hence, (32) is well formed, but (33) and (34) are ungrammatical:

(32)

qǐng	nǐ	bié	shēngqì
please	you	don't	angry

Please don't be angry.

(33)

*qǐng	nǐ	bu	–	yòng	gào	tā
please	you	not	–	use	sue	3sg

(Please, you don't need to sue him/her.)

(34)

*qǐng	nǐ	bu	–	bì	zháojí
please	you	not	–	necessary	anxious

(Please, you don't need to be anxious.)

The reason for the incongruity between the polite imperative form and the expressions *bu-yòng/bu-bì* is that sentences involving such expressions are not true direct commands, as the English translations of sentences (25)–(28) indicate. A sentence such as (25), meaning 'You don't need to dance', is only an indirect command. Strictly speaking, it is a statement. The imperative meaning of such a statement is inferred, not inherent. On the other hand, both *bié* 'don't' and *qǐng* 'please' have inherent imperative meaning. That's why *bié* 'don't' but not *bu-yòng/bu-bì* may co-occur with *qǐng* 'please'.

What is the status of *bu-yào*? We have noted that *bu-yào* literally means 'not-want'. If we place *bu-yào* in a sentence with a third person subject, then it can have only its literal meaning, as in

(35)

tā	bu	yào	chī	miàn
3sg	not	want	eat	noodle

S/He doesn't want to eat noodles.

If, on the other hand, we place *bu-yào* in a sentence with a first person plural subject, the sentence then has two interpretations: one is the first person plural command 'Let's . . .', and the other, a declarative sentence with *bu yào* meaning 'not want':

(36)   wǒmen   bu   yào   bàgōng
        we   not   want   strike

$$\begin{cases} \text{Let's not strike.} \\ \text{We don't want to strike.} \end{cases}$$

From the ambiguity of (36), we can see that *bu-yào* has two meanings: one is the imperative meaning 'don't', and one is the literal meaning 'not-want'. From now on, we should consider *bu-yào* as one word when it signifies the imperative 'don't'; but when it means 'not-want', of course, it is two separate words, *bu yào*. Since *bu-yào* has a negative imperative meaning, we can expect it to be able to co-occur with the polite imperative *qǐng*, as here:

(37)   qǐng   nǐ   bu-yào   wùhuì   wǒ
        please   you   don't   misunderstand   I

            –   de   yìsi
            –   GEN   meaning

Please don't misunderstand my meaning.

Indeed, *bié* and *bu-yào* are etymologically related. The former is merely a phonological fusion of the latter. No wonder they behave alike!

Bié can also occur in certain serial verb sentences in which the second clause functions as the direct object of the first verb phrase. The subject of this second clause may be, but need not be, a second person (you), as (38)–(41) show:

(38)   wǒ   zhǔzhang   <u>Lìsì   bié   chū   –   guó</u>
        I   advocate   Lisi   don't   exit   –   country

I have the opinion that Lisi shouldn't leave the country.

(39)   wǒ   –   de   yìsi   shì   <u>ni</u>
       I   –   GEN   opinion be   you

       <u>bié</u>   shuō   Zhōngwén
       don't   speak   Chinese

My opinion is that you shouldn't speak Chinese.

(40)   tā   mìngling   wǒ   bié   dǎ   –   lánqiú
       3sg   order   I   don't   play   –   basketball

SHe ordered me not to play basketball.

(41)   wǒ   shuō   tā   bié   tài   jīnzhang
       I   say   3sg   don't   too   tense

I say s/he shouldn't be too tense.

There is a condition controlling the occurrence of *bié* in the clause serving as the direct object: the main verb must be a verb of ordering, such as *mìngling* 'order', *jiào* 'direct', or a verb such as *zhǔzhang* 'advocate', *rènwei* 'feel', *xiǎng* 'think', which express a judgment or an opinion on the part of the subject, or a verb of saying, such as *shuō* 'say', *gàosu* 'tell'. The main verb can also be the copula *shì* 'be', as in (39), as long as the subject noun phrase signals an order, an opinion, or something advocated or said. To illustrate these conditions, let's consider the verb *zhīdao* 'know', which does not express a command or a judgment on the part of the subject and is not a verb of saying. If the direct object clause of *zhīdao* 'know' contains *bié*, clearly the sentence will be unacceptable:

(42)   *wǒ   zhīdao   tā   bié   chū   –   guó
        I   know   3sg   don't   exit   –   country

There are good reasons for these conditions: first, verbs of ordering specify that the following clause is a command, so it is natural that the negative imperative particle, *bié*, should be allowed to occur. The verbs of judgment have a mild imperative force, making it possible for their object clause to be a command. This accounts for the occurrence of *bié* in the object clauses of those verbs. The verbs of saying together with their complements are a form of indirect speech; that is, the complements themselves represent speech utterances. The semantic content of such verbs is rather neutral: such verbs allow any utterance, including commands, to occur as their clause objects (see section 21.2.1 of chapter 21 for further discussion). Finally, the copula as it is used in (39) is a linking verb. As long as the elements linked by the copula are compatible, the sentence will be appropriate. Thus, if the object of the copula is a command, the subject must signal a command, a judgment, or a saying.

In a similar way we can account for the *bié* 'don't' in (43) *a* and *b*:

(43) *a.*   tā   zuì   —   hǎo   bié   hē   jiǔ
           3sg   most —   good   don't   drink   wine

It's best for him/her not to drink wine.

b.   zuì   —   hǎo   tā   bié   hē   jiǔ
      most   —   good   3sg   don't   drink   wine

It's best for him/her not to drink wine.

The unacceptability of sentence (44) shows that the imperative quality of (43) *a* and *b* depends on the adverb *zuì-hǎo* 'most-good':

(44)   *tā   bié   hē   jiǔ
       3sg   don't   drink   wine

Zuì-hǎo is a sentential adverb in the sense that it sets a semantic frame for the rest of the sentence (see section 8.1 of chapter 8 on adverbs). The meaning of such an adverb makes it very clear that the sentence represents a judgment/suggestion on the part of the speaker; that is, it performs the same function as the verbs of judgment, signaling that the folː wing clause is a judgment/suggestion.

Finally, we should return to the first person plural command, which was discussed earlier in this chapter in the context of the negative imperative particle, *bié* 'don't'. We have seen that a negative first person command employs the negative imperative particle, *bié*; but we have not yet mentioned the affirmative first person command; 'Let's . . .'. The affirmative first person command typically uses the sentence-final particle, *ba*, which has the effect of soliciting agreement (see chapter 7). For example:

(45) wǒmen   qǐ   —   lai   ba
      we   rise —   come   SA

Let's get up.

(46) wǒmen   zǒu   ba
      we   go   SA

Let's go.

(47) wǒmen   niàn   Zhōngwén   ba
      we   study Chinese   SA

Let's study Chinese.

The sentence-final particle *ba* also may optionally occur in an ordinary second-person command, as in

(48) nǐ   shuì   —   jiào   ba
      you   sleep —   sleep SA

Go to bed, OK?

(49) nǐ   zǒu   —   zhe   qiáo   ba
      you   go   —   DUR   see   SA

Why don't you see as you go along, OK?

As a marker soliciting agreement, the sentence-final particle *ba* has the effect of softening the imperative force in the second person command.

To summarize this chapter on imperatives, we have seen that imperatives can be ordinary second person commands, in which case they can occur with such softening elements as *qǐng, láojià, máfan,* and the sentence-final particle *ba*, or they can be first person plural commands, which convey the idea of 'Let's . . .', in which case they generally occur with the sentence-final particle *ba*. Negative imperatives must occur with one of the special negative imperative particles *bié*, *bu-yào*, *bu-bì*, or *bu-yòng*. Finally, we have seen that imperatives, like other sentence types, can occur as the objects to certain verbs as well as with adverbs whose meanings involve ordering, saying, or judging.

Notes

1. This chapter has taken some ideas from Hashimoto (1969*b*; 1971*a*:77–81).
2. This is not to claim that a sentence with a third person subject can never take the negative imperative particle *bié*. See the analysis of examples (38)–(43) in this chapter.

CHAPTER 15

The bǎ Construction

The *bǎ* construction is a much-discussed topic in the grammar of Mandarin.[1] From a structural point of view, the *bǎ* construction is straightforward; in general, the direct object is placed immediately after *bǎ* and before the verb:

(1) subject   bǎ direct object   verb

Somewhat less easy to specify are what kinds of direct objects and what kinds of verbs occur in this construction, what can precede and follow the verbs, and what communicative function the construction serves. Examples (2)−(10) illustrate a variety of *bǎ* sentences. The *bǎ* noun phrase in each sentence is underlined:

(2)	kuài	yidiǎn	bǎ	zhèi	kuài	ròu	ná	—	zǒu
	fast	a:little	BA	this	piece	meat	take	—	go

Take this piece of meat away quickly!

(3)	nǐ	bǎ	tā	—	de	yìsi	jiǎng	—
	you	BA	3sg	—	GEN	meaning	talk	—

	chū	—	lái	le
	exit	—	come	CRS

You have explained what s/he meant.

(4) wǒ   bu   néng   bǎ   tā   —   de   bìmì
     I   not   can   BA   3sg   —   GEN   secret

     gàosu   nǐ
     tell   you

I can't tell you his/her secrets.

(5) tā   bǎ   fàntīng   shōushi   —   gānjing   LE
     3sg   BA   dining:room   tidy:up   —   clean   PFV/CRS

S/He tidied up the dining room.

(6) wǒ   bǎ   yǐzi   zǐxì-de   kàn   —   le   yixià
     I   BA   chair   carefully   see   —   PFV   once

I took a careful look at the chair.

(7) wǒ   jīntiān   bǎ   sān   —   běn   shū   dōu
     I   today   BA   three   —   CL   book   all

     mài   LE
     sell   PFV/CRS

I sold all three books today.

(8) tā   bǎ   shénme —   dōu   chī   —   guāng   LE
     3sg   BA   what   —   all   eat   —   gone   PFV/CRS

S/He ate up everything.

(9) tā   yǒu-de-shíhou   bǎ   yán   dāng   táng   chī
     3sg   sometimes   BA   salt   take:as   sugar   eat

S/He sometimes eats salt thinking it's sugar.

(10) nǐ   bǎ   jiǔ   màn-màn-de   hē
      you   BA   wine   slowly   drink

You drink the wine slowly!

In this chapter, we will discuss the nature of the noun phrase after *bǎ*, the message conveyed by the verb phrase in a *bǎ* sentence, and how these factors interact.

15.1 The *bǎ* Noun Phrase

The noun phrase following *bǎ*, which we will call the *bǎ* noun phrase, is generally *definite* or *generic*. (For a discussion of definite and generic, see section 4.2.5 of chapter 4). The *bǎ* noun phrase in sentence (2) above is a definite noun phrase with a demonstrative *zhèi* 'this'; those in (3)−(4) are definite noun phrases with possessor phrases; that in (9) is a generic noun phrase, referring to a class, *yán* 'salt'; and those in (5)−(8) and (10) are definite noun phrases with no marker of definiteness at all. What all these *bǎ* noun phrases share is that they are understood to refer to something about which the speaker believes the hearer knows; (6), for example, can be appropriately used only if the speaker believes that his/her listener knows what chair is being talked about. Similarly, for (7) to make sense, the speaker has to believe that the hearer knows what three books are being referred to.

In (9) the referent of *yán* 'salt' is generic. In other words, *yán* in sentence (9) does not refer to some salt or to any specific salt the hearer and the speaker know about; it refers to the type of entity called 'salt'. The speaker can assume that the hearer knows about the existence of 'salt' as a generic class of entity. For sentence (8) to be appropriately used, the hearer must know what delimits the set of items referred to by the pronoun *shénme-dōu* 'everything'. For example, it could be 'everything' in the refrigerator or 'everything' in the kitchen.

Sometimes, however, the *bǎ* noun phrase need only refer to something particular that the speaker has in mind but about which the hearer does not necessarily know. In such a case, the *bǎ* noun phrase is indefinite. Though such sentences are rare in actual speech, one should be aware that they can occur. Sentences (11)−(12) are examples:

(11)   wǒ   bǎ   yi   −   jian   shì   wàng   LE
        I   BA   one   −   CL   matter forget PFV/CRS

I forgot something (i.e., something in particular).

(12)   yǒu   rén   bǎ   yi   −   ge   zì
        exist   person BA   one   −   CL   character

        cā   −   diào   LE
        erase   −   off   PFV/CRS

Someone erased a (particular) character.

In general, however, when an object is indefinite, even though it refers to a specific entity, it cannot occur in a *bǎ* sentence, as the following examples show:

(13) *a.*

tā	mǎi	–	le	yi	–	liàng	chēzi
3sg	buy	–	PFV	one	–	CL	car

S/He bought a car.

b.

*tā	bǎ	yi	–	liàng	chēzi	mǎi	–	le
3sg	BA	one	–	CL	car	buy	–	PFV

(14) *a.*

tā	shā	–	le	liǎng	–	ge	rén
3sg	kill	–	PFV	two	–	CL	person

S/He killed two people.

b.

*tā	bǎ	liǎng	–	ge	rén	shā	LE
3sg	BA	two	–	CL	person	kill	PFV/CRS

We can see, then, that *bǎ* noun phrases are generally either definite or generic, that is, noun phrases whose referents are known by both speaker and hearer, though sometimes we find a *bǎ* noun phrase whose referent is a specific entity that the speaker has in mind but about which the hearer does not know.

15.2 Disposal

Grammarians studying *bǎ* sentences in Mandarin and written Chinese have been especially concerned with the question of why sentences such as those in (i) are acceptable, while sentences such as those in (ii) are unacceptable:

(i) Acceptable:

(15)

wǒ	bǎ	chá	–	bēi	nòng	–	pò	LE
I	BA	tea	–	cup	make	–	broken	PFV/CRS

I broke the teacup.

(16)

tā	bǎ	biāoyǔ	tiē	zài	qiáng	–	shang
3sg	BA	slogan	paste	at	wall	–	on

S/He posted the slogan on the wall.

(17)	nǐ	bǎ	kùzi	chuān	—	shang
	you	BA	pants	wear	—	ascend

Put on your pants!

(18)	bǎ	diànshì	guān	—	diào
	BA	TV	close	—	off

Turn off the TV!

(19)	wǒ	bǎ	jùzi	xiě	de	tài	cháng	le
	I	BA	sentence	write	CSC	too	long	CRS

I wrote the sentences too long.

(20)	tā	bǎ	gǔ	dǎ	de	wǒ	shuì	—
	3sg	BA	drum	hit	CSC	I	sleep	—

	bu	—	zháo	le
	can't	—	attain	CRS

S/He played the drums so that I couldn't sleep.

(ii) Unacceptable:

(21)	*tā	bǎ	xiǎo	māo	ài
	3sg	BA	small	cat	love

(S/He loves the kitten.)

(22)	*tā	bǎ	nǐ	xiǎng
	3sg	BA	you	miss

(S/He misses you.)

(23)	*wǒ	bǎ	nèi	—	jiàn	shìqing	liǎojiě
	I	BA	that	—	CL	matter	understand

(I understand that matter.)

(24)   *tā   bǎ   Zhāngsān   kàn   —   dào   LE
        3sg   BA   Zhangsan   see   —   arrive   PFV/CRS

(S/He was able to see Zhangsan.)

(25)   *tā   bǎ   gē   chàng   LE
        3sg   BA   song   sing   PFV/CRS

(S/He sang the song.)

(26)   *táo   —   shù   bǎ   huā   kāi   le
        peach   —   tree   BA   flower   bloom   CRS

(The peach trees are blooming.)

The question, of course, is: What is wrong with the sentences in (ii)? All of them involve definite *bǎ* noun phrases, and yet they remain ungrammatical. The essential clue to an explanation of the ungrammaticality of these sentences is provided by the Chinese grammarian Wang Li, who called the *bǎ* construction the "disposal" form.[2] In his words: "The disposal form states how a person is handled, manipulated, or dealt with; how something is disposed of; or how an affair is conducted" (translation by Li [1974:200−201]). We will follow Wang Li in using the term *disposal* to refer to this set of concepts; roughly, disposal has to do with what *happens to* the direct object. Now, when we apply this characterization of disposal to the analysis of the preceding examples, it becomes obvious that the concept of disposal is exactly what the sentences in (ii) are missing: they do not describe how an entity is handled or dealt with—or, in other words, disposed of. The first three, (21)−(23), contain verbs of emotion, *ài* 'love' and *xiǎng* 'miss', and a verb of cognition, *liǎojiě* 'understand'; none of these verbs affect their direct objects in the sense of disposal. Similarly, the verb *kàn-dào* 'able to see' in (24) is a simple perception verb, again implying no manipulation of or even attention to the direct object. Finally, the verbs *chàng* 'sing' and *kāi* 'bloom' in (25) and (26) are verbs whose meanings imply, not dealing with or handling their direct objects, but creating them: it is part of the *definition* of a song that it be sung and of a flower that it blooms, so sentences (25) and (26) do not convey any meaningful information about *what has happened* to the song or the flower.

The idea of disposal can also be inferred or understood in an implicit way. For example, while sentence (21), with *ài* 'love' as the verb, is not acceptable because 'love' does not carry the sense of disposal, sentence (27), which also uses the verb *ài* 'love', is perfectly acceptable:

(27)	tā	bǎ	xiǎo	māo	ài	de	yào	sǐ
	3sg	BA	small	cat	love	CSC	want	die

S/He loves the kitten so much that s/he wants to die.

The difference between (21) and (27) is that an expression has been added in (27). Notice that the verb of (27), *ài* 'love', is identical to the verb of (21). As far as the meaning of the *verb* is concerned, then, (27) has no more or less a sense of disposal than (21) does. The added expression *yào sǐ* 'want to die', however, hyperbolically creates an image that such intense love must have some effect on the 'small cat'. Thus, the disposal idea in (27) is not explicitly stated by the verb. The fact that the 'small cat' is dealt with in some sense is merely implied by the verb together with the added expression. An *implication* of disposal is, therefore, sufficient to warrant the use of the *bǎ* construction.

Let us consider another example. Recall (22), which is unacceptable because the verb, *xiǎng* 'miss', lacks the sense of disposal. On the other hand, though, (28), employing the same verb, is well formed:

(28)	tā	bǎ	nǐ	xiǎng	de	fàn	dōu	bu
	3sg	BA	you	miss	CSC	food	even	not

	kěn	chī
	willing	eat

S/He misses you so much that s/he won't even eat his/her meals.

Again, the difference between (28) and (22) is the presence of an added expression, which greatly exaggerates the degree of his/her missing you. It is as if one cannot help thinking that you are affected in some way when s/he misses you to such an extent that s/he can't even eat.

Sentences (29)−(31) are further examples of implied disposal:

(29)	wǒ	bǎ	tā	hèn	−	tòu	le
	I	BA	3sg	hate	−	through	CRS

I hate him/her so!

(30)	tā	bǎ	nèi	—	jiàn	shìqing	liǎojiě	de
	3sg	BA	that	—	CL	matter	understand	CSC

hěn	tòuchè
very	thorough

S/He understands that matter very thoroughly.

(31)	tā	zhōngyu	bǎ	zhèi	yi	tiān	pànwang
	3sg	finally	BA	this	one	day	hope

—	dào	LE
—	arrive	PFV/CRS

Finally this day has arrived through his/her hoping.

In (31), what is implied is that his/her hoping is so intense that it has made this day become real.

As stated in the beginning of this chapter, the general pattern for *bǎ* sentences is to put the direct object of the verb (see section 4.3.1.B for a discussion of direct objects) immediately after *bǎ*. In all of the examples so far, the *bǎ* noun phrase has been the direct object. There is another pattern, however, which can be schematized like this:

(32)   subject   bǎ   object₁   verb   object₂

This pattern schematizes what Lü (1948) called the "retained object" (*bǎo-liú bīn-yǔ*) construction. Consider sentence (33):

(33)	wǒ	bǎ	tā	bǎng	—	le
	I	BA	3sg	tie:up	—	PFV

liǎng	—	zhi	jiǎo
two	—	CL	foot

I tied up his/her two feet. (Literally: What I did to him/her was to tie up his/her two feet.)

Notice that in (33) the direct object of *bǎng* 'tie up' is *liǎng-zhi jiǎo* 'two feet'. Nevertheless, *tā* 's/he' is the noun that follows *bǎ*. The property of disposal, however, clearly is still the key to the interpretation of this sentence, as is suggested by its literal translation: 'What I *did to him/her* was to tie up his/her two feet'. Thus, the referent of the *bǎ* noun phrase, *tā* 's/he', is the one affected by the action, the one to which something *happens*, although the grammatical direct object of the verb, *bang* 'tie up', in (33) is *liǎng-zhi jiǎo* 'two feet'. Sentences (34)−(39), where the two objects are underlined, provide further illustration of this use of the *bǎ* construction:

(34)	wǒ	bǎ	<u>júzi</u>	bō	–	le	<u>pí</u>
	I	BA	orange	peel	–	PFV	skin

I peeled the orange. (Literally: What I did to the orange was to peel its skin).

(35)	wǒ	bǎ	<u>tā</u>	<u>érzi</u>	huàn	–	le	<u>xìngmíng</u>
	I	BA	3sg	son	change	–	PFV	name

I changed his/her son's name. (Literally: What I did to his/her son was to change his name.)

(36)	tā	bǎ	<u>táizi</u>	dǎ	–	le	<u>là</u>
	3sg	BA	table	apply	–	PFV	wax

S/He waxed the table. (Literally: What s/he did to the table was to apply wax to it.)

(37)	wǒ	bǎ	<u>bìlú</u>	shēng	–	le	<u>huǒ</u>
	I	BA	fireplace	start	–	PFV	fire

I started a fire in the fireplace. (Literally: What I did to the fireplace was to start a fire.)

(38)	tā	bǎ	<u>huǒ</u>	jiā	–	le	yi-diǎn	<u>yóu</u>
	3sg	BA	fire	add:on	–	PFV	a:little	oil

S/He added a little oil to the fire. (Literally: What s/he did to the fire was to add a little oil.)

(39)	wǒ	bǎ	<u>mén</u>	shàng	–	le	<u>suǒ</u>
	I	BA	door	ascend	–	PFV	lock

I locked the door. (Literally: What I did to the door was to bolt the lock.)

The more literal translations of sentences (34)−(39) clearly render the sense of disposal of the referent of the *bǎ* noun phrase. It has been observed that sentences of this type often show a possessive relationship between the *bǎ* noun phrase and the direct object of the verb, as in sentences (33)−(35). This possessive relationship, however, is not structurally specified, but rather is inferred, and it is not a necessary inference for the construction schematized by (32), as shown in (36)−(39).

Related to the type of *bǎ* sentences shown immediately above are those in which the *bǎ* noun phrase has a *part-whole relation* with the direct object of the verb. For example:

(40) wǒ   bǎ   píngguǒ   chī   —   le   sān   —   ge
       I   BA   apple   eat   —   PFV   three —   CL

I ate three of the apples.

(41) tā   bǎ   nèi   píng   jiǔ   hē   —   le
      3sg   BA   that   bottle wine   drink —   PFV

      yì   —   bàn
      one   —   half

S/He drank half of that bottle of wine.

(42) wǒ   bǎ   bìmi   xièlòu   —   le   bu   shǎo
       I   BA   secret leak   —   PFV   not   little

I leaked quite a bit of the secret.

The *bǎ* noun phrase in each of these sentences denotes a definite direct object with a fixed quantity, and the direct object of the verb refers to a part of that fixed quantity.

We have seen that the notion of disposal allows us to understand why some *bǎ* sentences are acceptable and some unacceptable. Let us further examine the nature of the *bǎ* construction with respect to the disposal notion.

First, we see that it accounts for why we never find *bǎ* with verbs such as *yǒu* 'exist', *xiàng* 'resemble', *xìng* 'be surnamed': these verbs never involve or imply anything happening to their direct objects.[3]

(43) *wǒ   bǎ   shū   yǒu
        I   BA   book   exist

(I have the book.)

(44)   *tā   bǎ   bàba   <u>xiàng</u>
       3sg   ba   father resemble

       (S/He resembles his/her father.)

(45)   *tā   bǎ   Wáng   <u>xìng</u>
       3sg   BA   Wang   be surnamed

       (S/He is surnamed Wang.)

(46)   *wǒ   bǎ   tā   xiàng   lǎohǔ
       I   BA   3sg   resemble   tiger

       (What I did to him/her was to resemble a tiger.)

(47)   *tā   bǎ   bàba   xiàng   de   yi   —   mó
       3sg   BA   father resemble CSC   one   —   mold

              —   yi   —   yàng
              —   one   —   manner

       (S/He resembles his/her father to the extent they are exactly the same.)

Second, the notion of disposal does not require purpose. In other words, the subject of a *bǎ* sentence may be an inanimate entity or some unspecified force or situation (see the next section, 15.3, for more discussion), or it may carry out an action accidentally.

(48) (inanimate subject)

       dà   shuǐ   bǎ   qiáo   chōng   —   zǒu   LE
       big   water   BA   bridge   wash   —   go   PFV/CRS

       The flood washed away the bridge.

(49) (unspecified situation as subject)

hǎoxiàng	yòu	yào	xià	yǔ ,	bǎ	wǒ
appears	again	will	descend	rain	BA	I

	qì	—	sǐ	LE
	angry	—	die	PFV/CRS

It appears that it's going to rain again, and that makes me so angry!

(50) (accidental mental activity)

tā	cōng-cong-máng-mang-de	bǎ	píbāo	wàng	LE
3sg	hurriedly	BA	wallet	forget	PFV/CRS

S/He was in a hurry and forgot his/her wallet.

(51) (accidental action)

háizi	bu	xiǎoxīn	bǎ	huā	—	píng
child	not	careful	BA	flower	—	vase

	nòng	—	pò	LE
	make	—	broken	PFV/CRS

The child accidentally broke the vase.

The above examples make it clear that disposal does not have to be purposeful; things can happen to entities without there being any willful action on the part of an instigator.

Third, disposal does not necessarily imply that the object is physically affected. This is most easily seen in cases where the *bǎ* noun phrase refers to something abstract, which cannot have something "happen" to it physically, as in (11) and (30) above. Still, such sentences do convey how that abstract thing has been dealt with. Here are two further instances:

(52)	tā	bǎ	nèi	—	ge	wènti	xiǎng	—
	3sg	BA	that	—	CL	problem	think	—

le	hěn	jiǔ
PFV	very	long

S/He thought about that problem for a long time.

(53)	lǚxíng	de	shíhou ,	tā	yào	bǎ	lù	—
	travel	NOM	time	3sg	want	BA	road	—

shang	—	de	fēngjǐng	huà	—
on	—	ASSOC	scenery	draw	—

xià	—	lái
descend	—	come

While s/he traveled, s/he wanted to draw pictures of the scenery along the way.

Sentence (53) is an interesting example: what happens to the scenery is nothing that affects *it* in any way, but rather that it gets translated into two-dimensional form onto the art paper. Sentence (54) displays similar characteristics:

(54)	nǐ	zuì	hǎo	bǎ	nǐ	—	de	yìsi
	you	most	good	BA	you	—	GEN	meaning

shuō	—	chū	—	lái
say	—	exit	—	come

You'd best say what you have in mind.

A fourth point about disposal is that it accounts for why *bǎ* is commonly used in imperatives: an imperative is a command to a listener to do something, and if a direct object known to the speaker and the hearer is involved, the listener is commanded to do something *to* the entity referred to by that direct object. The disposal function of the *bǎ* construction naturally fits such a role. Here are some examples:

(55) qǐng   nǐ   bǎ   zhèi   —   ge   píngguǒ   cā
      please   you   BA   this   —   CL   apple   rub

      —   yi   —   cā
      —   one   —   rub

   Please polish up this apple a little!

(56) nǐ   suíbiàn   bǎ   tā   —   de
      you   as:one:wishes   BA   3sg   —   GEN

                wénzhang   pīping   yīxià   ba
                article   criticize once   SA

   You can have a go at criticizing his/her article, OK?

(57) bié   bǎ   wǒ   —   de   dǎzìjī
      don't   BA   I   —   GEN   typewriter

                ná   —   zǒu
                take   —   away

   Don't take my typewriter away!

(58) bǎ   nǐ   —   de   chēzi   kāi
      BA   you   —   GEN   car   drive

                dào   hòumian qù
                to   back   go

   Drive your car around to the back!

A fifth point is that disposal helps explain the grammatical constraint against using *bǎ* with potential forms of resultative verb compounds (see section 3.2.3 of chapter 3). It has long been known to students of Mandarin that the resultative compound with a potential infix, whether affirmative or negative, cannot occur in the *bǎ* construction. For example, consider the resultative verb compound *xǐ-gānjing* 'wash-clean'; the affirmative potential infix for resultative compounds is *-de-*: *xǐ-de-gānjing* 'can wash-clean'; the negative potential infix is *-bu-*: *xǐ-bu-gānjing* 'cannot wash-clean'. Whereas the resultative verb compound itself can occur freely in the *bǎ* construction, the compound with either of the infixes *-de-* or *-bu-* cannot. That is, sentences (59) *a*—*c* are acceptable, but (59) *d* and *e* are not:

(59) *a.*

tā	bu	néng	bǎ	nèi	—	ge
3sg	not	can	BA	that	—	CL

xiāngzi	xǐ	—	gānjing
chest	wash	—	clean

S/He can't clean that chest.

b.

tā	xǐ	—	bu	—	gānjing
3sg	wash	—	can't	—	clean

nèi	—	ge	xiāngzi
that	—	CL	chest

S/He can't clean that chest.

c.

tā	xǐ	—	de	—	gānjing
3sg	wash	—	can	—	clean

nèi	—	ge	xiāngzi
that	—	CL	chest

S/He can wash that chest clean.

d.

*tā	bǎ	nèi	—	ge	xiāngzi
3sg	BA	that	—	CL	chest

xǐ	—	de	—	gānjing
wash	—	can	—	clean

(S/He can wash that chest clean.)

e.	*tā	bǎ	nèi	—	ge	xiāngzi
	3sg	BA	that	—	CL	chest

	xǐ	—	bu	—	gānjing
	wash	—	can't	—	clean

(S/He can't wash that chest clean.)

Sentences *a*, *b*, and *e* appear to be conveying similar messages, and sentences *c* and *d* seem to convey the same message. The unacceptability of *d* and *e* show, however, that *bǎ* is incompatible with the potential form of the resultative verb. Why?

As discussed in section 3.2.3 of chapter 3, sentences with the modal *néng* 'can' and with the potential forms of resultative verbs do not convey the same messages. *Néng* 'can' refers to the overall possibility of an event's taking place with respect to the subject's capabilities, but the potential form of a resultative verb compound refers to the success or failure of an action in achieving the result. Thus, in the case of (59) *a*, s/he may or may not have tried to wash the chest, but it is the speaker's judgment that s/he does not have the know-how to wash it clean. In such a case there is no problem in using *bǎ*, since (59) *a* claims that with respect to disposing of the box by washing it clean, s/he can't do it.

In the case of (59) *b*, on the other hand, the information being conveyed is that s/he cannot clean that box by washing it—in other words, that the action of 'washing' fails to achieve the result, which is 'clean'. Similarly, (59) *c* conveys the message that the action of 'washing' *can* achieve the result 'clean'. Thus, in both *b* and *c*, where the potential form of the resultative compound is used, the focus of the sentence is on the success or failure of *achieving a result* through an action, not on the action itself, which must bear the disposal meaning with respect to its object. This renders the meaning of the potential forms of resultative verbs incompatible with the meaning of the *bǎ* construction, which focuses on the disposal nature of the action verb.

Finally, the notion of disposal explains the fact that the negation of the *bǎ* construction involves placing the negative particle *bu* or *méi(yǒu)* 'not' immediately before *bǎ* rather than immediately before the verb. Structurally, the placement of the negative particle in the *bǎ* construction may be represented by the schema in (60):

(60)   subject   <u>bu/méi(yǒu)</u>   bǎ   direct object   verb

The question that arises from the position of the negative particle in the *bǎ* construction is: Why isn't the negative particle placed immediately before the verb—the order is shown in (61)—as it is in the negation of a non-*bǎ* sentence?

(61)   *subject   bǎ   direct object   <u>bu/méi(yǒu)</u>   verb

Let us answer this question by examining two examples:

(62) *a*.   wǒmen   <u>méi</u>   bǎ   Zhāngsān   qǐng   –   lái
            we   not   BA   Zhangsan   invite   –   come

     We didn't invite Zhangsan over.

    b.   *wǒmen   bǎ   Zhāngsān   <u>méi</u>   qǐng   –   lái
                  we   BA   Zhangsan   not   invite   –   come

In (62) *a*, the negative particle precedes *bǎ*. Thus the entire predicate lies in the scope of negation (see chapter 12 on negation for a discussion of scope). Given the scope of negation in (62) *a*, its meaning is something like this: 'It is not true that we invited Zhangsan over'. Now, let us look at (62) *b*. In (62) *b* the negative particle precedes only the verb; thus, only the verb lies in the scope of the negation. If we can represent the disposal function of the *bǎ* sentence by the paraphrase 'what we did to Zhangsan was . . .', then (62) *b* is trying to convey the message: 'What we did to Zhangsan was to not invite him over'; but such a message is nonsensical.[4] On the one hand, the *bǎ* construction signals how the referent of the *bǎ* noun phrase is dealt with as a result of the event named by the verb; on the other hand, the negation immediately preceding the verb signals that the event named by the verb does not occur. Thus, there exists an obvious inconsistency, and it is this inconsistency that renders (62) *b* ungrammatical.

Certain linguists have noted some apparent counterexamples to the principle that the negative particle must be placed before *bǎ* in the *bǎ* construction. Sentences in which a negative particle can follow the *bǎ* noun phrase are just those in which the combination *negative* + *verb* itself signals something happening to the direct object; in such cases, the inconsistency mentioned above in our discussion of (62) *b* disappears. For example:

(63)   tā   bǎ   wǒ   yidiǎn   dōu   <u>bu</u>   fàng
       3sg   BA   I   a:little even   not   place

               zài   xīn   –   shang
               at   heart –   on

    S/He didn't have me on his/her mind at all.

In (63), the phrase *bu fàng zài xīn-shang* 'not place at heart' has the idiomatic meaning of 'slighting'. Thus what (63) really means is that 'what s/he did to me was to slight me', and the disposal notion of the *bă* construction is not contravened by the negation of the verb *fàng* 'to place'. Few negative-plus-verb expressions can represent some sort of action or happening of the type shown in (63), and most of those that do have idiomatic meanings.

15.3 *bă* Sentences without a Subject

A *bă* sentence may be without a subject when the subject refers to either a noun phrase or a proposition that is understood from the context. If the understood subject refers to a noun phrase, it is simply a case of a zero pronoun (see chapter 24). In this section we will present some examples of *bă* sentences whose understood subjects refer to propositions. In (64)–(67) the proposition to which the understood subject of the *bă* sentence refers is given:

(64)	wŏ	cóng	mén	—	kŏu	chū	—
	I	from	door	—	mouth	exit	—

lai,	bă	Wángèr	xià	—	le
come	BA	Wanger	frighten	—	PFV

yi	—	tiào
one	—	jump

I came through the door, (and that) gave Wanger a scare.

(65)	zuótian	Lìsì	lái	—	le,	bă
	yesterday	Lisi	come	—	PFV	BA

Wángèr	gāoxing ·	de	shŏu	—
Wanger	happy	CSC	hand	—

wŭ	—	zú	—	dăo
dance	—	foot	—	jump

Yesterday Lisi came, (and that) made Wanger so happy that he was capering about.

(66) wǒ   zài   nàr   jiǎng   gùshi,   bǎ
      I   at   there   tell   story   BA

             tā   xiào   de   dùzi   dōu
             3sg   laugh   CSC   belly   all

      téng   le
      hurt   CRS

I was telling a story there, (and that) made him/her laugh so much that his/her belly hurt.

(67) zuótian   wǒmen   qǐng   –   kè,   bǎ
      yesterday we   invite –   guest   BA

             tā   chī   de   dùzi   dōu
             3sg   eat   CSC   belly   all

      zhàng   le
      bloat   CRS

Yesterday we treated (everyone, and that) made him/her eat so much that his/her belly was all bloated.

Sometimes the proposition is understood and need not have been explicitly expressed. For example, if we are discussing the way a friend has treated you, you can simply say:

(68) bǎ   wǒ   qì   –   sǐ   LE !
      BA   I   angry   –   die   PFV/CRS

It made me so mad!

Similarly, if one has been at a dull meeting until 8:00 P.M., one can exclaim:

(69) bǎ   wǒ   è   de   yào   –   mìng !
      BA   I   hungry CSC   want   –   life

It's made me so hungry I could die!

15.4 *bǎ . . . gěi*

A variant form of the *bǎ* construction involves the occurrence of the particle *gěi* immediately before the verb, as shown in (70):

(70)   subject   <u>bǎ</u>   direct object   <u>gěi</u>   verb

Sentences (71)–(73) are illustrations:

(71)	wǒ	<u>bǎ</u>	tā	—	de	tóu	<u>gěi</u>
	I	BA	3sg	—	GEN	head	GEI

	niǔ	—	guò	—	lai	LE
	twist	—	cross	—	come	PFV/CRS

I twisted his/her head around.

(72)	tā	<u>bǎ</u>	nèi	—	ge	rén	<u>gěi</u>
	3sg	BA	that	—	CL	person	GEI

	hài	—	kǔ	LE
	hurt	—	bitter	PFV/CRS

S/He hurt that person badly.

(73)	wǒ	<u>bǎ</u>	dàyī	<u>gěi</u>	tàng	—	hǎo	LE
	I	BA	coat	GEI	iron	—	done	PFV/CRS

I ironed the coat.

The addition of *gěi* before the verb has the effect of strengthening the disposal function of the *bǎ* construction. *Gěi* is not an obligatory element; (71)–(73) would be well-formed sentences without it. This variant form of the *bǎ* construction occurs fairly frequently, however. According to Wang Huan's survey of one short story, one-fifth of the *bǎ* constructions (four out of twenty) involve the use of *gěi*.[5]

15.5 When to Use the *bǎ* Construction

Putting together what we have described so far, we can cite two conditions under which it is appropriate to express a message in the form of a *bǎ* sentence.

(i) The *bǎ* noun phrase is *definite, specific, or generic*. In most cases, the *bǎ* noun phrase is the direct object of the verb; but it may also be a noun phrase directly affected by the disposal event signaled by the verb plus the direct object (e.g., [33]–[39]).

(ii) The message involves *disposal*, something happening to the entity referred to by the *bǎ* noun phrase.

These two conditions still leave a certain amount of flexibility, though; after all, in some instances a message could be expressed either by a *bǎ* sentence or in the non-*bǎ* form, as in (74):

(74) *a.*

wǒ	yǐjīng	mài	–	le	wǒ
I	already	sell	–	PFV	I

	–	de	qìchē
	–	GEN	car

I already sold my car.

b.

wǒ	yǐjīng	bǎ	wǒ	–	de
I	already	BA	I	–	de

	qìchē	mài	LE
	car	sell	PFV/CRS

I already sold my car.

What is the rule of thumb for deciding when to use *bǎ*? The decision is a relative one: the *more* a sentence fulfills conditions (i) and (ii), the *more likely* it is to appear in the form of a *bǎ* construction. Thus, while (74) *a* could be used simply to report on an event, (74) *b* would be more likely to be used in a discussion about what has happened to the speaker's car.

Similarly, suppose that you want to ask your friend to chop the onions for a dish you're making. If the onions are in the refrigerator or otherwise can't be seen, you might well use the non-*bǎ* form in your request:

(75) *a.*

qǐng	nǐ	qiē	–	qiē	cōng
please	you	cut	–	cut	onion

Please cut up the onions.

If, however, the onions stand out more in the speech context—for instance, if they are being pointed at or being held in your hand—it is more likely that the *bǎ* form would be used:

b.	qǐng	nǐ	bǎ	(zhèi)	—	xiē)
	please	you	BA	(this	—	PL)

		cōng	qiē	—	qiē
		onion	cut	—	cut

Please cut up (these) onions.

To take another example, if someone wants you to open the door, s/he can say either (76) *a* or (76) *b*:

(76) *a.*	qǐng	nǐ	lā	—	kāi	mén
	please	you	pull	—	open	door

Please open the door.

b.	qǐng	nǐ	bǎ	mén	lā	—	kāi
	please	you	BA	door	pull	—	open

Please open the door.

The second sentence, with *bǎ*, implies that the door is more obvious in the speech context and more immediate to our discussion. In other words, the more prominent the referent of the direct object is, the more appropriate it is to use a *bǎ* noun phrase to refer to it.

The second condition on the use of *bǎ*, the disposal condition, works in exactly the same way: the more the verb elaborates or specifies how the direct object is being handled or dealt with, the more appropriate it is to use *bǎ*. Looking once again at the pair (74) *a* and *b*, we see that, although the *bǎ* noun phrase is definite, the verb, *mài* 'buy', is minimally specified with regard to the disposal of the direct object *mài LE* 'sell PFV/CRS'.

(74) *a.*	wǒ	yǐjīng	mài	—	le	wǒ
	I	already	sell	—	PFV	I

		—	de	qìchē
		—	GEN	car

I already sold my car.

b.	wǒ	yǐjīng	bǎ	wǒ	—	de	
	I	already	BA	I	—	GEN	

	qìchē	mài	LE
	car	sell	PFV/CRS

I already sold my car.

If, however, more information about the disposal of the car, such as *-diào* 'off', is added to the verb, the *bǎ* version will be preferred:

(77) *a.*	wǒ	yǐjīng	bǎ	wǒ	—	de	qìchē
	I	already	BA	I	—	GEN	car

	mài	—	diào	le
	sell	—	off	CRS

I already sold off my car

b.	wǒ	yǐjīng	mài	—	diào	wǒ	—
	I	already	sell	—	off	I	—

	de	qìchē	le
	GEN	car	CRS

I already sold off my car.

And if we specify the disposal in even more detail, the non-*bǎ* form becomes unnatural, and only the *bǎ* form can be used:

(78) *a.*	wǒ	yǐjīng	bǎ	wǒ	—	de	qìche
	I	already	BA	I	—	GEN	car

	mài	gěi	wǒ	—	de	biǎogē
	sell	to	I	—	GEN	paternal:cousin

I already sold my car to my paternal cousin.

b. ? wǒ   yǐjīng   mài   wǒ   —   de   qìchē
      I   already   sell   I   —   GEN   car

      gěi   wǒ   —   de   biǎogē
      to   I   —   GEN   paternal:cousin

Let's look at another example. If we want to describe someone holding a bag of laundry, either the non-*bǎ* or the *bǎ* form can be used, since 'holding' does not strongly indicate disposal:

(79) *a.*   tā   bào   —   zhe   zāng   yīfu
            3sg   hold   —   DUR   dirty   clothes

S/He was holding dirty laundry.

b.   tā   bǎ   zāng   yīfu   bào   —   zhe
        3sg   BA   dirty   clothes   hold   —   DUR

S/He was holding the dirty laundry.

If, however, we change from 'holding' to 'picking up', using the resultative verb compound *bào-qǐ-lai* 'hold-rise-come', then the *bǎ* sentence immediately becomes the preferred form, since the message now conveys a much stronger sense of disposal of the laundry:

(80) *a.*   tā   bǎ   zāng   yīfu   bào   —
            3sg   BA   dirty   clothes   hold   —

            qǐ   —   lai   le
            rise   —   come   CRS

He picked up the dirty laundry.

b.   ?tā   bào   —   qǐ   —   lai
        3sg   hold   —   rise   —   come

        zāng   yīfu   le
        dirty   clothes   CRS

What we see, then, is that the less the message involves the prominence or the disposal of the object, the more likely the sentence is to be expressed in the non-*bǎ* form. We can express this generalization by means of a continuum:

bǎ	*bǎ*	*bǎ*	*bǎ*
impossible	unlikely	likely	obligatory

indefinite or nonreferential object	definite and highly prominent object
no disposal	strong disposal

We've seen examples of each point on this continuum. Starting at the left, we have examples such as (43) and (45), where the object is neither referential nor disposed of:

(43)	*wǒ	bǎ	shū	yǒu
	I	BA	book	have

(I have books.)

(45)	*wǒ	bǎ	Wáng	xìng
	I	BA	Wang	be:surnamed

(I am surnamed Wang.)

A little farther to the right along the continuum, we could place such examples as (81)–(83), which involve weak disposal and definite direct objects that are not highly prominent:

(81)	tā	bǎ	shǒubiǎo	kàn	—	yi	—	kàn
	3sg	BA	watch	see	—	one	—	see

S/He took a look at the watch.

(82)	tā	bǎ	wǒ	lā	—	zhe
	3sg	BA	I	pull	—	DUR

S/He was pulling at me.

(83)	wǒ	bǎ	qián	gěi	tā	le
	I	BA	money	give	3sg	CRS

I gave him/her the money.

Farther to the right along the continuum, where *bǎ* becomes more likely, are sentences with a *bǎ* noun marked by a demonstrative, which indicates that the *bǎ* noun is definite and highly prominent, or with resultative verb compounds (see section 3.2.3 of chapter 3), which elaborate the nature of the disposal of the *bǎ* noun:

(84)	kuài	yidiǎn	bǎ	zhèi	—	ge
	fast	a:little	BA	this	—	CL

	ròu	ná	—	zǒu
	meat	take	—	away

Quickly take this meat away!

(85)	wǒmen	bǎ	nèi	liǎng	—	ge
	we	BA	that	two	—	CL

	yǐzi	bān	—	jìn	—
	chair	move	—	enter	—

	lái	LE
	come	PFV/CRS

We moved those two chairs in.

Finally, at the extreme right of the continuum are sentences with highly prominent objects and a strong sense of disposal:

(86)	bié	bǎ	nǐ	–	de	péngyǒu
	don't	BA	you	–	GEN	friend

	dài	dào	lóushàng	qù
	take	to	upstairs	go

Don't take your friend upstairs.

(87)	wǒ	bǎ	dùzi	suō	–	le	liǎng	cùn
	I	BA	stomach	contract	–	PFV	two	inch

I contracted (my) stomach two inches.

(88)	tā	bǎ	zhǐ	–	mén	tī	–
	3sg	BA	paper	–	door	kick	–

	le	yi	–	ge	dòng
	PFV	one	–	CL	hole

S/He kicked a hole in the paper door.

Looking at *bǎ* sentences in this way, as resulting from the interaction of the prominence of the *bǎ* noun and the degree of disposal in the message, we can see a number of facts about the distribution of *bǎ* sentences in actual use become clear.

First, it is understandable why some grammarians and textbook writers have thought that the verb in a *bǎ* sentence cannot stand alone, but must be either preceded by some adverb or followed by some element, such as a perfective, directional, or resultative verb suffix or a complex stative clause. The reason that *bǎ* sentences always have verbs with those elements preceding or following them is that such elements serve to elaborate the nature of disposal.

Even more interesting is the question of what it is that can precede or follow the verb in a *bǎ* sentence. For example, we have seen that both the durative -*zhe* (see section 6.2 of chapter 6) and reduplicated verb morphemes signaling the delimitative aspect (see section 6.4 of chapter 6) can follow the verb in a *bǎ* construction, as in sentences (75) *b* and (79) *b* above. Neither the reduplication nor the durative suffix, however, enhances the disposal nature of the verb very much. This implies that *bǎ* sentences with a reduplicated verb or with the durative suffix on the verb should be rare. This is confirmed in one study of *bǎ* sentences found in colloquial essays, stories, and speeches:[6] out of eighty-three *bǎ* sentences, there were none whose verbs were reduplicated and only one whose verb was followed by *-zhe*. On the other hand, thirty-three of the eighty-three, or 40 percent, ended with a directional suffix, such as *xià* 'descend' or *qǐ-lái* 'come up', as in:

(89)	nǐ	kuài	qù	bǎ	tāmen	jiào
	you	fast	go	BA	they	call

	—	qǐ	—	lái
	—	rise	—	come

Go quickly and rouse them up.

And twenty-three of the eighty-three, or 28 percent, contained a directional phrase, as in:

(90)	Lǐsì	bǎ	Lǔsù	qǐng	dào	chuán	—	lǐ
	Lisi	BA	Lusu	invite	to	boat	—	in

Lisi invited Lusu inside the boat.

It is also true that when a simple verb is followed by only the perfective aspect suffix *-le*, there seems to be little communicative difference between the non-*bǎ* and the *bǎ* form, as, for example, in (73) *a* and *b*. In other words, V-*le* doesn't strongly favor the *bǎ* construction. Correspondingly, the study shows that only six, or 7 percent, of the eighty-three *bǎ* sentences ended with just V-*le*.

In an even more dramatic way, the results of the study correlate with what we have said about the definiteness of the object. We pointed out that it is possible to find an indefinite noun functioning as the *bǎ* noun if it refers to something specific. Since indefinite nouns are less prominent than definite ones, though, we expect that they should be rare in *bǎ* sentences. What the study revealed is that *all* of the eighty-three *bǎ* sentences had definite direct objects.

The numbers arrived at in this study of *bǎ* in real contexts provide striking confirmation of the two factors that we have said control the use of *bǎ*: the more prominent the object is and the more strongly the sentence expresses disposal, the more likely it is that the message will be expressed in the form of a *bǎ* construction.

Notes

1. For this chapter we have incorporated ideas from Wang (1947), Lü (1948), Wang (1957), Hashimoto (1971a), Li (1971, 1977), Cheung (1973), Huang (1974b), Li (1974), and Teng (1975a), as well as from unpublished work by Lin Shuang-fu and Mei Kuang.

2. In Mandarin, 'disposal form' is *chǔzhì shì* (see Wang [1947:160 ff.]). See also chapter 16 on the passive for more discussion of disposal.

3. In fact, strictly speaking, *shū* 'book' in sentence (43) is not a direct object at all (see chapter 7 on existential verbs).

4. Although the English sentence 'What we did to Zhangsan was to not invite him over' can convey a meaningful message when 'not invite him over' is inferred as a punishment, the disposal sense of the Mandarin *bǎ* sentence does not allow such an inference.

5. See Wang (1957:39).

6. This unpublished study was carried out by Grant Goodall.

CHAPTER 16

The bèi Construction

The term *passive* in Mandarin is generally applied to sentences containing the coverb *bèi* with the following linear arrangement (where NP = noun phrase):[1]

(1) NP_1 <u>bèi</u> NP_2 verb

For example:

(2) tā   bèi   jiějie   mà   LE
     3sg   BEI   elder:sister   scold   PFV/CRS

S/He was scolded by (his/her) older sister.

This type of construction has the direct object noun phrase, that is, the thing or person affected by the action of the verb, in sentence-initial position. This direct object noun phrase is followed by the passive coverb *bèi*, which introduces the agent of the action. We will call this the *bèi noun phrase*. The verb occurs in sentence-final position, as it does in the *bǎ* construction. Thus, in sentence (2), the first noun phrase, *tā* 's/he', is the direct object of the verb *mà* 'scold'; the *bèi* noun, *jiějie* 'older sister', is the agent, the one who did the scolding.

Schema (1), however, is not the only form in which the passive construction can occur. There are a number of variations. One important variation of (1) occurs when the agent, NP_2, is not present:

(3) NP_1 bèi   verb

For example:

(4)   tā   bèi   mà   LE
      3sg   BEI   scold   PFV/CRS

S/He was scolded.

(5)   wǒ   bèi   qiǎng   LE
      I   BEI   rob   PFV/CRS

I was robbed.

We will present other variations of (1) later in this chapter. At this point, the two forms of the passive construction represented by (1) and (3) will be the focus of our discussion. First we will talk about their use and function in Mandarin, and then we will discuss their grammatical characteristics.

16.1 Use and Function

16.1.1 Adversity

The *bèi* passive in Mandarin, like those of Japanese, Vietnamese, Thai, and other Asian languages, is used essentially to express an *adverse* situation, one in which something unfortunate has happened. For instance:

(6)   jiǎozi   bèi   (gǒu)   chī   —   diào   LE
      dumplings   BEI   (dog)   eat   —   down   PFV/CRS

The dumplings got eaten up (by the dog).

(7)   qiáo   bèi   (dà   —   shuǐ)   chōng   —
      bridge BEI   (big   —   water) wash   —

      zǒu   LE
      away   PFV/CRS

The bridge got washed away (by the flood).

(8)   tā   bèi   (gōngsi)   chèzhí   LE
      3sg   BEI   (company)   fire   PFV/CRS

S/He was fired (by his/her company).

(9)   nèi   —   zhi   niǎo   bèi   wǒ   —   de
      that   —   CL   bird   BEI   I   —   GEN

           érzi   fàng   —   zǒu   LE
           son   release   —   away   PFV/CRS

That bird was let go by my son.

(10)   wǒ   —   de   biǎo   bèi   tōu   —   diao   le
      I   —   GEN   watch   BEI   steal   —   away   CRS

My watch has been stolen.

(11)   nǐ   wèishenme   bèi   pǔ   le
      you   why   BEI   arrest   CRS

Why have you been arrested?

(12)   lǐngzi   bèi   tā   sī   —   pò   LE
      collar   BEI   3sg   tear   —   broken   PFV/CRS

The collar was torn by him/her.

(13)   qióng   rén   cháng   bèi   dìzhǔ   yā - pò
      poor   person   often   BEI   landlord   oppress

The poor are often oppressed by the landlords.

(14)   háizi   bèi   fùqin   mà   de   bu   zhīdào   zěnme
      child   BEI   father   scold   CSC   not   know   how

           bàn   LE
           do   PFV/CRS

The child was scolded by the father to such an extent that s/he didn't know what to do.

(15) tā   chángchang   bèi   tā   tàitai   dǎ
      3sg   often   BEI   3sg   wife   beat

He is often beaten by his wife.

(16) tā   yuànyi   bèi   rén   xiào
      3sg   willing   BEI   person   laugh

S/He is willing to be laughed at by people.

Once it is recognized that the major use of the *bèi* construction is to signal adversity, a number of interesting facts can be explained.

First of all, it has often been noted that the message carried by passive sentences with verbs of perception or cognition is unfortunate or pejorative, whereas the meanings of their verbs are neutral. Consider such verbs of perception or cognition as *kànjian* 'see', *fāxiàn* 'discover', and *tīng-dào* 'hear-arrive − able to hear'. They do not convey pejorative meaning by themselves or in nonpassive sentences, such as these:

(17) wǒ   kànjian   nǐ   le
      I   see   you   CRS

I saw you.

(18) Dā-ěr-wén fāxiàn   −   le   jìnhuà   −   lùn
     Darwin   discover −   PFV   evolution   −   theory

Darwin developed the theory of evolution.

(19) wǒ   tīng   −   dào   −   le   yǔzhòu   de   wéiyǔ
      I   hear   −   arrive −   PFV   universe   GEN   murmur

I heard the murmur of the universe.

The *bèi* constructions containing such verbs, however, have implications of adversity. Thus, (20) implies that Zhangsan shouldn't have been seen or didn't want to be seen, (21) implies that 'that matter' has a pejorative aspect to it, or should not have been found out, and (22) suggests that 'our conversation' should not have been heard:

(20) Zhāngsān   bèi   rén   kànjian   le
      Zhangsan   BEI   person   see   CRS

Zhangsan was seen by people.

(21) nèi   –   jian   shì   bèi   tā   fāxiàn   le
      that   –   CL   matter   BEI   3sg   discover   CRS

That matter was discovered by him/her.

(22) wǒmen   –   de   huà   bèi   tīng   –   dào   le
      we   –   GEN   speech   BEI   hear   –   arrive   CRS

Our conversation was overheard.

Second, it has been observed by practically all Chinese grammarians that the number of *bèi* constructions that do not express adversity is increasing, particularly in the written language of modern China. This increase in the nonadversity usage of the *bèi* constructions in modern Chinese is clearly due to the influence of the Indo-European languages, especially English. In fact, Chao calls such nonadversity *bèi* sentences "translatese." He states that "recently, from translating foreign passive verbs, 'by', or some equivalent in the Western language, is mechanically equated to *bèi* and applied to verbs of favorable meanings" (Chao [1968:703]). Elsewhere he explains that

> a Chinese translator . . . uses a preposition *bèi* 'by' whenever he sees a passive voice in the original verb, forgetting that Chinese verbs have no voice. . . . Once this sort of thing is done often enough, it gets to be written in originals, even where no translation is involved. . . . Such "translatese" is still unpalatable to most people and no one talks in that way yet, but it is already common in scientific writing, in newspapers, and in schools. [Chao (1970:155)]

According to another observer (Kierman [1969:74–75]),[2]

> a markedly increased use of the passive has perhaps been one of the striking syntactic trends in the development of Modern Chinese. . . . There has been a great deal of translation from foreign languages into Chinese during the past half century, including a perfect flood of Marxist material, which the Soviets translated and sold far below cost and which had a profound and continuing impact upon Chinese intelligentsia. The great majority of the translators were hacks, equipped with neither any real linguistic

sophistication nor even a very secure grasp of the languages involved and their stylistic niceties. They had learned another language in the most straightforward and mindless fashion: Here is a Russian verb *ispoljzovan* [which means 'is used, utilized']. What's the Chinese for that? *Bèi li-yòng* [where *liyòng* means 'to take advantage of someone or something for one's own benefit'] and ever thereafter, when the Russian *ispoljzovan* crops up, it is doggedly translated *bèi li-yòng*, with never a thought that there might be some possibility of recasting the sentence to put it into idiomatic Chinese, avoiding the passive. Such patterns become enshrined in ritually-admired literature and thence they are imitated in other literature and are read aloud; and in no time people are speaking that way, with no idea that they are participating in radical linguistic change.

Although in spoken Mandarin the *bèi* sentence, as Chao points out, is confined primarily to the expression of adverse messages, from the written language and "translatese" the nonadversity usage of the *bèi* passive has been extended into people's speech. This extension most naturally occurs with verbs representing usages borrowed or introduced into the language during the modern age, such as *xuǎn* 'elect', *jiěfàng* 'liberate', *fān(yi)* 'translate':

(23) Zhāngsān bèi rénmín xuǎn zuò   dàibiǎo   le
     Zhangsan BEI people elect serve:as representative CRS

Zhangsan has been elected by the people to be (their) representative.

(24) shěng   — chéng   bèi jiěfàng   le
     province — capital BEI liberate CRS

The provincial capital has been liberated.

(25) Losù   — de   shū   yǐjīng   bèi tā   fān
     Russell — GEN   book already BEI 3sg   translate

              — chéng   Zhōngwén le
              — become Chinese   CRS

Russell's book has already been translated into Chinese by him.

The mutual influence between the written and the spoken language is, of course, to be expected. In the case of the nonadversity usage of the *bèi* construction, the written language actually serves as a vehicle for the borrowing of a pattern from Indo-European languages into Mandarin.

The third point to be made is that it has been observed that the English passive often does not correspond to the *bèi* construction in Mandarin. In other words, what is normally best translated into an English passive sentence is often not a *bèi* sentence in Mandarin, and, conversely, an English passive sentence often does not translate into a *bèi* sentence in Mandarin. Here are some examples in which a Mandarin nonpassive sentence corresponds to an English passive sentence:

(26) *a.*   nèi   —   běn   shū   yǐjīng   chūbǎn   le
            that   —   CL   book   already publish   CRS

That book has already been published.

    b.   *nèi   —   běn   shū   yǐjīng   bèi   chūbǎn   le
                          that   —   CL   book   already BEI   publish CRS

(27) *a.*   nǐ   —   de   bāoguǒ   shōu   —   dào   le
            you —   GEN   package receive —   arrive CRS

Your package has been received.

    b.   *nǐ   —   de   bāoguǒ   bèi   shōu   —   dào   le
                          you   —   GEN   package BEI   receive —   arrive CRS

(28) *a.*   zhèi   —   ge   yǎnjiǎng   děi   jìlu   —   xià
            this   —   CL   lecture   must   record   —   descend

            —   lai
            —   come

This lecture should be recorded.

    b.   *zhèi   —   ge   yǎnjiǎng   děi   bèi   jìlu   —
                          this   —   CL   lecture   must   BEI   record   —

            xià   —   lai
            descend   —   come

(29) *a.*   tā   shuō   de   huà   rén   —   ren   dōu   dǒng
            3sg   say   NOM   speech   person   —   person   all   understand

What s/he said was understood by everyone.

b.	*tā	shuō	de	huà	bèi	rén	—	ren
	3sg	say	NOM	speech	BEI	person	—	person

dōu	dǒng
all	understand

As shown by the above examples, the *b* sentences in (26)−(29), which are the *bèi* sentences, are unacceptable because they do not convey a message of adversity. The *a* sentences in (26)−(29), which are normally considered the equivalents of the English passive sentence in translation either from English to Mandarin or vice versa, are topic-comment constructions in which the direct object of the verb is serving as the topic. In other words, when one wishes to say something about the direct object of the verb in Mandarin, one simply makes the direct object into a topic. Thus, the topic prominence of Mandarin together with the restriction of the *bèi* construction to adverse messages combine to reduce the usage of the passive in the language. Any student of Chinese who is also familiar with an Indo-European language will notice that the passive construction is much more rare in Mandarin speech and writing than in the speech and writing of the Indo-European languages.

Another situation in which English uses a passive and Mandarin does not is when the focus is on the agent of the transitive action verb. For example, if one is discussing a novel and wishes to make it clear that his/her mother is the author, one may choose a passive construction in English to convey the message, as in (30):

(30)   This novel was written by my mother.

The Mandarin counterpart of (30) will be (31) *a*, a *shì* . . . *de* construction (see section 20.3 of chapter 20 on the *shì* . . . *de* construction), but not (31) *b*, a *bèi* passive construction. Sentence (31) *b* is unacceptable because 'writing a novel', in general, does not have any pejorative implication, though, as was pointed out above, such sentences as (25) can be found in "translatese":

(31) *a.*	zhèi	—	běn	xiǎoshuō	shì	wǒ	mǔqin
	this	—	CL	novel	be	I	mother

xiě	de
write	NOM

This novel was written by my mother.

b.   **zhèi*   —   běn   xiǎoshuō   bèi   wǒ   mǔqin
     this   —   CL   novel   BEI   I   mother

xiě   LE
write   PFV/CRS

Sentences (32)–(34) provide some more examples, similar to (31), in which the Mandarin equivalent of an English passive is a *shì . . . de* construction:

(32) *a.*   zhèi   —   ge   fángzi   shì   Zhāngsān   shèjì   de
     this   —   CL   house   be   Zhangsan   design   NOM

This house was designed by Zhangsan.

b.   **zhèi*   —   ge   fángzi   bèi   Zhāngsān   shèjì   LE
     this   —   CL   house   BEI   Zhangsan   design   PFV/CRS

(33) *a.*   zhèi   —   ge   zhèngcè   shì   tā   tuījiàn   de
     this   —   CL   policy   be   3sg   recommend   NOM

This policy was recommended by him/her.

b.   **zhèi*   —   ge   zhèngcè   bèi   tā   tuījiàn   LE
     this   —   CL   policy   BEI   3sg   recommend   PFV/CRS

(34) *a.*   nèi   —   fu   huà   shì   tā   huà   de
     that   —   CL   painting   be   3sg   paint   NOM

That painting was painted by him.

b.   **nèi*   —   fu   huà   bèi   tā   huà   LE
     that   —   CL   painting   BEI   3sg   paint   PFV/CRS

The above examples illustrate that in Mandarin, it is the *shì . . . de* construction, not the *bèi* construction, which serves the function of placing the agent noun phrase in focus when the topic of the sentence is the direct object.

16.1.2 Disposal

In addition to adversity, the *bèi* construction also expresses disposal in the same manner as the *bǎ* construction does (see chapter 15 on the *bǎ* construction). That is, the *bèi* sentence describes an event in which an entity or person is dealt with, handled, or manipulated in some way. This is why, just as with the *bǎ* construction, *bèi* is not found with verbs that do not signal disposal, even if they have adverse meaning. The following sentences are, thus, unacceptable:

(35)	*Lǐsì	bèi	tā	hèn	—	le
	Lisi	BEI	3sg	hate	—	PFV

(Lisi was hated by him/her.)

(36)	*tā	bèi	qì	—	le
	3sg	BEI	anger	—	PFV

(S/He was angered.)

(37)	*wǒ	bèi	tā	tǎoyàn	—	le
	I	BEI	3sg	be:sick:of	—	PFV

(S/He was sick of me.)

Since the *bèi* passive conveys the notion of disposal precisely as the *bǎ* construction does, our description of the disposal function of the *bǎ* constructions is applicable as well to the *bèi* passive, which, of course, has the added function of signaling adversity. We will therefore not repeat that description here. Instead, we will provide a brief summary and examples of the main points concerning the notion of disposal as they apply to the *bèi* construction. For the details, the reader is referred to chapter 15 on the *bǎ* construction.

(i) Just as with *bǎ*, the *bèi* construction allows the affected entity to be a noun phrase other than the direct object:

(38)	wǒ	bèi	tā	bāng	—	le	yi	—	zhī	tuǐ
	I	BEI	3sg	tie	—	PFV	one	—	CL	leg

I had one leg tied up by him/her.

(ii) The *bèi* construction, like the *bǎ* construction, allows implied disposal, as in (39) which contains a complex stative construction clause (see chapter 22):

(39)	wǒ	bèi	tā	qì	de	tóu	dōu	hūn	le
	I	BEI	3sg	anger	CSC	head	all	dizzy	CRS

I was angered by him/her to such an extent that my head got dizzy.

(iii) The disposal nature of the *bèi* construction, as with *bǎ*, is incompatible with the potential infixes, whether positive or negative, of resultative verb compounds (see section 3.2.3 of chapter 3 on resultative verb compounds). For example:

(40)	*wǒ	bèi	tā	dǎ	—	de	—	sǐ
	I	BEI	3sg	beat	—	can	—	die

(I can be beaten to death by him/her.)

(41)	*nèi	—	ge	yǐzi	bèi	tā	nòng	—
	that	—	CL	chair	BEI	3sg	make	—

	bu	—	pò
	can't	—	broken

(That chair can't be broken by him/her.)

(iv) The disposal nature of the *bèi* sentence is incompatible with the negation of the verb only—that is, placing the negative particle, *bu/méi(yǒu)*, immediately in front of the verb so that only the verb lies in the scope of the negation (see chapter 12 on the scope of negation). The negative of a *bèi* sentence is formed by the placement of the negative particle in front of *bèi*, just as the negative particle is placed before *bǎ* in a *bǎ* sentence:

(42) *a*.	*wǒ	bèi	tā	<u>méi</u>	pīping
	I	BEI	3sg	not	criticize

b.	wǒ	<u>méi</u>	bèi	tā	pīping
	I	not	BEI	3sg	criticize

I wasn't criticized by him/her.

There is one notable difference between the *bǎ* construction and the *bèi* construction with regard to their shared disposal meaning: while the *bǎ* construction occurs freely as a command, the *bèi* construction cannot serve as a command except when it is negated with the negative imperative particle, *bié*. The reason is one of semantic incompatibility, in spite of the fact that the disposal meaning is generally conducive to the expression of commands. Recall that the first noun phrase of the passive construction is the direct object, not the agent, of the verb signaling disposal, whereas the first noun phrase of the *bǎ* construction is the agent of the verb signaling disposal. It makes sense to command the agent to carry out an action with a disposal meaning; but it is senseless to command the direct object with respect to the disposal action, because s/he or it has no control over the action. On the other hand, a command can be formed from a *bèi* sentence by the addition of the negative imperative particle, because commanding someone not to be the receiver of an action is tantamount to commanding him/her to do something to *avoid* an adverse experience. The following sentences are illustrations of this principle:

(43) *a.*

*(nǐ)	bèi	māo	zhua	—	le
(you)	BEI	cat	scratch	—	PFV

(be scratched by the cat)

b.

(ni)	bié	bèi	māo	zhuā	—	le
you	don't	BEI	cat	scratch	—	PFV

Don't get scratched by the cat.

So far we have shown that the passive construction with the particle *bèi* can best be understood in terms of its function of signaling adversity and disposal. We will next examine the structural properties of this construction.

16.2 Structural Properties

Several of the structural properties of the *bèi* construction have already been discussed in the preceding section, where its disposal meaning was presented. One of these structural properties concerns negation; another deals with the use of passive as a command. In chapter 8 on adverbs, the interaction between manner adverbs and the passive construction is described. The following structural properties of the *bèi* passive have not yet been mentioned, however.

16.2.1 Indirect Object Adversely Affected

The indirect object (see chapter 10) can represent the one adversely affected in a *bèi* sentence. Example (44) is a nonpassive sentence in which *wǒ* 'I' is the indirect object:

(44)	tāmen	wèn	−	le	<u>wǒ</u>	xǔduō	wèntí
	they	ask	−	PFV	I	many	questions

They asked me many questions.

The passive counterpart of (44) is (45), in which *wǒ* 'I' is adversely affected:

(45)	<u>wǒ</u>	bèi	tāmen	wèn	−	le	xǔduō	wènti
	I	BEI	they	ask	−	PFV	many	question

I was asked many questions by them (as a harassment).

Very few verbs that take both an indirect object and a direct object can occur in the *bèi* construction with the indirect object being adversely affected, however. The reason is that most of the verbs taking a direct and an indirect object cannot have an adverse meaning either explicitly or implicitly. A few other verbs that do occur in passive sentences with the adversely affected indirect object include *tōu* 'steal', *qiǎng* 'rob', *duó* 'snatch', *yíng* 'win'. Here is an example with *tōu* 'steal':

(46)	<u>tā</u>	bèi	péngyǒu	tōu	−	le	qián
	3sg	BEI	friend	steal	−	PFV	money

S/He was robbed of (his/her) money by a friend.

16.2.2 The *bèi* Noun Phrase Can Be Inanimate

The noun phrase immediately following *bèi* cannot refer to something that is being used by a person or an animate being to carry out an action; in other words, the *bèi* noun phrase cannot be an instrument noun phrase:[3]

(47)	*mén	bèi	<u>yàoshi</u>	dǎ	−	kāi	LE
	door	BEI	key	make	−	open	PFV/CRS

Inanimate noun phrases that can effect action on their own can occur as *bèi* noun phrases in the passive construction, however, as long as an adverse situation can be inferred. The following examples illustrate this phenomenon:

(48)	qìqiú	bèi	<u>fēng</u>	chuī	—	zǒu	LE
	balloon	BEI	wind	blow	—	away	PFV/CRS

The balloon was blown away by the wind.

(49)	bōli	bèi	<u>huǒ</u>	shāo	—	huà	LE
	glass	BEI	fire	burn	—	melted	PFV/CRS

The glass was melted by the fire.

(50)	nèi	—	jian	yīfu	bèi	<u>shuǐ</u>
	that	—	CL	clothing	BEI	water

	chōng	—	zǒu	LE
	wash	—	away	PFV/CRS

That dress was washed away by the water.

(51)	wūdǐng	bèi	<u>xuě</u>	gài	—	zhu	LE
	roof	BEI	snow	cover	—	firm	PFV/CRS

The roof was covered by snow.

16.3 *bǎ* and *bèi*

Bǎ and *bèi* can occur in the same sentence (see chapter 15 for a discussion of *bǎ*):

(52)	wǒ	<u>bèi</u>	tā	<u>bǎ</u>	wǒ	—	de
	I	BEI	3sg	BA	I	—	GEN

	dǎzìjī	dǎ	—	pò	LE
	typewriter	hit	—	broken	PFV/CRS

What happened to me was that my typewriter was broken by him/her.

As this example illustrates, the *bǎ* noun phrase must occur after the *bèi* noun phrase, and this is for a logical reason: the one who disposes of the typewriter is the *agent* (*tā* 's/he' in [52]), not the one affected (*wǒ* 'I' in [52]). Therefore, the agent, which is the *bèi* noun phrase, not the one affected, is the one that immediately precedes the *bǎ* noun phrase.

16.4 Variant Forms

At the beginning of this chapter, we mentioned the existence of variant forms of (1):

(1)   NP$_1$ bèi   NP$_2$ verb
          direct object   agent

One important variant form was already pointed out in (3), where the agent noun phrase is absent:

(3)   NP$_1$ bèi   verb
          direct object

The most common variant forms involve substituting *bèi* with *gěi, jiào, ràng*. Thus (53) is well formed with any of the four passive markers:

(53)   wǒ   ⎧ bèi ⎫   tā   tōu   —   le   liǎng   kuài   qián
                ⎪ gěi ⎪
                ⎨ jiào ⎬
                ⎩ ràng ⎭

          I   3sg   steal   —   PFV   two   dollar   money

     I had two dollars stolen by him/her.

Which of the four passive markers is preferred seems to depend on what dialect of Mandarin is being spoken. A distinction can be made, however, between *bèi* on the one hand and the last three markers in (53) on the other. *Bèi* has no meaning of its own. In other words, it is a function word, or a grammatical word. It has no meaning other than the function of occurring in the passive construction. The other three words, *gěi, jiào,* and *ràng*, besides being able to serve in the passive construction, are content words with independent meanings. *Gěi* is a verb meaning 'give', and it can also serve as the benefactive marker by immediately preceding the indirect object; *jiào* is a verb meaning 'call, be named, order'; and *ràng* is a verb meaning 'let, allow'. Hence, when *bèi* is used in a sequence such as

(54)   NP   <u>bèi</u>   (NP)   verb

the sentence unambiguously signals a passive construction. If, however, *gěi, jiào*, or *ràng* is used in place of *bèi* in (54), the sentence represented by the pattern given in (54) may be ambiguous. For example, (53) with *jiào* could mean, 'I told him/her to steal two dollars'; with *gěi*, it could mean, 'I stole two dollars for him/her'; with *ràng*, it could mean, 'I allowed him/her to steal two dollars'.

Jiào and *ràng* also differ from *bèi* in that the former two cannot occur as a replacement for *bèi* in (3), where the agent noun phrase is absent. Thus, (55) is unacceptable:

(55) *wǒ $\begin{Bmatrix} \text{jiào} \\ \text{ràng} \end{Bmatrix}$ tōu   —   le   liǎng   kuài   qián

      I   steal   —   PFV   two   dollar   money

(I was stolen two dollars.)

Speakers differ as to whether *gěi* may serve as a variant of *bèi* in pattern (3), where the agent is absent:

(56) ??wǒ <u>gěi</u>   tōu   —   le   liǎng   kuài   qián
      I   steal   —   PFV   two   dollar   money

I was stolen two dollars.

Two other variants of (1) involve the use of *jiào . . . gěi* and *ràng . . . gěi* in the following form:

(57)   NP$_1$ $\begin{Bmatrix} \text{jiào} \\ \underline{\text{ràng}} \end{Bmatrix}$ NP$_2$ <u>gěi</u>   verb

The following examples illustrate (57):

(58) Qín   cháo $\begin{Bmatrix} \text{jiào} \\ \underline{\text{ràng}} \end{Bmatrix}$ Hàn   cháo   <u>gěi</u>   miè   LE

      Qin dynasty   Han dynasty   overthrow   PFV/CRS

The Qin dynasty was overthrown by the Han dynasty.

(59) tā $\left\{\begin{array}{l}\text{jiào}\\\underline{\text{ràng}}\end{array}\right\}$ dí — bīng <u>gěi</u> shā LE

    3sg   enemy — soldier   kill   PFV/CRS

S/He was killed by the enemy soldier.

(60) fángzi $\left\{\begin{array}{l}\underline{\text{ràng}}\\\text{jiào}\end{array}\right\}$ tā <u>gěi</u> shāo LE

    house   3sg   burn   PFV/CRS

The house was burned by him/her.

The occurrence of *gěi* in addition to *jiào/ràng* in a sentence having the form of (57) seems to strengthen the disposal function of the construction. It is, therefore, not surprising that this *gěi* may also occur in the *bǎ* construction for the same function (see chapter 15 on the *bǎ* construction):

(61) tā <u>bǎ</u> nǐmen — de qiánchéng

    3sg BA you:PL — GEN future

    <u>gěi</u> dānwù LE

          ruin   PFV/CRS

S/He ruined your future.

Notes

1. This chapter has benefited greatly from ideas found in Wang (1957), Chu (1973), and in (unpublished) lectures given by Stephen Wallace (''Adversative Passives'') and Timothy Light (''Actively Passive'').
2. Kierman in turn credits these ideas to Paul Kratochvil. The comments in brackets have been added by us.
3. There isn't a grammatical category of instrument noun phrase in Mandarin. If a noun phrase is to denote an instrument, it is expressed grammatically as the direct object of the verb, *yòng* 'use', as in:

    (i) tā yòng yàoshi kāi mén

          3sg use key open door

    $\left\{\begin{array}{l}\text{S/He opens doors with keys.}\\\text{S/He uses keys to open doors.}\end{array}\right\}$

CHAPTER 17

Presentative Sentences

A *presentative sentence* performs the function of introducing into a discourse a noun phrase naming an entity. There are two ways in which this can happen: either the entity being introduced by this noun phrase can be claimed to exist or be located somewhere, as in (1), or it can be introduced by a verb of motion, as in (2):

(1)	chéng	–	li	yǒu	gōngyuán
	city	–	in	exist	park

There are parks in the city.

(2)	lái	–	le	yi	–	ge	kèrén
	come	–	PFV	one	–	CL	guest

Here comes a guest.

In most languages of the world, the noun phrase naming the entity being presented in a presentative sentence is indefinite. It represents new information, information that the speaker assumes the hearer does not have at the time, and it typically occurs after the main verb of the presentative sentence. These two properties are true of the noun phrase being presented by the Mandarin presentative sentence as well: in fact, since sentence-initial position is the position for topics in Mandarin, and since noun phrases introduced for the first time into discourse cannot be topics (see chapter 4, section 4.1.1), it is clear why a presented noun phrase must follow the main verb of the presentative sentence. Let's consider in greater detail the two ways in which a noun phrase can be presented.

17.1 Existential and Positional Verbs

An *existential sentence* is one that contains the existential verb *yŏu* or a verb of posture (see chapter 11, section 11.1.2.B), such as *zuò* 'sit', *tăng* 'lie', or *piāo* 'float', describing where something has been put or placed, as its main verb.[1] Existential sentences always signal the existence of the referent of a noun phrase, usually at some place, which we can call the *locus*. As with all presentative sentences, the noun phrase naming what exists comes immediately after the existential verb. The following are existential sentences with the verb *yŏu*; the locus is underlined twice, and the presented noun phrase is underlined once:

(3) (zài)   yuànzi   –   li   yŏu   yi
    at   yard   –   in   exist   one

    –   zhī   gŏu
    –   CL   dog

There's a dog in the yard.

(4) (zài)   chōuti   –   li   yŏu   hěn   duō   yóupiào
    at   drawer   –   in   exist   very   many   stamps

There are lots of stamps in the drawer.

(5) yŏu   yi   –   ge   rén   zài
    exist   one   –   CL   person   at

    wàimian   jiào   –   mén
    outside   call   –   door

There's someone outside knocking at the door.

The above examples show that a presentative sentence with an existential verb may have either one of the two following forms:

(6) *a.* existential verb   +   presented noun phrase   +   zài 'at'
        +   locus (verb phrase)

   b. (zài 'at')   +   locus + existential verb + presented noun phrase
        +   (verb phrase)

In both patterns, the presented noun phrase directly follows the existential verb, but in (6) *a* the locus follows the presented noun phrase and is introduced by the locative particle, *zài*, while in (6) *b*, the locus is in sentence-initial position. Sentences (3) and (4) are in the *b* form, and sentence (5) is in the *a* form. We may change the structure of (3) and (4) to *a* and the structure of (5) to *b*, as in the following:

(7)	yǒu	yi	–	zhī	gǒu	zài
	exist	one	–	CL	dog	at

	yuànzi	–	li
	yard	–	in

There is a dog in the yard.

(8)	yǒu	hěn	duō	yóupiào	zài
	exist	very	many	stamp	at

	chōuti	–	li
	drawer	–	in

There are lots of stamps in the drawer.

(9)	(zài)	wàimian	yǒu	yi	–	ge
	at	outside	exist	one	–	CL

	rén	jiào	–	mén
	person	call	–	door

There's someone outside knocking at the door.

There is a pragmatic difference between the pattern illustrated in (6) *a* and that represented in (6) *b*. In (6) *b*, the locus, occurring in sentence-initial position, must be definite in the sense that its existence must have already been established in the discourse context either linguistically or extralinguistically. It is in (6) *b*, but not in (6) *a*, that the locus takes on the function of a topic. For example, as an answer to question (10), (3), but not (7), is appropriate.

(10)	yuànzi	–	li	zěnme	zhème	chǎo?
	yard	–	in	how	so	noisy

How come it is so noisy in the yard?

The reason that (3) but not (7) is an appropriate answer to (10) is that question (10) has already established the noun *yuànzi-li* 'in the yard' as the topic and (3), but not (7), uses the same noun phrase as the topic. (See section 4.1.6 of chapter 4 for a discussion of locative phrases as topics.)

Sentences such as (5) and (9) constitute a special subtype of existential presentative sentences because they contain two verbs (here, *yǒu* ('exist' and *jiào-mén* 'knock at the door'). These sentences are termed *realis descriptive clause sentences* and, because they contain two verbs, are discussed in section 21.4.1 of chapter 21 on serial verb constructions.

Sentences (3)–(5) and (7)–(9) exemplified the use of the existential verb *yǒu* in existential presentative sentences. The following sentences illustrate the use of positional verbs in existential presentative sentences. Notice that these positional verbs can be followed by an aspect marker (see chapter 6) and that the locus always precedes the verb of posture in sentence-initial position. Again, the locus is underlined twice and that which exists is underlined once in the following examples:

(11)   bōli   —   shang   xiě   —   zhe
        glass   —   on   write   —   DUR

        sì   —   ge   zì
        four   —   CL   character

On the glass are written four characters.

(12)   zhuōzi   —   shang   fàng   —   le
        table   —   on   put   —   PFV

        hěn   duō   qiānbǐ
        very   many   pencil

There are a lot of pencils on the table.

(13)   shuǐ   —   li   piāo   —   zhe
        water   —   in   float   —   DUR

        yi   kuài   mùtou
        one   piece   wood

A piece of wood is floating in the water.

With the existential verb *yŏu*, it is also possible for the locus to be another referent rather than a location. That is, we can predicate the existence of one entity with respect to another; if that entity upon which the existence of another entity is predicated is animate, the sentence is understood as possessive, and the English translation typically shows the verb 'have':

(14) *a.*

tā	yŏu	sān	—	ge	háizi
3sg	exist	three	—	CL	child

S/He has three children.

b.

zhīzhū	yŏu	bā	—	ge	tuǐ
spider	exist	eight	—	CL	leg

Spiders have eight legs.

The difference between the English translations of sentences (14) *a* and *b* and those of sentences (3)–(5) should not keep us from seeing their essential similarity. In both types of examples, something is being claimed to exist; the difference is whether it is said to exist with respect to a place or to another entity. In fact, for some Mandarin sentences with *yŏu* 'exist', either a 'have' or a 'there is' translation is appropriate:

(15)

yi	—	nián	yŏu	wŭshí	—	èr
one	—	year	exist	fifty	—	two

—	ge	lǐbài
—	CL	week

⎰ There are fifty-two weeks in a year. ⎱
⎱ A year has fifty-two weeks (in it). ⎰

(16)

shūjià	—	shang	yŏu	yi	—
bookcase	—	on	exist	one	—

ge	dà	zhāngláng
CL	big	cockroach

⎰ There's a big cockroach on the bookcase. ⎱
⎱ The bookcase has a big cockroach (on it). ⎰

In most languages of the world, the same verb expresses both possession and existence, just as in Mandarin. We will refer to all these *yǒu* sentences as existential and will continue to gloss the verb *yǒu* as 'exist', even when it would translate into English as 'have'.

We have said that the existential verb in Mandarin is *yǒu*. It is also possible, however, to express existence with the copula verb *shì*.[2] Observe the following contrasting pairs:

(17) *a.*

wàimian	yǒu	yi	—	zhī	gǒu
outside	exist	one	—	CL	dog

There's a dog outside.

b.

wàimian	shì	yi	—	zhī	gǒu
outside	be	one	—	CL	dog

What's outside is a dog.

(18) *a.*

chōuti	—	li	yǒu	nǐ	—	de	yàoshi
drawer	—	in	exist	you	—	GEN	key

Your keys are in the drawer.

b.

chōuti	—	li	shì	nǐ	—	de	yàoshi
drawer	—	in	be	you	—	GEN	key

What's in the drawer are your keys.

(19) *a.*

qiánmian	yǒu	yi	—	ge	huāyuán
in:front	exist	one	—	CL	garden

In front there's a garden.

b.

qiánmian	shì	yi	—	ge	huāyuán
in:front	be	one	—	CL	garden

What's in front is a garden.

What determines the choice of *yǒu* 'exist' or *shì* 'be' in these existential sentences? As the translations suggest, there is a difference in their meanings. In the discussion of copula sentences (see A.2 in section 4.3.1 of chapter 4), it was pointed out that copula sentences serve to identify or characterize the referent of the subject noun phrase. In the *b* sentences in examples (17)–(19) above, then, the presented noun phrase is identifying or characterizing the locus; in order for this to happen, the speaker must believe not only that the listener already knows about the locus but that s/he has some reason to be interested in it and in what it is or what it has or what it looks like. The *a* sentences, on the other hand, are simply predicating the existence of the presented noun phrase at some locus in which the listener need not have had any interest.

This means, of course, that the two sentence types should be found in different kinds of speech contexts. For example, one would use (19) *b* to characterize or identify 'in front' with 'garden'. This could be either because all there is in front is a garden *(characterizing)*, or because the speaker is aware the hearer knows that something is in front and wishes to tell the hearer what it is *(identifying)*. Sentence (19) *a*, on the other hand, would not be appropriate under either of these circumstances, but could be used, for instance, as part of a description of a new house.

One way to understand the difference between the two sentence types is to consider their respective question counterparts:

(20)　lǐmian　　yǒu　　shénme ?
　　　　inside　　exist　　what

　　What's inside?

(21)　lǐmian　　shì　　shénme ?
　　　　inside　　be　　what

　　What is it that's inside?

The first question, with *yǒu*, does not necessarily imply that there is something inside. A possible and appropriate answer to (20) is:

(22)　lǐmian　shénme　dōu　méi　yǒu
　　　　inside　　what　　all　　not　　exist

　　There's nothing inside.

The second question with *shì*, however, presupposes that something is inside. Thus (22) is not an appropriate answer to (21).

Consider a speech context in which one is touring a factory and notices a great deal of noise coming from the frontmost building. It would be inappropriate for one to pose question (23), which employs *yŏu*. Question (24), which employs *shì*, would be preferable because the speech situation implies that the inquirer not only has a vested interest in the source of the noise but also presumes that there is something in front.

(23) <u>qiánmian</u>   <u>yŏu</u>   <u>shénme</u> ?
      in front   exist   what

    What's in front?

(24) <u>qiánmian</u>   <u>shì</u>   <u>shénme</u> ?
      in front   be   what

    What is it that's in front?

Imagine next, as a situation where *shì* would be inappropriate and *yŏu* would be preferred, that two people are trying to get from one yard to another at night. One could announce that s/he had found a gate by saying (25), where *zhèli* 'here' gives the location of *mén* 'gate', but the same sentence with *shì*, (26), would be odd for the speaker to use, because the hearer has no reason to expect that something exists at the locus *zhèli* 'here'.

(25) <u>zhèli</u>   <u>yŏu</u>   <u>mén</u>
     here   exist   gate

    Here's a gate.

(26) <u>zhèli</u>   <u>shì</u>   <u>mén</u>
     here   be   gate

    What's here is a gate.

To sum up, we can state that the existential verb *yŏu* as well as verbs of posture can be found in presentative sentences that predicate the existence of something at a certain locus. Now we'll look at presentative sentences in which something is introduced by a motion verb.

17.2 Verbs of Motion

The other way in which entities can be introduced into discourse is by means of a verb signaling motion. Typically in such a situation there is no locus named, but, as with the presentative sentences containing the existential verb or verbs of posture, the noun phrase being presented occurs immediately after the verb (the presented noun phrase is underlined once in the following examples):

(27) chū   —   lái   —   le   <u>yi</u>   —   <u>ge</u>   <u>kèren</u>
      exit —   come —   PFV   one   —   CL   guest

A guest has come out.

(28) táo   —   le   <u>sān</u>   —   <u>zhī</u>   <u>yáng</u>
      escape — PFV   three —   CL   sheep

Three sheep escaped.

(29) dào   —   le   <u>yi</u>   —   <u>pí</u>   <u>huò</u>
      arrise — PFV   one   —   batch merchandise

A shipment of merchandise has arrived.

(30) wǒmen —   de   wǎnhuì   zhǐ   lái   —   le
      we   —   GEN   party   only come —   PFV

      <u>Zhāngsan   gēn   Lǐsì</u>
      Zhangsan   and   Lisi

Only Zhangsan and Lisi came to our party.

The verbs of motion in presentative sentences are generally intransitive verbs, as the preceding examples show. In these sentences, the entity involved in the motion is the presented noun phrase, and the presentative noun phrase follows the verb. Not all intransitive verbs of motion, however, allow the noun phrase signaling the entity involved in the motion to be in the postverbal position, as the examples in (31) show (here the verbs of motion are underlined):

(31) a. *<u>tiào</u> —   le   yi   —   ge   xīshuài
         jump   —   PFV   one —   CL   cricket

b.   *<u>gǔn</u>   −   le   yi   −   ge   rén
        roll   −   PFV   one   −   CL   person

c.   *<u>pá</u>   −   le   yi   −   ge   lǎohǔ
        climb   −   PFV   one   −   CL   tiger

d.   *<u>fēi</u>   −   le   yi   −   ge   niǎo
        fly   −   PFV   one   −   CL   bird

e.   *<u>dǒu</u>   −   le   yi   −   ge   rén
        shake   −   PFV   one   −   CL   person

In order for these verbs to occur in presentative constructions where the presentative noun phrase refers to the entity in motion, the existential verb *yǒu* must be used, and the construction then becomes a serial verb construction, since two verbs are involved. For example, consider the intransitive verb of motion *dǒu* 'shake, tremble'; (32) is a presentative sentence with both the existential verb *yǒu* and the intransitive verb of motion *dǒu* 'shake, tremble':

(32)   yǒu   yi   −   ge   rén   dǒu   −   le
        exist   one   −   CL   person   shake   −   PFV

There was one person who shook.

The intransitive verbs of motion which do allow the noun phrase signaling the entity in motion to occur postverbally include *zǒu* 'leave', *chū* 'exit', *qù* 'go', *lái* 'come', *dǎo* 'topple', *qǐ* 'arise', *dào* 'arrive', *táo* 'escape', and all of the type (iii) directional verbs (see A.1 of section 3.2.3 in chapter 3). Here are some examples of presentative sentences with type (iii) directional verbs:

(33) *a.*   <u>shàng</u>   −   <u>lái</u>   −   le   sān   −   ge   rén
           ascend   −   come   −   PFV   three   −   CL   person

       Three people came up.

b.   <u>huí</u>   −   <u>qù</u>   −   le   wǔ   −
        return   −   go   −   PFV   five   −

               bǎi   −   ge   rén
               hundred   −   CL   person

       Five hundred people returned.

c. | jìn | — | lái | — | le | yi | — | ge |
|---|---|---|---|---|---|---|---|
| enter | — | come | — | PFV | one | — | CL |

dà	—	pàngzi
big	—	fat:person

A very fat person came in.

Finally, an intransitive verb of motion which forms a compound with either *lái* 'come', *qù* 'go', or a type (iii) directional compound always allows the noun phrase signaling the entity in motion to occur postverbally. Thus, example (31) *d* shows that *fēi* 'fly' does not allow the noun phrase signaling the entity in motion to occur after the verb, but *fēi-chū-lái* 'fly-exit-come = fly out' does, as in (34):

(34) | fēi | — | chū | — | lái | — | le |
|---|---|---|---|---|---|---|
| fly | — | exit | — | come | — | PFV |

yi	—	ge	wénzi
one	—	CL	mosquito

A mosquito flew out.

Notes

1. For more discussion of existential predicates, see Rygaloff (1973:chap. 8), Chu (1970), Teng (1979*a*), Hou (1979:chap. 3.3).
2. Some of the ideas on *shì* and *yǒu* discussed here are adapted from Chao (1948:153), Rygaloff (1973:191 ff.), and Van Valin (1975).

CHAPTER 18

Questions

18.1 The Four Types of Questions

It is always possible to turn a declarative statement into a question by using a slightly rising intonation pattern. In context, it is generally easy to identify such a question; for example, if A and B have been talking about whether A is going to go somewhere, and B says to A

(1)   nǐ   qù

         you   go

with a slightly rising intonation, A will typically take this as a question and not a statement or a command.

There are also, however, four grammatical devices that explicitly mark an utterance as a question. It is these four devices that will be discussed in the rest of this chapter.

The first device is the *question-word question*, in which the presence of a question word causes the construction to be a question. Question words in a language are the semantic equivalents of such English words as *who, what, where, which,* and so forth. An example in Mandarin is (2):

(2)   <u>shéi</u>   qù ?

       who   go

    Who'll go?

In the second device, the *disjunctive question*, the respondent is presented with a choice between two options. One type of disjunctive question is composed simply of two declarative sentences joined together by the morpheme *háishi* 'or'; for example:

(3)   nǐ   qù   <u>háishi</u>   tā   lái ?
        you   go   or   3sg   come

Will you go, or will s/he come?

We call each such sentence a *clause* when two or more of them combine to make a larger sentence. The two options presented to the respondent in (3) are clearly the two declarative clauses connected by the morpheme *háishi* 'or'. The answer is either (4) *a* or (4) *b*:

(4) *a*.   wǒ   qu
          I   go

I'll go.

b.   tā   lái
      3sg   come

S/He'll come.

The *tag question*, the third question-signaling device, is composed of a statement followed by an A-not-A form, such as *duì bu duì* 'right not right', *hǎo bu hǎo* 'good not good', *xíng bu xíng* 'OK not OK', *shì bu shì* 'be not be'.

The final device, called the *particle question*, is signaled by the presence of the question particle *ma* in sentence-final position, as in

(5)   nǐ   hǎo   <u>ma</u> ?
        you   well   Q

How are you? (Literally: Are you well?)

18.2 Question-Word Questions

18.2.1 Question Words in Questions

The following is a list of the most commonly used question words in Mandarin:

(6) shéi   'who'   năr, năli   'where'
     shénme   'what'   něi-CL   'which one'
     zěnme   'how, why'   něi-xiē   'which ones'
     zěnme-yàng   'how'   gànmá   'what for'
     wèishénme   'for what = why'
     duō   'how'
     duōshăo   'how much, how many'
     jĭ-CL   'how many'

In what follows, we will discuss and illustrate the use of each of these question words.

   In general, question words occur in the same position in the sentence as do nonquestion words that have the same grammatical function. For example, consider *shéi* 'who' and *shénme* 'what' in the following sentences:

(7) shéi   qĭng   Zhāngsān   chī   —   fàn ?
     who   invite Zhangsan   eat   —   food

     Who invited Zhangsan to eat?

(8) nĭ   qĭng   shéi   chī   —   fàn ?
     you   invite who   eat   —   food

     Whom did you invite to eat?

(9) shénme   shì   ài ?
     what   be   love

     What is love?

(10) nĭmen   zuò   shénme ?
      you   do   what

      What are you doing?

In (7), the question word *shéi* 'who' is the subject of the first verb and therefore occurs before the verb, as a subject usually does. In (8), however, the question word, *shéi*, 'who', is a pivotal noun (see section 21.3 of chapter 21), serving both as the direct object of the first verb and as the subject of the second verb; hence, it is placed just where a pivotal noun occurs, after the first verb but before the second verb. Similarly, *shénme* in (9), as the subject of *shì* 'be', occurs before it, while in (10) it is the direct object and so occurs postverbally.

In (9) and (10), *shénme* serves as a full-fledged noun, but it may also modify a head noun in a noun phrase. Examples (11) and (12) illustrate this usage of *shénme*:

(11) tā   shì   nǐ   –   de   <u>shénme</u> <u>rén</u> ?
      3sg   be   you   –   GEN   what   person

How is s/he related to you?

(12) <u>shénme</u> <u>dōngxi</u> zhème   xiāng ?
      what   thing   this   fragrant

What kind of thing is this fragrant?

Sentence (13) shows that *zěnme* occurs in the adverbial position, namely, before the verb, and is ambiguous, meaning either 'how' or 'why':

(13) nǐ   <u>zěnme</u>   xiě   xiǎoshuō ?
      you   {how}   write   novel
              {why}

{How do you write novels?}
{Why do you write novels?}

Sentence (14) shows that *zěnme* meaning 'why' may also occur in sentence-initial position:

(14) <u>zěnme</u>   nǐ   bu   qù   shàng   –   kè ?
      why   you   not   go   ascend   –   class

Why aren't you attending your class?

We can explain its position in both (13) and (14) in terms of these two meanings. 'How' and 'why' are both adverbial notions, but 'how' is a manner adverbial notion, pertaining to the manner in which the action of the verb is carried out, while 'why' is a sentential adverbial notion, requesting the respondent to provide a semantic frame for the entire sentence (see section 8.1 of chapter 8 on adverbs). Since sentential adverbs may occur either in sentence-initial position or in the "regular" preverbal adverbial position, but manner adverbs can occur only before the verb, *zěnme* unambiguously means 'why' when it occurs in sentence-initial position, as in (14), but it can mean either 'how' or 'why' in (13).

The question word *zěnme-yàng* is an unambiguous variant of *zěnme*, meaning 'how'. The suffix, *-yàng*, means 'manner'. Its presence rules out the other meaning, 'why', of *zěnme*. If *zěnme* in (13) is replaced by *zěnme-yàng*, the question is unambiguous:

(15)   nǐ   zěnme   —   yàng   xiě   xiǎoshuō ?
        you   how   —   manner write novel

How do you write novels?

Duō, another adverbial question word, means 'how' in the sense of 'to what extent'. It is found with adjectives and adverbs expressing properties that can be true to varying degrees (the same ones, in fact, that can be compared in a comparative sentence—see chapter 19):

(16)   tā   duō   gāo ?
        3sg   how   tall

How tall is s/he?

(17)   tā   duō   zǎo   shàng   —   bān ?
        3sg   how   early ascend   —   work

How early does s/he go to work?

Wèishénme is another sentence adverb question word. It means 'why', literally *wèi* 'for' plus *shénme* 'what'. Examples (18) and (19) show that, as expected, it too can occur in either of the two positions where sentence adverbs can appear:

(18) wèishénme   tā   bu   kāixīn ?
      why   3sg   not   happy

Why is s/he not happy?

(19)   tā   wèishénme   mà   wǒ   —   de   dìdi ?
       3sg   why   scold   I   —   GEN   younger:brother

Why did s/he scold my younger brother?

Gànmá is another word for 'what for'. Unlike *wèishénme*, however, because of its derivation from the verb phrase *gàn shénme* 'do what', it can occur as if it were a verb phrase in a serial verb construction, either before or after the "other" verb phrase:

(20) *a.*   nǐ   dài   shǒudiàntǒng   gànmá ?
             you   bring   flashlight   what:for

What did you bring a flashlight for?

    b.   nǐ   gànmá   dài   shǒudiàntǒng ?
           you   what:for   bring   flashlight

What did you bring a flashlight for?

The forms *nǎr/nǎli* 'where' are location question words and can occur wherever a locative noun phrase can occur:

(21)   tā   zài   nǎr   zuò   —   shì ?
       3sg   at   where   do   —   work

Where does s/he work?

(22)   nǎr   mài   chǎo   —   miàn ?
       where   sell   fry   —   noodle

What place sells fried noodles?

(23)   nǐ   qù   nǎr ?
       you   go   where

Where are you going?

There is no special question word meaning 'when' in Mandarin. The usual expression for 'when' is *shénme shíhou* 'what time', as in:

(24)   tā   shénme shíhou   lái ?
        3sg   what   time   come

   When will s/he come?

One may also use the expression *jǐ-diǎnzhōng* 'how:many—o'clock = at what hour':

(25)   tā   jǐ   —   diǎnzhōng lái ?
        3sg   how:many   —   o'clock   come

   At what hour will s/he come?

Jǐ-diǎngzhōng 'what time' demands a specific time, whereas *shénme shíhou* 'when' does not. Thus (26) is a reasonable answer for (24), but not for (25):

(26)   tā   xiàwǔ   lái
        3sg   afternoon   come

   S/He will come in the afternoon.

An answer to (25) must specify the hour. Consequently, the expression *jǐ-diǎnzhōng* is also used when one asks for the time:

(27)   qǐng   wèn   xiànzai   jǐ   —   diǎnzhōng ?
        please ask   now   how:many   —   o'clock

   May I ask, what is the time now?

The question words *duōshǎo* 'how many, how much', *jǐ-CL* 'how many', *něi-CL* 'which', and *něi-xiē* 'which-PL' usually modify the head noun in a noun phrase. In the cases of *něi-CL* 'which' and *jǐ-CL* 'how many', *CL* stands for the classifier that is appropriate for the noun that follows. These sentences serve as illustrations:

(28)   nǐ   yǒu   <u>duōshǎo</u>   qián ?
        you   exist   how:much   money

How much money do you have?

(29)   nǐ   dài   —   lai   —   le   <u>duōshǎo</u> rén ?
        you   bring   —   come   —   PFV   how:many   people

How many people did you bring?

(30)   nǐ   mǎi   —   le   <u>jǐ</u>   —   <u>ge</u>   ézi ?
        you   buy   —   PFV   how:many   —   CL   goose

How many geese did you buy?

(31)   nǐ   shuō   <u>něi</u>   —   <u>zhī</u>   bǐ   hǎo ?
        you   say   which   —   CL   pen   good

Which pen do you say is good?

(32)   nǐ   xǐhuan <u>něi</u>   —   <u>xiē</u>   niǎo ?
        you   like   which   —   PL   bird

Which birds do you like?

18.2.2 Question Words as Indefinite Pronouns

We have seen above that question words may be nominal or adverbial, or they may modify a head noun in a noun phrase. The nominal question words, however, may also function as indefinite pronouns denoting such notions as 'whoever', 'whatever', 'wherever', 'anyone', 'anything'. In this section, we will discuss the use of question words as indefinite pronouns in Mandarin.

A. *shéi* 'whoever'

(33)   <u>shéi</u>   zuì   —   le   jiu   fá   shí
        whoever   drink   —   PFV   then   fine   ten

                       kuài   qián
                       dollar   money

Whoever gets drunk will be fined ten dollars.

(34)   shéi   yào   hē   jiǔ   zhǐ   yào   fù
       whoever   want   drink   then   only   need   pay

       liǎng   kuài   qián
       two   dollar   money

Whoever wants to drink has to pay only two dollars.

(35)   jǐngchá   yào   zhuā   shéi   jiu   zhuā   shéi
       police   want   arrest   whoever   then   arrest   whoever

The police will arrest whomever they want to arrest.

As (33)−(35) show, it is the context that determines when the question word *shéi* is used as a question word and when it is used as an indefinite pronoun. The first clause containing *shéi* in each of the sentences (33)−(35) could be used independently as a question. In each of the above sentences, however, the clause containing *shéi* is accompanied by another clause. An important characteristic of (33)−(35) is that both clauses in each sentence refer to the indefinite pronoun. In (33), the understood direct object of the verb *fá* 'fine, penalize' in the second clause is coreferential with the indefinite pronoun of the first clause. In (34), the understood subject of the verb *yào* 'want' in the second clause is coreferential with the indefinite pronoun of the first clause. In (35) the indefinite pronoun *shéi* occurs simply as the direct object of both clauses.

B. *shéi-dōu/shéi-yě* 'everyone, anyone'

(36)   tā   shéi-dōu   bu   xìnren
       3sg   everyone   not   trust

{ S/He distrusts everyone.   }
{ S/He doesn't trust anyone.   }

(37)   shéi-dōu   yào   mǎi   piányi   dōngxi
       everyone   want   buy   inexpensive   goods

Everyone wants to buy inexpensive goods.

(38)   tā   <u>shéi-dōu</u>   yào   kǎowèn
       3sg   everyone   want   interrogate

S/He wants to interrogate everyone.

(39)   wǒ   <u>shéi-yě</u>   bu   rènshi
       I   everyone   not   recognize

I don't know anyone.

The two expressions, *shéi-dōu* and *shéi-yě*, are interchangeable. *Shéi* in these two expressions again stands for a nonspecific person. *Dōu* is the quantifier 'all', whose scope includes only the noun immediately preceding it (see section 8.2.2.F of chapter 8). *Yě* is an adverb meaning 'even' or 'also' (again, see section 8.2.2.F of chapter 8), and it, too, includes in its scope only the noun immediately preceding it.

In English, *anyone* is the negative counterpart of *everyone*. In other words, given an affirmative sentence containing *everyone*, such as (40):

(40) I like everyone.

the normal negative counterpart would be:

(41) I don't like anyone.

In Mandarin, though, there is no such variation; *shéi-dōu/shéi-yě* can be used in both negative and affirmative contexts, as here:

(42)   wǒ   shéi-dōu   xǐhuan
       I   everyone   like

I like everyone.

(43)   wǒ   shéi-dōu   bu   xǐhuan
       I   everyone   not   like

I don't like anyone.

An important property of *shéi-dōu/shéi-yě*, as shown in (36), (38), and (39), is that *they are positioned before the verb* even when they are the direct objects of their verbs. The reason for this property of *shéi-dōu/shéi-yě* is straightforward. The second component of these expressions is one of the adverbs *dōu* 'all' and *yě* 'even', which, as adverbs, occur only in preverbal position. Since they include only the noun phrase immediately preceding them in their scope, the first component, *shéi*, is forced to occur preverbally too.

The behavior of *shénme* in the following two sections, 18.2.2.C and 18.2.2.D, and the explanations for its behavior precisely parallel our description of *shéi* in sections 18.2.2.A and 18.2.2.B, respectively, so rather than repeating the description, we will merely provide examples for illustration purposes.

C. *shénme* 'whatever'

(44)   shénme   hǎo   wǒmen   jiu   sòng   qù   bówùguǎn
        whatever   good   we   then   send   go   museum

Whatever is good we will send to the museum.

(45)   nǐ   xiǎng   chī   shénme   jiu   mǎi   shénme
        you   desire   eat   whatever   then   buy   whatever

(You can) buy whatever you desire to eat.

(46)   nǐ   gěi   tā   shénme   tā   jiu   yòng   shénme
        you   give   3sg   whatever   3sg   then   use   whatever

S/He will use whatever you give him/her.

D. *shénme-dōu/shénme-yě* 'everything, anything'

(47)   wǒ   shénme-yě   bu   pà
        I   everything   not   afraid

I am not afraid of anything.

(48) zhèr   shénme-dōu   guì
      here   everything   expensive

Everything is expensive here.

(49) shénme-dōu   xíng
      everything   OK

Anything will do!

E. *năr* 'wherever', *năr-dōu* 'everywhere'

What has been said of *shéi* and *shénme* above applies exactly to *năr* 'where'. Hence, in (50) *năr* denotes 'wherever':

(50) năr   tiānqi   hăo   wŏmen   jiu   qù   năr
      wherever   climate good   we   then   go   wherever

We will go wherever the climate is good.

In (51), *năr-dōu* signifies 'everywhere':

(51) zhè   jĭ   tiān   năr-dōu   xià   –   yŭ
      this   few   day   everywhere   descend –   rain

These few days, it is raining everywhere.

18.3 Disjunctive Questions

Disjunctive questions with or without the morpheme *háishi* 'or' always present an either-or choice to the respondent. Two types of disjunctive questions exist. First, there are those composed of at least two constituents connected by *háishi* 'or', as in sentence (3), where the two disjoined constituents are declarative clauses:

(3)   nĭ   qù   háishi   tā   lái ?
      you   go   or   3sg   come

Will you go, or will s/he come?

The second category of disjunctive questions consists of an affirmative sentence followed by its negative counterpart, usually without *háishi* 'or'. This type of question is traditionally called the *A-not-A question*, where 'not' stands for one of the negative particles *bu* or *méi(yǒu)*. For example:

(52)   nǐ   qù   bu   qù ?
        you   go   not   go

    Will you go?

Let's consider each of these two types of disjunctive questions in turn.

18.3.1 Questions with Constituents Connected by *háishi*

This category of questions explicitly presents the respondent with a choice of two or more possible answers. The possible answers in each such question are connected by *háishi* 'or', and each possible answer may be called a *constituent*. The syntactic nature of the connected constituents may vary from question to question, but all such constituents within a question are of the same syntactic type. We have seen that in sentence (3) the connected constituents are clauses. Let's look at some other examples; the connected constituents are underlined in each sentence.

In (53) and (54), the constituents connected by the morpheme *háishi* are verb phrases. In (53), each verb phrase involves a verb and a direct object, whereas in (54) each verb phrase is a simple intransitive verb:

(53)   nǐ   mài   bàozhǐ   háishi   kāi   jìchéngchē ?
        you   sell   newspaper   or   drive   taxi

    Do you sell newspapers, or do you drive taxis?

(54)   nǐ   zǒu   háishi   pǎo ?
        you   walk   or   run

    Will you walk, or will you run?

In (55), the connected constituents are the direct objects, in (56), the subjects, and in (57), the verbs:

(55)   nǐ   mǎi   <u>zhèi   −   ge</u>   háishi   <u>nèi   −   ge</u> ?
       you   buy   this   −   CL   or   that   −   CL

Will you buy this one, or will you buy that one?

(56)   <u>Zhāngsān</u>   háishi   <u>Lǐsì</u>   jiǎng   −   huà ?
       Zhangsan   or   Lisi   talk   −   speech

Is Zhangsan talking, or is Lisi talking?

(57)   nǐ   <u>chǎo</u>   háishi   <u>zhēng</u>   zhèi   −   ge   qīngcài ?
       you   fry   or   steam   this   −   CL   vegetable

Do you fry or steam this vegetable?

Notice the difference between the connected constituents in (57) and those in (53) and (54): what is connected in (53) and (54) are the entire verb phrases, but what is connected in (57) are merely the verbs. In (58), the coverb phrases (see chapter 9) are connected by *háishi*; in (59), the adverbs (see chapter 8) are connected; in (60), it is the nominalized adjectives (see chapter 20) serving as the direct objects:

(58)   tā   <u>zài   zhèr</u>   háishi   <u>(zài)   nàr</u>   zhù ?
       3sg   at   here   or   (at)   there   reside

Does s/he live here or there?

(59)   tā   <u>jīntian</u>   háishi   <u>míngtian</u>   lái ?
       3sg   today   or   tomorrow   come

Is s/he coming today or tomorrow?

(60)   nèi   −   běn   −   shū   shì   <u>hóng   de</u>
       that   −   CL   −   book   is   red   NOM

         háishi   <u>bái   de</u> ?
         or   white   NOM

Is that book red or white?

Sentences (61) and (62) are examples of serial verb constructions (see chapter 21). In (61), the disjunction is in the first part of the serial verb construction, while in (62), the disjunction is in the second part of the serial verb construction:

(61) tā   guì   —   xia   —   lai   háishi
      3sg   kneel —   descend —   come   or

      zhàn   zài   nàr   qiú   Zhāngsān ?
      stand at   there beg   Zhangsan

    Does s/he kneel down to beg Zhangsan, or does s/he stand there to beg
    Zhangsan ?

(62) tā   guì   —   xia   —   lai   qiú   Zhāngsān
      3sg   kneel —   descend —   come   beg   Zhangsan

      háishi   bài   púsa ?
      or   worship Buddha

    Does s/he kneel down to beg Zhangsan, or does s/he kneel down to
    worship Buddha?

Sentences (61) and (62) can also be understood as examples of disjunction between a simple clause and a serial verb clause. Thus, (61) can also mean 'Does s/he kneel down, or does s/he stand there to beg Zhangsan?', whereas (62) can mean 'Does s/he kneel down to beg Zhangsan, or does s/he worship Buddha?'.

Finally, in (63), the connected constituents are the indirect objects (see chapter 10):

(63) nǐ   sòng   nèi   —   zhī   bǐ   gěi   wǒ
      you   give   that   —   CL   pen   to   I

      háishi   gěi   tā ?
      or   to   3sg

    Will you give that pen to me or to him/her?

We have implied that the number of disjoined constituents in this category of disjunctive questions may exceed two. Theoretically, there is no limit on the number of disjoined constituents, but practically, two is the most common number. In principle, each additional constituent could take on an additional conjunctive particle *háishi*. In the case of more than two disjoined constituents, however, speakers generally delete all occurrences of the disjunctive marker *háishi* preceding the last one, as in (64) *b*:

(64) *a*.

tā	jīntian	háishi	míngtian	háishi	hòutian	lai ?
3sg	today	or	tomorrow	or	day:after:tomorrow	come

Is s/he coming today, or tomorrow, or the day after tomorrow?

b.

tā	jīntian ,	míngtian ,	háishi	hòutian	lái ?
3sg	today	tomorrow	or	day:after:tomorrow	come

Is s/he coming today, tomorrow, or the day after tomorrow?

18.3.2 A-not-A Questions

The A-not-A question, as we have stated earlier, is a type of disjunctive question. The choice presented to the respondent is the choice between an affirmative sentence and its negative counterpart. *Háishi* 'or' can be used, but it is generally omitted.

In the formation of an A-not-A question, the general rule is to put the affirmative and then the negative version of the sentence together. For example, if one wants to ask whether *tā* 's/he' is at home, one takes the affirmative sentence:

(65)

tā	zài	jiā
3sg	at	home

S/He is at home.

and the negative sentence:

(66)

tā	bu	zài	jiā
3sg	not	at	home

S/He is not at home.

and puts them together, deleting the subject in the second clause:

(67)   tā   zài   jiā   bu   zài   jiā ?
       3sg   at   home   not   at   home

      Is s/he at home?

In addition to the obligatory deletion of the second subject, speakers also have the option of deleting the other repeated material in either clause except for the verb or the auxiliary; in general this material is deleted to avoid unnecessary repetition. For example, we could simplify (67) by deleting one of the words *jiā* 'home' to form either (68) or (69):

(68)   tā   zài   bu   zài   jiā ?
       3sg   at   not   at   home

      Is s/he at home?

(69)   ta   zài   jiā   bu   zài ?
       3sg   at   home   not   at

      Is s/he at home?

Although (67), (68), and (69) are all acceptable, the form illustrated by (68) is the preferred one.

The following general rule allows us to account for the form of all A-not-A questions:

(i) The affirmative and its negative counterpart (see chapter 12 on negation) are juxtaposed, the second subject must be deleted, and the repeated elements to the right of the first verb may be (and usually are) deleted.

There are three facts that constrain the way in which the deletion of repeated elements can take place: (*a*) in general, elements forming a semantic unit must be deleted together; (*b*) for Mandarin influenced by southern dialects, with a disyllabic verb or an auxiliary, deletion in the first clause may even include the second syllable of that verb or auxiliary; and (*c*) if the negative particle precedes any element other than a verb or an auxiliary, then deletion generally does not occur.

To illustrate, let us consider an A-not-A question in its full form and then see what can be deleted:

(70) nǐ   xǐhuān   tā   —   de   chènshān (háishi)
      you   like   3sg   —   GEN   shirt   or

      bu   xǐhuān   tā   —   de   chènshān ?
      not   like   3sg   —   GEN   shirt

Do you like his/her shirt?

Fact (*a*) says that elements forming a semantic unit must be deleted together. We can illustrate this by showing that since *tā-de chènshan* 'his/her shirt' forms a semantic unit, we couldn't delete just *chènshan* 'shirt' or just *tā-de* 'his/her', so (71)−(74) are all unacceptable:

(71) *nǐ   xǐhuān   tā   —   de   (háishi) bu   xǐhuān
      you   like   3sg   —   GEN   or   not   like

      tā   —   de   chènshān ?
      3sg   —   GEN   shirt

(72) *nǐ   xǐhuān   tā   —   de   chènshān (háishi) bu
      you   like   3sg   —   GEN   shirt   or   not

      xǐhuān   tā   —   de ?
      like   3sg   —   GEN

(73) *nǐ   xǐhuān   chènshān (háishi) bu   xǐhuān   tā   —
      you   like   shirt   or   not   like   3sg   —

      de   chènshān ?
      GEN   shirt

(74) *nǐ   xǐhuān   tā   —   de   chènshān (háishi) bu
      you   like   3sg   —   GEN   shirt   or   not

      xǐhuān   chènshān ?
      like   shirt

Instead, if any deletion takes place, *tā-de chènshān* 'his/her shirt' must be deleted as a unit:

(75)   ní   xǐhuān   bu   xǐhuān   tā   —   de   chènshān ?
        you   like   not   like   3sg   —   GEN   shirt

Do you like his/her shirt?

(76)   ní   xǐhuān   tā   —   de   chènshān   bu   xǐhuān ?
        you   like   3sg   —   GEN   shirt   not   like

Do you like his/her shirt?

According to fact (*b*), deletion in the first clause of an A-not-A question may even include deletion of the second syllable of the verb. To illustrate fact (*b*), let's look again at (70). If the deletion of repeated elements takes place in the first clause, then in Mandarin influenced by southern dialects—for instance, the Mandarin spoken in Taiwan—that deletion can include the *-huān* part of *xǐhuān* 'like':

(77)   ní   xǐ-   bu   xǐhuān   tā   —   de   chènshān ?
        you   like   not   like   3sg   —   GEN   shirt

Do you like his/her shirt?

Deletion of the second syllable of a disyllabic verb or auxiliary can take place only in the *first* clause of an A-not-A question and only when all the following material in that clause is also deleted. Consequently, (78) and (79) are unacceptable, even in Mandarin influenced by southern dialects:

(78)   *ní   xǐ-   tā   —   de   chènshān   bu   xǐhuān ?
        you   like   3sg   —   GEN   shirt   not   like

(79)   *ní   xǐhuān   tā   —   de   chènshān   bu   xǐ- ?
        you   like   3sg   —   GEN   shirt   not   like

A-not-A questions in which the second syllable of the verb or auxiliary in the first clause is deleted are extremely common in this kind of Mandarin. Here are three more examples in their shortened forms:

(80) nǐ   zhī-   bu   zhīdào   tā   shi   wǒ
      you   know   not   know   3sg   be   I

      —   de   dìdi ?
      —   GEN   younger:brother

      Did you know he is my younger brother?

(81) tā   kě-   bu   kěyi   chū   —   qu ?
      3sg   have:permission not   have:permission exit   —   go

      Does s/he have permission to go out?

(82) nǐ   rèn-   bu   rènshi   tā ?
      you   recognize not   recognize   3sg

      Do you recognize him/her?

Fact (*c*) says that deletion does not occur unless the negative particle precedes a verb or an auxiliary. To illustrate, let's consider an A-not-A question in which the negative particle in the second clause precedes, not a verb or an auxiliary, but a manner adverb:

(83) tā   màn-màn-de   pǎo   (háishi)   bu   màn-màn-de   pǎo ?
      3sg   slowly   run   or   not   slowly   run

      Does s/he run slowly?

Since the negated element is the adverb *màn-màn-de* 'slowly' rather than the verb, no deletion can occur in this sentence. Thus, (84) and (85) are unacceptable:

(84) *tā   màn-màn-de   pǎo   bu   màn-màn-de ?
      3sg   slowly   run   not   slowly

(85) *tā   màn-màn-de   bu   màn-màn-de   pǎo ?
      3sg   slowly   not   slowly   run

Another example would be a sentence in which the negative element precedes a coverb, such as *bǎ* (see chapter 15), as in:

(86)	tā	bu	bǎ	qián	gěi	wǒ
	3sg	not	BA	money	give	I

S/He won't give me the money.

Since fact (*c*) says that we cannot perform any deletion in an A-not-A question if the negative in the second clause precedes an element other than a verb or an auxiliary, the A-not-A question formed with (86) as its second clause would be (87), but not (88) or (89):

(87)	tā	bǎ	qián	gěi	wǒ	(háishi)	bu	bǎ
	3sg	BA	money	give	I	or	not	BA

	qián	gěi	wǒ ?
	money	give	I

Will s/he give me the money?

(88)	*tā	bǎ	qián	(háishi)	bu	bǎ	qián
	3sg	BA	money	or	not	BA	money

	gěi	wǒ ?
	give	I

(89)	*tā	bǎ	qián	gěi	wǒ	(háishi)	bu
	3sg	BA	money	give	I	or	not

	bǎ	qián ?
	BA	money

These examples clearly show that deletions in general cannot occur in A-not-A questions where the negative particle in the second clause precedes any element besides a verb or an auxiliary. This does not mean, however, that the long versions illustrated in (83) and (87) are the only ways to express these questions. It is always possible to add the copula verb *shi* 'be' (see A.2.2 in section 4.3.1 of chapter 4) and make an A-not-A question with it, and in the case of sentences such as (83) and (87) this is a particularly attractive option:

(90)   tā   shi   bu   shi   màn-màn-de   pǎo ?
        3sg   be   not   be   slowly   run

Is it the case that s/he runs slowly?

(91)   tā   shi   bu   shi   bǎ   qián   gěi   wǒ ?
        3sg   be   not   be   BA   money   give   I

Is it the case that s/he'll give me the money?

As discussed in chapter 4 and as indicated by our translations, sentences containing the copula *shi* are used only in certain situations, namely, when the proposition has already been brought up in the conversation. Now, sentences with adverbs and prepositional phrases often fall into this category; that is, for example, a sentence like (83) is typically used when both speaker and hearer know that s/he runs and the speaker simply wants to question whether s/he does it slowly. Consequently, questions with adverbs and prepositional phrases are ideal candidates for the alternative version with the copula *shi* 'be', as in (90); this is why a *shi bu shi* question is an especially useful alternative for questions such as (83) and (87).

The three facts given above, then, account for the way in which deletions of repeated material can occur in A-not-A questions. For the rest of our discussion, we will present our examples in their normal form, with the repeated elements already deleted.

Returning to the structure of the A-not-A question form in general, the rule given above in (i) suggests that the form of an A-not-A question is determined by the way negation works (again, for a discussion of negation, see chapter 12). For example, the negative counterpart of a sentence with an auxiliary verb is one in which the negative particle precedes the auxiliary and not the main verb:

(92)   tā   huì   dǎ   —   lánqiú
        3sg   know:how   hit   —   basketball

S/He knows how to play basketball.

(93)   tā   bu   huì   dǎ   —   lánqiú
        3sg   not   know:how   hit   —   basketball

S/He doesn't know how to play basketball.

(94)   *tā   huì   <u>bu</u>   dǎ   —   lánqiú
        3sg   know:how   not   hit   —   basketball

Thus, it follows that the A-not-A question composed of (92) and (93) must also have *bu* preceding the auxiliary and not the main verb; with deletion of repeated material, then, we get (95), but not (96):

(95)   tā   <u>huì   bu   huì</u>   dǎ -   lánqiú ?
        3sg   know:how   not   know:how   hit   basketball

        Does s/he know how to play basketball?

(96)   *tā   huì   <u>dâ   bu   dâ</u>   lánqiú ?
        3sg   know:how   play   not   hit   —   basketball

Similarly, since the negative counterpart of the coverb sentence (97) is (98), not (99),

(97)   tā   duì   nǐ   hǎo
        3sg   to   you   good

        S/He is good to you.

(98)   tā   duì   nǐ   <u>bu</u>   hǎo
        3sg   to   you   not   good

        S/He is not good to you.

(99)   *tā   <u>bu</u>   duì   nǐ   hǎo
        3sg   not   to   you   good

Then the A-not-A question form corresponding to (97) is (100) and not (101):

(100)   tā   duì   nǐ   <u>hǎo   bu   hǎo</u> ?
        3sg   to   you   good   not   good

        Is s/he good to you?

(101) *tā   duì   bu   duì   nǐ   hǎo ?
       3sg   to   not   to   you   good

Finally, let's illustrate this same point with a pair of serial verb sentences (see chapter 21):

(102) tā   zhīdao   wǒ   zài   Xiānggǎng
       3sg   know   I   at   Hong Kong

S/He knows that I am in Hong Kong.

(103) tāmen   jìn   dàxué   yǒu   wèntí
       they   enter   university   exist   problem

There are problems for them in getting into a university.

The negative versions of these sentences are (104) and (105), with the negative particle preceding the verb that takes the underlined clause as its direct object ([104]) or subject ([105]):

(104) tā   bu   zhīdao   wǒ   zài   Xiānggǎng
       3sg   not   know   I   at   Hong Kong

S/He does not know that I am in Hong Kong.

(105) tāmen   jìn   dàxué   méi   yǒu   wèntí
       they   enter   university   not   exist   problem

There are not problems for them in getting into a university.

The A-not-A questions combining the affirmative and negative versions, then, would be:

(106) tā   zhīdao   bu   zhīdao   wǒ   zài   Xiānggǎng ?
       3sg   know   not   know   I   at   Hong Kong

Does s/he know that I am in Hong Kong?

(107)	tāmen	jìn	dàxué	yǒu	méi	yǒu	wènti ?
	they	enter	university	exist	not	exist	problem

Are there problems for them in getting into a university?

With respect to A-not-A questions, the behavior of the negative particle *méi (yǒu)*, which denies completion, deserves special mention. Let's illustrate with a sentence containing the perfective aspect marker *-le*:

(108)	tā	mǎi	—	le	nèi	—	ge	fángzi
	3sg	buy	—	PFV	that	—	CL	house

S/He bought that house.

The negative counterpart of this sentence is one with the negative particle *méi(yǒu)*, which denies completion:

(109)	tā	méi(yǒu)	mǎi	nèi	—	ge	fángzi
	3sg	not	buy	that	—	CL	house

S/He didn't buy that house.

When we put these two together, we get (110):

(110)	tā	mǎi	—	le	nèi	—	ge	fángzi
	3sg	buy	—	PFV	that	—	CL	house

méi(yǒu)	(mǎi	nèi	—	ge	fángzi) ?
not	(buy	that	—	CL	house)

Did s/he buy that house?

In Mandarin influenced by southern dialects, however, as pointed out in the discussion in section 12.4 of chapter 12, a possible variant of (108) is (111), in which the perfective marker *yǒu* occurs instead of the northern Mandarin *-le*:

(111)	tā	yǒu	mǎi	nèi	—	ge	fángzi
	3sg		buy	that	—	CL	house

S/He bought that house.

With the affirmative variant (111) and the negative version (109), of course, we can form the A-not-A question (112):

(112)	tā	yǒu	méi	yǒu	mǎi	nèi	—	ge	fángzi ?
	3sg		not		buy	that	—	CL	house

Did s/he buy that house?

And for many speakers of Mandarin, (112) is a perfectly acceptable alternative to (110), even for those who find the affirmative sentence (111) odd.

In exactly the same way, both sentences (114) and (115) are possible A-not-A question counterparts to (113), with the experiential aspect marker -*guo* (see section 6.3 of chapter 6), but (115) is more acceptable to speakers of Mandarin influenced by southern dialects than to northern speakers:

(113)	tā	hē	—	guo	píjiǔ
	3sg	drink	—	EXP	beer

S/He has drunk beer before.

(114)	tā	hē	—	guo	píjiǔ	méi(yǒu)
	3sg	drink	—	EXP	beer	not
		(hē	—	guo	píjiǔ) ?	
		(drink	—	EXP	beer)	

Has s/he drunk beer before?

(115)	tā	yǒu	méi	yǒu	hē	—	guo	píjiǔ ?
	3sg		not		drink	—	EXP	beer

Has s/he drunk beer before?

To conclude our discussion of A-not-A questions, the examples we have considered illustrate the point that the structural properties of A-not-A questions can be predicted from, first, the facts concerning the deletion of repeated elements, and second, the behavior of negation.

18.4 Tag Questions

A statement can become a question by the addition of a short A-not-A question form of certain verbs as a tag to that statement. The most common tags are the ones illustrated in (116)−(119):

(116)   nǐmen   shi   jiǔ   —   diǎnzhōng   kāi   —
         you:PL   be   nine   —   o'clock   open   —

         mén   de ,   duì   bu   duì ?
         door   NOM   right   not   right

You opened at nine o'clock, right?

(117)   wǒmen   qu   chī   shuǐguǒ ,   hǎo   bu   hǎo ?
         we   go   eat   fruit   good   not   good

Let's go eat some fruit, OK?

(118)   gāi   nǐ   kāi   —   chē ,
         be:one's:turn   you   drive   —   vehicle

             xíng   bu   xíng ?
             OK   not   OK

It's your turn to drive, OK?

(119)   tā   zài   gēng   —   tián ,   shì   bu   shì ?
         3sg   DUR   plow   —   field   be   not   be

S/He is plowing the field, right?

Tag questions are functionally different from the other types of Mandarin questions in that they serve to seek confirmation of the statement that occurs before the tag. In the case of (119), for example, the speaker is requesting the respondent to confirm this statement:

(120)   tā   zài   gēng   —   tián
         3sg   DUR   plow   —   field

S/He is plowing the field.

18.5 Particle Questions

The particle question is structurally the least complex of all the question types. What signals the interrogative nature of this question type is the presence of a sentence-final particle, usually *ma*, which is destressed and has the neutral tone. For example:

(121)	tā	yòu	hē	jiǔ	yòu	chōu
	3sg	both	drink	wine	and	extract

		yān	ma ?
	–	smoke	Q

Does s/he both drink and smoke?

(122)	nǐ	néng	xiě	Zhōngguó	zì	ma ?
	you	can	write	Chinese	character	Q

Can you write Chinese characters?

(123)	nǐ	bǎ	Zhāngsān	dài	–	lái
	you	BA	Zhangsan	bring	–	come

		le	ma ?
	–	PFV	Q

Did you bring Zhangsan here?

(124)	tā	zài	nàr	sànbù	ma ?
	3sg	at	there	promenade	Q

Is s/he taking a walk there?

The sentence-final particle *ma* functions exclusively as a question marker. There are, however, two other sentence-final particles whose meanings allow them to function as question particles: *ba* and *ne*. Their use as question particles is discussed in detail in sections 7.2.1 and 7.3 of chapter 7; here we will simply present an example of each:

(125) (After Wanger says he was unhappy with the decision, Lisi asks him this.)

Zhāngsān	ne ?
Zhangsan	REx

How about Zhangsan?

(126)	tā	hěn	kāixīn	ba
	3sg	very	happy	SA

S/He is happy, isn't s/he?

For the remainder of this chapter, however, the term *particle question* will be used interchangeably with *ma question*.

18.6 Differences between A-Not-A Questions and Particle Questions

Of the four types of questions we have discussed in this chapter, one of them, the question-word type, can be functionally characterized as a request for specific information. The tag questions are seeking only confirmation. The other two, the A-not-A type and the particle type, on the other hand, are functionally similar in seeking an answer that confirms or denies the proposition in the question. What, then, is the difference between the two types of questions? In other words, when is an A-not-A question used, and when is a particle question used?[1]

To answer this question, let's consider two conversational examples together with their speech contexts. In the first example, imagine that A and B have met and exchanged greetings. The conversation in (127) then unfolds:

(127) A:	nǐ	hǎoxiàng	shòu	—	le	yìdiǎn
	you	seem	thin	—	PFV	a:little

You seem to have lost some weight.

B:	shì	ma ?	nǐ	kàn	wǒ	shòu
	be	Q	you	see	I	thin

	–	le	ma ?	wǒ	zìjǐ
	–	PFV	Q	I	self

	dào	bu	juéde
	on:the:contrary	not	feel

Is that so? Do you think I have lost weight? I haven't noticed it
myself.

Observe that B's response to A contains two particle questions. The conversation is
perfectly normal: A has made a statement, and B questions the validity of A's
statement. On the other hand, if we replace the particle questions in B's responses
with their A-not-A counterparts, the conversation becomes extremely awkward:

(128) A:	nǐ	hǎoxiàng	shòu	–	le	yidiǎn
	you	seem	thin	–	PFV	a:little

You seem to have lost some weight.

B:	??shì	bu	shì ?	??nǐ	kàn	wǒ
	be	not	be	you	see	I

	shòu	–	le	méiyou ?	wǒ
	thin	–	PFV	not	I

	zìjǐ	dào	bu	juéde
	self	on:the:contrary	not	feel

(Is that so? Do you think I have lost weight? I haven't noticed it
myself.)

The A-not-A questions in B's response are syntactically well formed and in
isolation would themselves be perfectly acceptable constructions. They are odd
merely in this particular speech context.

For the second example, let us construct the following context. Suppose you
have always known that Wang did not eat apples. One day, while having lunch

with him, you are surprised that he is having an apple for dessert; in other words, what he is doing goes against your assumption. Puzzled, you ask the question:

(129)   nǐ   chī   pǐngguo   ma ?
         you   eat   apple   Q

   Do you eat apples?

A question such as (129) is perfectly normal in this situation. Again, however, if it were in the A-not-A form, it would seem strange:

(130)   ??nǐ   chī   bu   chī   pǐngguo ?
         you   eat   not   eat   apple

   Do you eat apples?

What is clearly brought out by these examples is that if the speech situation is in conflict with the speaker's assumption and s/he wishes to ask a question to clarify the conflict, the A-not-A form cannot be used for the question. In (128), the context is one in which B's assumption, that s/he has not lost weight, conflicts with the speech situation in which A has asserted that B *has* lost weight. Wishing then to ask questions to clarify the conflict, B can pose the questions only in the particle form and not in the A-not-A form.

   At this point, we can make a general statement about the use of these two types of questions:

   (ii) The A-not-A question is used only in a *neutral context,* whereas the particle-question may be used in a *neutral* or a *nonneutral context.*[2] A neutral context is one in which the questioner has no assumptions concerning the proposition that is being questioned and wishes to know whether it is true. Whenever the questioner brings to the speech situation an assumption about either the truth or the falsity of the proposition s/he is asking about, then that context is nonneutral with respect to that question.

   Since principle (ii) states that the particle question may be used in either a neutral or a nonneutral context, it implies that in a neutral context one may use either a particle question or an A-not-A question to seek confirmation or negation of a proposition. That this is indeed correct is shown by the fact that, for example, as a greeting, one may use either the particle question:

(131)   (nǐ)   hǎo   ma ?
         (you)   good   Q

   How are you?

or the A-not-A question:

(132) (nǐ)   hǎo   bu   hǎo ?
       (you)   good   not   good

How are you?

The *a* and *b* sentences of the following examples are also equivalent in the contexts given:

(133) (Before preparing dinner for a guest, the speaker wishes to find
       out whether the guest drinks wine.)
    a.   nǐ   hē   jiǔ   ma ?
           you   drink wine   Q

Do you drink wine?

    b.   nǐ   hē   bu   hē   jiǔ ?
           you   drink not   drink wine

Do you drink wine?

(134) (After seeing a movie with a friend, the speaker wishes to find
       out whether the friend liked the movie.)

    a.   nǐ   xǐhuan   bu   xǐhuan   zhèi
           you   like   not   like   this

                           – ge   diànyǐng ?
                           – CL   movie

Did you like this movie?

    b.   nǐ   xǐhuan   zhèi   – ge   diànyǐng   ma ?
           you   like   this   – CL   movie   Q

Did you like this movie?

The speech contexts described for (133) and (134) are neutral, and since the two question forms are interchangeable in neutral contexts, either one can be used. In contrast, the contexts for (127) and (129) involved a conflict with the questioner's assumptions. In these two cases, then, only the *ma* question could be used.

In the light of this distinction, we can consider one further example:

(135)   ??nĭ   xìng   bu   xìng   Lĭ ?
          you   surname   not   surname   Li

    Do you have the surname Li?

This sentence seems strange even apart from any specific context. Why should this be so? Let us examine (135) in detail: the sentence inquires whether the hearer has the surname *Lĭ*. The most natural situation for making such an inquiry is that the questioner already has some inkling that the hearer's surname is *Lĭ* and wishes to confirm that assumption; the most natural reason for seeking confirmation is that the context offers conflicting information. In other words, the most normal situation in which question (135) might arise is precisely a *nonneutral* context. Since (135) is in the A-not-A form, principle (ii) predicts that it cannot be used in such a context.

In order to make (135) appropriate, we would have to conjure up an unusual speech context, such as this one: imagine a kidnap situation in which for some reason the kidnapper has tried to force the victim to take on the surname *Lĭ*. After pressuring the victim for some time, the kidnapper wishes to find out whether the victim has indeed adopted the surname *Lĭ*:

(136)   nĭ   xìng   bu   xìng   Lĭ ?
          you   surname   not   surname   Li

    Do you have the surname Li?

Sentence (136) could be used in this context because here there is no conflict between the speech context and any assumptions on the part of the questioner.

As additional confirmation of this distinction, let's look at rhetorical questions. The person asking a rhetorical question is not genuinely seeking an answer to it because s/he already knows the answer. This means that, by definition, rhetorical questions are cases of the speaker bringing an assumption to the speech situation. That is, the context for a rhetorical question is never a neutral one. The principle stated in (ii), then, correctly predicts that only the *ma* form can be used for rhetorical questions in Mandarin.[3] Thus, in the contexts provided, in (137) the assumption concerns the falsity of the proposition, while in (138) the assumption concerns the truth of the proposition. In both cases, the *ma* forms of these rhetorical questions are appropriate, but the A-not-A forms are not.[4]

(137) (The speaker knows that the hearer's children didn't go to school and thus is bringing to the speech situation an assumption that the proposition in the question is *false*.)

a.

jīntian	nǐ	—	de	háizi	zhēnde
today	you	—	GEN	child	really

qù	xuéxiào	le	ma?
go	school	CRS	Q

Did your children really go to school today?

b.

*jīntian	nǐ	—	de	háizi	zhēnde
today	you	—	GEN	child	really

qu	xuéxiào	le	méiyou?
go	school	CRS	not

(138) (The speaker sees that the hearer has returned and thus is bringing to the speech situation an assumption that the proposition in the question is *true*.)

a.

ou	nǐ	yǐjing	huí	—	lai	le	ma?
Oh	you	already	return	—	come	CRS	Q

Oh, are you back already?

b.

*ou	nǐ	yǐjing	huí	—	lai	le	méiyou?
Oh	you	already	return	—	come	CRS	not

To summarize, then, we can state that particle questions and A-not-A questions differ in the types of contexts in which they can be used: in a neutral context, either the A-not-A form or the particle question may be used, while in a nonneutral context, only the particle question is possible.

This "division of labor" is in fact quite natural. The A-not-A question explicitly presents the respondent with the choice between the affirmative and the negative versions of some proposition. Given that there is another question type in the language, it is reasonable that the A-not-A form would be the one used when the speaker is neutral and has no predisposition toward either the affirmative or the negative option in the disjunction. The form of an explicit disjunctive question, by presenting the hearer with a choice between two alternatives, thereby severely constrains the uses to which it can be put.

18.7 Questions Serving as Subjects or Direct Objects of a Verb

Chapter 21 on serial verbs discusses clauses and verb phrases functioning as the subject or direct object of another verb. Two of the four types of questions we have considered here can be subjects or direct objects of another verb.

Question-word questions, just as in English, can serve in this function. In the following examples, the question-word question that is the subject or direct object is underlined:

(139)   wǒ   bu   zhīdao   shéi   tōu   —   le
        I   not   know   who   steal   —   PFV

        wǒ   —   de   shǒu   —   biǎo
        I   —   GEN   hand   —   watch

I don't know who stole my watch.

(140)   nǐ   kàn   tā   xiě   shénme
       you   see   3sg   write   what

You see what s/he writes.

(141)   wǒ   jìde   nǐ   yǐqián   zhù   zài   nǎr
       I   remember   you   before   live   at   where

I remember where you lived before.

(142)   nǐ   tì   wǒmen   juédìng   zěnme
       you   for   we   decide   how

       —   yàng   fá   tā
       —   way   punish   3sg

You decide for us how to punish him/her.

(143)

wǒ	chá	—	chū	—	lai
I	investigate	—	exit	—	come

—	le	tā	zhuàn	—
—	PFV	3sg	earn	—

le	duōshǎo	qián
PFV	how:much	money

I found out how much money s/he makes.

(144)

shénme	rén	zuò	zōngtǒng	shi
what	person	serve:as	president	be

yi	—	jian	hěn
one	—	CL	very

zhòngyào	de	shì
important	NOM	matter

Who serves as president is a very important matter.

Disjunctive questions can also be subjects or direct objects of another verb phrase. In the following examples, (145) and (146) contain ordinary disjunctive questions, while (147) and (148) have A-not-A questions. Again, the disjunctive question serving as the subject or direct object is underlined.

(145)

wǒ	bu	xiǎode	shi	tā	qù
I	not	know	be	3sg	go

háishi	nǐ	qù
or	you	go

I don't know whether it's the case that s/he's going or you're going.

(146)

nǐ	jìn	dàxué	háishi	zuò
you	enter	university	or	do

shēngyi	méi	yóu	guānxi
business	not	exist	relevance

It doesn't matter whether you go to the university or do business.

(147)

wǒ	bu	zhīdao	tā	lái	bu	lái
I	not	know	3sg	come	not	come

I don't know whether s/he is coming or not.

(148)

tā	kěyi	bu	kěyi	chū
3sg	have:permission	not	have:permission	exit

	qu	shi	yi
—	go	be	one

	ge	wènti
—	CL	problem

Whether s/he can go out is a problem.

These examples show that both question-word questions and disjunctive questions can occur as the subject or direct object of a verb phrase. Particle questions, however, cannot. Contrast (149) and (150):

(149)

nǐmen	lái	bu	lái	méi	yǒu	guānxi
you:PL	come	not	come	not	exist	relevance

It doesn't matter whether or not you (plural) come.

(150)

*nǐmen	lái	ma	méi	yǒu	guānxi
you:PL	come	Q	not	exist	relevance

In (149) an A-not-A question serves as the subject of the verb phrase *méi yǒu guānxi* 'not have relevance'. Example (150) shows that the same question in its particle question form cannot serve as the subject of another verb phrase. Examples (151) and (152) show that the same is true of questions serving as direct objects:

(151)

nǐ	bu	zhīdao	tā	lái	bu	lái
you	not	know	3sg	come	not	come

You don't know whether or not s/he's coming.

(152)   nǐ   bu   zhīdao   <u>tā   lái</u>   ma

         you   not   know   3sg   come   Q

Do you not know that s/he's coming? (Cannot mean: You don't know whether or not s/he's coming.)

Tag questions also cannot occur as the subject or direct object of a verb:

(153)   *wǒ   zhīdao   <u>tā   lái   hǎo   bu   hǎo</u>

          I   know   3sg   come good   not   good

(154)   <u>*tā   lái   hǎo   bu   hǎo</u>   shì   duì   de

         3sg   come good   not   good   be   right   NOM

The reason the particle question cannot serve as the subject or direct object of a verb phrase is that the question particle *ma* is a sentence-final particle, and, like all other sentence-final particles (see chapter 7), it signals how the entire utterance to which it is attached is to be taken by the hearer. That is, just as a sentence-final *le* signals that the entire utterance to which it is attached is to be taken by the hearer as a currently relevant state, so, too, the sentence-final *ma* can signal only that the entire utterance to which it is attached is to be taken as a question to be answered by the hearer. This is why *ma* cannot just question the verb *lái* 'come' in (150) and (152); this is also why in (152) *ma* must be questioning the verb of the entire utterance, *zhīdao* 'know', as our translations indicate.

A tag question cannot serve as the subject or direct object of another verb for a similar reason: the tag question must be directly addressed to the listener, since it functions to seek confirmation of the statement that occurs before the A-not-A tag portion of the question. Because a question that serves as a subject or direct object of a verb cannot be addressed to the hearer as a question in its own right, tag questions cannot occur as subjects or direct objects.

18.8 Answers to Questions

Since questions seek answers, we need to discuss the forms in which these answers can occur.

The answers to question-word questions, of course, just as in English, provide the information requested:

(155) *a.* nǐ   <u>jǐ</u>   —   diǎnzhōng   xià   —   bān ?

         you how:many —   o'clock   descend —   work

        What time do you get off work?

b.	wǔ	—	diǎnzhōng
	five	—	o'clock

Five o'clock.

(156) A:	tā	gēn	shéi	niàn	—	shū ?
	3sg	with	who	study	—	book

Who does s/he study with?

B:	gēn	Lǐsì	niàn	—	shū
	with	Lisi	study	—	book

S/He studies with Lisi.

The answers to disjunctive and particle questions, however, are slightly more complex. Let's consider disjunctive questions first. Disjunctive questions present a choice to the listener. The natural response, then, is one of the options named in the question:

(157) A:	nèi	—	běn	shū	shi	hóng
	that	—	CL	book	be	red

	de	háishi	bái	de ?
	NOM	or	white	NOM

Is that book red or white?

B:	(shi)	hóng	de
	be	red	NOM

(It's) red.

(158) A:	tā	jīntian ,	míngtian ,	háishi
	3sg	today	tomorrow	or

	hòutian	lái ?
	day:after:tomorrow	come

Is s/he coming today, tomorrow, or the day after tomorrow?

B:	(tā)	jīntian	(lái)
	3sg	today	come

S/He's coming today.

Similarly, if the disjunction is of the A-not-A form, the natural answer is to choose either "A" or "not A." This also applies to tag questions, since they contain a tag in the A-not-A form:

(159) A:	nǐ	yào	bu	yào	chī	júzi ?
	you	want	not	want	eat	orange

Do you want to eat an orange?

B:	bu	yào ,	xièxie
	not	want	thank

No thanks.

(160) A:	tā	màn-màn-de	pǎo	háishi	bu
	3sg	slowly	run	or	not

	màn-màn-de	pǎo ?
	slowly	run

Does s/he run slowly?

B:	(tā)	màn-màn-de	pǎo
	3sg	slowly	run

(S/He) runs slowly.

(161) A:	nǐ	hē	bu	hē	jiǔ ?
	you	drink	not	drink	wine

Do you drink wine?

B:	(wǒ)	hē	jiǔ
	I	drink	wine

Yes.

(162) A: nǐ   yǒu   gāi   xǐ   de
             you   exist   should   wash   NOM

             yīfu ,   duì   bù   duì ?
             clothes   right   not   right

You have some clothes that need to be washed, right?

B: duì
      right

Right.

These examples show that to answer a disjunctive question of any type, including tag questions, the respondent chooses one of the options presented in the question, which s/he may then elaborate on, as illustrated in (159).

With a particle question, however, there are often several possible types of answers. Let's consider them in terms of a specific example. If the speaker asks the question in (163), the respondent can answer affirmatively with (164) *a*, *b*, or *c*, or negatively with (165) *a*, *b*, or *c*:

(163)   nǐ   xìng   Lǐ   ma ?
         you   surname   Li   Q

Are you named Li?

(164) *a*.   (wǒ)   xìng   Lǐ
              I   surname   Li

Yes.

b.   shì   (de)
        be   NOM

Yes.

c.   duì
        right

That's right.

(165) *a.*   bu   (xìng)   Lǐ
           not   surname   Li

      No.

     b.   bu   shì   (de)
           not   be   NOM

      No.

     c.   bu   duì
           not   right

      That's not right.

The *a* responses in (164) and (165) show that a particle question can be answered with the verb phrase named in the question or its negative counterpart. The *b* responses, however, show that a particle question can also be answered with *shì (de)* or *bu shì (de)* even if the questions themselves do not contain any *shì*. *Shì (de)* and *bu shì (de)* say, in effect, 'it is the case' and 'it is not the case', respectively. The *c* answers show that *duì* 'right' and *bu duì* 'not right' can also serve as answers to particle questions. The *b* and *c* answers, though, clearly cannot be responses to disjunctive questions of any type because a disjunctive question presents a choice. The double asterisk (**) in the examples below indicates that the answers cannot occur with the question given:

(166) A: nǐ   qù   háishi   tā   qù ?
           you   go   or   3sg   go

      Are you going, or is s/he going?

     B: **shì   (de)
           be   NOM

      Yes.

     C: **duì
           right

      That's right.

(167) A: nǐ   yào   bu   yào   dǎ   qiáo   —   pái ?
            you   want   not   want   hit   bridge —   card

Do you want to play bridge?

B: **bu   shì   (de)
      not   be   NOM

No.

C: **bu   duì
      not   right

That's not right.

Given the meanings of *shì (de)* and *bu shì (de)* as 'it is the case' and 'it is not the case', respectively, and of *duì* and *bu duì* as 'that's right' and 'that's not right', respectively, we can also understand how these answers are used in response to *negative* particle questions.[5] Needless to say, since an A-not-A question presents a neutral choice between an affirmative and its negative counterpart, the only way to express a negative question is with a question particle. As in English, negative questions are generally used when the situation causes us to question an earlier assumption. For example, if A knew that B goes to class every day at 9 A.M. and one morning finds B heading for the beach at that hour, s/he would say:

(168)   nǐ   bu   shàng   —   kè   ma ?
         you   not   ascend   —   class   Q

Aren't you going to class (i.e., I had assumed you would, since you generally do)?

To such a negative question, the affirmative responses in (172) *a* and *b* both affirm that 'it is the case' or 'it is right' that B is *not* going to class:

(169) *a*.   shì   (de)
              be   NOM

It is the case.

  b. duì
    right

  That's right.

The negative responses in (170) *a* and *b*, on the other hand, would say that 'it is *not* the case' or 'it is *not* right' that B is not going to class.

(170) *a.* bu shì (de)
     not be NOM

    It's not the case.

  b. bu duì
     not right

  That's not right.

In other words, in Mandarin, the answer to a particle question affirms or denies the statement to which the *ma* is added, regardless of whether that statement itself is affirmative or negative.

Notes

1. This section is adapted from Li and Thompson (1979*b*).
2. The nonneutrality of particle questions is mentioned by Chao (1968:800), Hashimoto (1971*a*:16), and Rygaloff (1973:54).
3. This point is due to Rygaloff (1973:54)
4. See also the discussion of negative questions in section 7 of this chapter.
5. This discussion is adapted from Chao (1968) and Elliott (1965).

CHAPTER 19

Comparison

19.1 Comparative Constructions

Comparative sentences in any language always involve comparing two things along some dimension. There are three types of relationships these two compared items can have to each other. With respect to the dimension along which they are being compared, one compared thing can be (1) *more* than the other (superiority); (2) *less* than the other (inferiority); or (3) the *same* as the other (equality). The basic pattern for all of these three sentence types in Mandarin is this:

(1)   X   comparison word   Y   (adverb)   dimension

What this formula says is that to express a comparative message in Mandarin, one must state the subject or topic (X), the item to which that subject or topic is compared (Y), and the predicate, which names the dimension along which the comparison is being made. The comparison morphemes for each of the three kinds of comparison are, first, *superiority: bǐ* (literally 'compare with'), as in (2):

(2)   tā   bǐ   nǐ   gāo
       3sg   compare   you   tall

        S/He is taller than you are.

second, *inferiority: méi(yǒu)* ('not') . . . *(nème)*, *bùrú* (literally 'not as') . . . *(nème)*, as in (3):

(3) tā $\begin{Bmatrix} \underline{méi(yǒu)} \\ bùrú \end{Bmatrix}$ nǐ (<u>nème</u>) gāo

    3sg $\begin{Bmatrix} not \\ not{:}as \end{Bmatrix}$ you (that) tall

S/He is not as tall as you are.

and, third, *equality: gēn* . . . *yíyàng* (literally 'with . . . same'), as in (4):

(4) tā <u>gēn</u> nǐ <u>yíyàng</u> gāo
    3sg with you same tall

S/He is as tall as you are.

Here are some examples illustrating various types of elements that can be compared: in (5)−(14) below, we will not gloss the comparison morphemes.

(5) tā $\begin{Bmatrix} bǐ \\ méi(yǒu)/bùrú \\ gēn \end{Bmatrix}$ nǐ $\begin{Bmatrix} (nème) \\ yíyàng \end{Bmatrix}$ dǎnxiǎo

    3sg you timid

S/He is $\begin{Bmatrix} \text{more timid than} \\ \text{not as timid as} \\ \text{as timid as} \end{Bmatrix}$ you are.

(6) tā $\begin{Bmatrix} bǐ \\ méi(yǒu)/bùrú \\ gēn \end{Bmatrix}$ nǐ $\begin{Bmatrix} (nème) \\ yíyàng \end{Bmatrix}$ xǐhuān Zhāngsān

    3sg you like Zhangsan

S/He $\begin{Bmatrix} \text{likes} \\ \text{doesn't like} \\ \text{likes} \end{Bmatrix}$ Zhangsan $\begin{Bmatrix} \text{more than} \\ \text{as much as} \\ \text{as much as} \end{Bmatrix}$ you do.

(7)   tā ⎰bǐ   ⎱   wǒ⎰   ⎱   zǎo   lái
         ⎨ méi(yǒu)/bùrú ⎬   ⎨ (nème) ⎬
         ⎩ gēn   ⎭   ⎩ yíyàng ⎭

      3sg   I   early   come

      S/He ⎰ arrived earlier than   ⎱   I did.
            ⎨ didn't arrive as early as ⎬
            ⎩ arrived as early as   ⎭

(8)   qù   ⎰ bǐ   ⎱   bu   qù   ⎰   ⎱   hǎo
            ⎨ méi(yǒu)/bùrú ⎬   ⎨ (nème) ⎬
            ⎩ gēn   ⎭   ⎩ yíyàng ⎭

      go   not   go   good

      Going is ⎰ better than   ⎱   not going.
               ⎨ not as good as ⎬
               ⎩ as good as   ⎭

(9) Zhāngsān   pǎo   de   ⎰ bǐ   ⎱   nǐ
                                ⎨ méi(yǒu)/bùrú ⎬
                                ⎩ gēn   ⎭

    Zhangsan   run   CSC   you

               (pǎo   de)   ⎰   ⎱   kuài
                              ⎨ (nème) ⎬
                              ⎩ yíyàng ⎭

               (run   CSC)   fast

    Zhangsan ⎰ runs faster than   ⎱   you do.
             ⎨ doesn't run as fast as ⎬
             ⎩ runs as fast as   ⎭

(10) wǒ   ⎰ bǐ   ⎱   zuótiān   ⎰   ⎱   shūfu
           ⎨ méi(yǒu)/bùrú ⎬   ⎨ (nème) ⎬
           ⎩ gēn   ⎭   ⎩ yíyàng ⎭

      I   yesterday   comfortable

I $\left\{\begin{array}{l}\text{feel better than} \\ \text{don't feel as good as} \\ \text{feel as good as}\end{array}\right\}$ (I did) yesterday.

(11)   tā $\left\{\begin{array}{l}\text{bǐ} \\ \text{méi(yǒu)/bùrú} \\ \text{gēn}\end{array}\right\}$ wǒ $\left\{\begin{array}{l}\text{(nème)} \\ \text{yíyàng}\end{array}\right\}$ wǎn

        3sg   I   late

                    chī   —   fàn

                    eat   —   food

        S/He eats $\left\{\begin{array}{l}\text{later than} \\ \text{not as late as} \\ \text{as late as}\end{array}\right\}$ I do.

(12)   xiàng $\left\{\begin{array}{l}\text{bǐ} \\ \text{méi(yǒu)/bùrú} \\ \text{gēn}\end{array}\right\}$ xióng bízi $\left\{\begin{array}{l}\text{(nème)} \\ \text{yíyàng}\end{array}\right\}$ cháng

        elephant   bear   nose   long

        Elephants $\left\{\begin{array}{l}\text{have longer noses than} \\ \text{don't have noses as long as (those of)} \\ \text{have noses as long as (those of)}\end{array}\right\}$ bears.

(13)   jīntiān $\left\{\begin{array}{l}\text{bǐ} \\ \text{méi(yǒu)/bùrú} \\ \text{gēn}\end{array}\right\}$ zuótiān $\left\{\begin{array}{l}\text{(nème)} \\ \text{yíyàng}\end{array}\right\}$ rè

        today   yesterday   hot

        Today is $\left\{\begin{array}{l}\text{hotter than} \\ \text{not as hot as} \\ \text{as hot as}\end{array}\right\}$ yesterday.

(14)   bàozhi   Xìnměi $\left\{\begin{array}{l} \text{bǐ} \\ \text{méi(yǒu)/bùrú} \\ \text{gēn} \end{array}\right\}$ wǒ   niàn

       newspaper Xinmei   I   read

              de $\left\{\begin{array}{l} \text{(nème)} \\ \text{yíyàng} \end{array}\right\}$ kuài

              CSC   fast

The newspaper, Xinmei reads $\left\{\begin{array}{l} \text{faster than} \\ \text{not as fast as} \\ \text{as fast as} \end{array}\right\}$ I do.

With comparison of superiority, to express the amount by which one entity exceeds the other, one places a phrase after the verb that conveys a measurable notion, as in:

(15)   wǒ   bǐ   nǐ   gāo   sān   cùn
        I   COMP   you   tall   three   inch

I am three inches taller than you are.

We can explain certain differences between Mandarin and English comparatives in terms of two important features of the comparative construction.

19.1.1 Dimension

The verb phrase that signals the dimension along which the two items are being compared must be capable of being quantified or measured. In other words, the verb phrase must be one of which we can ask, "To what extent?" This means that exactly those verbs that can occur with *hěn* 'very' can occur in verb phrases expressing dimension in a comparative construction. These include (1) Non-activity verbs, of which there are two types: (*a*) transitive—for instance, *xǐhuān* 'like', *ài* 'love', *hèn* 'hate' (see sentence [3]), and (*b*) intransitive—such as *hǎo* 'good', *shūfu* 'feel good' (see sentences [5], [7]); and (2) verb phrases containing measurable adverbs, such as *zǎo* 'early', *wǎn* 'late', *cháng* 'often' (see sentences [4], [8]). Just as it is semantically unacceptable to use *hěn* with an action verb, such as *pǎo-guò-lái* 'run over here', then, it is semantically unacceptable for such a verb to occur in a comparative construction:

(16) *tā   hěn   pǎo   —   guò   —   lái
   3sg   very   run   —   cross   —   come

(17) *tā   bǐ   wǒ   pǎo   —   guò   —   lái
   3sg   COMP   I   run   —   cross   —   come

Similarly, since one cannot be at home to a certain extent, a nonactivity predicate, such as *zài jiā* 'be at home', can neither be modified by *hěn* nor appear in a comparative construction:

(18) *tā   hěn   zài   jiā
   3sg   very   at   home

(19) *tā   bǐ   wǒ   zài   jiā
   3sg   COMP   I   at   home

19.1.2 Subject/Topic and the Standard of Comparison

The second important feature of comparative constructions has to do with the nature of X and Y in formula (1), which is repeated here:

(1)   X   comparison word   Y   (adverb)   dimension

The generalization about X and Y is that X must be the subject or the topic (see section 4.1 of chapter 4) of the verb phrase that expresses the dimension, and Y must be understood as the standard of comparison.

This generalization has several implications. First, nothing but subjects and topics can be compared. Thus, for example, direct objects cannot be compared at all, since, no matter where the direct object is placed, the sentence will not fit the formula. Thus, to express 'I like dogs better than cats', none of these sentences is acceptable:

(20) *a.*   *wǒ   xǐhuān   gǒu   bǐ   māo
    I   like   dog   COMP   cat

   b.   *wǒ   gǒu   bǐ   māo   xǐhuān
    I   dog   COMP   cat   like

c.	*gǒu	bǐ	māo	wǒ	xǐhuān
	dog	COMP	cat	I	like

The idea, to be expressible, must be stated in such a way that it conforms to the conditions given above. We can do this by comparing 'my liking of dogs' to 'my liking of cats' along the dimension *duō* 'much' with a complex stative construction (see chapter 22):

(21)	wǒ	xǐhuān	gǒu	bǐ	wǒ	xǐhuān	māo	xǐhuān
	I	like	dog	COMP	I	like	cat	like

	de	duō
	CSC	much

I like dogs better than cats.

Similarly, coverb phrases cannot be compared. Again, a sentence comparing such phrases is not acceptable:

(22)	*wǒ	xǐhuān	zài	chízi	—	li	bǐ	zài
	I	like	at	pool	—	in	COMP	at

	hǎi	—	li	yóuyǒng
	ocean	—	in	swim

(I like to swim in the pool more than in the ocean.)

This sentence is unacceptable because the compared phrase *zài chízí-lǐ* 'in the pool' is not the subject, and *yóuyǒng* 'swim' is not the verb for the compared phrase. Again, a complex stative construction, as given in (23), is needed to express in Mandarin the idea 'I like to swim in the pool more than in the ocean':

(23)	wǒ	xǐhuān	zài	chízi	—	li	yóuyǒng	bǐ
	I	like	at	pool	—	in	swim	COMP

	wǒ	xǐhuān	zài	hǎi	—	li	yóuyǒng
	I	like	at	ocean	—	in	swim

	xǐhuān	de	duō
	like	CSC	much

I like to swim in the pool more than in the ocean.

The grammatical generalization for the structure of comparative sentences, then, is:

(i) What is being compared in Mandarin must be stated grammatically in terms of the subject or the topic, and the verb phrase must characterize the dimension along which the comparison is being made.

Sometimes the comparative relationship between the terms X and Y is not directly specified, but must be inferred. For example, in the sentence

(24) wǒ   bǐ   zuótiān   shūfu
     I   COMP   yesterday comfortable

I feel better than I did yesterday.

where X is *wǒ* 'I' and Y is *zuótiān* 'yesterday', although *wǒ* 'I' is the subject of the verb *shūfu* 'feel good', we are of course not directly comparing *wǒ* 'I' and *zuótiān* 'yesterday'. Rather, what we understand from this sentence is that 'I today' am feeling better than 'I yesterday'. That is, speakers of Mandarin must sometimes infer what makes sense from a comparative sentence in which X and Y are not directly comparable. This kind of inferring is typical of everyday communication in any language.

A similar example requiring one to infer what is being compared is a sentence such as (9) above. If that sentence occurs with *bǐ* 'compare' and without the second occurrence of *pǎo de* in parentheses, it looks like this:

(25) Zhāngsān   pǎo   de   bǐ   nǐ   kuài
     Zhangsan   run   CSC   COMP   you   fast

Zhangsan runs faster than you do.

In (25), X is *Zhāngsān pǎo de* 'Zhangsan running' and Y is *nǐ* 'you'. Once again, though, a speaker of Mandarin would understand that sentence (25) is not comparing 'Zhangsan running' with 'you', but comparing 'Zhangsan running' with 'you *running*'. This second *pǎo de* 'running' after *nǐ* simply does not have to be explicitly mentioned in the sentence, although it may be, as sentence (9) illustrates.

19.2 Superlative

The superlative of a measurable verb phrase is expressed by the adverb *zuì* 'most' placed immediately before the verb or the measurable adverb of the verb phrase. If the measurable verb phrase is composed of an adjectival verb, *dǐng*

'most' may be used in place of *zuì*. Sentences (26)–(33) provide some examples
of the superlative:

(26) zhèi   —   tiáo   wéijīn   <u>zuì</u>   <u>hǎo</u>
      this   —   CL   scarf   most   good

This scarf is the best.

(27) nèi   —   ge   xióng   <u>dǐng</u>   <u>piàoliàng</u>
      that   —   CL   bear   most   pretty

That bear is the prettiest.

(28) zhèi   —   jiàn   shì   <u>zuì</u>   <u>máfan</u>
      this   —   CL   matter   most   troublesome

This matter is the most troublesome.

(29) jīntiān   <u>dǐng</u>   <u>lěng</u>
      today   most   cold

Today is the coldest.

(30) wǒ   <u>zuì</u>   <u>ài</u>   xiǎo   dòngwu
      I   most   love   small   animal

I love small animals the most.

(31) wǒ   <u>zuì</u>   <u>xīnshǎng</u>   gējù
      I   most   appreciate   opera

I appreciate operas the most.

(32) tā   <u>zuì</u>   <u>wǎn</u>   qǐ   —   chuáng
      3sg   most   late   rise   —   bed

S/He is the latest to get out of bed.

(33)　nǐ　　zuì　　zǎo　　xué　　Zhōngwén
　　　you　　most　　early　　learn　　Chinese

You are the first to learn Chinese.

The verbs in (26)–(29) are all adjectival verbs. They can occur with either *zuì* or *dǐng*. The verb phrases of (30) and (31) contain transitive nonactivity verbs, and the verbs in (32) and (33) are modified by measurable adverbs. For verb phrases such as those in (30)–(33), *zuì* is preferable to *dǐng*. In certain Mandarin dialects, however, *zuì* and *dǐng* are interchangeable, even in those verb phrases.

Just as in English, *zuì* can be used together with *yi* 'one' plus a classifier with the nonabsolute meaning 'a most':

(34)　tā　　shì　　yi　　　—　　ge　　zuì　　zhòngyào
　　　3sg　　be　　one　　—　　CL　　most　　important

　　　de　　lǐngdào　rényuán
　　　NOM　　lead　　personnel

S/He is a most important leader.

(35)　zhèi　　shì　　yi　　　—　　jiàn　　zuì　　tóu　　—
　　　this　　be　　one　　—　　CL　　most　　head　　—

　　　téng　　de　　shì
　　　hurt　　NOM　　matter

This is a most headache-causing matter.

It is important to note that (34) and (35) do not convey the messages of (36) and (37):

(36) S/He is one of the most important leaders.

(37) This is one of the most headache-causing matters.

The sentences that directly express (36) and (37) are given below:

(38)	tā	shì	zuì	zhòngyào	de	lǐngdào
	3sg	be	most	important	NOM	lead

	rényuán	zhǐyī
	personnel	one:of

S/He is one of the most important leaders.

(39)	zhèi	shì	zuì	tóu	—	téng
	this	be	most	head	—	hurt

	de	shì	zhǐyī
	NOM	matter	one:of

This is one of the most headache-causing matters.

CHAPTER 20

Nominalization

Every language has grammatical processes by which a verb, a verb phrase, a sentence, or a portion of a sentence including the verb can function as a noun phrase. These grammatical processes are called *nominalization*. Different languages, of course, may employ different strategies for nominalization. In Mandarin, nominalization involves placing the particle *de* after a verb, a verb phrase, a sentence, or a portion of a sentence including the verb.[1] In examples (1)–(3), the nominalization has been underlined:

(1)   zhèi   zhǒng   zhíwù   kěyǐ   dāng   –   zuò
          this   type   plant   can   take   –   be

                      chī   de
                      eat   NOM

      (One) can take this type of plant as food.

(2)   zhòng   shuǐguò   de   hěn   nán   guòhuó
          grow   fruit   NOM   very   difficult   make:living

      It is difficult for fruit growers to make a living.[2]

(3)   wǒmen   hézuò   de   wèntí   hěn   jiǎndān
          we   cooperate   NOM   problem   very   simple

      The problem concerning our cooperation is very simple.

In sentence (1), the verb, *chī* 'eat', is nominalized; in (2) what is nominalized is the verb phrase, *zhòng shuǐguǒ* 'grow fruit'; and in (3) a sentence, *wǒmen hézuò* 'we cooperate', is nominalized. Notice that in (3), the nominalized sentence, *wǒmen hézuò de*, immediately precedes the noun, *wèntí* 'problem'. The relation between the nominalized sentence and the following noun can be described as one of *modifier head noun*, where the head noun is *wèntí* 'problem' and the nominalized sentence serves as a modifier. Thus, as (1)–(3) illustrate, a nominalization can function either as a noun phrase ([1], [2]) or as a modifier of another noun ([3]). In the following sections, we will consider both of these functions, as well as a third one: the use of a nominalization after the copula verb *shi* (the *shi . . . de* construction).

20.1 A Nominalization Functioning as a Noun Phrase

Sentences (1) and (2) above provide examples of nominalizations functioning as noun phrases. Let us add to these two examples sentence (4):

(4)   nǐ   méi   yǒu   <u>wǒ   xǐhuān   de</u>
         you   not   exist   I   like   NOM

You don't have what I like.

What is nominalized in (4) is neither a verb phrase nor a sentence, but a part of a sentence consisting of a subject, *wǒ* 'I', and a transitive verb, *xǐhuān* 'like'. The direct object of the transitive verb, *xǐhuān*, is absent. Now, how do we know that the nominalized verb *chī de* 'eat NOM' in (1) should be interpreted as 'food (what is for eating)', but not as 'the one who eats'? How do we determine that the meaning of *zhòng shuǐguǒ de* 'grow fruit NOM' in (2) is 'fruit grower' and that the meaning of *wǒ xǐhuān de* 'I like NOM' in (4) is 'what I like'?

Let us lead up to a general answer to this question by again considering examples (2) and (4). The verb of the nominalized verb phrase in (2) is *zhòng* 'grow, plant'. *Zhòng* is a transitive verb, which means that it is always understood in terms of two participants, either overtly specified or else understood; in this case, the two participants are a subject, someone who does the planting, and a direct object, that which is planted. In the nominalization in (2), we see that the direct object is specified as *shuǐguǒ* 'fruit', but that the subject, who is doing the planting, is not specified. And now we notice that the interpretation of the nominalized verb phrase is precisely 'the fruit growers', that is, the ones who do the planting.

Similarly, in (4), the nominalized verb, *xǐhuān* 'like', is also a transitive verb whose meaning again includes two participants: someone who does the liking and what is liked. In the nominalized phrase in (4), however, the one who does the liking is specified (*wǒ* 'I'), but what is liked is not, and here the nominalized phrase *wǒ xǐhuān de* 'I like NOM' refers to what is liked.

With this analysis of the interpretation of these nominalizations, a pattern begins to emerge, which we can express in (i) and (ii):

(i) To be used alone as a noun phrase, a nominalization must contain a verb with at least one of its participants unspecified.

(ii) If there is only one participant unspecified, then the referent of the nominalization is the same as that of the missing participant.

The generalization provided in (i) and (ii), however, does not account for the meaning of the nominalized verb in (1). Here is sentence (1) again:

(1) | zhèi | zhǒng | zhíwù | kěyǐ | dāng | — | zuò |
     | this | type | plant | can | take | — | be |

chī	de
eat	NOM

(One) can take this type of plant as food.

Like *zhòng* 'plant' and *xǐhuān* 'like', the nominalized verb in (1), *chī* 'eat', is also a transitive verb, which implies that its meaning requires two participants—a subject, the one who does the eating, and a direct object, what it is that is eaten. This time, however, both participants are unspecified. The nominalized verb, *chī de* 'eat NOM', however, has the meaning 'food = what is to be eaten', and not 'the eaters'. This example suggests that a supplement to the generalizations (i) and (ii) is needed. The supplemental rule is stated in (iii):

(iii) If both the subject and direct object participants are unspecified in a nominalization, then that nominalization will generally be understood to have the same referent as the unspecified *direct object* participant of that verb.

In (1), then, the unspecified direct object participant of the verb *chī* 'eat' is 'what is eaten', and the nominalization *chī de* 'eat NOM' refers to that participant.

We can extend our consideration of generalizations (i)–(iii) to verbs that not only have subject and direct object participants but also inherently have indirect object participants as well (see chapter 10 for a discussion of indirect objects). For example, the meaning of the verb *mài* 'sell' requires the existence of three participants, either overtly specified or understood: the seller, the buyer, and the entity for sale. The simple sentence (5) serves as an illustration:

(5) Zhāngsān   mài   —   le   yi   —   jià
    Zhangsan   sell   —   PFV   one   —   CL

        fēijī   gěi   Lǐsì
        airplane   to   Lisi

    Zhangsan sold an airplane to Lisi.

In (5), *Zhāngsān*, the subject noun phrase, is the seller; *Lǐsì*, the indirect object noun phrase, is the buyer; and *fēijī* 'airplane', the direct object noun phrase, represents the entity for sale. Often the buyer is unspecified in a simple sentence involving the verb *mài* 'sell'. When the buyer is unspecified, it is either because the speaker and the hearer already know who the buyer is or because the speaker does not think that specifying the buyer is important. In other words, when the buyer is unspecified in a simple sentence, it is a matter of communicative strategy.

Having established that the verb *mài* 'sell' inherently has three participants, we will now consider various nominalizations involving *mài* as the verb:

(6)   mài   de   bù   rú   chū   —   zū   de   hǎo
       sell   NOM   not   as   exit   —   rent   NOM   good

    What is for sale is not as good as what is for rent.

(7)   wǒ   mài   de   shì   Zhōngguó   huò
       I   sell   NOM   be   China   product

    What I sell is Chinese merchandise.

(8)   mài   gěi   Lǐsì   de   shì   zuì   guì   de
       sell   to   Lisi   NOM   be   most   expensive   NOM

    What is sold to Lisi is the most expensive.

(9)   mài   qìchē   de   dàbàn   dōu   shì   hǎo   rén
       sell   car   NOM   majority   all   be   good   person

    Car sellers are mostly good people.

The principle given in (iii), that nominalizations with an unspecified direct object generally refer to the referent of that direct object, correctly accounts for the interpretation of sentence (8): the nominalization in (8) refers to what is sold. In (9), on the other hand, the direct object participant, *qìchē* 'car', is specified, but the subject—the seller—and the indirect object—the buyer—are unspecified. In this case, the nominalization refers to the seller, that is, the subject participant, but it cannot refer to the buyer, the indirect object participant. In sentence (7), both the direct object and the indirect object are unspecified, and in sentence (6), all three participants, the subject, the direct object, and the indirect object, are unspecified. Nevertheless the nominalizations in (6) and (7) refer to the direct object, namely, what is sold. It turns out, then, that the rule we need to supply in addition to (iii) in order to account for sentences (6), (7), and (9) is simply this:

(iv) A nominalization used alone as a noun phrase never refers to the indirect object participant.

The nominalization in (10) illustrates rule (iv): (10) is ungrammatical because the only unspecified participant of the verb in the nominalization is the indirect object.

(10)	*wǒ	mài	qìchē	de
	I	sell	car	NOM

Structurally, then, a nominalization functioning as a noun phrase consists of a portion of a sentence including the verb, followed by the particle *de*, where one of the participants normally associated with that verb is missing. The interpretation of the nominalization is governed by principles (i)−(iii), specifying to which of the missing participants the nominalization is understood to refer.

20.2 Nominalizations Modifying a Head Noun

A nominalization can also serve to modify a following noun; in such a construction the noun being modified is called the *head noun*. There are two types of constructions involving a nominalization modifying a head noun. Both have the form *nominalization + head noun*. One can be called a relative clause construction, while the other involves a complement to an abstract head noun.[3] We will discuss each of them separately.

20.2.1 Relative Clause Constructions

A *relative clause* in any language is a clause that restricts the reference of the head noun. A nominalization can be called a relative clause if the head noun that it modifies refers to some unspecified participant in the situation named by the nominalization.[4]

For example, if we take the nominalization in sentence (2), *zhòng shuǐguǒ de* 'grow fruit NOM', and place it in front of the head noun *nóngrén* 'farmers', we have the construction shown in (11):

(11)   zhòng   shuǐguǒ   de   nóngrén
         grow   fruit   NOM   farmer

         ⌣‾‾‾‾‾‾‾‾‾‾‾‾‾‾‾‾‾‾‾‾‾‾‾‾‾‾‾⌣   ‾‾‾‾⌣‾‾‾‾
         nominalization = relative clause   head noun

        (the) farmer(s) who grow fruit

In this expression, the head noun *nóngrén* 'farmer' refers to the unspecified subject participant of *zhòng* 'grow' in the nominalization, the one who does the growing. From now on, we will refer to a nominalization as a relative clause if its head noun refers to some participant in the event it describes.

The way in which the relative clause restricts the meaning of the head noun, as we just pointed out above, is that the head noun must be understood to refer to some participant of the verb in the nominalization. For example, consider (11) again. The nominalization in (11) is *zhòng shuǐguǒ de* 'grow fruit NOM'. Now *zhòng* 'grow' is a transitive verb; in this nominalization its direct object participant, *shuǐguǒ* 'fruit', is present, but its subject participant, that is, who it is that grows the fruit, is missing. Accordingly, the head noun *nóngrén* refers to this missing subject participant, so that 'the farmers' refers to the ones who grow fruit; the whole construction means 'the farmers who grow fruit'.

This example is similar:

(12)   tāmen   zhòng   de   shuǐguǒ
         they   grow   NOM   fruit

        the fruit that they grow

In (12), the nominalization is *tāmen zhòng de* 'they grow NOM'. This time, the subject participant is present (*tāmen* 'they'), but the direct object participant, namely, what it is that is grown, is missing, which means that the direct object participant is that participant to which the head noun *shuǐguǒ* 'fruit' refers. That is, the 'fruit' refers to 'what they grow' in the nominalization, giving 'the fruit that they grow' for the meaning of (12).

Now, though, let's suppose that the relative clause contains a verb with more than one unspecified participant. In such a case, the interpretation depends on what the head noun is. Consider a nominalization such as *pīping de* 'criticize NOM', which consists of the transitive verb *pīping* 'criticize', whose meaning requires two participants, one who gives the criticism, and one who receives it. Since under normal circumstances both of these participants must be human, if a relative clause contains a verb such as *pīping* 'criticize' with neither of its participants specified, and this clause modifies a head noun referring to a human being, such as *rén* 'person', the head noun could refer to *either* of these two participants; in other words, it would be ambiguous, as shown in (13):

(13) | zuótiān | pīping | de | rén | dōu |
      |---------|--------|-----|-----|-----|
      | yesterday | criticize | NOM | person | all |

	bu	zài	zhèlǐ
	not	at	here

{ The people who criticized (others) yesterday are all not here.
{ The people whom (others) criticized yesterday are all not here. }

Now consider another transitive verb, *yíng* 'win (in an argument or a bet)'. This time, the meaning of the verb requires a subject participant who must be human, the one who wins, and a direct object participant that is normally inanimate, such as *qián* 'money'.

Now, if *yíng* occurs in a relative clause with both of these participants unspecified, the semantic properties of the head noun will determine the interpretation of the construction *relative clause + head noun*. Let's look at examples (14) and (15):

(14) | jīntiān | yíng | de | qián | fù | fáng | — | zū |
      |---------|------|-----|------|-----|------|---|-----|
      | today | win | NOM | money | pay | house | — | rent |

The money (we) won today goes to pay the rent.

(15) | jīntiān | yíng | de | rén | yùnqì | hǎo |
      |---------|------|-----|-----|-------|------|
      | today | win | NOM | person | luck | good |

The people who won today had good luck.

In (14), the head noun, *qián* 'money', cannot refer to the missing subject participant, 'the ones who won', since 'money' can't do the winning; it can, however, refer to 'what was won'. The result is the meaning 'the money that (we) won today' for the relative-clause-plus-head-noun construction. In (15), on the other hand, the meaning of the head noun, *rén* 'people', allows it to refer to 'the ones who won'; hence the relative-clause-plus-head-noun construction in (15) would normally be interpreted as 'the people who won today'. Imagine, though, a circumstance in which the stakes at a gambling event are people. In such a context, sentence (15) would be, like (13), ambiguous, its other interpretation being 'The people whom (we) won today had good luck'.

So far we have been considering relative clauses in which either the subject or the direct object participant is missing from the nominalization. It is quite possible, however, for the head noun to refer to some other participant involved in the situation named by the relative clause, such as an instrument used, the location or time at which the event happened, or even the reason for which or the method by which it occurred. Here are some examples.

(i) Instrument:

(16)   xiūlǐ   shuǐ   —   guǎnzi   de   <u>jùzi</u>
        repair   water   —   pipe   NOM   saw

the saw with which to repair the water pipe

(17)   wǒ   xiě   xìn   de   <u>máobǐ</u>
        I   write   letter   NOM   brush:pen

the brush pen I write letters with

(ii) Location:

(18)   Zhāngsān   huà   huàr   de   <u>fángjiān</u>
        Zhangsan   paint   painting NOM   room

the room where Zhangsan does his painting

(19)   dēngshān   duì   pá   Xǐmǎlāyǎ
        mountaineering   team   climb   Himalaya

                            shān   de   <u>lùxiàn</u>
                            mountain NOM   path

the path by which the mountaineering team climbed the Himalayas

(iii) Time:

(20)	liàn	zúqiú	de	jìjié
	practice	soccer	NOM	season

the season when one practices soccer

(21)	wǒmen	xiǎo	de	shíhou
	we	small	NOM	time

the time when we were small (young)

(iv) Reason:

(22)	wǒ	lái	zhèr	de	yuángù
	I	come	here	NOM	reason

the reason why I came here.

(v) Method:

(23)	páshǒu	tōu	dōngxī	de	fāngfǎ
	pickpocket	steal	thing	NOM	method

the method by which pickpockets steal things

(24)	wǒmen	duìfu	Sūlián	de	shǒuduàn
	we	deal:with	Soviet:Union	NOM	tactic

the tactics that we use in dealing with the Soviet Union

In each of the above examples, the head noun refers to something in the nominalization. In (16), for instance, the head noun *jùzi* 'saw' refers to what one uses to repair the pipe with, while in (24), the head noun *shǒuduàn* 'tactic' refers to what we use to deal with the Soviet Union. Similarly, *fángjiān* in (18) refers to where Zhangsan paints.

In certain positions in the relative clause, a participant may not be unspecified, but must be represented by one of the pronouns in (25) in order for the head noun to refer to it.

(25) tā 'she, he, it'
      tāmen 'they'
      nàr/nàli 'there'

The positions where a pronoun must occur in a relative clause are given below.
  (i) Indirect object position:

(26)   wǒ   sòng   gěi   *(tā)   yi   —
        I   give   to   3sg   one   —

        běn   xiǎoshuō   de   rén
        CL   novel   NOM   person

    the person to whom I gave a novel.

(27)   wǒ   wèn   —   le   *(tāmen)   liǎng
        I   ask   —   PFV   they   two

        —   ge   wèntí   de   xuéshēng
        —   CL   question NOM   students

    the students of whom I asked two questions

 (ii) Following a coverb:

(28)   nǐ   bǎ   *(tā)   dài   —   chū
        you   BA   3sg   bring   —   exit

        —   lái   de   háizi
        —   come   NOM   child

    the child you brought out

(29)   wǒ   gēn   *(tāmen)   dǎ   —   qiú
        I   with   they   play   —   ball

        de   yùndòng   —   yuán
        NOM   exercise   —   person

    the athletes with whom I play ball

(iii) The pivotal noun phrase position (see chapter 21):

(30) nǐ   qǐng   *(tā)   hē   jiǔ   de   jiàoshòu
      you   invite 3sg   drink   liquor   NOM   professor

the professor whom you invited to drink

(31) wǒ   quàn   *(tā)   chū   —
      I   advise 3sg   exit   —

      guó   de   cānyìyuán
      country NOM   congressperson

the congressperson whom I advised to leave the country.

(iv) The locative noun phrase position after *zài*:

(32) Zhāngsān   zài   *(nàr)   zhǎng   —
      Zhangsan   at   there   grow   —

      dà   de   cūnzi
      big   NOM   village

the village where Zhangsan grew up

The relative clauses illustrated by (26)–(32) are marginal constructions in that they are rarely found in either speech or writing. Although they are not unacceptable, they appear awkward to many speakers of Mandarin.

To sum up our discussion of the relative clause, we observe that a relative clause construction always consists of a nominalization, and it always modifies a head noun by virtue of the fact that the head noun refers to some entity involved in the situation that is described by the relative clause.

20.2.2 A Nominalization Serving as the Complement to an Abstract Head Noun

In sharp contrast to the relative clause constructions we have just been considering, the most important characteristic of this noun complement construction is that the head noun is always abstract and does not refer to *any* entity, specified or unspecified, in the modifying clause. We have seen one example in sentence (3).

Here is (3) again, followed by some further examples of head nouns and their complements, with the head noun underlined:

(3)	wǒmen	hézuò	de	w<u>ènti</u>	hěn	jiǎndān
	we	cooperate	NOM	problem	very	simple

The problem concerning our cooperation is very simple.

(33)	tāmen	qù	Měiguó	xué	yī
	they	go	America	study	medicine

	de	<u>yìjiàn</u>
	NOM	opinion

the opinion that they should go to America to study medicine.

(34)	wǒmen	xiū	–	huì	de	<u>tíyì</u>
	we	adjourn	–	meeting	NOM	motion

the motion that we adjourn the meeting

(35)	wǒmen	zū	fángzi	de	<u>shì</u>
	we	rent	house	NOM	matter

the matter concerning our renting a house

(36)	Měiguó	zǒngtǒng	cízhí	de	<u>xīnwén</u>
	America	president	resign	NOM	news

the news that the president of the United States has resigned

In all these examples, the head noun is abstract and does not refer to any entity in the preceding nominalization. Rather, the nominalization modifies the head noun by specifying its "content." Thus, in (3), for example, the "content" of the problem is our cooperation.

The difference between the relative clause construction and the noun complement construction, then, is that in the former the head noun refers to something in the preceding nominalization, while in the latter it does not. In terms of this difference we can show how the two apparently similar constructions can be understood quite differently.

Let's illustrate with a pair of contrasting examples whose head noun is the same abstract noun, *yìjiàn* 'opinion':

(37) wǒ   tí   —   chū   —   lái   de   <u>yìjiàn</u>
      I   raise —   exit —   come NOM opinion

the opinion that I put forth

(38) fǎn   É   de   <u>yìjiàn</u>
      oppose   Russia NOM   opinion

the opinion that (we/someone) should oppose Russia

The phrase in (37) is a relative clause construction. The head noun *yìjiàn* 'opinion' refers to the unspecified direct object participant of *tí-chū-lái* 'put forth', in the preceding nominalization, namely, 'what I put forth'. The phrase in (38), on the other hand, is a noun complement construction. Here the head noun refers to nothing in the preceding nominalization. Instead, that nominalization names the content of the opinion, namely, that we/someone should oppose Russia.

20.3 The *shì* . . . *de* Construction

The *shì* . . . *de* construction is a special sentence type in which a nominalization is used. Structurally, it consists of a subject followed by the copula verb *shì* 'be' followed by a nominalization, as schematized in (39):

(39) subject   <u>shì</u>   nominalization[5]

Sentences such as (40) and (41) are examples:

(40) tā   shì   zuótiān   lái   de
      3sg   be   yesterday   come   NOM

The situation is that s/he came yesterday.[6]

(41) wǒmen   shì   cóng   Rìběn   zǒu   de
      we   be   from   Japan   go   NOM

The situation is that we left from Japan.

There are several features of this construction which set it apart from other sentences that superficially have the form of (39), such as (42):

(42)   bālā   shì   chī   —   de
        guava   be   eat   —   NOM

        Guavas are {to be eaten.}
                   {for eating. }

First, in a *shì . . . de* construction, the subject of the sentence must be the same as the missing subject participant in the nominalization. Thus, in (40), *tā* 's/he' is the same as the subject of *zuótiān lái de* 'yesterday came NOM', namely, the one who came yesterday'.

Second, the *shì . . . de* construction contains an adverbial word or phrase or an auxiliary verb giving the circumstances of the event in the nominalization. In (40), for example, *zuótiān* 'yesterday' names the temporal circumstances of the event in the nominalization.

Third, the *shì* 'be' in this type of construction can always be omitted—so sentence (43), without the *shì*, is an alternate form of (40) above:

(43)   tā   zuótiān   lái   de
        3sg   yesterday   come   NOM

        The situation is that s/he came yesterday.

Because the *shì* 'be' can always be omitted, from this point on we will put it in parentheses to indicate that it is optional.

Fourth, when a direct object occurs in the nominalization of the *shì . . . de* construction, an interesting reversal can take place: a sentence of the form

(44)   noun phrase   shì 'be'   verb   direct object   de

can occur with the direct object and the *de* in the opposite order:

(45)   noun phrase   shì 'be'   verb   de   direct object

For example, a sentence such as

(46) *a.*	tāmen	(shì)	bā	—	diǎnzhōng
	they	be	eight	—	o'clock

	kāi	<u>mén</u>	<u>de</u>
	open	door	NOM

The situation is that they opened at eight o'clock.

where the *de* follows the object, *mén* 'door', as in pattern (44), has an alternate form:

(46) *b.*	tāmen	(shì)	bā	—	diǎnzhōng
	they	be	eight	—	o'clock

	kāi	<u>de</u>	<u>mén</u>
	open	NOM	door

The situation is that they opened at eight o'clock.

where *de* precedes the direct object, *mén* 'door', as in pattern (45). Examples (46) *a* and *b* are essentially equivalent, and it makes little difference which one is used.

What the textbooks typically tell us about the meaning of these *shì . . . de* constructions is that the material between the *shì* and *de* is somehow being "emphasized," that the *shì . . . de* construction emphasizes the circumstances of the action. We can refine this idea of emphasis by showing that the *shì . . . de* construction serves to *characterize or explain a situation* by *affirming or denying some supposition*, as opposed to simply reporting an event.[7]

Let's contrast a pair of sentences for illustration:

(40)	tā	(shì)	zuótiān	lái	de
	3sg	be	yesterday	come	NOM

The situation is that s/he came yesterday.

(47)   tā   zuótiān   lái   LE
        3sg   yesterday   come   PFV/CRS

S/He came yesterday.

The important functional difference between (40) and (47) is that (47) describes an action, whereas (40) explains a situation. The best way to illustrate this difference is to see which sentence constitutes an appropriate answer to certain questions. Consider the question in (48):

(48) Why couldn't s/he speak English?

This question demands an explanation of a situation, but not a report of an event. Only (40), the *shì . . . de* construction, but not (47), can be used in an appropriate answer to question (48):

(49)   yīnwèi   tā   (shì)   zuótiān   lái   de
        because   3sg   be   yesterday   come   NOM

Because the situation is that s/he came yesterday.

On the other hand, consider this question:

(50) Has s/he arrived yet?

Question (50) demands information as to whether a certain event has occurred. Only the report of this event, but not the explanation of a situation, constitutes an appropriate answer to (50). Thus, (47), not (40), is an appropriate answer to (50):

(47)   tā   zuótiān   lái   LE
        3sg   yesterday   come   PFV/CRS

S/He came yesterday.

In general, the *shì . . . de* construction affirms or denies some assumption that is already in the air by clarifying what the situation is with respect to that assumption. For instance, in order for question (48) to be appropriate in a discourse, an assumption to the effect that 's/he couldn't speak English' must already be in the air. Sentence (49) then affirms that assumption by clarifying the situation with respect to it.

As another example, consider (51):

(51) (person on telephone to shipping company)

wŏmen	bu	shì	gōngsī ,	wŏmen
we	not	be	company	we

shì	sīrén	de
be	private	NOM

We're not a company—the situation is that we're private.

A natural context for this sentence would be one in which the shipping-company officer has just asked what kind of company the speaker represents. To explain the situation, the speaker uses the *shì . . . de* sentence (51) to deny the assumption that s/he is part of a company.

Let's consider another example.

(52)	wŏ	(shì)	gēn	nĭ	kāiwánxiào	de
	I	be	with	you	joke	NOM

The situation is that I'm joking with you.

(53)	wŏ	gēn	nĭ	kāiwánxiào
	I	with	you	joke

I am joking with you.

Sentence (53) would be an appropriate answer to a question such as (54):

(54) What's happening?

An appropriate context for (52), the *shì . . . de* construction, on the other hand, would be this: suppose that the speaker has made a statement as a joke, and the hearer, not knowing that the statement was a joke, is troubled by it and asks if the statement was correct. The speaker then utters (52) to deny that the statement was to be taken seriously, because (52) is suitable for reassuring the hearer that the situation they are in is merely a joking one.

Here are two more contrasting pairs as illustrations.

(55)   wǒmen   (shì)   bu   huì   qīfu
        we   be   not   likely   bully

        nǐmen   de
        you(PL)   NOM

The situation is that we aren't going to bully you.

(56)   wǒmen   bu   huì   qīfu   nǐmen
        we   not   likely   bully   you(PL)

We aren't going to bully you.

An appropriate context for (55) is one in which there is an assumption that the speakers might bully the hearers, and (55) denies the assumption by characterizing the entire situation as nonthreatening. Thus, the tone of (55) is more reassuring than that of (56). Sentence (56), on the other hand, is a neutral negative statement that could be, for instance, part of a proclamation made by an occupation force. It does not offer any *explanation* of the situation.

(57)   zhèi   —   ge   rén   hěn   wángù ,
        this   —   CL   person   very   stubborn

        wǒmen   (shì)   shuō   —   bu
        we   be   talk   —   can't

        —   fú   tā   de
        —   convince 3sg   NOM

        This person is very stubborn; the situation is that we can't convince him/her.

(58)   zhèi   —   ge   rén   hěn   wángù , wǒmen   shuō
        this   —   CL   person   very   stubborn we   talk

        —   bu   —   fú   tā
        —   can't   —   convince 3sg

        This person is very stubborn. We can't convince him/her.

The first impression a native speaker has about the functional difference between the *shì . . . de* construction of (57) and its non−*shì . . . de* variant, (58), is that the former is much more final than the latter in saying, 'We can't convince him/her'. In other words, (57) conveys the message that the speaker is sure to the point of being resigned to the fact that this person cannot be convinced. Sentence (58), however, does not imply such a message. This difference in the messages conveyed by the two sentences is again inferred from the general functional difference between the *shì . . . de* construction and its non−*shì . . . de* variant. The most natural context in which (57) would be used is one in which the issue of convincing the person had already been raised. In this situation, there would be an assumption that s/he could be convinced, and (57) would be used to clarify the situation with respect to that assumption; it explains that, contrary to the assumption, s/he can't be convinced, and so it sounds definitive: the question has been raised, and the answer is no. Sentence (58), on the other hand, states that the speaker cannot convince him/her, but does not characterize the situation with respect to any question or any assumption. The most likely context in which (58) would be used is not one in which the issue of convincing him/her had been discussed, but one in which the speaker is simply making a report about a mission. Thus, with normal intonation, it does not have the final definitive tone of (57).

Notes

1. There are other functions of *de* in Mandarin. See section 4.2.2 of chapter 4 on associative phrases, section 3.2.2 of chapter 3 on resultative verb compounds, section 8.2.1 of chapter 8 on manner adverbs, and chapter 22 on complex stative constructions.

2. In Mandarin, neither nouns nor nominalizations are marked for number. We have arbitrarily chosen either a singular or a plural interpretation for each of our examples rather than offering both options each time.

3. For further discussion, see Paris (1977).

4. There is another construction that is sometimes translated into English with a relative clause but bears no structural resemblance to the Mandarin relative clause construction we are discussing in this chapter. This construction is a type of serial verb sentence that is discussed and contrasted with the relative clause in section 21.4 of chapter 21:

(i)
tā	yǒu	yi	−	ge	mèimei	huì	jiǎng
3sg	exist	one	−	CL	sister	know	speak

Ménggǔ	huà
Mongolia	speech

S/He has a sister who knows how to speak Mongolian.

5. We have taken this idea from Paris (1979*a*).

6. The reason for this strange translation will be explained shortly.

7. We are grateful to Huang Shuan-fan for discussion of this point.

CHAPTER 21

Serial Verb Constructions

We will use the term *serial verb construction* to refer to a sentence that contains two or more verb phrases or clauses juxtaposed without any marker indicating what the relationship is between them.[1] What this means is that in Mandarin there are many sentences that all have the same form, namely, this (where NP = noun phrase, V = verb, and the NPs in parentheses are all optional):

$$(1) \quad (NP) \quad \underline{V} \quad (NP) \quad (NP) \quad \underline{V} \quad (NP)$$

but that convey different types of messages because of the meanings of the verbs involved and the relationships that are understood to hold between them. That is, the property they all share is that the verb phrases in the serial verb construction always refer to events or states of affairs which are understood to be related as *parts* of *one* overall event or state of affairs. The exact way in which they are related varies according to the meanings of the verbs in these verb phrases.

We can divide the types of meanings conveyed by serial verb constructions into four groups:

1. Two or more separate events
2. One verb phrase or clause serving as the subject or direct object of another verb
3. Pivotal constructions
4. Descriptive clauses

Let's look at them one by one.

21.1 Two or More Separate Events

One of the most obvious messages conveyed by the juxtaposition of two verb phrases or clauses is that of two separate events. As we mentioned just above, the verb phrases or clauses in a serial verb construction describe events that are always understood to be related in some way. In this type of serial verb construction, the two separate events may be understood to be related in one or more of the following four ways:

(i) Consecutive: One event occurs after the other.

(ii) Purpose: The first event is done for the purpose of achieving the second.

(iii) Alternating: The subject alternates between two actions.

(iv) Circumstance: The first verb phrase describes the circumstances under which the event in the second verb phrase or clause occurs.

Many sentences in this group can be understood in more than one way. In the examples below, we give the most natural translation(s) and put a (i), (ii), (iii), or (iv) after the translation to indicate which of the four relationships it represents. The verb phrases in each example are underlined.

(2) wǒ   mǎi   piào   jìn   —   qu
     I   buy   ticket enter —   go

    { I bought a ticket and went in. (i) }
    { I bought a ticket to go in. (ii) }

(3) tā   tiān   —   tiān   chàng   —   gē   xiě   —   xìn
     3sg   day   —   day   sing   —   sing write —   letter

Everyday s/he sings songs and writes letters. ([i], [iii])

(4) tā   shàng   —   lóu   shuì   —   jiào
     3sg   ascend —   stairs sleep —   sleep

S/He's going upstairs to sleep. (ii)

(5) hē   diǎn   jiǔ   zhuàng — zhuang   dǎnzi
     drink a:little wine strengthen — strengthen gall:bladder

⎧ Drink a little wine, and it will give you courage. (i) ⎫
⎨ Drink a little wine to give yourself courage. (ii)   ⎬
⎩ Get some courage by drinking a little wine. (iv)   ⎭

(6) wǒmen   yīnggai   xiǎoxīn   bu   shēng   —   bìng
     we   should   be:careful not   produce   —   sickness

We should be careful not to get sick. ([ii], [iv])

(7) wǒ   dìdi   kāi   —   chē   chū   —
     I   younger:brother drive   —   car   exit   —

           shì   LE
           affair   PFV/CRS

My younger brother had an accident while driving. ([i], [iv])

(8) wǒ   zhù   zài   zhèr   gēn   tāmen   dǎ   —   jiáodào
     I   live at   here   with   they   hit   —   interaction

⎰ I live here and have contact with them. ([i], [iv]) ⎱
⎱ I live here in order to have contact with them. (ii) ⎰

(9) wǒmen   zuò   huǒchē   qù   hǎo   ba ?
     we   sit   train   go   good SA

Let's go by train, shall we? ([ii], [iv])

(10) tā   qí   mǎ   chōu   —   yān
      3sg   ride horse extract —   smoke

⎧ S/He rode a horse and smoked. ([i], [iii]) ⎫
⎨ S/He rode a horse in order to smoke. (ii) ⎬
⎩ S/He rode a horse while smoking. (iv)   ⎭

(11) wǒmen | kāi | — | huì | kǎolǜ | nèi | — | ge | wènti
     we | hold | — | meeting | consider | that | — | CL | problem

We'll hold a meeting to consider that problem. ([ii], [iv])

(12) tā | zǒu | — | lái | zǒu | — | qù
     3sg | walk | — | come | walk | — | go

S/He walked back and forth. (iii)

(13) tāmen | yòng | shǒu | chī | — | fàn
     they | use | hand | eat | — | food

They eat with their hands. (iv)

(14) wǒ | yi | — | gc | rén | wǎnshang | chu | —
     I | one | — | CL | person | evening | exit | —

     qu | hěn | hàipà
     go | very | scared

I'm scared to go out alone at night. (iv)

(15) tā | niàn | — | shū | xīn | hěn | zhuān
     3sg | study | — | book | heart | very | engrossed

When s/he's studying, s/he's very engrossed. (iv)

(16) nèi | — | ge | lǎoshī | shuō | —
     that | — | CL | teacher | say | —

     huà | ài | zhuǎn-wén
     word | love | overuse:literary:words

That teacher loves to flaunt literary words when s/he talks. (iv)

In all of these examples, the meanings of the individual verb phrases determine which of the semantic relationships given in (i)−(iv) are possible, and the speech context determines which of these is most likely.

In the type of serial verb construction we are about to consider next, the two verb phrases are even more tightly bound to each other in that one of them is the subject or direct object of the other. Let's consider the ways in which this can happen.

21.2 One Verb Phrase/Clause Is the Subject or Direct Object of Another

21.2.1 The Second Verb Phrase/Clause Is the Direct Object of the First Verb

In this type of serial verb construction, the meaning of the first verb allows it to be followed by a direct object that is a verb phrase or a clause.[2] For example, the verb *yào* 'want' can be followed by a single verb phrase, as in (17), or by a whole clause, as in (18):

(17)	wǒ	yào	shàng	—	jiē
	I	want	ascend	—	street

I want to go out.

(18)	wǒ	yào	tā	guò	—	lai
	I	want	3sg	cross	—	come

I want him/her to come over here.

Here are some further examples. The verb whose meaning allows it to take a verb phrase or clause as a direct object is underlined twice, and the verb phrase or clause that is functioning as its direct object is underlined once.

(19)	tā	fǒurèn	tā	zuò	—	cuò	le
	3sg	deny	3sg	do	—	wrong	CRS

S/He denies that s/he was wrong.

(20)	tā	qíngyuàn	tā	—	de	háizi	niàn	—	shū
	3sg	prefer	3sg	—	GEN	child	study	—	book

S/He prefers his/her children to study.

(21) tā   zhǐ   zhuāng   bu   zhīdao
      3sg   only   pretend not   know

S/He's only pretending not to know.

(22) wǒ   pànwàng   nǐ   kuài   yidiǎn   bìyè
      I   hope   you   soon   a:little graduate

I hope you'll graduate a bit sooner.

(23) wǒ   kǒngpà   nǐ   láibují
      I   fear   you   can't:make:it:in:time

I'm afraid you can't make it in time.

(24) wǒ   yǐwei   nǐ   xìng   Hòu
      I   mistakenly:thought you   surname Hou

I mistakenly thought your surname was Hou.

(25) wǒ   méi   xiǎng   –   dào   nǐ   zhù   zài   Nánjīng
      I   not   think   –   arrive you   live   at   Nanjing

I didn't realize you lived in Nanjing.

(26) wǒ   jiānchí   wǒ   méi   fàn   –   fǎ
      I   insist   I   not   violate –   law

I insist that I didn't violate any law.

(27) wǒ   xíguàn   zǎodiǎn   chī   de
      I   be:accustomed breakfast eat   CSC

            fēicháng   shǎo
            extremely   little

I'm used to eating very little for breakfast.

(28)   tā   mèngxiǎng   zuò   yīngxióng
        3sg   dream   serve:as   hero

S/He dreamed that s/he would be a hero.

(29)   tā   hěn   jiǎngjiù   chuān   yīfu
        3sg   very   particular   wear   clothes

S/He's very particular about his/her clothes.

(30)   wǒmen   jìnzhǐ   chōu   —   yān
        we   prohibit   extract   —   smoke

We prohibit smoking.

In sentences of this type, the meaning of the first verb determines the type of verb phrase or clause that functions as its direct object, just as we would expect given that the meaning of a verb always determines the type of object it may take. For instance, just as the direct object of the verb *hē* 'drink' must be a liquid, the direct object of the verb *gǎndào* 'feel' must be a verb phrase:

(31)   wǒ   gǎndào   hěn   cánkuì
        I   feel   very   embarrassed

I feel very embarrassed.

The verb *juéde*, which can also be translated 'feel', however, has a broader meaning, including not only 'feel' as an emotion but also 'think that'. Therefore, while *juéde* can be used in a sentence like (32), it can also be used with an entire clause as its direct object, as in (33) *a*, which *gǎndào* cannot do:

(32)   wǒ   juéde   hěn   cánkuì
        I   feel   very   embarrassed

I feel very ashamed.

(33) *a*.   wǒ   juéde   nǐ   bu   yīnggāi   qù
            I   feel   you   not   should   go

I think that you shouldn't go.

b.	*wǒ	găndào	nĭ	bu	yīnggāi	qù
	I	feel	you	not	should	go

In a similar way, the meaning of the first verb imposes certain interpretations on the clause or verb phrase that is its direct object. Let's compare the meaning of the clause

(34)	wŏmen	dōu	qù	chī	jiăozi
	we	all	go	eat	dumpling

We'll all go eat dumplings.

when it is the direct object of *tíyì* 'suggest' and when it is the direct object of *méi xiăng-dào* 'didn't realize':

(35)	tā	tíyì	wŏmen	dōu	qù	chī	jiăozi
	3sg	suggest	we	all	go	eat	dumplings

S/He suggested that we all go eat dumplings.

(36)	tā	méi	xiăng	—	dào	wŏmen	dōu
	3sg	not	think	—	arrive	we	all

qù	chī	jiăozi
go	eat	dumplings

S/He didn't realize that we'd all gone to eat dumplings.

It is easy to see that, although the underlined objects in sentences (35) and (36) are exactly the same in form, because of the meaning of *tíyì* 'suggest', (35) leaves quite open the question of whether we went to eat dumplings, while (36), because of the meaning of *méi xiăng-dào* 'didn't realize', carries the implication that we did go to eat dumplings.

With verbs of saying, the verb-phrase or clause direct object can report the words that were spoken. Such constructions can be called *indirect discourse*. A feature of the serial verb construction expressing indirect discourse in Mandarin is the

optional occurrence of the verb *shuō* 'say, speak' before the object clause
representing the reported words:

(37)   tā   gàosu   wǒ   (shuō)   nǐ   tóu   téng
        3sg   tell   I   say   you   head   ache

S/He told me that you had a headache.

(38)   wǒmen   wèn   tā   (shuō)   Jiěfàng   Lù
        we   ask   3sg   say   Liberation Road

        zài   nǎr
        at   where

We asked him/her where Liberation Road was.

(39)   mèimei   lái   xìn   (shuō)   xià   —
        younger:sister arrive   letter   say   next   —

        ge   yuè   lái
        CL   month   come

(My) younger sister wrote (me) that she'd be here next month.

The only verb with which this *shuō* cannot be used for indirect discourse is *shuō*
itself:

(40)   tā   shuō   (*shuō)   tā   méi   zuò   gōngkè
        3sg   say   say   3sg   not   do   homework

S/He said s/he hadn't done his/her homework.

A *causative* sentence results from the juxtaposition of a verb meaning 'cause'
and a clausal direct object, as in (41):

(41)   zhèi   —   jian   shìqing   ⎧ shǐ ⎫   wǒ   hěn   nánguò
                                        ⎨ ràng ⎬
                                        ⎩ jiào ⎭

        this   —   CL   matter   cause   I   very   sad

This matter makes me very sad.

21.2.2 The First Verb Phrase/Clause Is the Subject of the Second Verb

In this type of serial verb construction, the meaning of the second verb allows it to occur with a clause or a verb phrase as its subject.[3] In the following examples, as before, the verb whose meaning allows it to take a clause or verb phrase as its subject is underlined twice, and the clause or verb phrase itself is underlined once:

(42)   dà   shēng   niàn   kèwén   kěyǐ   bāngzhù   fāyīn
      big   voice   read   lesson   can   help   pronunciation

Reading the lesson aloud can help one's pronunciation.

(43)   xué   Ménggǔ   —   huà   hěn   bu   róngyì
      study   Mongolia   —   speech   very   not   easy

It is not easy to learn Mongolian.

(44)   zài   zhèli   tíng   chē   fàn   —   fǎ
      at   here   stop   vehicle   violate   —   law

It is against the law to park here.

(45)   zuò   Zhōngguó   cài   tài   máfan   le
      make   China   dish   too   troublesome   CRS

Chinese cooking is too much trouble.

(46)   wǔ   —   ge   rén   zuò   yi
      five   —   CL   person   sit   one

      —   jià   mótochē   zhēn   wéixiǎn
      —   CL   motorcycle   real   dangerous

It's really dangerous for five people to ride one motorcycle.

(47)   nǐ   niàn   —   shū   hěn   yǒu
      you   study   —   book   very   exist

      —   chéngjiù   ba
      —   accomplishment   SA

Your studying is going well, right?

(48)

māma	chuān	duǎn	qúnzi	bu	hǎo	—	kàn
mother	wear	short	skirt	not	good	—	look

Mother doesn't look good in short skirts.

(49)

tā	bu	chī	xīguā	tài	kěxī	le
3sg	not	eat	watermelon	too	sad	CRS

It's too bad s/he doesn't eat watermelon.

(50)

nǐmen	chū	—	qu	hǎo
you:PL	exit	—	go	good

It would be good if you'd go outside.

(51)

tā	kǎo	dì	—	yī	míng
3sg	take:exam	ORD	—	one	name

tài	hǎo	le
too	good	CRS

It's terrific that s/he got the top honor in the exam.

(52)

tā	duìdai	shénme	rén	dōu	hěn	gōngjìng
3sg	treat	what	person	all	very	respectful

S/He treats everyone very respectfully.

Certain verbs that take a clause or a verb phrase as their subjects have the following curious property: these verbs can also occur in second position, directly following the subject or topic of the clause or in first position, preceding the verb phrase. In each of the following examples, the *a* and *b* forms have roughly the same meaning and can be considered to be optional variants; the verb taking a verb phrase or a clause as its subject, together with its modifiers, is underlined twice:

(53) *a.*

wǒmen	jiàn	—	miàn	hěn	nán	—	dé
we	meet	—	face	very	hard	—	obtain

It is rare that we see each other.

b. | wǒmen | hěn | nán | — | dé | jiàn | — | miàn |
|---|---|---|---|---|---|---|---|
| we | very | hard | — | obtain | meet | — | face |

It's rare that we see each other.

(54) a. | jiějué | zhèi | — | ge | wènti | hěn | róngyi |
|---|---|---|---|---|---|---|
| solve | this | — | CL | problem | very | easy |

It is very easy to solve this problem.

b. | zhèi | — | ge | wènti | hěn | róngyi | jiějué |
|---|---|---|---|---|---|---|
| this | — | CL | problem | very | easy | solve |

It's very easy to solve this problem.

(55) a. | zhǎo | gōngzuò | bu | tài | róngyi |
|---|---|---|---|---|
| seek | work | not | too | easy |

It is not very easy to find work.

b. | bu | tài | róngyi | zhǎo | gōngzuò |
|---|---|---|---|---|
| not | too | easy | seek | work |

It's not very easy to find work.

(56) a. | qù | Guìlín | bu | kěnéng |
|---|---|---|---|
| go | Guilin | not | possible |

It is not possible to go to Guilin.

b. | bu | kěnéng | qù | Guìlín |
|---|---|---|---|
| not | possible | go | Guilin |

It's not possible to go to Guilin.

Can a sentence contain both a clausal subject and a clausal direct object? Here is an example to show that it can:

(57)   tā   sòng   nǐ   dōngxi   bìng   bu
       3sg   give   you   thing   on:the:contrary   not

       biǎoshì   tā   ài   nǐ
       express   3sg   love   you

His/Her giving you things does *not* indicate that s/he loves you.

21.2.3 The Clause That Is a Subject or Direct Object Is a Question

Questions can occur as either subjects or direct objects of another verb phrase, just as declarative clauses can. Here is an example of each type:

(58) (subject)

       tā   huì   bu   huì   shuō   Tái
       3sg   know:how   not   know:how   speak   Taiwan

       —   yǔ   méi   guānxi
       —   language not   relevance

Whether s/he can or cannot speak Taiwanese is irrelevant.

(59) (direct object)

       tāmen   bu   xiǎode   shéi   bǎ   diàn
       they   not   know   who   BA   electricity

       —   dēng   guān   diào   LE
       —   light   close   off   PFV/CRS

They don't know who turned off the light.

Further discussion of questions serving as subjects or direct objects can be found in chapter 18.

In section 21.2, we have considered serial verb constructions in which one verb phrase or clause is the subject or direct object of another verb. Let us now move on to the third type of serial verb construction.

21.3 Pivotal Constructions

The defining characteristic of the *pivotal* construction is that it contains a noun phrase that is simultaneously the subject of the second verb and the direct object of the first verb.[4] That is, this noun phrase functions as a "pivot" relating the two verbs. We can schematize the relationships as in (60); the labeled arrows denote the relationships that hold between the two elements they connect, and the pivotal noun phrase is circled:

(60)   NP   V₁   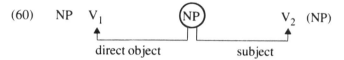   V₂   (NP)

The following examples are divided into two groups, which we will explain below; we have underlined the pivotal noun phrase.

(i) Group I:

(61)   wǒ   quàn   tā   niàn   yī
       I   advise   3sg   study   medicine

I advised him/her to study medicine.

(62)   pài   yi   —   ge   rén   lái
       send   one   —   CL   person   come

Send one person (to come) here!

(63)   wǒ   qiú   tā   dàibiǎo   wǒ
       I   beg   3sg   represent   I

I begged him/her to represent me.

(64)   wǒmen   wěituō   tā   bàn   yi   —   jian   shì
       we   entrust   3sg   do   one   —   CL   affair

We entrusted him/her to take care of an affair.

(65)   wǒ   qǐng   nǐmen   qù   chī   bīngjilíng
       I   invite   you:PL   go   eat   ice:cream

I invite you all to go have some ice cream.

(ii) Group II:

(66) wǒ   yuánliàng   nǐ   sī   —   huài   —
      I   forgive   you   tear —   ruin   —

            le   wǒ   —   de   shū
            PFV   I   —   GEN   book

I forgive you for tearing up my book.

(67) xiǎo   háizi   xiào   tā   shì   yi
      small   child   laugh   3sg   be   one

              —   ge   dà   pàngzi
              —   CL   big   fatso

The children laugh at him/her for being a big fatso.

(68) wǒ   gōngxǐ   tā   kǎo   —
      I   congratulate   3sg   take:exam   —

            jìn   Tái   —   Dà
            enter   Taiwan   —   University

I congratulated him/her on passing the entrance exam to Taiwan University.

(69) tā   pīping   wǒ   bu   yònggōng
      3sg   criticize   I   not   industrious

S/He criticized me for not being industrious.

The difference between groups I and II is a semantic one: the meaning of the first verb in each of the sentences in group I determines that the event expressed by the second verb is *unrealized*, that is, an event that *might happen*, while the first verb in each of the sentences in group II determines that the event expressed by the second verb is *realized*, or real as far as the subject of the first verb is concerned.[5] Thus, in the group I sentence (61), for example,

(61) wǒ quàn <u>tā niàn yī</u>
     I advise 3sg study medicine

I advised him/her to study medicine.

the event *tā niàn yī* 's/he study medicine' is unrealized. This interpretation of being unrealized is entirely due to the meaning of the verb *quàn* 'advise': we can't advise someone to do something that we know is already a reality. In the group II sentence (70), on the other hand,

(70) tā pīping <u>wǒ bu yònggōng</u>
     3sg criticize I not industrious

S/He criticized me for not being industrious.

the event *wǒ bu yònggōng* 'I not industrious' is a reality, at least as far as the subject *tā* 's/he' is concerned. Once again, this interpretation follows from the meaning of *pīping* 'criticize': we can't criticize someone for something unless we believe that that something is a reality.

The contrast between an unrealized and a realized interpretation can be illustrated by a minimal pair in which only the first verbs are different. Consider (71) *a* and *b*:

(71) *a*. (group I)

     tā mìngling <u>wǒ bāng jiějie — de máng</u>
     3sg order I help ·older:sister — GEN ∼

     S/He ordered me to help older sister.

     b. (group II)

     ta xièxie <u>wǒ bāng jiějie — de máng</u>
     3sg thank I help older:sister — GEN ∼

     S/He thanked me for helping older sister.

Both sentences contain the clause *wǒ bāng jiějie-de máng* 'I help older sister', and in both sentences *wǒ* 'I' is the pivotal noun phrase, functioning at once as the direct object of the first verb and as the subject of the second. The interpretation of this clause differs, however: in (71) *a*, 'helping older sister' is unrealized; it is a potential event that the speaker is being ordered to do. In (71) *b*, though, 'helping older sister' has already happened, at least in the mind of *tā* 's/he', who is thanking the speaker for doing it. The difference between the meaning of *mìnglìng* 'order' and that of *xièxie* 'thank' is precisely what causes this difference in the interpretation of the proposition that follows them.

Another interesting point about the first verbs in the sentences in group I: For the ones that have meanings related to giving commands or making suggestions, the clauses that follow are actually imperatives (see chapter 14 on imperatives). This can be demonstrated in two ways. First, this clause can occur with the word *qĭng* 'please', which is only used with imperatives:

(72)	tā	jiào	wŏmen	<u>qĭng</u>	shăo
	3sg	tell	we	please	little

	shuō	–	huà
	speak	–	speech

S/He told us please not to talk too much.

Second, if the clause is negative, then the imperative negatives *bié* or *bu-yào* 'don't' must be used:

(73) *a*.	tā	quàn	wŏmen	<u>bié</u>	zŏu
	3sg	advise	we	don't	leave

S/He advised us not to leave.

b.	*tā	quàn	wŏmen	<u>bu</u>	zŏu
	3sg	advise	we	not	leave

Clearly, the fact that the clauses following the first verb in certain of the sentences under group I have imperative or suggestive meanings is once again directly related to the meaning of those verbs.

21.4 Descriptive Clauses

The *descriptive clause* construction involves a transitive verb whose direct object is "described" by a following clause, as schematized in (74):

(74)

```
                              describes
               ┌──────────────┐
               ▼           ┌──┴──┐
   NP    V    NP    (NP)   V₂    (NP)
```

There are two types of descriptive clause constructions, which we will consider separately.

21.4.1 Realis Descriptive Clauses

This type of descriptive clause construction has the following properties: (1) the direct object of the first verb is always indefinite, and (2) the second clause provides an incidental description of this indefinite direct object.[6] This construction is a type of presentative sentence in that its function in discourse is to present or introduce a noun phrase to be described (see chapter 17 on presentative sentences).

In the following examples, we have underlined the descriptive clause once and the indefinite noun phrase it describes twice:

(75) | tā | yŏu | yi | – | ge | mèimei
| 3sg | exist | one | – | CL | younger:sister

hĕn | xīhuān | kàn | diànyǐng
very | like | see | movie

S/He has a younger sister who likes to see movies.

(76) | wŏ | pèng | – | dào | – | le | yi
| I | meet | – | arrive | – | PFV | one

– | ge | wàiguó | – | rén
– | CL | foreign | – | person

huì | shuō | Zhōngguo | – | huà
know:how | speak | China | – | speech

I met a foreigner who can speak Chinese.

(77)   wǒ   dǎ   —   pò   —   le
        I   hit   —   broken   —   PFV

<u>yi</u>   —   ge   chá   —
one   —   CL   tea   —

<u>bēi</u>   hěn   zhíqián
cup   very   valuable

I broke a teacup that is very valuable.

(78)   tā   chǎo   —   le   <u>yi</u>   —   ge   cài
       3sg   fry   —   PFV   one   —   CL   dish

<u>wǒ</u>   hěn   xǐhuān   chī
I   very   like   eat

S/He cooked a dish that I very much enjoyed eating.

The function of the serial verb construction with a realis descriptive clause is to introduce a new referent into the conversation and add some information about it. It is called a *realis* descriptive clause because the description provided by the second clause is *realized;* it is in the here and now of the ''real world,'' as opposed to the *irrealis* descriptive clause, shown in (79), which adds hypothetical or projected information about the noun phrase of the first clause.

(79)   wǒ   zhǎo   yi   —   ge   rén
       I   seek   one   —   CL   person

<u>bāng</u>   —   <u>máng</u>
help   —   ∼

I'm looking for someone to help (me).

Irrealis descriptive clause sentences are discussed in the following section, 21.4.2.

Semantically, the serial verb construction might appear to be rather similar to a relative clause construction (see section 20.2.1 of chapter 20), and in fact both types of constructions can be given the same English translation. The following examples are the relative clause analogues of (75)–(78), with the relative clauses underlined:

(80) tā   yǒu   yi   —   ge   hěn   xǐhuān
      3sg   exist   one   —   CL   very   like

      kàn   diànyǐng   de   mèimei
      see   movie   NOM   younger:sister

S/He has a younger sister who likes to see movies.

(81) wǒ   pèng   —   dào   —   le
      I   meet   —   arrive —   PFV

      yi   —   ge   huì   shuō
      one   —   CL   know:how   speak

      Zhōngguó   —   huà   de   wàiguo
      China   —   speech NOM   foreign

      —   rén
      —   person

I met a foreigner who can speak Chinese.

(82) wǒ   dǎ   —   pò   —   le
      I   hit   —   broken —   PFV

      yi   —   ge   hěn   zhíqían
      one   —   CL   very   valuable

      de   chá   —   bēi
      NOM   tea   —   cup

I broke a teacup that is very valuable.

(83) tā   chǎo   —   le   yi   —   ge
      3sg   fry   —   PFV   one   —   CL

      wǒ   hěn   xǐhuān   chī   de   cài
      I   very   like   eat   NOM   dish

S/He cooked a dish that I very much enjoyed eating.

The manner in which the realis descriptive clause and the relative clause provide information about the noun phrases they are describing, however, is different in a subtle but significant way: the message conveyed by the realis descriptive clause is that the property it names is entirely incidental, while the message conveyed by the relative clause is that there is a preestablished class of such items. By *preestablished* we mean that the item with the property in question is assumed or has already come up at some point in discussions between the speaker and the hearer; they can be said to have tacitly agreed on the existence of a class of items with this property. To see this more clearly, consider the minimal-pair examples (84) *a* and *b*, where just the realis descriptive clause and the relative clause are underlined:

(84) *a*. (descriptive clause)

wǒ	mǎi	—	le	yi	—	jiàn
I	buy	—	PFV	one	—	CL

yīfu	tài	dà
outfit	too	big

I bought an outfit that turned out to be too big.

b. (relative clause)

wǒ	mǎi	—	le	yi	—	jiàn
I	buy	—	PFV	one	—	CL

tài	dà	de	yīfu
too	big	NOM	outfit

I bought an outfit that was too big.

Both sentences assert that the outfit bought by the speaker was too big, but in (84) *a*, it simply happened or turned out to be too big, whereas for (84) *b* to be appropriate, the hearer and the speaker would have to have been discussing clothes that were too big, or the hearer would have to have known that the speaker was especially looking for an outfit that was too big. This is what we mean by saying that the relative clause sentence, but not the realis descriptive clause sentence, assumes that there is a preestablished class of such items, tacitly agreed upon by speaker and hearer; in this example, the agreed-upon class is the class of clothes that are too big.

For another example, consider sentences (85) *a* and *b*:

(85) *a.* (descriptive clause)

tā	yǎng	–	le	yi	–	tiáo
3sg	raise	–	PFV	one	–	CL

gǒu	wǒ	yào	mǎi
dog	I	want	buy

S/He has raised a dog, and I want to buy it.

b. (relative clause)

tā	yǎng	–	le	yi	–	tiáo
3sg	raise	–	PFV	one	–	CL

wǒ	yào	mǎi	de	gǒu
I	want	buy	NOM	dog

S/He has raised one of those dogs I want to buy.

The realis descriptive clause sentence, (85) *a*, asserts that s/he has raised a dog and that, as it happens, the speaker wants to buy it. The relative clause sentence, (85) *b*, on the other hand, claims that there exists, for the speaker and hearer, an understood class of dogs consisting of the dogs the speaker wants to buy, and s/he just happens to have raised such a dog.

The four pairs of examples we gave at the beginning of this section, (75)–(78) and (80)–(83), work in the same way. For example, we can best understand the difference between sentences (77) and (82) by translating them as follows:

(77)	wǒ	dǎ	–	pò	–	le
	I	hit	–	broken	–	PFV

	yi	–	ge	chá	–
	one	–	CL	tea	–

	bēi	hěn	zhíqían
	cup	very	valuable

I broke a teacup that happened to be very valuable.

(82)   wǒ   dǎ   —   pò   —   le
        I   hit   —   broken —   PFV

        yi   —   ge   hěn   zhíqían
        one   —   CL   very   valuable

        de   chá   —   bēi
        NOM   tea   —   cup

I broke one of those very valuable teacups.

As further confirmation of this distinction, we would predict that the realis descriptive clause is a more appropriate construction than the relative clause for expressing a specific, incidental description that is unlikely to describe a preestablished class of entities. Sentences (86) *a* and *b* bear out this prediction:

(86) *a*. (descriptive clause)

        nèibiān   yǒu   yi   —   kē   shù   wǒ
        there   exist   one   —   CL   tree   I

        yào   kàn   —   yi   —   kàn
        want   look   —   one   —   look

Over there is a tree I want to take a look at.

b. (relative clause)

        ?nèibiān   yǒu   yi   —   kē   wǒ   yào   kàn
        there   exist   one   —   CL   I   want   look

        —   yi   —   kàn   de   shù
        —   one   —   look   NOM   tree

Over there is one of the trees I want to take a look at.

The clause *wǒ yào kàn-yi-kàn* 'I want to take a look at' describes a specific and incidental event. In normal contexts, it is highly unlikely that the speaker and hearer would have agreed on a class of trees consisting of 'the trees I want to take a look at'. Therefore, the relative clause sentence, (86) *b*, is odd, but the descriptive clause sentence, (86) *a*, is perfectly plausible.

The contrast between the relative clause sentences (86) *b* and (87) further illustrates this point.

(87) (relative clause)

nèibiān	yǒu	yi	—	běn	wǒ
there	exist	one	—	CL	I

yào	yánjiu	de	shū
want	study	NOM	book

Over there is one of those books I want to study.

Unlike (86) *b*, sentence (87) is perfectly natural, because it is quite ordinary for one to be in a context (particularly among students and teachers) in which the existence of a class of books consisting of 'the books I want to study' is assumed by the participants of a discourse.

The structural property of descriptive clause sentences which accounts for their meaning of an incidental description, as opposed to the established-class meaning of relative clauses, is this: a realis descriptive clause sentence is actually no different from two sentences juxtaposed together, except that it is pronounced with one single intonation contour. Compare (75), for example, with (88), which is a sequence of two sentences:

(88)	tā	yǒu	yi	—	ge	mèimei ,
	3sg	exist	one	—	CL	younger:sister

	_____	hěn	xǐhuan	kàn	diànyǐng
	_____	very	like	see	movie

S/He has a younger sister. (She) likes to see movies.

(75)	tā	yǒu	yi	—	ge	mèimei
	3sg	exist	one	—	CL	younger:sister

	hěn	xǐhuān	kàn	diànyǐng
	very	like	see	movie

S/He has a younger sister who likes to see movies.

Because Mandarin makes extensive use of zero pronouns to refer to understood NPs (see chapter 24), the sequence in (88) is identical to that of sentence (75) in every way except that (75) is a single sentence, pronounced with a single intonation contour, while (88) is pronounced with two distinct falling contours broken by a pause in between. The semantic principles for interpreting sequences of sentences like (88) are exactly the same as those for interpreting a descriptive clause sentence like (75), though. This explains, then, the semantic contrast between the realis descriptive clause sentence and the relative clause sentence: semantically, a descriptive clause simply adds another assertion to the first one. A relative clause, on the other hand, is a *part* of the noun phrase naming the item in question, so it is natural that it allows the expression of a preestablished class of items with the property it names.

21.4.2 Irrealis Descriptive Clauses

Members of this category of the descriptive clause type of serial verb construction contain a noun phrase that is the direct object of the first verb and a following verb phrase that names an *unrealized (irrealis)* activity involving the direct object of the first verb. Thus, irrealis descriptive clauses are different from realis descriptive clauses in three ways: first, the direct object of the first verb in an irrealis descriptive clause is not necessarily an indefinite noun phrase: it can be definite, indefinite, or nonreferential; second, the verb of the irrealis descriptive clause always expresses an activity; and third, the irrealis descriptive clause always expresses an unrealized event. In the examples to follow, we have underlined the irrealis descriptive clause once and the noun phrase it describes twice:

(89)   wǒmen   zhòng   <u><u>nèi   zhǒng   cài</u></u>   <u>chī</u>
          we   raise   that   kind   vegetable   eat

We raise that kind of vegetable to eat.

(90)   wǒ   zhǎo   <u><u>xuéshēng</u></u>   <u>jiāo</u>
          I   seek   student   teach

I'm looking for students to teach   { (i.e., [i] students whom I can teach.)
                                      [ii] students who can teach
                                      someone else. }

(91)   wǒ   yǒu   qián   mǎi   shū
       I   exist   money   buy   book

I have money for buying books.

(92)   tā   gěi   –   le   wǒ   yi   wǎn
       3sg   give   –   PFV   I   one   bowl

       tāng   hē
       soup   drink

S/He gave me a bowl of soup to drink.

(93)   wǒ   yǒu   yīfu   xǐ
       I   exist   clothes wash

I have clothes to wash.

(94)   wǒ   měi –   (yǒu)   shíjiān   hē   chá
       I   not –   (exist) time   drink   tea

I don't have time to drink tea.

(95)   wǒ   méi   fázi   duì   lǎobǎn   jiāodài
       I   not   way   to   boss   report:back

I have no way to report back to the boss.

(96)   gěi   zhèi   –   ge   rén
       give   this   –   CL   person

       pái   yi   –   ge
       arrange one   –   CL

       shíjian chóngxīn   jiǎnchá !
       time   repeat   examination

Schedule a retest for this person!

(97)   zhèi   —   ge   cài   tài   xián
        this   —   CL   dish   too   salty

        le ,   méi   rén   chī
        CRS   not   person eat

This dish is too salty; there won't be anyone who will eat it.

(98)   tā   mǎi   nèi   —   běn   shū
        3sg   buy   that   —   CL   book

        gěi   nǐ   kàn
        to   you   look

S/He is buying that book for you to read.

(99)   tāmen   xūyào   jiāzi   jiā   hétáo
        they   need   pliers crack   walnuts

They need pliers with which to crack the walnuts.

21.5 Summary

We have seen that all serial verb constructions have the form given in (1) at the beginning of the chapter:

(1)   (NP)   <u>V</u>   (NP)   (NP)   <u>V</u>   (NP)

That is, there are at least two verbs (and various numbers of noun phrases) that are concatenated to express one overall event or state of affairs. The fascinating thing about these constructions is that although all of them have the same form, namely, that represented in (1), with no markers of any kind to signal how the two verb phrases are to be related to each other, speakers interpret them in different ways according to the meanings of their verbs. The interpretations are these:

1. Two separate events
    (i)   Consecutive: One event occurs after the other.
    (ii) Purpose: The first event is done for the purpose of achieving the second.
    (iii) Alternating: The subject alternates between two actions.

(iv) Circumstance: The first verb phrase describes the circumstances under which the event in the second verb phrase or clause occurs.

2. (i) One verb phrase/clause is the direct object of the other verb.

  (ii) One verb phrase/clause is the subject of the other verb.

3. Pivotal constructions

4. Descriptive clauses

  (i) Realis descriptive clauses.

  (ii) Irrealis descriptive clauses.

In each case, we have seen precisely how the various components of the meanings of the verbs determine the type of interpretation accorded to the entire serial verb construction.

Notes

1. For this section, we have drawn on Simon (1958), Tang (1972), Chan (1974), and Teng (1975*a*, 1975*b*), as well as some unpublished work of Teng Shou-hsin. For more discussion, see also our papers, Li and Thompson (1975*b*, 1978*a*, and 1978*b*).

2. For ease of presentation, we are assuming that clausal direct objects always follow their verbs and that clausal subjects always precede their verbs, since this is typically the case. The order can be reversed, however, as (i) and (ii) show:

  (i) (Clausal direct object preceding its verb; the clausal object is underlined.)

kàn	něi	—	ge	diànyǐng	wǒmen
see	which	—	CL	movie	we

hái	méi	juédìng
still	not	decide

  Which movie to see, we still haven't decided.

  (ii) (Clausal subject following its verb; the clausal subject is underlined.)

kěxī	tā	zài	kāi	—	dāo
pitiful	3sg	DUR	open	—	knife

  It's a pity that s/he is having an operation.

3. See n. 2 above.

4. We take the term *pivotal construction* from Chao (1968). See his discussion in section 2.13, pages 124–129, as well as Simon (1958:571–573).

5. The distinction being discussed here is also applicable in a limited sense to those serial verb constructions in which the second verb phrase or clause is the direct object of the first verb, though only a few verbs taking a verb phrase or a clause as a direct object require the event expressed by the second verb phrase or clause to be unrealized. These verbs include *yào* 'want', *xiǎng* 'wish', *xǐhuan* 'like'. For example, in the sentence

(i)   wǒ   ⎧ yào   ⎫   Zhāngsān   zhù   zài   zhèr
                  ⎨ xiǎng ⎬
                  ⎩ xǐhuan ⎭

         I   ⎧ want ⎫   Zhangsan   live   at   here
                 ⎨ wish ⎬
                 ⎩ like ⎭

         I   ⎧ want ⎫ Zhangsan to live here.
             ⎨ wish ⎬
             ⎩ like ⎭

the event expressed by the direct object clause *Zhāngsān zhù zài zhèr* 'Zhangsan live at here' is necessarily unrealized. Contrast (i) with (ii):

(ii)   wǒ   tīng   —   shuō   Zhangsan   zhù   zài   zhèr
         I   hear   —   say   Zhangsan   live   at   here

      I hear Zhangsan is living here.

In (ii), the event expressed by the same object clause, *Zhāngsān zhù zài zhèr* 'Zhangsan live at here', can be either realized or unrealized. The first verb in (ii), *tīng-shuō* 'hear-say', does not have any requirement as to whether the event expressed by the object clause is realized or unrealized.

6. This type of construction is also mentioned in Tai (1978:291–293).

CHAPTER 22

The Complex Stative Construction

The complex stative construction takes the form

(1)   clause   <u>de</u>   stative $\begin{Bmatrix} \text{clause} \\ \text{verb phrase} \end{Bmatrix}$

We will gloss the *de* that appears in this construction as *CSC* for 'complex stative construction'.[1]

22.1 Inferred Meanings

Speakers infer two types of meanings from such constructions, and which type is inferred depends on the meanings of the clauses themselves and the possible relationships between them. Let's look at each of these types before discussing the general properties of the construction.

22.1.1 Manner Inferred

A *manner* relationship between the two parts of a complex stative construction may be inferred when the stative verb phrase is an adjective. In other words, the adjective may be interpreted as a description of the manner in which the event described by the first clause of the complex stative construction occurs. Here are some examples; the stative clause or verb phrase, interpreted as expressing manner, is underlined:

(2)   Lǐsì   lái   de   <u>zhēn   qiǎo</u>
      Lisi   come   CSC   real   coincidental

It was really a coincidence that Lisi came.

(3) tā   dáyìng   de   bǐjiao   miánqiǎng
     3sg   accept   CSC   relatively   forced

S/He was rather reluctant to accept.

(4) tā   zǒu   de   hěn   màn
     3sg   walk   CSC   very   slow

S/He walks very slowly.

(5) wǒmen   shuì   de   hěn   hǎo
     we   sleep   CSC   very   good

We slept very well.

(6) tā   zǒu   de   fēicháng   zǎo
     3sg   leave   CSC   extremely   early

S/He left really early.

(7) tā   zhàn   de   hěn   wěn
     3sg   stands   CSC   very   steady

S/He stands very steadily.

(8) tā   chuān   de   hěn   piàoliang
     3sg   dress   CSC   very   beautiful

She dressed very beautifully.

Before considering the other inferred meanings for the complex stative constructions, we must digress very briefly to consider the functional difference between the manner adverbs discussed in chapter 8 on adverbs and the complex stative constructions with manner interpretations. Let's look at a minimal pair:

(9) (manner adverb)
     nǐ   kuài-kuài-de   pǎo
     you   quickly   run

Run quickly!

(10) (complex stative construction)

nǐ	pǎo	de	hěn	kuài
you	run	CSC	very	quick

You $\begin{Bmatrix} \text{run} \\ \text{ran} \end{Bmatrix}$ very quickly.

The difference is that the manner adverb sentence always refers to an *action*, while the complex stative construction always refers to a *state of affairs*. This is because the assertion in a complex stative construction is always the *stative* clause or verb phrase. Sentence (10) then, refers to your running being quick, either in general or at some particular time. In other words, (10) is a comment on the hearer's speed. Since it is stative, it cannot be a command. Sentence (9), on the other hand, refers to an action and is therefore a command.

Related to this difference is another characteristic of the complex stative construction: the event named in the first clause must be one that has already come up in the discussion or one that is "in the air." For example, if one says

(5)	wǒmen	shuì	de	hěn	hǎo
	we	sleep	CSC	very	good

We slept very well.

it must be the case either that someone has mentioned or asked the speaker about how well s/he and his/her friends slept or else that people are greeting each other the first thing in the morning. In either case, the event named in the first clause is already understood at the time sentence (5) is uttered. The same can be said about the event expressed by the first clause, *nǐ pǎo* 'you run', of (10). Sentence (9), on the other hand, does not represent an event that has already been mentioned or is "in the air." From these facts, it follows that only the manner adverb sentence can be used to answer a question such as that in (11) A, since the question does not imply that "his/her running" is already known:

(11) A :	tā	zài	zuò	shénme ?
	3sg	DUR	do	what

What is s/he doing?

B:	tā	zài	màn-màn-de	pǎo
	3sg	DUR	slowly	run

S/He is running slowly.

The complex stative construction, as in (12), cannot be used to answer the question in (11) A, because the function of (12) is to comment on the slowness of his/her running, something like 'When s/he runs/ran, it is/was very slow', whereas the question in (11) A asks, 'What is s/he doing?'

(12)   tā   pǎo   de   hěn   màn
        3sg   run   CSC   very   slow

S/He   {runs}   very slowly.
        {ran }

22.1.2 Extent Inferred

The inferred relationship between the two parts of a complex stative construction can also be one of *extent*; that is, the event in the first clause is done to such an extent that the result is the state expressed by the stative clause or verb phrase. Here are some examples, again with the stative verb phrase—this time interpreted as expressing extent—underlined:

(13)   tā   xiào   —   de   <u>zhàn</u>   —   <u>bu</u>   —
        3sg   laugh   —   CSC   stand   —   can't   —

                 <u>qǐ</u>   —   <u>lái</u>
                 rise   —   come

S/He laughed so much that s/he couldn't stand up.

(14)   tā   jiāo   de   <u>lèi</u>   <u>le</u>
        3sg   teach   CSC   tired   CRS

S/He taught so much that s/he is tired.

(15)   wǒ   kū   de   <u>yǎnjing   dōu   hóng   le</u>
        I   cry   CSC   eye   all   red   CRS

I cried so much that my eyes got all red.

(16)   tā   xiào   de   <u>wǒmen   dōu   buhǎoyìsi</u>
        3sg   laugh   CSC   we   all   embarrassed

S/He laughed so much that we all got embarrassed.

(17) | xiǎo | hái | zhǎng | de | wǒ | bu | rènshi | le |
      | small | child | grow | CSC | I | not | recognize | CRS |

The child has grown so much that I don't recognize him/her.

(18) | tā | gāoxing | de | shuì | — | bu | — | zháo |
      | 3sg | happy | CSC | sleep | — | can't | — | succeed |

| — | jiào |
| — | sleep |

S/He is so happy that s/he can't sleep.

(19) | nǐmen | zuò | — | wén | bu | yào | bǎ |
      | you:PL | do | — | composition | not | want | BA |

| jùzi | xiě | de | tài | cháng |
| sentence | write | CSC | too | long |

When you write essays, don't make the sentence too long.

(20) | wǒ | è | de | fa | — | huāng |
      | I | hungry | CSC | produce | — | panic |

I'm so hungry that I'm going crazy.

22.1.3 Either Manner or Extent Inferred

As we might expect, certain combinations of verb phrases in a complex stative construction allow either a manner or an extent inference. In examples (21) and (22), the (i) translation reflects the manner inference, while the (ii) translation reflects the extent inference:

(21) | wǒmen | chī | de | hěn | kāixīn |
      | we | eat | CSC | very | happy |

$\left\{\begin{array}{l}\text{(i) We ate very happily.} \\ \text{(ii) We ate to the point of being very happy.}\end{array}\right\}$

(22)	tā	kū	de	hĕn	shāng	—	xīn
	3sg	cry	CSC	very	hurt	—	heart

$\left\{\begin{array}{l}\text{(i) S/He cried very sadly.}\\ \text{(ii) S/He cried to the point of being very sad.}\end{array}\right\}$

22.2 General Structural Properties

One of the most striking structural properties of the complex stative construction manifests itself when the verb in the first clause is a transitive one with a direct object (see section 4.3.1 of chapter 4 on types of verbs). If the first clause contains a transitive verb and its direct object, the verb must be "copied" before the CSC *de*. In the following examples the two instances of the copied verb have been underlined twice:

(23)	tā	shuō	Tàiguó	—	huà	shuō	de
	3sg	speak	Thailand	—	speech	speak	CSC

fēichang	liúlì
extremely	fluent

S/He speaks Thai very fluently.

(24)	māma	xĭ	yīfu	xĭ	de	hĕn	gānjìng
	mother	wash	clothes	wash	CSC	very	clean

Mother washed the clothes very clean.

(25)	tā	qiē	yú	qiē	de	hĕn	zĭxì
	3sg	cut	fish	cut	CSC	very	meticulous

S/He cut the fish very carefully.

For further discussion of verb copying, see chapter 13.

Negatives and auxiliaries behave differently with respect to their position in a complex stative construction. If a complex stative construction contains a negative particle, it will occur before the stative verb phrase, never before the verb phrase of the first clause:

(26) *a.*

tā	kǎo	–	shì	kǎo	de	<u>bu</u>	hǎo
3sg	take	–	exam	take	CSC	not	good

S/He did not do well on the exam.

b.

*tā	<u>bu</u>	kǎo	–	shì	kǎo	de	hǎo
3sg	not	take	–	exam	take	CSC	good

c.

*tā	kǎo	–	shì	<u>bu</u>	kǎo	de	hǎo
3sg	take	–	exam	not	take	CSC	good

The position of the negative particle is predictable in terms of the scope of negative particles (discussed in section 12.1 of chapter 12): what follows the negative particle is what is being denied. The message in (26) is that the performance on the exam was not *good*, but not that *tā* 's/he' did not *take* the exam; thus, the negative particle *bu* must precede *hǎo* 'good', not *kǎo-shì* 'take the exam'.

Auxiliaries, on the other hand, in general can occur only before the first verb of the complex stative construction, as in:

(27) *a.*

tā	<u>néng</u>	tiào	de	hěn	gāo
3sg	can	jump	CSC	very	high

S/He can jump very high.

b.

*tā	tiào	de	<u>néng</u>	hěn	gāo
3sg	jump	CSC	can	very	high

There is, however, at least one auxiliary verb, *yīnggāi* 'should', which can occur in several positions in the complex stative construction:

(28) *a.*

nǐ	<u>yīnggāi</u>	fā	–	yīn	fā	–
you	should	produce	–	sound	produce	–

de	hěn	qīngchu
CSC	very	clear

You should pronounce very clearly.

b.	nǐ	fā	—	yīn	yīnggāi	fā	—
	you	produce	—	sound	should	produce	—

de	hěn	qīngchu
CSC	very	clear

You should pronounce very clearly.

c.	nǐ	fā	—	yīn	fā	—	de
	you	produce	—	sound	produce	—	CSC

yīnggāi	hěn	qīngchu
should	very	clear

You should pronounce very clearly.

Note

1. For further discussion of this construction, see C.-Y. Chen (1979).

CHAPTER 23

Sentence Linking

Even though it is sometimes useful to consider a single sentence in isolation in order to analyze its grammatical structure, in actual language use sentences occur in larger contexts, as part of dialogues, monologues, and conversations (as well as written paragraphs). In general, sentences spoken in close succession by one speaker or by several speakers will be related; otherwise, communication will break down. Often, however, the relationship is not made explicit; two sentences may simply be juxtaposed. For example, consider the two sentences in (1):

| (1) | wǒ | hěn | xǐhuān | chī | běifāng | cài , | chī |
| | I | very | like | eat | northern | food | eat |

| | Guǎngdōng | cài | juéde | méi | you | wèidao |
| | Canton | food | feel | not | exist | flavor |

I really like northern food; when I eat Cantonese food I feel it has no flavor.

These two sentences are obviously related in theme: they are both asserting something about the speaker's culinary tastes. No explicit relationship needs to be signaled in such cases. Sometimes, though, the speaker intends a sentence to be related to another one in a particular sense. In this chapter, we consider some of the ways in which Mandarin allows its speakers to link their sentences, either to other sentences, or, in some cases, to sentences uttered by their conversational partners.[1]

When a sentence is part of a larger sentence, it is called a *clause*. In the linking constructions to be considered in this chapter, we will refer to any sentence that is linked to another sentence as a clause.

There are essentially two kinds of linking: forward linking and backward linking. With *forward linking* we must talk about sentences containing at least two clauses, because the first clause is always dependent on the second clause for its meaning to be complete. With *backward linking,* on the other hand, the clause the speaker says is dependent on the previous clause for its meaning to be complete. Normally this previous clause is spoken by the same person, but in some cases it could be spoken by someone else engaged in the conversation.

In many sentences composed of two linked clauses, as we shall see, each of the two constituent clauses contains a linking element, the first clause having a forward-linking element and the second one a backward-linking element. For example, in the following sentence, each of the two underlined forms signals dependence of its clause on the other clause:

(2)	tā	suírán	méi	qián ,	kěshi	tā	háishi
	3sg	although	not	money	but	3sg	still

	hěn	kǎngkài
	very	generous

Although s/he has no money, s/he's still very generous.

We will discuss the two types of linking separately.

23.1 Forward Linking

With forward linking, as we have said, one clause is dependent on the following one. This dependence may be established in one of two ways, either by a specific linking element or by the speaker's intention. For example, in a sentence like

(3) C_1 C_2

jiǎrú	xià	yǔ ,	wǒmen	jiu	zài	wūli	chī	–	fàn
if	descend	rain	we	then	at	indoors	eat	–	food

If it rains, we'll eat indoors.

clause 1 (C_1) contains the forward-linking element *jiǎrú* 'if', whose function is to signal the dependence of C_1 on C_2 (clause 2) for its message to be complete.

The other kind of dependence is established by what we have called the speaker's intention. Here's an example:

(4)

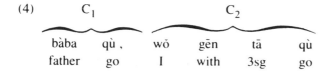

If father goes, I'll go with him.

With this type of dependence, C_1 has no explicit forward-linking word. In fact, in some contexts it could stand by itself and mean 'father is going', but in the context in which it precedes another clause, C_2, it is dependent for its meaning on C_2 because of the speaker's intention.

Let's look at each type of forward linking in detail.

23.1.1 Forward Linking with a Linking Element

There are three kinds of forward-linking elements:

A. Forward-linking elements in clause-final position

B. Adverbial forward-linking elements

    1. Movable forward-linking elements—can be positioned both after the topic/subject and in clause-initial position

    2. Nonmovable forward-linking elements—must be positioned either after the topic/subject or in clause-initial position

C. Perfective aspect

A. Forward-Linking Elements in Clause-Final Position

These kinds of linking elements come at the end of C_1, the first clause. The six most important ones are:

(5) de huà   'if'

     de shíhòu   'NOM time = when, while'

     yǐhòu   'after'

     yǐqián   'before'

     ne, me   pause particles (see section 4.1.1 of chapter 4 for a discussion of pause particles)

Here is an example of each:

(6)   nǐ   yǒu   qián   <u>de huà</u> ,   jiu   bu   huì
       you   exist   money   if   then   not   likely

       xiàng   wǒ   jiè   qián   le
       toward I   borrow money   CRS

If you had money, you wouldn't have to borrow money from me.

(7)   tā   xiǎo   <u>de shíhòu</u> ,   méi   rén   zhàogu   tā
       3sg   small   time   not   person care:for 3sg

When s/he was small, there was no one to take care of him/her.

(8)   xià   —   kè   <u>yǐhòu</u> ,   wǒ   jiu   qù   yóuyǒng
       descend —   class   after   I   then   go   swim

After I get out of class, I go swimming.

(9)   shàng   —   kè   <u>yǐqián</u> ,   wǒ   xiān   hē
       ascend —   class   before   I   first   drink

       yi   bēi   chá
       one   cup   tea

Before going to class, I first drink a cup of tea.

(10)   tā   lái   zhèr   <u>ne</u> ,   wǒ   xiǎng   yě   kěyǐ
       3sg   come   here   topic   I   think   also   can

As for his/her coming here, I think it's OK.

(11)   tā   bu   niàn   —   shū   <u>me</u> ,   wǒ   jiu
       3sg   not   study   —   book   topic   I   then

       bu   yǎng   tā
       not   support 3sg

If s/he doesn't study, I won't support him/her.

B. Adverbial Forward-Linking Elements

One group of adverbial forward-linking elements are of the movable-adverb type discussed in chapter 8. That is, they can occur either in sentence-initial position or after the subject or topic. The most important of these are:

(12) fēidàn
    búdàn   'not only'

    rúguǒ
    jiǎrú
    jiǎshǐ   'if'[2]
    yàoshi

    chúfēi   'unless'

    jíshǐ
    jiùshi   'even if'

    yàobushì   'if not that . . .'

    suīrán   'although'

    yīnwèi
    yóuyú   'because'

    wúlùn
    búlùn   'no matter whether'

    jìrán
    jìshi   'since'

    zhǐyào   'if only, as long as'

Here are a few examples:

(13) | tā | búdàn | huì | chàng | – | gē, | hái |
| --- | --- | --- | --- | --- | --- | --- |
| 3sg | not:only | know:how | sing | – | song | also |

	huì	tiào	bāléi	–	wǔ
	know:how	dance	ballet	–	dance

Not only can s/he sing, s/he also can do ballet.

(14)   yàoshi   jīntian   fàng   —   jià,   jiu   hǎo   le
        if   today   let:go   —   holiday   then   good   CRS

If today were a holiday, that would be good.

(15)   chúfēi   wǒmen   hěn   máng,   wǒmen   yídìng   lái
       unless   we   very   busy   we   certainly come

                kàn   nǐ
                see   you

Unless we're busy, we'll certainly come to see you.

(16)   jiùshi   zhème   piányi   tā   hái   bu   mǎi   ne
       even:if   this   cheap   3sg   still   not   buy   REx

Even if it's this cheap s/he still won't buy it.

(17)   huǒchē   yàobushì   tài   màn,   wǒ   zǎo   jiu
        train   if:not:that   too   slow   I   early   then

                dào   le
               arrive   CRS

If it weren't that trains are so slow, I would have arrived a long time ago.

(18)   wǒ   suīrán   hěn   xǐhuān,   kěshi   méi   qián
        I   although very   like   but   not   money

Although I like (it) very much, I have no money.

(19) yīnwèi   tiān   hēi   le,   suǒyǐ   wǒ   méi
      because   sky   black   CRS   so   I   not

               chū   —   qu
               exit   —   go

Because it had gotten dark, I didn't go out.

(20) wúlùn   tā   lái   bu   lái ,   wǒmen   yào
      no:matter 3sg   come   not   come   we   want

      zǒu   le
      go   CRS

No matter whether or not s/he comes, we have to leave.

(21) nǐ   jìrán   bu   xìn ,   nǐ   zìjǐ   qù   kàn   ba
      you   since   not   believe you   self   go   see   SA

Since you don't believe it, go look for yourself.

(22) zhǐyào   wǒ   nénggòu ,   wǒ   yídìng   hěn   lèyì
      as:long:as   I   can   I   certainly   very   glad

      bāng   nǐ   máng
      help   you   ~

As long as I can, I'll certainly be glad to help you.

We should note that the majority of these forward-linking movable adverbs require the occurrence of a backward-linking element in the clause that follows. The most common pairings of these linking elements are shown in (23):

(23) búdàn   'not only' $\left\{\begin{array}{l}\text{érqiě}\\\text{yě}\\\text{hái}\end{array}\right\}$ 'also'

$\left\{\begin{array}{l}\text{rúguǒ}\\\text{jiǎrú}\\\text{jiǎshǐ}\\\text{yàoshi}\end{array}\right\}$ 'if' $\left\{\begin{array}{l}\text{jiu}\\\text{yě}\end{array}\right\}$ 'then'
                                                                                                 'also'

$\left\{\begin{array}{l}\text{jíshǐ}\\\text{jiùshi}\end{array}\right\}$ 'even if' $\left\{\begin{array}{l}\text{yě}\\\text{hái}\end{array}\right\}$ 'still'

yàobushì   'if not that . . .' jiu   'then'

$$
suīrán \qquad \text{'although'} \quad \left\{ \begin{array}{l} \underline{dào} \\ \underline{kěshi} \\ \underline{hái(shi)} \end{array} \right\} \quad \begin{array}{l} \text{'but'} \\ \text{'but'} \\ \text{'still'} \end{array}
$$

$$
\left\{ \begin{array}{l} \underline{yīnwèi} \\ \underline{yóuyú} \end{array} \right\} \quad \text{'because'} \quad \left\{ \begin{array}{l} \underline{suǒyǐ} \\ \underline{jiu} \end{array} \right\} \quad \begin{array}{l} \text{'therefore'} \\ \text{'then'} \end{array}
$$

The other group of adverbial forward-linking elements are nonmovable (again, see chapter 8 on adverbs). They must occur after the topic or subject. Hence, they do not appear in sentence-initial position except when the topic is absent. There are four of them, all of which require an identical backward-linking element in the second clause. They are:

(24) <u>yòu</u> . . . <u>yòu</u> $\left\{ \begin{array}{l} \text{'both . . . and'} \\ \text{'not only . . . but also'} \end{array} \right\}$

<u>yě</u> . . . <u>yě</u> 'not only . . . but also'

<u>yuè</u> . . . <u>yuè</u> 'the more . . . the more . . .'

<u>yībiān</u> . . . <u>yībiān</u> 'while . . . V-ing . . . V-ing . . .'

The following examples illustrate their use:

(25)	píngguǒ	<u>yòu</u>	piányì	<u>yòu</u>	hǎo	–	chī
	apple	both	cheap	both	good	–	eat

Apples are both cheap and delicious.

(26)	nǐ	<u>yě</u>	kěyǐ	xué	Rìwén	<u>yě</u>
	you	not:only	can	study	Japanese	but:also

	kěyǐ	xué	Zhōngwén
	can	study	Chinese

You can learn not only Japanese but also Chinese.

(27)	nǐ	yuè	dà	—	shēng	shuō
	you	the:more	big	—	voice	talk

	—	huà	wǒ	yuè	tīng
	—	speech	I	the:more	listen

	—	bu	—	dǒng
	—	can't	—	understand

The louder you talk, the more I don't understand.

(28)	tā	yībiān	chī	píngguǒ	yībiān
	3sg	while	eat	apple	

	kàn	—	bào
	read	—	paper

S/He's eating an apple while reading the paper.

There is one nonmovable forward-linking adverb, occurring after the topic, which does not require an identical linker in the following clause. It is *yì* 'as soon as'. This linker, however, usually does occur with the linker *jiu* 'then' in the second clause. Sentence (29) is an example:

(29)	tā	yì	shuō,	wǒ	jiu
	3sg	as:soon:as	say	I	then

	dǒng	le
	understand	CRS

As soon as s/he mentioned it, I understood.

There is another group of nonmovable forward-linking adverbs that occur in sentence-initial position only, two of which typically occur with a backward linker in the second clause. They are given in (30):

(30) jíshǐ . . . yě 'even if . . . still'
     chufei 'unless'
     zhǐyǒu . . . cái 'only if . . . then'

The following sentences illustrate these nonmovable forward-linking adverbs.

(31) jíshǐ   tā   bu   lái ,   wǒmen   yě
      even:if   3sg   not   come   we   still

      děi   kāi   —   huì
      must   hold   —   meeting

Even if s/he does not come, we still have to hold the meeting.

(32) chúfēi   nǐ   gěi   wǒ   nèi   —
      unless   you   give   I   that   —

      běn   shū ,   wǒ   bu   xuǎn
      CL   book   I   not   select

      nèi   —   mén   kè
      that   —   CL   course

Unless you give me that book, I won't take that course.

(33) zhǐyǒu   tā   zhīchí   zhè   —   ge
      only:if   3sg   support this   —   CL

      jiànyì , wǒmen   cái   néng   chénggōng
      proposal we   then   can   succeed

Only if s/he supports this proposal can we succeed.

C. Perfective Aspect

Another forward-linking device is the use of the perfective aspect suffix -le with an unquantified direct object. As we pointed out in chapter 6, -le can be used only with bounded events, so that when it occurs in a clause with an unquantified direct object, it must be bounded by a clause signaling another event. For example:

(34) tā   chuān   —   shang   —   le   dàyī ,
      3sg   wear   —   ascend   —   PFV   coat

      jiu   chū   —   qu   sànbù
      then   exit   —   go   promenade

S/He put on his/her coat and went out for a stroll.

(35)	tā	hē	—	le	jiǔ,	jiu
	3sg	drink	—	PFV	wine	then
		shuì	—	zháo	le	
		sleep	—	succeed	CRS	

After s/he drank the wine, s/he went to sleep.

That is, the -le in C_1 signals dependence on C_2 in exactly the same way as do the other forward-linking elements that we have already discussed. As we point out in section 6.1.1 of chapter 6, the first clause in each of the above two sentences would be incomplete without a second clause or the clause-final le 'current relevant state', which indicates that the clause is relevant to the current discourse situation. In cases like this, then, we could say that the -le, in signaling boundedness, is serving as a forward-linking element. The relationship is one of sequentiality, though it is not signaled directly by the meaning of -le (as it is by a word such as yǐhòu 'after'), but rather is inferred from the boundedness meaning of -le together with the fact that the event named by the verb to which -le is attached is *not* bounded by anything in its own clause.

We've seen, then, that forward-linking elements include (1) sentence-final linking elements, which occur at the end of C_1, (2) adverbs occurring either at the beginning of C_1 or right after the topic or subject, and (3) the perfective aspect suffix -le. The meanings of all these elements convey a specific relationship between C_1 and C_2.

23.1.2 Forward Linking without a Linking Element

As we mentioned above (see sentence [4]), forward linking need not be overtly marked at all, but can occur simply by virtue of the speaker's intention that C_1 and C_2 be related. In such cases, the particular relationship between the two clauses is not signaled explicitly and must be inferred by the hearer from his/her knowledge of the situation and of what has been said to that point. Here is an example:

(36)	rénlèi	huó	zài	shì	—	shang,
	human:beings	alive	at	world	—	on
		bu	néng	bu	láodòng	
		not	can	not	labor	

$\left\{ \begin{array}{l} \text{Since} \\ \text{If} \\ \text{As long as} \end{array} \right\}$ human beings live in this world, they will have to do hard work.

The underlined clause, C_1, in (36) contains no explicit forward-linking element, which means that it is not dependent on C_2 in any formal way; that is, in other contexts C_1 could stand by itself to mean 'Human beings live in this world'. The relationship between C_1 and C_2 in (36) is not signaled by any overt element, but rather is inferred by the hearer from the knowledge s/he has of the world, the content of the two clauses in the sentence, and what has been under discussion up to that point. Since this relationship is inferred, any one of several messages are possible for the sentence as a whole, as indicated by the choices we suggest in our translations. Here are some further examples; C_1, which is underlined in each sentence, has no linking element:

(37) nǐ   bù   xiāngxìn ,   wǒ   zuò   gěi   nǐ   kàn
      you   not   believe   I   do   to   you   see

If you don't believe it, I'll do it for you to see.

(38) wǒ   shi   nǐ   −   de   péngyou ,
      I   be   you   −   GEN   friend

      cái   gàosu   nǐ   zhèi   −
      only:then   tell   you   this   −

      jian   shì
      CL   matter

It's only because I'm your friend that I'm telling you about this matter.

(39) wǒ   shuō   kěyǐ ,   jiu   kěyǐ
      I   say   can   then   can

{If / Once} I say it's OK, then it's OK.

(40) wǒ   sǐ   −   le ,   nǐ   zuì
      I   die   −   PFV   you   most

      hǎo   zài   jià
      good   again   marry

{If / When} I die, you'd better marry again.

(41) méi   −   yǒu   tāmen ,   jiu   méi   −
      not   −   exist   they   then   not   −

          yǒu   zhèi   −   ge   gōngsī
         exist   this   −   CL   company

{ [If it weren't for] them, we wouldn't have this company. }
{ [If we didn't have]   }
{   If they didn't exist, this company wouldn't exist.   }

(42) nǐmen   bu   zuò   −   gōng ,   wǒmen
      you:PL   not   do   −   work   we

            bu   fù   −   qián
           not   pay   −   money

If you don't work, we don't pay.

(43) wǒ   yǒu   shíjiān ,   yídìng   lái   kàn   nǐ
      I   exist   time   definitely come   see   you

{ When } I have time, I'll definitely come to see you.
{ If   }

(44) wǒ   yǒu   qián ,   jiu   kěyǐ   mǎi
      I   exist   money   then   can   buy

            hǎo   de   diànshì   −   jī
           good   NOM television   −   machine

If I had money, I could buy a good TV.

We have shown that the first clause in sentences like (37)–(44) exhibits forward linking without an overt linking element. The second clause, either by the message it conveys or by an explicit backward-linking element, is what determines the interpretation of the first clause. To see this point clearly, let's contrast (45) with (46):

(45)   wǒ   shì   Měiguó   rén ,   jiu
       I   be   America   person   then

       bu   huì   shuō   zhème
       not   will   speak   this

       zāo   de   Yīngwén
       rotten NOM   English

If I were an American, then I wouldn't be speaking such bad English.

(46)   wǒ   shì   Měiguó   rén ,   suǒyǐ   wǒ
       I   be   America   person   so   I

       xūyào   hùzhào   qù   Sūlián
       need   passport go   Soviet:Union

I am an American, so I need a passport to go to the Soviet Union.

As we can see, the underlined C_1 in these two examples is identical, yet in (45) it is interpreted to mean that I am *not* an American, while in (46) it is interpreted to mean that I *am* an American, just as it would if it were used by itself, say, in response to a question. The difference, of course, is in the inferences that can be drawn from the second clause in each of these examples. The second clause in (45) contains the backward-linking element *jiu*, which, as we shall see in the next section, can serve to shift the preceding clause into the hypothetical mode. Sentence (46), on the other hand, contains the backward-linking element *suǒyǐ*, whose meaning does not force any shift from the normal assumption that C_1 is an assertion of a true state of affairs.

Another type of forward linking without the use of an overt linking element is found in sentences in which C_1 contains a question word. As pointed out in chapter 18, question words can be used as indefinite pronouns marking a dependent relationship between two clauses:

(47) | shéi | zuì | — | le , | (jiu) | fá |
|------|------|-----|------|-------|------|
| who | drunk | — | PFV | (then) | fine |

	shí	kuài	qián
	ten	dollar	money

Whoever gets drunk will be fined ten dollars.

(48) | nǐ | gěi | tā | shénme , | tā | (jiu) | yòng | shénme |
|-----|-----|-----|----------|-----|-------|------|--------|
| you | give | 3sg | what | 3sg | (then) | use | what |

S/He will use whatever you give him/her.

(49) | nǐ | shuō | jǐ | — | diǎnzhōng , |
|-----|------|-----|------|--------------|
| you | say | how:many | — | o'clock |

	wǒmen	jiu	jǐ	—
	we	then	how:many	—

	diǎnzhōng	zǒu
	o'clock	leave

We will leave at whatever time you say.

In examples such as these, exactly as in the ones preceding them, the underlined C_1 does not contain any element that explicitly signals its relationship to C_2, and C_1 could stand on its own as a normal question, as in:

(50) | shéi | zuì | — | le ? |
|------|------|-----|------|
| who | drink | — | PFV |

Who got drunk?

The fact that C_1 is not interpreted as a question in (47) is due entirely to its dependence on C_2, which determines that the question word will be interpreted as an indefinite pronoun.

Forward linking in a clause without an explicit linking element is accomplished, then, by the speaker's intention to follow it with another clause in terms of which the material in the first clause can be appropriately understood.

23.1.3 The Semantics of Conditionals

One type of forward-linking construction deserves special mention. This is the conditional sentence, one that sets the conditions under which another proposition would be true.[3] In English, conditions are typically introduced by *if* or *unless*, but in Mandarin, as we have seen, the conditional clause may be introduced by a forward-linking adverb that signals "conditional," as in example (3) at the beginning of this chapter, or it may be expressed by forward linking with no linking element, as we saw in (4), (37), and (42).

There are essentially three important types of messages that conditional sentences can express. With illustrations drawn from English, these are:

(i) Reality—a conditional relation between two propositions referring to the so-called real world:

(51) If you heat water to 100 degrees, it boils.

(52) If you step on the brakes, the car slows down.

(53) If the sun comes out, we can go to the beach.

(54) If you finish this chapter, I'll take you out to dinner.

(55) If you can't swim, you'd better not go in the water.

(ii) Imaginative—expressing a proposition about an unreal or imagined situation, one that diverges from the real world:

(*a*) Hypothetical—what could be true in some imaginary world:

(56) If I saw the queen, I'd bow (I *could imagine* seeing the queen).

(57) If we moved, we could have a garden (I *could imagine* moving).

(58) If I were your father, I'd kick you out (I *could imagine* being your father).

(*b*) Counterfactual—what *could* have been true but *was not*:

(59) If you'd taken algebra, you would know this formula (but you *didn't* take algebra).

(60) If you'd listened to me, you wouldn't have suffered (but you
      didn't listen to me).

English makes grammatical distinctions among these three types of conditionals
in the auxiliary verbs and tense and aspect markers they can or must take, but
Mandarin has no such grammatical distinctions. Which type of message is conveyed by a Mandarin conditional construction is inferred by the hearer from the
proposition in the second clause and from his/her knowledge of the world and of
the context in which the sentence is being used. For example, clause (61) can be the
C_1 for all three types of conditionals, as shown in (62):

(61)	rúguó	nǐ	kàn	−	dào	wǒ	mèimei,	. . .
	if	you	see	−	arrive	I	younger:sister	

(62)	rúguó	nǐ	kàn	−	dào
	if	you	see	−	arrive

wǒ	mèimei,	nǐ	yídìng
I	younger:sister	you	certainly

zhīdào	tā	huáiyùn	le
know	3sg	pregnant	CRS

Reality: If you see my younger sister, you'll certainly know that she is
pregnant.

Imaginative hypothetical: If you saw my younger sister, you'd know
she was pregnant (I *could imagine* your seeing her).

Imaginative counterfactual: If you had seen my younger sister, you
would have known that she was pregnant (you *didn't* see her).

Although English makes a clear distinction among these three types of conditionals, it should be obvious that it is not necessary to do so, because the
interpretation of the sentence is always closely related to the context in which it is
spoken; the reality interpretation of sentence (62), for example, would be appropriate in a discussion of plans according to which the hearer actually expects to see
the speaker's sister. The hypothetical interpretation of (62) would be the natural
one in a conversation in which the speaker and the hearer are imagining whether the
hearer could tell that the speaker's sister was pregnant by looking at her. Both the

speaker and the hearer know that the hearer has not yet seen her but that it is within the realm of potential possibility. The counterfactual interpretation of (62), on the other hand, would be the one inferred in a conversation in which both the speaker and the hearer know that whenever the hearer has had a chance to see the speaker's sister, the hearer has not succeeded in seeing her; taking that fact as the starting assumption, of course, allows only the counterfactual interpretation of (62).

The three interpretations for (62) listed above make it clear, then, that although there are no grammatical markings in Mandarin to signal overtly which of these three types of conditionals is intended, there is no confusion because what is meant is clear from the context.

Let's now look at each of the three sorts of conditionals in more detail.

A. Reality

These conditionals express a relationship between two propositions in the real world; the second clause may make an assertion, a prediction, or a suggestion, or it may give a command or ask a question. Here are some examples:

(63) yàoshi   nǐ   bu   huì   yóuyǒng,   nǐ   bu
      if   you   not   know:how   swim   you   not

      yīnggāi   qù   huá   chuán
      should   go   row   boat

If you can't swim, you shouldn't go rowing.

(64) rúguǒ   nǐ   kàn   —   dào   wǒ   mèimei,   gēn
      if   you   see   —   arrive   I   younger:sister   with

      tā   dǎ   yi   —   ge   zhāohu
      3sg   hit   one   —   CL   greeting

If you see my younger sister, say hello to her.

(65) rúguǒ   yǒu   cǎihóng   chūxiàn,   wǒmen   jiu
      if   exist   rainbow   appear   we   then

      zhào   —   xia   —   lai
      photograph   —   descend   —   come

If a rainbow appears, let's take a picture of it.

(66)	jiǎshǐ	míngtiān	xià	—	yǔ,	wǒ	jiu
	if	tomorrow	descend	—	rain	I	then

	bu	shàng	—	bān	le
	not	ascend	—	work	CRS

If it's raining tomorrow, I won't go to work.

(67)	rúguǒ	nǐ	xǐhuān	chī	táozi,	nǐ	yídìng
	if	you	like	eat	peach	you	certainly

	yě	xǐhuān	zhèi	—	ge	shuǐguǒ
	also	like	this	—	CL	fruit

If you like peaches, you'll love this fruit.

When no linking element is present, there may be no formal distinction between a 'when' and an 'if' interpretation. A sentence presented earlier, (40), was one example:

(40)	wǒ	sǐ	—	le,	nǐ	zuì	hǎo	zài	jià
	I	die	—	PFV	you	most	good	again	marry

$\left\{\begin{matrix} \text{If} \\ \text{When} \end{matrix}\right\}$ I die, you'd better marry again.

Here is another:

(68)	tā	kāi	—	le	mén,	nǐ	jiu	jìn
	3sg	open	—	PFV	door	you	then	enter

	—	qu
	—	go

$\left\{\begin{matrix} \text{If} \\ \text{When} \end{matrix}\right\}$ s/he opens the door, you go in.

B. Imaginative

Imaginative conditionals, as we have said, are those used by a speaker who imagines a set of circumstances and then asks a question or makes an assertion based on this assumption. An imaginative conditional can have either a hypothetical or a counterfactual interpretation. As we've stated before, it is the context in which the sentence is used that determines the interpretation of the sentence. For example, consider (69):

(69)   rúguǒ   nǐ   gěi   qìchē   zhuàng   —   dǎo,
        if   you   BEI   car   hit   —   fall:over

        wǒmen   zěnme   bàn ?
         we   how   do

>   Hypothetical: If you were hit by a car, how would we manage (I *could*
>   *imagine* you being hit by a car)?
>   Counterfactual: If you had been hit by a car, how would we have
>   managed (you *weren't* hit by a car)?

The hypothetical interpretation would be appropriate, for example, as a response by a concerned family member to the announcement that someone has decided to deliver newspapers by riding a motorcycle in a congested urban area. The counterfactual interpretation, on the other hand, would be appropriate if a parent were admonishing a child who had just crossed the street without looking for oncoming traffic.

Here are three additional examples of sentences that can be interpreted either as hypothetical or counterfactual conditionals, depending on the context:

(70)   jiǎrú   nǐ   tīng   —   le   wǒ   —   de
        if   you   listen —   PFV   I   —   GEN

        huà,   jiu   bu   huì   chīkǔ   le
        speech then   not   likely suffer CRS

>   Hypothetical: If you listened to me, you would not suffer (I *could*
>   *imagine* you listening to me).
>   Counterfactual: If you had listened to me, you wouldn't have suffered
>   (you *didn't listen* to me).

(71)   jiărú   wŏ   yùbei   –   le   gōngkè, lăoshī   jiu
    if   I   prepare   –   PFV   homework teacher   then

    bu   huì   mà   wŏ
    not   likely scold   I

> Hypothetical: If I did my homework, the teacher wouldn't scold me (I *could imagine* doing my homework).
> Counterfactual: If I had done my homework, the teacher wouldn't have scolded me (I *didn't* do my homework).

(72)   jiărú   wŏ   shi   nĭ   fùqin,   wŏ   zăo   jiu
    if   I   be   you   father   I   early   then

    bă   nĭ   găn   –   chū   –   qù
    BA   you   chase   –   exit   –   go

    le
    CRS

> Hypothetical: If I were your father, I'd kick you out (I *could imagine* being your father).
> Counterfactual: If I had been your father, I would have kicked you out (I *wasn't* your father).

In this section we have isolated three types of messages for conditional sentences: reality, imaginative hypothetical, and imaginative counterfactual. The message that is actually conveyed by a given sentence depends crucially on the context in which it is used. In particular, the context involves the knowledge about the situation which the speaker and the hearer share.

23.2 Backward Linking

With backward linking, a clause is linked to the preceding clause. Unlike forward linking, however, where a speaker intends a relationship between a pair of clauses uttered by himself/herself, with certain linking elements, backward-linking clauses can be linked either to the speaker's own previous clause or to a clause that someone else has just said. *Kěshi* 'but' is such a backward-linking element. For example, in (73) one person uses *kěshi* 'but' to link his/her second clause with his/her own first clause:

(73) wǒ   běnlái   xiǎng   zǎo   yidiǎn   lái,   <u>kěshi</u>
      I   originally think   early   a:little come   but

            wǒ   méi   gǎn   —   shang   gōnggòng
            I   not   chase   —   ascend   public

            —   qìchē
            —   automobile

I had originally intended to come earlier, but I didn't catch the bus.

In (74), on the other hand, speaker B uses *kěshi* 'but' to link his/her proposition to what speaker A had just said:

(74) A: wǒ   yào   dá   tā   —   de   chēzi
         I   want   ride   3sg   —   GEN   vehicle

         qù   xuéxiao
         go   school

I want to ride in his/her car to go to school.

     B: <u>kěshi</u>   tā   —   de   chēzi   méi   yǒu
         but   3sg   —   GEN   vehicle not   exist

         qìyóu   le
         gasoline   CRS

But his/her car is out of gas.

Backward linking can be accomplished without any linking element, as we have seen in examples (36), (42), and (43), which contain neither forward-linking nor backward-linking elements. Backward linking can also, however, be expressed by adverbial elements in clause-initial position or by nonmovable adverbs. In what follows we will discuss two types of backward-linking elements separately.

23.2.1 Adverbial Backward-Linking Elements in Clause-Initial Position

Adverbial backward-linking elements must occur at the beginning of their clause. With the exception of *háishi* 'or', which can be used only in questions, adverbial backward linking can link a clause either to the speaker's own previous clause or to a clause someone else has just said. The most important adverbial backward-linking elements are these:

(75) bìngqiě
    érqiě   }   'moreover'

    kěshi
    dànshi
    búguò   }   'but, nevertheless, however'[4]
    ránér

    háishi   'or' (exclusive, used only in questions)

    huòshi
    huòzhě   }   'or' (inclusive)
    huòzheshì

    wèideshì   'in order to'

    shěngde   'so as to avoid'

    suǒyi   'so'

    yīnwèi   'because' (can also occur as a forward-linking element: see example [19])

Here are some examples.

(76)   zhèi   —   dòng   lóu   hěn   dà ,   bìngqiě
       this   —   CL   building   very   big   moreover

                     hěn   yǒumíng
                     very   famous

This building is very big, and it's also very famous.

(77) (discussing a friend's qualifications to organize a skit)

A:	wǒ	juéde	tā	hěn	nénggàn
	I	feel	3sg	very	capable

I feel s/he is very capable.

B:	érqiě	tā	hěn	yǒu	yǎn	—	xì
	moreover	3sg	very	exist	act	—	play

de	jīngyàn
NOM	experience

Moreover, s/he has a lot of acting experience.

(78)	tā	hěn	bèn ,	búguò	kǎo	—	shàng
	3sg	very	stupid	but	exam	—	ascend

dàxué	le
university	CRS

S/He's very stupid, but s/he passed the university entrance exam.

(79)	nǐ	yào	wǒ	bāng	nǐ	háishi	yào
	you	want	I	help	you	or	want

zìjǐ	zuò ?
self	do

Do you want me to help you, or do you want to do it yourself?

(80)	wǒmen	zài	zhèli	chī	huòzhe	chī	fàndiàn
	we	at	here	eat	or	eat	restaurant

dōu	xíng
all	OK

We can either eat here or eat out.

(81) tā qù Xiānggǎng wèideshi xué Guǎngdōng — huà

        3sg go Hong Kong in:order:to study Canton — speech

S/He went to Hong Kong in order to study Cantonese.

(82) nǐ kěyǐ yòng wǒ — de zìdiǎn , shěngde

        you can use I — GEN dictionary in:order:to:avoid

        nǐ mǎi le

        you buy CRS

You can use my dictionary, and then you won't have to buy one.

(83) zhù sùshè bǐjiao róngyi , yīnwei xuéxiào gài —

        live dormitory relatively easy because school build —

        le hěn duō xīn de sùshè

        PFV very many new NOM dormitory

It's easy to live in the dorm because the school has built a lot of new dorms.

23.2.2 Nonmovable Adverbs as Backward-Linking Elements

A few nonmovable adverbs (see section 8.2 of chapter 8), which occur immediately after the topic of clause, can also serve as backward-linking elements. Unlike most of the adverbial backward-linking elements in clause-initial position, the nonmovable adverbs that can function as backward-linking elements relate a clause only to the speaker's own previous clause, not to a clause that someone else has said. The most common backward-linking adverb is *jiù* 'then'. It is used in a number of examples in this chapter, including (3), (6), (8), (39), (41), and (45). Another nonmovable adverb that can function as a backward-linking element is *cái* 'only then', as in (84):

(84) tā juǎn — le tóufǎ cái piàoliang

        3sg curl — PFV hair only:then pretty

It's only when she curls her hair that she is pretty.

The third nonmovable adverb that can function as a backward-linking element is *dào* 'nonetheless'.[5]

(85)	tā	yīdiǎn	dōu	bu	cōngmíng ,	dào
	3sg	a:little	all	not	intelligent	nonetheless

	huì	tīng	—	huà
	know:how	listen	—	speech

S/He is not at all intelligent, but (s/he) knows how to be odedient.

In addition to the three nonmovable adverbs given above, there are four that occur as the second identical member of a correlative pair: *yòu, yě, yuè,* and *yìbiān*. For examples of these, see (25)−(28) above.

Notes

1. Some of the ideas for this chapter have been taken from Shaffer (1966), Chao (1968:sect. 2.2), and Tseng (1977), and from some unpublished research by Richard Te-lee Ch'i.
2. The semantics of conditional sentences deserve a special discussion; see section 23.1.3 below.
3. On the semantics of conditionals we have taken ideas from Schachter (1971).
4. There are slight differences in the kinds of contrast these words can be used to signal. For a discussion of the first three, see Ross (1978:201 ff.).
5. On *cái* and *dào*, see Tsao (1976).

CHAPTER 24

Pronouns in Discourse

24.1 Zero Pronouns

As we have indicated in chapters 2 and 4, a salient feature of Mandarin grammar is the fact that noun phrases that are understood from context do not need to be specified. Many languages have this property—for example, most American Indian languages, Japanese, and Korean—but it is sometimes difficult for speakers of Indo-European languages to grasp because the use of pronouns is so much more common in Indo-European languages, especially in English.[1]

Let's consider some examples. If the speaker is talking about how s/he spent the weekend, s/he might say:

(1)   Lù   Wényì   gēn   wǒ   qù   huá   —   chuán ,
        Lu   Wenyi   with   I   go   row   —   boat

            _____   diào   —   le   yi   —   ge   zhōngtóu   yú
                       catch   —   PFV   one   —   CL   hour   fish

Lu Wenyi and I went rowing, and (we) fished for an hour.

In response, the hearer could say:

(2)   _____   diào   —   zháo   —   le   _____   ma ?
                    catch   —   succeed   —   PFV   Q

Did (you) catch (anything)?

In each of the positions where we placed a blank in (1) and (2), a noun phrase is understood from what has already been said, and although English would use a pronoun in each of these positions, Mandarin, as indicated by the parenthetical elements in our translations, generally would not, but would leave the noun phrase completely unspecified. Although in terms of Mandarin grammar nothing is actually *missing* from these sentences—they are perfectly grammatical utterances in the appropriate contexts—we will continue to use blanks in the examples in this chapter simply for the sake of highlighting this particular difference between English and Mandarin. For convenience, we will call the blank, which stands for an understood noun phrase referent, a *zero pronoun*.

Here is a similar example:

(3) A: nèi   —   chǎng diànyīng   nǐ   juéde   zěnme
         that   —   CL   movie   you   feel   how

         —   yàng ?
         —   manner

How did you feel about that movie?

B: _____   yidiǎn   dōu   bu   xǐhuān _____
             a:little   all   not   like

(I) didn't like (it) a bit.

Again, because who is experiencing the disliking is perfectly clear from the discourse context, there is no need to specify that person with a noun phrase. The same can be said about the object of *xǐhuān* 'like', but an additional factor here is that the third person pronoun in Mandarin is rarely used to refer to an inanimate entity (see section 4.2.6 of chapter 4). Thus, the use of a third person pronoun here as the object of *xǐhuān* 'like', referring to 'that movie', would be inappropriate.

Here is an example that illustrates a zero pronoun for the understood referent ('books') and a normal pronoun, *wǒ* 'I', for the referent that could *not* be understood from context:

(4) A: zhèi   —   xie   shū   nǐ   yào   wǒ   fàng
         this   —   PL   book   you   want   I   put

         zài   nǎli ?
         at   where

Where do you want me to put these books?

B: gěi   wǒ   ———
      give   I

Give (them) to me.

The preceding zero pronoun examples have involved referents that are understood from having been mentioned in the discourse. Another situation in which a referent is understood is when it is ''general,'' or nonspecific; English uses *you* or *they* (or, more formally, *one*) in this function. Here are some examples:

(5)   diào   —   yú   ————   bu   néng   zháoji
       catch   —   fish   not   can   impatient

When (you) go fishing (you) can't be impatient.

(6)   zhèi   —   ge   hú   ————   kěyǐ   bu   kěyǐ
       this   —   CL   lake   can   not   can

              huá   —   bīng ?
              skate   —   ice

Can (one) skate on this lake?

(7)   Xīnhuá   Lù   ————   gài   —   le   hǎo
       Xinhua   Road   build   —   PFV   very

              duō   xīn   gōngyù
              many   new   apartment:buildings

On Xinhua Road, (they)'ve built a lot of new apartment buildings.

(8)   ————   yòu   xiū   lù   le
              again   repair   road   CRS

(They)'re fixing the road again.

One common situation in which noun phrases are unspecified is the *topic chain* (see section 4.1.8 of chapter 4 on topics), where a referent is referred to in the first clause, and then there follow several more clauses talking about the same referent but not overtly mentioning that referent. One very short example of the topic chain can be seen in (1) above, where the topic of the second clause is unspecified because it refers to the topic of the first clause. Here is another, slightly longer, example:

(9) A: wŏmen   dăsuàn   zuò   shénme   ne ?
          we   plan   do   what   REx

What shall we plan to do?

B: _____   xià   —   chē   yĭhòu ,   _____   xiān
             descend —   vehicle   after   first

    dào   Dàhuá   Fàndiàn ,   _____   xiūxi   yihuĭr ,
    arrive Dahua   Hotel   rest   a:while

    _____   chī   —   le   wŭ   —
             eat   —   PFV   afternoon   —

    fàn ,   jiu   _____   qù   kāi   —
    food   then   go   open   —

    huì ,   sàn   —   le   huì ,   _____
    meeting adjourn   —   PFV   meeting

    méi   shì   le ,   _____   kěyĭ   dào
    not   matter   CRS   can   to

    hú   —   biān   kàn   —   kan
    lake   —   side   see   —   see

    huòzhě   _____   gù   yi   —   ge
    or   hire   one   —   CL

    chuán   huá   —   hua
    boat   row   —   row

After (we) get off the train, (we)'ll go to the Dahua Hotel first and rest a while. After (we) eat lunch, (we)'ll attend the meeting. When the meeting ends, (we) have nothing to do, so (we) can go to the lake to look around, or (we) can rent a boat to row.

While the topic chain is a common situation exhibiting unspecified noun phrases, the zero pronoun, of course, does not always have to refer to the *topic* of the preceding clause. Here is an example: suppose, in the dialogue given in (9), that instead of talking exclusively about what *wǒmen* 'we' will do, speaker B had decided to talk about the Dahua Hotel, which is not the topic of the sentence in which it first appears. Then the response might have looked like this:

(10)

	xià	–	chē	yǐhòu,		xiān
——₁	descend	–	vehicle	after	——₂	first

dào	Dàhuá	Fàndiàn,	yàoshi		yǒu
arrive	Dahua	Hotel	if	——₃	exist

fángzi,	dāngrán		hěn	hǎo
room	of:course	——₄	very	good

After (we) get off the train, first (we)'ll go to the Dahua Hotel. If (they) have rooms, of course, (that) would be good.

Here, while the first two zero pronouns refer to the topic of the question *wǒmen* 'we', the third one refers to the Dahua Hotel ('if [they] have rooms' or 'if there are rooms [there]'), and the fourth one refers to the whole idea of their having rooms ('[that] would certainly be good').

Here is a similar example, in which the first zero pronoun refers to the topic, but the next one does not:

(11)

wǒ	shàng	xīngqi	gěi	Dàhuá	Fàndiàn	xiě
I	last	week	to	Dahua	Hotel	write

–	le	yī	–	fēng	xìn,
–	PFV	one	–	CL	letter

	qǐng	tāmen	bǎoliú	yí	–
——₁	invite	they	reserve	one	–

jiān	wūzi,	dào	xiànzài		hái
CL	room	to	now	——₂	still

méi	tōngzhī	wǒ
not	inform	I

Last week I wrote a letter to the Dahua Hotel, and (I) requested them to reserve a room. Up to now, (they) still haven't let me know.

The topic at the beginning of (11) is *wǒ* 'I'. The sense of the passage makes it clear that it was *I* (_____₁) who requested the hotel to reserve a room, and it was *they* (_____₂) who didn't get back to *wǒ* 'I'.

24.2 Pronouns

Pronouns often do occur in Mandarin conversation (see section 4.2.6 of chapter 4 for a discussion of pronouns); the question to be raised in the context of this chapter, of course, is this: If either a pronoun or a zero pronoun can occur, how does a speaker decide which is appropriate? While there exists no airtight, absolute answer to this question, a general guideline having to do with *highlighting* can be followed. That is, it is not enough just to say that whenever the referent can be understood or figured out, a zero pronoun can be used, because there are times when it would be quite obvious what the referent for a given pronoun would be if it were omitted, and yet it must be used. Let's consider an example. If one is describing a scene in which a gentleman had come into a room, one might say:

(12) wàibian jìn   —   lái   —   le   yi
      outside enter   —   come   —   PFV   one

      —   ge   rén   _____ liǎng —
      —   CL   person   two   —

      ge   hóng yǎnjing , yi   —   fù
      CL   red   eye   one   —   CL

      dà   yuán   liǎn , _____ dài   —
      big   round face   wear —

      zhe   yi   —   ge   xiǎo   màozi ,
      DUR   one   —   CL   small hat

      tā   xìng   Xià
      3sg   surname Xia

From outside came a person. (He) had two red eyes (and) one big round face, and (he) was wearing a small hat. He had the surname Xia.

In this discourse, the topic is the same from beginning to end, yet only the last clause contains a *tā* 'he'. Why? What is significant about this last clause is that it conveys a type of information that is unexpected in light of the information conveyed by the preceding clauses. All the other clauses in this passage describe the man as he appeared, while the final clause provides a piece of background information, something that is not connected with his appearance, as the clauses preceding it are. In this clause, then, but not in the others, we find the pronoun *tā*, highlighting the fact that the speaker has switched from describing his appearance to providing the background information concerning his name.

Here is an example of a different type, where a series of clauses offering descriptions precedes a clause referring to an action. Now, the action clause is the unexpected one, and it has the pronoun *tā* 'he':

(13)   Bái   Xiānsheng   zài   kètīng   —   lǐ   děng
        Bai   Mr.   at   living room   —   in   wait

        Lǐsì,   _____   dài   —   zhe   yǎnjìng ,
        Lisi   wear   —   DUR   glasses

        zài   nàr   kàn   bàozhǐ ,   _____   hǎoxiàng
        at   there   read   newspaper   seem

        yǒu   diǎn   bu   —   nàifán ,   tā
        have   a:little   not   patient   3sg

        shuō :   ". . . ."
        say   ". . . ."

Mr. Bai was waiting for Lisi in the living room. (He) was wearing glasses and reading a newspaper there. (He) seemed to be a bit impatient. He said: ". . . ."

In this example, all the clauses except the last one describe Mr. Bai's appearance, setting the scene in which he was waiting for Lisi. Then, in the last clause, an action ('He *said* . . .') is expressed, and here, even though it is obvious who the referent is, the *tā* cannot be omitted, because the sentence provides an unexpected type of information in the context of a series of clauses portraying Mr. Bai, and it is necessary to highlight the fact that the referent has not changed.

The role of highlighting can be seen even more clearly in the use of the first and second person pronouns. In general, a zero pronoun is used when there is no reason to highlight the reference to the speaker or the hearer, while the pronouns *wǒ*/ *wǒmen* 'I/we' or *nǐ*/*nǐmen* 'you/you all' are used when there is some reason to highlight the reference to the speaker or hearer. Let's clarify this principle by looking at some examples.

First, compare (14) *a* and *b*.

(14) *a.* _____ hǎo bu hǎo ?
        good not good

  How are (you)?

  b. <u>nǐ</u> hǎo bu hǎo ?
    you good not good

  How are you?

Sentence (14) *a* would be a natural greeting between two friends; sentence (14) *b*, on the other hand, could be used when two people are being introduced to each other for the first time, or when the speaker is greeting someone to whom s/he wishes to show respect or deference, or when the speaker has some reason to be genuinely inquiring about the health of the hearer. What all these contexts have in common is that in each of them the speaker has some reason to call attention to the fact that it is that particular person who is being addressed. In each case, it is simply more respectful to highlight that the question is being addressed to that hearer and to no one else.

Next, consider the following question with and without *wǒmen* 'we':

(15) *a.* _____ jīntiān wǎnshang chī shénme ?
        today evening eat what

  What are we having for supper tonight?

  b. <u>wǒmen</u> jīntiān wǎnshang chī shénme ?
    we today evening eat what

  What are we having for supper tonight?

Sentence (15) *a*, without the pronoun, would be most natural in the context of dinner preparations, such as if A and B are chatting in the kitchen near dinner time; in this context, there is no need to highlight the subject. If, however, A and B are in some setting other than that of dinner preparations, then (15) *b*, with the pronoun, would be the more appropriate way to seek the information. For example, question *b* would be appropriate if it is breakfast time and A wants to know what is for dinner so that s/he can decide what to pack for lunch, or if A and B are shopping for groceries at noon and A wants to know B's plans for dinner so that s/he can decide how many tomatoes to buy. In this situation, the pronoun serves to clarify the fact that it is indeed 'we' whose dinner plans are being referred to, since in this context, removed from the meal time and/or place, the referent of the zero pronoun might not be clear.

Let us look at another example involving questions. A clerk in a shop, upon seeing a customer, will say:

(16) _____ yào shénme ?
              want what

What do you want?

Once again, the question is entirely expected in the shop situation, there is no reason to highlight the reference to the hearer, and the pronoun would not be used. The question with the pronoun,

(17)   ni   yào shénme ?
      you   want what

What do you want?

however, would be used by the clerk, for example, to single out a specific shopper from a group of people, to address a revered older person, or as a request for clarification of the shopper's intentions.

Notice that, depending on the context and the people involved, the question with *nǐ* can sound either more concerned and friendly or more abrupt and rude. With (17), for example, if the shopkeeper uses it while waiting on a revered older person, then it sounds more concerned and friendly than (16), the question without *nǐ*. If the shopkeeper uses it to ask for clarification of the shopper's intentions, though, it can sound more rude and abrupt than (16). What this means is that the real difference between using and not using the pronoun is basically not a matter of such attitudes as greater or lesser friendliness or abruptness, but is, rather, a matter of the principle of highlighting, which we have been stressing, and it is this principle that allows differences in attitude to be expressed, depending on the situation. Of course, the abruptness or politeness accompanying such questions as (17) is also communicated through intonation, facial expression, volume, pitch of voice, and similar factors.

As a final example, consider a physician giving a medical examination to a patient. After the first one or two queries, the questions that the physician poses are likely to contain no subject pronoun referring to the hearer, once again because there is no reason to highlight the fact that the hearer is the one to whom the physician is referring. For example:

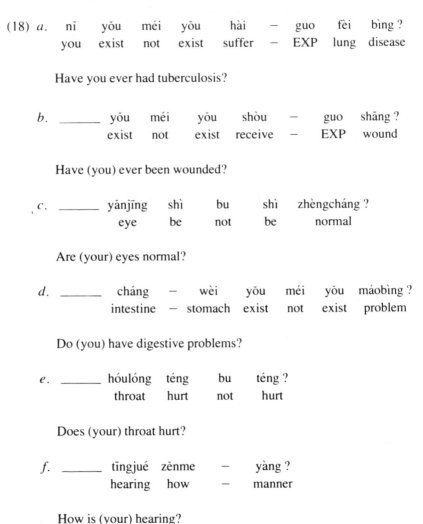

(18) *a.* nǐ   yǒu   méi   yǒu   hài   —   guo   fèi   bìng ?
           you   exist not   exist suffer —   EXP   lung   disease

Have you ever had tuberculosis?

b. _____ yǒu   méi   yǒu   shòu   —   guo   shāng ?
              exist not   exist receive —   EXP   wound

Have (you) ever been wounded?

c. _____ yǎnjīng   shì   bu   shì   zhèngcháng ?
              eye   be   not   be   normal

Are (your) eyes normal?

d. _____ cháng   —   wèi   yǒu   méi   yǒu   máobìng ?
              intestine —   stomach exist not   exist problem

Do (you) have digestive problems?

e. _____ hóulóng   téng   bu   téng ?
              throat   hurt   not   hurt

Does (your) throat hurt?

f. _____ tīngjué   zěnme   —   yàng ?
              hearing   how   —   manner

How is (your) hearing?

If pronouns are used in questions in which the referent is being highlighted, then it follows that, in general, ordinary information-seeking questions *will* contain pronouns in most contexts, since the context is neutral with regard to what the referent of the pronoun might be. This is, in fact, the case; it is difficult to imagine contexts in which questions such as the following will not have their pronouns:

(19) <u>nǐ</u>   xiǎode   bu   xiǎode   tā   yǒu   shénme   bìng ?
     you   know   not   know   3sg   exist   what   sickness

Do you know what his/her illness is?

(20) <u>nǐ</u>   tīng   shénme ?
     you   listen   what

What are you listening to?

(21) <u>nǐ</u>   chuān   jǐ   —   hào   xiézi ?
     you   wear   how:many   —   number   shoe

What size shoe do you wear?

(22) <u>nǐ</u>   xǐhuān   bu   xǐhuān   Bèiduōfēn   —   de
     you   like   not   like   Beethoven   —   GEN

         yīnyuè ?
         music

Do you like the music of Beethoven?

That is, since questions such as these are in no way expected in most contexts, the use of the pronoun highlights the fact that the subject of the question is indeed the hearer himself/herself. Thus, we would predict that if we could find a context in which there was no need to highlight the referent of the pronoun, the pronoun could be omitted. Taking (22) as an example, we suggest a context such as the following: after A and B have been listening to Beethoven for an hour, A could ask B question (23), which is (22) without the pronoun *nǐ* 'you':

(23) _____   xǐhuān   bu   xǐhuān   Bèiduōfēn   —   de
              like   not   like   Beethoven   —   GEN

         yīnyuè ?
         music

Do (you) like Beethoven's music?

Turning now to the occurrence of pronouns in *answers* to questions, we find the same principle at work: a first person pronoun is unusual in an answer to a question when it simply provides the information requested in the question, since there is generally no reason to highlight reference to oneself in answering a question. Thus, in exchanges such as the following, the answers would be highly unlikely to have the pronoun *wǒ* 'I':

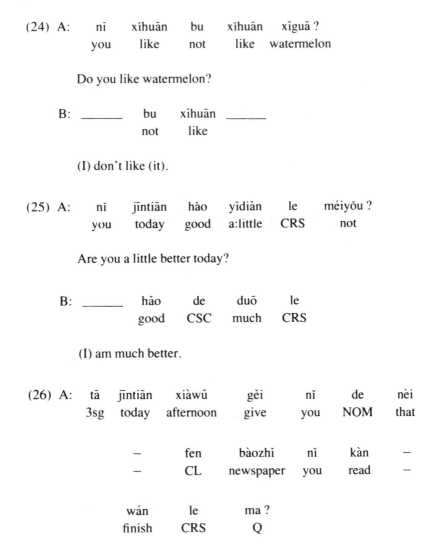

(24) A: nǐ   xǐhuān   bu   xǐhuān   xīguā ?
          you   like   not   like   watermelon

Do you like watermelon?

    B: _____   bu   xǐhuān   _____
                   not   like

(I) don't like (it).

(25) A: nǐ   jīntiān   hǎo   yīdiǎn   le   méiyǒu ?
          you   today   good   a:little CRS   not

Are you a little better today?

    B: _____   hǎo   de   duō   le
                   good   CSC   much   CRS

(I) am much better.

(26) A: tā   jīntiān   xiàwǔ   gěi   nǐ   de   nèi
          3sg   today   afternoon   give   you   NOM   that

          —   fen   bàozhǐ   nǐ   kàn   —
          —   CL   newspaper   you   read   —

          wán   le   ma ?
          finish   CRS   Q

Have you finished reading the newspaper s/he gave you this afternoon?

B: _____   kàn   –   wán   _____   le
               read   –   finish   CRS

(I)'ve read (it).

A contrast between zero pronoun and pronoun is possible, however, in other question-answer pairs. Consider the following: if A is at the station and needs to catch a train, s/he may ask B, a stranger, when the next train leaves:

(27) A: xià   –   yi   –   bān   huǒchē   shénme
            next   –   one   –   CL   train   what

            shíhòu   kāi ?
            time   leave

When does the next train leave?

B: *a.* _____   bu   xiǎode
                       not   know

(I) don't know.

b.   wǒ   bu   xiǎode
         I   not   know

I don't know.

The *a* answer, without the pronoun, is a simple, neutral response to the question. The *b* answer, with the pronoun, on the other hand, suggests that while *I* do not know, perhaps someone else does, and A should ask somebody else. Because it opens up this possibility, its message is somewhat softer and less abrupt than that of the *a* response; we again stress, however, that the less abrupt and softer effect is strictly a secondary feature derived from the fact that the speaker is highlighting reference to himself/herself.

Here is a similar example illustrating the contrast.

(28) A: tā   kànjian   nǐ   méiyǒu ?
            3sg   see   you   not

Did s/he see you?

B: *a.* _____ kànjian _____ le
                 see   CRS

(S/he) saw (me).

The pronouns *tā* 's/he' and *wǒ* 'I' may be omitted in B's response if it is intended as a straightforward answer to the question. If, on the other hand, the response is a preview to further unexpected material, the pronouns would be more likely to occur to highlight the fact that s/he did see me in spite of the circumstances mentioned in the following clause.

b.   tā   kànjian   wǒ   le ,   dànshi _____ lián
      3sg   see   I   CRS   but   even

      yí   −   jù   huà   dōu   méi
      one   −   sentence word   all   not

      gēn   wǒ   jiǎng
      with   I   speak

S/He did, but (s/he) didn't even say a single word to me.

The same principle can be seen to be at work in the choice of zero versus first or second person pronouns in exchanges that are not question-answer pairs. In the following dialogue, each occurrence of *wǒ* 'I' implies contrast; A2 conveys a contrast between A and others who have been to the auditorium, while B2 contrasts B's having been there with A's not having been there:

(29) A1:   tā   zài   shénme dìfang chàng   −   gē ?
          3sg   at   what   place   sing   −   song

Where is s/he singing?

B1:   zài   dàlítáng
      at   auditorium

In the auditorium.

A2: wǒ   hái   méi   qù   —   guo   dàlitáng
     I   still not   go   —   EXP   auditorium

I've never been to the auditorium.

B2: _____   méi   guānxi,   wǒ   qù   —   guo   _____
               not   matter   I   go   —   EXP

(That) doesn't matter, I've been (there).

Sometimes the speech situation relevant for determining whether to use a pronoun is the preceding discourse itself. Here is an example from an actual telephone conversation about moving (from Tsao [1977:216]):

(30) A1:   tā   yě   shuō   zuì   —   hǎo   néng
           3sg   also   say   most   —   good   can

           gǎnkuài   bān
           hurry   move

S/He also said it would be best to move sooner.

B1:   ha ,   a

Hum, hum.

A2: (i)   yě   kěnéng   jiù   shi   yuè   —   dǐ ,
             also   possible   just   be   month   —   end

     (ii)   xiànzài   _____   jiù   shi   děng   qiān
             now   just   be   wait   sign

        —   xià   —   lái ,
        —   descend —   come

     (iii)   yě   kěnéng   xià   —   ge   lǐbài ,
             also   possible   next   —   CL   week

(iv)	wǒ	xiǎng	dàgài	shì	yuè	—	dǐ
	I	think	probably	be	month	—	end

Possibly, the end of the month. (We) are just waiting for the signing. Next week is also possible. I think most probably the end of the month.

B2:	duì ,	yuè	—	dǐ	_____	bān	—
	right	month	—	end		move	—

	jiā ,	shì	ba
	home	be	SA

So, (you) will be moving at the end of the month, right?

In A2, clause (ii) is missing a first person plural subject 'we'. In the context of the discussion about when A's family should move, any comment, such as (ii), about the factors determining the timing would be expected and normal—hence the lack of a pronoun. In (iv), however, A is asserting her *opinion* about the probable timing of the move; here the contrast between what she thinks and what anyone else might think calls for highlighting the reference to herself; thus, the pronoun subject for *xiǎng* is obligatory. In fact, it is for this reason that first person subjects are nearly always expressed with verbs such as *xiǎng* 'think', *juéde* 'feel', *shuō* 'say'; these expressions typically offer the speakers subjective and personal assessment of the topic under discussion. The speaker's opinion in (iv) of example (30) is being implicitly contrasted with others' opinions, whereas the moving and the participants involved in it have been established as discourse topics and are not being contrasted with anything.

Finally, in B2, we find another case of zero referring to A and her husband; the reason that the pronoun *nǐmen* 'you:PL' does not appear there is precisely the same as the reason we just gave for which *wǒmen* 'we' does not appear in A2 (ii): in this situation, comments about the timing of the move are expected, and there is no special reason to highlight the subject.

Turning next to imperatives, we can see that the conditions governing the occurrence of second person pronouns are precisely the same as those governing the occurrence of pronouns in the questions, answers, and exchanges we have just been looking at. For example, suppose A has just poured a cup of hot tea, and B, not knowing it is hot, appears to be about to touch it; A might say:

(31) _____ bié pèng _____ !
            don't touch

Don't touch (it)!

In this context, such a command would be perfectly normal, and there would be no reason to use the subject pronoun *nǐ* 'you'. If it were used, it would imply that the hearer was being singled out and contrasted with others who might not be given the same warning, which is clearly not what is intended in this setting:

(32) <u>nǐ</u> bié pèng _____ !
     you don't touch

Don't you touch (it)!

Similarly, if A sees that B's shoes are soaked, s/he could say:

(33) _____ kuài qù huàn xiézi , _____ bié
            quick go change shoe   don't

            gǎnmào le
            catch:cold CRS

Hurry and go change your shoes—don't catch cold.

The command is normal and perfunctory in this setting; again, there would be no reason to use the pronoun.

What we have said so far provides a basis for understanding why first person pronouns are rarely omitted in statements that initiate conversation: at the beginning of a conversation, there are no assumptions about what the subject of the sentence is. Thus, if A wants to initiate a conversation by saying that s/he has a headache, it will be inappropriate for him/her to use the *a* form of (34); the *b* form, rather, is the appropriate one:

(34) *a.* _____ tóu — téng
            head — ache

(I) have a headache.

b.   wǒ   tóu   —   téng
         I   head   —   ache

      I have a headache.

Similarly, at the beginning of a conversation, sentences such as the following would also occur *with* the first person pronoun:

(35)   wǒ   yǒu   yi   —   ge   dìdi   mǎi
        I   exist   one   —   CL   younger:brother   buy

              —   le   yi   —   dòng   fángzi
              —   PFV   one   —   CL   house

      I have a younger brother (who) bought a house.

(36)   wǒ   zuótiān   jiàn   —   dào   Zhāngsān
        I   yesterday   see   —   arrive   Zhangsan

      I met Zhangsan yesterday.

(37)   wǒ   zhēn   dānxīn   tā   chū   —   le   shénme
        I   really   worry   3sg   exit   —   PFV   what

              shì   le
              affair   CRS

      I'm really worried about what might have happened to him/her.

(38)   lái ,   wǒmen   huá   —   quán ,   hǎo   bu   hǎo ?
       come   we   play   —   guess:fingers   good   not   good

      Come, let's play ''guess-fingers,'' OK?

What we have seen, then, in this chapter is that the decision to use a pronoun in referring to people and things depends not only on whether the referent is *understood*, but on whether there is reason to highlight the referent of the pronoun in the context in which it occurs.

24.3 Syntactic Constraints on Zero Pronouns

We have analyzed the discourse factors that determine the use of a zero pronoun or a pronoun in the preceding sections. The occurrence of a pronoun can, however, be required by the syntactic structure of a sentence. In other words, there are two syntactic environments in which a zero pronoun is not allowed, regardless of the discourse factors. First, the noun phrase occurring immediately after a coverb cannot be a zero pronoun (see chapter 9 for a discussion of coverbs). For example, (39)−(42) are unacceptable because the noun phrase occurring after the coverb in each sentence is a zero pronoun:

(39) *wǒ gēn _____ xué Yīngwén
       I   with   learn English

(40) *tā   bǎ   _____ dài   −   lái   LE
       3sg BA   bring −   come CRS/PFV

(41) *nǐ   cóng _____ zǒu ?
       you from   leave

(42) *Zhangsan gěi _____ xiū   shuǐ   −   guǎnzi
       Zhangsan for   repair water −   pipe

Second, the pivotal noun phrase in a serial verb construction cannot be a zero pronoun (see section 21.3 of chapter 21 on the pivotal construction). Sentences (43) and (44) are unacceptable because the pivotal noun phrase is a zero pronoun:

(43) *tā   mìnglìng _____ yòng dāozi
       3sg order   use   knife

(44) *wǒ quàn _____ bié hē   jiǔ
       I   urge   not drink wine

Note

1. This chapter has benefited from some comments made by James Tai and Talmy Givón. For much more detailed discussions of pronouns in discourse, see Li and Thompson (1979a) and Tai (1978).

References

Alleton, Viviane (1972). *Les adverbes en chinois moderne*. The Hague: Mouton.
——— (1973). *Grammaire du chinois*. Paris: Presses Universitaires de France.
——— (1977). "Les verbes auxiliaires de mode en chinois moderne." *CLAO* 1:31–41.
Anderson, C. J. M., and C. Jones (1974). *Historical Linguistics*. Amsterdam: North-Holland Publishing Co.
Baron, Stephen (1970). "Aspect *le* and Particle *le* in Modern Spoken Mandarin." M.A. thesis, Seton Hall University.
Cartier, Alice (1970). "Verbes et prépositions en chinois moderne." *La Linguistique* 6:91–116.
——— (1972). *Les verbes résultatifs en chinois moderne*. Paris: Librairie C. Klincksieck.
Chafe, Wallace L. (1976). "Givenness, Contrastiveness, Definiteness, Subjects, Topics, and Point of View." In Li (1976:25–55).
Chan, Stephen W. (1974). "Asymmetry in Temporal and Sequential Clauses in Chinese." *JCL* 2.3:340–353.
Chang, Roland Chiang-jen (1977). *Co-verbs in Spoken Chinese*. Taipei: Cheng Chung Book Co.
Chao, Yuen-ren (1948). *Mandarin Primer*. Cambridge, Mass: Harvard University Press.
——— (1968). *A Grammar of Spoken Chinese*. Berkeley and Los Angeles: University of California Press.
——— (1970). *Language and Symbolic Systems*. Cambridge: At the University Press.
Chen, Chung-yu (1979). "On Predicative Complements." *JCL* 7.1:44–64.
Chen, Gwang-tsai (1979). "The Aspect Markers LE, GUO, and ZHE in Mandarin Chinese." *JCLTA* 14.2:27–46.
Chen, Ruoxi (1976). *Yīn Xiàn-zhǎng* [Mayor Yin]. Taibei: Yuan-jing Publishing Co.
Cheng, C. C. (1973). *A Synchronic Phonology of Mandarin Chinese*. Monographs on Linguistic Analysis, no. 4. The Hague: Mouton and Co.
Cheng, Robert L., Ying-che Li, and Ting-chi Tang, eds. (1979). *Proceedings of Symposium on Chinese Linguistics, 1977 Linguistics Institute of the Linguistic Society of America*. Taipei: Student Book Co.

Cheung, Hung-nin Samuel (1973). "A Comparative Study in Chinese Grammars: The *ba*-Construction." *JCL* 1.3:343–382.

Ch'i, Te-lee (1974). "A Study of 'Verb-Object' Compounds in Mandarin Chinese." In Thompson and Lord (1974:87–106).

Chu, Chauncey C. (1970). "The Structures of *shì* and *yŏu* in Mandarin Chinese." Ph.D. dissertation, University of Texas.

——— (1973). "The Passive Construction: Chinese and English." *JCL* 1.2:437–470.

——— (1978). "Structure and Pedagogy—A Case Study of the Particles *zhe* and *ne*." *JCLTA* 13.2:158–166.

Comrie, Bernard (1976). *Aspect*. Cambridge: At the University Press.

D'Andrea, John (1978). "The Category AUX in Mandarin Chinese." M.A. thesis, University of Arizona.

Dressler, Wolfgang, ed. (1978). *Proceedings of the XIIth International Congress of Linguists*. Innsbruck: Innsbrucker Beitrage zur Sprachwissenschaft, Universitat Innsbruck.

Egerod, Søren (1967). "Dialectology." In *Linguistics in East Asia and South East Asia, Current Trends in Linguistics*, ed. T. Sebeok, vol. II, pp. 91–129. The Hague: Mouton.

Elliott, Dale (1965). "Interrogation in English and Mandarin." In *Project on Linguistic Analysis*, no. 11, pp. 56–117. Columbus: Ohio State University Department of Linguistics.

Forrest, R. A. D. (1948). *The Chinese Language*. London: Faber and Faber.

Givón, Talmy (1979a). *On Understanding Grammar*. New York: Academic Press.

———, ed. (1979b). *Discourse and Syntax*. Syntax and Semantics, vol. 12. New York: Academic Press.

Greenberg, Joseph H.(1963a). "Some Universals of Grammar with Particular Reference to the Order of Meaningful Elements." In Greenberg (1963b:73–113).

———, ed. (1963b). *Universals of Language*. Cambridge, Mass.: MIT Press.

Hagège, Claude (1975). *Le probleme linguistique des prépositions et la solution chinoise*. Paris: Editions Peeters.

Hashimoto, Anne Y. (1969a). "The Verb 'To Be' in Modern Chinese." In Verhaar (1969:72–111).

——— (1969b). "The Imperative in Chinese." *Unicorn* 4:35–62.

——— (1971a). "The Mandarin Syntactic Structures." *Unicorn* 8:1–149.

——— (1971b). "Descriptive Adverbials and the Passive Construction." *Unicorn* 7:84–93.

Hashimoto, Mantaro (1976). "Language Diffusion on the Asian Continent." *CAAAL* 3:49–66.

Hinds, John (1978). *Anaphora in Discourse*. Edmonton, Alberta: Linguistic Research.

Hopper, Paul J., ed. (1982). *Tense and Aspect: Between Semantics and Pragmatics*. Amsterdam: John Benjamins.

Howie, J. M. (1976). *Acoustical Studies of Mandarin Vowels and Tones*. Cambridge: At the University Press.

Huang, Shuan-fan (1966). "Subject and Object in Mandarin." In *Project on Linguistic Analysis*, no. 13, pp. 25–103. Columbus: Ohio State University Department of Linguistics.

——— (1974a). "Between Verbs and Prepositions." *Yŭyánxué Yánjiū Lùncóng* [Essays in linguistics], pp. 219–224. Taipei: Liming Book Co.

—— (1974b). "Mandarin Causatives." *JCL* 2.3:354–369.

—— (1978). "Historical Change of Prepositions and Emergence of SOV Order." *JCL* 6.2:212–242.

Kierman, Frank A., Jr. (1969). "Night-Thoughts on the Passive." *Unicorn* 5:72–78.

Kratochvil, Paul (1968). *The Chinese Language Today: Features of an Emerging Standard.* London: Hutchinson University Library.

Kwan-Terry, Anna (1979). "The Case of the Two *le's* in Chinese." *CAAAL* 10:39–55.

Lehmann, Winfred, ed. (1978). *Syntactic Typology.* Austin: University of Texas Press.

Li, Charles N., ed. (1975). *Word Order and Word Order Change.* Austin: University of Texas Press.

——, ed. (1976). *Subject and Topic.* New York: Academic Press.

Li, Charles N., and Sandra A. Thompson (1974a). "Co-verbs in Mandarin Chinese: Verbs or Prepositions?" *JCL* 2.3:257–278.

—— (1974b). "Historical Change of Word Order: A Case Study in Chinese and Its Implications." In Anderson and Jones (1974:199–217).

—— (1974c). "An Explanation of Word Order Change: SVO ——→ SOV." *Foundations of Language* 12:201–214.

—— (1974d). "A Linguistic Discussion of the 'Co-Verb' in Chinese Grammar." JCLTA IX.3:109–119.

—— (1975a). "The Semantic Function of Word Order in Chinese." In Li (1975: 163–195).

—— (1975b). "The 'Paratactic Relative Clause' in Mandarin Chinese." In *Asian Studies on the Pacific Coast*, pp. 1–8. Honolulu: University of Hawaii Department of East Asian Languages.

—— (1976). "Subject and Topic: A New Typology of Language." In Li (1976:457–489).

—— (1978a). "An Exploration of Mandarin Chinese." In Lehmann (1978:223–266).

—— (1978b). 'Grammatical Relations in Languages without Grammatical Signals." In Dressler (1978:687–691).

—— (1979a). "Third-Person Anaphora and Zero-Anaphora in Chinese Discourse." In Givón (1979b:311–335).

—— (1979b). "The Pragmatics of Two Types of Yes-No Questions in Mandarin and Its Universal Implications." In *Papers from the Fifteenth Regional Meeting of the Chicago Linguistic Society*, pp. 197–206. Chicago: University of Chicago Department of Linguistics.

—— (1979c). "Chinese: Dialect Variations and Language Reform." In Shopen (1979: 295–335).

Li, Charles N., Sandra A. Thompson, and R. McMillan Thompson (forthcoming). "The Discourse Motivation for the Perfect Aspect: The Mandarin Particle *le*." In Hopper (1982).

Li, Francis C. (1971). "Case and Communicative Function in the Use of *ba* in Mandarin." Ph.D. dissertation, Cornell University.

—— (1977). "How Can We Dispose of *Bǎ*?" *JCLTA* 12.1:8–13.

Li, Ying-che (1974). "What Does 'Disposal' Mean? Features of the Verb and Noun in Chinese." *JCL* 2.2:200–218.

Light, Timothy (1977). "Some Potential for the Resultative." *JCLTA* 12.1:27–41.

—— (1979). "Word Order and Word Order Change in Mandarin Chinese." *JCL* 7.2:149–180.

Lin, Wen-Liuh (1977). "Deictic Verbs and Directional Verbs in Chinese." M.A. thesis, Fu Jen University.

Lu, John H.-T. (1977). "Resultative Verb Compounds versus Directional Verb Compounds in Mandarin." *JCL* 5.2:276–313.

Lü Xiang (1948). "*Bǎ* Zì Yòng-fǎ Yánjiū" [Studies in the use of *ba*]. In *Zhōngguó Wénhuà Yánjiū Huìkān* [Studies in Chinese culture] no. 8, pp. 111–130.

Lu, Zhiwei (1965). *Hànyǔ de Gòucí Fǎ* [Chinese morphology]. Peking: Kēxué Chūbǎnshè.

Lyovin, Anatole (1972). "Comparative Phonology of Mandarin Dialects." Ph.D. dissertation, University of California, Berkeley.

Ma, Jing-heng S. (1977). "Some Aspects of the Teaching of *-Guo* and *-Le*." *JCLTA* 12.1:14–26.

Marney, John (1977). *A Handbook of Modern Chinese Grammar*. San Francisco: Chinese Materials Center.

Mei, Kuang (1972). "Studies in the Transformational Grammar of Modern Standard Chinese." Ph.D. dissertation, Harvard University.

Mullie, J. (1932). *The Structural Principles of the Chinese Language*. Peking: Bureau of Engraving and Printing.

Paris, Marie-Claude (1977). "Le morpheme 'de' et la relativation en mandarin." *CLAO* 2:65–76.

—— (1979a). *Nominalization in Mandarin Chinese*. Paris: Département de Recherches Linguistiques, Université Paris VII.

—— (1979b). "Some Aspects of the Syntax and Semantics of the *lián . . . yě/dōu* Construction in Mandarin." *CLAO* 5:47–70.

Peyraube, Alain (1977). "Adverbiaux et compléments de lieu en chinois." *CLAO* 1:43–60.

Rohsenow, John (1978). "Syntax and Semantics of the Perfect in Mandarin Chinese." Ph.D. dissertation, University of Michigan.

Ross, Claudia (1978). "Contrast Conjoining in English, Japanese, and Mandarin Chinese." Ph.D. dissertation, University of Michigan.

Rygaloff, Alexis (1973). *Grammaire Elémentaire du Chinois*. Paris: Presses Universitaires de France.

Schachter, Jacquelyn (1971). "Presupposition and Counterfactual Conditional Sentences." Ph.D. dissertation, University of California, Los Angeles.

Shaffer, Douglas (1966). "Paired Connectives in Modern Mandarin." Ph.D. dissertation, University of Texas.

Shih, Barbara M. (1966). "Negation in Chinese." M.A. thesis, Ohio State University.

Shopen, Timothy, ed. (1979). *Languages and Their Status*. Cambridge, Mass.: Winthrop Publishers.

Simon, Harry F. (1958). "Some Remarks on the Structure of the Verb Complex in Standard Chinese." *Bulletin of the School of Oriental and African Studies* 21:553–577.

Spanos, George (1977). "A Textual, Conversational, and Theoretical Analysis of the Mandarin Particle *le*." Ph.D. dissertation, University of Arizona.

—— (1979). "Contemporary Chinese Usage of LE: A Survey and a Pragmatic Proposal." *JCLTA*, 14.1:36–70, 14.2:47–102.

Tai, James H.-Y. (1973). "A Derivational Constraint on Adverbial Placement in Mandarin

Chinese.'' *JCL* 1.3:397 − 413.

——— (1978). ''Anaphoric Constraints in Mandarin Chinese Narrative Discourse.'' In Hinds (1978:279 − 338).

Tang, Ting-chi Charles (1972). *A Case Grammar of Spoken Chinese*. Taipei: Hai-Guo Book Co.

Teng, Shou-hsin (1973). ''Negation and Aspects in Chinese.'' *JCL* 1.1:14 − 37.

——— (1974*a*). ''Verb Classification and Its Pedagogical Extensions.'' *JCLTA* IX. 2: 84 − 92.

——— (1974*b*). ''Double Nominatives in Chinese.'' *Language* 50.3:455 − 73.

——— (1974*c*). ''Negation in Chinese.'' *JCL* 2.2:125 − 140.

——— (1975*a*). *A Semantic Study of Transitivity Relations in Chinese*. Berkeley, Los Angeles, and London: University of California Press.

——— (1975*b*). ''Predicate Movements in Chinese.'' *JCL* 3.1:60 − 75.

——— (1977). ''A Grammar of Verb Particles in Chinese.'' *JCL* 5.1:1 − 25.

——— (1979*a*). ''Modification and the Structures of Existential Sentences.'' In Cheng, Li, and Tang (1979): 197 − 210.

——— (1979*b*). ''Progressive Aspect in Chinese.'' *CAAAL* 11:1 − 12.

——— (1979*c*). ''Remarks on Cleft Sentences in Chinese.'' *JCL* 7.1:101 − 113.

Tewksbury, M. Gardner (1948). *Speak Chinese*. New Haven: Yale University Press.

Thompson, Sandra, and Carol Lord (1974). *Approaches to the Lexicon*, UCLA Papers in Syntax, no. 6.

Tsao, Feng-fu (1976). ''Expectation in Chinese: A Functional Analysis of Two Adverbs.'' In *Proceedings of the Second Annual Meeting of the Berkeley Linguistics Society*, pp. 360 − 374. Berkeley: Berkeley Linguistics Society.

Tsao, Feng-fu (1977). ''A Functional Study of Topic in Chinese: The First Step toward Discourse Analysis.'' Ph.D. dissertation, University of Southern California.

Tseng, David S.-D. (1977). ''A Study on the Chinese Equivalents of the English *And*.'' M.A. thesis, National Taiwan Normal University.

Van Valin, Robert (1975). ''Existential Locatives in Mandarin.'' Paper read at the Eighth International Conference on Sino-Tibetan Languages and Linguistics, October 1975, at the University of California, Berkeley.

Verhaar, John W. M., ed. (1969). *The Verb 'Be' and Its Synonyms*. Foundations of Language Supplementary Series, vol. 4. Dordrecht: D. Reidel Publishing.

Wang, Fred Fangyu (1967). *Mandarin Chinese Dictionary*. 2 vols. South Orange, N.J.: Seton Hall University Press.

Wang, Huan (1957). *Bǎ Zì Jù Hé Bèi Zì Jù* [*Bǎ* sentences and *bèi* sentences]. Shanghai:Xīn Zhīshī Chūbǎnshè. Translated into English in *Project on Linguistic Analysis*, ed. W. S.-Y. Wang, no. 4. Columbus: Ohio State University Department of Linguistics.

Wang, Li (1947). *Zhōngguó Xiàndài Yǔfǎ* [Modern Chinese grammar]. Shanghai: Zhōnghuá Shūjú.

Wang, William S.-Y. (1965). ''Two Aspect Markers in Mandarin.'' *Language* 41: 457 − 470.

Zee, Eric (1980). ''A Spectrographic Investigation of Mandarin Tone Sandhi.'' *UCLA Working Papers in Phonetics* 49:98 − 116.

Zhu, Dexi (1956). ''Xiàndài Hànyǔ Xíngróngcí Yánjiū'' [A study of adjectives in modern Chinese]. *Yǔyán Yánjiū* 1:83—112.

Notes on References

CAAAL = Computational Analyses of Asian and African Languages
CLAO = Cahiers de Linguistique Asie Orientale
JCL = Journal of Chinese Linguistics
JCLTA = Journal of the Chinese Language Teachers' Association
Unicorn is a journal published between the years 1966 and 1972 by the Chinese Linguistics Project at Princeton University under a Ford Foundation Grant.

For further references to materials in Chinese linguistics, see Yang, Paul Fu-mien (1974). *Chinese Linguistics: A Selected and Classified Bibliography*. Hong Kong: The Chinese University of Hong Kong.

Materials for the teaching of Mandarin which have influenced our thinking on Mandarin grammar and from which we have taken examples include:

Chao, Yuen-ren (1948). *Mandarin Primer*. Cambridge, Mass.: Harvard University Press.

DeFrancis, John (1963). *Beginning Chinese*. New Haven: Yale University Press.

——— (1964). *Intermediate Chinese*. New Haven: Yale University Press.

——— (1966). *Advanced Chinese*. New Haven: Yale University Press.

Dictionary of Spoken Chinese (1966). New Haven: Yale University Press.

Fenn, Henry C., and M. Gardner Tewksbury (1967). *Speak Mandarin*. New Haven: Yale University Press.

Pian, Rulan Chao (1961). *A Syllabus for Mandarin Primer*. Cambridge, Mass.: Harvard University Press.

Tewksbury, M. Gardner (1948). *Speak Chinese*. New Haven: Yale University Press.

Wang, Fred Fangyu (1967). *Mandarin Chinese Dictionary*. 2 vols. South Orange, N.J.: Seton Hall University Press.

Index

Compositor: Trend Western
Text: 10/13 Times Roman
Printer: Maple-Vail Book Manufacturing Group
Binder: Maple-Vail Book Manufacturing Group